T0331744

Collaboration and Student Engagement in Design Education

Richard Tucker
Deakin University, Australia

A volume in the Advances in Higher Education
and Professional Development (AHEPD) Book
Series

www.igi-global.com

Published in the United States of America by
    IGI Global
    Information Science Reference (an imprint of IGI Global)
    701 E. Chocolate Avenue
    Hershey PA, USA 17033
    Tel: 717-533-8845
    Fax: 717-533-8661
    E-mail: cust@igi-global.com
    Web site: http://www.igi-global.com

Library of Congress Cataloging-in-Publication Data

Names: Tucker, Richard, 1967- editor.
Title: Collaboration and student engagement in design education / Richard
  Tucker, editor.
Description: Hershey, PA : Information Science Reference, 2016. | Series:
  Collaboration and Student Engagement in Design Education | Includes
  bibliographical references and index.
Identifiers: LCCN 2016024299| ISBN 9781522507260 (hardcover) | ISBN
  9781522507277 (ebook)
Subjects: LCSH: Design--Study and teaching, Higher. | Architecture--Study and
  teaching. | Team learning approach in education.
Classification: LCC NK1170 .C65 2016 | DDC 745.4071/1--dc23 LC record available at https://lccn.loc.gov/2016024299

This book is published in the IGI Global book series Advances in Higher Education and Professional Development (AHEPD) (ISSN: 2327-6983; eISSN: 2327-6991)

British Cataloguing in Publication Data
A Cataloguing in Publication record for this book is available from the British Library.

For electronic access to this publication, please contact: eresources@igi-global.com.

Advances in Higher Education and Professional Development (AHEPD) Book Series

Jared Keengwe
University of North Dakota, USA

ISSN: 2327-6983
EISSN: 2327-6991

MISSION

As world economies continue to shift and change in response to global financial situations, job markets have begun to demand a more highly-skilled workforce. In many industries a college degree is the minimum requirement and further educational development is expected to advance. With these current trends in mind, the **Advances in Higher Education & Professional Development (AHEPD) Book Series** provides an outlet for researchers and academics to publish their research in these areas and to distribute these works to practitioners and other researchers.

AHEPD encompasses all research dealing with higher education pedagogy, development, and curriculum design, as well as all areas of professional development, regardless of focus.

COVERAGE

- Adult Education
- Assessment in Higher Education
- Career Training
- Coaching and Mentoring
- Continuing Professional Development
- Governance in Higher Education
- Higher Education Policy
- Pedagogy of Teaching Higher Education
- Vocational Education

IGI Global is currently accepting manuscripts for publication within this series. To submit a proposal for a volume in this series, please contact our Acquisition Editors at Acquisitions@igi-global.com or visit: http://www.igi-global.com/publish/.

The Advances in Higher Education and Professional Development (AHEPD) Book Series (ISSN 2327-6983) is published by IGI Global, 701 E. Chocolate Avenue, Hershey, PA 17033-1240, USA, www.igi-global.com. This series is composed of titles available for purchase individually; each title is edited to be contextually exclusive from any other title within the series. For pricing and ordering information please visit http://www.igi-global.com/book-series/advances-higher-education-professional-development/73681. Postmaster: Send all address changes to above address. Copyright © 2017 IGI Global. All rights, including translation in other languages reserved by the publisher. No part of this series may be reproduced or used in any form or by any means – graphics, electronic, or mechanical, including photocopying, recording, taping, or information and retrieval systems – without written permission from the publisher, except for non commercial, educational use, including classroom teaching purposes. The views expressed in this series are those of the authors, but not necessarily of IGI Global.

Titles in this Series

For a list of additional titles in this series, please visit: www.igi-global.com

Handbook of Research on Learner-Centered Pedagogy in Teacher Education and Professional Development
Jared Keengwe (University of North Dakota, USA) and Grace Onchwari (University of North Dakota, USA)
Information Science Reference • copyright 2017 • 451pp • H/C (ISBN: 9781522508922) • US $265.00 (our price)

Accelerated Opportunity Education Models and Practices
Rene Cintron (Louisiana Community & Technical College System, USA) Jeanne C. Samuel (Delgado Community College, USA) and Janice M. Hinson (University of North Carolina at Charlotte, USA)
Information Science Reference • copyright 2017 • 316pp • H/C (ISBN: 9781522505280) • US $180.00 (our price)

Preparing Foreign Language Teachers for Next-Generation Education
Chin-Hsi Lin (Michigan State University, USA) Dongbo Zhang (Michigan State University, USA) and Binbin Zheng (Michigan State University, USA)
Information Science Reference • copyright 2017 • 313pp • H/C (ISBN: 9781522504832) • US $185.00 (our price)

Innovative Practices for Higher Education Assessment and Measurement
Elena Cano (University of Barcelona, Spain) and Georgeta Ion (Universitat Autònoma de Barcelona, Spain)
Information Science Reference • copyright 2017 • 471pp • H/C (ISBN: 9781522505310) • US $215.00 (our price)

Handbook of Research on Study Abroad Programs and Outbound Mobility
Donna M. Velliaris (Eynesbury Institute of Business & Technology, Australia) and Deb Coleman-George (University of Adelaide, Australia)
Information Science Reference • copyright 2016 • 754pp • H/C (ISBN: 9781522501695) • US $335.00 (our price)

Setting a New Agenda for Student Engagement and Retention in Historically Black Colleges and Universities
Charles B. W. Prince (Howard University, USA) and Rochelle L. Ford (Syracuse University, USA)
Information Science Reference • copyright 2016 • 343pp • H/C (ISBN: 9781522503088) • US $185.00 (our price)

Handbook of Research on Professional Development for Quality Teaching and Learning
Teresa Petty (University of North Carolina at Charlotte, USA) Amy Good (University of North Carolina at Charlotte, USA) and S. Michael Putman (University of North Carolina at Charlotte, USA)
Information Science Reference • copyright 2016 • 824pp • H/C (ISBN: 9781522502043) • US $310.00 (our price)

Administrative Challenges and Organizational Leadership in Historically Black Colleges and Universities
Charles B. W. Prince (Howard University, USA) and Rochelle L. Ford (Syracuse University, USA)
Information Science Reference • copyright 2016 • 301pp • H/C (ISBN: 9781522503118) • US $170.00 (our price)

www.igi-global.com

701 E. Chocolate Ave., Hershey, PA 17033
Order online at www.igi-global.com or call 717-533-8845 x100
To place a standing order for titles released in this series, contact: cust@igi-global.com
Mon-Fri 8:00 am - 5:00 pm (est) or fax 24 hours a day 717-533-8661

Editorial Advisory Board

Table of Contents

Section 1
Teaching Collaboration: Team Building and the Andragogy of Teamwork in Design

Section 2
Evaluating Collaboration: Teaching Case Studies

Section 3
Preparing for Collaboration: Learning for Teamwork in Professional Practice

Detailed Table of Contents

Section 1
Teaching Collaboration: Team Building and the Andragogy of Teamwork in Design

Chapter 1
Richard Tucker, Deakin University, Australia

This chapter proposes an Input-Process-Output framework for understanding what impacts the effectiveness of teamwork when higher education students are collaborating on design assignments. The framework can help design educators integrate teamwork into their courses and better evaluate learning outcomes, and may also elucidate good practice for professional design teams. Explaining the genesis of the framework, the literature is assimilated on team effectiveness and predictors of team performance, including: definitions, dimensions and frameworks of team effectiveness in contexts far wider than design education. Informed by the challenges specific to teaching design, a 22-factor framework is proposed. The paper concludes with recommendations for teachers informed by the framework. The viability of the 22-factor model of team effectiveness is evidenced by national surveys across Australia, which are reported in summary here.

Chapter 2
Paola Gavilanez, Kwantlen Polytechnic University, Canada
Amber Ortlieb, Kwantlen Polytechnic University, Canada
Thomas Carey, Kwantlen Polytechnic University, Canada

Previous research on teaching and learning in the design disciplines has demonstrated the complex set of factors which need to be aligned in order for our students to be prepared for professional practice in teamwork. This chapter reports on ongoing work to extend this previous research, including integration with an institutional learning outcomes framework, incorporation of insights from beyond the design disciplines to engage student motivation in capability development, and a specific interest in the ways team teaching in design studios can contribute to the development of students' teamwork capability (in addition to advancing their development of design capability).

Chapter 3

Ju Hyun Lee, The University of Newcastle, Australia
Michael J Ostwald, The University of Newcastle, Australia
Ning Gu, University of South Australia, Australia

This chapter combines experimental data and established design theory to examine four issues associated with design cognition that contribute to an improved understanding of creativity and teamwork in design. Drawing on data developed from two parametric design experiments undertaken by the authors, this chapter investigates the implications of (i) cognitive space, (ii) design strategy, (iii) design productivity and (iv) spatial representation, for individuals, and by inference, for groups and educators. Through this process the chapter develops a deeper understanding of the cognitive challenges facing design teams and educators of those teams.

Chapter 4

Richard Tucker, Deakin University, Australia

This chapter considers a simple but important question: can students fairly assess each other's individual contribution to team designs? The chapter focuses on a key problem when using online self-and-peer assessment to individualising design grades for team assignments, namely rater bias – the possibility of students being biased when assessing their own and their peers' contributions. Three rater-bias issues are considered in depth: (1) self-overmarking; (2) gender bias and gender differences; and (3) out-group bias in the peer assessment of international students in multicultural cohorts. Each issue is explored via the analysis of eight years of quantitative data from the use of an online self-and-peer assessment tool. Evidence is found of self-overmarking and of out-group bias in nonhomogeneous cohorts. However, no evidence is found of gender bias. The chapter concludes with recommendations for design teachers around the assessment of individual contributions to teamwork using self-and-peer assessment.

Chapter 5

Neda Abbasi, Deakin University, Australia
Anthony Mills, Deakin University, Australia
Richard Tucker, Deakin University, Australia

This chapter examines conflict in student design teams. A review of literature is presented to understand conflict within student design teams and explore strategies to manage it. In addition, qualitative data on students' experiences of team conflict is analysed from two surveys offered to design students in 18 Australian Higher Education Institutions. Analysis of the survey found that "ignoring or avoiding to acknowledge team conflict" is a strategy commonly adopted by students, followed by "trying to resolve team conflict through discussion and improving communication" and "seeking support from teachers." Drawing upon these findings, the chapter makes recommendations on strategies to prepare students for conflict situations through a number of support models that design instructors might adopt, including both preventive and intervention strategies.

Section 2
Evaluating Collaboration: Teaching Case Studies

This chapter presents a case study of a large common first year unit/subject in a major Australian university. The unit introduces students to the theory and practice of design through a learning environment that is brief and intense; being delivered in block mode over just four days, and being free of other academic commitments. Students choose from one of two concurrent environments, either a camping field trip or an on-campus alternative, and work in mixed discipline groups of six to nine students, on two sequential design projects. Participant survey and reflective journal data are used to analyse student perceptions of the learning activities and to establish the pedagogical success of learning about collaboration through the act of collaborating; specifically through a project-based design environment. The data supports the hypothesis that groups that emotionally engaged with collaboration and collaborated more effectively achieved higher academic grades.

It is argued that 'design' is an essential characteristic of engineering practice, and hence, an essential theme of engineering education. It is suggested that first-year design courses enhance commencing student motivation and retention, and introduce engineering application content and basic design experience early in the curriculum. The research literature indicates that engineering design practice is a deeply social process, with collaboration and group interactions required at almost every stage. This chapter documents the evaluation of the initial and subsequent second offerings of a first-year engineering design unit at Griffith University in Australia. The unit 1006ENG Design and Professional Skills aims to provide an introduction to engineering design and professional practice through a project-based approach to problem solving. The unit learning design incorporates student group work, and uses self-and-peer-assessment to incorporate aspects of the design process into the unit assessment and to provide a mechanism for individualization of student marks.

This chapter presents an intervention in Design Thinking, a first year interdisciplinary design subject at the University of Technology Sydney. Over two iterations of this subject, researchers reframed the 'group work' component as critical collaboration, drawing from the momentum in the design professions for more participatory and collaborative processes and the increasing acknowledgement of design as being critical to sustainable human futures. The online self and peer assessment tool SPARKPlus was used to change the way students approached collaboration and then reflected on it following their experiences. In this model, self and peer assessment is used as a leaver to encourage critical thinking about collaboration, rather than as a hammer to enforce participation.

Chapter 9

CmyView is a research project that investigates how mobile technologies have the potential to facilitate new ways to share, experience and understand the connections that people have with places. The aim of the project is to theorise and develop a tool and a methodology that addresses the reception of architecture and the built environment using mobile digital technologies that harness ubiquitous everyday practices, such as photography and walking. While CmyView is primarily focused on evidencing the reception of places, this chapter argues that these activities can also make a contribution to the core pedagogy of architectural education, the design studio. This chapter presents findings of an initial pilot study with four students at an Australian university that demonstrates how CmyView offers a valuable contribution to the educational experience in the design studio.

Chapter 10

This chapter presents a project in which students taking an undergraduate course on Design Thinking participated in a university widening participation project, visiting local schools from a low socioeconomic status background and engaging the school students in a design exercise. The project aimed to draw on the value of service learning, learning through an engaged and socially meaningful task, with tertiary students learning to facilitate design, following principles of co-design, in a community of stakeholders, and secondary students gaining contact with university life, seeing an undergraduate perspective on design, and receiving education in design thinking. Tertiary students were asked to develop design thinking toolkits that would support their design facilitation process. The authors present the results of a study of the project, based on students' assignment submissions, and a focus group following the activity.

Chapter 11

Intercultural dialogue through design, globally known as "iDiDe" (pronounced i-dee-dee) was initiated by an Australian university in 2011 for architecture and built environment disciplines. Set within the context of international education and internationalisation, which are the focus of Australian universities this century, iDiDe offers a model of intercultural collaboration and student engagement. iDiDe is more than a generic international study tour. Firstly, there is collaborative academic leadership that comes from institutional partnerships between Australia and five Asian nations (Malaysia, Thailand, India,

Indonesia, Sri Lanka), secondly, intercultural dialogue and intercultural understanding underpin the pedagogical approach, and thirdly, iDiDe projects extend discipline specific learning into the realms of reality. This chapter is an expose of iDiDe. It seeks to determine what elements of the model contribute to intercultural collaboration and student engagement. Findings are evaluated for their impact upon participants. The potential for transformative learning and response to global citizenship are discussed along with future research.

Chapter 12

Ammon Beyerle, Here Studio, Australia & The University of Melbourne, Australia
Greg Missingham, The University of Melbourne, Australia

Two teaching experiences that structured individual student learning through the designed variation of group work opportunities are examined: a graduate architectural design studio and a repeated undergraduate course focused on methods and approaches for designing. The teaching approaches draw on participatory design and group learning theories. Group work was structured as a series of overlapping layers to bring about an individual learning experience and a shared studio experience of creativity. Various outcomes are read against an excerpt from Nancy's "The Inoperative Community" in Bishop's Participation (2006b). The discussion is a means to further explore common interests in designing design processes, in particular through developing collaborative learning in design, and a social-reflective practice in students. The authors are figuring yet another way of developing creativity wherein a student's skills, projects, and ideas come out of, and are intersected by a complexity of social processes, oppositions and the spectra that define them.

Chapter 13

Traci Rose Rider, North Carolina State University, USA
Elizabeth Bowen, North Carolina State University, USA

This chapter reviews the outline, process, and structure of the LEED Lab course at North Carolina State University (NCSU), which has engaged students from multiple colleges across the University. This chapter will specifically address NCSU's particular approach to teamwork in design education, using an existing building on NCSU's campus and an established assessment framework to provide context. With the LEED for Existing Buildings Operations and Maintenance as a guide, interdisciplinary teams of students worked together to establish recommendations for future operations. Additional teamwork opportunities included the engagement of a number of NCSU facilities departments, including Repairs and Renovation, Energy Services, Waste Reduction and Recycling, and others. Using examples of team-building exercises, integration with NCSU's Facilities Division, in-class hands-on exercises, and in-process photographs, this chapter will walk the reader through the opportunities and challenges of integrating non-traditional teamwork exercises into design education processes.

Section 3
Preparing for Collaboration: Learning for Teamwork in Professional Practice

Chapter 14

Nicole Wragg, Swinburne University of Technology, Australia
Carolyn Barnes, Swinburne University of Technology, Australia

Professional learning, where students gain skills and attributes relevant to their future work, is currently emphasised in tertiary education. Group work is promoted here for preparing students to work with clients and colleagues. We report on two capstone projects undertaken for external clients by teams of design students. In discussing the curricula and pedagogy of professional design education, the chapter addresses the value of group projects in developing graduates' work-readiness and insight into professional practice. Variances in approach, knowledge and perspective between colleagues, combined with differing needs and expectations across the designer-client-end-user divide, make goal setting and project resolution challenging in design. Project work approached from an expanded sense of the group and which delivers implementable proposals for clients provides graduating students with authentic learning around the demands of practice, stressing collaborative problem-solving based on knowledge of the design context and the wider relational systems surrounding industry practice.

Chapter 15

James Thompson, University of Washington, USA

Presenting narratives of three recent graduates of a U.S. Master of Architecture program, this study employs an interpretative-narrative approach to access and evoke the role that collaboration plays in the process of 'becoming a design professional'. Whereas ontological learning has been recognized as fundamental to life-long learning and development, research has yet to explore themes of self-authorship in relation to collaborative design experiences. In representing authentic voices of learners, the research presented in this chapter contributes to a deeper understanding of the ways in which aspiring design professionals make sense of their transformation from academic to professional selves. This will ultimately inform how design educators value and structure team-based design projects by providing a more holistic understanding of the role such projects might play in shaping individuals' identities.

Foreword

One of the great paradoxes in design education is that undergraduate students are encouraged to study and model the behaviors and attitudes of famous designers, but without being aware that such esteemed individuals rarely work in isolation. The vast majority of designers work in teams, as part of both the conceptualization and production processes. Even 'design-auteurs' or 'artist-designers' must still interact with, respectively, clients, consultants and contractors, or patrons, curators and publishers. As a result of this, collaboration is widely considered an essential part of the design process and a critical skill for developing a career in the design industries. However, while design practitioners and the professional bodies that represent them acknowledge the importance of groups and teams, there has been a general reluctance (either an unwillingness or inability) to emphasize the importance or team processes, or embed the development of team skills, in undergraduate design curricula. There are many reasons for this situation existing, but we cannot underestimate the general attitude, implicit in much design education and promulgated through the design media, that creativity is an individual trait.

One of the oldest myths about creativity is that it is found in the subconscious part of each person's mind, and it is only through engagement with a muse – a mystical teacher or source of inspiration – that a person's creative potential is unleashed. This conceit, often known as the 'romantic' model of creativity, stresses the importance of only one relationship, between teacher and student, and even then, the student is a strangely passive participant in the process. Parallels to this idea can be found in the historical apprenticeship and enculturation models of design education. In the former, the student is treated as either a passive vessel, waiting to be filled with knowledge, or as a tool, much like a pair of compasses, which is an extension of the master's hand. Through the apprenticeship model, the master transforms the student by passing on his or her own individual creativity and skills. The enculturation model, the historic antecedent of studio-based teaching, has a surprisingly similar educational transaction at its core. However, in its more recent and enlightened incarnation, it too stresses that creativity is innate to an individual, and education nurtures or draws it out, allowing the individual to reach their true potential. If such innate potential is not present, then a range of learnt strategies can be substituted.

There are certainly alternatives to these three models, including those which stress that creativity can be learnt if an appropriate context is available. Nevertheless, in the three classic models of design pedagogy and cognition, the relationships that exist are either between the teacher and student, or the student and the design. Neither of these acknowledge the critical importance of the team, in developing and applying creative skills. Indeed, a startling lacunae is uncovered if we seek to explain why so much has been written about teamwork, teambuilding and team operations in some fields (especially management and business), and design processes and creativity in others, but there is little or no overlap between the two.

It is in this context that Richard Tucker's book, *Collaboration and Student Engagement in Design Education*, is so significant. It offers a landmark contribution to design scholarship and pedagogy, focussing to the problem of educating students for an environment where groups, teams and collaborative modes of working are not only common, but essential. Tucker's book acknowledges the challenges that have beset previous attempts to introduce team-based creative processes in schools of design. For example, there have often been practical disincentives for schools to encourage (or require) their students to design in teams including the fact that design teachers are often in their positions by virtue of their capacity to design, rather than their ability to prepare people for understanding and improving interpersonal communication and relations. Conversely, where teamwork assignments do exist in schools, they are sometimes used opportunistically, as an efficient means of assessing work, rather than as an important learning occasion. Students themselves can strongly resist team projects and especially those where there is some level of creativity or innovation required. They often falsely assume that their creative potential will be somehow diminished through its contact with others. Further complicating the adoption of appropriate team-opportunities in design schools, there are often bureaucratic impediments to team projects, including the need to provide grades that differentiate between levels of contribution.

Across the 15 chapters in this book, these issues and others are discussed in detail and a range of practical solutions are proposed and demonstrated. Fundamentally, Tucker's book brings together a series of case studies, from a broad disciplinary and geographic base, which readers can use to improve the way they prepare students for a career in design. While some isolated studies on these topics have been published in the past, this book's scope and aspiration set it apart from all previous work on the topic. I strongly encourage readers to see what lessons they can adopt or adapt, and thereby understand that the gap that so often exists between design education and teamwork, can be bridged in many productive and exciting ways.

Michael J Ostwald
The University of Newcastle, Australia

Preface

WHY STUDY TEAMWORK?

The genesis of this book can be traced to the *Australian Learning Teaching Council* (ALTC) funded discipline scoping study *Understanding Architectural Education in Australasia* (Ostwald & Williams, 2008). In particular, it responds to *Recommendation 12,* which states "universities, students and employer groups are not only calling for more group work in professional programs, but also for each member of a group to be separately assessed and graded" (p.38). To address this recommendation, a further study was funded by the ALTC in 2011/13: *Enhancing and Assessing Group and Team Learning in Architecture and Related Design Contexts.*[1] The project sought to answer three key questions: "how do we teach teamwork skills in the context of design?; how do we assess teamwork skills?; and how do we fairly assess individual contribution to team designs?" To resolve these questions, *Enhancing and Assessing Group and Team Learning* gathered, developed, trialled and documented good-practice models of teaching design via collaboration and of assessing individual contributions to collaborative design. The project also investigated "how best to support through teaching and formative assessment (in a discipline where summative assessment still dominates) the learning of teamworking skills." These skills include those that are particularly needed to design collaboratively e.g. idea selection and development, shared understanding through graphic communication, and reflective practice; and those skills commonly needed for teamwork irrespective of field e.g. leadership, management, delegation, consensus seeking and the capacity to effectively handle conflict.

The research presented in this book is largely devoted to these learning and teaching issues. But while *Enhancing and Assessing Group and Team Learning* provided impetus for this book, it has been foreshadowed by the last ten years of my own research, which has charted evaluations of strategies for teaching and assessing teamwork. This work has been iterative in nature, developing research methodology for evaluating design teaching in an area where such methods have not commonly been used or documented. After all, most design teachers have been trained as designers and not researchers. This has certainly been true of the discipline of architecture, where my own path is shared by the great majority of educators in my field – from architect to teacher to researcher. The evolution of my own research on teaching design has been the classic one of learning from mistakes. Indeed, the research was first prompted by the urge to address early mistakes I had made in my own teaching.

At the final review of the very first design unit I had taught in which teamwork was a focus, a security guard was posted at the door of the studio to bar entry to an excluded student who had previously thrown a chair at a team mate's head during a heated design meeting. The incident was an extreme reflection of passions running high when students are designing in teams. A key reason for such conflict is that design is a highly subjective activity where there are as many solutions to a brief as there are designers, and where it is often difficult to clearly determine which solutions are best. From talking to students and reading their evaluations of my teaching, I came to realise that many students' teamwork experiences were negative and distressing. The poor evaluations for my own design subject echoed the almost universal unpopularity of team assignments in my school at that time.

This unpopularity reflected not only the problems students had with conflict but also the ad hoc nature of teamwork teaching and assessment in many design schools. This situation was not restricted to design schools, but was symptomatic of international trends throughout higher education of increasing numbers of teamwork assignments to reduce assessment workloads under the pressure of increasing staff-student ratios. Commonly, design assignments requiring students to collaborate were not devised to teach and assess teamwork or collaborative design skills, rather they were being used opportunistically to assess less work than would be produced by individuals. It was my firm belief that design subjects requiring substantial collaboration from students should assess design collaboration and teamwork skills, and thus should also teach these skills. But this belief prompted the question posed by *Enhancing and Assessing Group and Team Learning:* how do we best assess and teach teamworking in design? This question in turn prompts the question at the centre of *Collaboration and Student Engagement in Design Education*: what research methodologies and conceptual frameworks can we use to evaluate strategies for teaching and assessing design collaboration? As there is no straightforward answer to this question, we address it via fifteen recent research projects. These studies are conducted by design teachers who evidently believe, as I do, that design collaboration skills can be explicitly taught. But the andragogical approaches of design teachers are, as you will read in this book, many and varied and so we must be able to propose methods to evaluate the effectiveness of those teaching strategies.

THE CHALLENGES

It can be argued that design must always be a team [or collaborative] process. Design cannot advance without dialogue and collaboration: without criticism, feedback or confirmation. Design ideas cannot be tested and moved forward without the opinion of at least two people. Collaboration skills are essential in the design industry where large teams of professionals negotiate multiple design options. For instance, in the field of architecture the design process can include over fifty kinds of participants and consultants. Designers MUST be able to design as part of a team, yet design schools have historically largely failed to teach this essential professional competency. Moreover, research that evaluates strategies for teaching design collaboration or that puts foreword a conceptual framework for such evaluation has been minimal. Indeed, this book is the first that we are aware of that is dedicated to research on student collaboration in the context of design.

That is not to say that design schools do not require students to design collaboratively. On the contrary, the design students we surveyed in Australia and Canada have told us that there is far too much teamwork in their courses. In addition to the need to meet the requirements of the accrediting bodies of design courses, there are many reasons other than reducing assessment workloads for the ubiquitous use of teamwork assignments in design schools. Teamwork learning is seen as being more representative of work in a professional practice where design is nearly always a collaborative activity. Not only is collaborative design seen as more authentic, but it can result in ideas and knowledge being brought together for design outcomes that are superior to those that individual students might arrive at (Barber, 2004).

Educators also recognise that teamwork can lead to improvements in student learning due to a number of reasons: the development of interpersonal and critical thinking skills (Dochy, Segers, & Sluijsmans, 1999; Gokhale, 1995; Sluijsmans, Dochy, & Moerkerke, 1999), the promotion of inclusive learning (Cohen, 1994), moving students from passive to active learning (McGourty, Dominick, & Reilly, 1998), the ability to tackle more substantially-sized projects (Biggs, 1986), improved peer learning (van den Berg, Admiraal, & Pilot, 2006) and capacity for lifelong learning (Hanrahan & Isaacs, 2001).

But teamwork learning in design education is not without particular challenges requiring serious pedagogical consideration. In particular, three broad issues will be addressed in this book. First, many students leave academia without having been taught the knowledge and skills of how to design in teams. Second, the design of teaching, assessment and assignments needs to be informed by a clear understanding of what leads to effective teamwork (R Tucker, 2012). And third, in academic contexts there is a need to individually assess students, which means that most design assignments require individual submissions or, when students work in teams, require evaluation of individual contribution. This final issue is made even more difficult in design contexts because of the subjective nature of design evaluation and because of the difficulty of assigning authorship to a creative work, meaning that 'social-loafing' is difficult to detect. Thus, students state that by far their most crucial concern about teamwork is that they are assessed 'fairly' to recognise individual contribution, so that teammates cannot freeload on their efforts.

To sum up, this book will present research on how best to support through teaching and assessment the learning of teamworking skills in the design disciplines, and research on how to evaluate such teaching and assessment. We hope the studies will help design teachers develop and evaluate innovative approaches to collaborative studio-based learning in both multi-disciplinary and mono-disciplinary contexts.

THE CONTENT

This book is a collection of 15 studies investigating numerous and varied aspects of student collaboration and engagement when designing. Although many forms of collaboration are discussed, the majority of authors have focused on what they term *teamwork*. This prompts the question: is there a difference, when talking about the processes of designing and of learning how to design, between collaboration and teamwork? Certainly, all teamwork involves collaboration, but is all collaboration teamwork? One definition of teamwork used in the book, which differentiates group work from teamwork, would suggest not. For the distinction acknowledges the key difference between students collaborating on one assignment (teamwork) and students working together on individual assignments (group work). The process of designing commonly requires students to exercise both forms of collaboration.

An example of the use of both forms of collaboration can be drawn from architecture – the discipline that accounts for half of the 15 studies described in this book. When architecture students design collaboratively their work usually commences with context studies requiring them to collect information on a broad range of design influences. This may include a range of physical data (maps, views, climate, physiography, hydrology, flora and fauna, access etc.), and cultural data (design precedent, built heritage, habitation patterns, demographics etc.). To cover such a breadth of research, different areas of study are apportioned to different students, who then return to the group with this information to be shared. As this group work is carried out by individuals, it can also be assessed individually. If students are collaborating on one scheme, the proceeding design process is generally teamwork. The teamwork is then bookended by group work at the end of the project when students work on the production of presentation models and drawings. As the design phase of the collaborative process is normally teamwork, it follows that the majority of studies in this paper are focused on teamwork. But not all of this research is on teamwork, and indeed this is as it should be because a successful andragogy for teaching collaboration should always acknowledge, and sometime assesses, both teamwork and group work.

As its title implies, this book is also about engagement – what has been defined as representing both the time and energy students invest in educationally purposeful activities and the effort institutions devote to using effective educational practices (Kuh, 2003). While none of the 15 studies can be said to specifically focus on or measure levels of engagement, each of the ten case studies evaluate methods of engaging students with design learning, for designing collaboratively is by definition an activity that demands student engagement.

While *Enhancing and Assessing Group and Team Learning* was a learning and teaching investigation rather than research *per se*, it was designed to collect data that could be analysed. And so as well as teaching symposiums and focus groups with students, four survey instruments were distributed to teachers and students. The first two were pilot surveys circulated at the four partner universities participating in *Enhancing and Assessing Group and Team Learning* (Deakin University, The University of Newcastle, The University of Tasmania and Victoria University), and the second pair of surveys was nationally distributed to all design schools across Australia. The second student survey was also distributed to cohorts in the six Canadian schools of architecture. 28 teachers and 196 students completed the pilot surveys, and 40 teachers and 417 students completed the second pair of surveys. Data from *Enhancing and Assessing Group and Team Learning* directly informed two of the first five chapters of this book; including Chapter 1, which provides a conceptual *Framework for Understanding Effectiveness in Student Teams* – a framework that provides context for many of the other 13 chapters. Findings from the surveys have also been published elsewhere (see, for instance, (R. Tucker & Abbasi, in press).

CONTRIBUTORS AND THE ORGANISATION OF THE BOOK

During *Enhancing and Assessing Group and Team Learning*, symposiums were held with design-teachers who were passionate about teaching collaboration, and who represented the great majority of universities that teach design in Australia. Visits were also made to discuss the project with six schools in Canada:

- University of British Columbia School of Architecture and Landscape Architecture
- Faculty of Design at Kwantlen Polytechnic University
- University of Toronto, John H. Daniels Faculty of Architecture, Landscape and Design
- University of Waterloo, School of Architecture
- Université de Montréal École d'architecture
- McGill University School of Architecture, Montréal

From these exchanges grew a community-of-practice of sorts, or at least a connection between like-minded teachers. And while the call for chapters for this book was circulated globally, the vast majority of the 28 authors originate from this community. Indeed, this is the reason why 22 of the contributors are from Australian design schools, and 3 are from Canadian design schools.

The book is comprised of 15 chapters divided into three sections: (1) Teaching Collaboration – Team Building & the Andragogy of Teamwork in Design; (2) Evaluating Collaboration – Teaching Case Studies; and (3) Preparing for Collaboration – Learning for Teamwork in Professional Practice. Half of the chapters have a clear focus on the discipline of architecture. This was not an intentional bias, despite the fact that the editor studied, practiced and now teaches architecture. Indeed, we are confident that the findings of all the studies are relevant to all the design disciplines

The majority of chapters might be termed *case studies*, in that they focus on a particular case — a teaching strategy, a particular design course/subject, a particular design brief – that explores and evaluates a certain way of teaching students how to collaborate. The second section largely consists of case studies of undergraduate teaching. This section begins with three chapters evaluating examples of first-year teaching, and finishes with a study looking partly at a capstone unit (at the culmination of the second degree of an architecture program). In some of the other case studies, the cohorts discussed span disciplines and year levels. This is not the case, however, for the two case studies in the third section, which are both focused on teaching towards the end of programs that prepare students for professional collaboration in the workplace.

Section 1: Teaching Collaboration – Team Building and the Andragogy of Teamwork in Design

Focusing on teaching teamworking, in Chapter 1 Tucker proposes a 22-factor framework for understanding what impacts the effectiveness of teamwork when students are designing collaboratively. The framework is intended to help design educators integrate teamwork into their courses and better evaluate learning outcomes. The paper concludes with recommendations for teachers informed by the framework, covering aspects including: task structure, team formation, assessment and feedback, and teaching teamwork and team building skills. We have chosen this as our first chapter because it presents an overriding context for the many concerns discussed in the proceeding chapters.

Gavilanez, Ortlieb, and Carey report in Chapter 2 on integrating learning and teaching teamwork within an institutional learning outcomes framework. They write from the perspective of working at Kwantlen Polytechnic University, Canada – where teamwork learning has had an unusually core role, shaping curricula across the design disciplines. The research incorporates insights from beyond the design disciplines to engage student motivation in capability development, and the ways team teaching in design studios can contribute to the development of students' teamwork and design capabilities.

In Chapter 3, Lee, Ostwald and Gu examine the cognitive challenges facing design teams and educators of those teams. They argue that an improved understanding of creativity and teamwork in design can be arrived at by understanding the relationships between four issues associated with design cognition: (i) cognitive space, (ii) design strategy, (iii) design productivity and (iv) spatial representation.

Tucker focuses in Chapter 4 on a key problem when using online self-and-peer assessment to individualise design grades for team assignments, namely rater bias – the possibility of students being biased when assessing their own and their peers' contributions. Three rater-bias issues are considered: (1) self-overmarking; (2) gender bias and gender differences; and (3) out-group bias in the peer assessment of international students in multicultural cohorts. The chapter concludes with recommendations for design teachers.

In Chapter 5, Abbasi, Mills and Tucker deal with team building issues, in particular conflict in student design teams. A review of literature is presented to understand conflict within student design teams and explore strategies to manage it. Then, drawing upon the findings from two surveys offered to design students in 18 Australian higher education Institutions, recommendations are made for strategies to prepare students for conflict situations through a number of support models that design instructors might adopt, including both preventive and intervention strategies.

Section 2: Evaluating Collaboration – Teaching Case Studies

In Chapter 6, Crowther, Scott and Allen present the first of our Section 2 case studies. The study considers how novice design students, in Queensland, Australia, perceive design consideration. They evaluate a large common first year subject in which students work in mixed discipline groups of six to nine, on two sequential design projects. Survey and reflective journal data are used to determine the pedagogical success of learning about collaboration through the act of collaborating in project-based design. The study shows that groups that emotionally engaged with collaboration and collaborated more effectively achieved higher academic grades.

In Chapter 7, the second chapter focusing on self-and-peer-assessment, Palmer and Hall compare two offerings of a first-year engineering design subject at an Australian university in the state of Victoria. The subject provides an introduction to engineering design and professional practice through project-based problem solving, and uses group work with self-and-peer-assessment for individualization of marks. The authors find that the use of student group work for learning and practicing group work skills demands assessment that accounts for the effectiveness of group design activities as well as the quality of the resultant design artifact(s).

In Chapter 8, Crosby and Morgan also focus on self-and-peer-assessment, this time in a first year interdisciplinary design subject at an Australian university in New South Wales. Over two iterations of a subject, group work was reframed as critical collaboration; drawing from momentum in the design professions for more participatory and collaborative processes. The online self and peer assessment tool SPARKPlus was used to encourage critical thinking in students about collaboration by asking them to reflected on it following their experiences.

In Chapter 9, Garduño Freeman investigates how mobile technologies can facilitate new ways of sharing, experiencing and understanding people's connections with places. The chapter argues that CmyView, a mobile application and methodology that harnesses everyday practices such as photography and walking, can contribute to the core pedagogy of architectural education, the design studio. Garduño Freeman demonstrates that using CmyView enables students to work together, asynchronously, to understand how they each see their immediate urban environments in distinct ways. This helps students connect their own personal knowledge of architecture with their projective work in the design studio.

Bown, Gough and Tomitsch evaluate in Chapter 10 the teaching of participatory *design thinking*. Their students have visited local schools to engage children with design who are from areas of low socioeconomic status. The project aimed to draw on the value of service learning - learning through an engaged and socially meaningful task following principles of co-design. The authors show that service learning collaboration between university design departments and schools can mutually benefit both tertiary and secondary students.

In Chapter 11, Ang evaluates another model of participatory design learning, this time via intercultural collaboration between students from Australia and five Asian nations (Malaysia, Thailand, India, Indonesia, Sri Lanka). The chapter determines what elements of this model directly contribute to collaboration and student engagement. The potential for transformative learning and response to issues around global citizenship are discussed, along with future research.

In Chapter 12, Beyerle and Missingham present a comparative evaluation of two variations of teaching that structured individual student learning through group working. The teaching approaches draw on participatory design to develop collaborative learning and social-reflective practice in students. The authors describe means of developing creativity wherein a student's skills, projects, and ideas come out of, and are intersected by, a complexity of social processes, oppositions and the spectra that define them.

In Chapter 13, Rider and Bowen examine the outlines, process, and structure of design teaching at an US university that has engaged students from multiple colleges. Their approach to teamwork uses an established framework for assessing interdisciplinary teams. The chapter describes in detail the opportunities and challenges of integrating non-traditional teamwork exercises into design education processes.

Section 3: Preparing for Collaboration – Learning for Teamwork in Professional Practice

In Chapter 14, Wragg and Barnes evaluate the value of group learning for developing graduates' work-readiness and insight into professional practice. The two-capstone projects discussed stress collaborative problem-solving based on knowledge of the design context and the wider relational systems of industry practice. The authors show that project work approached from an expanded sense of the group, which delivers implementable proposals for clients, provides graduating students with authentic learning around the demands of practice.

Chapter 15 is appropriately positioned as our final chapter to reflect its position in the design curriculum of US architecture students transitioning to professionalism via the consideration of *Narratives of 'Becoming an Architect.'* In the study, Thompson explores themes of self-authorship in relation to collaborative design experiences. By providing a holistic understanding of the role collaboration might play in shaping individuals' identities, he aims ultimately to show how design educators might value and structure team-based design projects.

To conclude, we hope this book will appeal to and assist a global audience of educators, researchers and practitioners from across the design disciplines. We roughly estimate that there are 100,000 design teachers in 10,000 schools of design in the USA, Canada, UK, Australia and New Zealand alone. However, and crucially, many of the fundamental principles we present are applicable to teaching and learning across all fields of education, not just design. And so we ultimately hope that the book provokes further consideration of student collaboration and engagement across all disciplines, and encourages research that evaluates andragogical strategies for teaching teamworking.

Richard Tucker
Deakin University, Australia

REFERENCES

Barber, P. (2004). *Developing and assessing group design work: a case study.* Paper presented at the International Engineering and Product Design Education Conference, DELFT, Netherlands.

Biggs, J. (1986). Assessing student approaches to learning *'Research and development in higher education: volume 8: papers presented at the eleventh annual conference of the Higher Education Research and Development Society of Australasia, University of Auckland, Auckland, New Zealand, 24th-27th August 1985' edited by J Jones and M Hornsburgh, pages 241- 246. Sydney: Higher Education Research and Development Society of Australasia.*

Cohen, E. G. (1994). Restructuring the Classroom: Conditions for Productive Small Groups. *Review of Educational Research, 64*(1), 1–35. doi:10.3102/00346543064001001

Dochy, F., Segers, M., & Sluijsmans, D. M. A. (1999). The Use of Self-, Peer and Co-assessment in Higher Education: A review. *Studies in Higher Education, 24*(3), 331–350. doi:10.1080/03075079912 331379935

Gokhale, A. (1995). Collaborative Learning Enhances Critical Thinking. *Journal of Technology Education, 7*(1), 22–30. doi:10.21061/jte.v7i1.a.2

Hanrahan, S. J., & Isaacs, G. (2001). Assessing Self- and Peer-assessment: The students' views. *Higher Education Research & Development, 20*(1), 53–70. doi:10.1080/07294360123776

Kuh, G. D. (2003). What we're learning about student engagement from NSSE: Benchmarks for effective educational practices. *Change: The Magazine of Higher Learning, 35*(2), 24–32. doi:10.1080/00091380309604090

McGourty, J., Dominick, P., & Reilly, R. R. (1998, 4-7 November). *Incorporating Student Peer Review and Feedback into the Assessment Process.* Paper presented at the 28th Annual Frontiers in Education Conference, Tempe, Arizona. doi:10.1109/FIE.1998.736790

Ostwald, M. J., & Williams, A. (2008). *Understanding architectural education in Australasia. Retrieved from Strawberry Hills, N.S.W.: Schön, D. A. (1987). Educating the Reflective Practitioner.* San Francisco: Jossey-Bass.

Sluijsmans, D. M. A., Dochy, F., & Moerkerke, G. (1999). Creating a Learning Environment by Using Self-, Peer- and Co-Assessment. *Learning Environments Research, 1*(3), 293–319. doi:10.1023/A:1009932704458

Tucker, R. (2012). *Collaboration Down Under: investigating team learning in Australia in architecture and related design contexts* Paper presented at the Canada International Conference on Education (2012: Ontario, Canada) Ontario, Canada Tucker, R., & Abbasi, N. (in press). The Architecture of Teamwork: Examining Relationships between Teaching, Assessment, Student Learning and Satisfaction with Creative Design Outcomes *Journal of Architectural Engineering & Design Management.*

Valkenburg, R. (1998). Shared understanding as a condition for team design. *Automation in Construction, 7*(2-3), 111–121. doi:10.1016/S0926-5805(97)00058-7

van den Berg, I., Admiraal, W., & Pilot, A. (2006). Peer assessment in university teaching: Evaluating seven course designs. *Assessment & Evaluation in Higher Education, 31*(1), 19–36. doi:10.1080/02602930500262346

ENDNOTE

[1]   This project was led by myself (Tucker), and included three members of *Understanding Architectural Education* – Professor Michael Ostwald (who writes the foreword to this book), Professor Tony Williams and Louise Wallis.

Acknowledgment

The Australian Government Office for Learning and Teaching (OLT) provided support for the project that led to the book proposal submitted to IGI Global – *Enhancing and Assessing Group and Team Learning in Architecture and Related Design Contexts*. The views expressed in this book do not necessarily reflect the views of the Australian Government Office for Learning and Teaching. The editor would also like to acknowledge the contributions of the Editorial Advisory Board.

Peer feedback for the 15 chapters of this book was provided by a panel drawn from the 28 contributing authors and the EAB.

The editor would also like to thank the editorial and advisory contributions of Kim Roberts, and the unwavering support of Cat Tucker.

Section 1
Teaching Collaboration:
Team Building and the Andragogy of Teamwork in Design

Chapter 1
Teaching Teamwork in Design:
A Framework for Understanding Effectiveness in Student Teams

Richard Tucker
Deakin University, Australia

ABSTRACT

This chapter proposes an Input-Process-Output framework for understanding what impacts the effectiveness of teamwork when higher education students are collaborating on design assignments. The framework can help design educators integrate teamwork into their courses and better evaluate learning outcomes, and may also elucidate good practice for professional design teams. Explaining the genesis of the framework, the literature is assimilated on team effectiveness and predictors of team performance, including: definitions, dimensions and frameworks of team effectiveness in contexts far wider than design education. Informed by the challenges specific to teaching design, a 22-factor framework is proposed. The paper concludes with recommendations for teachers informed by the framework. The viability of the 22-factor model of team effectiveness is evidenced by national surveys across Australia, which are reported in summary here.

INTRODUCTION

Teamwork skills are essential in the design industry where practitioners negotiate often-conflicting design options in multi-disciplinary teams. Indeed, many of the bodies that accredit design courses explicitly list teamwork skills as essential attributes of design graduates e.g., the Australian Institute of Architects (AIA), Royal Institute of British Architects (RIBA), the National Council of Architectural Registration Boards (NCARB) of the United States and the Institution of Engineers, Australia (IEAust). In addition to the need of meeting the demands of the accrediting bodies, there are many reasons for the ubiquitous use of teamwork assignments in design schools. For instance, teamwork learning is seen as being representative of work in practice where design is nearly always a collaborative activity.

Learning and teaching in teamwork contexts in design education are not without particular challenges. In particular, two broad issues can be identified: first, many students leave academia without having been

DOI: 10.4018/978-1-5225-0726-0.ch001

taught the knowledge and skills of how to design in teams; second, teaching, assessment and assignment design need to be better informed by a clear understanding of what leads to effective teamwork and the learning of teamwork skills. In recognition of these issues, this paper sets out to elucidate the following questions: within the context of higher education design learning, what factors impact the effectiveness of student teamwork, and how might learning experiences be improved by recognising these factors? It is argued that an understanding of the factors that contribute to positive learning outcomes for students designing in teams will help design educators better support learning within teamwork contexts and the learning of teamworking skills.

In this chapter, a framework is proposed for understanding what impacts the effectiveness of student collaboration on team design assignments. The framework was first posited as part of a two-year Australian Office of Learning and Teaching (OLT) funded project: *Enhancing and assessing group and team learning in architecture and related design contexts*. The framework was informed by a literature review investigating what constitutes effective teamwork, what contributes to effectiveness in teams, what leads to positive design outcomes for teams, and what leads to effective learning in teams. The purpose of the framework is to identify the factors theoretically impacting effective teamwork, along with teaching responses and strategies that design educators might use to better support student learning. The validity of this multi-factorial *Framework of Effectiveness in Student Design Teams* was tested via surveys of educators' teaching practices and attitudes, and of students' learning experiences. 638 students and 68 teachers completed surveys: two pilot surveys for participants at the four partner institutions of the OLT funded project, which then informed two national surveys completed by participants from the majority of design schools across Australia. The data collected provided evidence for 22 factors impacting the effectiveness of student design teams. Pedagogic responses and strategies to these 22 teamwork factors were devised, tested and refined via case studies, focus groups and workshops. Analysis of the surveys also allowed for the determination of the relative importance of the 22 factors by analysing their correlations with ratings by teachers and students of their satisfaction with the outcomes of teamwork learning. Thus, the framework was not only intended to provide a checklist of the pedagogical issues that need to be considered, but it also allowed for the prioritization of these issues according to learning context and, importantly, to which of the issues have the greatest evidenced impacts on learning and team effectiveness. While the detailed description of this analysis and its findings is the subject of a previous publication ((Tucker et al. 2014)), and of a paper currently in authorship, a summary of these findings will be given in Section 7 of this chapter.

Instead, this chapter will focus on the theoretical basis of the framework. Thus, the literature will be reviewed in depth (Sections 1 to 4) on team effectiveness, approaches to defining highly performing teams and predictors of team performance. Considered in detail are five categories of factors impacting team performance that are informed by both workplace and educational contexts. As structured by these five categories, the *Framework of Effectiveness in Student Design Teams* proposed in Section 5 is based on an Input-Process-Output (IPO) model. The 22 factors, and teaching strategies they inform, are categorised according to three groups of input (Task Characteristics, Individual Level Factors and Team Level Factors), two groups of processes (Teaching Practice & Support Structures and Team Processes), and three categories of output (Task Performance, Teamwork Skills, and Attitudinal Outcomes). Eight of the 22 teamwork factors directly relate to the skills that need to be developed in students, one factor relates to design outputs, and the other 13 factors inform pedagogies that can be designed for better learning outcomes (see Figure 1).

Figure 1. IPO framework of effectiveness in student design teams

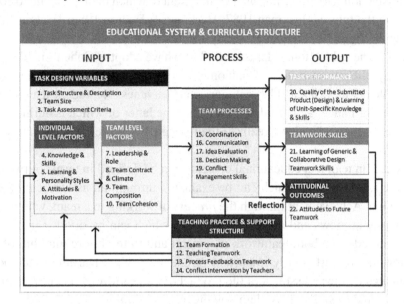

After a description of the framework, a summary of its pedagogic implications (Section 6) will be followed by recommendations (Section 7) summarised in table form and then discussed in greater detail pertaining to Teaching teamwork capabilities, Conflict and team diversity, and Pedagogic structure (Teamwork Learning across Curricula).

Before discussing the framework in detail, its genesis will be traced through its origins in the literature on team effectiveness. This explanation draws on a wide range of contexts, from work-teams in corporate settings, to professional design teams, to education outside of and within the design disciplines.

1. BACKGROUND: DEFINING TEAM EFFECTIVENESS

Irrespective of whether the context is professional or educational, team effectiveness can be defined in part by a team's final outcomes or 'production of designated products or services per specification' (Shea & Guzzo 1987b, 329). Team effectiveness in this sense is measured by the quality (and, in some instances, the quantity) of the team-produced outcomes. Yet such an outcome-focused definition overlooks the benefits of the processes that the team have undergone to produce the outcome (Hackman & Oldham 1980); processes that may in themselves be of value particularly in contexts of learning. Broader definitions of team effectiveness have been inclusive of notions of performance that relate to how well teams perceive they have worked together, and thus have considered the willingness of teams to collaborate together again. Thus, in a study of work teams, Sundstrom et al. (1990, 122) considered team effectiveness as consisting of 'performance' and 'viability,' where viability is the willingness of teammates to continue working together in the future. Similarly, Cohen (1997, 243) defines team effectiveness in terms of three dimensions, with the latter two seen to be equivalent to viability: (1) performance effectiveness or 'quantity and quality of outputs'; (2) team members' attitudes, and (3) behavioural outcomes. Other researchers have also referred to an attitudinal component of effectiveness that has two dimensions: (1)

team members' satisfaction with the team, and (2) the extent to which members tend to continue working together as a team in the future (Hackman 1987; Hackman & Walton 1986; Hackman & Morris 1975; Campion, Medsker & Higgs 1993; Hyatt & Ruddy 1997).

In the context of higher education, Adams et al. (2002) have adopted Cohen's model to describe team effectiveness by way of three measures of outcome: (1) performance, (2) behaviour and (3) attitude. While Deeter-Schmlez et al. (2002a, 117) categorise effectiveness in student teams according to two dimensions: 'task performance' and 'goal achievement,' the latter of which is defined as 'the extent to which team members believe they have realized their set goals' and reflects an 'internal evaluation of team effectiveness.'

Thus, effectiveness in teams in educational contexts can be defined in terms of two dimensions: (1) Performance on the assigned task, which can be evaluated through an assessment of *products* and/or *outcomes*; and (2) Goal Achievement through the *process* of working in a team, which can be evaluated through observation, interviews and questionnaires, and which can be divided into two aspects – (i) behaviour and (ii) attitudes (to both teamwork in general and to the future viability of the team). The processes of teamwork are particularly important for students when learning outcomes are expected beyond those evaluated by the assessment of the product of the teamwork; such as when, in design contexts, learning is required of skills in problem-solving, critical thinking, collaborative decision-making and conflict resolution. Clearly, a definition of team effectiveness in the context of design learning must address both measurable design outcomes and less quantifiable learning achievements gained via the process of designing in a team.

2. TEAM EFFECTIVENESS FRAMEWORKS IN PROFESSIONAL/WORK CONTEXTS

Frameworks for understanding team effectiveness have been developed around the definitions above. The 'Input-Process-Output (IPO) framework' is built upon a basic assumption that the group interaction process mediates between *input factors* – features of the team, the team task and its work context – and the *output* of the team (e.g. McGrath 1964; Cummings 1981; Gladstein 1984; Driskell, Hogan, and Salas 1987; Hackman 1987). In the IPO model, there are three levels of input variables: individual-level (i.e. member skills, attitudes and personality characteristics); group-level (structure, cohesion and group size); and environment-level (task characteristics, rewards and environmental stress). These input variables determine team outputs: performance outcomes (i.e. quality and time to reach solutions); and attitudinal outcomes (i.e. members' satisfaction and attitude change) resulting from team processes (Hackman 1987).

Adopting an IPO structure, Salas et al. (2004) developed an 'integrative framework' that acknowledges the roles of organizational context and, importantly, team member training through the inclusion of a feedback loop that informs subsequent teamwork. Here, four types of interrelated inputs shape team processes: individual, team and task characteristics, and work structure (Tannenbaum, Beard, & Salas 1992).

The 'ecological framework' widens the notion of a feedback loop by presenting a dynamic interrelationship between team effectiveness and the organizational context, its boundaries, and ongoing team development within that context. Building upon what is termed an 'ecological' perspective (Sundstrom and Altman 1989), work teams are considered within the environment of a symbiotic interrelationship between external surroundings and internal processes. Departing from the IPO approach (Gladstein 1984; McGrath 1964, 1984), this framework reflects the idea of team effectiveness as a continuous 'process' rather than an 'end-state' (Sundstrom, De Meuse, and Futrell 1990, 122).

Drawing upon the three frameworks above, how a team performs in the production of its outputs can be seen to be impacted by four groups of factors: three input factors – (1) task-related; (2) team- or group-level; (3) individual-level – and then (4) process-related factors. We shall now consider higher education research in relation to these four categories of factors.

3. FOUR CATEGORIES OF FACTORS IMPACTING TEAM EFFECTIVENESS IN EDUCATIONAL CONTEXTS

We have seen that the general literature on team effectiveness outside of educational contexts suggests that four categories of factors impact team outputs. Here we briefly consider the literature on team effectiveness in educational contexts to see how the four factors can be understood within the context of student teamwork learning. Through this it will become clear that each of these factors can be subdivided into sub-factors, some of which are pedagogical, some of which are related to the characteristics of teams, and some of which are related to the characteristics of the team members. Each will be numbered (Factor X) according to which factor it correlates with in our proposed 22-factor framework.

3.1 Task-Related

This category includes variables related to the design of team assignments, including the duration of the project, the sequences of tasks and their type and complexity. In relation to student teams, team size and criteria for assessing the products and outcomes of teamwork need to be examined.

3.1.1 Team Duration (Factor 1)

Research provides evidence for a relationship between team duration and the effectiveness of intervention strategies and team training. Team longevity has been found to be significantly associated with best team experiences, indicating that there is a higher chance of success for teams that are together longer (Bacon, Stewart, & Silver 1999b). Bradley et al. (2003) found that the effectiveness of intervention strategies to improve team performance is affected by the duration of team projects. In short-term teams (with the expectation of disbanding once the task was completed), interventions to encourage interpersonal relationships to increase team satisfaction and performance are far less effective when compared to long-term teams (that work together for an extended period of time and have the expectation of working together on future tasks) (Bradley, White, & Mennecke 2003). The results of a study by Hamlyn-Harris et al. (2006) showed a correlation between students' teamwork satisfaction and longer term mixed-gender teams. Similarly, Wong et al. (2004) suggest that in longer term projects members have the opportunity to become familiar with each other, allowing them to better capitalize on the socio-emotional communication skills of females.

3.1.2 Team Size (Factor 2)

Research on the relationship between team size and team effectiveness is mixed, sometimes conflicting, and findings vary between contexts. Some studies suggest an inverse relationship between team size and team performance, and decrease in individual performance as team size increases (Pfaff & Huddleston 2003; Ingham et al. 1974; Feichtner & Davis 1984; Salas et al. 1999). Others have found no significant relationship between team size and team performance (e.g. Bacon, Stewart, & Silver 1999b; Bacon, Stewart, & Stewart-Belle 1998). Watkin (2005) states that optimum team size is closely linked to the type of task or team project. Bacon et al. (1999b, 484) similarly acknowledge that not one size of team fits all tasks, stating that 'for some projects a group size of five is too small, whereas for others a size of three is too many.'

With design cohorts, the optimum team size varies with the context of teamwork. In studio based learning, when the required output is a designed artefact, we have found that three to five students appear to learn and design more effectively (Tucker et al. 2014).

3.1.3 Task Design (Factor 3)

Task design has a considerable influence on team processes, and should be clear about what is expected with regards to both product (the design artefact) and process (teamwork skills) (Tucker et al. 2014). The results of a study by Bacon et al. (1999b, 473) provided support for two hypothesis related to task design variables: (1) 'best teams will be more likely to say the instructor gave them sufficient instructions on outcomes (what the team was to submit or present) than will worst teams;' and (2) 'best teams will be more likely to say the instructor gave them sufficient instructions on process (how the team should perform its tasks) than will worst teams.' Task design should also foster 'positive interdependence' (Johnson & Johnson 1992), or what has been termed 'the quintessential quality that defines collaboration and transforms group work into teamwork' (Cuseo 2000, 7), by demanding both groupwork and teamwork.

3.2 Individual-Level

In this category, factors that individual members bring to the team are considered. These might include: age, gender, social and cultural backgrounds, level of education, motivation, attitude and personality type. For student teams, individual learning style is also considered an important variable.

3.2.1 Motivation, Attitude and Personality Type (Factors 5 and 6)

Drawing upon Morgan's findings that 'almost half the perceived problems of group work could be allocated to the 'poor motivation – general category'' (2002 cited in Watkins 2005, 5), Watkins (2005) refers to 'motivation' in individual students as an essential factor for student groups to work effectively.

Yellen et al. (1995) found a correlation between team members' personality types and group decision making, with extroverts being more effective than introverts for they are more comfortable about giving their opinions. Individual difference in terms of preference for teamwork was examined by Barr et al. (2005, 81) in a study of the 'Lone Wolf' phenomenon; 'identified by a preference to work alone, a dislike of group process and the ideas of others, and a proclivity to see others as less capable and effective.' The findings suggest the inclusion of lone wolves has negative impacts on team performance (Barr, Dixon,

& Gassenheimer 2005). In another study, Freeman (1996) found that an individual's attitude towards teamwork influenced Grade Point Average. While much research has considered the impact of learning styles on individual learning processes, only a few studies have considered how learning styles influence teamwork. Gardner and Korth (1998) found significant differences between learning styles and how teammates perceived group work; such that, accommodators, convergers and divergers preferred group work, whereas assimilators did not. While Yazici (2005) found that student's 'collaborative orientation' complemented their participation and helped them to compete, which in turn increased team performance. The influence of learning style was also found to vary with educational experience, gender and major, such that graduate students were more collaborative and independent learners (Yazici 2005).

3.3 Team- or Group-Level

In this category, factors related to a team or group as a whole are considered, including team composition, diversity, cohesiveness and shared goals, team climate and trust.

3.3.1 Team Composition (Factor 9)

While motivation or drive might be desired of all team members, uniformity of other individual characteristics might make for poor teamwork. Indeed, most researchers generally recommend teams composed of individuals with diverse personal characteristics i.e. personality types, gender, learning styles, attitudes and preferences (Martin and Paredes 2004; Bradley and Hebert 1997; Harrison et al. 2002).

Some researchers have studied the effect of the personality-type composition of teams on team performance (Bradley & Hebert 1997; Gorla & Lam 2004; Peeters-Baars 2006a; Peeters et al. 2006b). White (1984) suggested diversity in personality as a characteristic of successful teams. Gender mix within teams has been found to lead to a higher level of student satisfaction with teamwork for long-term projects (Hamlyn-Harris et al. 2006). Other research suggests that effects of 'surface-level' diversity i.e. age, race and gender, are weakened as team members continue working together and collaboration increases (e.g. Harrison et al. 2002). In another study, Jules (2007) found that demographic diversity may result in unfavourable team processes and outcomes, whereas diversity of team members' psychological characteristics, such as learning style, can lead to increased team effectiveness through diversity of thought.

3.3.2 Cohesiveness and Shared Goals (Factor 11)

In a study of the relationships between team conflict, conflict management, cohesion, and team effectiveness, Tekleab et al. (2009) found that team cohesion is positively related to perceived performance, satisfaction with the team, and team viability. Existence of a clear team purpose, set by the team itself, was found as a minimum requirement for effective student teams in an engineering classroom (Adams, Simon, & Ruiz 2002). Similarly, Deeter-Schmelz et al. (2002a) found that established shared goals have positive impacts on student team effectiveness. Furthermore, research evidences a strong connection between shared goals and task performance in teams (Yeatts and Hyten 1998). As Deeter-Schmelz et. al. (2002b) discuss, such research has shown: higher mean performance for teams with goals in comparison with teams with no goals (O'Leary-Kelly, Martocchio, & Frink 1994); goal setting leading to improved product quality (Longenecker, Scazzero, & Stansfield 1994); and a strong link between performance, team established goals, and level of agreement among members (Scott and Townsend 1994). Goal achievement is suggested to be more likely when members have a collective understanding of and shared commitment to team goals (Larson & LaFasto 1989; Erez & Zidon 1984; Locke & Latham 1990), and several researchers have highlighted the importance to team success of a shared vision (Burningham & West 1995) and a clear understanding of team objectives (Fowler 1995).

3.3.3 Team Climate and Trust (Factor 8)

A climate of inclusiveness and freedom, or what is referred to 'psychological safety,' is found to be conducive to teamwork (Adams, Simon, & Ruiz 2002). In a study of engineering student teams, psychological safety or 'an environment that allows members to take risk' was found as a minimum requirement for an effective team (Adams, Simon, & Ruiz 2002, unpaged). Consistent with this study, Dreu and Vianen (2001) suggest that team effectiveness is dependent upon opportunities provided for team members to safely voice opinions and ideas (e.g. Hackman 1987; Podsakoff, Aheame, & MacKenzie 1997; Steiner 1972; West, Borrill, & Unsworth 1998). Similarly, in research on university students, intra group trust and leadership emerged as two significant indicators of team effectiveness (Casperz, Wu, & Skene 2003).

3.4 Process-Related

This category of factors includes both internal and external processes affecting how team members interact and collaborate. Internal processes occur within a team, and include communication, collaboration, knowledge-sharing and conflict management between team members (Cohen 1997). In the context of education, external processes include teaching practices and support structures i.e. team formation methods, teaching teamwork skills, conflict interventions, and ongoing evaluation, feedback and assessment processes.

3.4.1 Internal Processes (Factors 15 to 19)

In a study of engineering student teams, Adams et al. (2002) found 'the existence of interdependence among team members' and 'the ability of members to resolve conflict' as two minimum requirements of a highly effective team. Etroo (2011, ix) refers to 'interdependency' as a major factor 'responsible for effective teamwork and team performance in the construction industry.' Dreu and Vianen (2001) found that team effectiveness improved when team members helped each other and coordinated activities together (e.g. Hackman 1987; Podsakoff, Aheame, & MacKenzie 1997; Steiner 1972; West, Borrill, & Unsworth 1998). In a study of the impacts of trust, task conflict, and collaboration on members' perceptions of team effectiveness across time, Chicchio (2011, 79, 87) concluded that collaboration is 'a key mechanism to integrated design teams' effectiveness,' which 'boosts the positive effect of trust and dampens the negative effect of task conflict, offering the opportunity to substantially improve performance.' Other researchers have similarly referred to 'open communication' as a characteristic of effective teams (Etroo 2011). Leadership and role-structure strategies are other internal processes that impact the performance of teams (Derbie 2008; Ferrante, Green, & Forster 2006).

The research provides evidence for relationships between conflict management, team performance and satisfaction with team experiences (Kankanhalli, Tan, & Wei 2007; Jehn 1995). While task conflict was often found to positively influence team performance, relationship conflict was linked to negative impacts on team performance (de Dreu 1997; Jehn 1995; Jehn 1997; Pelled, Eisenhardt, & Xin 1999;

Simons and Peterson 2000). The findings of a longitudinal study carried out by Tekleab et al. (2009) suggested that conflict management has a direct, positive effect on team cohesion and team cohesion is also positively related to perceived performance, satisfaction with the team and team viability. Behfar et al. (2008, 170) found that student teams that improved or maintained top performance over time adopted three common conflict resolution tendencies: 'focusing on the content of interpersonal interactions,' 'explicitly discussing reasons behind any decisions,' and 'assigning work to members who have the relevant task expertise'.

3.4.2 External Processes (Factors 11 to 14)

Four main external team processes are team formation, teaching of teamwork skills, conflict intervention and the provision of feedback and assessment. Three main approaches to team formation in educational contexts include self-selection, random assignment, and teacher assignment (Bacon, Stewart, & Silver 1999a). Three main benefits have been identified in 'self-selection': 'higher initial cohesion' (Strong & Anderson 1990); more effective interpersonal conflict management (Mello 1993); and improved team productivity (Gosenpud & Washbush 1991). Self-selected teams also have disadvantages: they are overly homogeneous (Jalajas & Sutton 1984-1985), thus lacking the advantages that diversity may offer (Bacon, Stewart, & Stewart-Belle 1998) and can lead to an inadequate combination of skills (Mello 1993). Another problem with self-selected teams is the tendency for stronger students to seek one another out, 'leaving the weaker ones to shift for themselves, which works to no one's benefit' (Oakley et al. 2004, 11). This leads to teams comprised of lesser ability students performing poorly in line with the 'self-fulfilling prophecy in the classroom' (Tucker & Rollo 2006). Thus some researchers recommend teacher assignment (e.g. Fiechtner & Davis 1992; Oakley et al. 2004; Tucker and Rollo 2006), to ensure well-functioning diverse groups within which 'the weak students get the benefit of seeing how good students approach assignments and they may also get some individual tutoring, while the strong students who do the tutoring may benefit even more' (Oakley et al. 2004)

Hamlyn-Harris et al. (2006) found a relationship between satisfaction with teamwork learning experiences, how teamwork skills are taught, students' levels of experience, and task duration. A two-day teamwork skills workshop was found to have a significant correlation with teamwork satisfaction for students in the final stages of their degree working on an eight-month project (Hamlyn-Harris et al. 2006). Similarly, significant correlations were found between design student satisfaction with the teaching of teamwork knowledge and skills and satisfaction with both teamwork outcomes and processes (Tucker & Abbasi 2014); a finding consistent with a previous study (Chapman & Auken 2001).

Conflict intervention is both an internal and external process: with on the one hand external intervention, usually by teachers in educational contexts, and on the other – internal conflict management carried out within the team by team members. While the importance of managing conflict in design teams is universally recognised (Behfar et al. 2008; Slimani et al. 2006; Klein 1991), there are conflicting suggestions about how precisely to deal with conflict. Some research suggests teams should be aided externally in resolving conflict early, while others suggest that a specific focus brought to conflict can have negative consequences by distracting team members from their tasks. Thus 'avoiding responses, which are associated with high team functioning and effectiveness because … allow team members to pursue task performance' (Dreu & Vianen 2001, 309). Scott (2010) suggests that when a work-based team requires external help in a conflict situation, managers can adopt one of four approaches; 'judging', 'counselling', 'negotiation' and 'mediation,' but that mediation is the most effective.

In teamwork assignments it is possible to assess students individually or to award a team mark. In design contexts, whichever of these two assessment models is used has a significant impact on the student learning experience (Tucker 2008). Transparency and perceived fairness of assessment is an important and contested issue in team design contexts for three primary reasons: first, designing collaboratively is a highly emotive activity; second, it is near impossible to avoid subjectivity in the evaluation of design (Christiaans 2002); and, third, the emotive nature of designing, and the difficulty of evaluating design, is further charged by the challenge of assigning authorship to a jointly-created work, meaning that 'free-riding' is difficult to detect.

Free-riding, otherwise known as social loafing, means that teamwork is subject to the 'Ringelmann effect,' where the combined output of the team is less than would be expected from combining the output of individual team members (Kravitz & Martin 1986). Free-riding may be due to problems of team discipline and/or domination of the team by the most assertive members (Brown 1995), meaning that teammates who are academically weaker or less motivated to contribute may become 'passengers' (Goldfinch & Raeside 1990). The problem of free-riding poses the question of how to encourage active participation by all team members (Cohen 1994). Self-and-peer-assessment (SAPA), often carried out via online systems, is a commonly used tool for discouraging free-riding by individualising student results from teamwork assignments (Freeman & McKenzie 2002; Goldfinch & Raeside 1990; Walker 2001; Raban & Litchfield 2006), as well as a means for providing formative feedback (Davies 2000; Mulder and Pearce 2007; Topping 1998). Moreover, iterative peer assessment has been shown to promote cooperative learning in architectural design studios (Shih, Hu, & Chen 2006).

Michaelsen et al. (2002) and Goltz et al. (2008) suggest that an essential element of team learning is frequent and immediate feedback on team processes or on how students might improve their teamwork skills. In the design studio, such feedback should designed to improve: shared understanding through effective oral and graphic communication of design ideas, communication that is inclusive of all team members, leadership, management, delegation, consensus seeking and the capacity to effectively handle conflict (Tucker & Abbasi 2014). Research suggests that feedback on teamwork should be continuous, occurring at multiple points during an assignment (Brooks & Ammons 2003; McKendall 2000). Hansen (2006) includes process feedback on teamwork as one of ten methods for improving the performance of student teams as well as the satisfaction of the students in those teams.

Before leaving the literature on team effectiveness in the context of higher education, it is worth noting the study work of Ohland and colleagues, who have describe the development of a web-based instrument that collects and analyses self- and peer-evaluation data (Ohland et al. 2012). It measures the same categories as the "Comprehensive Assessment of Team Member Effectiveness (CATME)" instrument developed by Loughry, Ohland, and Moore (Loughry, Ohland, & Moore 2007). The "instrument uses a behaviorally anchored rating scale to measure team-member contributions in five areas based on the team effectiveness literature" (Ohland et al. 2012, 1). The researchers found 29 specific types of team- member contributions "that clustered into five broad categories (Contributing to the Team's Work, Interacting with Teammates, Keeping the Team on Track, Expecting Quality, and Having Relevant Knowledge, Skills, and Abilities) (Ohland et al. 2012, 612). These "contributions" can be seen to be analogous to some of the individual level factors and team processes posited in our own framework. As the study focuses on peer evaluation, and thus team member effectiveness, it does not take into account the impact of pedagogy on team effectiveness.

4. TEAM EFFECTIVENESS IN PROFESSIONAL DESIGN COLLABORATION

Having reviewed the factors identified in the literature impacting, first, team effectiveness in general and, second, effectives in student teams; to complete our understanding of effectiveness in student design teams the factors specifically impacting the performance of design teams will be now discussed. Though it should be noted there is a paucity of research in this area.

Many of the characteristics of highly functioning teams, such as open communication (Derbie 2008; Etroo 2011), shared goals (Adams, Simon, & Ruiz 2002; Deeter-Schmelz, Kennedy, & Ramsey 2002a; Yeatts & Hyten 1998; Longenecker, Scazzero, & Stansfield 1994; Scott & Townsend 1994; O'Leary-Kelly, Martocchio, & Frink 1994) and positive interdependence (Campion, Medsker, & Higgs 1993; Campion, Papper, & Medsker 1996; Adams, Simon, & Ruiz 2002) are clearly applicable to design teams. Nevertheless, design teams face uniquely challenging issues. The measurement of design team effectiveness has proven to be a complicating matter, for while time and costs may be measured objectively, measuring quality remains problematic due especially to the difficulty of assigning the quality evaluator (i.e. design team members, design team leaders, supervisors, clients or independent raters) (Peeters et al. 2008, 440). In other words, it is difficult to objectively define what constitutes quality in a design or the process that created it.

In professional practice, where design collaboration is more often than not multi-disciplinary, design processes, and hence performance and team effectiveness, are significantly affected by tight deadlines, high technological standards, designers with strong influence on the team (Hales 1993; Cross & Clayburn-Cross 1996; Dorst 2003) and problems resulting from interactions of designers from different knowledge backgrounds and expertise (Busby 2001). Previous studies have provided insights into behavioural aspects of design collaboration by focusing on topics such as communication (Eckert & Stacey 2001; Stempfle & Badke-Schaub 2002), negotiation (Stumpf and McDonnell 2002), reflection (Valkenburg & Dorst 1998) and social processes (Cross & Clayburn-Cross 1996). In a study of factors influencing product development in collaborative design, Badke-Schaub and Frankenberger (2002) identify four mechanisms contributing the most to successful solutions: (1) experience and competence of the designers in the team; (2) availability of information (which is in part determined by the experience of the designers); (3) communication; and (4) group climate (which supports the open exchange of ideas between the designers and provides the opportunity for informal talk).

5. A FRAMEWORK FOR UNDERSTANDING EFFECTIVENESS IN STUDENT DESIGN TEAMS

In line with research and practice in the fields of work teams and organizational management (e.g. Cohen 1997; Sundstrom, De Meuse, & Futrell 1990), and in particular emerging research in educational contexts (e.g. Adams, Simon, & Ruiz 2002; Deeter-Schmelz, Kennedy, & Ramsey 2002a), a framework for understanding effectiveness in student design teams must include dimensions relating to both the products and processes of collaboration. Thus, the degree to which a student design team has performed well must be seen as a combination of (1) the quality of their final design (2) how effective the team processes have been. While the quality of the final product of teamwork may be readily assessed via criteria informed by learning objectives when designing team tasks, assessing the quality of team processes proves to be challenging. The difficulty of assessing the process-related dimensions of teamwork are linked to difficulties in defining for them criteria/standards/indicators and methods of evaluating the quality of team processes against those criteria. This issue will be briefly revisited in *Teaching teamwork capabilities* section of our recommendations.

We propose two broad categories of indicators for effective team processes in student teams. First, attitudinal outcomes i.e. students' attitudes to future teamwork and willingness or motivation to take on teamwork in the future (e.g. Hackman 1987; Hackman & Walton 1986; Hackman & Morris 1975; Sundstrom, De Meuse, & Futrell 1990; Campion, Medsker, & Higgs 1993; Hyatt & Ruddy 1997). Second, teamwork skills, which can be divided into two categories: (a) the particular skills needed to design collaboratively i.e. idea selection and development, shared understanding through graphic communication (Valkenburg 1998), and reflective practice (Schön 1987); (b) those skills commonly needed for group-and-team-work, irrelevant of field i.e. leadership, management, delegation, consensus seeking and conflict resolution.

To inform further pedagogic interventions, we have proposed a 22-factor model of team effectiveness (Figure 1) that combines the three types of framework reviewed earlier - (1) Input-Process-Output (IPO), (2) Integrative, and (3) Ecological. Three key interrelated categories of input are considered: (1) task-related factors; (2) individual level factors; and (3) team level factors.

Task-design variables include the types of tasks, their complexity, the structure of tasks (how they relate to each other, their durations and sequences), and the assessment criteria evaluating the quality of outcomes, which provide the grounds for enactment of individual and team level factors. Individual-level factors include the knowledge and skills that students bring to the team project, their learning styles, personalities, attitudes to learning, collaboration, motivation and expectations, which influence team level factors. Team-level factors include leadership approach and role structure, team contracts (which establishes rules and norms of teamwork), team composition (i.e. the degree of diversity or homogeneity of team members), team climate, shared goals and cohesiveness.

The three categories of 'Input' influence 'Outcome', both directly and indirectly through team processes (e.g. Cohen 1997). The group of influences called Internal Team Processes include coordination of tasks and responsibilities, communication, brainstorming, idea selection, decision-making, problem solving and conflict resolution. In addition to team internal processes, the role of external processes is acknowledged under the category of predictors called Teaching Practice and Support Structure, which includes team formation approaches, training and the explicit teaching of teamwork skills, monitoring and coaching of team processes, and conflict resolution interventions. These external processes have direct impacts on individual and team level factors as well as on team processes.

The framework consists of three categories of 'Outcome': (1) task performance i.e. the quality of the submissions and students' knowledge and skills of the content; (2) teamwork skills i.e. generic teamwork skills and collaborative design skills; and (3) attitudinal outcomes i.e. attitudes to teamwork and motivation for future collaboration. Our framework describes team effectiveness as a dynamic process rather than an end product or end-state (e.g. Sundstrom, De Meuse, & Futrell 1990; Sundstrom & Altman 1989). Thus, the two groups of outcome, teamwork skills and attitudinal outcomes influence the individual level factors of the student's next cycle of teamwork experience, and through this inform team level factors for subsequent team projects. The broader educational system and curricula structure are considered as the context within which student the team effectiveness cycle performs (e.g. Kozlowski & Ilgen 2006).

6. THE RELATIVE IMPORTANCE OF THE 22 FACTORS

As previously mentioned, a two-year Australian Office of Learning and Teaching (OLT) funded project developed and tested the viability of the *Framework of Effectiveness in Student Design Teams* via national surveys of teachers and of students across Australia, teaching symposiums, workshops and focus groups with students. These activities included the majority of design schools in Australia and covered the breadth of the design disciplines. The survey and its analysis are not the subject of this chapter and so are only referred to in passing here to elucidate the implications and understanding of the 22-factor framework. The survey, data collection and analysis methods and participants are detailed elsewhere (Tucker et al. 2014).

The survey allowed us to determine the relative importance of the 22 factors by analysing their correlations with student ratings for the statement: "I was satisfied with my teamwork learning experiences in this course/unit/subject." As we might have expected, the three outcomes of teamwork – the quality of the submitted design, the learning of teamwork skills and future attitudes – most strongly correlated with satisfaction with team learning. It is worth noting, however, that student satisfaction with their teamwork learning experience more strongly correlated with how highly they rated their learning of teamwork skills than with their satisfaction with design outputs. In a sense, this shows that students more clearly identified positive learning experiences with improved teamworking capabilities than with a successful end design-product, which is an encouraging finding for design educators aiming to teach teamworking. Team communication and cohesion were the factors rated by students as the next most important. Then came the pedagogic factors, with assessment rated the most important factor for teachers to design well, and the teaching of teamwork, task design and conflict intervention also seen as important.

RECOMMENDATIONS

From the findings of the survey and other activities of the OLT funded project that developed and tested the *Framework of Effectiveness in Student Design Teams,* we have published the following general recommendations for design teachers in relation to each of the 22 factors (Table 1 (Tucker et al. 2014, 19-23)).

While teachers should consider broad teaching strategies that acknowledge each of the 22 factors, it will be impractical in most circumstances to attend directly to all 22. Indeed, we only recommend such an exhaustive response to the framework if the subject being taught is one primarily focusing on teaching teamwork skills rather than, as is the case for most design contexts, when teamwork is merely the context for learning other skills and knowledge. Thus, for most team design assignments we suggest a pedagogic focus on the following three areas:

1. **Teaching Teamwork Capabilities:** For consistent and measurable outcomes in relation to successful teamwork, good design outcomes, improved teamwork capabilities and positive attitudes to future teamwork, design students should be taught the following six teamwork process skills: (1) coordination of tasks and responsibilities; (2) communication via speaking, writing, drawing, modelling; (3) idea generation, evaluation and selection; (4) decision making; (5) leadership; and (6) conflict management. Teachers need also to carefully design assessment and assignments to facilitate and encourage effective teamwork and the learning of these skills. While teamwork process skills are learned collaboratively, the educational intention is that individuals can apply these skills

Teaching Teamwork in Design

Table 1. Recommended teaching responses and strategies

Factor	Description	Recommended Teaching Responses/Strategies
Task Design Variables		
1. Task Structure and Description	Task structure i.e. duration, sequence and interrelationship of tasks has a considerable influence on team processes. Students should be clear about what is expected with regards to both product (the design artefact) and process (teamwork skills)	• Design task to foster positive interdependence. • Structure design assignments to require both independent individual contributions and collaboration. • Provide teams with an adequate description of outcomes and processes.
2. Team Size	Task structure and assessment need to be considered in relation to the size of team. There can be a relationship between the effectiveness of teamwork processes and team size	• Explore optimum team size in relation to task type. • Promote smaller teams in a 'conjunctive task', where every team member needs to contribute, to facilitate equal participation (Watkins 2005). • Consider three to five members, unless a large design task can be subdivided into appropriate smaller design packages. • Only expand to larger teams (six or above) at Masters level, when students have developed teamwork skills.
3. Task Assessment Criteria	Task assessment criteria need to be determined taking into account issues such as assessment of individual contributions, students' perception of fair assessment and assessment of both product and process of teamwork.	Differentiate between: • Task performance i.e. submitted product – usually a designed artefact; and • Teamwork skills. • Adopt appropriate methods of evaluating teamwork processes i.e. students' reflective statements and self-and-peer-assessment (SAPA). • Apply methods to ensure students' perceptions of fair assessment e.g. the use SAPA. • X
Individual Level Factors		
4. Knowledge and Skills	The differing levels of knowledge and skills in students about the task can influence the team performance and also the comparative performance of teams in cohorts.	Encourage a variety of skills and prior knowledge in all teams through adopting a teacher-assigned approach to team formation
5. Learning and Personality Styles	Learning styles of students can be reflected by student engagement in teamwork and may influence the types of task that teammates choose and how well they are able to complete them. The personality type of teammates can affect team processes with regards to many dimensions of communication.	• Encourage a diversity of personality types and learning styles in design teams. • Ask students to complete a simple learning style test and discuss the results at the outset of teamwork
6. Attitudes and Motivation	Attitudes to teamwork informed by previous experiences can correlate with motivation and thus engagement with team processes.	Require students to reflect on previous positive and negative experiences of teamwork at the outset of teamwork
Team Level Factors		
7. Leadership and Role	The leadership approach that student teams adopt and the ways that roles are structured and assigned in a team have impacts on the performance of teams.	• Assist students to assign roles within their teams at regular intervals and at different stages of the design process. • Encourage students to reflect on their roles at the end of each project stage. • Require students to discuss appropriate approaches to leadership in their teams.
8. Team Contract and Climate	The team contract, which establishes agreed ways of working together, can inform the leadership approach, role structure, team climate, shared goals and methods for dealing with conflict. Team climate determines how freely teammates are able to share opinions and ideas.	• Assist students to draw up and sign a team contract. • Promote a team climate of inclusiveness, freedom, interpersonal trust and mutual respect through communicating with students and encouraging them to adhere to the team contract.

continued on next page

Table 1. Continued

Factor	Description	Recommended Teaching Responses/Strategies
Task Design Variables		
9. Team Composition	Team composition including the range of individual differences in terms of age, gender, cultural background, past experience, personality and learning styles not only influences team processes and hence the team performance, but also the comparative performance of teams in cohorts.	• Ensure diversity in teams with regards to gender, culture and past experiences through adopting appropriate team formation methods. • Provide support for students to cope with diversity in teams.
10. Team Cohesion	Team cohesion is defined as "a dynamic process which is reflected in the tendency for a group to stick together and remain united in the pursuit of its goals and objectives" (Carron 1982, p. 124).	• Ensure team cohesion through positive interdependence. In addition to structuring tasks to allow for independent individual contributions and demand design collaboration, you can: (1) Apply 'jig-sawing" team membership (See (Frey, Fisher et al. 2009)); (2) Promote student-led reciprocal teaching; and (3) Encourage the use by teams of project work plans.
Teaching Practice and Support Structure		
11. Team Formation	Teachers have two basic ways to form teams: by forming the teams themselves or by allowing students to self-select. Both ways have pros and cons that teachers and students should be aware of.	• Consider forming single-sex teams, if a team cannot have at least two members of one sex. • For culturally diverse teams, try not to isolate single members of a culture that is different from the rest of their teammates. • Consider the location or where students live to facilitate out-of-class meetings. • Closely examine the consequences of team formation methods before adopting one.
12. Teaching Teamwork	Students are asked to work in teams in a large proportion of design assignments, but in most cases are taught little if anything about teamwork.	• Teach student both generic teamwork skills and collaborative design skills. • Provide basic training in teamwork skills for teaching staff. • Acknowledge the different characteristics of graduate and undergraduate students and determine the teaching style that suits each cohort.
13. Process Feedback on Teamwork	Team processes should be monitored continuously so that feedback can be regular and on both the product (the designed artefact) and the team processes that created the product.	• Create interim steps in a team design assignment for discussing individual and team progress. • Use SAPA or face-to-face discussions regularly as a tool for process feedback encouraging team members to give feedback on their own and their teammates' performance.
14. Conflict Intervention by the teacher	Even when taught conflict resolution skills, students need to be offered intervention strategies for problems that escalate. Teachers can model effective conflict resolution through such strategies.	• Offer teams intervention forums and try to resolve conflict at the team level. • Consider relocating individuals to other teams only as a very last resort e.g. in cases of bullying and harassment. • Preferably choose a neutral person to resolve the conflict e.g. a teacher who is not assessing the student's work.
Team Processes		
15. Coordination	The use of project plans (e.g. Gantt charts) produced at the beginning of assignments and then updated at regular intervals is one way to encourage coordination of tasks and responsibilities by teams.	• Encourage teams to coordinate tasks and responsibilities through the use of project plans. • Require students to submit revised and updated project plans regularly throughout the project. These should be assessed as part of final and interim submissions. • Gantt charts are a useful medium for recording work plans due to their common use in the construction and other design industries.
16. Communication	Interpersonal communication and team building skills are necessary for effectively functioning teams. For design, both oral and drawing interpersonal communications skills are important.	• Require teams to negotiate and agree on mediums and rules of communication. • Encourage students to consider the advantages of face-to-face communication for complex design negotiations. • Ensure students devise rules for communication via phone texts that recognise the limits and pitfalls of using it for discussing complex ideas. • Teach students the importance of graphic communication i.e. how to use thumbnails, diagrams and *partis* to communicate ideas.

continued on next page

Table 1. Continued

Factor	Description	Recommended Teaching Responses/Strategies
Task Design Variables		
17. Idea Evaluation	Idea evaluation in design teams involves generating, evaluating and developing ideas in a manner that is inclusive of all team members.	• Teach students techniques such as brainstorming for generating ideas in teams. • Teach students how to evaluate, test and refine ideas collaboratively. • Encourage constructive feedback skills by requiring students to "crit" their own work and the work of other teams. • Encourage collaborative design interpretation by asking teams to present the work of other teams.
18. Decision Making	Decision-making in a team requires an understanding of available strategies and selecting the approach that responds to the team task. The difficulty of making team decisions increases with team size.	• Teach students some common team decision-making models. • Encourage students to consider models other than democratic decision-making. • Support students to practice consensus-building skills and reflect on these teamwork processes in team or individual design journals.
19. Conflict Management Skills	Teams need to know how to recognise and productively resolve unhealthy forms of conflict.	• Teach students how to recognise and resolve conflict in a lecture and through a conflict management skills manual. • Support students to practice conflict management skills via role-play in workshops that recreate conflict scenarios.
Team Output		
20. Quality of the Submitted Product (Design) and Learning of Unit-Specific Knowledge and Skills	Task performance is evaluated by the quality of the submitted artefact (design) and the learning demonstrated of course-specific knowledge i.e. the skills and knowledge taught that are NOT related to teamwork (unless teamwork is the primary focus of the course).	• Ask students to differentiate between individual work and teamwork in interim review submissions. • Ensure the final submissions are team submissions and do not identify individual contributions. Use SAPA to individualise marks by generating multipliers of team marks.
21. Learning of Generic and Collaborative Design Teamwork Skills	Two broad areas of teamwork skills in design include: • Generic teamwork skills, which are the skills commonly needed for groupwork and teamwork, irrelevant of field e.g. leadership, management, delegation, consensus seeking and the capacity to effectively handle conflict; and • Collaborative design skills e.g. idea selection and development, shared understanding through graphic communication, and reflective practice (Schön 1987).	• Explore forms of artefact that present teamwork skills and ask students to submit these for assessment. • Allow students time to work together in class to practice and demonstrate teamwork skills. • Give students feedback on teamwork skills (preferably by teachers trained in teamwork).
22. Attitudes to Future Teamwork	A significant factor impacting team effectiveness is student attitudes to teamwork, which are heavily informed by previous experiences of teamwork.	• Require students to reflect on their experiences of teamwork in a reflective journal at the completion of assignments. • Encourage students to reflect on positive team experiences and the strategies that might lead again to these, and of negative team experiences and the strategies that might avoid these in future. • Require students to consider the skills they have learned and what skills they need to improve.

and improve them in subsequent contexts. Thus it makes sense to assess such skills individually. This assessment might have an individual focus – evaluating how a student has advanced their capability for teamwork (and other design skills) through learning from others on the team and from the overall team experience—and a collaborative focus—evaluating how a student has contributed to advancing the teamwork capability of others. For example, a designs assignment might specify 'dual goals' for each student team, with the Process goal being focused explicitly on the learning process of developing teamwork capabilities or other design skills by team members. In this way, some of the Process goals of a professional team can be subsumed as a secondary dimension of effectiveness on the Product goal. Moreover, individuals would then be able raise conflicts within the explicitly assessed context of learning teamwork skills, thus reducing the fear of negatively impacting the team environment or upsetting team members.

2. **Conflict and Team Diversity:** We recommend asking students to complete a simple learning style test and discussing the results at the outset of teamwork. Although past research on learning styles has come under heightened scrutiny due to the weight of evidence failing to support its validity as a predictor of learning behaviours (see, for instance, (Willingham, Hughes, & Dobolyi 2015)), these test are still useful to demonstrate to students how they vary in their response to different learning contexts and how some may be less comfortable with learning and/or designing collaboratively. While students need to be made aware of how such aptitudes may influence how they themselves and their teammates engage with team assignments, it should be noted that the surveys conducted as part of the aforementioned OLT project clearly indicated that learning styles (Kolb, in this instance) had little correlation with student satisfaction with team learning. However, we have found that an awareness in students of different mindsets towards different aspects of teamwork, and of different aptitudes between team members to the types problems they will need to resolve, can alleviate conflict by facilitating understanding, empathy and better communication. Students might also be made aware that their aptitude for teamwork can affect the attitudes they bring to team assignments. Negative attitudes to teamwork can have detrimental effects on team processes and on student's satisfaction with design outcomes unless students are mindful of differences between teammates.

3. **Pedagogic Structure (Teamwork Learning across Curricula):** Of the 22 factors in the framework, 13 are pedagogic and thus designed by teachers. Of the 13, task assessment, team formation methods, the use of self-and-peer-assessment, the teaching of teamwork skills, and teaching students how to design in collaboration were all found to statistically significantly impact learning outcomes in team contexts. Thus, these pedagogical factors require careful design.

While the need to contextualize the development of teamwork capability into authentic design settings is well-established; the challenges is how to develop that capability systematically so that every instructor is not charged with covering all the points in the framework. Thus we have recommended elsewhere (Tucker et al. 2014) that teamwork skill development can be scaffolded over the entire studio design stream based on a developmental continuum such as the Dreyfus model of skill acquisition: from Novice to Competence, Proficiency, to Expertise and finally to professional Mastery. The use of such a developmental continuum in tandem with assignments that emphasise some of the 13 pedagogic factors over others, depending on context and level, would facilitate the development of teamwork capabilities in a gradated, well-supported way.

Thus, for instance, at first-year level we have recommended that:

three teamwork skills are introduced at Novice level to teacher-assigned teams of two members only: Communication, Idea Development and Reflection. Then, at second-year level, teacher assigned teams of three to five members (studying within the same discipline) are introduced to four further skills: Coordination, Decision Making, Conflict Management, and Team Theory. (Tucker et al. 2014, 32)

Following the continuum, at final-year level students might then be required to design in multidisciplinary teams of five to 12 and be able to demonstrate mastery of all teamwork capabilities. Thus, at this level, students should have the knowledge to select their own teammates, and should have developed skills making it unnecessary for teachers to use pedagogic scaffolding to support teamwork—apart from appropriate assessment and formative feedback on teamwork processes.

FUTURE RESEARCH DIRECTIONS

While the framework has pedagogic implications, there are also research implications and gaps that must be addressed before the framework can be used to assess the causal relationships between team effectiveness and the 22 factors. For instance, while the surveys that tested the framework made use of existing scales where these were available, its overall validity needs to be established before it can be used to measure via further studies the impact of teaching interventions on teamwork outcomes and student learning.

CONCLUSION

To sum up, this chapter has described the genesis of a framework created for understanding the factors that impact the effectiveness of students designing in teams. The *Framework of Effectiveness in Student Design Teams* is based on the Input-Process-Output (IPO) framework for team effectiveness first proposed by McGrath in the mid-1960s. McGrath's IPO framework is built upon a basic assumption that the "group" interaction process mediates between input and output (e.g. McGrath 1964; Cummings 1981; Gladstein 1984; Driskell, Hogan et al. 1987). McGrath's IPO framework was contextualised in our literature review by relating its inputs and processes to analogous factors identified in the literature on teamwork in contexts of higher education and of design practice. The motivation for creating the framework was to identify what strategies both teachers and students might use to improve: teamwork learning experiences when students are asked to design in teams, the products of this teamwork, and the learning of teamwork skills.

It is intended that educators use the framework as a logic model describing linkages between their pedagogical goals (in terms of student capability, including knowledge, competencies and mindsets) and the pedagogical choices entailed in the instructional design of team assignments. The framework has the potential to inform research on the relationship between student design team outputs and the five categories of inputs and processes – task design, student individual characteristics, team characteristics, team processes and teaching practice and support structures. It may also reveal the relative importance to learning outcomes of these factors and/or groups of factors – a question that prior research has yet to conclusively establish.

REFERENCES

Adams, S., Simon, L., & Ruiz, B. (2002). A pilot study of the performance of student teams in engineering education.*Proceedings of the American Society for Engineering Education Annual Conference and Exposition,Montreal*.

Bacon, D. R., Stewart, K. A., & Silver, W. S. (1999a). Lessons from the Best and Worst Student Team Experiences: How a Teacher can make the Difference. *Journal of Management Education, 23*(5), 467–488. doi:10.1177/105256299902300503

Bacon, D. R., Stewart, K. A., & Silver, W. S. (1999b). Lessons from the Best and Worst Student Team Experiences: How a Teacher can make the Difference. *Journal of Management Education, 23*(5), 467–488. doi:10.1177/105256299902300503

Bacon, D. R., Stewart, K. A., & Stewart-Belle, S. (1998). Exploring predictors of student team project performance. *Journal of Marketing Education, 20*(1), 63–71. doi:10.1177/027347539802000108

Badke-Schaub, P., & Frankenberger, E. (2002). Analysing and modelling cooperative design by the critical situation method. *Le Travail Humain, 65*(44), 293–314. doi:10.3917/th.654.0293

Barr, T. F., Dixon, A. L., & Gassenheimer, J. B. (2005). Exploring the "Lone Wolf" Phenomenon in Student Teams. *Journal of Marketing Education, 27*(1), 81–90. doi:10.1177/0273475304273459

Behfar, K. J., Peterson, R. S., Mannix, E. A., & Trochim, W. M. K. (2008). The critical role of conflict resolution in teams: A close look at the links between conflict type, conflict management strategies, and team outcomes. *The Journal of Applied Psychology, 93*(1), 170–188. doi:10.1037/0021-9010.93.1.170 PMID:18211143

Bradley, J., White, B. J., & Mennecke, B. E. (2003). Teams and tasks: A temporal framework for the effects of interpersonal interventions on team performance. *Small Group Research, 34*(3), 358–387. doi:10.1177/1046496403034003004

Bradley, J. H., & Hebert, F. J. (1997). The effect of personality type on team performance. *Journal of Management Development, 16*(5), 337–353. doi:10.1108/02621719710174525

Brooks, C. M., & Ammons, J. L. (2003). Free riding in group projects and the effects of timing, frequency, and specificity of criteria in peer assessments. *Journal of Education for Business, 78*(5), 268–272. doi:10.1080/08832320309598613

Brown, R. W. (1995, November 1-4). Autorating: Getting Individual Marks from Team Marks and Enhancing Teamwork. *Paper presented at the 25th Annual Frontiers in Education Conference*, Atlanta, Georgia. doi:10.1109/FIE.1995.483140

Burningham, C., & West, M. A. (1995). Individual, climate, and group interaction processes as predictors of work team innovation. *Small Group Research, 26*(1), 106–117. doi:10.1177/1046496495261006

Busby, J. R. (2001). Error and distributed cognition in design. *Design Studies, 22*(3), 233–254. doi:10.1016/S0142-694X(00)00028-4

Campion, M. A., Medsker, G. J., & Higgs, C. A. (1993). Relations between work group characteristics and effectiveness: Implications for designing effective work groups. *Personnel Psychology, 46*(4), 823–850. doi:10.1111/j.1744-6570.1993.tb01571.x

Campion, M. A., Papper, E. M., & Medsker, G. J. (1996). Relations between work team characteristics and effectiveness: A replication and extension. *Personnel Psychology, 49*(2), 429–452. doi:10.1111/j.1744-6570.1996.tb01806.x

Casperz, D., Wu, M., & Skene, J. 2003. Factors influencing effective performance of university student teams. *Paper presented at the Learning for an unknown future:proceedings of the 2003 Annual International Conference of the Higher Education Research and Development Society of Australasia (HERDSA)*, Christchurch, New Zealand.

Chapman, K. J., & Auken, S. V. (2001). Creating Positive Group Project Experiences: An Examination of the Role of the Instructor on Students' Perceptions of Group Projects. *Journal of Marketing Education*, *23*(2), 117–127. doi:10.1177/0273475301232005

Chiocchio, F., Forgues, D., David, C., & Iordanova, I. (2011). Teamwork in integrated design projects: Understanding the effects of trust, conflict, and collaboration on performance. *Project Management Journal*, *42*(6), 78–91. doi:10.1002/pmj.20268

Christiaans, H.C.M. (2002). Creativity as a design criterion. *Communication Research Journal,* 14(1), 41-54.

Cohen, E. G. (1994). Restructing the Classroom: Conditions for Productive Small Groups. *Review of Educational Research*, *64*(1), 1–35. doi:10.3102/00346543064001001

Cohen, S. G. (1997). What Makes Teams Work: Group Effectiveness Research from the Shop Floor to the Executive Suite. *Journal of Management*, *23*(3), 239–290. doi:10.1177/014920639702300303

Cross, N., & Clayburn-Cross, A. (1996). Observations of teamwork and social processes in design. In N. Cross, H. Christiaans, & K. Dorst (Eds.), *Analysing design activity* (pp. 291–318). Chichester, US: John Wiley & Sons Ltd.

Cummings, T. G. (1981). Designing effective work groups. In P. C. Nystrom & W. H. Starbuck (Eds.), *Handbook of organizational design*. New York: Oxford University Press.

Cuseo, J. 2000. Collaborative and cooperative learning: Pedagogy for promoting new-student retention and achievement. *Paper presented at thePreconference workshop delivered at the 19th Annual Conference on The First-Year Experience*, Columbia, SC.

Davies, P. (2000). Computerized Peer Assessment. *Innovations in Education and Teaching International*, *37*(4), 346–355.

de Dreu, C. K. W. (1997). Productive conflict: The importance of conflict management and conflict issues. In C. de Drew & E. Van de Vliert (Eds.), *Using conflict in organizations* (pp. 9–22). London: Sage. doi:10.4135/9781446217016.n2

de Dreu, C. K. W., & Vianen, A. E. M. V. (2001). Managing relationship conflict and the effectiveness of organizational teams. *Journal of Organizational Behavior*, *22*(3), 309–328. doi:10.1002/job.71

Deeter-Schmelz, D. R., Kennedy, K. N., & Ramsey, R. P. (2002a). Enriching our understanding of student team effectiveness. *Journal of Marketing Education*, *24*(2), 114–124. doi:10.1177/0273475302242004

Dorst, K. (2003). *Understanding design. 150 reflections on being a designer*. Amsterdam, Netherlands: BIS Publishers.

Dreu, C. K. W. D., & Vianen, A. E. M. V. (2001). Managing relationship conflict and the effectiveness of organizational teams. *Journal of Organizational Behavior, 22*(3), 309–328. doi:10.1002/job.71

Driskell, J. E., Hogan, R., & Salas, E. (1987). Personality and group performance. In C. Hendrick (Ed.), *Group processes and intergroup relations* (pp. 91–112). Newbury Park, CA: Sage.

Eckert, C. M., & Stacey, M. K. (2001). Dimensions of communication in design. *Proceedings of the International Conference on Engineering Design, ICED01*, Glasgow (pp. 473-80).

Erez, M., & Zidon, I. (1984). Effect of goal acceptance on the relationship of goal difficulty to performance. *The Journal of Applied Psychology, 69*(1), 69–78. doi:10.1037/0021-9010.69.1.69

Etroo, F. (2011). *An assessment of teamwork among Ghanaian construction professionals*. Heriot-Watt University.

Feichtner, S. B., & Davis, E. A. (1984). Why some groups fail: A survey of students' experiences with learning groups. *The Organizational Behavior Teaching Review, 9*(4), 58–73.

Ferrante, C. J., Green, S. G., & Forster, W. R. (2006). Getting more out of team projects: Incentivising leadership to enhance performance. *Journal of Management Education, 30*(6), 788–797. doi:10.1177/1052562906287968

Fiechtner, S. B., & Davis, E. A. (1992). Why some groups fail: A survey of students' experiences with learning groups. In A.S. Goodsell, M.R. Maher & V. Tinto (Eds.), Collaborative Learning: A Sourcebook for Higher Education. National Center on Postsecondary Teaching, Learning, & Assessment, Syracuse University.

Fowler, A. (1995). How to build effective teams. *People Management, 1*(4).

Freeman, K. A. (1996). Attitudes toward work in project groups as predictors of academic performance. *Small Group Research, 27*(2), 265–282. doi:10.1177/1046496496272004

Freeman, M., & McKenzie, J. (2002). SPARK, a confidential web-based template for self and peer assessment of student teamwork: Benefits of evaluating across different subjects. *British Journal of Educational Technology, 33*(5), 551–569. doi:10.1111/1467-8535.00291

Gardner, B. S., & Korth, S. J. (1998). A framework for learning to work in teams. *Journal of Education for Business, 74*(1), 28–33. doi:10.1080/08832329809601657

Gladstein, D. (1984). Groups in Context: A Model of Task Group Effectiveness. *Administrative Science Quarterly, 29*(4), 499–517. doi:10.2307/2392936

Goldfinch, J., & Raeside, R. (1990). Development of a Peer Assessment Technique for Obtaining Individual Marks on a Group Project. *Assessment & Evaluation in Higher Education, 15*(3), 210–231. doi:10.1080/0260293900150304

Goltz, S. M., Hietapelto, A. B., Reinsch, R. W., & Tyrell, S. K. (2008). Teaching teamwork and problem solving concurrently. *Journal of Management Education, 32*(5), 541–562. doi:10.1177/1052562907310739

Gorla, N., & Lam, Y. (2004). Who should work with whom? Building effective software project teams. *Communications of the ACM, 47*(6), 79–82. doi:10.1145/990680.990684

Gosenpud, J. J., & Washbush, J. B. (1991). Predicting simulation performance: Differences between individuals and groups. In W. J. Wheatley & J. Gosenpud (Eds.), *Developments in business simulation & experiential exercises* (pp. 44–48). Stillwater, OK: Association for Business Simulation and Experiential Learning.

Hackman, J. R. (1987). The design of work teams. In J. W. Lorsch (Ed.), *Handbook of organizational behavior* (pp. 315–342). Englewood Cliffs, NJ: Prentice Hall.

Hackman, J. R., & Morris, C. G. (1975). In L. Berkowitz (Ed.), *Group tasks, group interaction process, and group performance effectiveness: A review and proposed integration* (pp. 47–99). Advances in experimental social psychologyNew York: Academic Press.

Hackman, J. R., & Oldham, G. R. (1980). *Work redesign. MA*. Reading: Addison-Wesley.

Hackman, J. R., & Walton, R. E. (1986). Leading groups in organizations. In P. Goodman (Ed.), *Designing effective work groups* (pp. 72–119). San Francisco: Jossey-Bass.

Hales, C. (1993). *Managing engineering design*. Harlow, UK: Longman Scientific & Technical.

Hamlyn-Harris, B. J., Hurst, B. J., Baggo, K. V., & Bayley, A. J. (2006). Predictors of team work satisfaction. *Journal of Information Technology Education*, *5*, 299–315.

Hansen, R. S. (2006). Benefits and problems with student teams: Suggestions for improving team projects. *Journal of Education for Business*, *82*(1), 11–19. doi:10.3200/JOEB.82.1.11-19

Harrison, D., Price, K., Gavin, J., & Florey, A. (2002). Time, teams, and task performance: Changing effects of surface and deep-level diversity on group functioning. *Academy of Management Journal*, *45*(5), 1029–1045. doi:10.2307/3069328

Hyatt, D. E., & Ruddy, T. H. (1997). An examination of the relationship between work team characteristics and effectiveness: A replication and extension. *Personnel Psychology*, *50*, 553–585. doi:10.1111/j.1744-6570.1997.tb00703.x

Ingham, A. G., Levinger, G., Graves, J., & Peckham, V. (1974). The Ringelmann effect: Studies of group size and group performance. *Journal of Experimental Social Psychology*, *10*(4), 371–384. doi:10.1016/0022-1031(74)90033-X

Jalajas, D. S., & Sutton, R. I. (1984-1985). Feuds in student groups, coping with whiners, martyrs, saboteurs, bullies, and deadbeats. *Organizational Behavior Teaching Review*, *9*(4), 217–227.

Jehn, K. A. (1995). A Multimethod Examination of the Benefits and Detriments of Intragroup Conflict. *Administrative Science Quarterly*, *40*(2), 256–282. doi:10.2307/2393638

Jehn, K. A. (1997). A qualitative analysis of conflict types and dimensions in organizational groups. *Administrative Science Quarterly*, *42*(3), 530–557. doi:10.2307/2393737

Johnson, D.W., & Johnson, R.T. (1992). Positive interdependence: Key to effective cooperation. In *Interaction in cooperative groups: The theoretical anatomy of group learning* (pp. 174-199).

Jules, C. (2007). *Diversity of Member Composition and Team Learning in Organizations*. Case Western Reserve University.

Kankanhalli, A., Tan, B. C. Y., & Wei, K.-K. (2007). Conflict and performance in global virtual teams. *Journal of Management Information Systems*, *23*(3), 237–274. doi:10.2753/MIS0742-1222230309

Klein, M. (1991). Supporting conflict resolution in cooperative design systems. IEEE Systems Man and Cybernetics, 21(6).

Kozlowski, S. W. J., & Ilgen, D. R. (2006). Enhancing the Effectiveness of Work Groups and Teams. *Psychological Science in the Public Interest*, *7*(3), 77–124. PMID:26158912

Kravitz, D. A., & Martin, B. (1986). Ringelmann Rediscovered: The original article. *Journal of Personality and Social Psychology*, *50*(5), 936–941. doi:10.1037/0022-3514.50.5.936

Larson, C. E., & LaFasto, F. M. J. (1989). *Teamwork: What Must Go Right/What Can Go Wrong*. Newbury Park, CA: Sage.

Locke, E. A., & Latham, G. P. (1990). Work motivation and satisfaction: Light at the end of the tunnel. *American Psychological Society*, *1*(4), 240–246.

Longenecker, C. O., Scazzero, J. A., & Stansfield, T. T. (1994). Quality improvement through team goal setting, feedback, and problem solving. *International Journal of Quality & Reliability Management*, *11*(4), 45–52. doi:10.1108/02656719410057944

Loughry, M. L., Ohland, M. W., & DeWayne Moore, D. (2007). Development of a theory-based assessment of team member effectiveness. *Educational and Psychological Measurement*, *67*(3), 505–524. doi:10.1177/0013164406292085

Martin, E., & Paredes, P. 2004. Using learning styles for dynamic group formation in adaptive collaborative hypermedia systems. *Paper presented at theProceedings of the 4th international conference on web-engineering*, Munich.

McGrath, J. E. (1964). *Social psychology: A brief introduction*. New York: Holt, Rinehart & Winston.

McGrath, J. E. (1984). *Groups: Interaction and performance*. Englewood Cliffs, NJ: Prentice-Hall.

McKendall, M. (2000). Teaching groups to become teams. *Journal of Education for Business*, *75*(5), 277–282. doi:10.1080/08832320009599028

Mello, J. A. (1993). Improving individual member accountability in small work group settings. *Journal of Management Education*, *17*(2), 253–259. doi:10.1177/105256299301700210

Michaelsen, L. K., Knight, A. B., & Dee Fink, L. (2002). *Team-based learning: A transformative use of small groups*. Praeger Pub Text.

Mulder, R. A., & Pearce, J. M. 2007. PRAZE: Innovating teaching through online peer review. *Paper presented at the24th Annual Conference of the Australasian Society for Computers in Learning in Tertiary Education*, Singapore.

O'Leary-Kelly, A. M., Martocchio, J. J., & Frink, D. D. (1994). A review of the influence of group goals on group performance. *Academy of Management Review*, *37*(5), 1285–1301. doi:10.2307/256673

Oakley, B., Felder, R. M., Brent, R., & Elhajj, I. (2004). Turning Student Groups into Effective Teams. *Journal of Student Centered Learning*, *2*(1), 9–34.

Ohland, M. W., Loughry, M. L., Woehr, D. J., Bullard, L. G., Felder, R. M., Finelli, C. J., & Schmucker, D. G. et al. (2012). The comprehensive assessment of team member effectiveness: Development of a behaviorally anchored rating scale for self-and peer evaluation. *Academy of Management Learning & Education*, *11*(4), 609–630. doi:10.5465/amle.2010.0177

Peeters, M. A. G., Rutte, C. G., van Tuijl, H. F. J. M., & Reymen, I. M. M. J. (2008). Designing in teams: Does personality matter. *Small Group Research*, *39*(4), 438–467. doi:10.1177/1046496408319810

Peeters, M. A. G., Van Tuijl, H. F. J. M., Rutte, C. G., & Reymen, I. M. M. J. (2006b). Personality and Team Performance: A Meta-Analysisy. *European Journal of Personality*, *20*(5), 377–396. doi:10.1002/per.588

Peeters-Baars, M. A. G. (2006a). *Design teams and personality: effects of team composition on processes and effectiveness*. TechnischeUniversiteit.

Pelled, L. H., Eisenhardt, K. M., & Xin, K. R. (1999). Exploring the black box: An analysis of work group diversity, conflict, and performance. *Administrative Science Quarterly*, *44*(1), 1–28. doi:10.2307/2667029

Pfaff, E., & Huddleston, P. (2003). Does it matter if I hate teamwork? What impacts student attitudes toward teamwork. *Journal of Marketing Education*, *25*(1), 37–45. doi:10.1177/0273475302250571

Podsakoff, P. M., Aheame, M., & MacKenzie, S. B. (1997). Organizational citizenship behavior and the quantity and quality of work group performance. *The Journal of Applied Psychology*, *82*(2), 262–270. doi:10.1037/0021-9010.82.2.262 PMID:9109284

Raban, R., & Litchfield. (2006, December 3-6). Supporting peer assessment of individual contributions in groupwork. *Paper presented at the23rd Annual Conference of the Australasian Society for Computers in Learning in Tertiary Education*, Sydney.

Salas, E., Rozell, D., Mullen, B., & Driskell, J. E. (1999). The effect of team building on performance, an integration. *Small Group Research*, *30*(3), 309–329. doi:10.1177/104649649903000303

Salas, E., Stagl, K. C., & Burke, C. S. (2004). 25 Years of Team Effectiveness in Organizations: Research Themes and Emerging Needs. In C. L. Cooper & I. T. Robertson (Eds.), *International Review of Industrial and Organizational Psychology* (pp. 47–91). New York: Wiley.

Schön, D. A. (1987). *Educating the Reflective Practitioner*. San Francisco: Jossey-Bass.

Scott, K. D., & Townsend, A. (1994). Teams: Why some succeed and others fail. *HRMagazine*, *39*(8), 62–67.

Scott, V. (2010). *Conflict Resolution at Work for Dummies*. Indianapolis, Indiana: Wiley Publishing, Inc.

Shea, G. P., & Guzzo, R. A. (1987b). Groups as human resources. In K. M. Rowland & G. R. Ferris (Eds.), *Research in personnel and human resources management* (pp. 323–356). Greenwich, CT: JAI Press.

Shih, S.-G., Hu, T.-P., & Chen, C.-N. (2006). A game theory-based approach to the analysis of cooperative learning in design studios. *Design Studies*, *27*(6), 711–722. doi:10.1016/j.destud.2006.05.001

Simons, T., & Peterson, R. (2000). Task conflict and relationship conflict in top management teams: The pivotal role of intragroup trust. *The Journal of Applied Psychology, 83*(1), 102–111. doi:10.1037/0021-9010.85.1.102 PMID:10740960

Slimani, K., Ferreira Da Silva, C., Médini, L., & Ghodous, P. (2006). Conflict mitigation in collaborative design. *International Journal of Production Research, 44*(9), 1681–1702. doi:10.1080/00207540500445198

Steiner, I. D. (1972). *Group Process and Productivity*. New York: Academic Press.

Stempfle, J., & Badke-Schaub, P. (2002). Thinking in design teams - an analysis of team communication. *Design Studies, 23*(5), 473–496. doi:10.1016/S0142-694X(02)00004-2

Strong, J. T., & Anderson, R. E. (1990). Free-riding in group projects: Control mechanisms and preliminary data. *Journal of Marketing Education, 12*(2), 61–67. doi:10.1177/027347539001200208

Stumpf, S. C., & McDonnell, J. T. (2002). Talking about team framing: Using argumentation to analyse and support experiential learning in early design episodes. *Design Studies, 23*(1), 5–23. doi:10.1016/S0142-694X(01)00020-5

Sundstrom, E., & Altman, I. (1989). Physical environments and workgroup effectiveness. In L. L. Cummings & B. Staw (Eds.), *Research in organizational behavior* (pp. 175–209). Greenwich, CT: JAI Press.

Sundstrom, E., de Meuse, K. P., & Futrell, D. (1990). Work Teams: Applications and Effectiveness. *The American Psychologist, 45*(2), 120–133. doi:10.1037/0003-066X.45.2.120

Tannenbaum, S. I., Beard, R. L., & Salas, E. (1992). Team building and its influence on team effectiveness: An examination of conceptual and empirical developments. In K. Kelley (Ed.), *Issue, Theory, and Research in Industrial/Organizational Psychology* (pp. 117–153). Amsterdam: Elsevier. doi:10.1016/S0166-4115(08)62601-1

Tekleab, A. G., Quigley, N. R., & Tesluk, P. E. (2009). A Longitudinal Study of Team Conflict, Conflict Management, Cohesion, and Team Effectiveness. *Group & Organization Management, 34*(2), 170–205. doi:10.1177/1059601108331218

Topping, K. (1998). Peer Assessment between Students in Colleges and Universities. *Review of Educational Research, 68*(3), 249–276. doi:10.3102/00346543068003249

Tucker, R. (2008). The Impact of Assessment Modes on Collaborative Group Design Projects. In S. Frankland (Ed.), *Enhancing Teaching and Learning through Assessment: Embedded Strategies and their Impacts* (pp. 72–85). Hong Kong: The Assessment Resource Centre, The Hong Kong Polytechnic University.

Tucker, R., Abbasi, N., Thorpe, G., Ostwald, M., Williams, A., Wallis, L., & Kashuk, S. (2014). Enhancing and assessing group and team learning in architecture and related design contexts. Sydney: Office of Learning and Teaching, Department of Education, Australian Government.

Tucker, R., & Abbasi, N. (2014). The architecture of teamwork: examining relationships between teaching, assessment, student learning and satisfaction with creative design outcomes. *Journal of Architectural Engineering and Design Management*.

Tucker, R., & Rollo, J. (2006). Teaching and Learning in Collaborative Group Design Projects. *Journal of Architectural Engineering & Design Management*, 2, 19-30.

Valkenburg, R. (1998). Shared understanding as a condition for team design. *Automation in Construction*, 7(2-3), 111–121. doi:10.1016/S0926-5805(97)00058-7

Valkenburg, R., & Dorst, K. (1998). The reflective practice of design teams. *Design Studies*, 19(3), 249–271. doi:10.1016/S0142-694X(98)00011-8

Walker, A. (2001). British psychology students' perceptions of group-work and peer. *Psychology Learning & Teaching*, 1(1), 28–36. doi:10.2304/plat.2001.1.1.28

Watkins, R. (2005). *Groupwork and assessment: The Handbook for Economics Lecturers*. Kingston University.

West, M. A., Borrill, C. S., & Unsworth, K. (1998). Team effectiveness in organizations. In C. L. Cooper & I. T. Robertson (Eds.), *International Review of Industrial and Organizational Psychology*. Chichester: Wiley.

White, K. (1984). MIS Project Teams: An investigation of cognitive style implications. *Management Information Systems Quarterly*, 8(2), 85–101. doi:10.2307/249346

Willingham, D. T., Hughes, E. M., & Dobolyi, D. G. (2015). The scientific status of learning styles theories. *Teaching of Psychology*, 42(3), 266–271. doi:10.1177/0098628315589505

Wong, Y. K., Shi, Y., & Wilson, D. (2004). Experience, gender composition, social presence, decision process satisfaction and group performance. *Proceedings of the ACM International Conference Proceeding Series*.

Yazici, H.J. (2005). A study of collaborative learning style and team learning performance. *Education+ training*, 47(3), 216-29.

Yeatts, D. E., & Hyten, C. (1998). *High-performing self-managed work teams: A comparison of theory to practice*. Thousand Oaks, CA, USA: Sage. doi:10.4135/9781483328218

Yellen, R. E., Winniford, M. A., & Sanford, C. C. (1995). Extroversion and introversion in electronically supported meetings. *Information & Management*, 28(1), 63–74. doi:10.1016/0378-7206(94)00023-C

KEY TERMS AND DEFINITIONS

Groupwork: A situations where a number of students work separately but in parallel on different aspects of a project and then combine their work.

IPO Framework: The 'Input-Process-Output (IPO) framework' is the basic assumption that the group interaction process mediates between *input factors* – features of the team, the team task and its work context – and the *output* of the team.

Mark Individualization: One possible outcome of SAPA is the calculation of a numerical scaling factor for each group member, which can then be applied to a common group mark to produce individual marks for each group member that attempt to fairly represent the contribution of each member to the assessable group task.

Self-and-Peer-Assessment (SAPA): At its most basic, SAPA involves students providing an evaluation for all group members, including themselves, of the individual contribution of each group member to the group work process. The SAPA evaluation may be used informal feedback, or formal and used as an element of the summative assessment for the group task. SAPA may be public or anonymous.

Team Effectiveness: In educational contexts can be defined in terms of two dimensions: (1) Performance on the assigned task, evaluated through an assessment of *products* and/or *outcomes*; and (2) Goal Achievement through the *process* of working in a team, which can be divided into two aspects – (i) behaviour and (ii) attitudes.

Teamwork: Joint work on an assigned project in a collaborative environment where members actively contribute to team cohesion and task achievement.

Chapter 2
Using a Value Cycle Framework to Analyze Teamwork Capability as a Learning Outcome in Interior Design Studio Courses

Paola Gavilanez
Kwantlen Polytechnic University, Canada

Amber Ortlieb
Kwantlen Polytechnic University, Canada

Thomas Carey
Kwantlen Polytechnic University, Canada

ABSTRACT

Previous research on teaching and learning in the design disciplines has demonstrated the complex set of factors which need to be aligned in order for our students to be prepared for professional practice in teamwork. This chapter reports on ongoing work to extend this previous research, including integration with an institutional learning outcomes framework, incorporation of insights from beyond the design disciplines to engage student motivation in capability development, and a specific interest in the ways team teaching in design studios can contribute to the development of students' teamwork capability (in addition to advancing their development of design capability).

INTRODUCTION

Teamwork skills are important for all higher education stakeholders. Superior teamwork skills enhance student employability and competitive edge for jobs in the design professions because teamwork is crucial for contemporary design practice. (Tucker et al., 2014, p.25)

DOI: 10.4018/978-1-5225-0726-0.ch002

Developing teamwork capabilities in design students is predicated on the industries' demand for practitioners to collaborate within interdisciplinary teams to achieve their project goals. This notion is specifically evidenced in the interior design associations' (e.g., Interior Designers of Canada [IDC], American Society of Interior Designers [ASID], Council for Interior Design Qualification [CIDQ]) definition and scope of interior designers which explicitly expresses collaboration with other practitioners (ASID, 2015; CIDQ, 2004; IDC, 2013). ASID extends the discussion beyond collaboration identifying that successful interior designers should be "good team leaders and good team players" with the ability to "negotiate and mediate when necessary" (ASID, 2015, para. 5).

Components of teamwork are acknowledged in five out of the 65 knowledge areas in the Interior Design Profession's Body of Knowledge conveyed as communication, critical listening, design communication methods, consultations with consultants, and multi-disciplinary collaboration (Guerin & Martin, 2010). Additionally, the 2017 professional standards of the Council for Interior Design Accreditation (CIDA) dictate student and program expectations of which six of the 123 standards (5a-5f) present specific teamwork outcomes (CIDA, 2015). In fact, CIDA standard number five describes collaboration as an intention to prepare students "to work effectively in teams and in leadership roles across disciplines" (CIDA, 2015, p. 17).

It is important that we not assume the mere occurrence of teamwork opportunities in our programs will assure successful development of the important knowledge, skills and attitudes comprising capability for effective teamwork. Teamwork experiences for students will only meet our expectations for development of teamwork capability when there is a constructive alignment of multiple instructional components working together.

For example, exposure to teamwork experiences does not guarantee student knowledge about effective teamwork practices. In fact, students did not perceive they had received teamwork instruction in several areas even though the faculty believed they had incorporated instruction (Webb & Miller, 2006).

Similarly, a study with interior design students by Gale et al. (2014) found that students' design studio experiences had led to less favourable attitudes toward teamwork over the course of their program:

Perhaps, the most interesting finding of this study was the . . . upper-division students reporting a more negative attitude toward collaborative learning than their lower-division peers . . . This presents an interesting dilemma to the interior design educator striving to prepare students to enter the profession with the desired competency of the ability to work collaboratively. This finding is perhaps even more troubling when considering the literature showing that upper-division interior design students have more realistic expectations of the type of work they will perform in the profession. (Gale et al., 2014, p.26)

As recent research with design studio courses has shown (Tucker & Abbasi, 2012, 2014a&b; Tucker et al., 2014, Tucker & Reynolds, 2006), a complex set of factors need to – and can – be aligned in order for our students to be prepared for professional practice in teamwork. This chapter reports on ongoing work to extend this previous research, including integration with an institutional learning outcomes framework, incorporate of insights from beyond the design disciplines to engage student motivation in capability development, and a specific interest on the ways team teaching in design studios can contribute to the development of students' teamwork capability (in addition to advancing their development of design capability).

BACKGROUND

The insights described in this chapter are results from an ongoing project in teaching and learning with interior design students. The project goals have evolved from an original motivation around the authors' personal teaching and research agendas for design studio courses to a broader role as an institutional pilot project (in the context outlined in the next section). As a result, this chapter will provide insights to readers sharing any of the following goals:

1. Improve the development of teamwork capability for students in our Interior Design program, with a specific interest in the role of team teaching in design studios.

As faculty members in a teaching-intensive university, the authors' primary responsibility is to develop students' capabilities for effective professional practice as well as their other roles as community members and global citizens. An important aspect of design studio work is the use of team teaching as a model in developing student capabilities for teamwork and collaboration. This approach reflects the insight that "we teach who we are" (Palmer, 2010, p. 188) so that *how we teach* becomes a key part of *what we teach*.

2. Contribute insights on team teaching in design studios with impact beyond our context to the larger design teaching community.

Previous research on developing teamwork capability in design studio courses, such as Tucker et al. (2014), had shown the complexity of the process and the potential interactions between various components. A preliminary scan of the available research literature identified few studies which tracked and demonstrated the impacts of team teaching in a design studio context (outlined below in the section on Impacts and Ongoing Work).

However, there was a strong intuitive consensus about its potential benefits. We wanted to understand the links between team teaching as an instructional method and the learning outcomes that our students achieve on these graduate attributes, both to enhance our teaching methods and to determine the return on investment from the teaching effort required.

3. Strengthen the institutional processes used to engage with program-level learning outcomes.

Much of the research evidence reviewed in this chapter does not refer to an institutional context. An institutional focus on program-level outcomes such as teamwork capability is a fairly recent development; much of the past work will have been developed independent of an effective institutional framework for consistent program learning outcomes. The work described in this chapter, by contrast, was commenced within – and supported – by an initiative to consistently advance program-level outcomes across the institution. That institutional context had implications for both the process and results of our review, and we expect this will increasingly be the case for other projects to advance research evidence and exemplary practices for teamwork capability.

The institutional framework being used for these institutional processes, described further in the next section, is a Learning Outcomes Value Cycle adapted from work by the Assuring Graduate Capabilities project in Australia (Oliver, 2015). This framework extends existing formulations of the learning and teaching process, which have focused on specifying, developing and assessing learning outcomes. In particular, the framework highlights the importance of related components of the instructional plan, such as motivating student engagement in developing their capability, documenting their achievement for stakeholders external to the program or Faculty (e.g., the university, employers and governments) and applying the assessment evidence in enhancing any of these components.

The work reported here became a test case for the university in applying this framework to constructive alignment of all these elements to develop student capability in a core graduate attribute. The immediate impact of this additional role for the project was to encourage – and require – investigation beyond the design studio environment, to find examples of disciplinary differences in developing student teamwork capabilities. As described further below, this process had the beneficial effect of providing a broader set of exemplary practices for us to consider in our teaching and scholarly agendas. (In addition, from the institution's perspective we were also demonstrating a contextualized approach to the overall University Graduate Attributes, in which each university Faculty would customize their program learning outcomes to fit their particular disciplinary and professional contexts).

The next section of the chapter provides an outline of the Learning Outcomes Value Cycle, along with further background about the approach to contextualizing institutional graduate attributes as program-level learning outcomes. The main section of the chapter then summarizes our review of research evidence and exemplary practices for developing student teamwork capability in design studio sources, structured around the extended Learning Outcomes Value Cycle framework. The closing section of the chapter highlights the insights this process yielded, for our own teaching and research goals and for the use of this kind of framework within our Faculty of Design and more broadly within the institution.

THE FRAMEWORK AND PROCESS FOR OUR ANALYSIS

The Learning Outcomes Value Cycle Framework

The institutional Learning Outcomes Value Cycle, for which our team teaching project was to be a test case, contains the following components:

- *Specify* the expected learning outcomes (course or program level, as customizations of the broader institutional level graduate attributes),
- *Engage* students by motivating the development of the capabilities,
- *Develop* and Demonstrate (with formative feedback) student capabilities,
- *Assess* (with summative evaluation) and *Document* the outcomes (for stakeholders external to the program, including the university, employers, prospective students and governments),
- *Enhance* our achievement in developing student capability, by applying the assessment evidence to constructive redesign for any of these elements as needed.

We describe next the motivation for the use of a structured framework to guide faculty work on program-level learning outcomes, the foundation underlying this particular framework, and the choice of Value Cycle to label the framework. This is followed by a description of the use of the framework to guide the process of reviewing research literature and exemplary practices to address the teamwork capability, as a test case for institutional use of a framework of this type in projects to advance teaching and learning.

Motivation: The institutional context for this work includes a university-wide initiative to update and advance program-level learning outcomes. The motivation for developing a structured framework of this type as part of that initiative came from awareness of the difficulties encountered elsewhere (Goff et al., 2015) when too much effort went into the description of multiple target outcomes and too little effort into demonstrating improvement in specific student outcomes as a result:

As a starting point, our students' learning experiences will benefit when we create clearer definitions for the outcomes we intend for them and for the ways we plan to measure their success. But that's only the beginning: the real value from our work on Learning Outcomes will come when we use the results from those Specifications and Assessments to help us identify areas where we can Enhance the student learning experience – and to share those results with colleagues as part of our scholarship in teaching and learning. (Carey, 2015, p. 5)

Development: The base for this institutional framework was a national project in Australia sponsored by the Australian Learning and Teaching Council (Oliver, 2011, 2013). The results from that project continue to evolve through their website on Assuring Graduate Capabilities (Oliver, 2015). The website collects research evidence and exemplary practices across the whole cycle of components from defining outcomes through developing and assessing them. The results are intended to enhance the teaching and learning experience by cycling back to applying the outcomes. In addition to mapping out the connections amongst the diverse components required to develop and assure program learning outcomes, this approach also emphasizes a focus on capability - including knowledge, skills and attitudes - as a broader notion than just competency (Oliver, 2013).

The framework from Assuring Graduate Capabilities was adapted for our university's context and needs through a few adaptations, such as the following:

- Minor revisions to fit with North American language use, e.g., replacing the use of "course" with "program", and "module" with "course";
- Separation of some components to highlight specific institutional priorities, e.g., separating activities to Engage from those to Develop in order to emphasize the importance of explicitly motivating student interest.

Value Cycle: The label Value Cycle for this institutional framework was intended to emphasize assessment for improvement of program-level learning outcomes. This would also indirectly address the other purposes of assessment, such as assessment for feedback to students and *assessment for* accountability for governments and other stakeholders. Of course, a cycle model is a simplification of what happens in actual teaching and learning: there is always a back-and-forth movement across these components, e.g., as particular learning activities raise issues about our understanding of what outcomes we are targeting, or as we discover that our proposed assessments are not revealing important aspects of student learning that we need to nurture.

Process for Analysis of Research Evidence and Exemplary Practice

One promising direction for institutional development of program-level learning outcomes is the creation of a high level statement of graduate attributes which is then contextualized at the Faculty and program level to yield learning outcomes. The institutional models for this direction include the University of Sydney (2011) and the University of Technology Sydney (2013), along with the underlying research which highlights the advantages of contextualized outcomes within a high level description of graduate attributes (Caspersen et al. 2014; Jones, 2013). As pursued within the author's institution, the practical impact for the work reported here was to encourage investigation of developments from other discipline areas which could be adapted to the target domain of design studio practice.

Two major reference points provide the central threads for the component-by-component analysis or research evidence and exemplary practice in the next section:

- The *Teaching Teamwork in Design* research and development program led by Richard Tucker at Deakin University has provided both exemplary resources – including a Teachers' Manual (Tucker & Abassi, 2014b), a Students' Manual (Tucker & Abassi, 2014a) and a Project Report (Tucker et al., 2014) – and research studies (Tucker, 2012; Tucker & Abassi, 2012, 2015) for the design studio context, with many of the same elements as our institutional Learning Outcomes Value Cycle framework.
- The *Transferable Integrated Design Engineering Education* (TIDEE) consortium from U.S. engineering schools (TIDEE, 2006) conducted a program of research and development in teamwork capabilities for engineering students which developed a set of exemplary resources (IDEALS, 2015) and research evidence (Davis et al., 2010, 2011, 2013; Davis & Ulseth, 2013; Gerlick et al., 2010; McCormack et al., 2012). In addition to the substantial body of insights and resources they have made available, this body of work appealed to us because it focused on 'engineering design' courses which had interesting similarities and differences with our design studio courses.

Following an extensive review of the two major reference points and their additional sources, a review of the research literature for teamwork capability development specific to Interior Design was undertaken. A further examination of selected research evidence from other discipline areas was also added to our review, with a particular focus on the Engage and Document components of the Framework as potential gaps in the Interior Design evidence and exemplars. These additional resources were identified as exemplars in the generic learning outcomes research literature or by scholars in teaching and learning from other disciplines, so the collection was more opportunistic than systematic. However, even this brief overview yielded transferable insights on developing student teamwork capability as well as highlighting similarities and differences in teamwork development across disciplines.

ANALYSIS OF RESEARCH EVIDENCE AND EXEMPLARY PRACTICES FOR TEAMWORK CAPABILITY

In this section of the chapter we review the research evidence and exemplary practices contributing to understanding the development teamwork capability with Design students in each of the framework components. Each section summarizes the evidence from the two main reference points and from additional references, and concludes with an outline of some of the application of the results to teaching teamwork in design studio courses with team-teaching as a model for student capability.

Specify: What Knowledge, Skills and Attitudes Are Students Expected to Achieve

Our analysis, of the available research for evidence and exemplary practices, demonstrated major agreement on many of the aspects of teamwork skills to be fostered in design studio courses (and elsewhere). Clear specification about the expected comprehension about principles and practices of effective teamwork was less common. Attitudes toward teamwork were frequently mentioned, but often without an explicit description by which the achievement could be assessed. The use of rubrics to specify a target level of achievement (and intermediate steps toward that level) was not typically included for any of the knowledge, skills or attitudes.

1. **Teaching Teamwork in Design Project:** The Student manual from this program of work outlines the following expectation for teamwork capability (Tucker & Abassi, 2014a, p. 7):

Six chief skills are required for effective teamwork:

Coordination of tasks and responsibilities (using, for instance, project work-plans and team contracts);

- *Communication via speaking, writing, drawing, modelling;*
- *Idea generation, evaluation & selection;*
- *Decision making;*
- *Leadership; and*
- *Conflict management.*

The matching Manual on Teamwork in Design for Teachers repeats this list and notes the implication for the course components:

Students therefore need to be taught these six skills. Teachers need to also carefully design assessment and assignments to facilitate and encourage effective teamwork. (Tucker & Abassi, 2014b, p. 8)

2. **Transferable Integrated Design Engineering Education:** Over the several years of the TIDEE program work, an explicit specification has been developed for the factors resulting in successful teamwork:

. . . team member behaviors and team processes contribute to constructive relationships, joint achievements, individual contributions, and information management that synergistically yield high team performance and successful project completion. (Davis et al., 2013, p. 6)

While the TIDEE description of teamwork success for engineering students contains many of the same components as the description above for design students, there are interesting implicit differences based on how professional teams function in these differing domains of knowledge and practice. For example, explicit role assignments are typical in the engineering context. Each team is expected to adapt a set of roles and responsibilities to reach their goals. Completing the engineering design project may entail roles assigned to specific performance or component and schedule aspects such as *Report Manager*; the team development goals may entail roles such as *Meeting Facilitator, Scribe, and Timekeeper* (Davis et al., 2013, p. 6). As another example, the specification for team processes in the engineering design case contains a much stronger emphasis on managing the information artifacts which provide rationale for the decisions and interfaces in the resulting product.

3. **Other Relevant References:** The differences noted above between various expectations for team-work are also identified in design disciplines as factors in thinking about spaces for collaboration and teamwork. For example, Augustin (2014) notes that interior designers creating workspaces for collaborative teamwork have to consider the impact of differing expectations for how teams function, including differences for the following types of teams:

A research team from IBM has identified six different types of collaborative groups (Matthews, Whittaker, Moran, & Yuen, 2011). The groups are distinguished by the goals they pursue and the assorted processes used to achieve those goals. They also differ in team longevity and leadership style. Group type number one are dynamic project teams who share a job-related objective and whose members may change during the course of a specific project. These dynamic project teams can be contrasted with stable project teams (the second type of collaborative group specified) who are also pursuing a job-related goal but whose membership stays the same throughout the course of the project. Committees (third type), in contrast are working to achieve a common objective, but that goal is secondary to their primary professional focus. Client–supplier groups are an ongoing type of team (fourth), organized to make it more likely that suppliers meet client needs. The fifth type of collaborative group is a community or collection of people who share interests or do similar jobs and who exchange information. The final collaborative groups identified by the IBM researchers are professional relationships. These associations were defined as between two individuals and as generally having little structure. Examples of this kind of collaborative group are mentor–mentee relationships or sets of individuals providing feedback to each other, perhaps on performance or ideas. (p.10)

This list of teams types reflects a different work context than the design studio setting, and more evidence about interior design work in teams across different settings would be valuable as a curriculum topic (and also in helping students to understand team structures and procedures). On the other hand, our students' education also needs to incorporate the knowledge that collaborative efforts from other work disciplines bring different expectations about team structure and engagement.

SUMMARY OF INSIGHTS AND ISSUES FOR TEAMWORK CAPABILITY AND TEAM TEACHING IN DESIGN STUDIOS

*   **Incorporating the Similarities and Differences in Teamwork**: Individual roles for teams in design vary from those in other disciplines. In interior design studio team projects for example, there

is often a fluid (rather than fixed) team leadership and work is not divided by task but by area to be designed. This requires a different type of team dynamics that includes similar levels of authority among members and clearer strategies for consensus on design decisions and conflict resolution. Our students should develop teamwork capability for working with professionals from other domains of knowledge and practice, and for their other roles (e.g., as community members and global citizens). There are initial steps in this direction, e.g., in the distinction between Generic teamwork skills and Collaborative Design skills in the Teachers Manual for Teaching Teamwork in Design (Tucker & Abbasi, 2014b, p. 5) and in the inclusion of "alternate teamwork approaches" and "deep understanding of multidisciplinary practice" as targets for an Expert level of student capability in the overall program report (Tucker et al., 2014, p. 34).

- **Expanding Definitions of Teamwork Capability to Include More Than Skills:** The discussion above about teamwork capability noted the need to go beyond competencies for teamwork to include knowledge and attitudes as learning outcomes (Oliver, 2013). Most of the research studies and exemplary practices examined in our review did not include exploration by students of how teams can function more effectively (and why); a notable exception was the work by Hynes (2015) described in the next section. This raises the question of how important such knowledge about teamwork functionality would be for design students, e.g., in supporting adaptation of their teamwork expectations for different settings.

Another aspect of potential importance is the development of productive attitudes to working in teams: as outlined at the beginning of this chapter, some efforts to engage students in teamwork have been shown to cause a more negative attitude toward working in teams (Gale et al., 2014). The issue of developing positive attitudes toward teamwork is explored in the review below of evidence and exemplars to motivate student engagement in the development of teamwork capability.

- **Using a Rubric Format to Specify Expected Levels of Achievement:** In North America there has been considerable effort invested in constructing rubrics to specify and assess levels of student achievement in particular learning outcomes criteria at the program level (Hughes & Jones, 2011). Many institutions are using variants of the rubrics for Valid Assessment of Learning in Undergraduate Education from the American Association of Colleges and Universities (AAC&U, 2010a), including a number of institutions who have customized the rubric for Teamwork (AAC&U, 2010b) (e.g., Gray, 2013). Given the variety of team expectations revealed in the research reviewed above, it is the rubric format rather than any particular set of content which is of most interest to us here.

Rubrics have traditionally been used more in Assessment, and there is a brief mention of assessment rubrics in the Teachers Manual for Teaching Teamwork in Design (Tucker & Abbasi, 2014b, p. 31). Our review identified some interesting research from other domains that suggested rubrics could be valuable as well in clarifying expectations for students (Cicek et al., 2015; Gray, 2013). As noted in the next section on engaging student interest in developing teamwork capability, this might be particularly helpful if the terminology in the rubric is linked to readiness for professional work (Hastie, Fahy, & Parrett,

2014), e.g., labelling milestones as demonstrating Foundational, Emerging, Developing and Professional capability rather than the AAC&U terminology of Benchmark, Milestones 2 and 3, and Capstone. There is further discussion of the issues and opportunities in rubric usage in the Assessment section below.

Engage Students by Motivating the Development of the Capabilities

1. **Teaching Teamwork in Design**: The project report *Enhancing and assessing group and team learning in architecture and related design contexts* (Tucker et al., 2014) recommends motivating students for capability development by listing expectations from professional bodies and industry:
   a. *Teamwork skills are essential in the design industry where practitioners negotiate often-conflicting design options in multi-disciplinary teams. Indeed, many of the bodies that accredit design courses explicitly list teamwork skills as essential attributes of design graduates (p. 5).*
   b. *Teamwork learning is seen as being representative of work in practice where design is nearly always a collaborative activity (p. 5).*
2. **Transferable Integrated Design Engineering Education:** An explicit Engagement model was developed in this program of work, built around twin goals of building an effective team and creating a successful product: "Teams have dual goals. Teams must work to advance simultaneously both team development and project completion. Over emphasis on one, at the cost of the other, will reduce team achievement" (Davis et al., 2013, p. 6).

The TIDEE recommendations for course design reflect this dual-goal structure - team development and project completion - throughout: specific activities and resources are included to *develop*, *demonstrate* and *assess* progress on both the team development goal and the project completion goal. Creating an effective team is framed as an engineering design assignment in its own right, with attention to "the specifications, inputs, feedback and control mechanisms, performance definitions and assessments" (Davis et al., 2013, p. 6). All students thus share some of the responsibility for their development of teamwork capability by other members of the team.

3. **Other Relevant Research with Design Students:** Much of the earlier research on developing teamwork capability with design students seems to have assumed a high degree of pre-existent student commitment to teamwork and to developing their own knowledge and capabilities (or at least does not refer to specific course components intended to engage student motivation for developing capability).
   a. For example, Russ and Dickinson (1999) draw on multiple sources to summarize the advantages of design teams that bring numerous perspectives to a design challenge. "Companies are increasingly using multidisciplinary teams to solve problems . . . This is understandable when collaboration increases design creativity, expedites the design process, generates greater amounts of work in a shorter period of time, and clarifies the task at hand" (p. 58). However, there is no account given of how evidence for these benefits was communicated to students in a compelling way. "Although the students encountered many of the typical problems associated with teamwork, the students seemed to understand that the experiences from this course were preparing them for the real world" (p. 58).

b. Another stream of thought around engaging student motivation for teamwork capability suggests that design students may have a stronger willingness or commitment to work in teams than other students (with an implicit or explicit suggestions that less effort may be required to engage their motivation for improving teamwork capability as an important goal in design studio courses). For example, Carmel-Gilfilen (2012) used an evaluation of design students' learning styles to conclude that they were predisposed to working in teams, based on their high scores on accommodating and diverging dispositions for learning.

Accommodating learners are best at feeling and doing . . . These learners are hands-on and rely on intuition to complete t asks rather than analytical abilities. Accommodating learners prefer to work in teams and often test multiple solutions. Diverging learners are best at feeling and watching . . . These learners are sensitive and emotional and often approach a task from many different perspectives . . . Diverging learners prefer to work in teams where they can listen carefully to all suggestions before deciding on a solution (p. 50).

Two issues with this approach weakened the argument that it would be any less important to build explicit engagement activities regarding teamwork capability into our design studio courses than would be the case in other domains of knowledge and practice. One issue was that past research on learning styles has come under heightened scrutiny in terms of its validity as a predictor of learning behaviours (Coffield et al., 2004; Pashler et al., 2008; Riener & Willingham, 2010). Secondly, there was no evidence presented that students who might in fact have a predisposition to engaging in teamwork would as a consequence also have a strong motivation to invest effort in further development of their teamwork capability.

c. The issue of addressing dual goals in a teamwork design project was approached in a different way in an assignment with interior design students Hynes (2015). While the assignment was undertaken by individual students rather than in a team, the task given to students was to design a space for team work. The assignment included the following description of the task:

Redesign the 2 interior design studios and resource room. Create a collaborative, cutting edge, learning environment for a minimum of 32 students and 2 instructors . . . It should be flexible to include spaces for group work, individual work, computer work, fabrication work, contemplation, hang-out, material and project storage, writable surfaces, and transparency. There should be space for all students and instructors to have a large combined (standing) class for a presentation/pin-up, but still be flexible for instructors to work with smaller groups and/or have separate classes of 16 each (as they are now) (Hynes, 2015, p. 5).

The assignment was carried out as a four-week project by individuals in order to test the impact of the project topic on student perceptions of teamwork (without the confounding factor of actually engaging as teams).

The purpose of this study was to explore the possibility that project content may influence a student's attitude towards teamwork in an interior design classroom:

- *Does it impact their confidence as a team member?*
- *Does it impact personal interest in teamwork?*
- *Does it impact their overall belief in its value or usefulness?*
- *Does it impact their perception of how teamwork is used in the profession?*

Measures in all 4 categories taken at two points indicate an increase in positive attitude towards teamwork after completion of the project assignment (Hynes, 2015, p. 13).

For interior design students, this approach might well serve to introduce some of the knowledge about different teams and how they collaborate, as preparation for students developing the skills in future teamwork assignments. (It should be noted, however, that the conclusions about the positive effects of the assignment tested only attitudes and not knowledge).

4. **Relevant Research from Other Disciplines:** Several of the studies we examined looked at specific issues in workplace teams for other professional disciplines, and how student attention could be directed to these issues within their course team experiences. This research from other professional areas demonstrated that specific issues for workplace teams could be included in an explicit curriculum for comprehension and motivation, and in included in the structure of project assignments for demonstration and capability development.

The contexts of these studies are sufficiently different from interior design that the conclusions on assignment design etc. do not easily generalize. However, the studies did raise questions about the need to develop explicit curriculum resources about teamwork issues in our own design domains, the extent to which a similar evidence base exists to identify workplace team issues of key importance in interior design and other design areas and how such issues can be incorporated into teamwork experiences within the constraints of an academic environment. For example, while perceived fairness in team composition and assessment has been shown to be an important factor for successful teamwork by architectural design students (Tucker & Abbasi, 2015; Tucker & Reynolds, 2006), there is a lack of evidence specific to design teams about the important of such factors in the workplace.

Some examples from these studies are briefly summarized below.

a. Work by Graen, Hui, and Taylor (2006) outlines an engineering design project assignment explicitly designed to help students learn teamwork in an intentionally challenging project. There was an explicit curriculum about knowledge of how project teams in engineering design function in the workplace, with a specific emphasis on Work Relationships versus Friendship Relationships and Fairness in Project Teams, and how the phases and deadlines of a project interact with these elements. These emphases were justified by the researchers as requiring students to focus on issues that were known to be critical for team success in the workplace, and which were unlikely to receive explicit attention in an instructional setting without strong design elements to direct student engagement.

A similar issue was raised by a study of developing teamwork capability with medical students (Aarnio, Nieminen, Pyörälä, & Lindblom-Ylänne, 2010): the key lesson from this study was the need to focus students' attention on the value of teamwork skills as applied in professional practice, not teamwork skills as applied within the academic context.

b.   Other research highlights the way our designs for student team projects need to reflect the values and principles about teamwork - such as procedural fairness - that students are expected to apply in the workplace. For example, Kidder and Bowes-Sperry (2012) examined the impacts of different team project designs on investment in teamwork development by management students. Amongst the measures used to determine success was the perceived fairness of the instructional design, based on the concept of procedural fairness in the workplace as a key factor in employee work engagement.

The researchers compared students' end-of-term reports on the perceived fairness of the project structure under several variations in the instructional design, and concluded that decisions made regarding the design of team projects can strongly influence the extent to which instructional designs are perceived as fair. For example, they reported that "class time devoted to the team project was perceived as beneficial [in terms of fairness], but telling students to work on the team project instead of coming to class was perceived negatively." (Kidder & Bowes-Sperry, 2012, p. 76).

SUMMARY OF INSIGHTS AND ISSUES FOR TEAMWORK CAPABILITY AND TEAM TEACHING IN DESIGN STUDIOS

The following ideas, insights and issues from the work in this section appear to hold the most promise for application to using team teaching as a model for teamwork capabilities:

- *Dual-goal engagement in student assignments*, around designing both a 'space' to develop teamwork capability and a solution to the project design assignment. There could be a link here to team teaching if the teachers are seen as developing roles, relationships and processes for their own teamwork in teaching. However, a team that has taught together before, or worked together on past team projects, may have already developed an implicit working arrangement that could make much of this effort unnecessary and artificial.
- *Motivating student interest through links to professional teamwork practice.* Team teaching might make a contribution in this area if the teachers were able to offer a richer or broader set of professional experiences as exemplars. The approaches listed above include acknowledgment of the constraints of a student setting as a simulation of a professional workplace. Other research has also noted that design studio courses are a "unique practice community that connects academic and professional contexts" and the need to therefore consider "the academic constraints on studio-based approaches to learning" (Brandt et al., 2011, p. 329).
- *Using data from student perception about issues like procedural fairness*, to better align design studio teamwork assignments with professional values and expectations.

Develop and Demonstrate Capabilities through Teaching and Learning Activities

Activities and resources for learning and teaching have been the focus of most of the research on developing student capabilities for teamwork. This section of the chapter presents only a brief summary of work from the design disciplines, as other chapters in the book report extensively on this area. The section outlines some developments from the design discipline that highlight the potential for team teaching to serve as a model of teamwork.

1. **Teaching Teamwork in Design:** The Manual on Teamwork in Design for Teachers (Tucker & Abbasi, 2014b) has made detailed recommendations for developing teamwork capabilities. Four Teaching Modules are proposed:

   Module 1: *Design and Prepare*
   Module 2: *Train and Engage Students*
   Module 3: *Monitor and Support Teams*
   Module 4: *Assess and Reflect. (p. 7)*

   The manual contains suggested procedures and recommendations for each of these modules.
   The Manual on Teamwork in Design for Teachers also makes the following recommendations regarding the role of teachers in providing formative feedback:

   Establish strategies to regularly monitor student team processes, identify problems and issues once they start emerging and provide students with necessary feedback and guidance on how to improve team processes. Monitoring team processes is particularly important in relation to preventing team conflict. Major monitoring strategies include keeping track of student team meetings and their effectiveness, online discussion forums and ongoing Self and Peer Assessment (SAPA) (p.37).

   The manual also provides the Ongoing Evaluation of Students' Team Experiences Tool (Tucker & Abbasi, 2014b, p. 38) and recommends using it in addition to team observation during class work and providing verbal feedback. Additionally, the suggestion is made that faculty intervene to help teams resolve conflict as it arises and monitor its progress. Specific preventive and intervention strategies are suggested; these include training in conflict resolution and tips on mediating conflict in teams.

2. **Transferable Integrated Design Engineering Education:** There is a similar set of curriculum resources and activities available from this program of work, summarized by Davis and Ulseth (2013). For example, sample module resources are presented for the following activities:

   a. Developing (initial) Shared Teamwork Expectations (p. 15),
   b. Defining Team Roles and Responsibilities (p. 16),
   c. Creating a Team Contract for use in reviewing and assessing team performance (p. 17),
   d. Providing Feedback on (individual) Member Contributions through a Team Member Citizenship Assessment (p. 18),
   e. Reviewing Team Processes against the expectations in the Team Contract (p. 19), and

f.   Evaluating Teamwork Achieved (p. 20).

These resources are also incorporated into an online system which manages the logistics of student use of the modules as well as individual and peer assessments (IDEALS, 2015). Including structured activities of this sort in class time represents a serious commitment, and begs the question of whether other classes are doing the same – it seems that some coordination across courses is required (which the authors point out, although in their context they assume only one design project team running for students in any given school term).

Many of the activities listed above to Develop student capability contain opportunities for formative feedback on the capabilities demonstrated. For example, as described by Davis and Ulseth (2013):

a.   "The instructor scores the feedback on the Team Member Citizenship Assessment, based on its quality, not the positive or negative nature of the feedback" (p. 18).

b.   "Instructors…score the quality of their team process revisions and offer suggestions to make additional process improvement" (p. 19).

Cognitive Apprenticeship: The instructional format recommended in the TIDEE work for facilitating development of teamwork capability employs the cognitive apprenticeship model, and deserves special mention here for its potential value in structuring team teaching to serve as a model for developing student capability:

. . . an instructional method that models and coaches development of skills, such as teamwork, along with thinking processes that enable these performance skills. The instructor models teamwork behaviors and provides explanations for the behaviors, followed by the learner practicing the same behaviors and describing thinking processes in increasingly challenging environments (Davis & Ulseth, 2013, p. 12).

As this instructor role relates directly to our longer-term interest in faculty team-teaching as a model of teamwork capability for students, the description of this process is of particular interest:

- Instructor demonstrates skill in a realistic context similar to that to be encountered in the future
- Instructor demonstrates and explains thinking processes associated with skill, including variations
- Learner practices skill in structured, coached environment
- Learner describes steps learned, for instructor checking
- Learner reflects on learning process to understand what helped and what hindered learning
- Learner is given more varied problems and identifies additional problems for which the skill is applicable. (Davis & Ulseth, 2013, p. 12)

Within the context of this cognitive apprenticeship model, some implications are drawn for instructors engaged in modeling teamwork capabilities (although team teaching as a format for this modelling is not mentioned):

Just as students need to learn teamwork skills, instructors need to learn and develop strong performances in mentoring the development of teamwork skills in students... It is expected that repeated practice of teamwork skills, reflection on teamwork learning, and initiative to address areas needing improvement by students will yield a spiral of teamwork growth that reaches significant levels of expertise before graduation. This requires a corresponding spiral of practice, reflection and improvement on the part of project mentors and instructors (Davis & Ulseth, 2013, p. 24).

While this program of work did emphasize the dual-goal concept for students developing a design project in parallel with developing their teamwork capabilities, the focus for faculty modeling capability was very much on the knowledge and skills for the design project.

3. **Other Relevant References:** To supplement the two main reference points, a further search was carried out for research specific to team teaching in design courses as an aid to developing student teamwork capability. The research identified in this review focused almost exclusively on teachers contributing from different design disciplines or professions, and not on the contribution of teaching teams as models of teamwork capability.

For example, Sadowska, Griffith, and Morgan (2009) reported on an experiment in design studio teaching with collaborative teaching by instructors in a U.K. Business school and an Australian College of Fine Arts. While the mix of "cross-continental, cross-cultural, cross-disciplinary" (p. 3) issues for students is highlighted, there is limited description of how the instructors developed their own teamwork and none about how this might have served as a model for students.

Another research project on teaching sustainability in design (Gürel, 2010) featured a "teaching scheme that utilised a team of instructors with varying degrees of knowledge and competence in different aspects of the topic, mediated the education of both the students and the instructors themselves" (p. 184). The focus of the study was an inter-professional understanding of sustainability: although students undertook team projects, there is no mention of how the instruction promoted teamwork capability and the questions asked of students post-course about contributions to student learning from the various course components did not include the team teaching aspect.

Recent work to develop teamwork capability with interior design students (Khodadad, 2013) has mentioned that in team teaching "professors model teamwork and the collaborative design process as a daily example of the roles and relationships between architects and interior designers" (p. 253). However, the results reported focus again on inter-professional aspects - "how students challenged their preconceived notions of their own discipline in relationship to the strengths and contributions of others within the design profession" (p. 254) – rather than the specific contributions of team teaching.

SUMMARY OF INSIGHTS AND ISSUES FOR TEAMWORK CAPABILITY AND TEAM TEACHING IN DESIGN STUDIOS

The concept of team teaching as a model is mentioned in several references as of potential importance, but no evidence was found about how well this might have been achieved in practice. However, the diverse set of methods and resources for developing student capability suggest ways that team teaching could be augmented and evaluated to better serve as a model for teamwork capability.

For example, several of the development approaches centered on creating artifacts to track team progress, e.g., a Team Contract and an Assessment of Teamwork Achieved (Davis & Ulseth, 2013).

Similar artifacts could potentially be used by teachers to track the development of their teaching team, especially if the team members are new to the concept of team teaching or to working together.

This could be a very explicit way for teachers to emphasize the importance of investing effort in team development in a professional context (although not the context in which students will be working). It may be more challenging for teachers to model for students a mindset seeking continuous improvement in capability for teamwork (as with other professional capabilities).

Assess (in Summative Evaluation) and Document Teamwork Capabilities

While the Assessment and Documentation of teamwork capabilities is an important part of the Learning Outcomes Value Cycle, the review of research evidence and exemplary practices did not reveal significant opportunities for team teaching to serve as a model for student teamwork capability through these activities. For completeness, the practices and resources in our two reference points for this component of the framework are outlined briefly below.

1. **Teaching Teamwork in Design:** The Manual on Teamwork in Design for Teachers (Tucker & Abbasi, 2014b) from this project recommends that faculty thoroughly consider the assessment of teamwork processes. It recommends students present their documented design process in digital, written or oral form as well as complete some form of peer-and-self assessment. Faculty should also assess teammates' contributions in order to provide fair individual marks. Differentiation between types of output should be clear:
   ○ *Task Performance, which should be assessed by teachers through an evaluation of the learning of course-specific knowledge represented by the submitted product – usually a designed artefact;*
   ○ *Teamwork process skills – both generic and collaborative design skills (p. 43).*

   Additionally, the project report *Enhancing and assessing group and team learning in architecture and related design contexts* (Tucker et al., 2014) identifies three areas of output that should be considered as part of the assessment process: "(a) Quality of the Submitted Product (Design) and Learning of Unit-Specific Knowledge and Skill, (b) Learning of Generic and Collaborative Design Teamwork Skills and Attitudes to Future Teamwork" (p. 23).

2. **Transferable Integrated Design Engineering Education:** In contrast to the formative feedback described in the previous section, the summative assessment in the TIDEE model focuses on the final Teamwork Achieved Assessment which describes the achievement of both the team and its individual team members: "The instructor scores each student's submission of the Teamwork Achieved Assessment, using a standard rubric" (Davis & Ulseth, 2013, p. 20). The Teamwork Achieved Assessment is prepared by the individual students (based on multiple iterations of self and peer- assessment of Teamwork Citizenship for individual members and of Teamwork Processes for the team as a whole).

3. **Documenting Teamwork Capability for External Stakeholders:** The review of exemplary practices and research evidence found very little consideration of new approaches such as micro-credentials for teamwork capability. The Manual on Teamwork in Design for Teachers (Tucker & Abbasi, 2014b) from this project doesn't provide specific recommendations on how to document

team capabilities. It does, however, suggest that faculty use portfolios, diaries and self-and peer assessments as artifacts to document quality and quantity of team member's contributions. This idea could be translated into artifacts to document team capabilities as well.

A search of the research literature on e-Portfolios yielded no examples of artifacts used to document the development of teamwork capability: although teamwork is frequently mentioned as an outcome that could be documented in an e-portfolio, it appears that what is actually documented is the occurrence of – and output from – team assignments (which as noted in the Introduction section are not always good indicators of teamwork capability).

There were instances of research studies where students use ePortfolios as a space in which to record reflections on their teamwork experiences (e.g., Bhika, Francis, & Miller, 2013). However, the exemplary instructional designs referenced above already contain explicit learning activities and artifacts for reflection on teamwork experiences in more structured ways. The recommendations from the Teaching Teamwork in Design program include providing class time three or four times throughout the course of the project to allow students to complete the provided "Ongoing Evaluation of Students' Team Experiences" (Tucker & Abbasi, 2014b, p. 38). The Teachers Manual cites the following benefits for this ongoing evaluation:

Summary of Insights and Issues for Teamwork Capability and Team Teaching in Design Studios

- Traditionally, assessment in design studios includes specific rubrics for the assessment of the creative design process. Students are assessed for their ability to properly document design decisions resulting in final project solutions. The research evidence and exemplary practices reviewed in this section suggest that a dual-goal assignment structure requires that assessment of the creative design process during team assignments should include how process as a team activity differs from the activity of an individual and how it impacts project outcomes.
- There were examples of effective use of explicit criteria for assessing teamwork capability in both the major reference points and in other sources. However, the review did not identify examples of a rubric format (with explicit levels of capability) used to assess teamwork with design students. Work in other domains suggests significant value for such structured rubrics for assessment (e.g., Hughes & Jones, 2011; Gray, 2013; González-Fernández et al., 2014), so this appears to be a promising area for further investigation.
- As in the other sections of this review, questions remain as to how the ways team teachers reflect on and assess teamwork experiences in teaching could serve as a model for students in developing capability. For example, could such work be shared with students in ways that convey the importance – to us and to them – of ongoing development of teamwork capability in new contexts?

ENHANCING THE DEVELOPMENT OF TEAMWORK CAPABILITY: APPLYING THE RESULTS TO OUR TEACHING, RESEARCH AND INSTITUTIONAL GOALS

This section highlights how the structured review of research evidence and exemplary practices has impacted the instructional goals stated in the introduction, with a focus on the authors' adaptations of the results for teaching – at the course (module) and program levels. The next section describes the impact of the research review on our further scholarly work as well as a very brief summary of some of the implications at the institutional level.

Enhancing Initiatives to Advance Teaching

1. At the level of an individual design studio course or module, several key enhancements stand out as particularly promising in developing knowledge, skills and attitudes for effective teamwork:

    a. *Integrating more effective methods of engaging student motivation for the development of teamwork capability.* The dual-goal project assignment of TIDEE for engineering design can be adapted for Interior Design by posing the challenge of creating a 'virtual space' of roles and processes to support more effective teamwork.

    b. *Expanding the direct instructional activities focused on teamwork capability.* Augmenting previous process and resources models for design studios (e.g., Tucker et al. 2014) with ideas from other disciplines (e.g., TIDEE) could enhance the learning outcomes achieved by students. For Interior Design students in particular, it is also easy to conceive how an assignment to design a physical space for more effective teamwork (Hynes 2015) would require students to develop a stronger knowledge base about team effectiveness.

    c. *Adapting the artifacts supporting team activity to enable team teaching as a more visible model.* A first step in this direction can be undertaken largely as a background activity: members of a teaching team can experiment by using some of the teamwork artifacts designed for use by students in their own teamwork development, assessment and enhancement – without sharing the results with students until the initial efforts have proven effective!

    d. *Establishing team teaching as a model for students of teamwork capabilities in action.* Team-teaching faculty who are experienced team players should find ways to use their own interactions in team development and collaboration as models for student reflection and learning. This may require some degree of formalization for those interactions within online course spaces, and could include some or all of the following to illustrations of teamwork capabilities and practices:

        i.   Distributing workload for best use of each team member's skills and resources;
        ii. Communication in verbal, written and graphical form;
        iii. Sharing of leadership roles;
        iv. Resolving disagreements; and
        v.   Iterative reflection on practice as a team for future improvement.

Attitudes towards teamwork will improve if students are allowed time to reflect on the impact of these in action (as seen in class exemplified by their teachers) and how they can apply them in their own work.

Strengthening the achievement of teamwork capability in these ways implies an intentional redirection of student effort. That is, if students are investing more time and energy in developing more effective teamwork, some other learning activities in the course or module will receive less of their attention. The immediate effect for a reallocation of student effort could be a decline in some other outcome.

An argument can be made that more effective teamwork developed early in a program can free up time later for attention to be redirected to professional capability specific to the discipline (although this challenge was not addressed in any of the research studies or exemplary practices reviewed). It is worth noting that the use of a teamwork-oriented assignment along the lines of Hynes (2015) appears to avoid this challenge, by replacing an existing design task with an equivalent one generating value for the additional goal of developing teamwork capability

2. The potential tradeoff in outcomes raised in the previous paragraphs is just one example of the interactions across courses or modules which need to be addressed and coordinated at a program level.

    a. At the program level, some formal structure for progressive development of teamwork capability needs to be envisioned. Some of this happens now in less formal ways: for example, the challenge of working in inter-professional teams is typically not addressed until students have achieved substantial experience with teams of other design students in their own discipline area.

    b. Developing specific milestones for teamwork capabilities in each year of a program could provide students with opportunities to reflect on previously acquired knowledge and skills, and to intentionally enhance their capabilities through building on these skills.

    c. If the efforts of individual instructors are not coordinated, there is a danger that students may have multiple exposures to the same resources and evaluations which may cause "resource fatigue". Using some of the research evidence and exemplary practices outlined above, a program could instead design progressively richer resources for knowledge, skills and attitudes in teamwork to align with increasingly challenging team assignments.

FUTURE RESEARCH DIRECTIONS

Enhancing Initiatives to Advance Scholarship

The research review highlighted four issues in interpreting results from research studies on developing teamwork capability:

*   Some studies were explicit about the model for effective teamwork being applied, including a number cited earlier in the section on specifying the teamwork capability students were expected to achieve. Other studies left this implicit, which makes it more difficult to interpret the results on the effects of various approaches to teaching and learning for that capability. Such studies were not dropped from the research review if their model of effective teams, and therefore of teamwork capability, was not clear.

*   The review also highlighted a lack of precision in some studies about the distinction between three attitudinal elements: a willingness to work in teams, a willingness to commit effort to making teams work effectively and a willingness to commit effort to developing team work capability (e.g., Smith 2013).

*   A number of research studies were not explicit about the learning activities and resources used to support the development of teamwork capability. This made it difficult to interpret conclusions along the lines of "students preferred…" or "students made negative comments about…" since the complex interaction of factors producing these student responses could not be tracked.

- Finally, in a number of studies dealing with a coherent student cohort there was no evident consideration given to the impact of student experiences in concurrent courses or modules which might be taken at the same time by a large subset of the students providing data. This made it difficult to interpret claims about the impact of specific course features on the development of teamwork capability, as a positive or negative effect might have been influenced by teamwork experiences or learning opportunities beyond those within the course being examined.

Amongst the research topics identified in the review as gaps in the available evidence base, two stood out as particular promising for further study:

- The Introduction section outlined the chapter authors' interest in investigating the impact of team-teaching on students' teamwork capabilities and exploring how to maximize its positive impact, with a particular focus on how the teaching teams' interactions and processes might serve as a model for teamwork capability. The review did not identify exemplary practices or research evidence on this particular aspect, so it appears to be a fruitful area for systematic study.
- Documenting teamwork capabilities developed in both formal and informal learning contexts seems to be an area that has not been addressed in a systematic way. What would be an appropriate and acceptable format for the design profession, the accreditation bodies and the educational institutions? How can we incorporate insights on the integration of emerging tools to "curate, credential and carry forward" (Oliver 2015) evidence about teamwork capability?

It should be noted, however, that any future scholarly work done on this capability should be built on the basis methodological and pedagogical discoveries in this chapter being applied in the classroom to address issues highlighted above prior to developing new research. We recognize that our original intent to develop a scholarly research agenda around the impact of team teaching requires that we first implement a number of the approaches highlighted in this chapter (and elsewhere in this volume) so that any such research study builds on the exemplary practices, research evidence and promising innovations already identified.

In addition, the chapter authors' use of a structured framework in a review of research evidence and exemplary practice provided an opportunity for the review to be an act of creative inquiry in its own right, "exploring the deep underlying assumptions "of our design education community as well as "an opportunity for self-inquiry" (Montuori, 2005).

Enhancing Initiatives to Advance Learning Outcomes at the Institutional Level

The work reported in this chapter also had impacts at the institutional level due to the project's role as a test case for the framework. We list here brief illustrative comments on this experience:

- Adaptations were made to the pilot institutional framework components as a result of the work reported in this study acting as a test case[1].
- The most valuable aspects of the institutional framework for the work described in this chapter were the Engage and Enhance components[2].

- In the work reported in this chapter, the university's interest in contextualized outcomes led to investigation of other discipline areas to evaluate what insights could be shared across disciplinary boundaries, which proved to very illuminating[3].

It is also important to also note that this review has not considered any of the larger institutional issues around promoting and supporting a Learning Outcomes Value Cycle as an approach to institution-wide curriculum renewal in an institutional strategy for teaching and learning (Oliver, 2013).

CONCLUSION

While team projects have been a part of the interior design curriculum for a long time, teaching of teamwork capabilities has not been formally included in the curriculum, neither has it been formally assessed in the past. It is clear that without proper training in teamwork, students may not be able to overcome the challenges generated by designing in teams and they won't be able to resolve the issues and conflicts that arise. Design curricula should include planned instruction on team capabilities as well as formal assessment on it.

Faculty involvement in team processes has frequently been unstructured in the past and often occurred on an 'as needed' basis when conflict in teams reached a critical stage. Teaching of teamwork capability requires a more planned and proactive involvement, which includes evaluation and reflection on team processes on a regular basis. Team teaching could be one way to augment this process, if the teaching approach is intentionally structured to parallel and support student engagement with the practices, processes and resources in the instructional design.

The previous section emphasized the impacts of the review results on the authors' immediate goals in teaching and scholarship. It is important to note the preliminary nature of the "next steps" outlined there – as local "conclusions" about promising directions which will be subject to further assessment and enhancement.

REFERENCES

Aarnio, M., Nieminen, J., Pyörälä, E., & Lindblom-Ylänne, S. (2010). Motivating medical students to learn teamwork skills. *Medical Teacher*, *32*(4), e199–e204. doi:10.3109/01421591003657469 PMID:20353320

American Association of Colleges and Universities [AAC&U]. (2010a). *Valid Assessment of Learning in Undergraduate Education*. Retrieved from https://www.aacu.org/value

American Association of Colleges and Universities [AAC&U]. (2010b). *Teamwork VALUE Rubric*. In T.L. Rhodes (Ed.), *Assessing Outcomes and Improving Achievement: Tips and tools for Using Rubrics*. Association of American Colleges and Universities. Retrieved from https://www.aacu.org/value/rubrics/teamwork

American Society of Interior Designers [ASID]. (2015). *Becoming an interior designer*. Retrieved from https://www.asid.org/content/becoming-interior-designer#.VgcaLKSFOM8

Augustin, S. (2014). Designing for Collaboration and Collaborating for Design. *Journal of Interior Design, 39*(1), ix–xviii. doi:10.1111/joid.12020

Bhika, R., Francis, A., & Miller, D. (2013). Faculty professional development: advancing integrative social pedagogy using ePortfolio. *International Journal of ePortfolio, 3*(2), 117-133.

Brandt, C. B., Cennamo, K., Douglas, S., Vernon, M., McGrath, M., & Reimer, Y. (2013). A theoretical framework for the studio as a learning environment. *International Journal of Technology and Design Education, 23*(2), 329–348. doi:10.1007/s10798-011-9181-5

Carey, T. (2015). Defining learning outcomes is just the beginning: Exploring a learning outcomes value cycle for KPU. *Teaching Matters@KPU,* 8. Retrieved from http://www.kpu.ca/sites/default/files/ Teaching_and_Learning /INSTL-newsletter_Sep2015_Issue4.pdf

Carmel-Gilfilen, C. (2012). Uncovering pathways of design thinking and learning: Inquiry on intellectual development and learning style preferences. *Journal of Interior Design, 37*(3), 47–66. doi:10.1111/j.1939-1668.2012.01077.x

Caspersen, J., Frølich, N., Karlsen, H., & Aamodt Per, O. (2014). Learning outcomes across disciplines and professions: Measurement and interpretation. *Quality in Higher Education, 20*(2), 195–215. doi:1 0.1080/13538322.2014.904587

Cicek, J. S., Ingram, S., Sepehri, N., Burak, J. P., Labossiere, P., & Mann, D. Topping A. (2015). Rubrics as a Vehicle to Define the Twelve CEAB Graduate Attributes, Determine Graduate Competencies, and Develop a Common Language for Engineering Stakeholders. *Proceedings of the Canadian Engineering Education Association.* Winnipeg MB: Canadian Engineering Education Association.

Coffield, F., Moseley, D., Hall, E., & Ecclestone, K. (2004). *Learning styles and pedagogy in post-16 learning: a systematic and critical review.* London: The Learning and Skills Research Centre.

Council for Interior Design Accreditation. (2015). *Final draft professional standards 2017: August 2015.* Retrieved from http://accredit-id.org/wp-content/uploads/2014/10/Professional-Standards-2017-final-draft-August-2015.pdf

Council for Interior Design Qualification [CIDQ]. (2004). *Definition of interior design.* Retrieved from http://www.ncidqexam.org/about-interior-design/definition-of-interior-design/

Davis, D., Trevisan, M., Gerlick, R., Davis, H., McCormack, J., Beyerlein, S., & Brackin, P. et al. (2010). Assessing team member citizenship in capstone engineering design courses. *International Journal of Engineering Education, 26*(4), 771.

Davis, D., Trevisan, M., Leiffer, P., McCormack, J., Beyerlein, S., Khan, M. J., & Brackin, P. (2013). Reflection and metacognition in engineering practice. In M. Kaplan, N. Silver, D. LaVaque-Manty, & D. Meizlish (Eds.), *Using reflection and metacognition to improve student learning: Across the disciplines, across the academy.* Sterling, VA: Stylus Publishing, LLC.

Davis, D., Trevisan, M. S., Davis, H. P., Beyerlein, S. W., Howe, S., Thompson, P. L., & Khan, M. J. et al. (2011). IDEALS: A model for integrating engineering design professional skills, assessment and learning.*Proceedings of the American Society for Engineering Education Annual Conference*. Vancouver, Canada: ASEE.

Davis, D.C., & Ulseth, R.R. (2013, June). Building Student Capacity for High Performance Teamwork. *Paper presented at 2013 ASEE Annual Conference*, Atlanta, Georgia. Retrieved from https://peer.asee.org/19274

Gale, A. J., Martin, D., Martin, K., & Duffey, M. A. (2014). The burnout phenomenon: A comparative study of student attitudes toward collaborative learning and sustainability. *Journal of Interior Design*, *39*(1), 17–31. doi:10.1111/joid.12022

Gerlick, R., Davis, D., Brown, S., & Trevisan, M. (2010). Reflective practices of engineering capstone design teams.*Proceedings of the American Society for Engineering Education Annual Conference*. Louisville, KY: American Society for Engineering Education.

Goff, L., Potter, M. K., Pierre, E., Carey, T. T., Gullage, A., Kustra, E., . . . Van Gaste, G. (2015). Learning outcomes assessment: A practitioner's handbook. Higher Education Quality Council of Ontario, Research Report 13/14- 008. Retrieved from http://www.heqco.ca/SiteCollectionDocuments/heqco.LOAhandbook _Eng_2015.pdf

González-Fernández, M. J., García-Alonso, J. M., & Montero, E. (2014). The Use of a Rubric-Based Method to Assess Teamwork Skill Development. A Case Study in Science and Engineering Courses. *Proceedings of the New perspectives in science educationConference* (p. 409). Rome: Edizioni Libreriauniversitaria.

Graen, G. B., Hui, C., & Taylor, E. A. (2006). Experience-based learning about LMX leadership and fairness in project teams: A dyadic directional approach. *Academy of Management Learning & Education*, *5*(4), 448–460. doi:10.5465/AMLE.2006.23473205

Gray, P. J. (2013). Developing Assessment Rubrics in Project Based Courses: Four Case Studies. *Proceedings of the9th International CDIO Conference, Cambridge, Massachusetts*.

Guerin, D., & Martin, C. (2010). *The interior design profession's body of knowledge and its relationship to people's health, safety, and welfare*. Retrieved from http://www.idbok.org/PDFs/IDBOK_2010.pdf

Gürel, M. Ö. (2010). Explorations in teaching sustainable design: A studio experience in interior design/architecture. *International Journal of Art & Design Education*, *29*(2), 184–199. doi:10.1111/j.1476-8070.2010.01649.x

Hastie, C., Fahy, K., & Parratt, J. (2014). The development of a rubric for peer assessment of individual teamwork skills in undergraduate midwifery students. *Women and Birth; Journal of the Australian College of Midwives*, *27*(3), 220–226. doi:10.1016/j.wombi.2014.06.003 PMID:25042349

Hughes, R. L., & Jones, S. K. (2011). Developing and assessing college student teamwork skills. *New Directions for Institutional Research*, *2011*(149), 53–64. doi:10.1002/ir.380

Hynes, W. (2015). Impacting student attitudes towards teamwork.*Proceedings of the 3rd International Conference for Design Education Researchers* (p. 1002). Alto Finland: Cumulus Association.

IDEALS Learning System. (2015). *Integrated Design Engineering Assessment and Learning System (IDEALS).* Retrieved from https://ideals.tidee.org/

Interior Designers of Canada. (2013). *An interior designer's scope of work.* Retrieved from http://www. idcanada.org/english/for-the-public/an-interior-designers-scope-of-work.html

Jones, A. (2013). There is nothing generic about graduate attributes: Unpacking the scope of context. *Journal of Further and Higher Education, 37*(5), 591–605. doi:10.1080/0309877X.2011.645466

Khodadad, N. (2013). Fostering the connection: examining the impact of team-teaching and collaboration within an interdisciplinary design studio (Panel session). *Proceedings of Interior Design Educators Council 2013 Annual Conference*, Indianapolis, IN: Interior Design Educators Council.

Kidder, D. L., & Bowes-Sperry, L. (2012). Examining the influence of team project design decisions on student perceptions and evaluations of instructors. *Academy of Management Learning & Education, 11*(1), 69–81. doi:10.5465/amle.2010.0040

Matthews, T., Whittaker, S., Moran, T., & Yuen, S. (2011). Collaboration personas: A new approach to designing workplace collaboration tools.*Proceedings of the SIGCHI Conference on Human Factors in Computing Systems* (pp. 2247-2256). ACM: New York.

McCormack, J., Beyerlein, S., Davis, D., Trevisan, M., Lebeau, J., Davis, H., & Leiffer, P. et al. (2012). Contextualizing professionalism in capstone projects using the IDEALS professional responsibility assessment. *International Journal of Engineering Education, 28*(2), 416.

Montuori, A. (2005). Literature review as creative inquiry: Reframing scholarship as a creative process. *Journal of Transformative Education, 3*(4), 374–393. doi:10.1177/1541344605279381

Oliver, B. (2011). *Good practice report: Assuring graduate outcomes.* Australian Learning and Teaching Council. Retrieved from http://www.olt.gov.au/resource-assuring-graduate-outcomes-curtin-2011

Oliver, B. (2013). Graduate attributes as a focus for institution-wide curriculum renewal: Innovations and challenges. *Higher Education Research & Development, 32*(3), 450–463. doi:10.1080/07294360. 2012.682052

Oliver, B. (2015). *Assuring Graduate Capabilities.* Retrieved from http://www.assuringgraduatecapabilities.com/ about.html

Palmer, P. J. (2010). *The courage to teach: Exploring the inner landscape of a teacher's life.* New York, NY: John Wiley & Sons.

Pashler, H., McDaniel, M., Rohrer, D., & Bjork, R. (2008). Learning styles concepts and evidence. *Psychological Science in the Public Interest, 9*(3), 105–119. PMID:26162104

Riener, C., & Willingham, D. (2010). The myth of learning styles. *Change: The magazine of higher learning, 42*(5), 32-35.

Russ, R., & Dickinson, J. (1999). Collaborative design: "Forming, storming, and norming. *Journal of Interior Design, 25*(2), 52–58. doi:10.1111/j.1939-1668.1999.tb00344.x

Sadowska, N., Griffith, S., & Morgan, T. (2009, April). Mind the gap: A collaboration in design teaching and learning between UK and Australia.*Proceedings of the 8th European Academy Of Design Conference*. Aberdeen, Scotland: The Robert Gordon University.

Smith, K. M. (2013). Recognition of problem insufficiency: A proposed threshold concept emergent in student accounts of memorable interior design educational experiences. *Journal of Interior Design, 38*(4), 37–54. doi:10.1111/joid.12018

Transferable Integrated Design Engineering Education [TIDEE]. (2006). *About the Project*. Retrieved from http://www.tidee.wsu.edu/

Tucker, R. (2012). Collaboration down under: Investigating team learning in Australia in architecture and related design contexts, In C.A. Shoniregun, & G.A. Akmayeva (Eds.), *CICE 2012: Proceedings of the Canada International Conference on Education*, Guelph, Canada (pp. 324-329). Infonomics Society.

Tucker, R., & Abbasi, N. (2012). Conceptualizing teamwork and group-work in architecture and related design disciplines, *in ASA 2012: Building on knowledge, theory and practice. Proceedings of the 46th Annual Conference of the Architectural Science Association*, Architectural Science Association, Gold Coast (pp. 1-8).

Tucker, R., & Abbasi, N. (2015). The architecture of teamwork: Examining relationships between teaching, assessment, student learning and satisfaction with creative design outcomes. *Architectural Engineering and Design Management, 11*(6), 405–422. doi:10.1080/17452007.2014.927750

Tucker, R., Abbasi, N., Thorpe, G., Ostwald, M., Williams, A., Wallis, L., & Cashuk, S. (2014). Enhancing and assessing group and team learning in architecture and related design contexts. Office for Learning and Teaching, Department of Education. Sydney: N.S.W.; Retrieved from http://dro.deakin.edu.au/eserv/DU:30069902/tucker-enhancing-2014.pdf

Tucker, R., & Reynolds, C. (2006). The impact of teaching models, group structures and assessment modes on cooperative learning in the student design studio. *Journal for Education in the Built Environment, 1*(2), 39–56. doi:10.11120/jebe.2006.01020039

Tucker, T., & Abbasi, N. (2014a). *Manual on teamwork in design for students*. Retrieved from http://www.teaching-teamwork-in-design.com/manual-on-teamwork-in-design-for-students.html

Tucker, T., & Abbasi, N. (2014b). *Manual on teamwork in design for teachers*. Retrieved from http://www.teaching-teamwork-in-design.com/manual-on-teamwork-in-design-for-teachers.html

University of Sydney. (2011). *Graduate Attributes Policy*. Retrieved from https://www.itl.usyd.edu.au/graduateAttributes/policy.htm

University of Technology Sydney. (2013). *Graduate Attributes and the UTS Graduate Profile Framework*. Retrieved from http://www.iml.uts.edu.au/learn-teach/attributes.html

Webb, J. D., & Miller, N. G. (2006). Some preparation required: The journey to successful studio collaboration. *Journal of Interior Design, 31*(2), 1–9. doi:10.1111/j.1939-1668.2005.tb00407.x

KEY TERMS AND DEFINITIONS

Cognitive Apprenticeship: A learning process in which learners utilize cognitive and metacognitve skills and practices to develop understanding and capability through the demonstration, support, and examples of a capable mentor.

Constructive Alignment: An outcomes-based approach to the design of learning, intended to align outcomes, assessments and teaching and learning activities to support learners in constructing their own understanding and competence.

Graduate Attributes: The characteristic knowledge, skills and mindsets of students completing any of a university's programs, expected to be transferable beyond across disciplinary contexts.

Learning Outcomes: Specifications of what the *learner will know and be able to do* by the end of a course (module) or program. At the program level, Learning Outcomes can be a discipline or program-specific contextualization of the more general institutional Graduate Attributes.

Value Cycle: The process by which activities of an enterprise generate improved value for its stakeholders.

ENDNOTES

[1]   For example, the Develop and Demonstrate component was originally two separate components (as was the Assess and Document component). There was an institutional rationale for both of these divisions based on emerging use of co-curricular activities or ePortfolios for demonstrating or documenting capability. When the review did not identify any resources on demonstrating capability where were not already included in the resources reviewed for developing capability, it was recommended that these components be merged in the institutional framework to make it easier to use.

[2]   Having an explicit focal point around engaging student motivation for capability development led to a more systematic search for research studies and exemplary evidence in this area, and sensitized the authors to the important of this aspect of the learning outcomes value cycle. The Enhance component helped to focus effort on programs of work which developed increasing rich resources and activities through a series of research and development iteration, bringing the second of our two major reference points into the foreground.

[3]   The use of an institution-wide rubric for institutional graduate attributes appears to be most advanced in the U.S., whereas the use of contextualized learning outcomes at the program and Faculty levels appears to be most advanced in Australia and elsewhere. These approaches need not be mutually exclusive.

Chapter 3
Cognitive Challenges for Teamwork in Design

Ju Hyun Lee
The University of Newcastle, Australia

Michael J Ostwald
The University of Newcastle, Australia

Ning Gu
University of South Australia, Australia

ABSTRACT

This chapter combines experimental data and established design theory to examine four issues associated with design cognition that contribute to an improved understanding of creativity and teamwork in design. Drawing on data developed from two parametric design experiments undertaken by the authors, this chapter investigates the implications of (i) cognitive space, (ii) design strategy, (iii) design productivity and (iv) spatial representation, for individuals, and by inference, for groups and educators. Through this process the chapter develops a deeper understanding of the cognitive challenges facing design teams and educators of those teams.

INTRODUCTION

A design team is, by definition, made up of a group of individuals, working with either a singular vision, or in a managed way, to produce an outcome that draws on the strengths and abilities of each member. Whereas many linear or controlled tasks, even complex ones, can be undertaken by teams with a reasonable level of consistency and transparency, the design process is not such a task. Design involves multiple, simultaneous activities and processes, some of which are learnt and are seemingly well documented and understood, while others are more intuitive, contingent and subliminal. Problematically, design is largely an internalized cognitive system, involving conceptual, creative and strategic thought processes, which are not always clear, even to the designer. However, the real difficulty arises when these processes must be communicated to others, either verbally or using some means of representation (drawings and

DOI: 10.4018/978-1-5225-0726-0.ch003

models). In combination, these factors make the process of designing in a team, and of teaching people to design in teams, a difficult one.

Under normal circumstances, one solution to improving this situation would be to conduct detailed empirical observations of the team design process and develop lessons from this research to support people to learn relevant skills and abilities. However, despite extensive empirical research into the actions of individual designers, equivalent cognitive research into team-processes in design is rare, and results tend to be difficult to generalize (Stempfle & Badke-Schaub, 2002). Furthermore, there are also two distinct impediments to producing useful research into team design processes. First, researchers have demonstrated that there are significant communication barriers, both linguistic and cognitive, in the design process, which complicate any empirical approach to the topic (Valkenburg & Dorst, 1998). Second, the environment in which the design process occurs—the creative and communicative platform, media or system—also has an impact on the way people work (Visser, 1993; Bilda & Demirkan, 2003). Given the paucity of research into the cognitive processes that occur in design teams, and the difficulty of overcoming these two challenges of language and environment, an alternative approach to this issue is needed. One such alternative is to examine the findings of past empirical research into the way individuals design, and consider what these studies might imply for teamwork and education. Furthermore, should these results take into account individual differences in terms of linguistic barriers and use an environmental setting for their experiments that is optimized for teamwork, then the results from individuals could provide a useful catalyst for thinking about the cognitive aspects of designing in teams.

This is the approach taken in the present chapter, which reviews the results of past experimental research undertaken by the authors to consider the significance of their findings for design teams. The data used in the chapter are derived from selected patterns of design cognition presented by individuals, but which have deeper implications for teams and for educators. The data have been developed from two small but detailed protocol studies of the actions and thoughts of designers who are working towards solutions to a project brief. Importantly, both studies were undertaken using parametric environments as a common testing platform. This is significant because even though the studies were of individuals, such environments are optimized for team processes and to enable the development of a Computer Supported Collaborative Workplace (CSCW) (Cross & Clayburn Cross, 1995; Grudin, 1994; Ibrahim & Rahimian, 2010). Indeed, a critical aspect of design in parametric environments is its capacity to facilitate the sharing and managing of design information in a way which previous design environments have been unable to achieve (Lawson, 1980; Kolarevic, 2003). In contrast, advanced parametric applications—like Grasshopper, CATIA and Generative Components—support parallel processes, allowing multiple people to work together, sharing coding and visualization roles to solve design problems (Holzer, Hough, & Burry, 2007). The other important factor which allows the results of these past studies to be usefully generalized for consideration in teams, is that one of the studies focuses on linguistic issues. That study, the last presented in this chapter, is explicitly concerned with the way language affects cognition and communication in design.

Therefore, this chapter revisits selected results from two previous experiments by the authors, to draw out issues that are potentially significant for teams and for the education of designers. However, the findings of this past research are about particular, high-level cognitive, creative, spatial and linguistic issues in design. As such, they do not have an easy or direct application in undergraduate education, but they are pertinent to the longer-term development of strategies to support teamwork in design.

This chapter commences by reviewing literature on design cognition and creativity in the context of teamwork. This review identifies four areas that are potentially significant and for which there is consistent data available from studies in the same parametric test environment. The four themes are: cognitive space, design strategy, design productivity and spatial representation. Thereafter the chapter describes the method used to collect the data examined throughout the chapter. All of the studies use protocol analysis, a standard method for studying design cognition (Akin & Lin, 1995; Eastman, 1969; Suwa, Purcell, & Gero, 1998). Protocol studies typically involve rigorous and detailed observations of the actions of small numbers of participants working under controlled conditions. Data are then compared mathematically and statistically to identify patterns in different people's design approaches. Protocol studies fundamentally gain their credibility through the rigor of their analysis, not through their sample size. Then the chapter investigates specific results that are relevant to the four themes, before offering thoughts about future research and a conclusion

BACKGROUND

The primary reason why design in teams is potentially so problematic is that design is an innately creative process. Design is not a straightforward, linear exercise; it is subjective, recursive and heuristic. It is difficult enough for expert designers to work in teams, let alone novices because they are still developing their creative and communicative skills. The pivotal role of creative thinking in the design process is also why teaching people to work in teams on design projects is problematic from a design cognition perspective. However, it is widely agreed that creativity is an essential component of the design process (Glanville, 1999; Boden, 2004; Hasirci & Demirkan, 2007; Maher, 2010). Furthermore, various cognitive activities have been shown to contribute significantly to creative thinking and discovery processes in design, leading to what has become known as "creative cognition" (Finke, Ward, & Smith, 1992). Importantly in the present context, creativity is also recognized as being potentially the product of either an individual or a collective (Fischer, Giaccardi, Eden, Sugimoto, & Ye, 2005).

Parametric environments have also been repeatedly linked to creative processes, by virtue of their capacity to support rapid exploration of design options. In parametric environments, designers continuously explore concepts using mathematical algorithms to shape design. This in turn may require a designer to evolve and then select a design among a hundred or more unfamiliar forms that fulfill the required parameters. Past research has argued that this type of exploration is a critical part of the creative process (Blosiu, 1999; Iordanova, 2007). This is why parametric environments have been repeatedly tied to both creative and collaborative outcomes, although the experimental evidence associated with these factors is more complex (Lee, Gu, & Ostwald, 2013; 2015; Lee, Gu, & Williams, 2014).

In this background section to the chapter we identify four areas where evidence starts to suggest connections between the actual cognitive processes of individual designers, and the potential issues faced by design teams and educators. The first of the four areas identified for analysis is "cognitive space".

Design is often described as an iterative process that involves searching through two complimentary but different cognitive spaces; "problem space" and "solution space" (Maher & Poon, 1996). Design problem defining behavior is a core and measurable cognitive indictor within the design process (Coley, Houseman, & Roy, 2007). However, past research suggests that designs that have been rated highly in terms of creativity rarely arise from problem-solving activities in isolation, they also require a designer to shift mindsets, and enter a different cognitive space where solutions are produced and opportunities tested (Maher & Poon, 1996; Dorst & Cross, 2001). Thus, design is regarded as a "co-evolutionary" process, which needs to shift backwards and forwards between these two cognitive spaces for a creative product to be produced (Dorst & Cross, 2001). Significantly, Stempfle and Badke-Schaub (2002) frame their analysis of communication in design teams using four operations in cognitive space. These cognitive operations are "generation" and "exploration" to widen a problem space, and "comparison" and "selection" to narrow this space. These cognitive operations can also be mapped to "divergent" and "convergent" thinking processes (Guilford, 1967). By aligning the cognitive operations of designers within particular "spaces" (problem or solution) mutual interactions and productive relationships in a team may be supported. This message is reflected in the argument that the establishment and sharing of creative processes and activities in a socially enriched environment enables the co-evolutionary potential in design (Giaccardi, 2004, 2005; Fischer et al., 2005). Thus, the way in which members of teams move between problem and solution spaces would appear to be key to understanding and improving their collective performance.

The second area of interest identified in past research is concerned with "design strategy". A design strategy is a cognitive approach to achieving an outcome (von der Weth, 1999). Design strategies define sub-goals which limit or enable certain operations. They are linked to personal preferences and habits and contribute to defining designers' thought processes (Lee et al., 2014). Past research has demonstrated that expert and novice designers use different problem decomposition strategies for design thinking (Ho, 2001). Specifically, experts use a "working-forward" search strategy seeking opportunities, while novices adhere to the "working-backward" strategy of attempting to solve specific challenges. Experts tend to establish sub-problems or reformulate problems in their pursuit of inventiveness (Lindström, 2006), whereas the working-backward strategy is often reliant on trial and error (Ahmed, Wallace, and Blessing 2003). However, Kruger and Cross (2006) warn that while a solution-driven strategy may produce a more creative outcome, it is likely to be of a lower level of quality. In contrast, a problem-driven design strategy often provides a more balanced solution between quality and creativity. The fact that there are different cognitive strategies at work in the average design process is what is significant here. People develop such strategies through experience and education, but they are rarely, if ever, asked to examine the strategies they personally use or those employed by fellow team members.

The third area of interest raised in past research is concerned with "design productivity". This area is associated with the effectiveness and efficiency of a cognitive process that is either individually or collectively undertaken (Goldschmidt, 1995). Costa and Sobek (2004) argue that generating ideas and defining problems at a system level results in the highest positive correlation with increased productivity in a team. Economy of thought is also directly associated with levels of creativity (Perkins, 1981), while efficiency is associated with both creativity and expertise (Goldschmidt, 1995). In order to analyze design processes with a focus on productivity, Goldschmidt developed a method called linkography, for recording, visualizing and analyzing connections between actions, ideas or events (Goldschmidt, 1990, 1995). This method is useful for understanding the relationship between the creative qualities of ideas, their level of integration in the design process and the functioning of design groups (Van der Lugt, 2000). Such is the importance of this way of conceptualizing the effectiveness of design cognition, that mathematical methods have been developed for interpreting linkograph data (Kan & Gero, 2008). Specifically, "forelink" entropy measures in the linkograph, represent idea generation opportunities in the design process, whilst "backlink" entropy measures relate to opportunities associated with enhancements or responses to design (Kan & Gero, 2008). Entropy calculations are based on Shannon's (1948) information theory, which relates to the average information per symbol in a set of symbols with a priori probabilities in linkographs. Design productivity is therefore, a way of understanding and calculating the effectiveness or efficiency of different cognitive approaches to design, whether individual or collaborative.

The final area of importance for examining individual and group processes is associated with spatial representation. A critical part of the design process involves employing spatial relational terms to communicate various relationships between elements, sub-elements and objects in space (Hegarty & Kozhevnikov, 1999; Tenbrink & Ragni, 2012). Spatial representation may differ from other forms of cognitive representation because of the impact of individual perceptual processes and experiences (Schwartz & Heiser, 2006). However, the difference in mental models, naturally induced by using particular linguistic terms, has been shown to have consequences for problem solving and for teamwork (Munnich, Landau, & Dosher, 2001). Specifically, cross-linguistic differences in spatial thinking have been observed which suggest that language influences both conceptual development and communication between team members (Bowerman, 1996; Levinson, 1996; 2003). While this issue, the reliance of spatial representational approaches on language, has direct implications for international or multi-lingual design teams, linguistic issues also complicate all cognitive processes, leading to concerns about the capacity to engage team members in a transparent process.

Collectively, there are multiple experimental and theoretical indications that these four aspects of design cognition— space, strategy, productivity and representation—are potentially significant for the way teams operate as part of the design process, and especially for understanding how creativity is accommodated and supported in this process.

RESEARCH METHOD

The results presented in this chapter were developed using standard protocol analysis techniques; the most widely used and accepted approach for researching cognition in design (Suwa et al., 1998; Chai & Xiao, 2012; Coley et al., 2007). Each study recorded the activities and verbalized thoughts of a series of designers, working on an identical project brief, in the same environment, using the same tools (parametric software) and in a similar timeframe. Two video cameras were used, one providing a view of the designer's overall activities and the other recording the computer screen on which they were working. All participants undertook a "practice-run" as part of the briefing process for the experiment and to get used to "thinking-aloud" while they designed. The brief used in the experiment was for the conceptual design of a high-rise building and the completed computational design models were collected at the end of the experiment. After each experiment was completed, the participant was interviewed and asked to retrospectively reflect on and explain their thoughts and activities, whilst watching the video of their design session. This resulted in three sources of information—video, audio and retrospective explanation—about each participant's design process. Full descriptions of the experimental set-up are contained in the authors' past publications (Lee et al., 2013; 2014; 2015).

Once the recording process was completed the analysis commenced with the detailed coding of all activities and behaviors (Table 1). The chosen coding scheme consists of three levels of cognitive activities: physical, perceptual and conceptual (Suwa et al., 1998). Furthermore, because designing in parametric environments involves both geometric and algorithmic activities, the physical and perceptual levels in the coding scheme were sub-divided into two categories. Thereafter, each activity from every experiment was coded into one of 17 potential codes, all linked to a timeline and sequence, to describe each participant's design process.

As a brief explanation of the codes, the "physical" level includes activities such as creating shapes using either geometric or algorithmic tools. The "perceptual" level includes assessing forms or algorithms

Table 1. Parametric design coding scheme

Level	Category	Code	Description
Physical	Geometry	G-Geometry G-Change	Create geometries without an algorithm Change existing geometries
	Algorithm	A-Parameter A-Change Parameter A-Rule A-Change Rule A-Reference	Create initial parameters Change existing parameters Create initial rules Change existing rules Retrieve or get references
Perceptual	Geometry	P-Geometry	Attend to existing geometries
	Algorithm	P-Algorithm	Attend to existing algorithms
Conceptual	Problem-Finding	F-Initial Goal F-Geometry Sub Goal F-Algorithm Sub Goal	Introduce new ideas (or goals) based on a given Design brief Introduce new geometric ideas Introduce new algorithmic ideas
	Solution-Generating	G-Generation	Make generation (or variation)
	Solution-Evaluating	E-Geometry	Evaluate primitives or existing geometries
		E-Parameter E-Rule E-Reference	Evaluate existing parameters Evaluate existing rules Evaluate existing references

(Lee et al., 2013)

and the conceptual level consists of three categories of actions: problem-finding, solution-generating and solution-evaluating (Gero & Neill, 1998). While cognitive activities of the conceptual level can be largely interpreted as problem-solving processes, problem- selection and evaluation processes are equally as important as parts of an integrated process for supporting design creativity and are reflected in the categorization of this level (Dacey & Lennon, 1998). The solution-generating action is essential to capturing the generative aspect of a parametric design. The process of making variations is used to extend the boundaries of the designer's knowledge and the state-space of possible solutions, both of which are key to producing creative works (Gero, 1996; Liu & Lim, 2006).

Once the coding was complete, the designs produced in the experiments were all independently evaluated using the standard consensual assessment technique (CAT) (Amabile, 1983). In accordance with this technique an expert panel, made up of experienced members who are familiar with the design domain and the techniques for producing the design, assess the output of each experiment. Four criteria were used for the assessment: novelty, usefulness, complexity, and aesthetics (Hennessey & Amabile, 1999). For the results reported here, three design experts assessed each design using a seven-point Likert scale. In this way, an additional point of comparison was developed, whereby the different design cognition behaviors could be linked to levels of creativity and usefulness.

CHALLENGES FOR DESIGN COGNITION IN TEAMS

Cognitive Space

This section investigates the results of a study involving four designers (D1-4) and the way they shift between cognitive spaces as part of the design process. All four designers used parametric software and two were highly experienced designers and users of the software (D1 and D2), while the other two were less experienced (D3 and D4). In the expert panel assessment using the CAT, the level of creativity exhibited in D2's design was assessed as being the highest and D1's design achieved the second highest overall score but had the highest result for usefulness. In contrast, D3's and D4's designs had the lowest assessed creativity overall.

Table 2 shows the coding results for the percentage of the frequency weighted by time duration of each code. On average, throughout the design experiment, the coverage of "physical" activities accounts for 45.3% (geometry: 5.5%, algorithm: 39.8%); "perceptual" accounts for 6.2%; and "conceptual" accounts for 48.5% (problem-finding: 11%, solution-generating: 5.5%, solution-evaluating: 32%).

The conceptual level of the coding allows for the identification of two cognitive spaces: the problem space (through the "Problem-finding" code) and the solution space (through "Solution-generating" and "Solution-evaluating" codes). The frequency coverage of "Problem-finding" in the experiment showed that two designers' cognitive activities occurred largely in the problem space (D1 and D3) and that one of these (D1) was rated highly for creativity, seemingly confirming the view that problem-driven processes can provide a balance between quality and innovation (Kruger & Cross, 2006). In contrast, D2 produced more cognitive activities in the solution space, having the highest frequency coverage of "Solution-generating" and "Solution-evaluating" behaviors (combination of 49.9%). The frequency coverage of "G-Generation" for D2 was also the highest (13%) and D2's protocol had the second highest frequency coverage of "A-Change Parameter" (4.7%). Complementing the solution-driven process, "G-

Table 2. The percentage of coding results

Level	Category	Code	D1	D2	D3	D4	Mean	SD
Physical	Geometry	G-Geometry	2.0	0.0	6.4	1.3	2.4	2.8
		G-Change	0.5	0.0	8.8	3.0	3.1	4.0
	Algorithm	A-Parameter	4.9	0.1	3.0	2.9	2.7	2.0
		A-Change Parameter	10.0	4.7	1.6	1.0	4.3	4.1
		A-Rule	24.7	20.0	16.5	19.0	20.0	3.5
		A-Change Rule	6.0	12.2	2.9	26.9	12.0	10.3
		A-Reference	0.0	0.2	0.0	2.8	0.8	1.3
Perceptual	Geometry	P-Geometry	2.8	1.8	1.0	0.4	1.5	1.0
	Algorithm	P-Algorithm	3.2	4.0	2.8	8.6	4.7	2.6
Conceptual	Problem-finding	F-Initial Goal	3.0	0.2	1.4	1.1	1.4	1.2
		F-Geometry Sub Goal	7.0	2.5	10.7	2.3	5.6	4.0
		F-Algorithm Sub goal	4.1	4.4	6.4	1.0	4.0	2.2
	Solution-generating	G-Generation	4.0	13.0	1.9	3.0	5.5	5.1
	Solution-evaluating	E-Geometry	19.4	17.3	18.1	8.8	15.9	4.9
		E-Parameter	0.8	0.0	0.0	0.0	0.2	0.4
		E-Rule	7.6	19.5	18.5	17.9	15.9	5.5
		E-Reference	0.0	0.1	0.0	0.0	0.0	0.1
	Sum		100	100	100	100	100	-

(Lee et al., 2013)

Generation" and "A-Change Parameter" codes may have enabled D2 to generate more design variations. D2's model had the highest creativity score as assessed using the CAT. This too is consistent with past research which indicates that design strategies adopting a solution-driven process can lead to higher levels of perceived creativity (Kruger & Cross, 2006). This has implications too for the design team, which is arguably more able to rapidly generate and test new concepts (Cross & Clayburn Cross, 1995; Visser, 1993). Meanwhile, the solution-evaluating activities as cognitive processes can be perceived as a useful part in the "reflection-in-action" (Schön, 1984) theory.

But what does this mean for designing in teams and for education? First, it stresses the importance of not allowing students to let a single cognitive space dominate their design processes. Students and practitioners should learn to recognize and understand when they are over-emphasizing either the problem-defining or solution-seeking aspects in their own processes. Second, solution- generating and evaluating practices are both critical for creativity and are also effective in groups. But student designers rarely have the right tools to evaluate their own work, let alone that of others, and the value of solution generation lies in a combination of its breadth and accessibility. Such cognitive skills are only rarely taught in contemporary design education for individuals, but they may be more important for working in design teams.

Design Strategy

The data developed in the previous section can also be re-examined to identify any patterns in the design strategies used. For this purpose, a separate coding scheme is employed: "Analysis–Synthesis–Evaluation" (Jones, 1992). The "Analysis" (An) activity decomposes a problem into sub-problems, corresponding to the problem-finding category in Table 1 "Synthesis" (Sy) refers to the re-composition of sub-problems into different forms, including the physical (Sy_p) and the solution-generating levels (Sy_g). "Evaluation" refers to testing the performance of new structures, being equivalent to the solution-evaluating category in the coding scheme. In this section we consider two levels of evaluation, algorithmic evaluation (Ev_a) and geometric evaluation (Ev_g) as a means of illuminating different cognitive design strategies.

While Sy_p and Ev_g were the dominant activities over time in the data, occurrences of both An and Sy_g codes differ more significantly between the four participants (See Figure 1). In particular, the Sy_g—generative synthesis—within D2's protocol occurred at regular intervals throughout the time

Figure 1. Patterns of different levels of design thinking (Ev_a: Evaluation (Algorithm), Ev_g: Evaluation (Geometry), Sy_g: Synthesis (Generative), Sy_p: Synthesis (Physical), and An: Analysis)

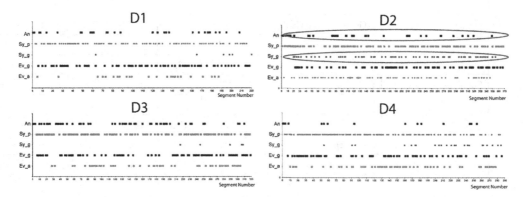

period. The analysis codes also appear regularly in the protocols of both D1 and D2. The problem space is based on "analysis", whilst the solution space highlights "synthesis" (generative level). Based on this understanding, it can be observed that D2 used a design strategy highlighting both the problem and the solution spaces, and was assessed through the CAT as producing the most creative design. Conversely, the An and Sy_g codes do not occur regularly in the protocols of D3 and D4, which may be a feature of the more novice approach to problem-solving. The Sy_g codes only appear towards the end of D3's protocol, while the A_n code rarely occurs in D4's protocol, which only features Sy_p and Ev_a codes. Neither of these features have evidently enhanced creativity in the design process and CAT, where D3's and D4's designs were rated as less creative. In contrast, D1's protocol shows the regular use of "analysis" with a small number of activities encoded as making generation (Sy_g) compared to D2. As the problem space in this study is based on "analysis", while the solution space relates to the generative aspects of design, these features imply that D1 adopted a problem-driven strategy rather than a solution-driven strategy to produce the design.

In order to investigate the four designers' problem decomposition strategies in more detail, the research illustrates the three cognitive activities of "analysis" over time (See Figure 2). "An-Initial Goal" refers to the definition of a main problem, while the other two codes introducing sub-goals deal with sub-problems. A closer examination of Figure 2 reveals that only D1 produces "An-Initial Goal" at the beginning, middle and end of the protocol. D1 also sequentially decomposes the problem into geometric sub-problems and then algorithmic sub-problems. This is consistent with Ho's (2001) explicit problem-decomposing strategy and may also be in line with the problem-driven strategy (Kruger & Cross, 2006) that produces balanced results in terms of both overall solution quality and creativity. In contrast, D3 and D4 tended to use an implicit problem-decomposing strategy, a strategy often adopted by novices (see Figure 2). In particular, D3 produced "An-Initial Goal" at the beginning but did not sequentially relate this goal to the geometric and algorithmic sub-problems. Rather, D3 tended to stop to solve each problem as it emerged. This implies a lack of a working-forward search strategy needed in an effective design process. D4 produced "An-Initial Goal" at the beginning and end of the protocol but rarely dealt with sub-problems. Thus, both D3 and D4 adopted either unsystematic or backward-working search strategies, whereas, D1 and D2 explicitly decomposed the initial problem into both geometric and algorithmic sub-problems. Furthermore, as revealed in Figure 3, D2 regularly used the generative synthesis (Sy_g) activity suggesting that D2's design strategy kept sight of both the problem and the solution, although the generation of solutions was typically linked to sub-problems as shown in Figure 1 (see also sequential sub-problems in Figure 2).

Figure 2. Three cognitive activities of "analysis" over time
(Lee et al., 2014)

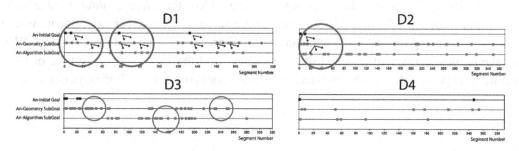

Figure 3. Two parametric design strategies
(Lee et al., 2014)

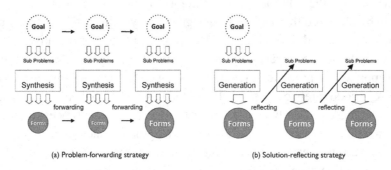

Stempfle and Badke-Schaub (2002) recommend that designers must be taught to reflect on their own cognitive strategies when dealing with design problems. In order to support the development of designers' cognitive skills, the findings in this section suggest two effective strategies: problem-forwarding strategy and solution-reflecting strategy (See Figure 3). Designers may often use both strategies to produce creative solutions, but focusing on one or other strategy could be more effective in achieving different qualities in the outcomes, and mixing cognitive and learning styles across a larger team. The problem-forwarding strategy, as a specific problem-driven approach, focuses on "analysis" and explicitly decomposes the initial problem into both geometric and algorithmic sub-problems. The solution-reflecting strategy highlights the generation of variations and reflection-in-action is a powerful strategy to effectively perform design activities. In order to achieve a comprehensive solution, the solution-reflecting strategy often leads to the production of variations and reflecting on the variations recursively. These reflective and self-evaluative processes, as the previous section suggests, are difficult to instill in young designers. Especially given, as Stempfle and Badke-Schaub (2002) observe, that criticism of a team's approach to design mostly produces unfavorable reactions, which can undermine useful self-reflection. Educators, therefore, need to emphasize the importance of continuous self-reflection, or formative guidance and assessment rather than its more summative variant.

Design Productivity

This section draws on the results of a second protocol study, this time with four different participants, two Australians (A1 and A2) and two Swedes (S1 and S2). The test environment, the data recording systems and the project brief are unchanged. However, a different coding system is used to investigate specific "moves" made as part of the design process, and which can be used to measure levels of cognitive efficiency and effectiveness.

Once every action observed in the experiments were coded, the average duration of each coded segment was calculated as 13.2 seconds and the average value of the number of segments was 300.5. Table 3 shows the coding results of the parametric design processes of the four participants. S1's protocol has the highest number of encoded segments (360), and the shortest average time of segments (10.7 seconds). This indicates that S1 produced clear and rapid cognitive activities. In contrast, A2 has

Table 3. Coding results of the parametric design process (Lee, Ostwald, & Gu, 2015)

Designer	Time	Number of segments	Coded segments	Average time of segments
A1	47 m 54.7 s	220	208 (94.5%)	13.0 s
A2	1 h 27 m 8s	319	277 (86.8%)	16.5 s
S1	1 h 4 m 22 s	360	347 (96.4%)	10.7 s
S2	1 h 3 m 12 s	303	278 (91.7%)	12.5 s
Mean	1 h 5 m 42 s	300.5	277.5 (92.3%)	13.2 s
SD	16 m 9.9 s	58.8	56.7	2.4 s

the smallest percentage of the encoded segments (86.8%) and therefore took more time to complete a cognitive activity. A2 also produced many unnecessary (not-encoded) activities. On average, 92.3% of segments were encoded in the entire process-oriented coding scheme. A2 and S2 each produced a larger number of geometric activities, because both drew shapes more often in the design environment and then imported them into the algorithmic editor. Both also struggled with the development of algorithmic rules so that they evaluated them more often (E-Rule), which accounts for over 16% of their time, and were more limited in generating behaviors (G-Generation). Conversely, the two Australians undertook more perceptual activities while the two Swedes tended to evaluate existing parameters more often. This confirms that there are potential differences in their approaches to design.

While the data discussed this far in this section is about the frequency of activities, this in isolation is no direct reflection on quality. A person who has a lower level of activity may still produce a quality design, and a highly active and seemingly decisive designer may produce a low quality work. To gain a better sense of the nature of the activity, a linkography analysis is undertaken of the data identifying four distinct moves that can be connected to outcomes. The moves are, "introducing geometric/algorithmic ideas", "creating algorithmic components (as a unit)", "modification activities", and "evaluation activities". These correlate to Goldschmidt's (1995) "link-intensive" or "critical moves" (CM) in the design process. A CM is an activity that has an overall positive effect on the outcome of the process. As such, a CM also serves as a sound indicator of cognitive productivity.

Figure 4 shows the linkography analysis of the experimental data and each link index, which is the number of links divided by the number of moves (Goldschmidt & Tatsa, 2005). Notably, the link indexes

Figure 4. Linkography and link index of the four design sessions

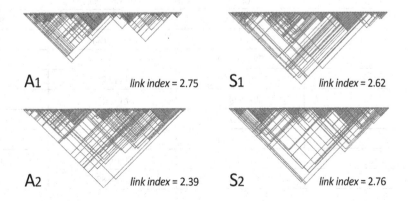

65

of A1 (2.75) and S2 (2.76) are higher than the others in their language groups. Goldschmidt and Tatsa (2005) argue that there is a correlation between such a high link index value and productivity. Furthermore, moves that are particularly rich in critical links also serve as a useful indicator of quality of productivity.

Table 4 shows critical moves with more than five, six and seven links within the session. A1's protocol develops the highest values in the percentages of the CMs over the total number of moves, while S1's produces the lowest. The link indexes in Figure 4, and the figures listed in Table 4, suggest that A1's design session may be most productive, and both A1 and S2 are more productive than the others in their language groups, according to the accepted rationale (Goldschmidt, 1995; Kan & Gero, 2008). This also indicates that S1's design activities (shown in Table 3.) which feature the highest number of moves, do not actually contribute to its productivity in terms of idea generation. This last result is why analyzing the number of actions is not sufficient, in itself, to measure the productivity of a design session.

To assist in interpreting the data, forelinks generally set up solutions to problems whereas modification activities are those which occur when designers revisit and change previous decisions. However, changing the original can also signal a new forelink. The fact that there is a degree of recursion in this process is not problematic, as long as the modification activities are rare, and the corrections lead to solutions, not more corrections. An important backlink is associated with the "evaluation activity"; a move wherein designers evaluate their work. "Evaluating geometries" is one of the dominant activities in all four protocols. Because parametric design may generate unexpected solutions, which must be evaluated in terms of both their geometries and scripts. The last two out of the four distinct moves strongly relate to creative cognition in parametric design such as "transitions between cognitive spaces" and "reflection" that are captured by the previous sections. That is, these moves support productivity as well as creative cognition in this particular environment.

For design teams, the message is that forelink-type activities, which produce measurable and assessable outcomes, will support an efficient and effective design process. Backlink-type activities are also valuable, if they are to critically assess a previous stage, or to revise an assumption, rule or parameter, which is otherwise blocking progress. A lack of activity, or an excessive focus on past stages, may reduce

Table 4. Critical moves with more than five, six and seven links within the two design sessions

	Link	CM5 (CM5%)	CM6 (CM6%)	CM7 (CM7%)
A1	Forelinks	44 (20.0%)	40 (18.2%)	35 (15.9%)
	Backlinks	19 (8.6%)	10 (4.6%)	9 (4.1%)
	Total	63 (28.6%)	50 (22.7%)	44 (20.0%)
A2	Forelinks	51 (16.0%)	39 (12.2%)	34 (10.7%)
	Backlinks	24 (7.5%)	15 (4.7%)	9 (2.8%)
	Total	75 (23.5%)	54 (16.9%)	43 (13.5%)
S1	Forelinks	51 (14.2%)	44 (12.2%)	41 (11.4%)
	Backlinks	20 (5.6%)	7 (1.9%)	5 (1.4%)
	Total	71 (19.7%)	51 (14.1%)	46 (12.8%)
S2	Forelinks	48 (15.8%)	43 (14.2%)	36 (11.9%)
	Backlinks	31 (10.2%)	20 (6.6%)	13 (4.3%)
	Total	79 (26.0%)	63 (20.8%)	49 (16.2%)

cognitive productivity and potentially undermine the capacity of an entire team to complete a project. However, activity should not be praised just for its own sake, it must consist of more forward links or progressive actions, than backward links, or recursive actions.

Spatial Representation

The final category considered in this chapter uses the same data and experimental basis as the previous section—two Australians (A1 and A2) and two Swedish (S1 and S2) designers. However the focus of this section is on language and in particular on the way spatial relations are constructed and represented. This is significant for two reasons, first transparent communication is critical for a productive team process, and second, basic spatial relations are core to design.

When examining the recorded data, especially the spoken word, the impact of language is clearly evident in the descriptions of objects and their relationship to other objects. For this reason, the coding used in this section identifies four categories of spatial representation: "relation", "object", "directness", and "syntactic format" (Table 5).

The "relation" category divides the spatial terms of each protocol into three sub-classes: local relation, global relation and demonstrative pronouns. Local relation and global relation highlight the use of the prepositional phrases to indicate location, while demonstrative pronouns such as "there" and "here" replace the longer or more detailed descriptions of place or time.

The "object" category in the coding identifies the number of objects involved in each description. This includes consideration of the axial structure of the reference object (Munnich et al., 2001) and the impact of functional relationships between entities on spatial description choices (Coventry & Garrod, 2004).

While spatial terms differ widely, projective terms (left, right, front, behind, above, below), are often used in spatial reasoning tasks and have repeatedly been noted as potential linguistic constraints in communication and construction of ideas (Tenbrink & Ragni, 2012). Such linguistic constituents necessarily encode "directness" as well as the distinctions which underlie linguistic expressions used when referring to spatio-temporal configurations (van der Zee & Slack, 2003).

The "syntactic format" coding focuses on how speakers frame their spatial descriptions syntactically. This is because word order and information structure are important for the mental reasoning process

Table 5. Coding scheme identifying spatial representation

Category	Subclass	Description
Relation	L-Relation G-Relation D-Pronoun	Local relation (e.g. the usage of projective terms (left, right, front)) Global relation (e.g. the usage of compass-based terms like north) Demonstrative pronouns (e.g. the use of here, there)
Object	1-Object 2-Object M-Object	Describe one object Describe two objects Describe multiple objects
Directness	Direct Indirect	Express a direct relationship between objects e.g. the usage of "beside"
Syntactic format	L-st-R st-R-L st-L	Locatum (L) - Spatial term (st) – Relatum (R) Spatial term - Relatum - Locatum Spatial term – Locatum

(Lee et al, 2015)

(Hörnig, Oberauer, & Weidenfeld, 2006). Speakers tend to adhere to syntactic formats that are appropriate for the information structure chosen for descriptions (Tenbrink & Ragni, 2012). For example, the sentence, "a bedroom is to the right of the entrance", is encoded as "L-st-R" because it consists of a "locatum" (bedroom), a spatial term (to the right of), and a "relatum" (entrance).

Table 6 shows the results produced using the coding scheme for data derived from experiments undertaken by two Swedish (S1 and S2) and two Australian (A1 and A2) designers. Data for the two Swedish speakers suggest higher frequencies of demonstrative pronouns than those of the Australians. This may be because it is less onerous for speakers to use demonstrative pronouns than to provide a full prepositional phrase. The instructions for the think-aloud protocol collection method may also affect the incidence of demonstrative pronouns. Nonetheless, this outcome may be caused by linguistic differences or habits. As for "Object", the data identifies only the small number of objects that are in spatial relationships (L or G relation). Interestingly, A1, a slightly more experienced designer, produced the most frequent terms and clauses associated with spatial representation, while the less experienced designers, in particular A2, produced the least.

With the rise of international, interdisciplinary teams in the architecture and construction industries, the past assumption that design is a universal language has come under increasing scrutiny. Language is at the core of any design team, and past research (Boroditsky, 2001; Gleitman & Papafragou, 2005) has revealed that language, as a system, is both a reflection of the way we think and of our socio-cultural differences and values. Furthermore, language is a facilitator to bridge between individual knowledge and the larger body of experience held by the team (Dong, 2005). Burleson and Caplan (1998) describe that the communication process as consisting of four components: perceiving others and defining social situation; producing messages; interpreting and responding to the messages of others; coordinating interaction with others. These components draw on the individual's social information-processing capacity. Although the research in this section only deals with spatial description and representation, the results demonstrate the spatial differentiation, terms and clauses can be regarded as an indicator of "productivity", which is also related to individual cognitive differences. That is, the individual fluency of spatial representation can impact on social design process and cognition. Collectively, this suggests that for effective teams to design collaboratively, educators need to pay special attention to verbal literacy in the design process (Jara, 2014).

Table 6. Spatial representation of the four protocols

Category	Subclass	A1	A2	S1	S2	Mean	SD
Relation	L-Relation	27	7	7	7	12	10
	D-Pronoun	10	3	6	18	9.25	6.5
Object	1-Object	3	0	0	0	1.5	0.75
	2-Object	3	0	0	1	1.41	1
Directness	Direct	1	1	0	1	0.75	0.5
Syntactic format	L-st-R	24	3	1	16	11	10.92

(Lee et al., 2015)

FUTURE RESEARCH DIRECTIONS

This chapter draws on a combination of empirical data developed by the authors and grounded theory to identify aspects of design cognition which require future research and consideration to support the development of effective design teams. One such area is design communication. One of the clear advantages of teams over individuals in the design process is that they provide an opportunity to combine a broad range of skills and approaches (Cross & Clayburn Cross, 1995; Fischer et al., 2005; Prather & Middleton, 2002; Safoutin & Thurston, 1993). But at the same time, there is also a potential loss of efficiency and productivity in the group due to the problems of communication, which are necessarily exacerbated in groups (Hackman & Morris, 1975; Steiner, 1972). Developing a communication-based technique for supporting interdisciplinary design teams (Safoutin & Thurston, 1993) is a core factor for improving productivity and performance in design teams, and educational strategies are needed to accommodate this. Furthermore, coordination and management skills—to support identifying, avoiding and resolving conflicts—are also part of the effective team process for design (Cross & Clayburn Cross, 1995). Some of these skills and abilities are already taught to design students, but rarely as they are integral to the design process. Educators should investigate including these issues as part of any future curriculum renewal to support design team.

A second area for future research arises from a consideration of two themes developed previously in this chapter as part of the examination of design space and design strategy. In both cases, design researchers have been able to identify clear cognitive patterns in an individual's work, and which can, in turn, be connected to levels of experience, creativity and usefulness. But how do novice designers became aware of the processes they are using, and how can they learn to adapt them to be more effective? This is a challenge for educators, who traditionally teach design through a mentoring process, often as part of a studio environment. In the conventional design studio, cognitive processes are often marginalized in favor of supporting students to achieve an outcome, using whatever means they can. Or else, if cognitive aspects of design are mentioned at all, they are typically framed as problem-solving activities, without any distinction being made between the multiple different approaches to defining, testing and solving problems. It is normally only mature designers and teachers who can identify when people are using a "working-forward" search strategy seeking opportunities, or a "working-backward", trial and error strategy, attempting to solve specific challenges. Experienced designers and teachers will also often be aware when students are adopting divergent and convergent approaches to design, but it is rare for this to be imparted to the students themselves. Yet, it is likely that some level of self-awareness of both cognitive space and strategy is necessary for teams to design effectively. Future research is required to not just identify these different cognitive properties, but how to teach students to be aware of their own tendencies when they design.

CONCLUSION

The first of the four areas of cognitive design practice examined in this chapter is the co-evolutionary process, which shifts between problem and solution spaces and is central to the production of creative and useful designs. While grounded theory in design cognition holds that the individual must evolve his or her design proposal in both spaces, the implications for designing in teams, and teaching students to work in this way, are twofold. First, there is a need to raise students' awareness of the differences between problem- defining and solving behavior on the one hand, and solution- finding and testing on the other. The two are complimentary, not identical. The former is focused on the difficulties inherent in a design program or client brief, while the latter is concerned with the opportunities offered by valid solutions. The second implication of this realization is that in a team, it may not be strictly necessary for every member to inhabit the same cognitive space, but rather to know when to transfer their ideas to someone inhabiting an alternative.

The second area considered in this chapter has parallels to the first. The problem-forwarding strategy is driven by limiting the negative impact of impediments, while the solution-reflecting strategy is concerned with ensuring positive impact. Although cognitive processes may be influenced by a variety of factors (such as personal experiences and design environments) this research identifies the solution-reflecting strategy as important for both individuals and teams. For educators, the key to strengthening skills in solution-reflecting lies in developing effective self-critical and team-critical capacities.

Productivity is a significant theme when considering design cognition in teams. From the results reported in this chapter, it is clear that modification and evaluation activities produced "backlinks" in the parametric design environment. These critical moves were also related to the transitions between cognitive spaces and the solution-reflecting strategy. This implies that facilitating creative cognition would be an important contribution to effective design performance as well as productivity in the design process. Similarly, these four critical moves can also be utilized to support creative and productive co-creation for design teams.

Data which were coded in accordance with linguistic content raised a problem for design teams that has been previously examined by various researchers. Given that communication is one of the most important factors for design teams to increase their productivity and performance, linguistic issues must be the subject of further research and development. In particular, the almost complete reliance of the design process on basic spatial terminology indicates that the problems are not just about large-scale language barriers—say between native English and native Swedish speakers—but rather that designers construct their ideas linguistically as well, and that these constructions must also be communicated to other teams members.

Ultimately, Goldschmidt (1995) suggests that each designer actually operates "as a team of one", bringing their learnt, practiced and evolved cognitive skills to bear on a particular design challenge. This is the fundamental dichotomy when talking about design cognition in the context of teams. Arguably a paradigm shift is needed in design cognition which takes into account the practices and behaviors identified in group activities, not just as parallel disconnected processes, but as a collectively intelligent process. The efforts of educators can certainly assist in the meantime, mostly through developing critical and reflective skills in students, but not focusing on the design itself, but rather on the process taken to produce that design.

REFERENCES

Ahmed, S., Wallace, K. M., & Blessing, L. M. (2003). Understanding the differences between how novice and experienced designers approach design tasks. *Research in Engineering Design*, *14*(1), 1.

Akin, Ã., & Lin, C. (1995). Design protocol data and novel design decisions. *Design Studies*, *16*(2), 211–236. doi:10.1016/0142-694X(94)00010-B

Amabile, T. M. (1983). *The social psychology of creativity*. New York: Springer-Verlag. doi:10.1007/978-1-4612-5533-8

Bilda, Z., & Demirkan, H. (2003). An insight on designers' sketching activities in traditional versus digital media. *Design Studies*, 24(1), 27–50. doi:10.1016/S0142-694X(02)00032-7

Blosiu, J. O. (1999). Use of synectics as an idea seeding technique to enhance design creativity. *Paper presented at the IEEE SMC '99 Conference on Systems, Man, and Cybernetics*, Tokyo. doi:10.1109/ICSMC.1999.823365

Boden, M. A. (2004). *The Creative Mind: Myths and Mechanisms* (2nd ed.). London: Routledge.

Boroditsky, L. (2001). Does Language Shape Thought?: Mandarin and English Speakers' Conceptions of Time. *Cognitive Psychology*, 43(1), 1–22. doi:10.1006/cogp.2001.0748 PMID:11487292

Bowerman, M. (1996). Which way to the present? Cross-linguistic differences in thinking about time. In J. Gumperz & S. Levinson (Eds.), *Rethinking linguistic relativity* (pp. 145–176). Cambridge, MA: Cambridge Univ. Press.

Burleson, B. R., & Caplan, S. E. (1998). Cognitive complexity. In J. C. McCroskey, J. A. Daly, M. M. Martin, & M. J. Beatty (Eds.), *Communication and personality: Trait perspectives* (pp. 233–286). Cresskill, NJ: Hampton Press.

Burry, M. (2011). *Scripting Cultures: Architectural Design and Programming*. London: John Wiley and Sons.

Chai, K.-H., & Xiao, X. (2012). Understanding design research: A bibliometric analysis of Design Studies (1996-2010). *Design Studies*, 33(1), 24–43. doi:10.1016/j.destud.2011.06.004

Coley, F., Houseman, O., & Roy, R. (2007). An introduction to capturing and understanding the cognitive behaviour of design engineers. *Journal of Engineering Design*, 18(4), 311–325. doi:10.1080/09544820600963412

Costa, R., & Sobek, D. K. (2004). How process affects performance: an analysis of student design productivity. *Paper presented at theASME '04 International Design Engineering Technical Conferences and Computers and Information in Engineering Conference*, Salt Lake City, Utah USA. doi:10.1115/DETC2004-57274

Coventry, K. R., & Garrod, S. C. (2004). *Saying, seeing and acting: The psychological semantics of spatial prepositions*. Psychology Press.

Cross, N., & Clayburn Cross, A. (1995). Observations of teamwork and social processes in design. *Design Studies*, 16(2), 143–170. doi:10.1016/0142-694X(94)00007-Z

Dacey, J. S., & Lennon, K. H. (1998). *Understanding creativity: the interplay of biological, psychological, and social factors*. San Francisco: Jossey-Bass.

Dong, A. (2005). The latent semantic approach to studying design team communication. *Design Studies*, 26(5), 445–461. doi:10.1016/j.destud.2004.10.003

Dorst, K., & Cross, N. (2001). Creativity in the design process: Co-evolution of problem-solution. *Design Studies, 22*(5), 425–437. doi:10.1016/S0142-694X(01)00009-6

Eastman, C. M. (1969). Cognitive processes and ill-defined problems: a case study from design*Proceedings of the 1st international joint conference on Artificial intelligence* (pp. 669-690). Washington, DC: Morgan Kaufmann Publishers Inc.

Finke, R. A., Ward, T. B., & Smith, S. M. (1992). Creative cognition: Theory, research, and applications. Cambridge, MA: MIT Press (Bradford Book).

Fischer, G., Giaccardi, E., Eden, H., Sugimoto, M., & Ye, Y. (2005). Beyond binary choices: Integrating individual and social creativity. *International Journal of Human-Computer Studies, 63*(4-5), 482–512. doi:10.1016/j.ijhcs.2005.04.014

Gero, J. S. (1996). Creativity, emergence and evolution in design. *Knowledge-Based Systems, 9*(7), 435–448. doi:10.1016/S0950-7051(96)01054-4

Gero, J. S., & Neill, T. M. (1998). An approach to the analysis of design protocols. *Design Studies, 19*(1), 21–61. doi:10.1016/S0142-694X(97)00015-X

Giaccardi, E. (2004). *Principles of Metadesign: Processes and Levels of Co-creation in the New Design Space. (PhD)*. Plymouth, UK: University of Plymouth.

Glanville, R. (1999). Researching design and designing research. *Design Issues, 15*(2), 80–91. doi:10.2307/1511844

Gleitman, L., & Papafragou, A. (2005). Language and thought. In K. J. Holyoak & R. G. Morrison (Eds.), *Cambridge handbook of thinking and reasoning* (pp. 633–661). New York: Cambridge University Press.

Goldschmidt, G. (1990). Linkography: Assessing Design Productivity. In R. Trappl (Ed.), *Cybernetics and system '90, World Scientific* (pp. 291–298). Singapore: World Scientific.

Goldschmidt, G. (1995). The designer as a team of one. *Design Studies, 16*(2), 189–209. doi:10.1016/0142-694X(94)00009-3

Goldschmidt, G., & Tatsa, D. (2005). How good are good ideas? Correlates of design creativity. *Design Studies, 26*(6), 593–611. doi:10.1016/j.destud.2005.02.004

Grudin, J. (1994). Computer-supported cooperative work: History and focus. *Computer, 27*(5), 19–26. doi:10.1109/2.291294

Guilford, J. P. (1967). *The Nature of Human Intelligence*. New York: McGraw-Hill.

Hackman, J. R., & Morris, C. G. (1975). In L. Berkowitz (Ed.), *Group tasks, group interaction process, and group performance effectiveness: A review and proposed integration* (Vol. 8, pp. 1–55). Advances in experimental social psychologyNew York: Academic Press.

Hasirci, D., & Demirkan, H. (2007). Understanding the effects of cognition in creative decision making: A creativity model for enhancing the design studio process. *Creativity Research Journal, 19*(2-3), 259–271. doi:10.1080/10400410701397362

Hegarty, M., & Kozhevnikov, M. (1999). Types of visual–spatial representations and mathematical problem solving. *Journal of Educational Psychology, 91*(4), 684–689. doi:10.1037/0022-0663.91.4.684

Hennessey, B., & Amabile, T. (1999). Consensual assessment. In M. Runco & S. Pritzker (Eds.), *Encyclopedia of creativity* (pp. 346–359). San Diego, CA: Academic Press.

Ho, C.-H. (2001). Some phenomena of problem decomposition strategy for design thinking: Differences between novices and experts. *Design Studies, 22*(1), 27–45. doi:10.1016/S0142-694X(99)00030-7

Holzer, D., Hough, R., & Burry, M. (2007). Parametric Design and Structural Optimisation for Early Design Exploration. *International Journal of Architectural Computing, 5*(4), 625–643. doi:10.1260/147807707783600780

Hörnig, R., Oberauer, K., & Weidenfeld, A. (2006). Between reasoning. *Quarterly Journal of Experimental Psychology, 59*(10), 1805–1825. doi:10.1080/17470210500416151 PMID:16945861

Ibrahim, R., & Rahimian, F. P. (2010). Comparison of CAD and manual sketching tools for teaching architectural design. *Automation in Construction, 19*(8), 978–987. doi:10.1016/j.autcon.2010.09.003

Iordanova, I. (2007). Teaching Digital Design Exploration: Form Follows. *International Journal of Architectural Computing, 5*(4), 685–702. doi:10.1260/147807707783600807

Jara, C. (2014). Verbal literacy in the design process: Enthusiasm and reservation. *Paper presented at theARCC/EAAE 2014 International Conference on Architectural Research Conference*, Honolulu, USA.

Jones, J. C. (1992). Design methods (2nd ed.). New York: Van Nostrand Reinhold.

Kan, J. W. T., & Gero, J. S. (2008). Acquiring information from linkography in protocol studies of designing. *Design Studies, 29*(4), 315–337. doi:10.1016/j.destud.2008.03.001

Kolarevic, B. (2003). *Architecture in the Digital Age: Design and Manufacturing*. London, New York: Spon Press.

Kruger, C., & Cross, N. (2006). Solution driven versus problem driven design: Strategies and outcomes. *Design Studies, 27*(5), 527–548. doi:10.1016/j.destud.2006.01.001

Lawson, B. (1980). *How designers think* (E. ed.). Westfield, NJ: Architectural Press.

Lee, J. H., Gu, N., & Ostwald, M. J. (2013). Architectural Design using Algorithmic Scripting: An Application of Linkographic Analysis Techniques. In *Cutting Edge:47th International Conference of the Architectural Science Association* (pp. 133-142). Hong Kong: Architectural Science Association.

Lee, J. H., Gu, N., & Ostwald, M. J. (2015). Creativity and parametric design? Comparing designer's cognitive approaches with assessed levels of creativity. *International Journal of Design Creativity and Innovation, 3*(2), 78–94. doi:10.1080/21650349.2014.931826

Lee, J. H., Gu, N., & Williams, A. (2014). Parametric design strategies for the generation of creative designs. *International Journal of Architectural Computing, 12*(3), 263–282. doi:10.1260/1478-0771.12.3.263

Lee, J. H., Ostwald, M. J., & Gu, N. (2015). Multi-cultural design communication: Exploring both cognitive and linguistic characteristics in the design process. In Y. Ikeda, C. M. Herr, D. Holzer, S. Kaijima, M. J. Kim. M, A, Schnabel (Eds.), CAADRIA 2015: Emerging Experience in Past, Present and Future of Digital Architecture (pp. 531-540). Hong Kong: The Association for Computer-Aided Architectural Design Research in Asia (CAADRIA).

Levinson, S. C. (1996). Frames of reference and Molyneux's question: Crosslinguistic evidence. In P. Bloom & M. Peterson (Eds.), *Language and space* (pp. 109–169). Cambridge, MA: MIT Press.

Levinson, S. C. (2003). *Space in Language and Cognition: Explorations in Cognitive Diversity*. Cambridge University Press. doi:10.1017/CBO9780511613609

Lindström, L. (2006). Creativity: What Is It? Can You Assess It? Can It Be Taught? *International Journal of Art & Design Education*, *25*(1), 53–66. doi:10.1111/j.1476-8070.2006.00468.x

Liu, Y.-T., & Lim, C.-K. (2006). New tectonics: A preliminary framework involving classic and digital thinking. *Design Studies*, *27*(3), 267–307. doi:10.1016/j.destud.2005.11.008

Maher, M. L. (2010). Evaluating Creativity in Humans, Computers, and Collectively Intelligent Systems. *Paper presented at the DESIRE'10: Creativity and Innovation in Design*, Aurhus, Denmark.

Maher, M. L., & Poon, J. (1996). Modeling Design Exploration as Co-Evolution. *Computer-Aided Civil and Infrastructure Engineering*, *11*(3), 195–209. doi:10.1111/j.1467-8667.1996.tb00323.x

Munnich, E., Landau, B., & Dosher, B. A. (2001). Spatial language and spatial representation: A crosslinguistic comparison. *Cognition*, *81*(3), 171–208. doi:10.1016/S0010-0277(01)00127-5 PMID:11483169

Perkins, D. N. (1981). *The mind's best work*. Cambridge, MA: Harvard University Press.

Prather, L. J., & Middleton, K. L. (2002). Are N+1 heads better than one?: The case of mutual fund managers. *Journal of Economic Behavior & Organization*, *47*(1), 103–120. doi:10.1016/S0167-2681(01)00172-X

Safoutin, M. J., & Thurston, D. J. (1993). A communications-based technique for interdisciplinary design team management. *IEEE Transactions on* Engineering Management, *40*(4), 360–372.

Schön, D. A. (1983). *The Reflective Practitioner: How Professionals Think in Action*. New York: Basic Books.

Schön, D. A. (1984). The architectural studio as an exemplar of education for reflection-in-action. *Journal of Architectural Education*, *38*(1), 2–9. doi:10.1080/10464883.1984.10758345

Schwartz, D. L., & Heiser, J. (2006). *Spatial Representations and Imagery in Learning. The Cambridge handbook of: The learning sciences* (pp. 283–298). New York, NY, US: Cambridge University Press.

Shannon, C. E. (1948). A mathematical theory of communication. *The Bell System Technical Journal*, *27*(3), 397–423. doi:10.1002/j.1538-7305.1948.tb01338.x

Steiner, I. D. (1972). *Group Processes and Productivity*. New York: Academic Press.

Stempfle, J., & Badke-Schaub, P. (2002). Thinking in design teams - an analysis of team communication. *Design Studies*, *23*(5), 473–496. doi:10.1016/S0142-694X(02)00004-2

Suwa, M., Purcell, T., & Gero, J. (1998). Macroscopic analysis of design processes based on a scheme for coding designers' cognitive actions. *Design Studies, 19*(4), 455–483. doi:10.1016/S0142-694X(98)00016-7

Tenbrink, T., & Ragni, M. (2012). Linguistic Principles for Spatial Relational Reasoning. In C. Stachniss, K. Schill, & D. Uttal (Eds.), *Spatial Cognition VIII* (Vol. 7463, pp. 279–298). Springer Berlin Heidelberg. doi:10.1007/978-3-642-32732-2_19

Valkenburg, R., & Dorst, K. (1998). The reflective practice of design teams. *Design Studies, 19*(3), 249–271. doi:10.1016/S0142-694X(98)00011-8

Van der Lugt, R. (2000). Developing a graphic tool for creative problem solving in design groups. *Design Studies, 21*(5), 505–522. doi:10.1016/S0142-694X(00)00021-1

van der Zee, E., & Slack, J. M. (2003). *Representing Direction in Language and Space.* Oxford University Press. doi:10.1093/acprof:oso/9780199260195.001.0001

Visser, W. (1993). Collective design: A cognitive analysis of cooperation in practice. *Paper presented at the 9th International Conference on Engineering Design ICED '93*, Zurich, Switzerland (*Vol. 1*).

von der Weth, R. (1999). Design instinct?—the development of individual strategies. *Design Studies, 20*(5), 453–463. doi:10.1016/S0142-694X(99)00021-6

KEY TERMS AND DEFINITIONS

Algorithm: A set of programming scripts consisting of parameters and rules to generate geometries in parametric design. There are two types of script editors, text-based editors (e.g. Maya Script Editor and Python) and graphical algorithmic editors (e.g. Grasshopper).

Cognitive Space: An analogical organization consisting of two, three or higher dimensions to describe and categorize cognitive activities and thoughts.

Creative Cognition: The mental processes and structures that contribute to creative thinking and discovery.

Design Process: A series of activities or steps that designers use in creating a design outcome.

Design Productivity: The effectiveness and efficiency of design thinking and design processes.

Design Strategy: A pattern or plan of design activities to achieve a design goal or goals. It includes the designer's preferences and habits that contribute to identifying designers' thinking processes.

Geometry: A shape and its properties that are related to points, lines, surfaces, solids, etc.

Parametric Design: The process of exploring and generating design variations using parametric rules. It conventionally occurs in specific software modeling and algorithmic scripting environments.

Spatial Representation: The description of spatial relationships such as the location of objects in space, their directions and their movements.

Chapter 4
Prejudicial Evaluation:
Bias in Self–and–Peer–Assessments of Teamwork Contributions to Design

Richard Tucker
Deakin University, Australia

ABSTRACT

This chapter considers a simple but important question: can students fairly assess each other's individual contribution to team designs? The chapter focuses on a key problem when using online self-and-peer assessment to individualising design grades for team assignments, namely rater bias – the possibility of students being biased when assessing their own and their peers' contributions. Three rater-bias issues are considered in depth: (1) self-overmarking; (2) gender bias and gender differences; and (3) out-group bias in the peer assessment of international students in multicultural cohorts. Each issue is explored via the analysis of eight years of quantitative data from the use of an online self-and-peer assessment tool. Evidence is found of self-overmarking and of out-group bias in nonhomogeneous cohorts. However, no evidence is found of gender bias. The chapter concludes with recommendations for design teachers around the assessment of individual contributions to teamwork using self-and-peer assessment.

INTRODUCTION

In teamwork assignments it is possible to assess students as individuals or to award a team mark, and whichever of these two assessment models is used can have, especially for design cohorts, a significant impact on the student learning experience. Assessment recognising individual contribution is pivotal in this context because of the highly emotive nature of designing, and because of the difficulty of assigning authorship to a creative work meaning 'free-loading' is difficult to detect. Thus, for students designing in teams it is crucial that they are assessed 'fairly' to recognise individual effort. This chapter considers in depth therefore a simple but important question: can we assess individual contributions to team designs through self-and-peer assessment (SAPA)? Specifically, the chapter focuses on a key problem when using self-and-peer assessment to individualise design grades for team assignments, namely rater bias – the possibility of students being biased when assessing their own and their peers' contributions.

DOI: 10.4018/978-1-5225-0726-0.ch004

The chapter reviews ten year's of research by the author on the use of self-and-peer-assessment in higher education contexts, specifically in built environment teaching, and focused on students learning to design in teams. Three rater-bias issues are considered in depth that teachers should be aware of: (1) self-overmarking; (2) gender bias and gender differences; and (3) out-group bias in multicultural cohorts. Each issue is explored via the analysis of eight years of quantitative data from the use of an online SAPA tool. The chapter concludes with recommendations for design teachers around the assessment of individual contributions to teamwork using SAPA.

BACKGROUND

The impetus for the research presented in this chapter comes from nearly 15 years of teaching architecture students how to design in teams. Early experiences during this period were not always positive for the author or his students. It became increasingly clear that many students did not enjoy team- or group-work, and felt that far too many of their assignments across their curricula required them to work with their peers. The common complaint from students was not about the relevancy of teamwork learning as preparation for professional practice, but that they felt that most teamwork in their courses was for the benefit and convenience of their teachers rather than the students. This opinion reflected the fact that with rapidly increasing student-to-staff ratios, many teachers were attempting to reduce assessment and face-to-face time demands by teaching and assessing groups rather than individuals. As face-to-face time demands are high for design teachers, were one-to-one feedback has always been a common pedagogy, these problems were acute in studio education. Thus, rather than spreading their time thinly over a large number of individual projects, an increasing number of design teachers were setting group projects to allow for longer and more in-depth review sessions on a smaller number of assignment submissions. Commonly in such contexts student teams are required to submit one design per team, and each team member receives the same grade. Furthermore, students communicated that they were more often than not taught very little about how to design in teams.

Such negative feedback from students prompted the author to research if their discontent was supported by data. Early research participated in by students from the courses enrolled in by students from the author's institution clearly evidenced that unfair assessment was the key complaint, closely followed by poorly designed pedagogies failing to reflect the demands of teamwork and the skills and capabilities students needed to learn to successfully work in teams (R. Tucker, 2008; R. Tucker & Reynolds, 2006; R. Tucker & Rollo, 2006). As one student complained, 'it is easy to free-ride in a group and, unfairly, it is us, the hard workers, that have to carry the lazy ones'. It became clear to the author that a mechanism would have to be built into the assessment of team-design assignments that rewarded those working hard while penalizing those who were not. During the next couple of years software was developed to individualise grades for team assignments using self-and-peer-assessment conducted anonymously online. The tool, a particular type of SAPA known as Self-and-Peer-Assessment-Continuous-Assessment (SAPCA)), requires students to rate each other's weekly contributions to team design assignments. Rather than the category-based approach that rates teamwork on explicit multiple dimensions, SAPCA uses the holistic approach to peer assessment, for research has demonstrated that students are more supportive of this method and that their teamwork may be improved using it (Lejk & Wyvill, 2002).

As discussed elsewhere (Tucker, Fermelis, & Palmer, 2009), in a two-year study SAPCA was shown to be robust under the most testing of educational conditions. It was used and evaluated by around two thousand students, in highly culturally diverse cohorts, from two courses based in two faculties, on four campuses, and at two offshore partnership campuses. Up to fourteen different teachers were involved at any one time in the delivery of one of the courses. The study found SAPCA to "promote reflective learning by giving students weekly formative evaluation of their team-working, thus enhancing the motivation for participation" (Tucker, 2011, p. 78), and provide "a "pressure valve;" allowing teams to function harmoniously, despite unequal levels of skill and contributions, and allowing students to be tolerant of different learning and assessment aspirations in team members" (op. cit.).

In parallel to research on SAPCA, the author was also leading a project on the *Academic Acclimatisation Difficulties of International Students of the Built Environment* (Tucker & Ang, 2007). This study found that, at the participating institution, average marks in team design projects for Year 1, 2 and 3 students who were classified (via their source of funding) as *international* was far lower than for domestic students. It was also clear from logged observations of participation in design discussions that there was a "hierarchy of engagement in group discussions in studio suggesting that international students are not comfortable with communicating architectural ideas within a collaborative design team" (R Tucker & Ang, 2007, p. 209). As Tang also suggests, we concluded that when students are participating in studios and not communicating in their mother tongue, tutors need to provide them with the procedural knowledge of "how to participate in group discussions, how to express and justify their ideas, and how to give a receive constructive criticism " (Tang, 1996, p. 199), and that while the students who were the subjects of our research clearly struggled with participation, their struggle was "entirely in line with their language difficulties when viewed relative to the similar difficulties of home students" (Tucker & Ang, 2007, p. 213).

These findings raised a further concern in light of the fact that the students participating in the research were using SAPCA to evaluate the contributions of their peers. Namely, might the lower marks of the students classified as international be reflected, and thus partly explained by, any form of outgroup bias in the peer ratings. While raising the spectre of racism amongst the students was a sensitive issue and one with implications difficult to discuss, never mind resolve, it would be naïve to think that Australian students were not susceptible to the same type of biases that all of us can be when we interact with others we view as different to ourselves. Of course, this possibility suggested that biases other than those relating to cultural origin should also be considered, with gender being the obvious factor to also consider in a field – education for the professions of the built environment – that had until only very recently been clearly dominated numerically by males.

After 8 years of many instructors using SAPCA, enough data existed to firmly determine if peer-rater bias was indeed a problem that needed to be addressed in the context of design. Thus the SAPCA data was compared for domestic versus international students, and males versus females. A further bias, and one commonly raised by students when asked to give feedback about using SAPCA, was also considered – self leniency, or the likelihood that students might rate their own contributions higher that their teammates'.

Thus this chapter will present three delineated studies on rater bias with regards to: (1) self-leniency, (2) gender and (3) cultural origin (domestic versus internationally funded students). Each study will commence with a review of the literature on the specific bias being investigated. It should be noted that little detail is given about the types of assignments that the students were working on in their teams. While readers may be interested in what the students were designing and how they were being supported in learning how to design in teams, the author posits that the types of biases that are being investigated are little impacted by variations in the nature of the tasks that were completed. In summary with respect to this issue, all the participants were working on assignments for courses in built environment degree programs, the majority were studying architecture, and the greater majority were undergraduates. Around 55% of the students were completing team assignments as part of a design studio, while the rest were in related courses running parallel to their design studios. Around 40% were enrolled in a design studio headed by the author and so here it might also be added that they were being specifically taught how a team of three to five might design one building (which in most cases was a multiple dwelling, with attached offices for an architectural practice, informed by the precepts of passive solar design – a detailed description of this studio has been published as part of a project funded by the OLT (Tucker et al., 2014) Appendix G: Case Study Design 2B)).

Before moving on to the three studies, the literature will now be summarised on the general benefits and problems of using SAPA to individualise marks for team assignments.

THE BENEFITS OF ASSESSING INDIVIDUAL CONTRIBUTIONS TO TEAMWORK USING SELF-AND-PEER-ASSESSMENT

It has been suggested (e.g., (Barber, 2004; Freeman, Hutchinson, Treleaven, & Sykes, 2006; L. Johnston & L. Miles, 2004; R. Tucker & Rollo, 2006)) that students and teachers alike recognise that successful teamwork and outcomes for team assignments are contingent on the issue of assessment that student's perceive as fairly rewarding individual contributions. Without design assessment that recognises individual contributions some students can lack motivation to engage with team learning and to contribute to teamwork. Watson (2005) suggests that motivation is an essential factor for student groups to work effectively, and Morgan reports that "almost half the perceived problems of group work" can be due to poor motivation ((Morgan, 2002) as quoted in Watson (2005) p.5). Student motivation and attitudes to teamwork impact on both the effectiveness of the teams they are working in and on their learning.

Student self-and-peer assessment is often proposed as a solution to the motivation and assessment issues in team and group work assessment (for instance, (Dochy, Segers, & Sluijsmans, 1999a; Falchikov, 1988; Topping, 1998; Tucker et al., 2009). Peer assessment can be defined as a process by which each student evaluates the extent to which each of their teammates has exhibited certain traits, performed specific tasks or accomplished particular objectives (Kane & Lawler, 1978). When using peer assessment it is common to also require students to self-assess their own contributions to encourage reflection on the value of these contributions in comparison to those of teammates. Self-and-peer-assessment can be: qualitative and/or quantitative; formative and/or summative; informal and/or formal; and periodic or one-off (Dochy, Segers, & Sluijsmans, 1999b). Advocates of SAPA suggest that it can increase student engagement, with consequential improvement in learning through a number of mechanisms, including: giving increased responsibility, autonomy and power to students (Nancy Falchikov & Goldfinch, 2000; Taras, 2008); if students know that their contribution is to be assessed there will be less 'free-riding' (Lucy Johnston & Lynden Miles, 2004); it encourages students to consider the learning objectives and performance levels required of assessment (McGourty, Dominick, & Reilly, 1998); encouragement of reflective thinking (Dochy et al., 1999b; Mark Freeman & McKenzie, 2002; McGourty et al., 1998); and giving feedback to others encourages students to improve their own performance (Davies, 2000; Mark Freeman & McKenzie, 2002; McGourty et al., 1998; Sluijsmans, Dochy, & Moerkerke, 1999). In addition to student benefits, SAPA allows teachers to individualise grades in teamwork assignments (Mark Freeman & McKenzie, 2002; Goldfinch & Raeside, 1990; Raban & Litchfield, 2006; Walker, 2001), as well as a means for providing formative feedback (Davies, 2000; Mulder & Pearce, 2007; Topping, 1998).

Rater Bias Problems When Assessing Individual Contributions To Teamwork Using Self-and-Peer-Assessment

A key issue with students assessing each other's contributions to teamwork is that it depends on student honesty when self-interest and other forms of prejudice might corrupt such honesty. Farh et al. (1991, p. 368) report that peer appraisal is likely to be influenced by "virtually every form of rater bias that has been documented with supervisor and self-appraisals;" including halo (e.g., assessing favourably on all criteria when an individual excels in one or two), leniency, race and gender, while, as an example, Gómez et al. (2000) report on team members being evaluated higher when they are perceived to be in an in-group rather than an out-group when age, nationality and gender are variables. In this chapter three studies are reported that consider three of these issues: self-leniency, race and gender. The first and third studies are discussed here for the first time, while the second study is a summary of work previously published (Tucker, 2013).

Before detailing these studies, a description is given of how SAPA was employed in these studies, which was via the use of a particular model of SAPA developed by the author and known as SAPCA – self-and-peer-continuous-assessment.

Procedure: Making Assessments and the Individualisation of Team Scores Using SAPCA

The description of SAPCA in Tucker, R., Fermelis, J., & Palmer, S. (2009) is summarised in this section. On completion of the assignments, teachers awarded each team's submission a team mark that was then individualised using SAPCA ratings if there was evidence of significant unequal contributions by team members. Throughout the team assignments, students were required to make weekly holistic ratings of their own and their teammates' contributions to process. Students made assessments via a password-protected web site accessed within an online learning environment. They were informed that the ratings should reflect whether teammates had fulfilled a number of obligations: attending meetings and tutorials, actively communicating with teammates, participating in decision-making, completing their designated tasks to the required standard and/or form, meeting deadlines and sharing the workload. This information was provided in an instructional document to ensure consistency of rating advice between cohorts. However, as the instructors for many of the classes varied widely, the framing of what counts as 'good teamwork,' and the priming of students with these values before assessment, would likely be inconsistent between cohorts.

Students made three different types of assessment. The first is a holistic relative contribution (C) score for each team member. The total of the C scores a student awards must add up to the total number of members in the team. Thus, for example, if it is believed that all teammates contributed equally then the student awards all teammates (including themselves) a rating of 1. The intent of this first measure is to encourage students to consider the question of workload contribution. The second measure requires students to rate the quality of teammates' contributions (labelled "performance" (P)) on a five-point Likert scale ranging from 1 for "Inadequate" to 5 for "Excellent." While the Likert evaluation asked students to consider the quality as opposed to the quantity of each other's contributions, it was translated into a numeric value that was used in combination with the quantitative relative contribution assessment to produce a holistic rating of each member's contribution. A third qualitative measure, which seeks comments to justify and explain the first two ratings, has two purposes: firstly, to elucidate for the assessing teachers ratings, anomalies and unexpected final evaluations; and secondly, to develop in students evaluation, feedback and reflective skills.

At the end of each weekly self-and-peer-assessment, and at the conclusion of the team assignment, the software calculated for every student a multiplicative scaling factor (MSF). The MSF, which a student sees at the end of each weekly assessment and then at the completion of the assignment, indicates how peers' ratings of that student compared to the mean rating for the team. Trials have indicated that a range of greater than 0.3 in MSFs within any team should trigger further investigations into the evenness of student contributions. These investigations can include reference to the SAPCA qualitative comments and discussions with tutors and students. If SAPCA MSFs are verified by investigation then students within each team with a greater than 0.3 MSF range will have their mark individualised through the multiplication of the team mark by the MSF. Thus, if the team receives 80%, and a student receives a MSF of 0.95, the student will be awarded 0.95 x 80 = 76%.

Participants

Participants: Studies 1 and 3

For Studies 1 and 3, peer assessment ratings were made using SAPCA in six different courses at two Australian universities in four different degree programs. In total, 1,523 students participated in the study; making a total 18,814 assessments of their own and their peers' contributions to group work. The sample size makes these studies the largest published analysis we are aware of of rater biases in self-and-peer assessment. The six courses were chosen in order to allow for the examination of the possibility of bias in a diverse range of contexts. The six courses were from three different built environment discipline areas. Some of the team assignments were of a short duration that required students to make only one assessment of each other's contributions, while others were longer requiring students to make multiple periodic ratings (up to nine ratings for a nine-week project). In some cohorts there was a fairly even gender split, in others there were a far greater proportion of males. For some cohorts the students self-selected teammates while for others their teachers allocated them to teams. For one cohort the peer assessments themselves were worth 15% of course marks and were evaluated by teachers. In the other courses the students were induced to use SAPCA by penalising them assignment marks for missing ratings. But for all the courses the method for obtaining the peer ratings was precisely the same, using the same online software as described in Section 3.1.

Participants: Study 2

For Study 2, which looked for out-group bias where the in-group was domestic students and the out-group international students, only three of the six cohorts used in Studies 1 and 3 were examined. For these three cohorts, grades were available for teamwork and individual work, thus allowing a comparison of individual grades between domestic and international students. In total, 479 students participated in the study; making a total 8,502 assessments of their own and their peers' contributions to group work. International students were very much in the minority in these three cohorts, representing only 7.5% of students (36 out of 479). As all self-and-peer-assessments were obtained from all the cohorts in the same manner, data from the three cohorts was combined.

Method

Method: Study 1

In Study 1 (Section 4.1), for each assessment the holistic relative contribution score (C) and individual performance score (P) were averaged (whereby the Likert performance score was given a numeric value to make it equivalent in value to the relative contribution score). In order for ease of comparison and analysis, this average ((P+C)/2) was multiplied by a scale factor to produce a SAPCA rating out of 100. Thus, students in the sample received SAPCA ratings between a "perfect" 100 and a low of 16.7. Each student rated each of their peers between one and seven times – depending on the cohort and, usually, on the duration of the team assignment. The peer mark received by each individual from a particular rater was determined by averaging the total peer scores received from that rater. For each cohort, we then compared peer assessment ratings for the cohort as a whole to self-assessment ratings for the cohort as a whole.

Method: Studies 2 And 3

For studies 2 and 3, SAPCA ratings out of 100 were generated as described above in Section 3.3.1. The second study on gender may be seen as a follow-up investigation to the 1997 study of Falchikov and Magin, and one that therefore adopts the same methodology. Both studies consider gender bias in peer marking of group process work. Thus, as in the Falchikov and Magin study, for each group of students in our sample a matrix is generated that can be divided in to four sub-groups. As Falchikov and Magin explain (388-89) (see Figure 1);

The top left sub-group provides raw scores received by female students from female raters (F X Fr); the bottom left for scores received by females from male raters (F X Mr); the top right for scores received by males students from female raters (M X Fr); and the bottom right for scores received by males from male raters (M X Mr).

Figure 1. Averaged marks for the 4 sub-groups
(Praveen Aggarwal & O'Brien, 2008, p. 389)

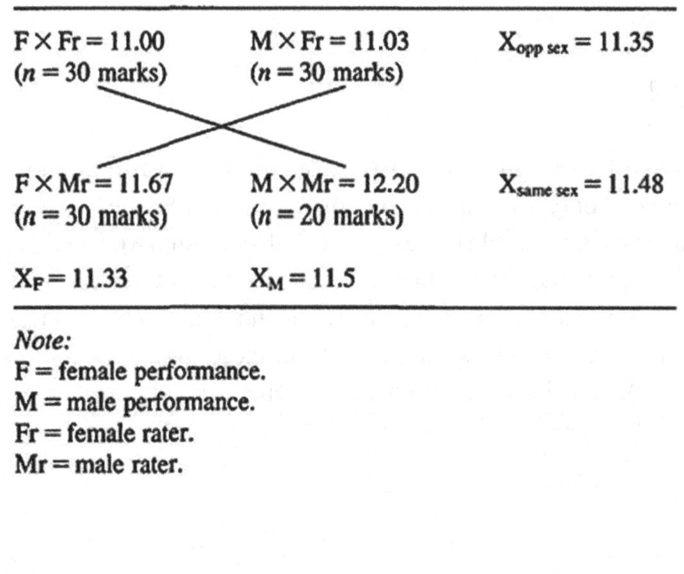

$F \times Fr = 11.00$	$M \times Fr = 11.03$	$X_{opp\ sex} = 11.35$
($n = 30$ marks)	($n = 30$ marks)	
$F \times Mr = 11.67$	$M \times Mr = 12.20$	$X_{same\ sex} = 11.48$
($n = 30$ marks)	($n = 20$ marks)	
$X_F = 11.33$	$X_M = 11.5$	

Note:
F = female performance.
M = male performance.
Fr = female rater.
Mr = male rater.

The averaged marks from these sub-groups are then calculated as $X_{opp\,sex}$, $X_{same\,sex}$, X_F, and X_M. Thus, we can calculate the gender difference as the difference between X_F, and X_M, and the gender bias as the difference between $X_{opp\,sex}$ and $X_{same\,sex}$.

For Study 3, on out-group bias, the same methodology is adapted from Falchikov and Magin that is used in Study 3. However, in Study 2 the two groups are domestic and international students (rather than male and female students).

SELF-OVERMARKING IN SELF-AND-PEER-ASSESSED CONTRIBUTIONS TO TEAMWORK

Background

As reported in Topping (1998), and in Dochy, Segers et al. (1999a), many studies have questioned the accuracy of student self-assessments. Falchikov (1986) found that younger students less reliable self assessors and that more able students are more likely to undermark themselves. Boud and Falchikov (1989) analysed studies published between 1932 and 1988 that had compared student self-ratings to teacher ratings, and reported stronger students underrating themselves and weaker students overrating themselves. Shore, Shore and Thornton reported that validity was weaker for self-ratings than peer ratings (1992), and Fulham and Stringfield (1994) found peer assessment to be more reliable than self-assessment. Wright (1995) found that self-assessment yielded lower marks, and similarly Lennon (1995) found that self-assessment correlated with undermarking and clustering around the median.

The first study considered the extent to which the inclusion of self-ratings can affect the reliability of SAPA (Zhang, Johnston, & Kilic, 2007). While previous research on the effect of including self-rating in SAPA has consistently found that self-rating is different from peer rating (N. Falchikov, 1991; Lejk & Wyvill, 2002), conflicting findings are reported on how self-ratings compare with peer ratings. Johnston and Miles (L. Johnston & L. Miles, 2004) and Zhang et al. (2007) all found that students inflated their self-ratings of their contribution to group project, whereas Falchikov (1991) found that when self-ratings were compared with peer ratings there was no greater tendency for self-raters to overmark or undermark. Irrespective of these conflicting results, it is clear that when completing self-and-peer-assessments group members have an incentive to exaggerate their own contributions (Tu & Lu, 2005). This study seeks to determine whether this problem is indeed significant, for when biases such as these exist any valid peer assessment methodologies should take into account these biases.

The experience of a decade of assessing teamwork learning within the context of design assignments in architectural education has informed the basis for the hypothesis discussed in this paper; namely that students significantly self-overmark in self-and-peer-assessments and that this overmarking should be compensated for in assessment procedures. Based on our own findings published elsewhere (Tucker, 2013) that males are generally more generous on the whole when making peer assessment of contributions to teamwork, we also hypothesise that males will tend to self-overmark more than females.

Findings

As all self-and-peer-assessments were obtained from all the cohorts in the same manner, we are able to combine cohorts to examine peer- and self-ratings overall. Eighteen participants were removed from the combined data because they had been enrolled in more than one of the cohorts being studied and thus were more aware of the issue of self-overmarking. Thus, there were 1505 students in total (603 female, 902 male) who constituted 368 groups.

An independent t-test was conducted to compare the mean ratings for individual contributions to teamwork given to each student compared to the mean ratings they gave to themselves. Peer ratings (M=74.04, SD=11.80) were significantly lower than self-ratings (M=79.31, SD=8.09; t(2665) = 17.099, ρ<0.000. The effect size statistic is moderate at $\eta^2 = 0.056$.

An independent t-test was also conducted to compare the mean self-ratings for individual contributions to teamwork given by female students compared to the mean self-ratings given by male students. There was no significant difference in female self-ratings (M=78.94, SD=8.10) compared to male self-ratings (Table 1) (M=79.58, SD=8.08; t(1120) = 1.307, ρ<0.192. The effect size statistic is very small at $\eta^2 = 0.002$.

Discussion

There are two primary findings from the analyses of peer ratings in these varying contexts (Table 2):

- **First:** In all but one of the six courses, and in the data combined, self-ratings were significantly higher than peer ratings. Thus our first hypothesis is supported.
- **Second:** In the analysis of all the cohorts combined, there was no significant difference between male self-ratings and female self-ratings. In two of the courses there were significant gender differences but these findings were reversed: for one the male self-ratings were significantly higher while for the other the female self-ratings were significantly higher. Thus our second hypothesis that males would overrate more than females was not generally supported.

We can also observe a number of other trends in the data from comparing the results against the pedagogical context of each cohort (Table 2). First, there is a slight tendency for the difference between self and peer ratings to be lower as the number of ratings made by students increases. For example, we note that the in sixth cohort where students assessed each other only once at the end of the assign-

Table 1. Peer and self-assessments for all cohorts

All Cohorts	Averaged Mark Mean SD		Averaged Mark Mean SD	
Given By:	**All Self-Ratings**		**All Male Self-Ratings**	
(number of marks)	79.31	8.09	79.58	8.08
	1122		647	
	All Peer-Ratings		**All Female Self-Ratings**	
(number of marks)	74.04	11.80	78.94	8.10
	3786		475	
Mark difference	+5.27		+0.64	
Significance Effect size (Eta squared)	p = 0.000 $\eta^2 = 0.039$		p = 0.192 $\eta^2 = 0.002$	

Table 2. Comparison of results in different contexts

Cohort	1	2	3	4	5	6
Mean self-rating minus mean peer-rating	+4.78	+5.05	+3.23	+4.58	+3.57	+10.18
Significance Effect size (Eta squared)	$P<0.000$ 0.005	$P<0.000$ 0.039	n/s 0.001	$P<0.000$ 0.051	$P<0.000$ 0.068	$P<0.000$ 0.104
Mean male self-rating minus female self-rating	-2.88	+1.27	+2.84	+0.09	+3.4	-1.05
Significance Effect size (Eta squared)	n/s 0.002	n/s 0.008	$P<0.05$ 0.042	n/s 0.001	$P<0.05$ 0.00003	n/s 0.003
Year level	1	1	2	1	2	3
% males	53%	55%	64%	77%	87%	64%
No. of SAPCA periods	7	3	7	1	9	1
% worth of teamwork	30%	30%	65%	25%	100%	40%
Course subject area	Comms	Design	Design	Tech	Tech	Tech

ment, the mean self-rating 10.18 marks higher than the mean peer rating. This trend suggests that the employment of multiple self-and-peer-assessments may help reduce the effect of self-rater bias. This suggestion aligns with our own experience that the accuracy of the MSFs indicated by SAPA increases as the number of assessment increases. Second, comparing results with year level offers no evidence to challenge Griffee's (1995) general conclusion that there is no difference between self-ratings and year of study. Third, there appears to be no relationship between the difference in male and female self-ratings and the proportions and males and females in a cohort. This finding does not support the possibility suggested by Falchokov and Magin (1997) that gender differences might be greatest when where there are disproportionate numbers of males or females in a class. Finally, nor does the data suggest relationships between self-rater bias, gender bias, subject of study and the worth of the teamwork assignments.

As the evidence in favour of significant self-overmarking in our findings is strong, it is clear that if self-and-peer-assessments are to be validly used to individualise student's marks for team assignments then students should gain no benefit from exaggerating their own contributions. Thus, while we suggest that students are required to self-rate due to the reflective value of self-rating, we advise against including self-ratings in the calculation of MSFs. Thus, each student's MSF is simply: total of an individual's ratings awarded by other students divided by the total of all peer ratings. In our own SAPCA tool we display to teachers both the MSF *without* the self-rating (displayed as "self" in the screen shot below) and the MSF *with* the self-rating (displayed as "self"). We also display the self-range: the difference between the two values. This self-range can be viewed as a measure of how "self-inflated" an opinion a student has of their contribution, or what might be described as a measure of their deception. This measure can be useful to know when instructors are making further investigations into team dynamics if there are conflicts among teammates or if students question their SAPCA ratings.

In a sense, the combination of the over-rating scores and the MSFs (the self scores) could be said to provide an indicator of social loafing to teachers. In the hope for more accurate ratings, greater accountability and thus a subsequent decrease in social-loafing, we have recently made it clear to our students that the SAPCA display that teachers can access each week indicates a measure of student over-marking.

Our intuitive sense from talking to students is that this has indeed led to greater honesty, suggesting that further research might usefully investigate this possibility.

A sense of openness and honesty among team members is of course important, because this can help create a team climate of inclusiveness, freedom, interpersonal trust and mutual respect (termed "psychological safety"), which in turn supports the open exchange of ideas between students. Such a climate correlates with effective teamwork, and can be further facilitated through teacher communication. Indeed, we suggest that students are given the opportunity, if they want it, to openly discuss in their teams self-and-peer-assessment ratings with their teachers, because this enhances a climate of honesty and defuses unhealthy team conflict in the presence of an impartial observer.

GENDER BIAS AND GENDER DIFFERENCES IN PEER ASSESSMENTS OF CONTRIBUTIONS TO GROUP WORK

Background

Females in education have repeatedly been shown to gain higher marks than males (Ahern, 2007). Moreover, teamwork is widely considered to be the preferred pedagogy of women as compared to men (Alge, Wiethoff, & Klein, 2003) and why some studies have shown females to rate higher on teamwork skills (Alfonseca, Carro, Martín, Ortigosa, & Paredes, 2006; Amason, 1996; Amason & Sapienza, 1997; Anderson, 1988). Such research, and the experience of a decade of assessing teamwork learning within the context of architectural education, has informed the basis for the hypothesis discussed in this study. Namely that, in peer assessments of contributions to group assignments, female students might rate higher than their male equivalents, but that this difference is not due to gender bias.

As reported by Johnson and Smith (1997), studies on gender effects on performance appraisal have provided mixed results; with some evidence of gender related bias (e.g., (Bacon, Stewart, & Silver, 1999; Drazin & Auster, 1987), while other research has failed to find such effects (Bacon, Stewart, & Stewart-Belle, 1998; Badke-Schaub & Frankenberger, 2002; L. Shore & Thornton III, 1986). Findings from studies on the specific influence of gender in learning environments are uneven (Arnett, 1993), reflecting that the effect of gender in the classroom is complex and dependent on the nature of the assessed task. In an overview of gender bias on peer assessment, relating to the reliability of both teacher and peer marking, Falchikov and Magin (2008) cite examples of same-sex subjects being both favoured and disfavoured. Falchikov and Magin (2008) observed in their own analysis of two case studies, one involving 67 students and the other 169 students, slight biases towards females independent of the gender of the assessor. However, they found no reports at the time of other studies employing cross-sex/same-sex analysis of marks to determine gender bias in peer assessment of students' contributions to group work. Thus, it was concluded three years later (Nancy Falchikov & Goldfinch, 2000, p. 318), that this issue "deserves the attention of researchers. Gender effects are present in a wide variety of social and academic situations, and it is possible they may also play a role in peer assessment."

Since the Falchikov and Magin overview, as I have reported elsewhere (REF) research in this area has been limited and mixed. In peer assessment of individual performance in group-work in chemical engineering courses, Kaufmen and Felder (2000) observed men to give teammates slightly higher ratings and to receive slightly higher ratings from their teammates. In contrast, May and Gueldenzoph (2006) found that females received higher peer evaluation scores, whether being rated by other females or males, but that as males scored lower grade point averages (GPA) these lower peer evaluations could be a function of lower ability or performance rather than because of gender bias. Similarly, Baker (2008) found that women received higher peer ratings than males but that this may have been because their quiz scores were higher. Both the May and Baker studies echo the much earlier findings of Sherrard and Raafat (1994), who found that women received higher peer evaluations but also had much higher GPA scores.

Menchaca, Resta and Awalt (2002) saw the peer ratings of females remaining high over time while those of off-campus males decreased, but related this to differences in attitudes to on-line learning between race rather than gender. In a study of peer assessment of oral presentations, Langan et al. (Langan et al., 2005) also detected gender differences, finding that males tended to grade other male speakers slightly higher than female speakers while female assessors were uninfluenced by speaker gender. Gatfield (1999) detected no gender effects in student satisfaction with peer assessment and group projects in Australian undergraduates while, in contrast, Wen and Tsai (2006) found that male students had more positive attitudes to peer assessment. In a review of six studies of peer assessment, Topping (2008) found more positive attitudes toward peer assessment amongst male students.

Gender differences have also been found in self-assessment. For instance, Pope (2005) suggested that females are more stressed than males by self-assessment, and in a study of first-year medical students, Rees (2003) found that 72.7% of females underestimated their performance while 73.3% of males overestimated themselves. In another study of medical students, Lind et al. (2002) also found males to overestimate and females to underestimate their own performances, when in reality female students were statistically outperforming their male peers. Both of these studies are in line with Das (1998), who found gender as a highly significant variable in negative self evaluation of problem-based learning amongst women.

As peer assessments in our study were made on-line via a Learning Management System, it is worth also noting the gender differences that Barrett and Lally (1999) found in engagement with web-based learning contexts. In this study, men's contributions to on-line discussions were typically more numerous, longer and including greater levels of social exchange than those of women, although women appeared to be more interactive than men.

Findings

As all peer ratings were obtained from all the cohorts in the same manner, we are able to combine cohorts to examine peer ratings overall. Eighteen participants were removed from the combined data because they had been enrolled in more than one of the cohorts being studied. Thus, there were 1505 students in total (603 female, 902 male) who constituted 368 groups.

Results

Results are shown in Table 3. An analysis of the impact of gender on peer ratings shows there was a statistical difference at the $p<0.05$ level in peer ratings received by males compared to those received by females [$F(1, 3784) = 15.568$, $p=0.000$]. The mean rating was 1.54 higher for females. However, the effect size was very small at $\eta^2 = 0.004$. There was also a statistical difference at the $p<0.05$ level between the peer ratings given by males compared to those given by females [$F(1, 3784) = 6.649$, $p=0.010$], with males being the more generous markers.

Table 3. Peer assessment for all cohorts

All Cohorts	Averaged Peer Mark Mean SD		Average of Marks Given by Female Raters Mean SD		Average of Marks Given by Male Raters Mean SD	
Received by:						
Female students (number of marks)	74.96	10.48	74.83	10.71	75.10	10.22
	1510		765		745	
Male students (number of marks)	73.42	12.57	72.08	12.84	74.12	12.37
	2276		776		1500	
Mark difference (F-M)	+1.54		+2.75		+0.98	
Significance Eta squared	$p = 0.000$ $\eta^2 = 0.004$		$p = 0.000$ $\eta^2 = 0.013$		not significant $\eta^2 = 0.002$	

Note:

Same sex: Mean = 74.36 SD = 11.84 N = 2265

Opposite sex: Mean = 73.56 SD = 11.72 N = 1521

Difference = 0.80 Effect size η^2 = 0.001, Significance $p<0.05$

Comparing the peer ratings received by females when rated by females to the peer ratings received by males when rated by females showed a statistical difference at the $p<0.05$ level in peer ratings received [$F (1, 2120) = 20.899$, $p=0.000$]. The effect size was small at $\eta^2 = 0.013$.

Comparing the peer ratings received by females when rated by males to the peer ratings received by males when rated by males showed there was no statistical difference at the $p<0.05$ level in peer ratings received [$F (1, 2243) = 3.516$, $p=0.000$].

Comparing the difference between same sex ratings and mixed gender ratings on the peer ratings received by students showed a statistical difference at the $p<0.05$ level in peer ratings given by both groups [$F (1, 3784) = 4.208$, $p=0.040$]. However, the effect size virtually zero at $\eta^2 = 0.001$ and hence had very little discernable influence on the variance of scores.

A one-way between-groups analysis of variance (ANOVA) comparing the peer ratings in the four gender/rated-rater pairings showed a statistical difference at the $p<0.05$ level in peer ratings received [$F (3, 3782) = 10.448$, $p=0.000$]. Despite reaching statistical significance, the actual difference in mean scores between the four groups was quite small. The effect size, calculated using eta squared, was small at 0.010. Post-hoc comparisons using the Dunnett T3 test indicated that: Group 1 (females rating females) was significantly different from Group 3 (males rating females); the mean score for Group 2 (females rating males) was significantly different from Group 3; and the mean score for Group 4 (males rating males) was significantly different from Group 3.

Discussion

There are five primary findings from the analyses of peer ratings in all these varying contexts:

- **First:** Females received marginally higher marks than the males for peer assessments of individual contributions to teamwork. In the two largest cohorts, and for all the cohorts combined, the difference in marks was significant. Although in all three of these cases the effect sizes were small, this finding supports previous research suggesting that females in education gain higher marks than males (Ahern, 2007), it aligns with the widely held view that teamwork is the preferred pedagogy of women as compared to men (Alge et al., 2003), and reinforces previous studies that have shown that females rate higher on teamwork skills (Alfonseca et al., 2006; Amason, 1996; Amason & Sapienza, 1997; Anderson, 1988).

- **Second:** Males were significantly more generous than females when giving peer ratings. We suggest that these first two findings may be related. For as Falchikov and Magin suggest, slight female peer assessment advantage in group work contexts may be explained by females' superior group maintenance behaviors and other teamwork skills. It might therefore be speculated that males may be acknowledging and compensating for inferior teamwork skills in their greater generosity when making peer assessments.

- **Third:** There was statistical significance between same sex ratings and the mixed gender ratings, with same sex ratings being marginally higher. However, the effect size was very small and hence had very little discernable influence on the variance of scores.

- **Fourth:** The data indicates no relationship between overall mean ratings and the total number of ratings made. Neither does the data indicate correlation between year level, which is an indicator of familiarity with the process of self-and-peer-assessment because students are required to use SAPCA in multiple courses throughout the curriculum, and overall ratings.

- **Fifth:** Falchokov and Magin (1997) suggested that gender differences might be greatest when where there are disproportionate numbers of males or females in a class, and the significant difference found in this case study could be seen as evidence of this. However, in cohorts 4 and 5 there were greater proportions of males (77% and 87% respectively), but no significant differences between same-gender and mixed-gender ratings. Thus, there would seem to be little evidence in our data of gender effects due to the gender mix of cohorts.

OUT-GROUP BIAS IN THE PEER ASSESSMENT OF INTERNATIONAL STUDENTS IN MULTICULTURAL COHORTS

Our third study considers the possibility that when students are assessing each other's contributions to teamwork using SAPA, they might be influenced by in-group favouritism (also known as in-group–out-group bias, in-group bias, or intergroup bias). In other words, they might demonstrate a pattern of favouring team members of their in-group. Specifically, this study considered whether home students, who comprised 92.5% of the cohort and thus the clear in-group, might be biased against international students.

Background

The numbers of international students attending Australian universities has expanded over the last decade. As reported in Australian Education International (2010), the Asian countries supply the majority of students, "with over 33% of international higher education students coming from East Asia, over 34% from the rest of Asia (that is, over two thirds from Asia) and less than 33% from the rest of the world" (Choi & Nieminen, 2012). A range of experiences is associated with international students' transition into the Australian education system, including: heightened physical and emotional upheaval due to displacement and difficulties acclimatizing to a new environment, feelings of anxiety, loss of control, lack of confidence, insecurity, stress, isolation, frustration and anger. Sawir (2005) found that transition difficulties affect the performance of international students in their studies and impact negatively on their learning experiences. Wong (2004) identified three challenges faced by Asian students who have studied abroad – different learning styles, cultural barriers and language problems. Burns also found that, compared to local students, overseas students had significantly greater difficulties adjusting to academic requirements relating to study methods, independent learning, participation, time management, and language skills (Burns, 1991).

While it is argued that the internationalisation of cohorts can help develop in staff and students, both domestic and international, intercultural competencies for effective working in international contexts, a number of studies have presented strong evidence of minimal intercultural contact in culturally diverse cohorts (Halualani, Chitgopekar, Morrison, & Dodge, 2004; Pettigrew, 1998; Quintrell & Westwood, 1994), meaning the opportunities for learning from positive interactions are limited. De Vita (2007) concluded from a wide-ranging review of the literature on internationalization that "the ideal of transforming a culturally diverse student population into a valued resource for activating processes of international connectivity, social connectivity and intercultural learning is still very much that, an ideal" (p. 165). Leask and Carroll (2011) go further when discussing the experiences of international national students, describing a campus environment "where those who are perceived as belonging to cultural and linguistic minorities are locked into the status of 'outsider', either unwilling or unable to engage with the dominant majority" (p.648). Leask's studies in Australia and Sweden found that international students encountered attitudes and actions in domestic students that made it difficult to actively learn and socialise across cultures.

While group learning in culturally diverse teams is seen as presenting opportunities for positive intercultural learning (Glauco De Vita, 2001), research into learning and team-working in culturally diverse versus mono-cultural groups is inconclusive (Kimmel & Volet, 2012). While De Vita's (2002) and Watson et al.'s (Watson, Johnson, & Zgourides, 2002) findings evidence the benefits of diverse groups, Wright and Lander (2003) have found shortcoming in the intercommunication of culturally diverse groups. Kimmel and Volet (2012, p.157) found that "language proficiency, academic competencies, and cohort characteristics" play an important role in intercultural learning, and that "students' own attitudes towards intercultural interactions may be affected by the quality of close peers' experiences in culturally diverse groups (extended contact effect)." International students are often unprepared for and disadvantaged by the high levels of language skills demanded of them, both written and oral. These demands are heightened in teamwork contexts, where deficiencies in interpersonal and language skills can be conspicuous. Moreover, for Asian students in particular, experience-informed learning style preferences do not foster aptitudes for group problem solving. As Wong explains (2004, p. 162), "generally, Asian students do not have much experience in teamwork. They found it difficult to work in a team especially with members that are not cooperative and unreliable. There is a preference to work individually so that they can have full control of the final product." Koehne (2005) describes ethnic (her terminology) students in Australian cohorts feeling excluded in teamwork, an experience described as being positioned as "other" that is accentuated when domestic students form mono-cultural teams are asked to self-select teammates. Further afield, Trahar and Hylans (2011) report staff and students describing difficulties with group work in multi-cultural cohorts in the UK, such as "communication issues, unequal commitment to the group and over-talking or interrupting" (p. 629). These difficulties are linked to what Haigh (2008) describes as "chauvinistic resistance to the intrusion of, if not outside ideas, then outside ways of doing things" (p. 282).

The specific context of our own study, which is building design, presents a particularly acute language and interpersonal communication challenges for international students. Whilst it can be argued that the communication of a student's design work, which is presented largely in graphic or modelled mediums, should not rely on words, if the design is not orally explained well to peers and teachers this can adversely affect learning outcomes and assessment. It is, after all, expected that architects should be capable of 'selling' an idea - and good communication and negotiation skills are accepted to play a significant role in this.

Oral communication and interpersonal skills are at the forefront of design programmes, but they are commonly the skills that international students of design have trouble learning and demonstrating - especially when this learning takes place collaboratively (see Tucker & Ang, 2007). Cohen highlights (1994), that where extensive mutual exchange of ideas and strategies is desired, limited participation of out-group students, ie., those seen as 'other,' may impede interaction.

Research suggests the problems of Asian international students, who are usually seen as belonging to the out-group in teams, can be linked to the group psychology of co-operative learning (Biggs & Watkins, 1996; Chan, 2001; Wong, 2004; Zhen Hui, 2001), with regards to issues of hierarchy, status, face and shame. For if learning preferences have been informed by a cultural emphasis on respect for authority such as is common in Asian society (Li, 2003), it can be expected that their classroom behaviour will reflect this emphasis. Classroom behaviour in Asia tends therefore to have moral as well social connotations explaining why, as Ballard and Clanchy suggest (1991, p. 16), "many of our Asian students find it repugnant to join in spirited arguments in the classroom where Australian students are questioning the point of view of their teacher." This preference for tutor-centred knowledge transmission, which maintains the 'passivity' of learning style characteristic of the former education of many Asian students (Ballard & Clanchy, 1991), is heightened not only by time-constraints but also by the social dynamics of group work. For the students admitted to being far less likely to present their point of view if this opened them to tutor criticism that they did not have time to defend - a situation they felt was confronting in the context of group discussions. Reticence during group discussions is largely a result of language difficulties and shame avoidance. The attitudes to group learning can be understood via the significance of status recognition to co-operative learning to suggest that student perceptions of unequal status make small collaborative design groups less productive in terms of inequitable interaction and unequal cooperative learning outcomes. Thus, as Cohen has stated (1994, p. 24), inequities in participation informed by marked identity characteristics, such as race and gender within cooperative groups, must be considered in heterogeneous settings. For if the participants "have pre-existing stereotypes about lesser competence of minorities and women confirmed in their group experience, then the effects of cooperation are far less desirable than many proponents of the technique would have us believe."

Findings

In order to see whether there was an actual difference between the performance of international students and domestic students in the specific learning contexts of the three course cohorts, an independent t-test was conducted to compare the mean grades awarded to international students for their individual assignments compared to the mean grades awarded to domestic students for their individual assignments. For each all three cohorts, the students were enrolled in a course for which they completed both a teamwork assignment and an individual assignment. There was no significant difference between individual grades between these two groups. Although it is worth noting that the individual grades of international students

(M=70.03, SD=13.02) were generally higher than those of domestic students (M=68.65, SD=13.78). Thus it can be said that academic aptitude in the courses is a variable that has been controlled for. In other words, there is no significant difference between the abilities of domestic and international students in these contexts.

Results are shown in Table 4. An analysis of the impact of cultural origin on peer ratings shows there was a statistical difference at the $p<0.05$ level in peer ratings received by international students compared to those received by domestic students $[F (1, 1939) = 6.659, p=0.010]$. The mean rating was 4.42/100 higher for domestic students. However, the effect size was very small at $\eta^2 = 0.003$. There was no significant difference between the peer ratings given by international students compared to those given by domestic students $[F (1, 1939) = 3.107, p=0.078]$, although international students were slightly more generous.

The next analysis directly considered whether domestic students peer assess international students lower than they peer assess fellow domestic students. Comparing the peer ratings received by international students when rated by domestic students to the peer ratings received by domestic students when rated by domestic students showed a statistical difference at the $p<0.05$ level in peer ratings received $[F (1, 1764) = 33.850, p=0.000]$. The mean rating was 6.025/100 higher for domestic students, and the effect size was small at $\eta^2 = 0.020$.

The next analysis considers whether international students peer assess international students lower than domestic students. Comparing the peer ratings received by international students when rated by international students to the peer ratings received by domestic students when rated by international students showed no significant difference $[F (1, 173) = .023, p=0.880]$, with the mean peer rating only 1.07/100 higher for domestic students.

Comparing the difference between same culture ratings and mixed culture ratings on the peer ratings received by students showed no statistical difference $[F (1, 1939) = 3.107, p=0.078]$ with the mean peer rating only 2.26/100 higher for mixed culture ratings.

Table 4. Peer assessment for all cohorts

All Cohorts	Averaged Peer Marks Given by All Students Mean SD		Averaged Peer Marks Given by International Students Mean SD		Averaged Peer Marks Given by Domestic Students Mean SD		Averaged Individual Marks	
Received by:								
International students (no. of marks)	73.76	11.37	78.35	7.51	71.12	12.37	70.03	13.02
	153		56		97		36	
Domestic students (no. of marks)	77.30	16.58	79.43	53.04	77.14	9.75	68.65	13.78
	1788		119		1669		443	
Mark difference (D-I)	+4.42		+1.08		+6.02		-1.38	
Significance Eta squared	p = 0.000 $\eta2 = 0.003$		Not significant		p = 0.000 $\eta2 = 0.02$		Not significant	

Note:
Same Culture: Mean = 76.82, SD = 10.00, N = 1766
Opposite Mean: Mean = 79.09, SD = 43.88, N = 175
Difference = 2.27, Not significant

A one-way between-groups analysis of variance (ANOVA) comparing the peer ratings in the four cultural-origin/rated-rater pairings showed a statistical difference at the $p<0.05$ level in peer ratings received [F (3, 1937) = 5.32, $p=0.001$]. Despite reaching statistical significance, the actual difference in mean scores between the four groups was quite small. The effect size, calculated using eta squared, was small at 0.008. Post-hoc comparisons using the Dunnett T3 test indicated that: the mean peer rating for Group 1 (domestics rating domestics) was significantly different from Group 3 (domestics rating internationals), with domestics rating domestics 6.02/100 higher than they rated internationals; and that the mean rating for Group 3 (domestics rating internationals) was significantly different from Group 4 (internationals rating internationals), with domestics rating internationals 7.23/100 lower than internationals rated internationals.

Discussion

A number of findings can be drawn from the analyses of peer ratings in all three courses:

- There is no significant difference between the overall academic performance of international students and domestic students in the specific learning contexts of each unit when individual assignment grades are used as the measure of this performance. In fact, international students slightly outperformed domestic students in their individual assignments. However, the data does not elucidate whether there is a difference, perceived or actual, in the teamworking abilities of international and domestic students, and the lack of evidence on this represents a knowledge gap requiring further research.
- The analysis clearly shows that domestic students peer assess international students significantly less favourably than they assess their fellow domestic students.
- The analysis shows that international students peer assess their fellow international students more or less equally to domestic students.
- These three findings together – that domestics peer assess internationals lower then fellow domestics, that both groups performed equivalently in individual assignments, and that internationals assessed both groups equally – strongly suggests that some form of out-group bias is prejudicing the peer assessment of international students by domestic students, for it is only domestic students that perceive the performance of international students being inferior.
- Thus our first hypothesis is supported, namely that international students are being unfairly disadvantaged in peer assessment by out-group bias against them.
- While issues of cultural diversity in teams were discussed with students in these cohorts, it appears more work is needed in this area. The study also suggests that peer ratings of international students ought to be used with caution for individualising marks for teamwork, and that multicultural cohorts need to be educated about the consequences of out-group bias.

However, caution should be used when interpreting these results, for it is all too easy to jump to the straightforward conclusion of racial prejudice against the out-group international students biasing the peer assessment of these students by the in-group domestic students. For there are of course other possibilities that might explain this mechanism. It is possible, for instance, that domestic students perceive that international students exhibit inferior teamworking skills, and that the understanding of what are these teamwork skills differs between domestic and international students. The peer ratings of domestic students might also reflect perceptions of lesser participation by international students not comfortable with contributing to discussions not in their mother tongue.

Despite the low opinions held by domestic students of the teamwork contributions of their international teammates, it is worth noting that international students' ratings of their teamwork learning experiences, which were obtained and analysed in a related but different project funded by the Australian Office of Learning and Teaching (OLT) (R. Tucker et al., 2014), differ little from those of domestic students. So even though there appears that perceptions of international students by domestic students are influenced by prejudice, this dynamic is not degrading the teamwork learning of international students.

RECOMMENDATIONS

As has been recommended elsewhere, "task assessment, team formation methods, the use of self-and-peer-assessment, the teaching of teamwork skills, and teaching students how to design in collaboration all significantly impact learning outcomes in team contexts"(R. Tucker et al., 2014, p. 9). Thus, these pedagogical factors require careful design in both design and non-design units. Moreover, analysis of the quantitative data of the three studies informs a number of specific recommendations in relation to the use of SAPA to individualise grades in team design assignments:

- In line with other studies on peer assessment, we have found that SAPA is an effective method for individualising marks that students see as fair and transparent, and that its use therefore enhances student motivation to learn and engage with teamwork.
- Students should gain no benefit from exaggerating their own contributions. Thus, while students should be required to self-rate due to the reflective value of self-rating, self-ratings should be excluded from the calculation of MSFs.
- Students should be given the opportunity to openly discuss in their teams self-and-peer-assessment ratings with their teachers, because this enhances a climate of honesty and defuses unhealthy team conflict.
- Improved team climate and reduced unhealthy conflict can be achieved by: asking teams to draw up team contracts, teaching students conflict management skills, and providing conflict intervention strategies.
- Both the teachers and teammates of international students (especially those non-fluent in the domestic tongue) should be encouraged to acknowledge and compensate for the difficulties these students might have with communication and integration. Moreover, we suggest that international students should not be isolated with culturally dissimilar teammates, unless they are comfortable with this.
- Peer ratings of international students ought to be used with caution for individualising marks for teamwork, and multi-cultural cohorts need to be educated about the consequences of out-group bias.

A further recommendation is far broader and deals with how SAPA as an assessment strategy can support the learning goals of design education. It is clear that assessment should not only be about providing grades, but should also drive learning. As concluded by the 2012 OLT funded project *Assessing creativity: Strategies and tools to support teaching and learning in architecture and design*, any assessment task should "purposefully link the choice of assessment type with the outcomes that are being assessed and... correlate the assessment type with appropriate assessment support tools and enablers which, over the duration of the students' degree, will develop the aspired skills and knowledge identified by the professional body" (Williams, Askland, & Boud, 1996, p. 24). In line with this recommendation, we have found SAPA should ideally be closely harnessed to learning and teaching teamworking capabilities. Thus it should not stand alone purely as a rating tool, but instead be incorporated into the studio-learning environment as a feedback mechanism that informs and openly encourages reflection among teammates. For instance, it is strongly recommended that for teams where SAPA evidences unequal contributions, teammates should be given the opportunity to openly discuss with each other and their teacher how they will address the feedback given to them via SAPA. This encourages honesty, which in turn can improve team climate and cohesiveness, and often leads to better planning and management of team objectives – all team skills and characteristics that lead to improved teamworking capabilities. Indeed, SAPA might be directly linked to ratings for tasks that students identify in project plans and guidelines for collaboration that they identify in team contracts. In this way SAPA might then be used to assess teamworking capabilities as well as individualising contributions.

A final statistic is worth commenting on with regards to the use of SAPA for team design assignments is the contrast we found in SAPCA informed individualisation rates between the design units and the lecture-based theory units taught in parallel to design. For while only 17% of students had their marks individualised in the theory units, 37% of the design students had their marks individualised. This contrast might be significant for design instructors, for it suggests that the use of SAPA to alleviate the problems caused by poor contributions to teamwork might be far greater when the product being assessed by instructors is a team created design. The reasons for this can only be speculated upon, but it might be suggested that free riding is far easier when the product is not a written piece for it is more straightforward to ascribe individual authorship to constituent components of collaborative writing than it is to credit "elements" of a collaborative design to individuals.

FUTURE RESEARCH DIRECTIONS

As evidence in this third study on out-group bias was strong, and as the study has few parallels, the need for further research in this area is obvious. In particular, two significant gaps in the data need to be addressed in future research:

- **First:** The delineation between *domestic* and *international* students according to funding source is blunt and reveals nothing of the true nature of the cultural differences in the cohorts, for national citizenship (which informs the funding source of students) is clearly quite different to cultural origin. This blunt delineation in the especially culturally diverse cohorts of Australia (where even the domestic students come from a wide range of immigrant cultures) gives no understanding of who precisely is rating who in a team. Thus, for instance, the data does not account for students who are international but ostensibly not perceived as 'other' (i.e., Caucasian, English-speaking students from outside Australia), or for students who are domestically funded but who may be recent immigrants and thus perceived as 'other.'
- **Second:** As the data is purely quantitative the reasons for the rating differences can only be speculated upon.

CONCLUSION

Before summarising conclusions specific to each study, some wider conclusions might be drawn form an overview of all studies. In particular, Farh's proposition stated at the beginning of this chapter might be reflected on within the context of student teamwork in higher education; namely that peer appraisal might be influenced by "virtually every form of rater bias that has been documented with supervisor and self-appraisals" (1991, p. 368). While a lack of gender informed bias might suggest the world has moved on in this respect, especially in the context of the design disciplines where the gender balance of cohorts has become far more balanced in recent years, the remaining two studies appear to confirm that other forms of bias indeed impact peer assessment.

In summary, the first study shows that self-leniency is indeed an issue when design students are comparing their own contributions to those of their teammates, for self-ratings in our large sample were significantly higher than peer ratings. This finding is consistent with Johnston and Miles (L. Johnston & L. Miles, 2004) and Zhang et al. (2007), who all found that students inflated their self-ratings, but contradicts Falchikov (1991) who found no greater tendency for self-raters to overmark or undermark.

The second study found that females received marginally higher peer ratings than males, and that males were significantly more generous than females when giving peer ratings for design. These two findings might be explained by the superior group maintenance behaviours and other teamwork skills that Falchikov and Magin suggest are demonstrated by females; skills which males may be acknowledging and compensating for in their more generous assessments. Unlike Falchokov and Magin (1997), there was little evidence in the data of gender effects due to the gender mix of cohorts. Overall, our finding of little evidence of gender differences in self-assessments supports the finding of Falchikov and Magin (1997) that gender biases have no impact on the validity and reliability of self-and-peer-assessment. We also agree with Falchikov and Magin's suggestion that multiple peer assessments appear to cancel same/ opposite gender bias effects. Finally, it should be noted that while the data allowed for the consideration of gender balance within cohorts, it did not allow for analysis of the effect of gender balance within the student teams. This is a gap in the data that future research might address to elucidate the gender dynamics of design teams.

The third study found that: domestics peer assess internationals lower then fellow domestics, both groups performed equivalently in individual assignments, and internationals assessed both groups equally. This strongly suggests that out-group bias is prejudicing the peer assessment of international students by domestic students. These findings are consistent with attitudes discovered in multicultural cohorts by Leask and Carroll (2011). However, while the data presented in the chapter clearly shows that out-group bias is happening when SAPA is used in design cohorts for individualising team grades, the data does not indicate why and how this bias is occurring and thus does little to inform how the problem might be addressed. Moreover, as discussed above, the delineation between *domestic* and *international* students in our data reveals little of the nature of the cultural differences in Australian design cohorts. These issues would benefit greatly from further research, for only by talking with students and looking closely at the cultural differences between teammates will we be able to understand the mechanisms behind the peer ratings and thus how any bias might be addressed.

REFERENCES

Aggarwal, P., & O'Brien, C. L. (2008). Social Loafing on Group Projects: Structural Antecedents and Effect on Student Satisfaction. *Journal of Marketing Education, 30*(3), 255–264. doi:10.1177/0273475308322283

Aggarwal, P., & O'Brien, C. L. (2008). Social loafing on group projects: Structural antecedents and effects on student satisfaction. *Journal of Marketing Education, 30*(3), 255–264. doi:10.1177/0273475308322283

Ahern, A. (2007). What are the perceptions of lecturers towards using cooperative learning in civil engineering? *European Journal of Engineering Education, 32*(5), 517–526. doi:10.1080/03043790701433152

Alfonseca, E., Carro, R. M., Martín, E., Ortigosa, A., & Paredes, P. (2006). The impact of learning styles on student grouping for collaborative learning: A case study. *User Modeling and User-Adapted Interaction, 16*(3-4), 377–401. doi:10.1007/s11257-006-9012-7

Alge, B. J., Wiethoff, C., & Klein, H. J. (2003). When does the medium matter? Knowledge-building experiences and opportunities in decision-making teams. *Organizational Behavior and Human Decision Processes, 91*(1), 26–37. doi:10.1016/S0749-5978(02)00524-1

Amason, A. (1996). Distinguishing effects of functional and dysfunctional conflict on strategic decision making: Resolving a paradox for top management teams. *Academy of Management Journal, 39*(1), 123–148. doi:10.2307/256633

Amason, A., & Sapienza, H. (1997). The effects of top management team size and interaction norms on cognitive and affective conflict. *Journal of Management, 23*(4), 496–516. doi:10.1177/014920639702300401

Anderson, D. (1988). The process of learning. 2nd ed. Sydney: Prentice- Hall, 1987: review. Forum of Education; 47(2), 103-105.

Arnett, B. (1993). Education and human development at future workstations. *Paper presented at the TeleTeaching '93 Conference*, Trondheim, Norway.

Bacon, D. R., Stewart, K. A., & Silver, W. S. (1999). Lessons from the Best and Worst Student Team Experiences: How a Teacher can make the Difference. *Journal of Management Education, 23*(5), 467–488. doi:10.1177/105256299902300503

Bacon, D. R., Stewart, K. A., & Stewart-Belle, S. (1998). Exploring Predictors of Student Team Project Performance. *Journal of Marketing Education, 20*(1), 63–71. doi:10.1177/027347539802000108

Badke-Schaub, P., & Frankenberger, E. (2002). Analysing and modelling cooperative design by the critical situation method. *Le Travail Humain, 65*(44), 293–314. doi:10.3917/th.654.0293

Baker, D. (2008). Peer assessment in small groups: A comparison of methods. *Journal of Management Education, 32*(2), 183–209. doi:10.1177/1052562907310489

Ballard, B., & Clanchy, J. (1991). *Teaching students from overseas: a brief guide for lecturers and supervisors*. Melbourne: Longman Cheshire.

Barber, P. (2004). Developing and assessing group design work: a case study. *Paper presented at the International Engineering and Product Design Education Conference*, DELFT, Netherlands.

Barrett, E., & Lally, V. (1999). Gender differences in an on line learning environment. *Journal of Computer Assisted Learning, 15*(1), 48–60. doi:10.1046/j.1365-2729.1999.151075.x

Biggs, J., & Watkins, D. (1996). The Chinese learner in retrospect. In D.A. Watkins & J.B. Biggs (Eds.), The Chinese learner: cultural, psychological and contextual influences (pp. 269-285). Hong Kong: Comparative Education Research Centre (CERC) and Melbourne: Australian Council for Educational Research (ACER).

Boud, D., & Falchikov, N. (1989). Quantitative Studies of Student Self-Assessment in Higher Education: A Critical Analysis of Findings. *Higher Education, 18*(5), 529–549. doi:10.1007/BF00138746

Burns, R. B. (1991). Study and Stress Among First Year Overseas Students in an Australian University. *Higher Education Research & Development, 10*(1), 61–77. doi:10.1080/0729436910100106

Chan, C. K. K. (2001). Promoting learning and understanding through constructivist approaches for Chinese learners. In D.A.W. & J.B. Biggs. (Eds.), Teaching the Chinese learner: psychological and pedagogical perspectives (pp. 181-203.). Hong Kong: Comparative Education Research Centre Melbourne Vic: Australian Council for Educational Research.

Choi, S. H. J., & Nieminen, T. A. (2012). Factors influencing the higher education of international students from Confucian East Asia. *Higher Education Research & Development, 32*(2), 161–173. doi:10.1080/07294360.2012.673165

Cohen, E. G. (1994). Restructuring the Classroom: Conditions for Productive Small Groups. *Review of Educational Research, 64*(1), 1–35. doi:10.3102/00346543064001001

Das, M., Mpofu, , Dunn, , & Lanphear, . (1998). Self and tutor evaluations in problem based learning tutorials: Is there a relationship? *Medical Education, 32*(4), 411–418. doi:10.1046/j.1365-2923.1998.00217.x PMID:9743805

Davies, P. (2000). Computerized Peer Assessment. *Innovations in Education and Teaching International, 37*(4), 346–355.

De Vita, G. (2001). *The use of group work in large and diverse business management classes: Some critical issues.* Paper presented at the The International Journal of Management Education. doi:10.3794/ijme.13.11

De Vita, G. (2002). Does assessed multicultural group work really pull UK students' average down? *Assessment & Evaluation in Higher Education, 27*(2), 153–161. doi:10.1080/02602930220128724

De Vita, G. (2007). Taking stock: An appraisal of the literature on internationalising HE learning. In *Internationalising higher education* (pp. 154-167).

Dochy, F., Segers, M., & Sluijsmans, D. (1999a). The use of self-, peer and co-assessment in higher education: A review. *Studies in Higher Education, 24*(3), 331–350. doi:10.1080/03075079912331379935

Dochy, F., Segers, M., & Sluijsmans, D. M. A. (1999b). The Use of Self-, Peer and Co-assessment in Higher Education: A review. *Studies in Higher Education, 24*(3), 331–350. doi:10.1080/03075079912 331379935

Drazin, R., & Auster, E. (1987). Wage differences between men and women: Performance appraisal ratings vs. salary allocation as the locus of bias. *Human Resource Management, 26*(2), 157–168. doi:10.1002/hrm.3930260204

Falchikov, N. (1986). Product Comparisons and Process Benefits of Collaborative Peer Group and Self-assessment. *Assessment & Evaluation in Higher Education, 11*(2), 146–166. doi:10.1080/0260293860110206

Falchikov, N. (1988). Self and peer assessment of a group project designed to promote the skills of capability. *Programmed Learning and Educational Technology, 25*, 327–339.

Falchikov, N. (1991). Group process analysis: self and peer assessment of working together in a group. In S. Brown & P. Dove (Eds.), *Self and peer assessment*. Birmingham: SCED Publications.

Falchikov, N., & Goldfinch, J. (2000). Student Peer Assessment in Higher Education: A Meta-Analysis Comparing Peer and Teacher Marks. *Review of Educational Research, 70*(3), 287–322. doi:10.3102/00346543070003287

Falchikov, N., & Magin, D. (1997). Detecting gender bias in peer marking of students' group process work. *Assessment & Evaluation in Higher Education, 22*(4), 385–396. doi:10.1080/0260293970220403

Farh, J., Cannella, A., & Bedeian, A. (1991). The impact of purpose on rating quality and user acceptance. *Group & Organization Management, 16*(4), 367–386. doi:10.1177/105960119101600403

Freeman, M., Hutchinson, D., Treleaven, L., & Sykes, C. (2006). Iterative learning: self and peer assessment of group work. *Paper presented at the Proceedings of the 23rd annual ascilite conference: Who's learning? Whose technology?,* The University of Sydney.

Freeman, M., & McKenzie, J. (2002). SPARK, a confidential web-based template for self and peer assessment of student teamwork: Benefits of evaluating across different subjects. *British Journal of Educational Technology, 33*(5), 551–569. doi:10.1111/1467-8535.00291

Furnham, A., & Stringfield, P. (1994). Congruence of self and subordinate ratings of managerial practices as a correlate of supervisor evaluation. *Journal of Occupational and Organizational Psychology, 67*(1), 57–67. doi:10.1111/j.2044-8325.1994.tb00549.x

Gatfield, T. (1999). Examining student satisfaction with group projects and peer assessment. *Assessment & Evaluation in Higher Education, 24*(4), 365–377. doi:10.1080/0260293990240401

Goldfinch, J., & Raeside, R. (1990). Development of a Peer Assessment Technique for Obtaining Individual Marks on a Group Project. *Assessment & Evaluation in Higher Education, 15*(3), 210–231. doi:10.1080/0260293900150304

Gómez, C., Kirkman, B., & Shapiro, D. (2000). The impact of collectivism and in-group/out-group membership on the evaluation generosity of team members. *Academy of Management Journal, 43*(6), 1097–1106. doi:10.2307/1556338

Griffee, D. T. (1995). *A Longitudinal Study of Student Feedback: Self-Assessment*. Course Evaluation and Teacher Evaluation.

Haigh, M. (2008). Internationalisation, planetary citizenship and Higher Education Inc. *Compare: A Journal of Comparative Education, 38*(4), 427–440. doi:10.1080/03057920701582731

Halualani, R. T., Chitgopekar, A., Morrison, J. H. T. A., & Dodge, P. S.-W. (2004). Who's interacting? And what are they talking about?—intercultural contact and interaction among multicultural university students. *International Journal of Intercultural Relations, 28*(5), 353–372. doi:10.1016/j.ijintrel.2004.08.004

AE International. (2010). International student numbers, 2009. Retrieved from http://aei.gov.au/AEI/PublicationsAndResearch/Snapshots/2010022610_pdf.pdf

Johnson, C., & Smith, F. (1997). Assessment of a complex peer evaluation instrument for team learning and group processes. *Accounting Education, 2*, 21–40.

Johnston, L., & Miles, L. (2004). Assessing contributions to group assignments. *Assessment & Evaluation in Higher Education, 29*(6), 751–768. doi:10.1080/0260293042000227272

Johnston, L., & Miles, L. (2004). Assessing contributions to group assignments. *Assessment & Evaluation in Higher Education, 29*(6), 751–768. doi:10.1080/0260293042000227272

Kane, J. S., & Lawler, E. E. (1978). Methods of peer assessment. *Psychological Bulletin, 85*(3), 555–586. doi:10.1037/0033-2909.85.3.555

Kaufman, D., Felder, R., & Fuller, H. (2000). Accounting for individual effort in cooperative learning teams. *Journal of Engineering Education-Washington, 89*(2), 133–140. doi:10.1002/j.2168-9830.2000.tb00507.x

Kimmel, K., & Volet, S. (2012). University Students' Perceptions of and Attitudes Towards Culturally Diverse Group Work Does Context Matter? *Journal of Studies in International Education, 16*(2), 157–181. doi:10.1177/1028315310373833

Koehne, N. (2005). (Re) construction: Ways international students talk about their identity. *Australian Journal of Education, 49*(1), 104–119. doi:10.1177/000494410504900107

Langan, A., Wheater, C., Shaw, E., Haines, B., Cullen, W., Boyle, J., & Lockey, L. et al. (2005). Peer assessment of oral presentations: Effects of student gender, university affiliation and participation in the development of assessment criteria. *Assessment & Evaluation in Higher Education, 30*(1), 21–34. doi:10.1080/0260293042003243878

Leask, B., & Carroll, J. (2011). Moving beyond 'wishing and hoping': Internationalisation and student experiences of inclusion and engagement. *Higher Education Research & Development, 30*(5), 647–659. doi:10.1080/07294360.2011.598454

Lejk, M., & Wyvill, M. (2002). Peer Assessment of Contributions to a Group Project: Student attitudes to holistic and category-based approaches. *Assessment & Evaluation in Higher Education, 27*(6), 569–577. doi:10.1080/0260293022000020327

Lennon, S. (1995). Correlations between tutor, peer and self assessments of second year physiotherapy students in movement studies. *Enhancing student learning through peer tutoring in higher education. Section, 3*, 66–71.

Li, M. (2003, November 29 – December 3). Culture and classroom communication: a case study of Asian students in New Zealand language schools ·*Educational research, risks and dilemmas. Proceedings ofNZARE/AARE Conference*, Auckland New Zealand. Association for Research in Education.

Lind, D., Rekkas, S., Bui, V., Lam, T., Beierle, E., & Copeland, E. III. (2002). Competency-based student self-assessment on a surgery rotation. *The Journal of Surgical Research, 105*(1), 31–34. doi:10.1006/jsre.2002.6442 PMID:12069498

May, G., & Gueldenzoph, L. (2006). The effect of social style on peer evaluation ratings in project teams. *Journal of Business Communication, 43*(1), 4–20. doi:10.1177/0021943605282368

McGourty, J., Dominick, P., & Reilly, R. R. (1998, November 4-7). Incorporating Student Peer Review and Feedback into the Assessment Process. *Paper presented at the28th Annual Frontiers in Education Conference*, Tempe, Arizona. doi:10.1109/FIE.1998.736790

Menchaca, M., Resta, P., & Awalt, C. (2002). Self and Peer Assessment in an Online Collaborative Learning Environment.

Morgan, P. (2002). Supporting staff to support students: the application of a performance management framework to reduce group working problems. Retrieved from http://www.business.heacademy.ac.uk/resources/reflect/conf/2002/morgan

Mulder, R. A., & Pearce, J. M. (2007). *PRAZE: Innovating teaching through online peer review.Paper presented at the24th Annual Conference of the Australasian Society for Computers in Learning in Tertiary Education*, Singapore.

Pettigrew, T. F. (1998). Intergroup contact theory. *Annual Review of Psychology, 49*(1), 65–85. doi:10.1146/annurev.psych.49.1.65 PMID:15012467

Pope, N. K. L. (2005). The impact of stress in self- and peer assessment. *Assessment & Evaluation in Higher Education, 30*(1), 51–63. doi:10.1080/0260293042003243896

Quintrell, N., & Westwood, M. (1994). The influence of a peer-pairing program on international students' first year experience and use of student services. *Higher Education Research & Development, 13*(1), 49–58. doi:10.1080/0729436940130105

Raban, R., & Litchfield. (2006, December 3-6). Supporting peer assessment of individual contributions in groupwork. *Paper presented at the23rd Annual Conference of the Australasian Society for Computers in Learning in Tertiary Education*, Sydney.

Rees, C. (2003). Self assessment scores and gender. *Medical Education, 37*(6), 572–573. doi:10.1046/j.1365-2923.2003.01545.x PMID:12787384

Sawir, E. (2005). Language difficulties of international students in Australia: The Effects of prior learning experiences. *International Education Journal, 6*(5), 567–580.

Sherrard, W. R., & Feraidoon, R. (1994). An empirical study of peer bias in evaluations: Students rating students. *Journal of Education for Business, 70*(1), 43–47. doi:10.1080/08832323.1994.10117723

Shore, L., & Thornton, G. III. (1986). Effects of gender on self-and supervisory ratings. *Academy of Management Journal, 29*(1), 115–129. doi:10.2307/255863

Shore, T. H., Shore, L. M., & Thornton, G. C. (1992). Construct validity of self-and peer evaluations of performance dimensions in an assessment center. *The Journal of Applied Psychology, 77*(1), 42–54. doi:10.1037/0021-9010.77.1.42

Sluijsmans, D. M. A., Dochy, F., & Moerkerke, G. (1999). Creating a Learning Environment by Using Self-, Peer- and Co-Assessment. *Learning Environments Research, 1*(3), 293–319. doi:10.1023/A:1009932704458

Tang, C. (1996). Collaborative learning: the latent dimension in Chinese students' learning. In D.A. Watkins & J.B. Biggs (Eds.), The Chinese learner: cultural, psychological and contextual influences (pp. 183-204). Hong Kong: Comparative Education Research Centre (CERC) and Melbourne: Australian Council for Educational Research (ACER).

Taras, M. (2008). Issues of power and equity in two models of self-assessment. *Teaching in Higher Education, 13*(1), 81–92. doi:10.1080/13562510701794076

Topping, K. (1998). Peer Assessment between Students in Colleges and Universities. *Review of Educational Research, 68*(3), 249–276. doi:10.3102/00346543068003249

Trahar, S., & Hyland, F. (2011). Experiences and perceptions of internationalisation in higher education in the UK. *Higher Education Research & Development, 30*(5), 623–633. doi:10.1080/07294360.2011.598452

Tu, Y., & Lu, M. (2005). Peer-and-self assessment to reveal the ranking of each individual's contribution to a group project. *Journal of Information Systems Education, 16*(2), 197.

Tucker, R. (2008). The Impact of Assessment Modes on Collaborative Group Design Projects. In S. Frankland (Ed.), *Enhancing Teaching and Learning through Assessment: Embedded Strategies and their Impacts* (Vol. 2, pp. 72–85). Hong Kong: The Assessment Resource Centre, The Hong Kong Polytechnic University.

Tucker, R. (2011). The architecture of peer assessment: Do academically successful students make good teammates in design assignments? *Assessment & Evaluation in Higher Education*, 2011, 1–11.

Tucker, R. (2013). Sex does not matter: Gender bias and gender differences in peer assessments of contributions to group work. *Assessment & Evaluation in Higher Education, 39*(3), 293–309. doi:10.1080/02602938.2013.830282

Tucker, R., Abbasi, N., Thorpe, G., Ostwald, M., Williams, A., Wallis, L., & Kashuk, S. (2014). *Enhancing and assessing group and team learning in architecture and related design contexts (D. o. Education, Trans.)* (p. 109). Sydney: Office of Learning and Teaching, Department of Education, Australian Government.

Tucker, R., & Ang, S. (2007). The Academic Acclimatisation Difficulties of International Students of the Built Environment. *The Emirates Journal for Engineering Research, 12*(1), 1–9.

Tucker, R., Fermelis, J., & Palmer, S. (2009). Designing, Implementing and Evaluating a Self-and-Peer Assessment Tool for E-learning Environments. In C. Spratt & P. Lajbcygier (Eds.), *E-Learning and Advanced Assessment Technologies: Evidence-Based Approaches* (pp. 170–194). Hershey, PA, USA: IGI Global. doi:10.4018/978-1-60566-410-1.ch010

Tucker, R., & Reynolds, C. (2006). The Impact of Teaching Models on Collaborative Learning in the Student Design Studio. *Journal for Education in the Built Environment, 1*(2), 39–56. doi:10.11120/jebe.2006.01020039

Tucker, R., & Rollo, J. (2006). Teaching and Learning in Collaborative Group Design Projects. *Journal of Architectural Engineering & Design Management, 2,* 19-30.

Walker, A. (2001). British psychology students' perceptions of group-work and peer. *Psychology Learning & Teaching, 1*(1), 28–36. doi:10.2304/plat.2001.1.1.28

Watkins, R. (2005). *Groupwork and assessment: The Handbook for Economics Lecturers.* Kingston University.

Watson, W. E., Johnson, L., & Zgourides, G. D. (2002). The influence of ethnic diversity on leadership, group process, and performance: An examination of learning teams. *International Journal of Intercultural Relations, 26*(1), 1–16. doi:10.1016/S0147-1767(01)00032-3

Wen, M., & Tsai, C. (2006). University students' perceptions of and attitudes toward (online) peer assessment. *Higher Education, 51*(1), 27–44. doi:10.1007/s10734-004-6375-8

Williams, A., Askland, H. H., & Boud, D. (1996). Assessing creativity: Strategies and tools to support teaching and learning in architecture and design. *Resource Library, 1995,* 1994.

Wong, J. (2004). Are the Learning Styles of Asian International Students Culturally or Contextually Based? *International Education Journal, 4*(4), Retrieved from http://iej.cjb.net

Wright, L. (1995). All students will take more responsibility for their own learning. In S. Griffiths, K. Houston, & A. Lazenblatts (Eds.), Enhancing student learning through peer tutoring in higher education (Vol. 1, pp. 90-92). Coleraine, Northern Ireland: University of Ulster.

Wright, S., & Lander, D. (2003). Collaborative group interactions of students from two ethnic backgrounds. *Higher Education Research & Development, 22*(3), 237–251. doi:10.1080/0729436032000145121

Zhang, B., Johnston, L., & Kilic, G. B. (2007). Assessing the reliability of self- and peer rating in student group work. *Assessment & Evaluation in Higher Education, 33*(3), 1–12.

Zhen Hui, R. (2001). Matching teaching Styles with learning Styles in East Asian Context. *Foreign language College.* Retrieved from http:iteslj.org/Techniques/Zhenhui-TeachingStyles.html

KEY TERMS AND DEFINITIONS

Domestic Students: In Australia (and in our data set) a student is an Australian domestic student if they are (a) An Australian citizen, (b) An Australian permanent resident (holders of all categories of permanent residency visas, including humanitarian visas), or (c) A New Zealand citizen.

International Students: In Australia (and in our data set) a student is an international student if they are (a) A temporary resident (visa status) of Australia, (b) A permanent resident (visa status) of New Zealand, or (c) A resident or citizen of any other country.

Groupwork: A situations where a number of students work separately but in parallel on different aspects of a project and then combine their work.

Mark Individualization: One possible outcome of SAPA is the calculation of a numerical scaling factor for each group member, which can then be applied to a common group mark to produce individual marks for each group member that attempt to fairly represent the contribution of each member to the assessable group task.

Self-and-Peer-Assessment (SAPA): At its most basic, SAPA involves students providing an evaluation for all group members, including themselves, of the individual contribution of each group member to the group work process. The SAPA evaluation may be used informal feedback, or formal and used as an element of the summative assessment for the group task. SAPA may be public or anonymous.

Team Effectiveness: In educational contexts can be defined in terms of two dimensions: (1) Performance on the assigned task, evaluated through an assessment of *products* and/or *outcomes*; and (2) Goal Achievement through the *process* of working in a team, which can be divided into two aspects – (i) behaviour and (ii) attitudes.

Teamwork: Joint work on an assigned project in a collaborative environment where members actively contribute to team cohesion and task achievement.

Chapter 5
Conflict Resolution in Student Teams:
An Exploration in the Context of Design Education

Neda Abbasi
Deakin University, Australia

Anthony Mills
Deakin University, Australia

Richard Tucker
Deakin University, Australia

ABSTRACT

This chapter examines conflict in student design teams. A review of literature is presented to understand conflict within student design teams and explore strategies to manage it. In addition, qualitative data on students' experiences of team conflict is analysed from two surveys offered to design students in 18 Australian Higher Education Institutions. Analysis of the survey found that "ignoring or avoiding to acknowledge team conflict" is a strategy commonly adopted by students, followed by "trying to resolve team conflict through discussion and improving communication" and "seeking support from teachers." Drawing upon these findings, the chapter makes recommendations on strategies to prepare students for conflict situations through a number of support models that design instructors might adopt, including both preventive and intervention strategies.

INTRODUCTION

Conflict is a significant challenge of teamwork that can have impact on student team effectiveness. Individuals come from different social, cultural and cognitive backgrounds and have different expectations, motives, opinions, personalities, values and preferences. These individual differences make conflict

DOI: 10.4018/978-1-5225-0726-0.ch005

inevitable within teams. While conflict can be beneficial to team functioning and outcomes, it is critical to constructively manage it to ensure effective team performance. The impacts of conflict on teams of students designing together can be particularly acute because design, even without interpersonal conflict, is a highly emotive and subjective activity. These impacts are accentuated by the difficulty of assigning authorship to a design, which means that 'social-loafing', a chief cause of team conflict, is difficult to detect. Added to these issues is a lack of the type of team hierarchy that can ease decision-making in professional contexts, and also a lack of experience in students of managing conflict. Thus it is not uncommon that conflict in student design teams can become a significant barrier to effective learning and teaching.

This chapter examines conflict in student design teams via a review of the literature exploring: (1) definitions, types and determinants of conflict in teams; (2) distinguishing features of conflict in student teams and key considerations; and (3) approaches to conflict resolution and managing emotions. This review is followed by an analysis of qualitative data on experiences of team conflict from two surveys offered to design students in 18 Australian universities. The two surveys (a pilot then a nationally distributed survey), which were administered as part of a project funded by the Australian Government Office for Learning and Teaching (OLT), addressed questions about students' perceptions and experiences of teamwork in design. More than 400 comments were recorded and coded under different themes. It was found that students acknowledge there is "constructive" conflict in the form of differences of opinions that can be beneficial to team performance. As it was hypothesised, the presence of non-contributing and non-committed team members is the most often referred to cause of conflict. Almost half the comments in the pilot survey suggested that students commonly make an effort to address the problem of non-contributing team members and often come to a solution. It was found that student satisfaction with the outcomes and processes of their teams was highly correlated with: (1) the presence of social-loafers in teams; and (2) student perceptions of whether assessment was fair.

The chapter concludes with presenting ways to support student teams to manage team conflict, with both 'preventive strategies' and 'interventive strategies' explored.

BACKGROUND

In this section the following will be discussed: definitions of conflict, the role of conflict management in team performance, and different types of team conflict and their common antecedents. Approaches to conflict management in teams in professional and business organisations are also reviewed before the relevance of these approaches to educational contexts is studied.

Defining Conflict in Teams

Smith (1966, p.511) defines conflict as "a situation in which the conditions, practices, or goals for the different participants are inherently incompatible." Similarly, Tedeschi *et al.* (1973, p.232) define conflict as "an interactive state in which the behaviours or goals of one actor are to some degree incompatible with the behaviours or goals of some other actor or actors." De Dreu and Weingart (2003, p.741) offer another definition of conflict as "the process resulting from the tension between team members because of real or perceived differences." Common to these definitions is that conflict is the result of "incompatibility or opposition in goals, activities, or interaction among the social entities" (Rahim, 2015, p.16).

Reviewing a number of recent definitions of conflict, Baron (1990, p.199) identifies five elements of conflict common to different definitions:

1. Conflict includes opposing interests between individuals or groups in a zero-sum situation;
2. Such opposed interests must be recognized for conflict to exist;
3. Conflict involves beliefs, by each side, that the other will thwart (or has already thwarted) its interests;
4. Conflict is a process; it develops out of existing relationships between individuals or groups and reflects their past interactions and the contexts in which these took place; and
5. Imply actions by one or both sides that do, in fact, produce thwarting of others' goals.

Generally, three types of team conflict have been studied in recent research: task, affective, and process conflicts (Jehn & Mannix, 2001). Task conflict has to do with disagreements in relation to team tasks; including procedures, goals, and decisions (Jehn, 1994). Affective conflict, or what can also be described as relationship or emotional conflict, is characterized by anger and hostility among team members. Process conflict is caused by disagreement about approaches to team tasks and team processes. Research has distinguished affective or emotional conflict from task conflict (Eisenhardt, Kahwajy, & Bourgeois III, 1997; Pelled, 1996; Pelled & Adler, 1994; Pelled, Eisenhardt, & Xin, 1999), and from process conflict, (Jehn, 1997) in order to explain the different findings about the impacts of these different types of conflict on team performance.

Determinants of Team Conflict

Research has examined the causes of conflict in student teams in order to better understand strategies that can support students to work together in effective teams and to minimise the possibility of conflict situations evolving (Harper & Nagel, 2014). Common antecedents of conflicts in student teams are differences between teammates in relation to: expected outcomes (grades), deliverables, roles, learning and problem solving styles, values, available resources (e.g. time and other personal commitments), and basic personality characteristics (Dool, 2010). Generally, the causes of conflict in teams have to do with lack of team effectiveness attributes that characterise highly functioning teams. Examples of some common issues that may lead to team conflict are outlined in Table 1.

One of the common conflict factors in student teams is the presence of non-committed team members, namely free-riders and social-loafers. Morris and Hayes (1997, p.3) describe a free-rider as "the nonperforming group member who reaps the benefit of the accomplishments of the remaining group members without little or no cost to him/herself."

Freeman and Greenacre (2011, p.7) have looked at social loafing from another perspective referring to a less well defined phenomenon in literature, namely struggling students, who "have difficulty contributing in class because, when compared with the rest of the cohort, they are marginally behind in their understanding of the material" and whose "marginally lower skill levels require more time to be spent on studying and thus delays the student's initial ability to contribute." To prevent struggling students receiving punishments targeted at social loafers, which may limit their ability to learn, it is important to use strategies to assist students in teams distinguish between non-contributing social loafers and contributing struggling low ability students (Freeman & Greenacre, 2011).

Table 1. Key characteristics of effective teams and relevant causes of team conflict

Team Features	Conflict Factors
1. Dynamic exchange of information and resources Team members communicate effectively sharing resources and information.	Lack of efficient communication i.e. face-to-face and virtual communications
2. Coordination of tasks Team members coordinate tasks to be completed in order to achieve team goals.	Lack of a clear team project plan i.e. division of tasks (who should do what and when)
3. Interdependence Team members rely on each other to complete the team project.	Lack of efficient collaboration
4. Ongoing adjustment to changes and task demands Team members are aware of the team dynamics and progress, and hence able to adjust to changes and emerging task demands.	- Lack of clear team goals - Inefficient team meetings
5. Shared authority and joint accountability for team outcomes Team members are equally committed to completion of team project and share the same level of expectations and standards of quality of team product.	- Non-committed and/or dominating team members - Distrust and hostility among team members

Adopted from (McGourty & De Meuse, 2001)

Influences of Team Conflict

Conflict is not always detrimental to teamwork. Indeed, teams may benefit from constructive conflict that capitalises on controversy by allowing team members to express their disagreement and criticism (Crossley, 2006; Kirchmeyer & Cohen, 1992; Tjosvold & Deemer, 1980). Research suggests that such constructive conflict in teams encourages interpersonal relationships, promotes involvement in the group or team, enhances quality and creativity in decision making, and fosters commitment to team decisions (Johnson & Johnson, 1994).

The findings of a longitudinal study carried out by Tekleab *et al.* (2009) suggest that conflict management has a direct, positive effect on team cohesion and team cohesion is also positively related to perceived performance, satisfaction with the team, and team viability. In organisations, Rahim (2015) lists some of the 'functional' outcomes of conflict; including: (1) stimulating innovation, creativity and change; (2) improving decision making processes; (3) finding alternative and synergistic solutions to common problems; (4) enhancing individual and group performance; and (5) encouraging individual and group to articulate and clarify their position and look for new approaches. 'Dysfunctional' outcomes of conflict in organizations include: (1) leading to job stress, burnout and dissatisfaction; (2) reducing communication between individuals and groups; (3) creating a climate of distrust and suspicion; (4) damaging relationships; (5) reducing job performance and affecting commitment and loyalty to the organization; and (6) increasing resistance to change (Rahim, 2015, pp.6-7).

Of the three types of conflict – task, affective, and process – studies suggest that task conflict may support team functioning (Eisenhardt et al., 1997; Jehn, 1995; Zhang, Chen, & Guo, 2009). One reason that may account for the positive relationship between task conflict and team performance is the opportunity afforded for considering alternatives before arriving at a solution (Pelled et al., 1999). Focusing on the impacts of conflict on an individual team member's behaviours, Kurtzberg and Mueller (2005) also suggest that task conflict has a positive relationship with individual creativity. Contrary to these findings, other researchers have found that task conflict does not always have functional outcomes for teams (De Dreu & Weingart, 2003; Jehn, Chadwick, & Thatcher, 1997) and the relationship between task conflict and team performance may be influenced by it being complicated and evolved into affective and process conflicts (Hansen, 2015; Jehn & Chatman, 2000; Lira, Ripoll, Peiró, & González, 2007; Simons & Peterson, 2000). Task conflict may also lead to reduced motivation to participate in teamwork due to increased stress and dissatisfaction (Gamero, González Romá, & Peiró, 2008; Jehn, 1994; Shaw et al., 2011). In functionally diverse teams, Lovelace *et al.* (2001, p.779) suggest that the effect of task conflict on team performance "depended on how free members felt to express task-related doubts and how collaboratively or contentiously these doubts were expressed." Similarly, in a study of 208 Norwegian and Danish management teams, Hansen (2015) points to a positive association between task and relationship conflict suggesting that "task conflict and its effects must be considered in light of the presence of relationship conflict." The author concludes that

... task conflict has a tendency to elicit relationship conflict. The challenge is therefore how management teams can engage in open and direct task discussions, without eliciting destructive relationship conflicts (Hansen, 2015, p.ii).

The other two types of conflict – affective and process – have been generally found to negatively influence team performance (De Wit, Greer, & Jehn, 2012). Affective or relationship conflict, for example, was found to negatively influence team performance and member satisfaction in student teams (Jehn et al., 1997) and work teams (De Dreu & Weingart, 2003; Jehn, 1997), mainly due to the resulting anxiety, time and energy spent on emotional hostility and disagreement (Pelled et al., 1999). Other research has found a more complicated relationship between affective conflict and team performance. Jehn (1995, p.276), for example, suggests that the negative effects of relationship conflict on team performance may not be always significant "because the members involved in the conflicts choose to avoid working with those with whom they experience conflict."

Research suggests that the impacts of conflict on team performance and members' satisfaction and behaviour are moderated by factors related to individuals and team processes i.e. task characteristics shaping the uncertainty, complexity and routineness of tasks, group diversity, group conflict norms, emotions, and conflict management processes (Jehn & Bendersky, 2003). For instance, De Dreu and Weingart have considered the impact of conflict on three types of highly complex teams: 'project groups' that are engaged in different tasks ranging from planning and executing to decision-making, and that deal with the most complex and uncertain tasks; 'decision-making groups' that work on tasks requiring consensus building on matters that have no right or wrong answers; and 'production groups' that plan and execute tasks to meet defined standards and deal with the least complex and most routine tasks. They found that in 'project groups' and 'decision-making groups' (and also hybrids of these two groups), conflict has a stronger negative relationship with team performance than in 'production groups' (De Dreu & Weingart, 2003). In other words, the negative impact of conflict becomes greater as the complexity of the tasks increases.

Absence of conflict in a team can be a sign that the group is experiencing "groupthink" (Janis, 1972); "the condition in which a group makes defective decisions through conformity pressures in order to avoid disagreement and reach quick compromises" (Crossley, 2006, p.37). The conventional belief that views conflict as detrimental to teamwork is reflected in student interpretation of effective collaboration as "implying the need to avoid conflict and engage in concurrence-seeking in order to maximize their grades" because conflict is regarded negative and detrimental to group productivity (Crossley, 2006, pp.33-34). Simply put, there are constructive conflicts that commonly lead to enhanced team processes and higher quality team products. The key is management and resolution of conflict situations, but this can only be achieved if team members have conflict management skills.

Approaches to Conflict Resolution

A starting point to mitigate conflict in student teams is seen as addressing the problem of social loafers or non-committed team members. Morris and Hayes (1997, pp.3-4) suggest that social loafing arises mainly due to failure to assess individual team members' contributions to the team project, meaning instructors emphasise the evaluation of the 'product' of teamwork rather than "the processes students go through, and the skills developed through this learning experience, to achieve output." Adopting fair assessment strategies and monitoring and managing student team processes may then be considered to mitigate and eventually eliminate social loafing in student teams (Morris & Hayes, 1997).

Freeman and Greenacre (2011) point to corrective responses and promoting constructive behaviours as other strategies to deal with social loafing. These corrective responses include giving feedback about the undesirability of social loafing and building a sense of regret for non-contribution, and should be implemented by contributing team members "who are most able to recognize a student not contributing and who have an interest in prompting participation." The contributing team members may also be empowered to tackle social loafing through constructive behaviours by "setting mutually agreed deadlines and standards, setting progress deadlines, establishing progress reporting procedures, among others" (Freeman & Greenacre, 2011, p.7).

Other researchers recommended the use of diary methods, i.e. reflective journals, minute books, and weekly e-mail updates to instructors, to help student teams overcome the challenge of social loafers (Dommeyer, 2007; Dommeyer & Lammers, 2006; Freeman & Greenacre, 2011). These tools can provide evidence of where the conflict started and help support students in managing and resolving the conflict at the intervention phase. While Dommeyer's and Lammers's (2006) experiment found that the use of both group and individual diaries failed to control social loafing in a group project, the use of individual diaries was seen to make the majority of the class, namely the non-loafers, more aware of and less tolerant of their loafing partners. Freeman and Greenacre (2011, p.14) argue that regardless of the nature or form of the diary tool itself, the instruction that students may receive about the different tools and assessment of these tools should reflect "the fact that they not only serve the purpose of documenting tasks but also of documenting learning experiences and experiences of group dynamics."

As the last resort, when every effort to resolve team conflict fails, the team may be offered the opportunity by the instructor to disintegrate or to sack the non-contributing team members. Some researchers have argued that this option may be considered with caution to balance the realities of practice and professional contexts with educational commitments to equal opportunities and inclusion (Orr, 2010; Smart & Dixon, 2002).

DESIGN STUDENTS' EXPERIENCES AND PERCEPTIONS OF TEAM CONFLICT

This section presents the qualitative data collected through two surveys, one pilot and one national survey, on student teamwork experience. The surveys were designed for a project examining teaching and assessment of team learning in architecture and other design-related disciplines (2012-2014), which was funded by the OLT. It was hypothesised that one of the key causes of team conflict would be the presence of team members who make no or little or poor quality contribution to teamwork. Given this, the pilot survey asked students to describe the ways that they dealt with non-committed and non-contributing team members. In the national survey, the issue of team conflict was directly addressed with students being asked to reflect on whether or not they had experienced conflict in their teams, and if yes, to provide details about the conflict situations, the possible causes and the ways that they dealt with those situations.

The Surveys

The pilot survey, made available in 2012 to students enrolled in architecture, construction and other built environment disciplines at four Australian universities, asked for ratings of satisfaction with: (1) team working processes; (2) outcomes of their teamwork; (3) team size; (4) the teaching they received about teamwork; (5) the level of feedback they received on their team working during the assignment; (6) the method by which their team was formed; (7) whether they considered that the product of their teamwork was fairly assessed to recognise individual contributions to the teamwork; and (8) whether at least one teammate had made little or no contribution to teamwork. The pilot survey responses analysed for this chapter were for the question:

P1. If you had members in your team who made no or very little contribution to the teamwork, how did you deal with them?

The national survey, made available in 2013 to design students enrolled in design disciplines at all Australian universities, aimed to test the validity of a "Framework of Effectiveness in Student Design Teams" that was developed in the first year of the project. The survey consisted of 143 items divided into six sections: (1) student demographics; (2) the overall teamwork experience in the degree program; (3) the teamwork experience in the last course/unit/subject; (4) quantitative questions relating to the 22 dimensions of teamwork; (5) qualitative questions on the teamwork experience in the last subject; and (6) questions to establish students' Kolb learning styles. The question in the National Survey that provided the data for this chapter was:

N1. Do you think that your team had a problem with conflict? If yes, how did you deal with this and what effect did it have?

196 students completed the pilot survey. It was found that student satisfaction with the outcomes and processes of their teams was correlated most highly with the presence of social-loafers in teams, followed by their perceptions of whether assessment of teamwork was fair. 417 students completed the national survey. While detailed findings of the quantitative data from the national survey will be published elsewhere, it should be noted that the factors that most strongly correlated with satisfaction with team learning in design contexts were factors that can be seen to mitigate conflict – effective team communication, team cohesion and then fair assessment.

The following sections will focus on the qualitative data from the two survey questions listed earlier.

Students' Views on Team Conflict, Contributing Factors and Strategies to Deal with It

129 students' comments were recorded to the pilot survey question (P1) on strategies to deal with non-contributing team members. 226 useable students' comments were recorded to the question related to team conflict in the national survey (N1). From these comments, students' views on the causes of team conflict and the strategies that they adopted to resolve or manage conflict were identified. A common theme in the comments was the need to differentiate between constructive conflict (difference of opinions) and destructive conflict (affective conflict or personality clashes). Students' comments suggested that they acknowledge the difference between constructive conflict or difference of opinions and the conflict that harms team performance. Comments suggested that students most often resolved difference of opinions through "mutual investigation of all courses of action possible," "voting with margins of error," "discussing the different design solutions," "a democratic process," asking team members to "back up their opinion with logic" before further considering it, and taking "things forward diplomatically or logically."

While constructive conflict or difference of opinions can assist in making better design decisions, there are conflict situations in student teams that can harm team performance significantly if they are not resolved. Students' comments addressed some of the negative impacts of unresolved team conflict, including:

- Dissatisfaction with team experiences and loss of motivation to work in the team

The effect our conflict had meant that no one wanted to work on our projects (Undergraduate male student).

- Climate of tension and hostility in the team and emotional stress for team members

There were also some bitter words and some hostility in the group and friendships end (Postgraduate female student).

- Detrimental effects on team processes i.e. decision making

... the effect was slow progression, further resulting in one member making firm decisions without confiding in group discussion beforehand (obviously causing more problems) (Postgraduate female student).

Causes of Team Conflict

The most common cause of team conflict was found to be the presence of non-contributing team members or unequal contributions (37 REF) (Table 2).

Three other causes of team conflict were: (1) differences that team members bring to the team i.e. personal differences and differences in terms of understanding, level of commitment and expectation as well as differences in the quality of the portions of work submitted by each team member (22 REF); (2) dominant team members (10 REF); and (3) miscommunication or lack of communication (9 REF). Clearly, lack of face-to-face interaction was a factor that further led to miscommunication and made it challenging to resolve conflict.

Table 2. Causes of conflict in student design teams, data from the national survey

Causes of Team Conflict	NO REF
Non-Contributing Team Members	37
We had issues with members not pulling their weight, and not responding to attempts for meetings and discussion about the work (Male postgraduate student).	
Differences	22
Clearly academic levels and commitment levels between team members were highly different. There is no doubt that the committed students were high achievers, but their mark was averaged down due to the less dedicated students 'last minute work' (Male undergraduate student).	
Dominant Team Members	10
I think there were too many hot-headed, 'I like to be right' people within the group and then one individual who was laid back which just caused too many conflict (Male undergraduate student).	
Miscommunication or Lack of Communication	9
My team did have a conflict when there was no communication. I was asked to do over 90% of the work for the first 4 weeks as the other member had other commitments. I sent her regular updates ... She often did not reply to these messages and did not show any sign of concern. Come week 6, she was unhappy with the results and accused me of excluding her from the project (male undergraduate student).	

Authors

Strategies to Manage Team Conflict

When asked to provide further details on the strategies adopted to deal with team conflict, students referred to two common approaches (Table 3): (1) ignoring or avoiding to acknowledge team conflict (38 REF); and (2) trying to resolve team conflict through discussion and improving communication (30 REF).

In many cases, the team conflict was not voiced or acknowledged and students chose to ignore it due to a range of reasons, in particular, not insulting their peers or not risking the submission of the final team product. However, as some of the comments under this theme suggest, failure to acknowledge conflict does not always lead to successful outcomes. Students also recognised that failure to address non-contribution might be an acceptable method of avoiding conflict, and one that may often have little impact on the quality of the submitted design – albeit at the expense of extra workload for some team members. Indeed, the quantitative data from the national survey backed up this perception, where it was found that unequal contribution between team members did not strongly correlate with reduced quality of design (as indicated by grades and student satisfaction with the design). Another common method that students adopted to deal with conflict was discussing the issues as a team, cooperating towards resolution, and improving communication. However, 19 survey respondents stated that they would seek support from teachers when facing conflict situations in their teams. This was the case for difficulty in making design decisions, namely constructive conflict, and for other team conflict situations caused by issues such as non-contributing team members.

Other conflict management behaviours that could be identified from student comments include: acknowledging conflict even though the team may not reach resolution (12 REF); consensus via voting (11 REF); and adopting an accommodating or compromising approach (11 REF). However, adopting a compromising or accommodating approach did not always guarantee quality work or satisfied team members.

Table 3. Strategies to manage team conflicts, data from the pilot and national survey

	Strategies to Manage Team Conflict	No REF	Sample Comments
1	Ignoring/Avoiding to Acknowledge Team Conflict	38	We did not choose to have a major confrontation with the other half of the team. This was due to the fact it would merely become a major insult to their skills in design and drawing which was an unnecessary stress. Any work they DID produce had to be redone later by either me or my other team member (Undergraduate male student).
2	Trying to resolve team conflict through discussion and improving communication	30	We overcome many of our minor conflicts simply by communicating with each other … We sat down and talked and worked until it was solved (Postgraduate female student).
3	Seeking support from teachers	19	Minor conflict in the projects' initial stages - however, quickly resolved (within ten minutes) by means of external opinions and liaisons (Undergraduate female student).
4	Acknowledging conflict even though the team may not reach to ultimate conflict resolution	12	I tried to accept their suggestion in terms of design and I tried to sit down with them to have a discussion on that. However, the person who dominated kept going with his own idea without respecting us. Also the due day of assignment push us to follow his direction (Undergraduate male student).

Authors

This was dealt with all other members retracting opinions and ideas, so as not to cause more conflict … we were able to produce a project, but not to the detail or degree that could have been obtained by working effectively together towards our common goal (Postgraduate male student).

Other student comments pointed to four strategies for lessening the possibility of conflict: division of tasks and workload i.e. making it clear who was doing what (4 REF); using a "Team Contract" that establishes ground rules at the beginning of a project (4 REF); one team member acting as mediator or leader in team disagreements (4 REF); and firing non-contributing team members (2 REF). Students suggested other ways of preventing conflict from developing when it starts, such as exercising "tolerance and restraint," adopting a "forget and forgive" approach, cooperating and trying to "be transparent about everything" and prioritising team task and processes ahead of personality differences.

It is good to be transparent about everything. However, the focus on the task should always come first, before any petty arguments between members. If everybody cooperates, things can go on very efficiently despite internal conflicts (Postgraduate female student).

Intervention by instructors was considered as the last resort due to the negative team climate it creates by putting students in the difficult position of reporting on their teammates.

SUPPORTING STUDENTS TO MANAGE TEAM CONFLICT

In many cases, constructive conflict due to differences of team members' perspectives, design ideas and opinions can lead to more effective decision-making, better decisions and improved design outcomes. While such conflict cannot be avoided and may even be beneficial to the team performance, students need to develop skills to constructively manage and resolve team conflict. This section integrates the findings of the literature review and qualitative study to recommend strategies to help students manage and resolve team conflict.

The strategies educators might use to support students in team conflict situations will be discussed under two contextual categories: (1) preventing negative conflict from developing; and (2) making proper interventions to assist teams in resolving conflict when it emerges.

Preventive Strategies

When planning a course with teamwork components, educators should consider strategies to prevent conflict as well as strategies to apply if any conflict emerges. Two key methods are recommended for avoiding conflict: (1) requiring teams to establish at the commencement of a project ground rules for teamworking; and (2) monitoring teams during the project.

Set Up the Grounds for Student Teamwork

A series of preparation tasks before students start working on the team project can significantly prevent conflict in student teams. In particular, educators should address two issues at the outset of a team project: (1) adopting and clearly explaining an appropriate team formation approach; and (2) providing students with instruction on effective teamwork processes.

Examine Team Formation Approaches

In respect to team conflict, educators need to closely examine team formation criteria because students' perceptions of why they are working with a particular team of peers can have an impact on team climate during the early stages of team building. Teachers have two basic ways to form teams: by forming the teams themselves or by allowing students to self-select. Both ways have pros and cons that teachers and students should be aware of. Regardless of the broad method of team formation that the instructor may choose, it is important that the selection and team composition criteria and processes are clearly explained to students. Students must understand the reasons for the methods chosen, why this is appropriate for the tasks required for designing and how this will lead to the best learning outcomes. This is particularly important if students are denied their preferred method of team formation – self-selection. Put simply, students must have trust in the team formation method so that they might develop trust with the people they are working with. This can be achieved, for instance, by bringing examples of situations from real-world workplaces where team members' own preferences for teammates may not be a priority meaning they may have to work with a group of people who are selected by their manager.

While team formation and the research on its impacts could easily be the subject of a dedicated chapter, a number of recommendations have been made from a study of student design teams (Tucker et al., 2014):

- Consider forming single-sex teams, if a team cannot have at least two members of one sex;
- For culturally diverse teams, try not to isolate single members of a culture that is different from the rest of their teammates;
- Consider the location or where students live to facilitate out-of-class meetings; and
- Closely examine the consequences of team formation methods before adopting one.

Provide Instruction on Effective Teamworking

Of course, it is wrong to assume that once students are put in teams they will instantly start working as an effective and harmonious team. To facilitate team building and setting up the ground rules for working together that help mitigate conflict, students should receive appropriate training on generic teamwork skills (i.e., those that are non-discipline specific) and basic team processes that will be required throughout the different stages of team development; including how to: (1) establish team goals and purposes; (2) assign team roles and responsibilities; (3) develop a project plan; (4) develop a team contract; (5) run an effective team meeting; (6) communicate effectively in teams; and (7) manage team conflict (Bacon, Stewart, & Silver, 1999; Buckenmyer, 2000).

Educators should consider instruction on these skills at the different phases they will be required. For example, a 'team building session' at the beginning of the course may provide students with instructions about establishing a team contract, rules of productive team meetings, principles of constructive communication etc. Another session may be provided a while after student teams have started working together when conflicts and problems begin to surface. In such a 'conflict management session', educators should raise student awareness about conflict. It is recommended that four topics may be addressed: (1) understanding team conflict and antecedents to it; (2) developing and testing appropriate conflict resolution approaches; (3) communication, verbal and non-verbal, and its essential role in preventing and managing conflict in teams; and (4) awareness and management of cultural diversity.

On the second of these topics, Thomas and Kilman (1974) suggest that in any conflict situation students need to be aware of the approaches that they adopt to face and resolve the conflict. Their research identifies five different approaches that teams may adopt to address conflict: (1) avoidance; (2) accommodating; (3) competing; (4) compromising; and (5) collaborating. Here, *avoidance* is characterised by team members accepting ideas and solutions without any rigorous discussion and assessment of pros and cons, team meetings being ended with no clear idea on what has happened and what should be expected next, and the same problems repeatedly coming to attention. When *accommodating*, team members sacrifice their needs and interests to avoid conflict, tend to back down on their positions, are overly polite and uncomfortable about expressing their ideas and feelings, and the decisions made are poor as the priority is keeping all team members happy rather than finding the optimum solution to the problem. Teams that are *competing* have members who neglect team goals because they are overly obsessed with satisfying their own needs and thus fail to consider alternatives and opinions other than their own. There is a hostile environment within such teams because members blame each other when things go wrong, and often subgroups can develop. *Compromising* is meeting everyone halfway and is similar to *accommodating*. *Compromising* often leads to a lowest-common-denominator solution because decisions are made via voting or taking into account something of every team member's position, instead of engaging in discussion and ongoing critique to reach the best solution. *Collaborating* is very likely to result in the most effective management of conflict, helping the team to reach an optimal and creative solution, where every team member feels free to express their ideas and interests while ensuring that other members also meet their needs. Thomas and Kilman (1974) recommend that students need to be taught and practice skills to move towards a collaborating style in managing and resolving team conflict.

Monitor Team Processes

An important part of preventing conflict in teams is monitoring team processes by teachers. Team processes should be monitored continuously so that feedback can be regular and on both the product (the designed artefact) and the team processes that created the product. Monitoring can include attending and noting progress and teamworking in student team meetings, checking in on online discussion forums, and the use of ongoing self-and-peer-assessment (SAPA). Students should also be encouraged to reflect on team processes regularly – within their teams and as an individual. Not only so that they can identify how to improve teamwork skills, but also so that they are able to discuss and manage conflict early within the team. They should also be encouraged to seek help from teachers when conflict reaches a stage that is significantly affecting the team's outputs and processes.

It is possible when employing SAPA to expose students to qualitative (peer comments) and/or quantitative feedback (peer ratings). Instructors should consider and compare the benefits of these different reflective formative feedback components in light of the pedagogic aims of the team assignments they have designed and balanced against the impacts on conflict that this feedback might have. It has been shown that students are less resistant to receiving and giving quantitative over qualitative feedback (Tucker et al., 2009), for in small teams there are problems of maintaining anonymity when qualitative peer feedback comments are made visible because students are able to determine through elimination who has written what. As well as leading to conflict, this can discourage students from making accurate and honest assessments. It has been found that when used appropriately to provide feedback during a team project, ongoing SAPA can mitigate conflict by providing a "pressure valve" that allows teams to function harmoniously, despite unequal levels of skill and contributions, by allowing students to become more tolerant of the differential learning and assessment aspirations of their peers.

Interventive Strategies

This section examines how design educators can help student teams to manage conflict situations. There are two critical issues that educators need to consider here: (1) their role in supporting teams to resolve or manage the conflict; and (2) the nature of team conflict.

Facilitate Conflict Management

Even when taught conflict resolution skills, students need to be offered intervention strategies for problems that escalate. Teachers can model effective conflict resolution through such strategies. When a team seeks help with a conflict situation, the educator may decide to adopt one of four approaches (Scott, 2010): (1) judging, which is about listening to what each party has to say and then deciding or commenting on who is right and who is wrong; (2) counselling, which involves actively and empathetically listening to what each party has to say without commenting or taking any action; (3) negotiation between the parties involved, taking into account their alternative solutions until they reach a compromise partially satisfying each party; and (4) mediation, which includes guiding the conversation between the parties involved as they work towards understanding each other and reaching a solution that works best for all of them. In order to effectively support student teams to resolve or manage conflict, it has been found that it is important that educators try to play the role of a mediator (Scott, 2010). In doing so, six steps need to be taken:

1. Familiarise yourself with the issue/s to be addressed before the conflict resolution session i.e. who is involved and what is the conflict about. Team members may be asked to come to the session with an agenda or a list of topics to be addressed;

2. Prepare students for the conflict resolution session by clarifying for them the purpose of the session, your role and a set of ground rules e.g. 'be open-minded', 'use proper language' and 'listen actively';

3. Give each team member an opportunity to share his/her points of view;

4. Negotiate the solutions, brainstorm the suggestions and discuss how the solutions might work for each team member;

5. Take a break from the session, or set up a private meeting, when the student team seem to make no progress at negotiating the conflict and emotions are intense during the session; and

6. "Craft agreement" and "monitor follow-through." Bring the student team together after the break and ask them to share the solutions. Start to narrow down the solutions and work out the agreement among team members on the actions to be taken, team members' responsibilities in this relation and the deadlines (Scott, 2010, p.14).

Three key recommendations have been made for conflict intervention in student design teams (Tucker et al., 2014):

-   Offer teams intervention forums and try to resolve conflict at the team level;
-   Consider relocating individuals to other teams only as a very last resort e.g. in cases of bullying and harassment; and
-   Preferably choose a neutral person to resolve the conflict e.g. a teacher who is not assessing the students.

Develop a Comprehensive Understanding of the Nature of Conflict in Student Teams

To summarise, educators need to understand three key different types of conflict and offer students recommendations on how to act in each conflict situation (Table 4).

FUTURE RESEARCH DIRECTIONS

A key finding of our study is that students usually adopt an ignoring or avoiding to acknowledge team conflict approach. Future research needs to pinpoint the causes behind students' reluctance to acknowledge and deal with conflict, and the impacts of these avoidance strategies compared to those of others that students adopt in team conflict situations. In this light, further research might also study the impacts of teaching teamwork skills on students' abilities to understand and acknowledge team conflict and adopt more proactive strategies to manage and resolve it. Such research will be necessary to elucidate the relationship between the prevalence of negative conflict situations and lack of team working capabilities.

In relation to one of the conflict prevention strategies that we have suggested in this chapter, 'monitoring team processes', examining the effectiveness of SAPA as a formative feedback mechanism for team design projects would also be informative i.e. the criteria or what should be assessed by students, when and how often to conduct SAPA throughout a team project, and how to best incorporate SAPA

Table 4. Three key different types of conflict in student teams, causes and conflict resolution recommendations

Types of Conflict	Recommendations for STUDENT
1. Affective Conflicts	
Relationship or emotional conflict that is characterized by anger and hostility among team members	Remain polite and respect other team members. Understand that the issue is with what a team member is doing and how he/she is doing it. Criticise the action and the approach instead of attacking your teammate. If you are being criticised, avoid taking it personally.
2. Task and Process Conflict	
Disagreements in relation to team tasks including procedures, goals, decisions, approaches to team tasks and team processes	Focus on the facts. Adopt a problem-solving approach. Avoid allowing personality differences and characteristics to affect the discussion.
3. Interest-Based Conflicts	
Differences in needs, values, goals and access to information	Seek for common grounds and try to build solution upon them. Find the interest that your team members may all share.

adopted from (McGourty & De Meuse, 2001)

results to individualise student marks. Little is also known about the role of design teachers in mitigating team conflict and assisting student to resolve conflict. Future research needs to test the effectiveness of teacher intervention strategies in team conflict situations, and identify good practice examples of conflict intervention in design contexts.

CONCLUSION

Conflict resolution and management is an important factor influencing team effectiveness. Conflict in student teams is inevitable. Team members come from different social, cultural and cognitive backgrounds and have different expectations, motives, ideas and opinions, personalities, values and preferences, and these differences can lead to conflict. However, conflict in teams is not always a negative process but can "enhance the quality of decision making and actually increase the overall cohesiveness of the team" (McGourty & De Meuse, 2001, p.32). While conflict can be beneficial to the team functioning and outcomes, it is difficult to avoid it within student teams, and can have very negative impacts. It is critical therefore to constructively manage it in order to ensure effective team performance.

In the research reported in this chapter, more than 400 comments were recorded and coded under different themes. It was found that students acknowledge there is a "constructive" type of conflict that can be beneficial to team performance i.e. differences of opinions and making design decisions/choices (21 REF). As it was hypothesised, the presence of non-contributing and non-committed team members is the most referred to cause of conflict by students. Comments in the pilot survey suggest that students are keen to address the problem of non-contributing team members. The national survey found that "ignoring or avoiding to acknowledge team conflict" is a strategy commonly adopted by many students (61 REF), followed by "trying to resolve team conflict through discussion and improving communication" (30 REF) and "seeking support from teachers" (28 REF).

The instructor can play a significant role in mitigating the impacts of the greatest cause of team conflict – free-riding or social loafing. The key issue here is how to detect social loafing and how to address it. As Ruel and Bastiaans (2003, pp.2-3) suggest, performance cannot always act as a good measure of social loafing as it "does not necessarily lower the overall group performance, that is if the group performance equals the performance of the best students in that group." It is important that students are provided with a good understanding of the phenomenon of social loafing and how to distinguish between non-contributing social loafers and non-contributing struggling students in their teams. Students need to be given skills to constructively address the problem of social loafing and avoid destructive behaviours such as excluding the loafing students from team communications and processes. When social loafing is not resolved with such constructive strategies, and contributing students continue to practice destructive behaviours, it becomes imperative for teachers to apply intervention strategies.

Teachers are encouraged to develop teamwork pedagogies that place onus on teamworking as well as on the design to be submitted. Through this, students can learn the importance of adopting and maintaining strategies to assure effective team processes, and thus not be confined to the assumption that "there was absolutely no time to deal with conflict. Like a real life project it was all about product, not process" (Quote from an undergraduate male student). Teachers need also to think about strategies that allow for the monitoring of team processes so that conflict can be identified and addressed early. Thus, while students should feel at ease to seek help with conflict, the unenviable situation might be avoided where students feel they must choose to/not to "complain about others students" and hence be "judged by their friends" (Quote from an undergraduate female student).

REFERENCES

Bacon, D. R., Stewart, K. A., & Silver, W. S. (1999). Lessons from the Best and Worst Student Team Experiences: How a Teacher can make the Difference. *Journal of Management Education, 23*(5), 467–488. doi:10.1177/105256299902300503

Baron, R. A. (1990). Conflict in organizations. In K. R. Murphy & F. E. Saal (Eds.), *Psychology in organizations: Integrating science and practice* (pp. 197–216). Hillsdale, NJ: Lawrence Erlbaum Associates Inc. Publishers.

Buckenmyer, J. A. (2000). Using Teams for Class Activities: Making Course/Classroom Teams Work. *Journal of Education for Business, 76*(2), 98–107. doi:10.1080/08832320009599960

Crossley, T. (2006). Letting the drama into group work: Using conflict constructively in performing arts group practice. *Arts and Humanities in Higher Education, 5*(1), 33–50. doi:10.1177/1474022206059996

De Dreu, C. K. W., & Weingart, L. R. (2003). Task versus relationship conflict, team performance, and team member satisfaction: A meta-analysis. *The Journal of Applied Psychology, 88*(4), 741–749. doi:10.1037/0021-9010.88.4.741 PMID:12940412

De Wit, F. R. C., Greer, L. L., & Jehn, K. A. (2012). The paradox of intragroup conflict: A meta-analysis. *The Journal of Applied Psychology, 97*(2), 360–390. doi:10.1037/a0024844 PMID:21842974

Dommeyer, C. J. (2007). Using the diary method to deal with social loafers on the group project: its effects on peer evaluations, group behavior, and attitudes. *Journal of Marketing Education, 29*(2), 175–188. doi:10.1177/0273475307302019

Dommeyer, C. J., & Lammers, H. B. (2006). Students' attitudes toward a new method for preventing loafing on the group project: The team activity diary. *Journal of College Teaching and Learning, 3*, 15–22.

Dool, R. (2010). Managing conflict in online multicultural student teams. *Journal of Education, Information, and Cybernetics, 2*(2).

Eisenhardt, K. M., Kahwajy, J. L., & Bourgeois, L. J. III. (1997). Conflict and strategic choice: How top management teams disagree. *California Management Review, 39*(2), 42–62. doi:10.2307/41165886

Freeman, L., & Greenacre, L. (2011). An examination of socially destructive behaviors in group work. *Journal of Marketing Education, 33*(1), 5–17. doi:10.1177/0273475310389150

Gamero, N., González-Romá, V., & Peiró, J. M. (2008). The influence of intra-team conflict on work teams' affective climate: A longitudinal study. *Journal of Occupational and Organizational Psychology, 81*(1), 47–69. doi:10.1348/096317907X180441

Hansen, R. S. (2015). *The relationship between task conflict, task performance and team member satisfaction: the mediating role of relationship conflict.* (Master), University of Oslo. Retrieved from https://www.duo.uio.no/bitstream/handle/10852/44744/The-relationship-between-task-conflict--task-performance-and-team-members-satisfaction---the-mediating-role-of-relationship-conflict--Hansen-2015-.pdf?sequence=11&isAllowed=y

Harper, S. R., & Nagel, R. L. (2014). A study on conflicts during an interdisciplinary capstone design experience. *International Journal of Collaborative Engineering, 1*(3-4), 256–273. doi:10.1504/IJCE.2014.063354

Janis, I. L. (1972). *Victims of 'Groupthink.* Boston: Houghton Mifflin.

Jehn, K. A. (1994). Enhancing effectiveness: An investigation of advantages and disadvantages of value-based intragroup conflict. *The International Journal of Conflict Management, 5*(3), 223–238. doi:10.1108/eb022744

Jehn, K. A. (1995). A Multimethod Examination of the Benefits and Detriments of Intragroup Conflict. *Administrative Science Quarterly, 40*(2), 256–282. doi:10.2307/2393638

Jehn, K. A. (1997). A qualitative analysis of conflict types and dimensions in organizational groups. *Administrative Science Quarterly, 42*(3), 530–557. doi:10.2307/2393737

Jehn, K. A., & Bendersky, C. (2003). Intragroup conflict in organizations: A contingency perspective on the conflict-outcome relationship. *Research in Organizational Behavior, 25*, 187–242. doi:10.1016/S0191-3085(03)25005-X

Jehn, K. A., Chadwick, C., & Thatcher, S. M. (1997). To agree or not to agree: The effects of value congruence, individual demographic dissimilarity, and conflict on workgroup outcomes. *The International Journal of Conflict Management, 8*(4), 287–305. doi:10.1108/eb022799

Jehn, K. A., & Chatman, J. A. (2000). The Influence of Proportional and Perceptual Conflict Composition on Team Performance. *The International Journal of Conflict Management, 11*(1), 56–73. doi:10.1108/eb022835

Jehn, K. A., & Mannix, E. A. (2001). The Dynamic Nature of Conflict: A Longitudinal Study of Intragroup Conflict and Group Performance. *Academy of Management Journal, 44*(2), 238–251. doi:10.2307/3069453

Johnson, D. W., & Johnson, F. P. (1994). *Joining together: Group Theory and Group Skills*. Needham Heights, MA: Allyn and Bacon.

Kirchmeyer, C., & Cohen, A. (1992). Multicultural Groups Their Performance and Reactions with Constructive Conflict. *Group & Organization Management, 17*(2), 153–170. doi:10.1177/1059601192172004

Kurtzberg, T. R., & Mueller, J. S. (2005). The influence of daily conflict on perceptions of creativity: A longitudinal study. *The International Journal of Conflict Management, 16*(4), 335–353.

Lira, E. M., Ripoll, P., Peiró, J. M., & González, P. (2007). The roles of group potency and information and communication technologies in the relationship between task conflict and team effectiveness: A longitudinal study. *Computers in Human Behavior, 23*(6), 2888–2903. doi:10.1016/j.chb.2006.06.004

Lovelace, K., Shapiro, D. L., & Weingart, L. R. (2001). Maximizing cross-functional new product teams' innovativeness and constraint adherence: A conflict communications perspective. *Academy of Management Journal, 44*(4), 779–793. doi:10.2307/3069415

McGourty, J., & De Meuse, K. P. (2001). *The Team Developer: an assessment and skill building program / Student guidebook*. New York: Wiley.

Morris, R., & Hayes, C. (1997). Small group work: are group assignments a legitimate form of assessment? *Paper presented at the Learning Through Teaching:Proceedings of the 6th Annual Teaching Learning Forum*, Perth, Australia, Murdoch University.

Orr, S. (2010). Collaborating or fighting for the marks? Students' experiences of group work assessment in the creative arts. *Assessment & Evaluation in Higher Education, 35*(3), 301–313. doi:10.1080/02602931003632357

Pelled, L. H. (1996). Demographic diversity, conflict, and work group outcomes: An intervening process theory. *Organization Science, 7*(6), 615–631. doi:10.1287/orsc.7.6.615

Pelled, L. H., & Adler, P. S. (1994). Antecedents of intergroup conflict in multifunctional product development teams: A conceptual model. *IEEE Transactions on* Engineering Management, *41*(1), 21–28.

Pelled, L. H., Eisenhardt, K. M., & Xin, K. R. (1999). Exploring the black box: An analysis of work group diversity, conflict, and performance. *Administrative Science Quarterly, 44*(1), 1–28. doi:10.2307/2667029

Rahim, M. A. (2015). *Managing conflict in organizations*. Transaction Publishers.

Ruel, G., & Bastiaans, N. (2003). Free-riding and team performance in project education. *International Journal of Management Education, 3*(1), 26–37.

Scott, V. (2010). *Conflict Resolution at Work for Dummies*. Indianapolis, Indiana: Wiley Publishing, Inc.

Shaw, J. D., Zhu, J., Duffy, M. K., Scott, K. L., Shih, H., & Susanto, E. (2011). A contingency model of conflict and team effectiveness. *The Journal of Applied Psychology*, *96*(2), 391–400. doi:10.1037/a0021340 PMID:20939655

Simons, T., & Peterson, R. (2000). Task conflict and relationship conflict in top management teams: The pivotal role of intragroup trust. *The Journal of Applied Psychology*, *83*(1), 102–111. doi:10.1037/0021-9010.85.1.102 PMID:10740960

Smart, J., & Dixon, S. (2002). The discourse of assessment: Language and value in the assessment of group practice in the performing arts. *Arts and Humanities in Higher Education*, *1*(2), 185–204. doi:10.1177/1474022202001002005

Smith, C. G. (1966). A comparative analysis of some conditions and consequences of intra-organizational conflict. *Administrative Science Quarterly*, *10*(4), 504–529. doi:10.2307/2391573

Tedeschi, J. T., Schlenker, B. R., & Bonoma, T. V. (1973). *Conflict, power and games*. Chicago: Aldine.

Tekleab, A. G., Quigley, N. R., & Tesluk, P. E. (2009). A Longitudinal Study of Team Conflict, Conflict Management, Cohesion, and Team Effectiveness. *Group & Organization Management*, *34*(2), 170–205. doi:10.1177/1059601108331218

Thomas, K. W., & Kilman, R. H. (1974). *The Thomas-Kilman Conflict Mode Instrument*. Tuxedo, NY: Xicom.

Tjosvold, D., & Deemer, D. K. (1980). Effects of controversy within a cooperative or competitive context on organizational decision making. *The Journal of Applied Psychology*, *65*(5), 590–595. doi:10.1037/0021-9010.65.5.590

Tucker, R., Abbasi, N., Thorpe, G. R., Ostwald, M. J., Williams, A. P., & Wallis, L. (2014). *Enhancing and Assessing Group and Team Learning in Architecture and Related Design Contexts*. Retrieved from http://www.olt.gov.au/system/files/resources/ID11_2004_Tucker_Report_2014.pdf

Tucker, R., Fermelis, J., & Palmer, S. (2009). Designing, Implementing and Evaluating a Self-and-Peer Assessment Tool for E-learning Environments. In C. Spratt & P. Lajbcygier (Eds.), *E-Learning and Advanced Assessment Technologies: Evidence-Based Approaches* (pp. 170–194). Hershey: Information Science Reference. doi:10.4018/978-1-60566-410-1.ch010

Zhang, X., Chen, Z., & Guo, C. (2009). The opening" black box" between conflict and knowledge sharing: A psychological engagement theory perspective. *Paper presented at the42nd Hawaii International Conference on System Sciences*.

KEY TERMS AND DEFINITIONS

Affective/Relationship/Emotional Conflict: Conflict characterized by anger and hostility among team members.

Conflict: The situation in which "the conditions, practices, or goals for the different participants are inherently incompatible" (Smith, 1966, p.511).

Interest-Based Conflicts: Conflict caused by the differences in needs, values, goals and access to information.

Interventive Strategies: Proper interventions that teachers make to assist teams in resolving conflict when it emerges.

Preventive Strategies: Strategies that educators might use to prevent the negative conflict from developing.

Process Conflict: Conflict caused by disagreement about approaches to team tasks and team processes.

Self-And-Peer-Assessment (SAPA): At its most basic, SAPA involves students providing an evaluation for all group members, including themselves, of the individual contribution of each group member to the group work process. The SAPA evaluation may be used informal feedback, or formal and used as an element of the summative assessment for the group task. SAPA may be public or anonymous.

Social Loafing: The situation when individuals fail to contribute completely or contribute less than their fair share when they work in a team as opposed to when they work alone.

Task Conflict: Conflict caused by disagreements in relation to team tasks; including procedures, goals, and decisions (Jehn, 1994).

Team Effectiveness: Team Effectiveness in educational contexts can be defined in terms of two dimensions: (1) Performance on the assigned task, evaluated through an assessment of products and/or outcomes; and (2) Goal Achievement through the process of working in a team, which can be divided into two aspects – (i) behaviour and (ii) attitudes.

Teamwork: Joint work on an assigned project in a collaborative environment where members actively contribute to team cohesion and task achievement.

Section 2
Evaluating Collaboration:
Teaching Case Studies

Chapter 6
Perceptions of Collaboration Amongst Novice Design Students

Philip Crowther
Queensland University of Technology, Australia

Andrew Scott
Queensland University of Technology, Australia

Tom Allen
Queensland University of Technology, Australia

ABSTRACT

This chapter presents a case study of a large common first year unit/subject in a major Australian university. The unit introduces students to the theory and practice of design through a learning environment that is brief and intense; being delivered in block mode over just four days, and being free of other academic commitments. Students choose from one of two concurrent environments, either a camping field trip or an on-campus alternative, and work in mixed discipline groups of six to nine students, on two sequential design projects. Participant survey and reflective journal data are used to analyse student perceptions of the learning activities and to establish the pedagogical success of learning about collaboration through the act of collaborating; specifically through a project-based design environment. The data supports the hypothesis that groups that emotionally engaged with collaboration and collaborated more effectively achieved higher academic grades.

INTRODUCTION

Collaboration is a critical aspect of professional practice in all design disciplines, and similarly so in design education. As such it is an important learning outcome of the design unit (subject) reported on in this chapter. This case study explores a large 'common' first-year unit in a School of Design at a major Australian university, and seeks to expose students' perceptions of their multi-disciplinary collabora-

DOI: 10.4018/978-1-5225-0726-0.ch006

tive experiences. Limited evidence to date suggests that the experience is highly enjoyed by students though the value of the learning experience is less clear. This research hypothesises that students do learn about collaboration through deep engagement; they learn about collaboration through collaborating. In the context of design education, Shon (1984, p. 4) makes the interesting distinction between knowing about something and knowing how to do something; the theoretical and the practical. This study asks the question: is an intense experience of collaboration a successful mode in which students can learn about collaboration, and what are the lasting perceptions taken away from the experience. It will study *how* students collaborated in order for them to learn *about* collaboration. This will provide valuable understanding from a pedagogical point of view, as well as a professional one.

Collaboration is an important aspect of the signature pedagogy of design (Schulman 2005, p. 54). The problem-based learning activities of the unit being studied here rely heavily on collaboration as a mode of learning by doing; an important characteristic of the signature pedagogy (Shreeve, Sims, & Trowler, 2010). If what students learn (learning outcomes) is embedded in how they learn it (context and doing) then further research into that context is important (Laurillard & McAndrew, 2002). A constructivist theory of learning supports this view of students creating their own mental models from their experiences (Jonassen & Reeves, 1996, p. 695). This research seeks to understand the mental models that students are constructing, especially around the topic of collaboration, and to understand those models using established pedagogical frameworks.

This research study provides new knowledge about student perceptions of design collaboration and generalizable pedagogical knowledge about student collaborative processes in design education. It has the potential to significantly improve our understanding of collaboration as a pedagogical process in our design education context, and through this allow us to adapt our practices to improve student learning. In the context of design education, Shon (1984, p. 4) makes the interesting distinction between knowing about something and knowing how to do something; the theoretical and the practical. This research project seeks to answer the question; what can students learn about collaboration by doing collaboration?

Analysis of the case study offers two researched understandings of the collaborative activities that the students experienced. Firstly a theoretical analysis of the activities using three significant pedagogical frameworks (Delahaye, 2005; Laurillard, 2002; Honey & Mumford, 1992) to explain the breadth and depth of the structured program, and to support an assertion that this form of collaboration offers greater opportunity for constructivist learning. Secondly the chapter presents an empirical study, through several data sources, of student perceptions of trans-disciplinary collaboration, as experienced through the program. Evidence from this analysis similarly supports the success of the program in enabling student learning. Comparisons are made between the field trip setting and the less immersive and more familiar on campus setting; and also between groups of students who received high grades and those who received lower grades.

Student perceptions have been gathered using an on-line survey and asked students to reflect on their experiences of collaboration and engagement during the unit activities. The survey has used a five point Likert scale ('strongly disagree' to 'strongly agree') for responses to questions pertaining to experiences of collaboration and engagement during the block-delivery activities. Data from the survey was cross referenced with students' visual journals in which they reflected on their learning experience of both design and collaboration. In general student perceptions of the collaborative experience were positive and support the hypothesis that students can learn about design and collaboration by doing design and collaboration.

BACKGROUND

Collaboration in Design

The importance and significance of collaboration in the design professions is well understood and well established (Kvan, 2000). "Team collaboration and innovation in design are emerging as decisive factors in determining and maintaining global competitiveness for firms and countries" (Maldonado, Lee, Klemmer & Pea, 2007, p. 490). In order to successfully complete complex tasks, such as designing a new mobile phone, an innovative service, or a building, requires numerous specialist professionals, each with their own unique knowledge base and perspective. The interactions of such a group can be characterised as multi-disciplinary, and it can occur through processes of cooperation, coordination and collaboration. These three processes have increasing levels of interaction with collaboration being the most complex and interdependent state of group activity. This is especially so in group design activity where the interdependence of team members is critical to the achievement of shared goals. Mattessich and Monsey (1992) offer one of the most thorough definitions of collaboration which highlights this difference. They note that collaboration requires a greater level of trust in which authority is shared and determined through a joint process. Most significant is that collaboration connotes a relationship in which all members of a team share a common goal, as opposed to the separate but related goals of cooperation.

"Collaboration is a mutually beneficial and well-defined relationship entered into by two or more organisations [or individuals] to achieve common goals. The relationship includes a commitment to: a definition of mutual relationships and goals; a jointly developed structure and shared responsibilities; mutual authority and accountability; and sharing of resources and rewards" (Mattessich & Monsey, 1992, p. 11). Collaboration requires "a higher sense of working together in order to achieve a holistic creative result. It is a far more demanding activity, more difficult to establish and maintain, than simply completing a project as a team" (Kvan, 2000, p. 410). In order to be successful a collaborative project must have clear and shared outcomes in which members of the group also share some level of interdependency alongside a clear understanding of those outcomes and the interdependencies (Kvan, 2000, p. 410).

While in a professional design context there may be a hierarchy of command or instruction, and a lead designer, true collaboration implies a flatter, non-hierarchical, approach in which "collaborative work is marked by shared decision making, the give and take of ideas exchanged and explored, the integration of multiple perspectives and a synthesis that integrates hitherto isolated ideas" (Poggenpohl, 2004, p. 144). The volume of information and specialist knowledge is simply too great for just one designer, with just one perspective, to develop high quality creative solutions to the complex and wicked problems of contemporary industrialised society. Collaboration allows the whole to be greater than the sum of the parts, and certainly greater than any individual contribution; "collaboration co-constructs new knowledge that goes beyond any knowledge possessed by a single member in isolation" (Donato, 2004, p. 287). "Collaborative success can therefore be said to be achieved when we have accomplished something in a group which could not be accomplished by an individual" (Kvan, 2000, p. 410).

Collaboration in Education

There are numerous studies that have demonstrated the educational advantages of collaborative learning activities, and "increasingly we recognise that knowledge is created socially" (Poggenpohl, 2004, p. 144). Such advantages have been variously attributed to a number of factors including opportunities to explain one's ideas and reasoning, sharing knowledge and understanding, observing peers and their strategies for learning, opportunities for peer to peer critiques, and the ability to engage in rich debate about ideas and processes. Much of this research has illustrated that on average collaborative learning environments lead to better learning outcomes than individual learning environments (Barron, 2000, p. 405). The benefits of collaborative learning lie in processes of articulation, communication, problem solving, disagreement, negotiation, assertions and denials; all leading to an increased level of understanding (Barros & Verdejo, 2000, p. 221).

In the formalised learning environments of contemporary society we see that for the student "knowledge is commonly socially constructed, through collaborative efforts toward shared objectives or by dialogues and challenges brought about by different persons' perspectives" (Pea, 1993, p. 48). These dialogues and different perspectives are often those of the teachers or the authors of texts or the directors of rich media. They can however equally be the dialogues and perspectives of other students. It is for this reason that collaboration with peers offers great opportunity for knowledge development. While teachers and instructors can facilitate formal learning with stated learning outcomes, interaction with one's peers facilitates informal learning since "the key to acquiring tacit knowledge is shared experience (e.g. observation, imitation and practice)" (Dorta, Lesage & Di Bartolo, 2012, p. 99). For the student "it is above all through interacting with others, coordinating his/her approaches to reality with those of others, that the individual masters new approaches" (Doise, 1990, p. 46).

Just as collaboration in the professions allows groups to successfully tackle increasingly complex issues, "collaborative learning allows the students to approach more complex problems, and to express designs, critics and arguments to partners, which promotes a reflection type that leads to learning. In collaborative environments of design learning, the design process is seen as a task in which the individuals share a common objective (to design) in which they need to work in groups (to collaborate). It is the process that students follow that leads them to learn." (Bravo, Redondo, Ortega & Verdejo, 2006, p. 153).

The success of collaborative group work as a learning environment for students has been researched by many educators at many different educational levels from early years at school to higher education. "Collaborative learning research has paid close attention to the study of pupils' interactions during peer-based work in order to analyse and identify the cognitive advantages of joint activity" (Barros & Verdejo, 2000, p. 221). These cognitive advantages, fostered by this social context of learning, have been identified and studied by other researchers who have noted that "collaboration was effective in improving group processes, group project performance, individual student achievement, and confidence in complex problem solving" (Lou, 2004, p. 49).

Collaborative Problem Solving in Design

"Knowledge is socially constructed through interaction with others and with the context. An effective way of learning, therefore, is to engage learners in the collaborative problem solving of real-world problems" (Lou, 2004, p. 50). While the characterisation of designing as problem solving is a gross oversimplification, there is value in reviewing the literature on collaborative problem solving, as many of the desirable characteristics of such are relevant to a successful learning environment for collaborative design. These include learning environments which are; situated, learner centred, integrated, authentic and relevant, and which involve active participation, critical thinking, multiple perspectives, and learning by doing (Nelson, 2013). A wide ranging review of educational practices in project-based and problem-based pedagogy has identified four principles for the design of successful learning activities using these modes of delivery: learning appropriate goals, scaffolding that supports student and teacher learning, opportunities for self-assessment and revision, and social organisations that promote participation and a sense of agency (Barron et al., 1998). While these four principles might reasonably apply to any form of pedagogy, it is important to note the significance of social organisations in the development of successful learning activities in a project-based pedagogy.

The act of collaboration activates a range of unique learning process: opportunities to share insights, debate different perspectives, explain one's own thinking, critique of other's ideas, and observation of other's strategies and thinking (Barron, 2003). This research in to the advantages of collaborative problem-based learning is also supported by students' perception of the advantages of collaboration in design projects, which has been shown to include playing different roles within the group, preparation for professional practice after graduation, working with people with different perspectives, and skill development in teamwork (O'Brien, Soibelman & Elvin, 2003, p. 90).

Further to this the group activities of collaborative learning provide unique opportunities that support active reflective learning. "Small group interactions, opportunities to contribute, peer review, and having access to data about how others have thought through the same problem are all methods" that have been shown to support active reflective learning (Barron et al., 1998, p. 285). This relationship between social interaction and the quantity and quality of reflective learning has also been noted and researched by Maldonado, Lee, Klemmer and Pea (2007, p. 491). They found a strong correspondence between team dynamics and the type and frequency of reflective learning recorded in student logbooks. This link or relationship between social organisation and reflective learning and self-assessment is interesting and relevant to the research project presented in this chapter; as is the use of logbooks (or journals) for students to record reflections about their learning.

Problem-based or project-based learning environments, as typically applied in a design education context, work well to accommodate a range of learning opportunities or affordances. Laurillard's (2002) framework for the analysis of learning environments identifies the critical learning activities of: apprehending, investigating, discussing, experimenting, and synthesising. Analysis of the design studio and its use of project-based or problem-based learning, has shown how effective the typical design studio is in facilitating all of Laurillard's affordances (particularly including the social activity of discussing) and enhancing student learning (Crowther, 2013). In a typical design studio environment "the combination of instruction (lectures and discussions), action (collaborative design project), and reflection (individual and group process critique), has proven an effective model for collaborative design education" (O'Brien, Soibelman & Elvin, 2003, p. 91).

The design studio is an ideal pedagogical model for collaborative learning and the creation of zones of proximal development. The project-based or problem-based approach provides opportunity for immersion in the active participation and materiality of design (the "doing" as espoused by Schon, 1984) and the collaborative support and instruction that facilities learning and development (the "social environment" described by Vygotsky, 1978). Learning by doing has been well explored as a strategy for studio based education by Schon (1984). His ideas of learning *about* design (the development of knowledge), learning *to* design (the development and application of skills) and learning to *become* an architect (the transformative pedagogy in which learning is identified as changing as a person) are all enhanced by collaborative activity (Dorta, Lesage & Di Bartolo, 2012). It is reasonable to summarise that "on average, group work leads to better problem-solving and learning outcomes" (Barron, 2003, p. 308).

CASE STUDY

This chapter reports on research into the activities of a 'common' first year unit (subject) experienced by students (number = 469) from six different design disciplines in a major Australian university. The participating disciplines were: architecture, fashion design, industrial design, interactive and visual design, interior design, and landscape architecture. This common unit provides an accelerated experience of a collaborative design process and concludes before the middle of the first semester, early enough to have a bearing on other discipline design units. It follows an intensive block-delivery model wherein a four week lecture program precedes an intensive programme of collaborative design activities. The lecture programme introduces a range of topics including design process, design ideation, reflection and group dynamics. Heufler's (2004) model of design function (Table 1) is used as a basis for the design exercises that follow.

The intensive program takes place over just four days in the semester during a 'project week', free from other classes, in which students collaborate in multi-disciplinary teams to design and create. Students are given the choice of two concurrently delivered immersive learning environments; one on campus and the other in the form of a camping field trip isolated from the routine distractions of university and home. In both environments forced proximity plays an important role in team development, though to differing degrees between the two environments.

Students were randomly assigned to mixed discipline teams of six to nine students. As a team they were required to respond to two sequential design provocations by designing and constructing two artefacts, each with significantly different goals, and each taking just one and a half days to complete. While each of these artefacts is assessed at the time (20% weighting each) and students given immediate feedback, the major assessment item of the unit (60% weighting) is an individually completed journal that visually and textually records the activities and the experiences and provides explicit evidence of direct student self-reflection.

The two project-based design exercises each take place over approximately one and a half days. The first deals with the more physical and quantifiable aspects of design; it asks the students to design and construct a device that will raise both a flag and a two kilogram payload, each and separately to a maximum height. The artefact must also exhibit structural integrity and aesthetic expression, which is to say practical and aesthetic function. The second exercise deals with the less tangible qualitative aspects of design by adding symbolic function to the design brief; it asks students to design and construct a form of sculptural installation that expresses the idea of 'lightness'. Both projects are assessed using a criterion referenced assessment matrix with the criteria of practical function, structural stability, appropriate material usage, aesthetic development, and for the second project, appropriateness of symbolic expression.

Table 1. Design function

Experience	**Function**
Physical experience	Practical function
Sensory experience	Aesthetic function
Social experience	Symbolic function

after Heufler (2004)

In both activities the students are limited to using only the provided materials: cane, timber dowels, light-weight fabric, strings, sticky tape, and in the case of the second exercise glow-sticks for an evening presentation. During the activities a number of staff circulate amongst the teams and offer formative feedback on work in progress, as is typical in a traditional design studio environment. Students receive summative assessment and feedback shortly after the completion of each exercise; feedback on the first exercise is given before the start of the second exercise such that students can learn from the first exercise, and respond to feedback and potentially improve their performance in the second activity. Unlike typical student design projects this happens in an accelerated cycle spanning only three days for both projects together, creating an intensive and iterative experience of the design process. The group activities provide opportunities for students to engage in the 'active processing and questioning of ideas' (Sale, 2001, p. 58) and to 'actively construct ideas and generate meaning' (Toohey, 1999, p. 55).

While working on the design projects, and again after the projects have been concluded, students are individually expected to record their activities in their visual journals and record reflections on their activities, the activities of other students in their team, and of other teams. The use of student's reflective critiques of collaborative work has been used successfully to engage students in transformative learning (O'Brien, Soibelman & Elvin, 2003). The student reflections from this case study are discussed later in this chapter.

Theoretical Analysis of the Collaborative Program

The project-based activities of this case study have been analysed using three pedagogical frameworks for understanding student learning activities; the seven steps of a learning project developed by Delahaye (2005), the five fundamental steps of learning activity proposed by Laurillard (2002), and the four stages of the learning cycle from Honey and Mumford (1992). These three theoretical frameworks are presented in Table 2. While each of these frameworks articulates the learning activities and affordances of many types of pedagogical environments or situations, it is noteworthy that all focus heavily on experience and activity, and that both Delahaye and Laurillard explicitly identify stages of collaboration in their structures, with the activities of: discussion, collaboration, negotiating, debating, and interaction. Analysis of the learning activities of the case study here shows good alignment with all three of these pedagogical frameworks.

This analysis of the case study activities was used to assist in the development of the survey tool used in this research. Key aspects of the three frameworks were developed into terms in the survey questions put to student participants. In this way the theoretical analysis informs the research and provides guidance in assessing the success of the pedagogical program in facilitating learning about collaboration through the act of collaborating in a project-based learning environment.

Analysis of Survey Data

Despite the longevity of this pedagogical approach (this mode of delivery has been used for over eight years), there had to date been no systematic research into the student perception of the value of the collaborative experience. Anecdotal evidence, anonymous student feedback (through the university system), and the quality of the student assignments, suggests that the learning experience is valuable and valued by the students. This research study sought to gather rigorous evidence of student perceptions through a survey of students who had recently completed the block-delivery experience, and from the students

Table 2. Stages of the case study project-based activities

Case Study	Seven Steps of a Learning Project (Delahaye, 2005, p. 310)	Five Learning Activities (Laurillard, 2002, pp. 90 & 191)	Four Stages of the Learning Cycle (Honey & Mumford, 1992)
Students were given the design briefs for Projects 1 and 2.	Project is explicitly defined	Attending and apprehending: clarify structure of argument and nature of the evidence	Have an experience
Guided exploration of site, context, and resources for Project 1 and 2.	Investigate the work situation/site; review the context and stakeholder	Exploring and investigation: selecting and negotiating tasks and goals	
Theoretical framework for design process and collaboration discussed during lectures program prior to site visit. Heufler's (2004) model of design function (practical, aesthetic and symbolic) was used to frame the projects.	Develop and review theories and concepts		Review the experience
Reflective practice (for action, in action, on action) encouraged for lectures and design projects. Formative and summative feedback given at the conclusion of each project.	Critical thinking, action, and critical reflection	Experimenting and practicing: goals against which students can compare intrinsic feedback to modify their next actions	Conclude from the experience
Supervised team work during four-day intensive off-campus activity.	Discussion and collaboration with teachers and peers	Discussing and debating: generate questions that require students to use experience at the interactive task level	
Each project runs for 1½ days allowing two complete design-build-assess cycles.	Repeat steps 1 to 5		
Students individually report on their perceptions of their group's design process via sketches and written reflections in their Design Journal. Reflections on the lecture programme are encouraged to draw comparisons between theory and practice.	Finalise and produce report, output/design	Synthesising, articulating and expressing: reflecting on comparison between theories and practice	Plan the next steps

own visual journals in which they reflected upon their collaborative experiences both at the time of the activities and after the event.

All of the students who participated in the unit were approached via email, several weeks after completion of the unit, inviting them to participate in a short on-line survey about their experiences of collaboration. A total of forty two students responded to the survey, representing 9% of the total student cohort from this unit. The survey sample of student respondents were a close match with the makeup of the overall cohort, both in respect to distribution of disciplines represented, and in respect to the session attended (the two field trip/camping sessions, and the on-campus located session).

The survey asked students to respond to questions using a five point Likert scale from 1 being "strongly disagree" to 5 being "strongly agree". The averages (means) and standard deviations are presented in Table 3 arranged from the strongest positive response to the strongest negative response. It is worth noting that the strongest responses (furthest away from a neutral response of 3) are all positive; the top six in Table 3. These questions/responses are discussed later.

Further analysis of the survey results was conducted to ascertain if there was any statistically significant difference between the responses of groups of students based on session attended, and/or grades/results for the unit. A series of *t*-tests were conducted on the data (unless noted otherwise, all tests were

Table 3. Student perceptions of collaborative activities (on a five point Likert scale: 1 being strongly disagree, 5 being strongly agree) n = 42

	Question	Mean	SD
1	I normally enjoy interacting with other students in the classroom	3.98	0.94
2	Working with students from other disciplines, with different skills, was helpful	3.95	1.03
3	Working with other students helped me to understand collaboration	3.79	0.87
4	Working with students from other disciplines, with different skills, helped me to learn	3.71	0.94
5	The block-delivery (intensive) mode of this unit helped me to learn	3.71	1.20
6	Having designated team roles and responsibilities helped create better outcomes	3.71	0.83
7	I felt my voice was heard and I was able to contribute effectively	3.67	1.30
8	We worked better as a team on the second project	3.62	1.25
9	Our team collaborated well	3.57	1.13
10	Being in close proximity with other students helped us to work as a team	3.55	1.04
11	I normally enjoy working in groups	3.45	0.99
12	I felt more motivated working on a group (than on my own)	3.45	1.13
13	I felt that I was part of a learning community	3.45	1.13
14	My group worked effectively as a team	3.43	1.21
15	Some group members did not help much with the projects	3.40	1.27
16	We voted to make decisions	3.40	1.19
17	I enjoyed working in this group	3.38	1.25
18	There was trust among team members which helped making good design decisions	3.38	1.10
19	I was pleased with how our group worked	3.34	1.26
20	Close proximity and deadline pressures led to a united team	3.33	1.00
21	We shared the work fairly evenly	3.00	1.10
22	Building small mock-ups allowed our team to reach decisions more easily	2.83	1.06
23	Making decisions as a team was easy	2.81	1.19
24	We nominated a team leader	2.40	0.94
25	I was reluctant to put forward my views and opinions in our team environment	2.38	1.06
26	Decisions were made by a nominated team leader	2.31	0.90

two tailed and assumed unequal variance). A significance level of probability $p<0.05$ was adopted; as is generally appropriate for psychological statistics. Results from this analysis are presented in Table 4.

Firstly analysis was conducted to investigate any difference between the responses of students who attended the field trip sessions and those who attended the on-campus sessions. Anecdotal evidence from several years of teaching in this unit suggested that students who attended the field trip collaborated better in teams, and also performed better in their visual journal (and therefore also performed better in the unit overall). However analysis of the survey data did not support this hypothesis. The average grade achieved for the visual journal (the individual component of assessment in this unit) by students attending the field trip sessions was 5.65 while that of students attending the on-campus session was 5.58; there being no statistically significant difference when analysed by t-test. Analysis of the overall grades

Table 4. Unpaired sample t-test statistics and probabilities: low grades compared to high grades (showing only questions where p<0.05) n = 42

Question	Overall Grade for the Unit					
	Low Grades (5 and Below on 7 Point Scale)		High Grades (6 and Above on 7 Point Scale)			
	Mean	SD	Mean	SD	*t* Value	*p* Value
I normally enjoy working in groups	2.94	1.18	3.77	0.71	2.47	0.018
I felt more motivated working in a group than on my own	2.94	1.06	3.77	1.07	2.42	0.020
Grade for "Visual Journal"						
	Low grades (5 and below on 7 point scale)		High grades (6 and above on 7 point scale)			
	Mean	SD	Mean	SD	*t* Value	*p* Value
I normally enjoy working in groups	3.11	1.20	3.74	0.69	2.02	0.050
I felt more motivated working in a group than on my own	3.05	1.13	3.78	1.04	2.16	0.037
Grade for "Project One"						
	Low grades (5 and below on 7 point scale)		High grades (6 and above on 7 point scale)			
	Mean	SD	Mean	SD	*t* Value	*p* Value
I enjoyed working in this group	2.90	1.22	3.86	1.11	2.63	0.012
My group worked effectively as a team	2.95	1.20	3.90	1.04	2.75	0.009
I was pleased with how our group worked	2.90	1.30	3.80	1.06	2.42	0.020
Decisions were made by a nominated team leader	2.67	0.97	1.95	0.67	2.75	0.009
Making decisions as a team was easy	2.38	1.02	3.24	1.22	2.47	0.018
There was trust among team member which helped making good design decisions	3.05	0.92	3.71	1.19	2.03	0.049
Grade for "Project Two"						
	Low Grades (5 and Below on 7 Point Scale)		High Grades (6 and Above on 7 Point Scale)			
	Mean	SD	Mean	SD	*t* Value	*p* Value
I felt more motivated working in a group than on my own	2.94	1.00	3.83	1.09	2.75	0.009
We worked better as a team on the second project	2.83	1.20	4.21	0.93	3.96	0.0003
Working with other students helped me to understand collaboration	3.44	0.98	4.04	0.69	2.17	0.036

for the unit gave identical average results of 5.74. Attendance on the field trip sessions did not appear to provide any advantage to the students' academic achievement; in contrast with anecdotal expectations. While this is pedagogically reassuring, it does not support the hypothesis that the field trip experience has additional academic value in promoting better collaboration.

Similar analysis using *t*-tests was conducted for each of the survey questions, comparing student groups who attended the field trip and those who did not. Again despite expectation that those students on the field trip would have had a more successful collaborative experience, and would have experienced stronger teams that worked better together, the data did not support this view. None of the questions relating to the collaborative experience returned test results that were significant. Student perceptions of their collaborative activities and experiences were relatively similar between the two cohorts.

Secondly analysis was conducted to investigate any difference between the responses of the groups of students based on their academic achievement in the unit. Students with high grades (6 and 7 on a 7 point scale) were compared with students with low grades (5 and below on a 7 point scale). Analysis using *t*-tests was conducted between these student groups for overall grades in the units, grades for the visual journal (the individual assessment item), and grades for the two projects (each being a group assessment item). Table 4 shows those questions/responses that showed statistically significant differences at $p<0.05$. The implications of this, for future pedagogical development of collaborative environments, are discussed later in this chapter.

Analysis of Student Visual Journals Data

As part of their learning activities, and as the major individual assessment item of the unit (60%), all students completed a visual journal in which they recorded the activities, their designs and those of others, and their reflections on the experience, both at the time of the activities (during the block delivery mode) and in the few days immediately afterwards. Students were directed to record and reflect upon the activities using the four Rs model:

- Report (describe) an idea or experience and explain why it is important to design.
- Relate the issues/experience to their own practice or discipline knowledge.
- Reason about the idea or experience to show understanding of how things work in design.
- Reconstruct their understanding and show how what they have learned affects them as a designer.

Analysis of the student' reflections identified a number of recurring themes, including decision making, group cohesion, group communication, prototyping, rust, conflict, and the intensity of the learning experience.

Journal reflections showed how decision-making, leadership and delegation were bound up with ideas of authority within the team. Some students were uneasy with appearing bossy even though they felt a desperate need to fill a leadership vacuum in order to propel the design process forward. "We all took on different roles which was interesting to see. I always take on the project manager type of role. I hope I wasn't too bossy and rude. I think we needed someone overseeing the whole plan though" (N91031). It could be argued that a focus on creating specific roles and responsibilities along with team-building and confidence-building within a group at the beginning of collaboration would help group outcomes by giving the coordinator and other team roles greater confidence in both delegating and/or completing their specific tasks. Whilst greater confidence may improve efficiency, students highlighted people skills and the manner in which delegation was handled as an important factor in collaboration. "I need to work on my people skills. I think I got a little stressed out, but people don't respond to stress. People respond to happy, positive encouragement" (N91031). "It could be clearly seen that the team with the best group dynamics produced stronger designs than those with poor group dynamics" (N91708).

Group cohesion and effective communication was identified as essential for good team dynamics. Better communication was perceived to have a direct influence on the level of collaboration and the improvement of the end result of a design project. Student reflective journals pointed to four key findings in regards to communication:

- Good communication leads to cohesion.
- Lack of communication creates frustration.
- Miscommunication can result in misalignment of project goals and bad time management.
- Confusion creates tension.

Student reflective comments were very clear about the perceived value of communication and group cohesion in achieving successful collaboration, and therefore successful design outcomes. "We had good cohesion because we had good communication" (N94815). "The two key areas that I believe to be most valuable to team dynamics – cohesion and communication" (N94654). "In comparison to project 1, our group indicated better communication which had a direct influence on the end result of project 2" (N94514).

Prototyping and testing was seen by students as an important element which led to better results, encouraged participation and allowed team members to come to an agreement. It was also observed how more successful groups had created varied iterations of their design and prototyped and tested them, whilst less successful groups discovered the flaws in their outcomes when it was too late to make further improvements. Testing or prototyping was seen as a successful strategy for achieving better group agreement and more productive collaboration. "When disagreements arose, we would do mock ups and trials of both to test different opinions to try to encourage creativity, but also to encourage participation" (N94717). "If I were to complete the group exercise again, I would ensure that we completed some prototyping as some of the other groups were far more successful for completing a prototype" (N94481).

The ability for all students in a group to voice their opinion, and feel comfortable in doing so, was highlighted as a key factor in determining project success. A culture trust and listening to other team member's suggestions was identified as a valuable trait for group cohesion and success. Brainstorming was used as a tool to allow all team members to contribute and then set goals based on an aligned understanding. When there was a lack of trust within a team, group cohesion was affected negatively. "I think the key is for everyone to feel like their opinion is valuable so any group work will run a lot smoother if I try to encourage this" (N94717). "I personally believe that one of the most important skills I learnt from block delivery was being able to work with and understand a range of different personalities. By appreciating and respecting others' opinions and beliefs about a task and considering all possibilities it is much easier to come up with a successful design that accounts for all constraints" (N94604). "It's important to have an 'equal' share of thoughts and ideas. If one person 'dictates' the design process, there will be frustration by other team members, having a major impact on the design" (N94368).

The forced proximity, pressure and intensity of block delivery effected team collaboration in a number of ways. Not only did the forced proximity help to unite some teams, but the intensity was seen as an effective working method to motivate those with a tendency to procrastinate. "Because of the intensity of the week it allowed everyone to stay focused and reduced the stress I would often feel when doing an assignment. One of the things I suffer from is procrastination and I often leave things to the last minute. The nature of this camp eliminated any chance I had to procrastinate" (N94815). However, it was also noted that exhaustion and tiredness had a negative effect on groups, with some group members lowering participation later in the activities as a result of this.

Some students noted how collaboration and team success was negatively affected by ego, with low academic results being attributed to an inability of all in the group to listen to other people's ideas and see the value in them. Unproductive conflict was also attributed to individual student ego with team collaboration suffering due to the favouring of one's own ideas. "Some people were a little too attached to their ideas which caused unnecessary conflict. This caused friction in our group and made things super awkward" (N94759). "One of the problems we faced was the inability to not only listen to one another but to also value each other's ideas equally. This in my opinion was the biggest problem as I believe this heavily impacted on our low [academic] result" (N94943).

Overall, there is strong evidence to suggest that when teams contain focused, driven and enthusiastic students, collaboration is improved as this behaviour is then reflected in other team members' behavior. The data from the journals concurred with the data from the survey with evidence that students who had a positive emotional response to collaboration were academically more successful.

DISCUSSION OF RESULT

The results from the survey questions (Table 3) show strong support for collaborative activity as a learning experience. The four questions with the most positive response all relate to the value of working with other students, either as an enjoyable or motivating experience or as a successful experience for learning. In the comparisons of students with high grades and students with low grades (Table 4) the questions/responses that showed statistically significant differences were mostly related to experiential aspects of motivation, enjoyment, pleasure, and trust. That is to say those students who had a positive emotional response, and who found collaboration to be motivating and enjoyable, generally performed better in their academic grades. These findings are supported by data and analysis from the students' visual journals, as presented above. It is important to note that in the visual journals, students were providing positive feedback about motivation and enjoyment before they had received their final assessment for the journal or the unit. That being noted, while there is a strong link between these emotional aspects of the experience and academic grades, we cannot conclude that this is causal.

Intrinsic Feedback

Not only did the question "working with other students helped me to understand collaboration" return a high positive result overall, but it also showed a statistically significant difference between the students who received high grades and those who received lower grades on the second design project. This could suggest that students who learned best about collaboration from the experience of collaboration on the first design project applied what they had learned in order to collaborate better on the second project and hence achieve a higher grade. The positive and significant response to this question implies that there has been successful intrinsic feedback, about collaboration, in the project based activities. Again the feedback in the reflective journals supports this implication. While it could be suggested that students who performed better on the second project had simply learned the assessment regime better, the significant differences in the assessment tasks and the criteria for assessment would make this unlikely.

Formalised learning in a university context is usually a process of externalisation in which "tacit knowledge becomes explicit, taking the shape of metaphors, analogies, concepts, hypotheses, or models" (Nonaka & Takeuchi, 1995, p. 64). Expanding upon these conceptual models with physical experiences, such as the physical collaboration of group project work, adds an aspect of internalisation in which the previously conceptual knowledge becomes experiential through "learning by doing" (Nonaka & Takeuchi, 1995, p. 69). These physical experiences mean that students engage with a dynamic relationship between the three aspects of learning: knowledge, thinking, and doing (Sale, 2001, p. 49). The way in which students know about collaboration, think about collaboration, and do collaboration, recognises the fact that "thinking is an active process, which requires a pedagogy that is interactive and collaborative" in itself (Sale, 2001, p. 55). Student perception, through the reflective journals and the survey, supports the hypothesis that students are learning about collaboration by collaborating.

Emotional Engagement

When data from the survey is compared with data from the visual journals we found that the correlation between those students who responded very positively to aspects of enjoyment, motivation, and supporting learning, and who also received higher academic grades, is also supported by comments from the same students made at the time of collaborating. That is to say that even before the students were aware of their academic grades they had positive reflections on their collaborative experience. Typical comments from this group of high achieving students, contemporaneous with the collaborative experiences, included the following: "the experience of working in a multidisciplinary group is positive" (N94022), "our overall feel and vibe was fun and enthusiastic" (N94375) "I am really pleased with my group and how we worked" (N94803). To some extent this alleviates validity concerns that students were responding positively to their experience of collaboration only after, or because, they knew they had achieved high academic grades.

While there are several studies that have shown that good grades or marks do not necessarily indicate successful collaboration of the students who received them (Maldonado, Lee, Klemmer & Pea, 2007, p. 497), the results from the survey data presented here do suggest that students who enjoy collaboration and are motivated by working with other students do achieve higher grades. We can also see from the survey data that groups in which the decisions were made collaboratively as a team achieved significantly higher grades, and those groups in which decisions were made by a team leader achieved significantly lower grades, again showing that successful collaboration can be linked to higher academic achievement.

Intensity

If a positive emotional response is valuable for helping students learn about collaboration, then clearly the creation of an enjoyable learning environment is important to the success of the experience. The survey results, and visual journals, suggest that some students approach collaborative projects with apprehension, possibly due to negative past experiences of collaboration. The approach employed by the unit in this case study is to ask students to undertake a challenging group task in a short period of time. The combination of challenge and intensity appear to be important. A task which is challenging but achievable will build the student's confidence, both in their own abilities and in the ability of the group to meet future challenges. This suggests that the design of the task and the approach of the teaching team should work hand-in-hand to nurture confidence. A generosity in the assessment scheme may assist in this but tasks which are perceived as easy by students may backfire.

Time pressure creates a sense of urgency that discourages procrastination and encourages a shared purpose that builds group cohesion and group trust. Collaboration experiences may be unsatisfying when group members have incompatible approaches to scheduling: those who prefer to complete tasks well before a deadline are likely to be frustrated by those who wait until the last minute. An intense, short project may sidestep this issue by forcing the whole group to complete tasks immediately, in a sense at the last minute. Another aspect of intensity is the creation of immersion in the task, possibly approaching a sense of *flow* (Csikszentmihalyi, 1996), leading to fewer distractions and an increase in productivity.

Attendance on the field trip sessions, as opposed to the on-campus session, did not appear to provide any advantage to the students' academic achievement. While this is reassuring from a pedagogical point of view (the learning experiences of all sessions would appear to result in identical or near identical academic achievement) it does not support a hypothesis that there are academic advantages in the field trip experience due to its isolation from distractions, and its more intense level of collaborative social interaction. The degree of success in achieving less tangible experiential elements such as socialization and enculturation to design education norms are harder to assess and may be fruitful to explore in future research.

FUTURE RESEARCH DIRECTIONS

While this research has supported some assertions as to the value of collaborative learning in a design context, it has also shown that some previously held assumptions, about the value of the field trip experience as a unique learning environment, are not supported by this data. There are quite likely other, less tangible, benefits to the social experience of collaboration in a learning context that is outside of the campus experience; indeed much of the literature on collaboration speaks to such intangible benefits. Future research would wisely focus on such areas and investigate the indirect benefits of social networks in collaborative learning environments. It is also worth noting that the analysis conducted for this case study is all based on data collected during the collaborative learning activities or shortly afterward. A study of student perceptions and academic achievements in the longer term, two or three years later, may reveal longer lasting benefits of the collaborative experiences of this unit.

Certainly the current program, of block delivered collaborative design exercises, can be considered successful by most measures, both in terms of students learning about design and learning about collaboration. While the program of activities appears to have facilitated such learning, there is more to be investigated around the qualities of the physical environment that supports it.

CONCLUSION

The data and findings from the student survey and visual journals all points to the success of this case study program as a collaborative learning experience. This data also reinforces the analysis of the program as a successful learning project, as presented in the analysis of Table 2. Traits and activities that are explicit in the three pedagogical models were repeatedly referenced by students in their reflections: critical thinking, collaboration, apprehension, negotiation, experimenting, intrinsic feedback, discussion and debating, expression, reviewing and planning, and having an experience. This case study has shown good alignment of the program with established theoretical models.

Qualitative analysis, from the coding of the data in the student visual journals, and quantitative analysis of data in the student surveys, both supported a number of findings:

- The physical location of the activities (field trip or on-campus) did not affect academic results
- The physical location of the activities (field trip or on-campus) did not affect the students' perceptions of their collaborative experiences
- Students who indicated that they had a more positive emotional experience of collaboration generally performed better academically
- Students who indicated that they understood collaboration better through the act of working with other students generally performed better in the second project

Findings from this research support the notion that successful collaboration is achieved through a joint process where authority is shared (Mattessich and Monsey, 1992) and a non-hierarchical approach is adopted (Poggenpohl, 2004, p. 144). This research also supports the notion and success of learning about collaboration through the act of experiencing collaboration; there is a strong correlation, both qualitatively and quantitatively, between the understanding of collaboration (as evidenced in visual journals), the student perceptions of collaboration (in the data of the survey), and the success of actually collaborating in practice (as assessed through academic performance).

Short, intensive collaborative experiences can be useful in learning about collaboration. Intensive-mode delivery encourages a more positive experience of collaboration through forced proximity. This sidesteps some of the factors that typically lead to negative group collaborations such as poor group attendance, misaligned time usage, and other commitments which distract group members. Social loafing can still occur but it is more conspicuous in an intensive mode and therefore peer group pressure tends to mitigate it somewhat. Emotional engagement and enjoyment appear to be significant factors in learning about collaboration. This suggests that positive experiences build group cohesion and therefore trust and confidence in the group. Effective communication as a team can create better group cohesion and project results while early prototyping and testing helps students to reach an agreement and create better project results. Good 'people skills' was also identified as an intrinsic element to team success and good collaboration.

This study has explored the distinction between the theory of knowing about something, in this case understanding collaboration, and the practical application of knowing how to do something, in this case being able to collaborate (Shon, 1984, p. 4). We can conclude that design students tend to be experiential learners, even novice design students. Learning about collaboration through collaborative experiences suits them.

REFERENCES

Barron, B. (2000). Achieving Coordination in Collaborative Problem-Solving Groups. *Journal of the Learning Sciences*, 9(4), 403–436. doi:10.1207/S15327809JLS0904_2

Barron, B. (2003). When smart groups fail. *Journal of the Learning Sciences, 12*(3), 307–359. doi:10.1207/S15327809JLS1203_1

Barron, B. J., Schwartz, D. L., Vye, N. J., Moore, A., Petrosino, A., Zech, L., & Bransford, J. D. (1998). Doing with understanding: Lessons from research on problem-and project-based learning. *Journal of the Learning Sciences, 7*(3-4), 271–311. doi:10.1080/10508406.1998.9672056

Barros, B., & Verdejo, M. F. (2000). Analysing student interaction processes in order to improve collaboration. The DEGREE approach. *International Journal of Artificial Intelligence in Education, 11*(3), 221–241.

Bravo, C., Redondo, M. A., Ortega, M., & Verdejo, M. F. (2006). Collaborative environments for the learning of design: A model and a case study in Domotics. *Computers & Education, 46*(2), 152–173. doi:10.1016/j.compedu.2004.07.009

Crowther, P. (2013). Understanding the signature pedagogy of the design studio and the opportunities for its technological enhancement. *Journal of Learning Design, 6*(3), 18–28. doi:10.5204/jld.v6i3.155

Csikszentmihalyi, M. (1996). *Creativity: flow and the psychology of discovery and invention.* New York: Harper Collins Publishers.

Delahaye, B. L. (2005). *Human Resource Development: Adult Learning and Knowledge Management.* Brisbane: John Wiley & Sons.

Doise, W. (1990). The development of individual competencies through social interaction. In H. C. Foot, M. J. Morgan, & R. H. Shute (Eds.), *Children helping children* (pp. 43–64). Chichester: J. Wiley & sons.

Donato, R. (2004). 13. Aspects of Collaboration in Pedagogical Discourse. *Annual Review of Applied Linguistics, 24*, 284–302. doi:10.1017/S026719050400011X

Dorta, T., Lesage, A., & Di Bartolo, C. (2012). Collaboration and design education through the interconnected HIS. *Physical Digitality:Proceedings of the eCAADe* (Vol. 2, pp. 97-105).

Heufler, G. (2004). *Design basics.* Zurich: Niggli Verlag.

Honey, P., & Mumford, A. (1992). *The manual of learning styles.* Maidenhead: Peter Honey.

Jonassen, D., & Reeves, T. C. (1996). Learning with technology: Using computers as cognitive tools. In D. Jonassen (Ed.), *Handbook of research for educational communications and technology: a project of the Association for Educational Communications and Technology.* New York: Macmillan Library Reference.

Kvan, T. (2000). Collaborative design: What is it? *Automation in Construction, 9*(4), 409–415. doi:10.1016/S0926-5805(99)00025-4

Lauche, K., Bohemia, E., Connor, C., & Badke-Schaub, P. (2008). Distributed collaboration in design education: Practising designer and client roles. *Journal of Desert Research, 7*(3), 238–258. doi:10.1504/JDR.2008.024193

Laurillard, D. (2002). *Rethinking university teaching: A conversational framework for the effective use of learning technologies* (2nd ed.). London, New York: Routledge. doi:10.4324/9780203304846

Laurillard, D., & McAndrew, P. (2002). Virtual Teaching Tool: Bringing academics closer to the design of e-learning. In S. Banks, P. Goodyear, V. Hodgson and D. McConnell (Eds.) *Network Learning 2002: A Research Based Conference on e-Learning in Higher Education and Lifelong Learning*. Retrieved from http://kn.open.ac.uk/public/document.cfm?docid=7243

Lou, Y. (2004). Learning to solve complex problems through between-group collaboration in project-based online courses. *Distance Education, 25*(1), 49–66. doi:10.1080/0158791042000212459

Maldonado, H., Lee, B., Klemmer, S. R., & Pea, R. D. (2007). Patterns of Collaboration in Design Courses: Team dynamics affect technology appropriation, artefact creation, and course performance. *Proceedings of the 8th international conference on Computer supported collaborative learning* (pp. 490-499). International Society of the Learning Sciences. doi:10.3115/1599600.1599690

Mattessich, P. W., & Monsey, B. R. (1992). *Collaboration: What Makes It Work*. St. Paul, MN: Amherst H. Wilder Foundation.

Nelson, L. M. (2013). Collaborative Problem Solving. In C. M. Reigeluth (Ed.), *Instructional-design theories and models: A new paradigm of instructional theory 2* (pp. 241–267). Hoboken, Pennsylvania: Taylor and Francis.

Nonaka, I., & Takeuchi, H. (1995). *The knowledge-creating company: How Japanese companies create the dynamics of innovation*. Oxford: Oxford university press.

O'Brien, W., Soibelman, L., & Elvin, G. (2003). Collaborative design processes: An active and reflective learning course in multidisciplinary collaboration. *Journal of Construction Education, 8*(2), 78–93.

Pea, R. D. (1993). Practices of distributed intelligence and designs for education. In G. Salmon (Ed.), *Distributed cognitions: Psychological and educational considerations* (pp. 47–87). Cambridge: Cambridge University Press.

Poggenpohl, S. H. (2004). Practicing collaboration in design. *Visible Language, 38*(2), 138–157.

Sale, D. (2001). Designing a 'Thinking Curriculum' in the Classroom. *Curriculum and Teaching, 16*(1), 45–57. doi:10.7459/ct/16.1.04

Schon, D. A. (1984). The Architectural Studio as an Exemplar of Education for Reflection-in-Action. *Journal of Architectural Education, 38*(1), 2–9. doi:10.1080/10464883.1984.10758345

Shaffer, D. W. (1997). Design, collaboration, and computation: The design studio as a model for computer supported collaboration in mathematics.*Proceedings of the 2nd international conference on Computer support for collaborative learning* (pp. 253-258). International Society of the Learning Sciences. doi:10.3115/1599773.1599804

Shreeve, A., Sims, E. A. R., & Trowler, P. (2010). A kind of exchange: Learning from art and design teaching. *Higher Education Research & Development,29*(2), 125–138. doi:10.1080/07294360903384269

Shulman, L. S. (2005). Signature pedagogies in the professions. *Daedalus, 134*(3), 52–59. doi:10.1162/0011526054622015

Toohey, S. (1999). *Designing courses for higher education.* Buckingham: Society for Research into Higher Education/Open University.

Vygotsky, L. S. (1978). *Mind in society: The development of higher psychological processes.* Cambridge, Massachusetts: Harvard university press.

KEY TERMS AND DEFINITIONS

Block Delivery: Delivery of teaching content and learning experiences in a relatively short period of time, perhaps three or five weeks, in contrast to the typical three of four-month duration of standard university semesters.

Intensive Mode: A concentrated learning experience typically spanning one or more days uninterrupted by other activities or distractions; usually employed to create focused, highly immersive and engaging student experiences.

Multi-Disciplinary: Describing an activity, or a collaborative team, that includes representatives of more than one discipline or profession, working together.

Project Based Learning: A teaching method in which students learn by working over a period of time on a complex, 'wicked' problem with no specific right or wrong answer; can be similar to, or sometimes referred to, as Problem Based Learning.

Reflective Journal: A diary like journal in which students record their thoughts about learning activities after the activity. For design students these are often heavily biased to visual recording.

t-**Test:** Also referred to as "Students *t*-Test, is a statistical method of identifying significant difference between two groups of participants/data; by analyzing means and standard deviations.

Chapter 7

An Evaluation of Group Work in First-Year Engineering Design Education

Stuart Palmer
Deakin University, Australia

Wayne Hall
Griffith University, Australia

ABSTRACT

It is argued that 'design' is an essential characteristic of engineering practice, and hence, an essential theme of engineering education. It is suggested that first-year design courses enhance commencing student motivation and retention, and introduce engineering application content and basic design experience early in the curriculum. The research literature indicates that engineering design practice is a deeply social process, with collaboration and group interactions required at almost every stage. This chapter documents the evaluation of the initial and subsequent second offerings of a first-year engineering design unit at Griffith University in Australia. The unit 1006ENG Design and Professional Skills aims to provide an introduction to engineering design and professional practice through a project-based approach to problem solving. The unit learning design incorporates student group work, and uses self-and-peer-assessment to incorporate aspects of the design process into the unit assessment and to provide a mechanism for individualization of student marks.

INTRODUCTION

It is often argued that 'design' is an (perhaps the) essential characteristic of engineering practice, and hence, an essential theme of engineering education (Atman, Kilgore, & McKenna, 2008; Dym, Agogino, Eris, Frey, & Leifer, 2005; Schubert, Jacobitz, & Kim, 2012). Some authors claim a level of consensus regarding the elements of engineering design (Hubka & Eder, 1987), and a range of normative framings of engineering design can be found (Dym et al., 2005; Howard, Culley, & Dekoninck, 2008; Salter & Gann, 2003; Schubert et al., 2012). Comparative definitions also exist that position engineering design

DOI: 10.4018/978-1-5225-0726-0.ch007

in relation to other types of design, i.e., architectural design and computer programming (Lloyd & Scott, 1994). It is often claimed that, "Design requires unique knowledge, skills, and attitudes common to all engineering disciplines, and it is these attributes that distinguish engineering as a profession." (Atman et al., 2008, p. 309) Hence it is not surprising to see engineering design identified as a key element of engineering education:

Engineering design is a critical element of engineering education and a competency that students need to acquire. (Atman et al., 2007, p. 359)

... the purpose of engineering education is to graduate engineers who can design, and that design thinking is complex. (Dym et al., 2005, p. 103)

Typically, exposure to aspects of design are distributed throughout the undergraduate engineering curriculum (Davis, Gentili, Trevisan, & Calkins, 2002). Student design projects have long been used as a key pedagogical element for the development of engineering student design skills and knowledge. Traditionally, these have taken two complementary forms:

- **Final-Year Design Courses:** Open referred to as 'capstone' design courses (Dutson, Todd, Magleby, & Sorensen, 1997); and
- **First-Year Design Courses:** Often referred to as 'cornerstone' design courses.

Cornerstone design courses arose as a response to perceptions that first-year engineering curricular, historically loaded with math, physics and other theoretical foundation studies, often left commencing students wondering what engineers actually do. It is suggested that first-year design courses enhance commencing student motivation and retention, and introduce engineering application content and basic design experience early in the curriculum (Dym et al., 2005).

Computer-Aided Design (CAD) has been a part of engineering design since the 1960s, and by the 1990s developments in low-cost computer hardware and electronic communications made CAD a ubiquitous element of engineering design (Salter & Gann, 2003). CAD was traditionally associated with the production of design drawings and other documentation, but CAD can be used in all phases of the engineering design process (Hubka & Eder, 1987). Even if only for the documentation of engineering design concepts, CAD plays an important role as an enabler of group design work via the formal representation of design information in a standard and unambiguous form that minimizes errors in the sharing of design concepts between members of the design team (Brereton & McGarry, 2000). In engineering education, evidence of the close association between engineering design and CAD can be observed in the commonly found pairing of training in the use of CAD systems combined with introductory engineering design theory and practice in a single unit of study.

There is evidence that experienced engineers carry out design activities in qualitatively different ways to novice or less experienced engineers. And, if engineering students are considered as 'student engineers', a similar growth in sophistication in engineering design output has been observed between junior and senior students. As part of a longitudinal investigation into undergraduate engineering student design performance, data were collected on how both freshmen (commencing) and senior students conducted design exercises (Atman, Cardella, Turns, & Adams, 2005; Atman, Chimka, Bursic, & Nachtmann, 1999). It was observed that senior student performance was better than freshman performance with respect to several design elements, with senior student design behavior tending to be more sophisticated than freshmen, and seniors tending to produce higher quality design solutions. The authors noted a number of implications for appropriate teaching strategies for first-year engineering design students to encourage them to iterate through all the steps in the design process, develop multiple alternatives and gather information.

Engineering design is, in most cases, performed by groups of individuals who, "must know how to discuss, deliberate and negotiate with others if their individual proposals and claims are to be taken into account and have meaning." (Bucciarelli, 2002, p. 220) Baird, Moore, and Jagodzinski (2000) note, "… engineering design is not a mechanistic process which can be fully described in a manual, but a complex and elaborate socially-mediated activity of which much is tacit." (p. 333) In ethnographic studies of the engineering design processes in two engineering firms, Bucciarelli (1988) observed that, "… different participants think about the work on the design in quite different ways. They do not share fully congruent internal representations of the design. In this sense the design at any time in the design process is more than the sum, or simple synthesis, of its participants' interpretation. In this sense it is a social construction." (p167) Bucciarelli (2002) further observed that compromise and mediation may be required between design group members to bring a complex engineering design to resolution - "Different participants work in different domains on different features of the system; they have different responsibilities and more often than not, the creations, findings, claims and proposals of one individual will conflict with those of another. Negotiation and trade-offs are required to bring participants' efforts into coherence." (p. 220) In a different ethnographic study of engineering design processes, Lloyd (2000) concluded that, "… a design process is as much about key social points—a particular meeting, a talk with the customer, a chat among several engineers … It was also of note that activities which are often thought of as individual—drawing, sketching, listing requirements, etc.—add to the narrative of a particular design project by producing objects for communication and discussion, and these objects contribute to the ongoing discourse. There can be very few parts of an engineering design process that are not socially explored." (p. 371)

So, while much literature observes engineering design as 'simply' a technical process of optimization, in reality it is deeply social activity that helps organize the process to transform design requirements into reality (Lloyd, 2000). The more complex the engineering design process, the more important conversations with other designers become (Salter & Gann, 2003). For these reasons, as well as a practical response to large class sizes, engineering design projects commonly involve student group work. The terms 'group work' and 'teamwork' are commonly used interchangeably in the research literature, however some authors make a technical distinction between group work and teamwork. The essential difference is typically expressed as, the former encompasses situations where a number of students work separately on different aspects of a project and then combine their work with minimal consideration, whereas the latter situation involves on-going joint work in a collaborative environment where members actively contribute to team cohesion and task achievement (Oakley, Felder, Brent, & Elhajj, 2004). Student engineering design projects might conceivably include both of these modes of work at different phases. While cognizant of the distinction in terminology, for simplicity, hereafter the authors will refer generically to group work.

There is a range of established methods for assessing group work generically, however assessment that reflects a student's contribution as an effective group member is still not well-developed in many engineering pedagogies, which typically focus on individual performance (Dym et al., 2005). As noted by Atman et al. (1999), in assessing engineering design, both the quality (however defined) of the final design artefact, as well as the nature of the design processes used by students, are of interest. It is important to explicitly assess both of these aspects, as a post facto evaluation of the final design output reveals little about the design processes from which it arose (Bucciarelli, 1988; Dym et al., 2005). One approach to the evaluation and assessment of individual contributions to a group design effort is through the use of peer review (Dutson et al., 1997). One comprehensive form of student peer review is self-and-peer-assessment (SAPA) (Tucker, Fermelis, & Palmer, 2009).

At its most basic, SAPA involves students providing an evaluation for all group members, including themselves, of the individual contribution of each group member to the group work process. If group members are aware that their group contribution is to be assessed there may be less 'free-riding' (Johnston & Miles, 2004) and the requirement of providing performance feedback to other group members may make one focus on improving one's own performance (Davies, 2000; Freeman & McKenzie, 2002). Additionally, SAPA provides a mechanism for the individualization of student results, typically using the student SAPA ratings to compute an individual scaling factor for each group member that is then used to convert the overall mark for the group output into marks for each student (Freeman & McKenzie, 2002; Willey & Gardner, 2007). While the presence of an explicit process for individualization of marks may promote good group work behaviors, it is observed that the individualization factors typically derived through SAPA don't generally lead to dramatic modification of individual marks (Johnston & Miles, 2004).

There exists a range of pedagogical models, badged with a range of names, for teaching engineering design, for example: problem-based learning (Al-Abdeli & Bullen, 2006; Atman et al., 1999); design-based learning (Gómez Puente, van Eijck, & Jochems, 2011); conceive-design-implement-operate (CDIO) (Agouridas, 2007; Cárdenas, 2009; Dym et al., 2005); problem-oriented project-based learning (Gómez Puente et al., 2011; Kolmos, 2002); social design based learning (Cárdenas, 2009); and project-oriented, design-based learning (Chandrasekaran, Stojcevski, Littlefair, & Joordens, 2013). However, generically, one of the most common is project-based learning (PBL) (Agouridas, 2007). There are many case studies of PBL in the research literature, but they are often simple descriptions of the course learning designs – detailed evaluations are much rarer (Helle, Tynjälä, & Olkinuora, 2006). This chapter draws on previously reported evaluations of the initial and subsequent second offerings of a first-year engineering design unit at Griffith University in Australia, provides a theoretical context for the unit, and consolidates the evaluation findings. The unit 1006ENG Design and Professional Skills aims to provide an introduction to engineering design and professional practice through a project-based approach to problem solving. The unit learning design incorporates student group work, and uses self-and-peer-assessment to incorporate aspects of the design process into the unit assessment and to provide a mechanism for individualization of student marks. This chapter presents the rationale and context for 1006ENG, the detailed results from the two evaluations, and conclusions regarding student engagement in collaborative engineering design activities in a first-year unit.

PROJECT-BASED LEARNING FOR ENGINEERING DESIGN EDUCATION

A wide range of aims and practices are claimed under the banner of PBL (Helle et al., 2006), and the significant blurriness in the activities variously represented as PBL make a strict definition difficult (Thomas, 2000). However, in the related literature it is possible to infer a general agreement that PBL contains the following elements (Frank, Lavy, & Elata, 2003; Helle et al., 2006; Macías-Guarasa, Montero, San-Segundo, Araujo, & Nieto-Taladriz, 2006; Prince & Felder, 2006):

- Teaching staff take a supporting rather than leadership role;
- Students generally work in groups/teams to complete a design project;
- Solution of a problem or completion of a task that requires students to complete a number of educational activities that direct their learning;
- Generally, the project would involve the creation of a tangible artefact – a design, a physical model, a report, a thesis, a computer model, etc.;
- The project is non-trivial and often multidisciplinary in nature, requiring work over an extended period of time; and
- The completion of the project often includes a reporting element, either a written document and/or oral presentation.

It is useful to differentiate project-based learning from problem-based learning – the latter being a related but distinct popular group-based learning method. Problem-based learning is a pedagogy originating in medical education, where important theoretical learning is developed through the consideration (generally by student groups) of real-world scenarios that present typical 'problems' commonly encountered in professional practice (Boud & Feletti, 1998; Dym et al., 2005). Problem-based learning is also used in discipline areas such as business and law, where complex, expert decision-making is also a routine element of professional practice, and where it is used as a teaching method it may also be referred to as 'PBL'. Hereafter in this chapter in the context of engineering design education, the authors use PBL to refer to project-based learning with the characteristics described above. The benefits for student learning attributed to PBL (Doppelt, 2005; Frank et al., 2003; Helle et al., 2006; Macías-Guarasa et al., 2006; Mills & Treagust, 2003; Thomas, 2000) include:

- Experience of problem solving and the design process;
- Experience and development of group work skills;
- Coping with incomplete and imperfect information;
- Exposure to the multi-disciplinary and systems nature of design problems;
- Experience of authentic engineering problems and professional practices;
- Self-motivation and student ownership of the problem, solution and learning;
- Development of self-regulation, agency, commitment and competence;
- Development of reflective thinking skills; and
- Development of written, oral and other communication skills.

It is claimed that PBL can provide students with experiences in both divergent thinking (the generative, conceptual, know-how aspects of engineering design) and convergent thinking (the analytical, knowledge, know-why aspects of engineering design) (Dym et al., 2005). The nature of PBL makes it an important pedagogical strategy in engineering education – design can be the context for learning, an inductive mode of learning and teaching can be employed, and authentic engineering problems can be posed to students. In addition, PBL is a common pedagogy employed in secondary and primary schools internationally, hence it is a form of learning that will be familiar to many first-year engineering students (Mills & Treagust, 2003; Thomas, 2000).

Griffith University in Queensland Australia offer a number of Engineering programs on their Gold Coast and Nathan campuses. Both undergraduate and postgraduate programs are available. At an undergraduate level, three years full-time (240 credit points) Bachelor of Engineering Technology and four years full-time (320 credit points) Bachelor of Engineering with Honours programs are offered. Moreover, the flexibility of these programs presents part-time study opportunities. Double degrees and postgraduate programs offer further engineering study options. At the Gold Coast campus, only Bachelor of Engineering with Honours programs and Double degrees are offered at an undergraduate level. The five (current, 2015) Bachelor of Engineering with Honours program offerings on the Gold Coast are:

- Civil Engineering;
- Mechanical Engineering;
- Electrical and Electronic Engineering;
- Mechatronic Engineering; and
- Electronic and Biomedical Engineering.

These five programs have a common first year that includes '1006ENG Design and Professional Skills', a first-year PBL unit (see Figure 1).

As an element of the initial offering of 1006ENG it was decided to undertake a detailed evaluation of the unit. As part of the evaluation, enrolled students were surveyed to gauge their previous exposure to PBL learning experiences, and to assess their perceptions of the conduct of 1006ENG, with a particular focus on the group work aspects of the unit. Approval to conduct the survey was sought and obtained from the Griffith University Human Research Ethics Committee (GUHREC). During the development of the survey questionnaire, an independent and experienced member of the academic staff was invited to review the draft questionnaire, and based on their feedback it was refined to enhance its face validity. The questionnaire sought responses from students relating to:

- Respondent demographic information;
- Prior experience with PBL;
- Prior perceptions of key pedagogic elements of 1006ENG;
- Perceptions of the experience of aspects of 1006ENG; and
- Open-ended comments on the 'best aspects' and 'needs improvement' elements of 10065ENG.

The questionnaire that was used to collect the data is given in the Appendix. The questionnaire was administered during the final week of the semester. As required by the GUHREC approval, the questionnaire was anonymous and voluntary. Following analysis of the initial survey data, a number of refinements were made to the learning design for 1006ENG for the second unit offering. The evaluation survey was repeated for the second unit offering to collect additional student feedback, and to assess the impact of the learning design changes.

Figure 1. Bachelor of engineering with honors: common first year at Gold Coast campus

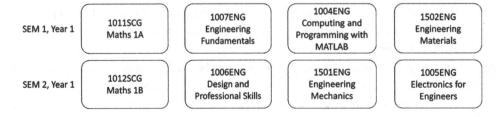

EVALUATION OF PBL IN FIRST-YEAR ENGINEERING AT GRIFFITH UNIVERSITY

1006ENG Initial Offering

The first implementation of 1006ENG Design and Professional Skills in 2010 (Palmer & Hall, 2011) aimed to provide a greater focus on learner-led activities in Griffith's undergraduate engineering programs on the Gold Coast campus. In this unit the learning design attempted to move away from instructor-led activities that were theoretical and prescriptive to self-directed student tasks. The initial offering of the unit focused on developing engineering design skills (and the relevant graduate attributes) in three core engineering disciplines:

- Mechanical engineering;
- Electrical/electronic engineering; and
- Civil engineering.

These three core disciplines were fundamental to all Gold Coast campus offerings at that time (and are still relevant now). They underpinned all of the program offerings at the time Design and Professional Skills was introduced in 2010 and remain the central focus of the five current undergraduate offerings mentioned above.

A lecture series was used to support the engineering design and professional skills activities. Three design project activities were embedded in the unit, one activity for each of the core disciplines. The mechanical offering focused on the design and build activity of a mousetrap racer; the electrical/electronic project required the students to design and build a small linear accelerator; and the civil design project focused on the construction of a geometric scale model of an urban development. It has been proposed that the use of a series of 'mini' design projects can enhance PBL, particularly at the foundation level where it provides students multiple opportunities to experience and develop project skills (Frank et al., 2003; Macías-Guarasa et al., 2006). These three design activities each required a group-based submission for a preliminary and a final design report (3 x 25% of the unit). To assist students to understand the expectations for each of these design projects, a rubric was provided. The rubric clearly articulated the assessment criteria and the corresponding levels of quality, ranging from low quality (poor) to high quality (excellent). The rubrics were introduced as an efficient feedback mechanism for a large student cohort and as a means to communicate design project expectations. The rubrics also provided an opportunity for students to make realistic evaluations about their own performance and that of the other group members, especially in the context of a using SAPA as an element of the assessment.

Students were permitted to choose the members of their groups, and were requested to reflect on the performance of all group members, and to include with their final project report a SAPA rating for each group member, including themselves. In this instance, the primary intention of the SAPA rating was to provide a mechanism for individualization of the assessment for each member in the group design projects. Students were provided with a rubric guide for making their SAPA ratings: ratings were out of 10, with up to 2 marks awarded for participation/attendance, 4 marks for the quantity of work produced and 4 marks for perceived quality of the work. Provision of SAPA ratings by students was optional, and non-submission of a rating was taken as an implied equal rating for group members. The individualized design report mark was calculated using Equation 1.

$$\text{Final Report Mark} \times \frac{\text{Total Peer Assessment Mark (for student in question)}}{\text{Total Peer Assessment Mark (for best performing student)}} \tag{1}$$

In addition, students were required to provide individual CAD drawings for one of the projects (15% of the unit) and were supported in this activity with basic CAD classes (with an attendance 'hurdle' requirement to encourage student participation, but no summative marks). Moreover, an oral presentation on one of the design projects was required. The presentation was performed in a group, but students were marked individually. The unit therefore considered a broad-based design curriculum with embedded professional skills activities (for example group work, and written and oral communication). Table 1 summarizes the assessment design.

Table 2 gives a summary of the demographic and other information about the survey respondent group for which the corresponding information was known about the entire enrolled 1006ENG class. The overall response rate from the initial survey group was 30.4 per cent – 72 out of a unit enrolment of 237. For the demographic dimensions of gender and enrolled program, the exact, two-sided version of Fisher's test was used to compare the proportions of respondents and the entire enrolled class, to assess the representativeness of the survey respondent group. Fisher's exact test provides a test of the contingency (association) between two kinds of classification. The test is suitable even when sample sizes are small, and, it makes no assumptions about the source data other than that the variable categories (i.e., gender and student group, enrolled program and student group, etc.) are not associated. If there were non-respondents in any category the sum of the frequencies will be less than 72. Table 3 gives the mean and standard deviation for student responses to the questionnaire scale items. As noted in the Appendix, all questionnaire scale items were rated by students on a scale of 1(minimum agreement) to 5 (maximum agreement). For all statistical testing presented, the authors use a p value of less than 0.01 to indicate a significant result – that is, it is demanded that the probability of the observed statistical test result occurring by chance alone be less than one in one hundred before the result is classified as significant. The respondent open-ended comments were analyzed to identify common themes which were tallied and ranked, as show in Table 4.

Table 2 shows that, based on Fisher's exact test, there was no significant difference between the respondent sample and overall enrolled student population on the demographic dimensions of gender and enrolled program. The relatively large number of respondents and good match on known demographic

Table 1. Summary of 1006ENG unit assessment design

Assessment Item	Marks Weighting	Description
Preliminary design report for Project 1	3	Group mark
Final design report for Project 1	22	Group mark plus SAPA
Preliminary design report for Project 2	3	Group mark
Final design report for Project 2	22	Group mark plus SAPA
Preliminary design report for Project 3	3	Group mark
Final design report for Project 3	22	Group mark plus SAPA
CAD drawings for Project 1, 2 or 3	15	Individual mark
Oral presentation for Project 1, 2 or 3	10	Group delivery, but individual mark

Table 2. Demographic and other information about the initial survey respondent group

	Sample	Population	Significance / etc.
Number of Respondents	72	237	30.4%
Gender			Fisher's exact test $p > 0.33$
Female	8	18	
Male	63	219	
Enrolled Program			Fisher's exact test $p > 0.35$
Engineering	50	176	
Engineering Technology	6	19	
Engineering with Advanced Studies	6	13	
Engineering / Science	3	6	
Engineering / Information Technology	1	2	
Engineering / Business	3	9	
Other	0	12	
Previous Experience with PBL?			
Yes	29		42.7%
No	33		48.5%
Not sure	6		8.8%

characteristics provides some confidence that the respondent sample is representative, and that inferences about the overall enrolled student group can be made based on the respondent data. About one half of respondents indicated having no previous experience with PBL, suggesting that providing clear information to the class about the purpose and processes of PBL would be very important. Examining Table 3 shows that many of the mean ratings for the questionnaire scale items are similar. In a similar investigation of PBL in an 'early years' context (first and second year of an engineering program), the overall mean rating for enjoyment reported by students was 3.79 (out of 5) (Edward, 2004) – similar to the 3.46 observed here for the 'overall' scale item. Based on estimating 99 per cent confidence intervals

Table 3. Mean ratings for scale items from the initial survey respondent group

Questionnaire Item	Mean	Std Dev
Do you enjoy working in groups/teams?	3.43	0.93
Do you enjoy giving oral presentations?	2.65	1.21
Did you understand what you needed to do for the design project assignments?	3.51	0.86
Were you able to find the information you needed to complete the design project assignments?	3.72	0.84
Did your group work well together on all design project assignments?	3.36	1.24
Was your group presentation successful?	3.53	0.93
Were you satisfied with the designs produced by your group?	3.67	0.95
Overall, was 1006ENG an enjoyable learning experience?	3.46	0.96
Did 1006ENG increase your knowledge of engineering design & professional skills?	3.63	0.98

Table 4. Themes from open-ended comments ranked by frequency for initial survey respondent group

Best Aspects	Frequency	Needs Improvement	Frequency
Group work	18	More time on project work	11
Hands on / practical	16	More instruction on CAD	11
No exam	11	Better explanation of expectations	10
Projects enjoyable	7	Less emphasis on group marks	5
Less lectures	6	Smaller groups	4
CAD	5	More background on principles behind projects	4
Mousetrap car	4	More even participation on groups	3
Variety of projects	4	Faster feedback	3
Meeting new peers	4	Spread assessment due dates better	3
Helpful staff	3	More consistency in marking	2
Exposure to engineering work	3	Unit more organized	2
Group shared workload	2	Support for design report writing	2
Independent studies	2	More lectures	2
Linear accelerator	1	Guidelines for group operation	1
Regular assessment	1	More feedback	1
Problem solving	1	More help from demonstrators	1
Appropriate difficulty	1	Choice in projects	1
Group motivated me to work	1	Relate projects better to discipline areas	1
Develop group skills	1	More scope for variation in designs	1
Presentation	1	Fewer projects	1
Workload	1	Workload too heavy	1
Presentation skills	1	Blind peer review not 'blind'	1
Good resources	1	More general support for students	1
Project guides comprehensive	1	Minimize/drop lectures	1
Civil project	1	Prize for best mousetrap racer	1
Engineering reporting	1	Activities to meet peers prior to group selection	1
Design work	1		

for the mean ratings given in Table 3, only one item is significantly different from the rest – the scale item 'Do you enjoy giving oral presentations?' is significantly lower than all others. Previously in the literature it has been noted that many engineering students report not enjoying public speaking (Beer, 2002). Additionally, a similar result as was observed here was also observed in another first-year engineering design unit – students found the experience enjoyable but disliked oral presentations the most (Hanesian & Perna, 1999). While it was observed that the scale item for enjoyment of oral presentations produced the lowest mean rating, the mean rating for the scale item 'Was your group presentation successful?' was significantly higher. This provides some evidence that the procedures adopted for the oral presentation element of the unit helped students work through the development and delivery of their oral presentations as a learning activity in a productive way.

A test was undertaken to determine if there were any significant differences in the mean ratings given to any scale items by different groups of student respondents, i.e., mean rating difference by: gender; enrolled program; intended study major; and previous PBL experience. An analysis of variance (ANOVA) test was used to compare the mean ratings of all questionnaire scale items against each respondent category. The ANOVA test assumes that the distribution of values in each category is approximately normal, and that the variance of the values in each category is approximately the same. The ANOVA test is relatively robust to departures from normality in the test data, and Levene's test of homogeneity of variance can be used to assess if the variance is significantly different between respondent categories. In all cases, Levene's test of the homogeneity of variance indicated no significant difference in the variance of scale item ratings between categorical groups. In many cases the mean ratings were essentially identical between respondent groups, and the ANOVA tests showed that there were no significant differences in mean scale item ratings between any groups. This provides some evidence that most students were able to participate in, and experienced, the unit in essentially the same way, regardless of gender, enrolled program, previous experience with PBL, etc. Other investigations have also found that PBL/design projects can be a supportive pedagogy for diverse engineering student cohorts to participate equitably (Du & Kolmos, 2009; Lumsdaine, Shelnutt, & Lumsdaine, 1999).

Some of the 'best aspects' themes reported by students are also found in the literature on student evaluations of PBL, including:

- Students perceived group work as valuable (Dym et al., 2005);
- Use of 'real world' practical applications (Edward, 2004; Mills & Treagust, 2003);
- Assessment moved from summative examination to assessed project work;
- Exposure to aspects of professional engineering and engineering work; and
- Experiencing helpful teaching and support staff (Frank et al., 2003).

Likewise for some of the 'needs improvement' themes:

- High time demands of project work;
- Issues with group members who did not pull their weight (Mills & Treagust, 2003);
- Need for an introduction to, and preparation for, group work; and
- Need for instruction on engineering/design report writing (Frank et al., 2003).

1006ENG Second Offering

Following the initial offering of the unit in 2010, some revisions were made to the unit learning design in response to the 'Needs Improvement' issues identified by students (see Table 4) (Hall, Palmer, & Bennett, 2012). To provide 'more time on project work' and less emphasis on 'group marks', the unit was restructured and only two projects (the mechanical and civil engineering projects) were offered. This was a reduction from the original three projects. This reduction allowed students to become more involved in each of the two projects, whilst also facilitating a reduction of the overall weighting of 'group marks'. The geometric scale model of an urban project development was offered as the first of the two projects and the mousetrap racer project second. While the intention was to offer the initial three projects on a rotating basis in the future, changes in the administration of the unit have seen only the mechanical engineering and civil engineering project pair used in subsequent offerings of 1006ENG. Furthermore, there was a redistribution of the marks with a higher proportion on offer for the second project (the civil project was worth 25% and the mechanical project was worth 35% of the available unit marks (see Table 5). This approach allowed the students to reflect on their initial performance and consider where they might be able to improve for the project with the greater percentage weighting. To address the need for 'More Instruction on CAD' summative assessment items for the basic tuition classes were included (worth 10% of the unit) and there was a requirement to submit CAD drawing for both design projects (worth 20% of the unit). A total of 30% of the unit marks was therefore available for the CAD component. The oral presentation remained unchanged in its structure. To address the student request for 'a better explanation of the expectations', a single point of contact (i.e. the Unit Chair / Course Convener) was instituted for all technical and administrative issues related to the design projects. Previously, an academic staff member was directly responsible for technical aspects of each project, whilst the Unit Chair was responsible for all administration issues.

A limitation of the initial SAPA system for individualizing student marks (see Equation 1) was that students were not able to attain an individual mark for the final design reports that was higher than the overall report mark assigned by the marking tutor. So while low performing students might have their report mark scaled down, a student who contributed a more significant share of the group design work could never score higher than the tutor's overall mark for the report. In the second offering of 1006ENG a revised SAPA strategy was used, adapted from Willmot and Crawford (2004). In the revised scheme, a weighting factor was derived for each group member based on the total SAPA score they received from the group divided by the mean group SAPA score, as given in Equation 2, and this weighting factor was applied to 50 per cent of the final report mark as assessed by the tutor, producing an individualized report mark as given by Equation 3.

$$Wf = \left(\frac{\sum SAPA}{\text{mean} \left(\sum SAPA \right)} \right) \tag{2}$$

Final Report Mark $(0.5 + 0.5Wf)$ (3)

This presented the opportunity for higher performing students (as assessed by the group members via SAPA) to achieve individual marks that were more representative of their contributions to the design

Table 5. Summary of revised 1006ENG unit assessment design

Assessment Item	Marks Weighting	Description
Preliminary design report for Project 1	3	Group mark
Final design report for Project 1	22	Group mark plus SAPA
Preliminary design report for Project 2	3	Group mark
Final design report for Project 2	32	Group mark plus SAPA
CAD drawings for Project 1 and 2	30	Individual mark
Oral presentation for on Project 1 or 2	10	Group delivery, but individual mark

project. It was an attempt to provide a fairer distribution of group work marks. Table 5 summarizes the revised assessment design.

Adopting a similar data analysis methodology to that used above for the initial offering of 1006ENG, Table 6 gives a summary of the demographic and other information about the survey respondent group for which the corresponding information was known about the entire enrolled 1006ENG class. The overall response rate from the follow-up survey group was 80.1 per cent – 205 out of a unit enrolment of 256. For the demographic dimensions of gender and enrolled program, the exact, two-sided version of Fisher's test was used to compare the proportions of respondents and the entire enrolled class, to assess the representativeness of the survey respondent group. If there were non-respondents in any category the sum of the frequencies will be less than 205. Table 7 gives the mean and standard deviation for student responses to the questionnaire scale items. The respondent open-ended comments were analyzed to identify common themes which were tallied and ranked, as show in Table 8.

Table 6 shows that, based on Fisher's exact test, there was no significant difference between the respondent sample and overall enrolled student population on the demographic dimensions of gender and enrolled program. The large number of respondents, the high response rate and the good match on known demographic characteristics again provides confidence that the respondent sample is representative, and that inferences about the overall enrolled student group can be made based on the respondent data. About one half of respondents indicated having either no previous experience with PBL or where unsure, confirming the previous finding that providing clear information to the class about the purpose and processes of PBL is very important. Examining Table 7 shows that, as for the initial offering of 1006ENG, while the mean rating for most scale items are similar, the mean rating for the scale item 'Do

Table 6. Demographic and other information about the follow-up survey respondent group

	Sample	Population	Significance / etc.
Number of Respondents	205	256	80.1%
Gender			Fisher's exact test $p > 0.52$
Female	18	22	
Male	185	234	
Enrolled Program			Fisher's exact test $p > 0.167$
Engineering	151	190	
Engineering Technology	10	15	
Engineering with Advanced Studies	2	14	
Engineering / Science	4	6	
Engineering / Information Technology	4	8	
Engineering / Business	7	11	
Other	4	12	
Previous Experience with PBL?			
Yes	100		49.3%
No	76		37.4%
Not sure	27		13.3%

Table 7. Mean ratings for scale items from the follow-up survey respondent group

Questionnaire Item	Mean	Std Dev
Do you enjoy working in groups/teams?	3.56	0.96
Do you enjoy giving oral presentations?	2.80	1.22
Did you understand what you needed to do for the design project assignments?	3.96	0.77
Were you able to find the information you needed to complete the design project assignments?	4.07	0.76
Did your group work well together on all design project assignments?	3.76	1.00
Was your group presentation successful?	3.67	0.88
Were you satisfied with the designs produced by your group?	3.84	0.92
Overall, was 1006ENG an enjoyable learning experience?	3.82	0.84
Did 1006ENG increase your knowledge of engineering design & professional skills?	3.86	0.96

Table 8. Themes from open-ended comments ranked by frequency for follow-up survey respondent group

Best Aspects	Frequency	Needs Improvement	Frequency
Group work	31	More instruction on CAD	33
Hands on / practical	31	Nothing	22
Projects enjoyable	31	Improve CAD section	20
Helpful staff	30	Better explanation of expectations	9
No exam	13	More time in laboratories	8
Design work	13	Too much CAD work	7
CAD	12	Delete/improve oral presentation	7
Presentation	10	Grouping system / management	6
Mousetrap car	9	More even participation on groups	5
General	9	Choice in projects	5
Explanation of theory	9	Workload too heavy	5
Exposure to engineering work	7	CAD software problems	5
Fair group assessment	6	Civil project	4
Less/Quick lectures	5	Match CAD to projects (timings)	3
Problem solving	5	Spread assessment due dates better	2
Variety of projects	3	More feedback	2
Meeting new peers	3	Less CAD marks	2
Workload	2	Too much/hard assessment	2
Civil project	2	Better explanation of Matlab	2
Research skills	2	SAPA system unfair	2
Feedback	2	Others (21) (single response)	1
Well organized / clear expectations	2		
Develop group skills	1		
Engineering reporting	1		
Others (4) (single response)	1		

you enjoy giving oral presentations?' is significantly lower than all others – comparatively speaking, once again, students had an aversion to public speaking.

Comparing the results Table 7 to those in Table 3, it can be seen that the mean rating for each scale item was higher in the follow-up offering of 1006ENG. A t-test of means was used to compare the mean ratings obtained in the initial and follow-up offerings, for each of the questionnaire scale items. Like the ANOVA test, the t-test assumes that the distribution of values in each group is approximately normal, that the variance of the values in each group is approximately the same, and the t-test is relatively robust to departures from normality in the test data. As for the ANOVA test, Levene's test of homogeneity of variance can be used to assess if the variance is significantly different between respondent groups. Only two scale items had significantly different variances between the initial and follow-up offerings – 'Did you understand what you needed to do for the design project assignments?' and 'Did your group work well together on all design project assignments?' For these two scale items, a modified t-test based on the Welch statistic was used. Welch's t-test is similar to a standard t-test, except that the test statistic t and the associated degrees of freedom (F – a test parameter based on the sample sizes) are computed using methods that account for unequal sample variances. Based on the appropriate t-test, there were three questionnaire scale items that had significantly higher mean ratings in the follow-up offering of 1006ENG compared to the initial offering, these were:

- "Did you understand what you needed to do for the design project assignments?" ($F_{112.9} = 15.8$; $p < 0.0002$);
- "Were you able to find the information you needed to complete the design project assignments?" ($F_{276} = 10.7$; $p < 0.0013$); and
- "Overall, was 1006ENG an enjoyable learning experience?" ($F_{275} = 8.9$; $p < 0.0032$).

SOLUTIONS AND RECOMMENDATIONS

How students engage with the learning activities in, and their overall perception of, a unit of study is powerfully influenced by the design of the assessment (James, McInnis, & Devlin, 2002). While the mean ratings for the two questionnaire scale items "Did you understand what you needed to do for the design project assignments?" and "Were you able to find the information you needed to complete the design project assignments?" were relatively high in the initial offering, in the follow-up offering they were significantly higher again. In fact, they had the highest mean ratings, and also had the smallest standard deviations of all scale items in the follow-up offering, suggesting that students were generally in agreement about their high ratings of these two scale items. The change to a single point of contact for academic advice in relation to the unit, and the reduction in the number of design projects (from three to two) giving more time to devote to each project, may have contributed to significantly higher mean ratings observed for the first two scale items above. A clearer understanding of assessment expectations and how to locate the information necessary to complete the design projects are both likely to be of importance to students, and may contribute to students' enjoyment of, and overall perception of, the unit.

Comparing the open-ended comments in Table 4 and Table 8 from the initial and follow-up offerings of 1006ENG provides some insight into the impact of changes made to the unit learning design. In the 'best aspects' category, there is a striking consistency in the highest ranked themes between the two unit offerings – seven of the top ten themes, and four of the top five themes, are identical. This provides some evidence that the questionnaire has reliably elicited student perceptions about 1006ENG. Turning to the 'needs improvement' category, the highest ranked theme in the initial offering ('More time on project work') is absent in the follow-up offering, suggesting that the reduction from three to two design projects has been favorably perceived by students. In the follow-up offering, the second most frequently reported 'needs improvement' theme ('Nothing') is an explicit indication by students that nothing needs improvement, providing some additional evidence that the changes to the unit learning design have been well received by many students.

Table 4 and Table 8 show many themes relating to group work. If the numerous group work-related threads in the 'needs improvement' column in Table 4 were summed, then 'group work' would be both the most commonly reported positive and negative item in the student open-ended comments received for the first offering of 1006ENG. Similarly, the scale item in Table 3 with the largest standard deviation (and second largest standard deviation in Table 7) is 'Did your group work well together on all design project assignments?'. These results point to the complex and multi-faceted nature of student group work. While students were permitted to self-select their group membership, a number of respondents indicated 'meeting new peers' was one of the best aspects of the unit. Engineering design is not totally represented by an individual working alone at a desk (Bucciarelli, 2002) – much 'real' engineering design work is conducted in a group environment (Dym et al., 2005). It has been shown that engineering designers do benefit from periods of time working alone to concentrate intensely on design problems and engineering work (Salter & Gann, 2003). However, engineering design is a social activity that is as much about discussion between engineers as it is about technical specifications (Lloyd, 2000). It is essential that engineering students are exposed to the importance of group work in the engineering design process, but also to the processes and experience of group design work, so that they can develop skills and strategies for the successful negotiation through the social aspects of engineering design practice.

FUTURE RESEARCH DIRECTIONS

In Table 8, two of the three highest ranking 'needs improvement' items in the follow-up offering relate to the CAD aspects of the 1006ENG. This result is despite a significant increase in both the tuition time and assessment weighting given to CAD in the follow-up unit offering. In fact, inspection of the themes in Table 8 shows that many of the student 'needs improvement' comments relate to CAD. However, both Table 4 and Table 8 also show that some students perceived the CAD elements of 1006ENG to be the best aspect of the unit. The situation regarding CAD in 1006ENG is clearly complicated, and requires additional careful consideration in future offerings of the unit.

While not at the top of the list in the 'needs improvement' column in Table 4 or Table 8, some issues relating to group work and assessment are apparent. The SAPA system for individualization of student marks in group work was an overt part of the unit, and informal feedback indicated that some students appreciated the SAPA system and consequent moderation of individual marks. However, students do want to know that their work has been assessed fairly, and especially so for group work where both relative and absolute equity in assessment issues come to the fore (James et al., 2002). Student use of the SAPA system was optional. There is scope to reconsider the operation and integration of the SAPA system in the unit, and how student use of the SAPA system might be improved. The authors believe that there would be significant value for student learning and development in strengthening the self-reflection aspects of the unit. This would ideally include additional guidance about the purpose, value and process of self-reflection, and allocating some specifically identified assessment weighting to a self-reflection task. The open-ended student comments collected in both years of the evaluation are a rich data set that has not yet been analyzed in full detail. Additional research work is planned to identify appropriate methods for the analysis of this textual data, both across and between the two unit offerings, to gain further insights into the experiences of students enrolled in 1006ENG, and the contributors to the numerical ratings provided by students on the questionnaire scale items.

CONCLUSION

This chapter documents the evaluation of the initial and subsequent second offerings of a first-year engineering design unit at Griffith University in Australia. The unit 1006ENG Design and Professional Skills aims to provide an introduction to engineering design and professional practice through a project-based approach to problem solving. The unit learning design incorporates student group work, and uses self-and-peer-assessment to incorporate aspects of the design process into the unit assessment and to provide a mechanism for individualization of student marks. This chapter presents the rationale and context for 1006ENG, the detailed results from the two evaluations, and conclusions regarding student engagement in collaborative engineering design activities in a first-year unit.

Following the initial unit offering, an evaluation suggested a number of revisions to the unit learning design. In response to the initial evaluation, a number of specific changes were made to the unit, and the evaluation process was repeated at the completion of the second unit offering to gauge the impact of these changes on the student perceptions of the unit. The evaluations revealed that students (in both the initial and second offering) generally enjoyed the experience, but that the second offering was found to be a significantly more enjoyable learning experience. Students in the second offering also reported a significantly better understanding of what they needed to do for the design projects and where to find the requisite information. The oral presentation aspect of the initial and second offerings received the lowest satisfaction rating. The inclusion (and delivery) of the CAD component of the unit was seen as a positive aspect by some students, but many others commented on it negatively. The best aspects of the PBL unit and those aspects needing further improvement were similar to the findings of other investigations documented in the literature.

The research literature indicates that, while there are individual aspects to engineering design practice, it is also a deeply social process, with collaboration and group interactions required at almost every stage. As an authentic educational strategy in the preparation of engineering students for this aspect of professional practice, and as a pragmatic educational strategy in response to large class sizes, student group work is used widely, and is particularly common in the form of group design projects. The use of student group work generally, especially where it contributes directly to summative assessment results, requires a method for the equitable assessment of individual student contributions. In the context of engineering design education, the use of student group work as a strategy for learning and practicing group work skills demands an assessment scheme that accounts for the effectiveness of group design activities as well as the quality of the resultant design artifact(s). Self-and-peer-assessment is one common strategy for the equitable assessment of group work. The evaluations presented in this chapter reveal the complex nature of group engineering design exercises. In agreement with the research literature, the students both highly valued group work, but also identified issues relating to being adequately prepared for group work and ensuring equitable contributions from group members. The refinement of the group work aspects of 1006ENG will remain a focus in future unit evaluations.

For the continuous improvement of engineering design education, on-going evaluation of design studies are essential (Davis et al., 2002), and the introduction of a new unit of study in engineering design is a key event that should trigger such evaluation. Dutson et al. (1997) note extensive anecdotal reporting of the value of engineering design education, but that a more objective assessment is required, and that formal evaluation should be undertaken. They also note that students are a key stakeholder group in design education, and that they should be included in any formal evaluation. While additional evaluation data can be drawn from sources such as the staff involved in the teaching of design units and existing institutional teaching evaluation systems, here the authors have employed a purpose-designed evaluation instrument for surveying student perceptions. The specific details of the instrument are unlikely to suit the evaluation needs of design studies units in other disciplines/contexts, however the authors recommend the use of a similar instrument structure based on the following rationale for the intended use of the data obtained:

- Respondent demographic information – where the survey respondents are a subset of the unit enrolment, it may be possible to assess the representativeness of the respondent sample based on similarity of demographic makeup; and it may be possible to compare responses to important survey items from different demographic groups to determine if different student groups experience aspects of unit in different ways.
- Assessment of prior experience – familiarity with topic knowledge and/practice may influence student survey responses, and a diagnostic assessment of the level of student prior experience may help plan/optimize unit teaching approaches.
- Assessment of prior perceptions – existing perceptions may influence student responses to new learning experiences, and a knowledge of entry perceptions may allow an assessment of the impact of the unit learning activities on student perceptions.
- Perceptions of learning activities – numerical response scales for the rating of student perceptions of key elements of the unit learning design that are of interest for the evaluation – in the case presented here student group work aspects were central to the evaluation.
- Open-ended comments – qualitative/text data can provide a valuable supplemental source of triangulation and explanation for other quantitative data obtained in the evaluation process.

The authors offer this survey instrument structure as a useful model for those interested in the evaluation of student collaboration in design education in particular, but also student perceptions of aspects of design education more generally.

REFERENCES

Agouridas, V. (2007, June 11-14). Towards the systematic Definition of Project-Based Design Modules. *Paper presented at the 3rd International CDIO Conference*, MIT, Cambridge, Massachusetts, USA.

Al-Abdeli, Y., & Bullen, F. (2006, December 10-13). Connecting teaching and research through problem based learning in thermal and automotive engineering. *Paper presented at the17th Annual Conference of the Australasian Association for Engineering Education*, Auckland.

Atman, C. J., Adams, R. S., Cardella, M. E., Turns, J., Mosborg, S., & Saleem, J. (2007). Engineering Design Processes: A Comparison of Students and Expert Practitioners. *The Journal of Engineering Education, 96*(4), 359–379. doi:10.1002/j.2168-9830.2007.tb00945.x

Atman, C. J., Cardella, M. E., Turns, J., & Adams, R. (2005). Comparing freshman and senior engineering design processes: An in-depth follow-up study. *Design Studies, 26*(4), 325–357. doi:10.1016/j.destud.2004.09.005

Atman, C. J., Chimka, J. R., Bursic, K. M., & Nachtmann, H. L. (1999). A comparison of freshman and senior engineering design processes. *Design Studies, 20*(2), 131–152. doi:10.1016/S0142-694X(98)00031-3

Atman, C. J., Kilgore, D., & McKenna, A. (2008). Characterizing Design Learning: A Mixed-Methods Study of Engineering Designers' Use of Language. *The Journal of Engineering Education, 97*(3), 309–326. doi:10.1002/j.2168-9830.2008.tb00981.x

Baird, F., Moore, C. J., & Jagodzinski, A. P. (2000). An ethnographic study of engineering design teams at Rolls-Royce Aerospace. *Design Studies, 21*(4), 333–355. doi:10.1016/S0142-694X(00)00006-5

Beer, D. F. (2002, September 17-20). Reflections on why engineering students don't like to write - and what we can do about it. *Paper presented at theIEEE International Professional Communication Conference*, Portland, Oregon. doi:10.1109/IPCC.2002.1049119

Boud, D., & Feletti, G. (1998). *The challenge of problem-based learning* (2nd ed.). London, Stirling: Psychology Press.

Brereton, M., & McGarry, B. (2000). An observational study of how objects support engineering design thinking and communication: implications for the design of tangible media. *Paper presented at theSIGCHI conference on Human Factors in Computing Systems*, The Hague, The Netherlands. doi:10.1145/332040.332434

Bucciarelli, L. L. (1988). An ethnographic perspective on engineering design. *Design Studies, 9*(3), 159–168. doi:10.1016/0142-694X(88)90045-2

Bucciarelli, L. L. (2002). Between thought and object in engineering design. *Design Studies, 23*(3), 219–231. doi:10.1016/S0142-694X(01)00035-7

Cárdenas, C. (2009, October 18-21). Social design in multidisciplinary engineering design courses. *Paper presented at the39th IEEE Frontiers in Education Conference*, San Antonio, Texas. doi:10.1109/FIE.2009.5350878

Chandrasekaran, S., Stojcevski, A., Littlefair, G., & Joordens, M. (2013). Project-oriented design-based learning: Aligning students' views with industry needs. *International Journal of Engineering Education, 29*(5), 1109–1118.

Davies, P. (2000). Computerized Peer Assessment. *Innovations in Education and Teaching International, 37*(4), 346–355.

Davis, D. C., Gentili, K. L., Trevisan, M. S., & Calkins, D. E. (2002). Engineering Design Assessment Processes and Scoring Scales for Program Improvement and Accountability. *The Journal of Engineering Education, 91*(2), 211–221. doi:10.1002/j.2168-9830.2002.tb00694.x

Doppelt, Y. (2005). Assessment of Project-Based Learning in a MECHATRONICS Context. *Journal of Technology Education, 16*(2), 7–24.

Du, X., & Kolmos, A. (2009). Increasing the diversity of engineering education – a gender analysis in a PBL context. *European Journal of Engineering Education, 34*(5), 425–437. doi:10.1080/03043790903137577

Dutson, A. J., Todd, R. H., Magleby, S. P., & Sorensen, C. D. (1997). A Review of Literature on Teaching Engineering Design Through Project-Oriented Capstone Courses. *The Journal of Engineering Education, 86*(1), 17–28. doi:10.1002/j.2168-9830.1997.tb00260.x

Dym, C. L., Agogino, A. M., Eris, O., Frey, D. D., & Leifer, L. J. (2005). Engineering Design Thinking, Teaching, and Learning. *The Journal of Engineering Education, 94*(1), 103–120. doi:10.1002/j.2168-9830.2005.tb00832.x

Edward, N. S. (2004). Evaluations of introducing project-based design activities in the first and second years of engineering courses. *European Journal of Engineering Education, 29*(4), 491–503. doi:10.1080/03043790410001716284

Frank, M., Lavy, I., & Elata, D. (2003). Implementing the Project-Based Learning Approach in an Academic Engineering Course. *International Journal of Technology and Design Education, 13*(3), 273–288. doi:10.1023/A:1026192113732

Freeman, M., & McKenzie, J. (2002). SPARK, a confidential web-based template for self and peer assessment of student teamwork: Benefits of evaluating across different subjects. *British Journal of Educational Technology, 33*(5), 551–569. doi:10.1111/1467-8535.00291

Gómez Puente, S. M., van Eijck, M., & Jochems, W. (2011). Towards characterising design-based learning in engineering education: A review of the literature. *European Journal of Engineering Education, 36*(2), 137–149. doi:10.1080/03043797.2011.565116

Hall, W., Palmer, S., & Bennett, M. (2012). A longitudinal evaluation of a project-based learning initiative in an engineering undergraduate program. *European Journal of Engineering Education, 37*(2), 155–165. doi:10.1080/03043797.2012.674489

Hanesian, D., & Perna, A. J. (1999, November 10-13). An evolving freshman engineering design program- The NJIT experience. *Paper presented at the 29th Annual Frontiers in Education Conference*, San Juan, Puerto Rico. doi:10.1109/FIE.1999.839284

Helle, L., Tynjälä, P., & Olkinuora, E. (2006). Project-Based Learning in Post-Secondary Education – Theory, Practice and Rubber Sling Shots. *Higher Education, 51*(2), 287–314. doi:10.1007/s10734-004-6386-5

Howard, T. J., Culley, S. J., & Dekoninck, E. (2008). Describing the creative design process by the integration of engineering design and cognitive psychology literature. *Design Studies, 29*(2), 160–180. doi:10.1016/j.destud.2008.01.001

Hubka, V., & Eder, W. E. (1987). A scientific approach to engineering design. *Design Studies*, *8*(3), 123–137. doi:10.1016/0142-694X(87)90035-4

James, R., McInnis, C., & Devlin, M. (2002). *Assessing Learning in Australian Universities*. Melbourne: Centre for the Study of Higher Education and The Australian Universities Teaching Committee.

Johnston, L., & Miles, L. (2004). Assessing contributions to group assignments. *Assessment & Evaluation in Higher Education*, *29*(6), 751–768. doi:10.1080/0260293042000227272

Kolmos, A. (2002). Facilitating change to a problem-based model. *The International Journal for Academic Development*, *7*(1), 63–74. doi:10.1080/13601440210156484

Lloyd, P. (2000). Storytelling and the development of discourse in the engineering design process. *Design Studies*, *21*(4), 357–373. doi:10.1016/S0142-694X(00)00007-7

Lloyd, P., & Scott, P. (1994). Discovering the design problem. *Design Studies*, *15*(2), 125–140. doi:10.1016/0142-694X(94)90020-5

Lumsdaine, E., Shelnutt, J. W., & Lumsdaine, M. (1999, June 20-23). Integrating Creative Problem Solving and Engineering Design. *Paper presented at the ASEE Annual Conference & Exposition*, Charlotte, NC.

Macías-Guarasa, J., Montero, J. M., San-Segundo, R., Araujo, A., & Nieto-Taladriz, O. (2006). A project-based learning approach to design electronic systems curricula. *IEEE Transactions on Education*, *49*(3), 389–397. doi:10.1109/TE.2006.879784

Mills, J. E., & Treagust, D. F. (2003). Engineering Education – Is Problem-Based or Project-Based Learning the Answer? *Australasian Journal of Engineering Education*, *3*(2), 2–16.

Oakley, B., Felder, R. M., Brent, R., & Elhajj, I. (2004). Turning student groups into effective teams. *Journal of Student Centered Learning*, *2*(1), 9–34.

Palmer, S., & Hall, W. (2011). An evaluation of a project-based learning initiative in engineering education. *European Journal of Engineering Education*, *36*(4), 357–365. doi:10.1080/03043797.2011.593095

Prince, M. J., & Felder, R. M. (2006). Inductive Teaching and Learning Methods: Definitions, Comparisons, and Research Bases. *The Journal of Engineering Education*, *95*(2), 123–138. doi:10.1002/j.2168-9830.2006.tb00884.x

Salter, A., & Gann, D. (2003). Sources of ideas for innovation in engineering design. *Research Policy*, *32*(8), 1309–1324. doi:10.1016/S0048-7333(02)00119-1

Schubert, T. Jr, Jacobitz, F., & Kim, E. (2012). Student perceptions and learning of the engineering design process: An assessment at the freshmen level. *Research in Engineering Design*, *23*(3), 177–190. doi:10.1007/s00163-011-0121-x

Thomas, J. W. (2000). *A Review of Project Based Learning*. San Rafael, California: The Autodesk Foundation.

Tucker, R., Fermelis, J., & Palmer, S. (2009). Designing, Implementing and Evaluating a Self-and-Peer Assessment Tool for E-learning Environments. In C. Spratt & P. Lajbcygier (Eds.), *E-Learning Technologies and Evidence-Based Assessment Approaches* (pp. 170–194). New York: IGI Global. doi:10.4018/978-1-60566-410-1.ch010

Willey, K., & Gardner, A. (2007, December 9-13). Building better teams at work using self and peer assessment practices. *Paper presented at theEighteenth Annual Conference of the Australasian Association for Engineering Education*, Melbourne.

Willmot, P., & Crawford, A. (2004, October 16-21). Online peer assessed marking of team projects. *Paper presented at theInternational Conference on Engineering Education*, Gainesville, Florida.

KEY TERMS AND DEFINITIONS

Cornerstone Design Course: A (typically) first-year design-based unit of study that provides foundation design knowledge, skills and practice. The term is derived as a counterpoint to 'capstone' design courses that traditionally occur and the end of a program of study with the intention as a context to integrate previous studies in the context of a realistic major design project. It is suggested that first-year design courses enhance commencing student motivation and retention, and introduce engineering application content and basic design experience early in the curriculum.

Engineering Design: Most simplistically, the method used by engineers for the realization of technical systems through the processes of (a) Eliciting and documenting client requirements and constraints; (b) Analysis of task requirements; (c) Generation of conceptual design alternatives; (d) Evaluation and selection of optimal solution; (e) Technical embodiment design; (f) Detailed design of system solution elements; and (g) Implementation of the solution system.

Group Work: Collaborative student work where a number of students work separately on different aspects of a project/task and then combine their work, often with limited consideration or attempt at integration.

Learning Design: The intentions of the designers of a unit of study, encompassing (a) The intended student learning outcomes; (b) The assumed prerequisite student knowledge; (c) The planned sequence of learning activities; (d) The unit learning resources; (e) The unit assessment activities that document student mastery of the learning outcomes; and (f) The required student support systems.

Mark Individualization: One possible outcome of SAPA is the calculation of a numerical scaling factor for each group member, which can then be applied to a common group mark to produce individual marks for each group member that attempt to fairly represent the contribution of each member to the assessable group task.

Project-Based Learning: A learning and teaching pedagogy that typically has the following characteristics (a) Teaching staff take a supporting rather than leadership role; (b) Students generally work in groups/teams to complete a design project; (c) Solution of a problem or completion of a task that requires students to complete a number of educational activities that direct their learning; (d) Generally, the project would involve the creation of a tangible artefact – a design, a physical model, a report, a thesis, a computer model, etc.; (e) The project is non-trivial and often multidisciplinary in nature, requiring work over an extended period of time; and (f) The completion of the project often includes a reporting element, either a written document and/or oral presentation.

Self-and-Peer-Assessment (SAPA): At its most basic, SAPA involves students providing an evaluation for all group members, including themselves, of the individual contribution of each group member to the group work process. The SAPA evaluation may be used informally as feedback, or formally as an element of the summative assessment for the group task. SAPA may be public or anonymous.

Student Evaluation of Teaching: The process of surveying students, typically at the end of a teaching period, to ascertain their perceptions of particular aspects of the learning and teaching environment. Such surveys may incorporate quantitative ratings and/or qualitative, open-ended comment responses from students.

APPENDIX

1006ENG Design and Professional Skills – PBL Questionnaire

1.1 Please state your age in years AND months

1.2 Please indicate your gender

1.3 Please indicate your enrolled program code

1.4 Please indicate your intended study major

1.5 Please indicate your Griffith tertiary entrance score

2.1 Before commencing 1006ENG, had you previously participated in PBL activities? [Y/N/?]

2.2 Do you enjoy working in groups/teams? [1-5]

2.3 Do you enjoy giving oral presentations? [1-5]

3.1 Did you understand what you needed to do for the design project assignments? [1-5]

3.2 Were you able to find the information you needed to complete the design project assignments? [1-5]

3.3 Did your group work well together on all design project assignments? [1-5]

3.4 Was your group presentation successful? [1-5]

3.5 Were you satisfied with the designs produced by your group? [1-5]

3.6 Overall, was 1006ENG an enjoyable learning experience? [1-5]

3.7 Did 1006ENG increase your knowledge of engineering design & professional skills? [1-5]

4.   What were the best aspects of 1006ENG? [Free text comment]

5.   What could be improved about 1006ENG? [Free text comment]

Chapter 8
Levering Critical Collaboration:
The First Year Interdisciplinary Design Experience

Alexandra Lara Crosby
University of Technology Sydney, Australia

Adam C. Morgan
University of Technology Sydney, Australia

ABSTRACT

This chapter presents an intervention in Design Thinking, a first year interdisciplinary design subject at the University of Technology Sydney. Over two iterations of this subject, researchers reframed the 'group work' component as critical collaboration, drawing from the momentum in the design professions for more participatory and collaborative processes and the increasing acknowledgement of design as being critical to sustainable human futures. The online self and peer assessment tool SPARKPlus was used to change the way students approached collaboration and then reflected on it following their experiences. In this model, self and peer assessment is used as a leaver to encourage critical thinking about collaboration, rather than as a hammer to enforce participation.

INTRODUCTION

The process of synthesizing ideas from disparate disciplines is unfamiliar and uncomfortable. But it is precisely in that discomfort that the seeds of creativity lie, and if the group can continue to play the believing game— not insisting on certainty, closure, or judgments— participants may ultimately move to new truths and imaginative solutions (Strober, 2010, p. 165).

It is widely accepted that design involves interdisciplinary collaboration, whether a visual communicator is working with a programmer, a fashion designer with a photographer, or a product designer with a team of engineers. Due to the changing nature of social problems and the complex range of responses that are required to make sense of them, design is becoming increasingly interdisciplinary and collab-

DOI: 10.4018/978-1-5225-0726-0.ch008

orative. In higher education, "newer perspectives of learning have begun recognising that learning is less a solitary act and more about the collaboration with others to pool knowledge, experiences, skills and tools" (McMahon & Amatullo, 2013, p. 1) as traditional, individual-focused methods are being challenged. How to best teach design collaboration, however, in a way that is at once caring and critical, remains somewhat of a wicked problem.

This chapter explores how design curricula can address the complexity of learning critical collaboration. We argue that the consideration of critical collaboration is important in the creation of a learning context that is more accurately representative of the dynamic role of design professions and that provides opportunities for increased inclusiveness. We use the term critical collaboration to draw together the learning processes of critical reflection and collaborative design. In our case study, this is achieved through the design of an online self and peer assessment integrated with a reflective writing task in a first year interdisciplinary design subject.

Within the interdisciplinary design studies program at the University of Technology Sydney, where the authors work[1], this emphasis on critical collaboration has enabled an opening up of the curriculum to include previously neglected aspects of design thinking such as the understanding of place through the Aboriginal notion of country (Crosby, Hromek, & Kinniburgh, 2015) and the gender bias of discourses on creativity (Potur & Barkul, 2009). We argue that genuine and critical collaborative scenarios create more authentic learning environments for design students to explore challenging concepts and to take the necessary creative risks to develop as designers and social risks to develop as human beings.

As the research for this chapter, we have been reframing group work as critical collaboration in Design Thinking, one of the first year subjects in the interdisciplinary design studies program that includes a three-day design camp on Cockatoo Island in Sydney. Firstly, we encouraged a change in the way the students approached their group assessment by priming them for critical collaboration and using the design of a manifesto as a preparatory studio exercise. Secondly we used SPARKPlus, a tool for self and peer assessment to improve the way students reflected on their collaboration following the camp. In an effort to act as facilitators of critical collaboration, rather than enforcers, we have also shifted the way we use the online platform–from a hammer to a lever, by allowing for students to comment on their direct experience of interdisciplinary design. This paper evaluates the effectiveness of this intervention over two iterations of the Design Thinking subject in 2015.

The chapter is structured in four parts. We begin with a background that covers the concept of critical collaboration in relation to interdisciplinary design studies; an explanation of the first year subject within which we work; and a discussion of our self and peer assessment practices with a focus on qualitative online feedback. Secondly we present the intervention. Here we provide a short description of our method describing the interventions we made in the subject of Design Thinking as well as the way we collected and analysed the results. This section is divided by the two iterations of this intervention. In short, our project has been to align the criteria for assessing collaboration with the student experience of doing it; to prime students before their experience of collaboration and reflection; and to observe and analyse the results of this change over two semesters. Thirdly, we provide a discussion of the results collected, focusing on the way students have articulated critical collaboration and providing an example of a group's learning path from manifesto to reflection in the form of a vignette. Finally, summarised by two recommendations, we discuss the implications of -these data in relation to critical design, by focusing on the student voice, the interplay of design educators with a tool such as SPARKPlus, and the expanded notions of design that are implicated in the teaching of design for the future.

BACKGROUND

Critical Collaboration in Interdisciplinary Design Studies

In this chapter we employ the idea of critical collaboration as a way to help students develop their skills in what is commonly referred to as 'group work' in university settings. Drawing from recent scholarship of critical design practice (Barab, Thomas, Dodge, Squire, & Newell, 2004; DiSalvo, 2009; Dunne & Raby, 2013), we build on generic principles of good collaboration (such as the valuing of diverse ideas, having a common purpose, trust, and sharing decision-making) to consider the specificity of collaboration to design practice.

We define critical collaboration as a way that students can approach working together. While critical collaboration requires reflection, it also involves using design skills to act on that reflection in a critical way. Critical thinking can be used to challenge preconceptions about the role of collaboration in learning, design, and indeed everyday life. Critical collaboration can be used to co-create alternatives. We use the idea of critical collaboration as a way of positioning group work in broader discussions about design pedagogy, the future of the design profession, and interdisciplinary creative practice. In other words, the design thinking studio, and subsequent interdisciplinary design studies subjects, is meant to foster critical thinking and critical making between students of different design disciplines through design collaboration.

Broadly, our work joins that of other design scholars in addressing the distinctiveness of the studio learning and teaching experience for creative practice outcomes. In our pedagogical work on critical collaboration, we view collaborative studio space as "distinctive in the professions and pervasive in the curriculum of the visual and performing arts, architecture and design disciplines across institutions" (Peterson, Frankham, McWhinnie, & Forsyth, 2015, p. 72). Zehner et al. (2009) describe the design studio as "an investigative and creative process driven by research, exploration and experimentation, and critique and reflection" (p. vi). To this list we add collaboration.

Ostergaard and Summers (2009) define collaborative design as "a collection of agents (human or artificial) that are working towards a *common shared goal* using shared resources or knowledge" (58). They summarise various ideas around collaborative design practice into a 'taxonomy' which consists of six categories. The categories include team composition, communication, distribution, design approach, information and the nature of the problem. We build on this taxonomy in our definition of critical collaboration aligning it with our commitment to Interdisciplinary design at UTS. Interdisciplinary design learning provides the space for first year students to begin to participate and describe particular types of collaboration across disciplinary differences that are increasingly important to design practice. It has been argued that these environments are more representative of work in professional practice by design scholars such as Ezio Manzini who discuss how the future of design can only be understood in the context of collaborative practice (Manzini, 2013). He says "designers are becoming part of a growing number of actors to work together to generate wide and flexible networks that collaboratively conceive, develop and manage solutions" (Manzini, 2013, p. 215).

The ability to work in teams and the skills of reflecting on that team work are important for all professions and there is a reported gap between the level of teamwork skills required by employers and the level developed by students during their undergraduate courses (Martin, Bryan, Case, & Fraser, 2005; Meier, Williams, & Humphreys, 2000). In Design professions this gap has particular resonance. Graduates are expected to be able to work across the disciplinary boundaries of their education. As design educators, we know that collaboration is a skill that graduates need in professional practice, but interdisciplinary collaboration is not often the emphasis of university assessment. In this chapter, we argue that feedback mechanisms and assignments need to be informed by what students themselves identify as effective teamwork and inclusive interaction.

Design Thinking at UTS

Design Thinking is an interdisciplinary first year foundation subject in the School of Design at University of Technology Sydney. The phrase 'design thinking' has been the subject of many heated articles and books. Although opinions differ as to the value of design thinking dicourse (in both design and non design contexts), there is some consensus about the process, which includes ideation, iteration, observation, framing and prototyping. There is also, as Bill Moggridge argues, strong connections between the ideas of design thinking and interdisciplinary collaboration so that "the power of intuitive creative processes can be harnessed to stimulate innovation, solve difficult problems and develop new opportunities" (Moggridge 2010).

In the School of Design at UTS, the subject sits within a suite of subjects that begin in first year with Researching Design History and continue in second year with Design Lab A, a speculative exercise in design futuring. In their third and final year of the interdisciplinary stream, students take part in an innovative combination of industry and global studios. These studios are the culmination of critical collaboration skills developed throughout the interdisciplinary program. In all subjects, SPARKPlus is used as a way to lever reflection on collaboration and develop skills in critical collaboration. The interdisciplinary design studies program is dynamic and responsive. While the intervention discussed in this paper focuses on a first year subject, we contextualize it within other work we are doing in second and third year subjects to redesign the experience of self and peer assessment.

Each time it runs (twice a year) Design Thinking includes up to 300 students from six design disciplines (Animation, Fashion and Textile Design, Interior and Spatial Design, Integrated Product Design, Photography and Situated Media and Visual Communication Design) who come together to build core skills in critical creativity, collaboration and reflection in a studio setting.

A central focus of the subject is Design Camp where students are encouraged to develop their capacity for self-reflection as described by Donald Schön in *The Reflective Practitioner*. Self-reflection can enable designers to evaluate options based on anticipated futures and historical understandings (Fry, Dilnot & Stewart, 2015) but more importantly it can enable students to question their own assumptions and the implications of these to other actors in design networks. Students are also encouraged to critique the work of others in the context of group design projects. To cultivate their reflective skills, students are urged to continually sketch, testing and trying out concepts and ideas, through documentation (actively observe) and visualisation (mapping). These largely ethnographic skills form the basis of group work projects that take place at camp.

The site of Design Camp is Cockatoo Island, a UNESCO World Heritage site in the middle of Sydney Harbour that possesses a rich history that can be traced back to the use of the island as a meeting place by the Aboriginal peoples of the Eora nation (Figure 1). However, Cockatoo Island is also well known for its convict and industrial heritage. Given its location and up until recently inaccessibility, the site is deliberately unfamiliar to students and aims to take them out of their comfort zones. On the island, students work collaboratively in interdisciplinary groups of four or five to explore the hidden, un-noticed, unexpected features of the island. For example, in the first on site assessment, a mapping

Figure 1. Cockatoo Island is a UNESCO world heritage site in Sydney harbor

challenge, students creatively record their observations through experimental map-making. Whilst in the Inhabitation challenge, students are encouraged to work with the limitations and possibilities of the island to provoke critical and creative thinking about human needs and the way designers might address them in the future. These needs are addressed by creatively re-purposing an assortment of "materials' provided by the school. Such strategies for creative thinking have long been associated with design processes that aim to develop innovative responses to 'complex and wicked problems like climate change and peak everything, crisis-prone democratic and economic systems, overburdened health and transport systems" (Tonkinwise, 2014, p. 6).

In Design Thinking, students are primed for critical collaboration in the weeks leading up to design camp. We use the term prime as it has appeared in social change contexts to explain the way participants can be primed to understand certain issues before a participatory or co design process begins (Crompton, 2010). In previous years, student groups were asked to create a group charter, used across the university to improve student experience of group work (IML, 2002). This charter has been developed into a design manifesto task in current iterations of Design Thinking.

While design students at UTS have many group projects during their degree, their first encounter with a sustained group work setting is on the island during Design Thinking and their first encounter with the idea of critical collaboration is leading up to camp. Group work is often difficult for students and requires support if they are to develop reflective skills. To prime students for camp we have developed a protocol (in the form of a manifesto unit of the subject) that enables students to first identify key skills such as listening as well as develop common values and goals (Ostergaard & Summers, 2009). The design manifestos given to students as examples of critical collaboration are sometimes historical (for example the Futurist Manifesto, the Communist Manifesto and the First Things First Manifesto) but also include contemporary examples that articulate the ways designers can collaborate with objects, tools and environments, (for example the Repair Manifesto, First Things First 2000 and the Permaculture Design Principles). During their first experience of a collaborative design context at university, students need shared communication and a collaborative framework for sharing the same goals. For Mao-Lin Chiu "collaborative design is an activity that requires participation of individuals for sharing information and organizing design tasks and resources" (Chiu 2002, p. 187). Students create their own manifestos in groups that help them position their collaboration as it is happening. In other words, the student manifestos prime the students to form 'designerly' relationships with the site, its weather, its history, its flora, fauna, its built environment, their teachers and each other.

Self and Peer Assessment in Design Thinking

In 2014, online self and peer assessment called SPARKPlus was included in Design Thinking. SPARK-Plus is an online tool centred round students making judgements. The tool's original, and most widely used, mode is its group contribution mode (Freeman & McKenzie, 2001; 2002). This is where students make judgements about their own and their peers' contribution to collaborative efforts. In short, after an assessment, students log into the system and rate their own and peers' contribution against criteria. Students may also be required to provide feedback to their peers in a textbox. This textbox can also be set to be inward facing, where students are required to make confidential comments about their peers. Students usually are given one week 'to SPARK'. Once the window closes, an algorithm is applied to the ratings so that two factors are produced for each student. One relates to the student's self-assessed ratings of criteria compared with his or her peers' ratings (the SA/PA factor). The second relates to student's received ratings and how these compare to all members' received ratings. This is called the Relative Performance Factor (RPF), which can then be used to moderate marks to reflect each individual's contribution to the group effort.

Typically, SPARKPlus in contribution mode is used in subjects at UTS to deal with perceptions of inequity in student groups, particularly the inequity associated with free riding (Morris & Hayes, 1997; Thompson & McGregor, 2009). As most of the group work that students do is expected to take place outside of class time, teaching staff find it difficult to make judgements on each student's contributions. Before the ubiquity of the internet, this problem was addressed by students completing an end-of-project proforma, where students rated their own and peers' contribution (Goldfinch, 1994; Goldfinch & Raeside, 1990). Ratings were collated and used by the teacher to make judgements of equity, and to moderate if required. SPARKPlus is essentially an online version of this once paper-based proforma. As ratings are made within the system, calculations are made automatically.

When students log in to SPARKPlus, they are first required to rate their own performance on a set of criteria. These can be selected from a standard set (e.g. suggesting ideas, helping the group to function well as a team), or written specifically for the collaborative task requirements. Students are then required to rate each of their peers' performance against the criteria on a scale ranging from 'well below average' to 'well above average'. Students are also typically provided with a textbox so they can give feedback to each of their peers, which reads "feedback for [peer name inserted]".

From the authors' experience with SPARKPlus in other subjects, a number of problems exist in the 'standard' set up. First, the standard criteria are generic and particularly decontextualized. Second, students do not always engage with the feedback option as hoped. Many students leave the box blank. Others write inappropriate and poorly phrased comments, which cannot be published. The standard setup, however, can be overridden. Contextualised criteria can be used. The textbox can also be changed, whereby (a) the student is given specific instructions on what needs to be written in the field, and (b) these written comments can be withheld from publishing. That is, the students can be instructed to make comments about, rather than for, their peers.

REDESIGNING SELF AND PEER-ASSESSMENT TO ENHANCE STUDENTS' REFLECTION

Method

Over two iterations of Design Thinking, our intervention has redesigned the experience of using SPARK-Plus and reframed group work as critical collaboration with a focus on priming students through manifesto design. These changes, and their effect on student engagement with the self and peer assessment process, are outlined below.

In exploring the impact of our intervention, we have analysed multiple data sets including student comments collected in SPARKPlus over two semesters, comments from tutors collected during focus groups and interviews, and reflective writing by students in their final (individual) assessment. We have also observed and documented students in the subject both in studios on campus and during the camp.

Iteration 1: Autumn Semester 2015 (290 Students)

In its first redesign, the generic SPARKPlus criteria (e.g., attended meetings), were replaced with ones that related specifically to the collaborative task. These were:

1. Contributed to group identity (through creation of the group charter, preparation before camp etc.)
2. Included other group members in group discussions and decisions and engaged with their ideas
3. Participated in the group's progress over 3 days of camp (e.g. by embracing and working with difference, keeping to schedule, dealing with friction etc.)
4. Contributed to producing submission materials and presentation

The textbox was also set to be inward facing, and required students to provide justifications for their ratings. The instructions were:

Use this box to make a comment about this student if your ratings of him/her are above or below average (ie. WB, BA, AA, WA). You need to justify your lower or higher than average ratings for this person. This comment will not be made public to the student.

These instructions were written to address an issue we had noticed in the data collected over previous years in other subjects, where students rate various peers extremely high or low, without any reason given for these ratings. Students were introduced to SPARKPlus in their final lecture before the camp. They were also given a demonstration on how to use SPARKPlus. The rating period began immediately after the camp finished and closed one week later. Over 90% of the students 'SPARKed', which was very successful outcome given it was largely a non-compulsory requirement. As it was not specified in the subject outline it could not be mandated.

After the camp finished, a tutor meeting was held to read and discuss the SPARKPlus results.[2] Each tutor present was given a profile of each of their students. This profile contained their spark scores (RPF and SA/PA), along with any comments written about them by their peers. Tutors found these profiles particularly interesting and made comments such as: "wow, these are so insightful, I never knew that the other group members felt this way about this student". Other tutors agreed. As the tutors inspected the profiles, one noted how many of the comments appeared to be phased as though the student was justifying, which of course was the intended design and was followed by some students. For example, one student wrote:

I gave [student name] slightly lower ratings because he was less forthcoming with ideas and not so keen to have input or participate in the process, and he provided few materials for our project.

Another wrote:

I have rated [student name] in a higher average range than some of the others because when nobody wanted to write the text piece for the escape map, we decided to work as a team and during this process [student name] stood out as contributing the most. This happened not only in the escape map but also the memory map.

However, through discussion and comparison at the tutor meeting, it became apparent that many students had deviated away from the 'please justify your ratings' instructions. Many had provided a critique of their peers, outlining in detail what they had done, and how this impacted on their group.

For example, one student wrote:

[student name] was incredible in the way in which she could listen to what we all had to say and would be willing to use her own time for the good of the group. [student name] has this extreme creative quality to her which makes her helpful to work collaboratively with and fun to be around. [student name] at times would take control of situations to ensure the most was gained from an idea of one of the group members and contributed fully to the assessment at hand. [student name] has this amazing ability to compromise and to merge ideas together in a way that allows an even greater idea to be conceived. [student name] was a huge asset to the group and the group would have not stuck were it not for her creative instincts.

Another wrote:

[student name] was a very quiet and conscientious girl who listened very carefully and thought deeply about everyone's opinions. She thoroughly did the tasks that were asked of her and whenever there was friction in the group with ideas, she was happy to go with whichever idea. [student name] contributed greatly for a peaceful group atmosphere and struggled greatly with the language barrier and as such her ideas weren't communicated in a large group. Interesting I found that she flourished in a 1:1 person situation and was more capable of expressing great and interesting solutions to work issues. Working with her has been a positive and interesting experience and I thoroughly enjoyed teaming up with her. She has a hidden ability to draw ideas out of others and encourage them to materialize their ideas into the world. Without her, the third project idea would not have happened and I personally don't think the others have noticed this because she's quiet and feels uncomfortable to speak her ideas out to the group.

To get her ideas across, I told the group her ideas later after a one-on-one talk with her so that she could still feel like she contributed to the group.

Some students were also making specific reference to their peer's disciplinary background, and how this contributed to design collaboration. For example:

[student name]'s course knowledge from her studies in Interior design brought a great deal of knowledge that other members did not have, for example she had studied decibel readings within her course, and she had also looked at the term 'heterotopia' in a much deeper way than the other members of our group. In that way, she was crucial in the development of the sound map, because she helped us figure out how to map the experience of our senses. She essentially led the way with the sound map in the beginning of the process, and once we had collaboratively decided upon our concept, [other student name] and [other student name] worked together on that map. In that way, [student name] was vital in our construction of one map, however, she did not have as much contribution to the networks map, which was one that mostly [other student name] and I had worked on. I do not see this as a problem because of her significant contributions in other aspects of the group work, and her eagerness to work together and collaborate; she was extremely helpful to the group.

Another wrote:

[student name] was an enthusiastic and extremely valued member of our group. She worked hard constantly over the duration of the camp constantly broadening and developing concepts and ideas. [student name] always put forward ideas and drew upon these and other peoples when coming up with concepts and designs. She successfully drew upon her own practice as a spatial and interior design student and taught us quite a bit about what she was learning about. [student name] was respectful and encouraging towards everyone in the group, I thoroughly enjoyed working with her.

It became apparent that many students were reflecting quite deeply about their peers in SPARKPlus. We realised that the textbox in SPARKPlus was providing a platform for students to critique their peers, even though they were not required to do so in a way that appeared to be an exercise in critical collaboration. Some tutors also noted that the quality of the students' final reflective essay had overall improved compared to previous years. This was suggested to be due to students making 'richer' reflective comments about their peers. SPARKPlus was therefore helping students to reflect on their peers at an individual level, which was helping them to also write their reflective essay. It appeared to be acting as priming tool in the reflective writing process. However, it was realised that the instructions for the text box should be changed so as to better help guide students to reflect on their peers — particularly from a disciplinary perspective, which is a key aspect of the Design Thinking subject. It was also realised that any re-design of this text box should involve the tutoring team again. Their insights and opinions at this meeting were invaluable.

Iteration 2: Spring Semester 2015, 230 Students

The second set of changes began with a 3 hour workshop, where tutors from Design Thinking were invited to participate in the SPARKPlus redesign in the subject. This workshop was funded by a First

Table 1. Summary of changes made to scale description and criteria over two iterations

Previous Peer Assessment Criteria (Autumn 2015)	Tutor Developed Criteria (Spring 2015)
Scale Description WB, BA, AA, WA	**Scale 1 = Very Poor to 5 = Very Good**
1. Contributed to group identity (through creation of the group charter, preparation before camp etc.)	1. Contributed to establishing the group through creation of the manifesto, planning and preparation before camp etc.
2. Included other group members in group discussions and decisions and engaged with their ideas	2. Contributed to a positive group culture by including all group members in group discussions and decisions and engaging with their ideas
3. Participated in the group's progress over 3 days of camp (e.g. by embracing and working with difference, keeping to schedule, dealing with friction etc.)	3. Acted like something was at stake in the project, invested in the group
4. Contributed to producing submission materials and presentation	4. Participated in the group's progress over 3 days of camp (e.g. by attending, keeping to schedule, dealing with conflict, accepting feedback etc.)
	5. Contributed to the resolution of ideas, producing submission materials and presenting

Year Experience Teaching and Learning Grant, which paid the tutors for their attendance and catering expenses. [3] Background was given and a number of collaborative activities were designed to facilitate the re-design. Working in groups, the tutors were invited the re-write the criteria (and the scale). They were also invited to re-write the text box instructions, so as to better help students to reflect on their peers and their group processes. Small changes were made to the criteria*, and the scale was changed to 1 = very poor to 5 = very good (Table 1).

Large changes were made to the textbox. Following a plenary discussion, it was decided that the text box instructions should read:

Use this text box to reflect upon what you learnt about group work while working with [peer name]. You may wish to consider:

- What skill sets they brought from their discipline
- How this influenced the group
- How this influenced you

Note: Teaching staff will only have access these comments. Other members of your group will not see these comments.

From the tutors' suggestions and discussions that followed, it was decided that the textbox needed to focus on the student and their learning about groupwork. Although their peers' disciplinary background was important, it was the learning that needed to be encouraged via SPARKPlus. The changes were made and implemented. Students were, once again, briefed about SPARKPlus in their last lecture before the camp. Due to the workshop, tutors were also better able to explain SPARKPlus to their students. Indeed, they could say that they were involved in its design.

Of the 239 students (92%) who completed SPARKPlus in the week following camp, the vast majority critiqued their peers as instructed. Further, the quality of these critiques was considerably better than the 2014 cohort. These 2015 students had (a) written more text, (b) were more specific in terms of disciplinary background critiquing, and (c) written more about what they had learned from their peers. For example, one student wrote:

[Student name] brought various skills from visual communication that were an important contribution in the creation of our team's maps. Her attention to detail, sensitivity to craft, and graphic sensibility, contributed to creating our Networks map. For example, this was seen in detailing the outline of the map, and carefully placing thread to indicate particular connections. I learnt that having clear group communication and having similar project goals allows you to trust your team members in carrying out particular tasks--you know that the work they produce will be on par with what the group has envisaged.

Another wrote:

Along with her knowledge of fashion, and especially colour theories, "[student name] brought an extremely positive and collected outlook to our group which i found to be greatly influential within our group. [Student name's] methods of working collaboratively enabled us to move past points of conflict and progress with the project. Especially in our "thermometer" map, Eliza applied the elements of her design discipline which would enable us to convey our concept in the most clear and concise manner possible, while also ensuring our map would be aesthetically pleasing. From working with [student name], i gained a greater understanding of the importance of being able to accept the varying views of my peers and in this, reaching a satisfactory compromise. More often than not, [student name] would ask us to illustrate our ideas as this was easiest for her to understand, rather than a verbal description. In this i learned that in group work, we must be versatile in our production process to account for each individuals way of working.

For a different peer, this same student from above wrote:

[Student name] is an animation student which, as we very quickly discovered, is quite different from interior and spatial design, in regards to how we produce our work. Because of this, [student name] and I often had conflicting perspectives on how we would approach a design problem. This was an extremely valuable learning curve for myself as i began to realise that in group work, people will inevitably have opposing ideas for how they desire a project to be presented, however this is a positive thing, rather that negative as I had initially thought. Throughout the three days spent working with [student name], I became increasingly aware of how it is important to integrate the ideas of the individuals within a group in order to produce the strongest possible project. This was evident in my very precise and structured way of working, which contrasted with [student name]'s more aesthetic based design approach. Thus, we were able to reach a mid-point between our two design methods to produce maps which were direct in their message and purpose, yet still interesting and aesthetically pleasing to look at.

As shown above, the final two comments, written by the same student, show the depth of the critique, and how different they are. They are clearly tailored. Such tailored critiquing is very common in the comments made by students in the 2015 cohort.

DISCUSSION

Instructors who had marked reflective assessments over more than two years noted that after using the criteria that they helped develop, the reflective writing assessment was 'quicker to mark' and essays tended to be more 'well written', 'clearer' and 'deeper.'

Students enrolled during the Spring semester also commented in class that using SPARKPlus helped them write their essay. Overall, marks for essays improved over the two semesters, assessed against the same criteria by the same tutors. We are confident from these data that our approach to incorporating SPARKPlus into our program as a lever for critical self-reflection rather than as an enforcer of participation works best in this context of first year interdisciplinary studies.

In Design Thinking, students are now introduced to SPARKPlus in their final lecture before camp. They are given a demonstration on how to use SPARKPlus. The rating period begins immediately after the camp finishes and closes one week later. The participation rate is generally well over 90%, which was very successful outcome given it is largely a non-compulsory requirement. We have chosen not to make SPARKPlus compulsory as we want students to view SPARKPlus as an available tool to help them write their required reflective task. Whether or not they choose to use this tool may indeed be viewed as an engagement with critical collaboration.

With the changes to SPARKPlus that are outlined in the previous section and implemented in 2015, the lecture series that supports the subject was also changed to include two lectures on critical collaboration that referred directly and indirectly to these criteria. Due to the workshop, tutors were also better able to explain SPARKPlus to their students and to connect the lectures to the 'group work' demands of the subject. Indeed, they could confidently say that they were involved in the design of this curriculum.

Following this iteration, tutors again noted a great improvement from 2014 to 2015 in the quality of the students writing in their third assessment, a reflective essay on critical collaboration. It was suggested that this improvement was due to students making 'richer' reflective comments about their peers. SPARKPlus was therefore thought to be helping students to reflect on their peers at an individual level, which was helping them to also write their reflective essay. SPARKPlus appeared to be acting as priming tool in the reflective writing process and contributing to the broader learning objectives of Design Thinking.

While the intervention sketched out in previous section may seem very deliberate, and designed from the top down, through the writing of the curriculum, the use of learning technologies and the formal assessment of the experience of collaboration, it is in fact the students themselves who are developing language to articulate their own collaborations. The comments from SPARKPlus reinforce what we already know as educators: it is through reflective practice that students must discover how to actually design in teams.

Seagulls and Manifestos

This section uses a vignette of student work from Design Thinking to illustrate what happens when manifestos are used to prime students for critical collaboration, and self and peer assessment is used as a lever in the teaching of critical collaboration. When Design Thinking was held in Autumn in 2015, camp fell in mid-October. While wildlife had not been a concern in planning of the event, it was discovered on arrival at Cockatoo Island that October is the height of the seagull nesting season.

The Sydney Harbour Federation Trust Makes This Clear on Their Website

Seagull breeding season is on now and we would like to kindly remind our visitors to keep an eye out for seagulls protecting their nests and young. During this time, seagulls can become quite aggressive, engaging in magpie-like swooping behaviour, however it is important to remember that seagulls are defending their young not attacking people.

If you are on the island and enter the territory of a nesting seagull, please be mindful of the following:

- *Do not provoke the birds*
- *Do not try to touch nests or pick up eggs*
- *Avoid nesting sites where possible, and take an alternative route*
- *If possible, wear a hat* (http://www.cockatooisland.gov.au/events/disruptions-to-access)

During the exploration stage of the camp, when students are encouraged to use active observation methods and undertake a dérive to explore the island many students developed an interest in the seagulls and their nests. Observing, drawing and documenting the behaviour of the gulls became one way the students could interact with the site. One group in particular (students work in groups of 4-5 from at least three disciplines) struggled with the first stage of collaboration, each focusing on their own line of enquiry and, according to their tutor, having difficulty exchanging ideas and choosing one to work on. These were students from different courses who may have little or no contact outside this subject. According to their tutor, the students regrouped and reflected on this process on the second day. At this stage they used their manifesto to work on a critical collaborative approach, rather than assuming it would 'just happen'. Their manifesto, titles 'Divertimento' articulated a number of goals, such as 'We strive to face challenging forms and complex ideas; we will work off the strong points of all our members'.

Considering how design collaboration might include non-human actors, such as the seagulls, and the limited materials they were given[4], the group worked on a wearable design for seagull season. They made a suit and hat and a percussive wand that could be used when traversing the island during seagull breading season. In their presentation the students explained that the aim of their design was to bring awareness to people about the territorial needs of the gulls as well as to protect people from harm without disrupting the environment or harming the fauna.

They talked about how, in order for them to come up with an idea they could all work on together, they needed to step 'in and out' of collaborative mode, in other words, they needed a critical approach to collaboration and to use their skills in reflection. In their reflections through SPARKPlus, these group members made the following comments about their peers:

[Student name] was great at using her photography skills to capture photos of our progress but was also very involved in solving design problems we encountered. She was particularly great in solving structural problems we had in our designs.

[Student name] used her skills as a fashion designer to sew and cut the neon wings to fit the model. She also added flair to the costume by adding colourful streamers. She helped with the little details of the project making it look even better.

When we were discussing ideas [Student name] always had a pen in her hand. We were able to look back at her notes and reflect what we could do better as a group for the assignment.

[Student name] used her skills as an animator to suggest how to design the neon wings so she could move easily and freely when walking.

Following their participation in SPARKPlus, these students completed their reflective writing task and made the following comments, acknowledging the difficulties working together and responding positively to their learning. Because of the demands of the task (i.e. it is a piece of academic writing rather than an open online platform), the language used tends to be more formal and less about the individual team members than the collaborative process generally:

We had a few bumpy parts in our collaboration, but the experience ended on a high note. I would definitely like to work with these group members if we had the chance to do so again. ... we were able to build a work ethic and find our own team dynamic.

Another wrote:

Despite the challenges we faced, the team was able to successfully work together to design an object for cockatoo island.

They also pointed to the importance of the manifesto in the journey:

It is important to note that each team member was equally responsive and very much invested in producing a team name and manifesto to which I believe lead a great deal to our team bonding before the camp.

These comments, and many others from the most recent iteration of camp, pointed to importance of priming students for collaboration, the ways that student can develop skills in critical collaboration, and they way that online self and peer assessment can lead into reflective writing on collaboration. With each iteration of Design Camp (twice a year) there are around forty groups of students from different disciplinary programs that go through a similar journey. Their learning can be understood as the first experience in a potentially long career of critical collaboration.

RECOMMENDATIONS

Our research leads us to make two recommendations for those interested in improving the experience of group work for design students in their first year of study:

1. For first year design cohorts, integrate SPARKPlus use with a reflective writing task.
2. Prime students with a frame for collaboration. We used critical collaboration as the frame and the creation of manifestos as the lead in activity for their assessment.

The stories told in this chapter represent an ongoing project to improve the learning experience of students in their first year of design school. The variables are many–from the teaching team, to the size of the cohort, to the weather. Despite this sprawling and iterative collaborative process, we are able to make these two general recommendations to those using SPARKPlus or a similar tool in teaching design collaboration.

Firstly, we recommend integrating the use of SPARKPlus with a reflective writing task. Part of this means being inclusive and iterative in determining criteria for students to evaluate their peers and making sure these are connected to the demands of assessed reflection. We suggest as far as possible to match these criteria to assessment criteria.

Secondly, we recommend priming students with a sensible frame for collaboration rather than leaving them in the 'wilderness' of group work. Whichever frame is used, it needs to provide students a way to articulate collaboration, keeping in mind that it is the student voice that is most important. We would encourage empowering students to talk about their own experiences as much as possible in class, in formal assessments, and through peer assessment tools. Our approach has been to make use of student peer feedback to identify 'leaders' or 'champions' of collaboration (sometimes these were not the 'leaders' of groups as being able to articulate how interdisciplinary collaboration happened is not necessarily identified as a leadership quality by other students). Such an approach celebrates and rewards students who attempt to define critical collaborative for themselves, contributing to the development of values. We recommend this over the more commonly taken approach to using such data as a punitive tool to punish non-participation, nor as a way to adjust marks.

While first year students are only beginning to define design and to identify as designers, they are expected to develop sophisticated positions and identities in later years. Data from our SPARKPlus redesign indicate that first year students already have nuanced language to describe collaboration and design practices. By identifying and encouraging such language at the earliest possible opportunity, design academics can help students prepare for the complex questions of design in the future.

FUTURE RESEARCH DIRECTIONS

Given that design professions and practices are becoming more collaborative and participatory, and that technologies that catalyse this trend continue to emerge, strategies for teaching teamwork across the design disciplines, that go beyond the recommendations in the previous section are increasingly important. The case in this chapter presents just the beginning of work that needs to be done to better understand how students learn in groups and how teachers and curricula can best support this learning.

A number of questions have arisen from this study, which will direct our continuing work. These can be summarised as follows:

- How does structured organisation facilitate design communication and consequently contribute to the success of the design project? In this study we did not compare SPARKPlus comments with the results of the reflective writing task, nor with the results of the group design project task.
- How do the types of comments recorded in SPARKPlus (and more generally the types of participation with the tool) correlate to categories of students? For example: different types of learners, gender difference, international and domestic students, students from different design disciplines.

- How does participation in SPARKPlus vary across design school subjects? And consequently how do students from different design disciples understand, articulate and *do* collaboration differently?
- How does SPARKPlus need to be implemented differently in different subjects across the university? How do design students articulate collaboration differently from students enrolled in other degrees?
- How can SPARKPlus help us identify and intervene early in mental health issues, particularly during students' transition to university?
- How can SPARKPlus be used to lever critical collaboration over the three to four years of a design degree? How does this learning relate to the development of particular graduate attributes?

CONCLUSION

Our results have taught us a great deal about the how students articulate design collaboration, the interplay of design educators with a tool such as SPARKPlus, and the expanded notions of design that are implicated in the teaching of design for the future. We have also gained better insight into how students collaborate and what they value from their peers' contribution. For example, students value when peers are critical of each other's suggestions. They also value when their peer 'teaches' them things from what they have learnt (from their particular course of study or elsewhere).

Our own critical collaboration as educators has taught us that we need to remain responsive and agile. The use of educational technologies such as SPARKPlus is relational and requires constant tweaking and rethinking. The work discussed here is part of the ongoing critical collaboration design of the subject and the subjects that follow the first year experience continuing to prepare students for their future design careers.

Overall, the re-design of SPARKPlus in Design Thinking through this intervention has been successful, although there are many factors we are yet to consider. From their own comments, it is clear that students are using the tool to reflect in depth on their peers and be more mindful of their own roles in critical collaboration. Further, as one of the questions related to their manifestos, SPARKPlus is linking the experience before they even stepped foot on the island.

It is now providing the platform to help students consider each peer individually and to link this peer's actions to their own learning and experiences of group work. It is also helping the students to write their reflective essays in a much more nuanced way, where individual instances can be better drawn upon. This is a very non-standard way to employ SPARKPlus, but is a highly effective one based on the high quality comments made by students.

We are sure that the role of critical reflection is important in collaborative design research and practice as well as to teaching design. Gaining a deeper understanding of individual contributions and the contributions of team members might create more productive and progressive design environments and contribute to expanded notions of design that include human and non-human actors as collaborators.

ACKNOWLEDGMENT

The authors would like to acknowledge the support of Dr Kathy Egea, UTS First Year Experience Coordinator. We would also like to acknowledge the input of Dr Jacqueline Kasunic to the writing of this chapter. We would also like to acknowledge the contribution of the many hundreds of students who participated. Finally, we would like to acknowledge the talented and invaluable first year interdisciplinary teaching team: Dr Christine Dean; Dr Tom Lee; Ella Barclay; Clare Cooper; Clare Britton; Dr George Catsi; Paul Sutton; Chris Bowman; Dr Bert Bongers; Jennifer Hagedorn, Lin Wei, Melissa Silk, Técha Noble, Dr Francis Maravillas, Dr Kirsten Seale, Dr Kate Scardifield, Tessa Zettel and Cathy Lockhart.

REFERENCES

Adams, R. S., Daly, S. R., Mann, L. M., & Dall'Alba, G. (2011). Being a professional: Three lenses into design thinking, acting, and being. *Design Studies*, *32*(6), 588–607. doi:10.1016/j.destud.2011.07.004

Amatullo, M., Becerra, L., & Montgomery, S. (2011). Design matters case studies: Design education methodologies as a tool for social innovation. *Paper presented at theAnnual Conference of the National Collegiate Inventors and Innovators Alliance*, Washington, D.C.

Barab, S. A., Thomas, M. K., Dodge, T., Squire, K., & Newell, M. (2004). Critical design ethnography: Designing for change. *Anthropology & Education Quarterly*, *35*(2), 254–268. doi:10.1525/aeq.2004.35.2.254

Chiu, M. (2002). An organisational view of design communication in design collaboration. *Design Studies*, *23*(2), 187–210. doi:10.1016/S0142-694X(01)00019-9

Crosby, A. L., Hromek, M. J., & Kinniburgh, J. (2015, August). Making space: Working together for Indigenous design and architecture curricula. *Paper presented at theIndigenous Content in Education Symposium*. Adelaide, Australia.

DiSalvo, C. (2009). Design and the construction of publics. *Design Issues*, *25*(1), 48–63. doi:10.1162/desi.2009.25.1.48

Dunne, A., & Raby, F. (2013). Speculative Everything: Design, Fiction, and Social Dreaming. Cambridge, MA, USA: MIT Press.

Egea, K., McKenzie, J., & Griffiths, N. (2013). Achieving academic engagement: Supporting academics to embed first year transition pedagogies in the curriculum.*Proceedings of the 16th International First Year in Higher Education Conference*. Wellington, New Zealand.

Freeman, M., & McKenzie, J. (2001). Aligning peer assessment with peer learning for large classes: The case for an online self and peer assessment system. In. D. Boud, R. Cohen & J. Sampson (Eds.), Peer Learning in Higher Education: Learning from & with Each Other (pp. 156-169). London: Kogan Page.

Freeman, M., & McKenzie, J. (2002). SPARK, A confidential web-based template for self and peer assessment of student teamwork: Benefits of evaluating across different subjects. *British Journal of Educational Technology*, *33*(5), 551–569. doi:10.1111/1467-8535.00291

Fry, T., Dilnot, C., & Stewart, S. (2015). *Design and the Question of History*. London: Bloomsbury.

Goldfinch, J. (1994). Further developments in peer assessment of group projects. *Assessment & Evaluation in Higher Education*, *19*(1), 29–35. doi:10.1080/0260293940190103

Goldfinch, J., & Raeside, R. (1990). Development of a peer assessment technique for obtaining individual marks on a group project. *Assessment & Evaluation in Higher Education, 15*(3), 210–231. doi:10.1080/0260293900150304

IML. (2002). *Enhancing Experiences of Group Work: A Resource Kit for Managing and Motivating Student Groups. Sydney.* Sydney: Institute for Interactive Media and Learning, University of Technology.

Kift, S. (2009). *Articulating a Transition Pedagogy to Scaffold and to Enhance the First Year Student Learning Experience in Australian Higher Education: Final report for ALTC Senior Fellowship Program.* Strawberry Hills, NSW: Australian Learning and Teaching Council.

Law, J. (2009). Actor network theory and material semiotics. In B. S. Turner (Ed.), *The New Blackwell Companion to Social Theory* (pp. 141–158). Chichester, England: Wiley-Blackwell. doi:10.1002/9781444304992.ch7

Martin, R. M., Maytham, B., Case, J., & Fraser, D. (2005). Engineering graduates' perceptions of how well they were prepared for work in industry. *European Journal of Engineering Education, 30*(2), 167–180. doi:10.1080/03043790500087571

McKenzie, J., & Egea, K. (2015, July). Sustaining an institutional first year experience strategy: A distributed leadership approach. *Paper presented at the Students, Transitions, Achievement, Retention & Success (STARS) Conference,* Melbourne, Australia.

Meier, R. L., Williams, M. R., & Humphreys, M. A. (2000). Refocusing our efforts: Assessing non-technical competency gaps. *The Journal of Engineering Education, 89*(3), 377–385. doi:10.1002/j.2168-9830.2000.tb00539.x

Moggridge, B. (2010). Design Thinking: Dear Don. *Core 77 online design journal.* Retrieved from http://www.core77.com/posts/17042/design-thinking-dear-don-17042

Morris, R., & Hayes, C. (1997, February). Small Group Work: Are group assignments a legitimate form of assessment? In Pospisil, R. and Willcoxson, L. (Eds.), Learning Through Teaching (pp. 229-233). *Proceedings of the 6th Annual Teaching Learning Forum,* Murdoch University, Perth.

Ostergaard, K. J., & Summers, J. D. (2009). Development of a systematic classification and taxonomy of collaborative design activities. *Journal of Engineering Design, 20*(1), 57–81. doi:10.1080/09544820701499654

Peterson, J. F., Frankham, N., McWhinnie, L., & Forsyth, G. (2015). Leading creative practice pedagogy futures. *Art. Design & Communication in Higher Education, 14*(1), 71–86. doi:10.1386/adch.14.1.71_1

Potur, A. A., & Barkul, Ö. (2009). Gender and creative thinking in education: A theoretical and experimental overview. *Journal of ITU A|Z, 6*(2), 44-57.

Schön, D. (1983). *The Reflective Practitioner: How Professionals Think in Action.* New York: Basic Books.

Senge, P. M., Scharmer, C. O., Jaworski, J., & Flowers, B. S. (2005). *Presence: An Exploration of Profound Change in People, Organizations, and Society.* New York: Doubleday.

Strober, M. H. (2010). *Interdisciplinary Conversations: Challenging Habits of Thought.* Palo Alto, CA: Stanford University Press.

Thompson, D., & McGregor, I. (2009). Online self and peer assessment for groupwork. *Education + Training, 51(5/6),* 434 - 447.

Tonkinwise, C. (2014). What is Design Studies good for? *Design and Culture, 6*(1), 5–44. doi:10.2752 /175470814X13823675225036

Zehner, R., Forsyth, G., Musgrave, E., Neale, D., de la Harpe, B., Peterson, F., & Frankham, N. with Wilson, S., & Watson, K. (2009). *Curriculum Development in Studio Teaching Volume One, STP Final Report.* Sydney: Australian Learning and Teaching Council. Retrieved from http://online.cofa.unsw. edu.au/studioteaching/

KEY TERMS AND DEFINITIONS

Critical Collaboration: The way reflection can be used to challenge preconceptions about the role of collaboration in learning, design, and indeed everyday life. We use the idea of critical collaboration as a way of positioning group work in broader discussions about design pedagogy, the future of design, and interdisciplinary creative practice.

Design Thinking: The first year core interdisciplinary subject at the UTS School of Design, for all design degrees.

Interdisciplinary: While Interdisciplinary has a range of applications, in this chapter it refers to a learning space where students from a range of design disciplines are able to learn together.

Priming: The way participants (students) can be primed to understand certain issues before a participatory or co design process begins.

SPARKPlus: An online tool for self and peer assessment. It enables students to rate their own and their peers' contribution to a team task or individual submission.

ENDNOTES

[1]   Alexandra Crosby is the current Course Director of Interdisciplinary Design Studies at UTS and was the subject coordinator of Design Thinking in 2014 and 2015. Adam Morgan is a lecturer at the Institute for Interactive Media and Learning and worked closely on the subject Design Thinking from 2011 to 2015.

[2]   In previous years SPARK data was not read by tutors, only subject coordinators.

[3]   While critical collaboration has been a focus of Design Thinking since the first iterations of the subject almost ten years ago, the project of analysing data to improve the use of SPARKPlus only begun in 2013. This project was supported by a First Year Experience grant in 2015. The aim of this grant was to align our use of SPARKPlus with the First Year Curriculum Principles of 'Evaluation and Monitoring', 'Assessment' and 'Diversity' (Kift, 2009). The UTS strategy for transition including the grant process is explained in detail in Egea, McKenzie, & Griffiths (2013) and McKenzie & Egea (2015).

Chapter 9
Informal Networked Learning as Teamwork in Design Studio Cmyview:
Using Mobile Digital Technologies to Connect with Student's Everyday Experiences

Cristina Garduño Freeman
Deakin University, Australia

ABSTRACT

CmyView is a research project that investigates how mobile technologies have the potential to facilitate new ways to share, experience and understand the connections that people have with places. The aim of the project is to theorise and develop a tool and a methodology that addresses the reception of architecture and the built environment using mobile digital technologies that harness ubiquitous everyday practices, such as photography and walking. While CmyView is primarily focused on evidencing the reception of places, this chapter argues that these activities can also make a contribution to the core pedagogy of architectural education, the design studio. This chapter presents findings of an initial pilot study with four students at an Australian university that demonstrates how CmyView offers a valuable contribution to the educational experience in the design studio.

INTRODUCTION

The design studio is a particular pedagogical space that is central to the education of architects and designers. Within this mode of learning students undertake and practice solving design problems within the built environment, by drawing on, and synthesizing knowledge from, other disciplinary areas. The studio reflects the architectural discipline's primary concern with the production of buildings and is consequently an intellectual space where the educational tensions between the academy, the profession

DOI: 10.4018/978-1-5225-0726-0.ch009

and practice are often played out. The studio is often used as an exemplar of the value of problem-based learning, and in particular, Schön's theories of professional knowledge and reflective practice. However it is not without critique: it is seen to dominate in the architectural curriculum; its open format presents complex social dynamics and inconsistencies within assessment; its insularity and sense of disconnection from society's views of the built environment, as well as students own experiential knowledge about the world in which they live. The role of collaboration and teamwork as essential skills for professional practice are increasingly being recognised. This chapter describes the application of research focused on finding new and innovative ways to assess, experience and collaborate on the concept of social value of architecture and the built environment to the pedagogy of the design studio. Essentially, the chapter considers how the *reception* of architecture can contribute to the learning outcomes of students undertaking design studio, where the focus is on the production of architecture.

CmyView is a project that investigates how mobile technologies have the potential to facilitate new ways to share, experience and understand the connections that people have with places. This connection is described as social value in the field of heritage, sense of place in urban geography and place attachment in environmental psychology and is one part of the reception of architecture. The project is in the initial pilot phase and its central aim is to theorise and develop a tool and methodology that addresses social value. Strategically, CmyView aims to harness ubiquitous everyday practices, such as *photography* and *walking* that are commonly facilitated by mobile digital technologies. A prototype mobile application that is currently in development will be publicly launched in late 2016. For this chapter, a small study was carried out with architectural students at an Australian University, in order to investigate and focus upon the effects of *sharing experiences* of places, as a form of collaborative informal networked learning around social value. Students used the CmyView methodology to document their own walks, as well as to share in the experiences of other's walks. They also completed two short surveys to discuss how these experiences could enhance their understanding and observations of the built environment.

The chapter positions the theoretical contribution that CmyView can make to architectural education by drawing upon the literature on the pedagogy of the design studio, teamwork in design, informal learning networks and visual culture, and then discusses these ideas in relation to the preliminary findings from the student study. In particular the chapter makes a contribution to the scholarship of teaching and learning by considering the crucial role of *sharing* in order to incorporate the *reception* of architecture and the built environment in the teaching of its *production* within the pedagogical framework of the design studio.

BACKGROUND

Architectural Education and the Profession of Architecture in Australia

To understand the centrality of the design studio, and its significance as space where educational and professional priorities play out, it is important to review its historical roots. The formalisation of architectural education in Australia is intimately linked to the rise of architecture as a profession and this connection is still evident in the regulation of the title Architect - in Australia, graduates who have been awarded a degree in architecture may not use the title 'Architect' until they are fully registered with the Board of Architects, as decreed in the Architects Act 2003. Notably, registration involves a period of professional practice undertaken after graduation from university, supervised by a senior registered architect, as well as further training and examination (NSW Board of Architects, 2014a, 2014b). Like other professional degrees, architectural education is not only subject to university regulations, but also to professional standards set by external organisations, making it a complex pedagogical space.

The first universities in Australia were established in the early 1850s but it took some years before architectural education was brought into the university system. In Australia, training for architects, as for most professionals, took place within institutes of technology such as the Sydney School of Arts and the Working Men's College. Otswald and Williams (2008a) report that the first universities established in Australia were The University of Sydney in 1850 and The University of Melbourne in 1853. While they do not make an exhaustive account of all the technical institutes that offered education in architecture during the early years of university education in Australia, they specifically note that the Sydney School of Arts, which later became the Sydney Technical College, and the Working Men's College, (which later became the Royal Melbourne Institute of Technology) were offering architecture courses around 1878. These technical institutions offered programs in architecture but their courses, unlike those of today, were not bound by a guiding set of principles or standards that determined the skills and attributes graduates should possess on graduation. In fact, it was not until 1896 that the first Australian qualification in architecture - a diploma - was even awarded (Donaldson & Morris, 2001, p. 9). The first university level architectural qualification was not established until 1907 at The University of Melbourne.

The architectural profession was working on establishing its presence through state level associations during the same period that saw the formalisation of architectural education. The first of these, the Victorian Architect's Association, was formed in May 1851. The federation of the various state associations into the national body, that was known as the Royal Australian Institute of Architects, took place some years later in 1930. Today the national body has become the Australian Institute of Architects. The shift by architects towards collective professionalization and the formalising of education, was not unique to architecture. John Maxwell Freeland argues in *The Making of a Profession* that architects were motivated to develop educational frameworks and professional associations in order to gain social status. He notes that at this time design-engineers were accorded a higher socioeconomic status and therefore considered 'professionals' because they were educated within the framework of a 'science of construction'. In contrast, architect-builders had a lower social status because they were trained on site and therefore more closely aligned with tradespeople. Freeland states that in these conditions:

Education and registration did come together intimately in the work of the [state] Institutes...in the 1880's when the final heave was being made to lift the practice of architecture from its old trades-builder connections to the purer realms of unsullied professionalism. (Freeland, 1971, p. 203)

The connection of social status with the framework of education and professionalization of architects provides the background for the contemporary design studio program. Typically, in Australia, a mix of academics and practicing architects teach the design studio; a situation observed in at least four universities in Australia: The University of Sydney, University of New South Wales, University of Technology, Sydney and Deakin University.[1] The integration of practicing architects with academics in architectural studio education emulates the historical precedent of 'on-site' training or indeed, a form of apprenticeship. The tension between architecture as an academic pursuit and as a practical skill has influenced the way programs are delivered. These range from the more typical full-time study architectural degrees through to cooperative education programs that take place between universities and architectural practitioners. The first degree at The University of Melbourne (Ostwald & Williams, 2008a, p. 14) operated under the cooperative mode, as did the Bachelor of Architecture offered in the 1990s at the University of Technology, Sydney.

Whilst most universities have given up this dual mode of delivery, perhaps due to the increasing pressures of mass education and research output, it is still in place today within the graduate process of registration. To become registered architects, and be eligible to sit the registration exam, students must complete the required professional practice activities. While design competencies are considered in the AACA's 'National Competency Standards in Architecture', the registration process is focused on the legal implications of the practice of architecture, such as preparation of architectural drawings, coordination of documentation, establishing the building site conditions and assessing the regulatory context, preparing evaluations and feasibility studies, co-ordinating specialists and administering the building contract (Architects Accreditation Council Of Australia (AACA), 2000a, 2000b). However, design, a highly contested and subjective area of architectural practice, remains contained within the educational setting of the design studio.

The Design Studio as a Central Educational Experience

The Design Studio is a core pedagogy within architectural education. In their 2008 review of architectural education in Australia, Michael J Ostwald and Anthony Williams observe that almost half of the curriculum at a typical school of architecture in Australia is devoted to the subject of design. However, they note that this emphasis on design is not in line with the needs of the profession which places a greater emphasis on construction and management skills in professional practice (Ostwald & Williams, 2008a, p. 18). Nonetheless, with half the curriculum of many architecture courses devoted to design studio, both staff and students tend to see design as the central skill of architecture, adding to the multiple roles this pedagogy plays in education, practice and the profession.

The Design Studio curriculum is founded on a problem-based approach to learning, a unique modality first introduced within architectural education (Webster, 2004). The precursor of the design studio, the atelier, emerged from the Académie des Beaux-Arts and then the École des Beaux-Arts in France during the 17th, 18th and 19th centuries (Ostwald & Williams, 2008b, p. 12). In the atelier, groups of students learned to design through practice by responding to competition briefs. Students emulated professional practice by working in a space not unlike the artist's studio, under the supervision of a 'master architect'. During the day they developed their ideas, which were later critiqued by the master architect in the evening. While they may have worked on individual proposals, critique of these would have been collaborative. This form of discussion and critique continues to be embedded within the design studio, through the 'design jury' that is used to assess student's design proposals and projects at the culmination of each studio program. The model is also central to the weekly studio setting in the form of the 'desk crit' where a tutor engages directly with a student via conversation and drawing to evaluate and offer feedback on their design proposal. The atelier differentiates itself as a distinct model of education, from the previous on site apprenticeship model of architectural education (Ostwald & Williams, 2008a), by distancing itself from the physical act of making buildings at 1:1 scale, and moving indoors into the educational setting of the university. Architecture in the studio is mediated through drawings and models and arguably, the shift away from on-site training, has disconnected architectural education from the everyday experience of architecture and the built environment.

Problem-based approaches to student learning have been widely theorised within the architectural profession, as well as within scholarship of teaching and learning. Most influential is educational psychologist Donald Schön's 1983 seminal book *The Reflective Practitioner: How Professionals Think in Action* where he capitalises on the intertwined nature of the architectural profession and architectural education. In *The Reflective Practitioner* Schön proposes an epistemology of practice where he theorises on the intuitive forms of knowledge drawn upon by professionals as part of their work. To describe this form of knowledge, Schön coined the term 'Reflection in Action'. He had based his investigations on the activities of professionals such as architects, psychotherapists, engineers, planners, and managers (Schön, 1983, p. viii). Schön's theory argues that these kinds of professionals must posses an additional type of knowledge to the accepted technical or scientific knowledge, in order to solve non-standard problems. He suggests that professionals use intuitive forms of knowledge coupled with reflective processes to deal with situations they had not previously encountered. This intuitive knowledge, or knowing-in-action, as Schön argues, is implied without being stated. That is, it is tacit. The design studio is underpinned by an acknowledgement that to practice architecture (and other design professions for that matter) requires skills in synthesis and that the knowledge required cannot simply be imparted through traditional knowledge transfer activities, and therefore requires action as a means to develop this skill (Webster, 2004, p. 102).

Key to Schön's theory and the conceptualisation of reflective practice is the valuing of personal experience as a form of knowledge for learning. This aligns with the concept of social value from the field of heritage, which seeks to acknowledge the uses associations and meanings that people have with places (ICOMOS Australia, 2013. Article 1.2). While the concept of reflection-in-action has been widely addressed as a theory that connects students' design practice in the studio with their practice once they move out into the professional field, it has not been discussed as a pedagogical framework for the informal learning activities that happen outside of the studio. Students enrol in architectural education to learn and become skilled in the practice of architecture, yet their existing experience and embodied knowledge of the spatial world is not usually acknowledged. This chapter argues that students, like all individuals in society, observe, connect ideas and move through the built environment as members of the broader public. In other words, they arrive at universities with some form of spatial knowledge, one that is more readily understood as an informal experiential kind of knowledge in the *reception* of architecture. As has already been noted, reflection-in-action is well theorised in terms of the *production* of architecture. But its value and application to the *reception* of architecture and the consequent influence of this on the design studio, the educational setting for practicing the *production of architecture* has not been considered.

Reception and Teamwork in Architecture

Architecture, as well as many design disciplines, is not an individual activity, but one that requires working with others to solve complex problems and enable their realisation. However, the design studio reflects the architecture's concern with the production of buildings and individual authorship (Stead & Garduño Freeman, 2013), rather than on the reception of buildings and teamwork. Architecture has historically focused on the process and reasoning of the production of buildings, on architects and their oeuvres, intellectual movements and aesthetic styles rather than the public perceptions of places and buildings in everyday life. Similarly, the emphasis on authorship has also constructed an idealised notion of the architect as singular, white, male - evident in popular characterisations, such as Howard Roark in Ayn Rand's the Fountainhead and in commendation systems, such as the Pritzker Prize (Heynen, 2012; Stead, 2006) rather than the architect as team member skilled in the processes of collaboration. Reception, has been the domain of literary, media and cultural studies and teamwork the domain of organizational management and general education literature (Tucker & Abbasi, 2012). There are of course exceptions. Post-occupancy surveys that address the environmental sustainability of buildings could constitute a form of reception, as could architectural criticism or even architectural historiography, in the way it understands architectural works as having distinct meanings for particular groups at particular times. Teamwork, while strictly defined as members working together to produce a common output while sharing leadership and goals, involves group work, collaboration, peer learning and sharing. And both the reception of architecture and conceiving of architects as member of a team challenges the status quo, even though reception seeks to understand how others experience architecture, and teamwork, as Richard Tucker and Neda Abbasi argue, "is the linchpin of design practice" (2012).

The concern is to address how a collaborative approach to the reception of architecture can make a contribution to architectural education and in particular within the pedagogical space of the design studio. In their book on design education titled *Design Expertise*, Byran Lawson and Kees Dorst note the way in which design students appear to forget their own first hand knowledge of architecture and the built environment (Lawson & Dorst, 2009). To exemplify this they cite one of their students who was working on a multi-occupancy residential building, Lawson describes the way in which the student designed the entry to a dwelling with no landing to separate the stairs and the entry. When this issue with the planning arrangement was pointed out, the student agreed that this would indeed be problematic. The student was then queried on their observation of a similar situation in real life - it became clear that they had not been encouraged to draw upon and value their personal experience as a repository of knowledge about the architectural world (p. 249). This anecdote demonstrates the way informal learning and observation about the built environment is a rich source of knowledge for students, yet it also reveals the disconnection that can be often observed between a student's experiences and individual reception of the built environment, and their understanding of the requirements in order to produce building. One of the intentions of CmyView is enabling the student to create a bridge between their knowledge of the existing world and the one they are designing through collaboration, thereby increasing their skills and understandings of architecture, and of each other's views about architecture in a meaningful way.

Teamwork, in its strict definition, is less easily identified when considering the informal learning that occurs in the reception of buildings. This is especially so when they are enabled by mobile technologies because collaboration, particularly if it is asynchronous and mediated by technology, operates on several levels. While an individual may be carrying out an independent task, for example taking a photograph of the Sydney Opera House and posting it on Flickr, that same task can also contribute to a group repository of photographs on the same building, and further, those members of the group may together negotiate the associated meanings of this place (Garduño Freeman, 2010). Online interactions are dynamic and fluid and while social media platforms are initially designed to be used in particular ways, they are also open to new uses typified as a form of co-creation (Carvalho & Goodyear, 2014). With the higher rate of adoption of mobile digital technologies, social media and augmented interactions as ubiquitous to every-day life and the experience of the built environment, understanding the informal learning opportunities and experiences enabled through these is becoming increasingly important. *CmyView* seeks to explore how such dynamic and fluid forms of *collaboration* around the *reception* of architecture can contribute to the learning experiences within the studio – perhaps be understood as a form of place-based networked learning, an emerging area of research (Carvalho, Goodyear, & de Laat, 2016).

CMYVIEW

This section of the chapter describes CmyView and argues that the experiences central to its methodology, in particular the idea of *sharing embodied experiences* of the built environment through walking and photography can act as a platform for students to develop important spatial and visual analytical skills with their peers, gain a broader understanding of the aspects which communities and the broader public value in places, and contextualise spatial ideas pertinent to design studio within the real context of the built environment. It does this by describing the experiences facilitated by the app and their theoretical underpinnings, and presenting initial findings from a pilot study that tests the preliminary aspects of the app and the conceptual methodology with four students at an Australian University.

The advent of new internet and communication technologies are blurring existing conceptions and definitions of community and audience, of education and entertainment and of communication and participation. Digital media projects that seek to connect communities, people and place through participatory cultures are an emerging area of creative design practice and interdisciplinary scholarly research. Social media is increasingly recognised as a means to gain insight on society and culture through shared visual phenomena (Burgess, 2009; van Dijck, 2008, 2011, 2013; Van House & Ames, 2007; Van House & Churchill 2008; Van House et al., 2004). This is exemplified in projects such as *Murmur* (CFC Media Lab, 2003), *Sydney Sidetracks* (Barnes), *Mappiness* (MacKerron & Mourato), *Geocaching* (Groundspeak Inc, 2000-16), *Long Time, No See?* (Armstrong, Sade, & Thomas, 2012-13) and *City Souvenirs* (Seisler & Bosque, 2010) that collect and engage with the societal values of places, and exemplify a shift towards creative, situated and embodied methods for qualitative and creative research.

Mappiness, a project by Dr. George MacKerron at the London School of Economics, maps people's emotions alongside geographical location and social context to better understand wellbeing and urban climate. While *Sydney Sidetracks*, an ABC project by Sarah Barns, delivers archival audio material through mobile technologies in order to resituate history in place, and in the present. In contrast *City Souvenirs* is an on-going art project in which Nicole Seisler and Liene Bosque facilitate public walks during which participants are encouraged to make porcelain imprints of architecture. The porcelain imprints, facilitate conversations between participants, and videos of the walks are then posted online. Such explorative social projects that engage with experiences people have in the built environment, through visual, material and narrative exchanges, are only possible on a widespread scale because of digital media. These projects underscore the way digital media is commonplace within the social interactions and engagements that take place everyday.

The Mobile Application: Collecting and Sharing Experiences of Places

CmyView aims to deliver a mobile application tool that collects data in order to enable a better understanding and evidencing of people's experiences and connections with place. The methodology of the mobile application will employ *walking, photography* and *audio recordings*, thereby combining embodied and creative methods in order to become integral to existing everyday practices. The application will facilitate two kinds of participation: The first experience will allow people to *map* their own walks and then *share* them on CmyView. Using spatial mapping technology, the app will track the route walked and connect this with photographs taken by the participant during the journey. Each photograph is described as a 'view' and is described as something significant or of interest to the individual. The number of 'views' depends on the distance walked; the further an individual walks the more views that can be made. Making the number of views available dependent on the distance walked is an important incentive to users to move through the built environment. It also increases the focus on choosing something significant, rather than taking photographs in a limitless way. After each view has been made, users are asked to make an audio recording describing why the view was taken and what in the view was significant to them. This is a reflective process that makes Schön's notions of reflection in action an explicit part of the experience. The use of audio recordings also is important; it permits the physical experience of walking to continue while also recording. This is in contrast to the discontinuity required if comments were typed in textually. The app will then package the route, the photos and audio recordings into a shareable audio-photo-walk that others can share and participate in.

The second experience enables people to *engage* in one of the walks that has been contributed. In this version of the experience the app enables individuals to *see* the built environment through someone else's eyes. In this mode the walk becomes a visual treasure hunt where the photographs and comments of the contributor act as signposts that guide the experience, and the audio recordings describe the way the other person sees the built environment. The audio recordings here also play a role in enabling emotion to be communicated, and to create a level of intimacy that is more difficult to achieve via textual means. By engaging in one of the shared walks it is intended participants will gain an understanding of how others experience the world, what is important to them, how they value the built environment and consider how this affects their own views. Collecting and sharing, and engaging in walks on CmyView can be done individually or in groups, but the app enables all users to collaborate in documenting the *reception* of the built environment. In doing so, it offer participants several important ways of experiencing architecture and the built environment that compliments the constraints of the design studio (Figure 1).

CMYVIEW: PILOT AND METHODOLOGY

The preliminary app and methodology of CmyView was tested in September 2015 with four students enrolled in design studio at an Australian university. The aim of this small pilot was to gain information on the task (walking, photographing and making audio-recordings) and the reaction of users during the two experiences. While the numbers of the study were limited, data was collected in a variety of forms in order to gain a sound understanding of the potential of the project. The results discussed below, whilst promising, should be seen as initial insights into the potential of CmyView to contribute to architectural

Figure 1. Conceptual diagram by the author, which explains how CmyView a social media app can share people's views about the places they care about

education. It is intended to develop the app into a full prototype stage and conduct more extensive testing in 2016 with approximately 50-100 individuals.

Students were asked to undertake two walks, one to 'collect' views and the second to 'share' views. The students went out during a design studio session to the local environment that surrounds the university campus. The walks were not related to the design studio project. Students were then instructed to take an individual walk (approx. 30 minutes) and make between 6-12 views of aspects they felt were significant to them. A neutral stance was important in order to enable students to capture aspects both positive and negative (or simply interesting or odd). Because the app prototype is still in development, students made the walk using the native camera application of an iPad and recorded their audio on the 'voice memos' app. Photographs, audio recordings, and geo location identifiers of each participant's walk were collected as data. Students then completed a short 5-10 minute online survey of open-ended questions about their experience.

The second walk was undertaken a week later at the same time of day. The data collected the previous week had been manually entered into an existing app that enables the design and sharing of custom walking tours titled 'TourBuddy'. Each student's walk from the previous week was set up on Tourbuddy as an individual route where the photographs had geo location identifiers so that they could be re-contextualised in the built environment. Each student selected one of the other's walks to undertake and was asked to find each of the photographs taken in the surrounding environment to the campus and to listen to the audio recordings for each of the walk's views. This too, was completed individually. After this second walk, students were again asked to complete a short 5-10 minute online survey of open-ended questions about their experience (Figure 2).

Walks and Photographs as an Educational Modality

Walking is central to human existence.[2] In *Wanderlust*, Rebecca Solnit (2000) offers a cultural history of walking where she articulates the ways in which walking is embedded in daily life. Solnit explores the way walking intersects with the sacred in the form of the pilgrimage, its use as a type of mediation, and its centrality to landscape forms such as the labyrinth. She describes the way it can help us think in new

Figure 2. How the pilot tests were carried out using alternative software.

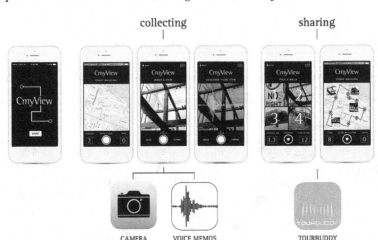

ways or simply become a form of transport to reach a destination. Walking is an embodied experience, both as an activity and biologically in terms of its effects on our anatomical evolution. Walking is a way to increase fitness and a means to unclutter the mind. Walking gives entry into many different kinds of experiences, and critically, situates such questions as the significance of place in situ, rather than in the realm of memory where it resides in the design studio. Embodied engagements, such as walking, are already recognised to have a significant impact on creativity and reflective thinking (Barns, 2011; Bendiner-Viani, 2005; Middleton, 2010; Oppezzo & Schwartz, 2014). Marily Oppezzo and Daniel L. Schwartz state that being physically active through walking can change our mental state and increase creativity, during and for a period afterwards (2014, p. 1148). This increase in creativity coupled with the simultaneous experiencing of place and reflecting on its personal value has the potential to encourage architecture students to connect the activity of design with their own personal experiences of architecture and the built environment.

New research in the social sciences also offers valuable arguments for developing creative and reflective ways to understand people's sense of their own identity or attitudes to specific issues. Rather than the traditional approaches, such as questionnaires or focus groups to understand peoples' ideas about their identity, Professor of Media, Art and Design, David Gauntlett, argues that creative practices, such as making things or in this case taking photographs, can offer a reflective process for individuals that gives a richer and deeper understanding of the social processes taking place (Gauntlett, 2007, 2011; Gauntlett & Holzwarth, 2006). Traditional approaches to sociology frame the dynamic and complex socio-cultural processes of the connections between people and place as singular direct responses to the physical environment. Further as already highlighted earlier, architecture, and traditional research methods, tend to overlook the critical role that visual representations play in *forming* and *informing* our ideas about the built environment (Garduño Freeman, 2010, 2013; Rattenbury, 2002; Stead & Garduño Freeman, 2013). So by making representations of architecture and the built environment whilst being in place, participants in CmyView are required to reflect on what is of value, why and for whom. Taking photographs might at first seem a thoughtless process, but when framed as a creative task much like the design studio brief, it can become an opportunity for sharing views and developing a better understanding of place.

A further aspects of architectural practice needs to be taken into account to evaluate walking and sharing photographs as a way of connecting the tasks of the design studio with students' experiential knowledge of the built environment. While it may appear contradictory, architectural practice is not the practice of making buildings; architects do not do the physical labour of construction. Rather, they make drawings, that is, representations, for others to carry out this work. This conflation has consequences for the way in which representations and built architectural objects are inextricably entwined and 'slippery'. As Kester Rattenbury observes:

Architecture's relationship with its representation is peculiar, powerful and absolutely critical. Architecture is driven by belief in the nature of the real and the physical: the specific qualities of one thing – its material, form, arrangement, substance, detail – over another. It is absolutely rooted in the idea of 'the thing itself'. Yet it is discussed, illustrated, explained – even defined – almost entirely through its representations. (Rattenbury, 2002, p. xxi)

The conflation between the built architectural object and its representation in drawings, models and even gestures is perhaps, nowhere more prevalent than in the design studio. Discussions between tutors and students in the design studio about the qualities, characteristics and value of design proposals and existing architectural precedents, occur entirely through representations. Part of the pedagogical premise of CmyView is to use representations as a means to connect students' observations outside the studio, with the discussions and decisions that take place within it. Ostwald and Williams note that educational researchers argue that the emphasis on design studio within architectural education is necessary because this skill takes time to mature (2008a). Design requires students to develop the ability to synthesise creative ideas with technical and theoretical knowledge, and one way to assist this development is for them to make connections between the representations that are so central to architectural practice and education, and their own experiences of architecture within the built environment.

The development of digital photography and its incorporation into mobile communication devices has made photographs a ubiquitous part of everyday culture. Whilst photographs have always played a social role (Chalfen, 1987), their value as mementos has expanded to include their use as messages:

When pictures became a visual language conveyed through the channel of a communication medium, the value of individual pictures decreases while the general significance of visual communication increases. A thousand pictures sent over the phone may now be worth a single word: 'see!'. Taking, sending and receiving photographs is a real-time experience and, like spoken words, image exchanges are not meant to be archived (Van House et al., 2005). Because of their abundance, these photographs gain value as 'moments', while losing value as mementoes. (van Dijck, 2008, p. 59)

Photography is a performance of seeing and representing. In the process of taking a photograph the photographer frames a picture, making decisions about what to include and exclude from the frame. Recording a comment about that image and then curating a collection of images relating to a walk requires a process of reflection on the experience of the physical act of walking through space. Such an open ended process of playful reflection-in-action (Schön, 1985) about the individual's experience of the built environment, offers an informal learning experience that can contribute to their understandings of the *production* of architecture in the design studio.

COLLECTING: REFLECTION-IN-ACTION THROUGH RECEPTION

In the CmyView pilot, each of the students undertook a distinct route in the urban environment that surrounds the university campus. (See Figure 3). However, three out of four students walked towards the waterfront area, only one student kept directly away from this. This is interesting because there is a significant difference in urban quality between the 'leisure' zone of the waterfront, which is very well maintained and has several tourist attractions, and the more 'urban' areas of the city without vistas and 'things to see'. To develop a better understanding of what drew each student's attention, their route needs to be coupled with photographs and comments, in other words, their 'views'.

The views made by each of the students who participated in the CmyView pilot all displayed quite distinct visual approaches to 'seeing' the built environment (See Figure 4). Their individual perspectives were not readily drawn from the photographs alone, but from the combined photograph and audio recording. One student repeatedly questioned why areas of the city were left unused, unkempt or in disrepair observing: "So its three thirty in the middle of the working week, middle of the working day. Why is there only one car in this carpark? It's meant to be the city...well not really a city but a town.

Figure 3. Student pilot of CmyView 'collecting' walks

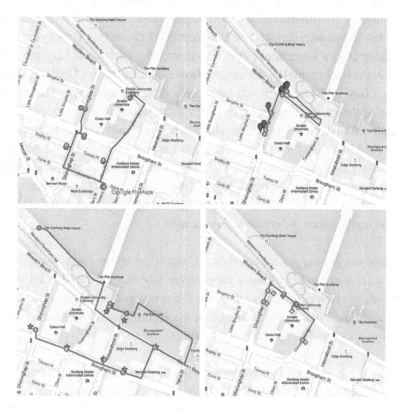

Figure 4. Photographs from student pilot of CmyView 'collecting' walks
From top: questioning, heritage and icons, aesthetics and composition and re-observing the everyday

Why is it so empty? Just makes no sense…". Another focused on taking photographs and commenting on architectural examples that traditionally constitute heritage and iconic symbols of the area. After photographing the waterfront area this student commented "I chose this view because I think it is very iconic of what Geelong is as a waterfront city or town, um, the iconic and very recognisable sculpture pieces that you see in the background of the image show that tie back the Geelong waterfront and what we all know to be the Bay". The third student had a very different approach. The student was drawn to make views because of the images' aesthetic qualities, both in terms of composition, colour, form and light. The photographs taken depicted lights, trees backlit by the sunset and architectural and urban details. The student commented that they "like[d] this image because it showed repetition and harmony and it was orderly and its [was] also very dynamic". The final student took images of aspects of the city that he noticed because of the activity of participating in the CmyView pilot, areas that were commonplace experiences to them, but that became interesting through the act of photography. This was most clearly expressed in the first image taken, where they commented:

This first view I found interesting for the exercise in that it's a space I would walk through, probably every day um but its [sic] not until you have an exercise like this where like this where you stop and think about it that I really appreciate the old and new I suppose you see through the old beams and then the clean sort of white plasterboard and then also in the right hand corner you the um the light which is backlit up the beam… I thought was really interesting.

What is clear from these walks and photographs is the distinct approach to 'seeing' the built environment that each student has, and the value of a reflective exercise in observation. It drew out their own knowledge through reflection-in-actions and validates their existing experience of the built environment. The task of walking, taking photographs and making audio recordings resulted in students documenting their own visual perspective on the built environment as a form of visual critique. From a pedagogical perspective, it was also valuable to understand how students perceive the built environment and what aspects they value when given an open opportunity, as opposed to a directed task to solve a design problem.

Schön's theories of reflective practice can not only be used to describe the messy creative processes that are at the centre of the practice of design (Kinsella, 2007, p. 103), but can also be a valuable framework for understanding the importance of embodiment, both in the studio and, by extension, in the activities prompted by CmyView. The work of Inger Mewburn (2009, 2011) situates the use of 'gesture' as central to the design studio. Her study of the role of physical movement in describing designs alongside drawings, models and collaborative imagining between students and tutors brings to light the overlooked role of embodiment as an essential component of the studio. Mewburn both challenges Schön's theory of reflection-in-action and adds to it, by introducing the idea of 'embodiment' and 'performativity' as components of the design studio pedagogy. Mewburn's work demonstrates the contribution that students' embodied experiences using drawings and models to explain their idea contributes to their learning. David Kirsch, a scholar of embodied cognition argues for the potential of the connection between our minds, bodies and technologies. He asserts that humans think with their bodies as well as their brains. Tools enable interactions that are likely to change perception and therefore thinking. Kirsch states that "the concepts and beliefs we have about the world are grounded in our perceptual-action experience with things, and the more we have tool mediated experiences the more our understanding of the world is situated in the way we interact through tools" (Kirsh, 2013, p. 3:3). In other words, the knowing gained by doing (both formally in the studio and informally as part of everyday life) is more powerful than the passive consumption of information.

In the CmyView first post walk survey, students were asked about their experience. Their responses indicate that their conscious focus was on 'seeing' and 'observing' the built environment in the immediate surrounds to the campus. The activity of taking photographs was central to enabling them to 'see'. One student commented that taking photographs made them "actually consider more deeply why I noticed the things I did and what significance those places had", another stated: "I was much more conscious of the environment that I was walking through. What was I seeing, what was happening and most importantly for me why was this happening, why was this here?". Students saw the task of taking photographs as an active process of making representations that allowed them to document their reception of the places they visited thereby seeing familiar places in a new way. Interestingly their responses to the value of walking as part of the collecting experience in the pilot study were less explicit. One student commented "By walking and paying a closer attention on little aspects that intrigue us, makes you critique the one dimensionality of the views you take for granted every day". Students' understanding of the effect of walking on creativity appeared to be implicit rather than explicit. Overall, students reported that the collecting CmyView exercise could contribute to their design studio learning as "a great source of inspiration for design" and that it could "potentially encourage you to be more critical of your understanding in your studio research or drawings you read". Another interesting outcome was the way the experience was seen as a scaffolded exercise that contributed to their presenting skills: "in a way it is like presenting your design at final review. You must think about what it is you are saying and how you compose the view. It links to how clearly are you able to communicate with words and a graphic a story". Whilst the first CmyView walk where students mapped their views was not a typical design studio activity, students were clearly able to make connections with how it could extend their learning, experience, knowledge and criticality beyond the boundaries of the studio.

SHARING: INFORMAL NETWORKED LEARNING AS TEAMWORK

Engaging through informal learning networks may be seen as a contentious definition of teamwork. As has already been noted, teamwork is usually distinguished from groupwork, where members focus on a common outcome (Tucker & Abbasi, 2012). However, in an informal setting mediated by digital technologies, activities, intentions, interactions and negotiations occur more fluidly, and an individual task, such as the collecting of views from the CmyView pilot study, may then be used to achieve a team goal, such as understanding others' experiences of the built environment. Central to both teamwork and informal networked learning is the idea of *sharing*. Whilst students may not be focused on developing a design outcome, the synchronous and asynchronous experiences shared and enabled by mobile technologies and digital platforms offer a less pressured and more conversational space for collaboration. This, one might argue, offers a way for students to see the world through each other's eyes – that is, to share their experiences outside the studio in order to develop a critical discourse and an understanding about people's diverse experiences of the built environment within the pedagogy of the studio. Without sharing, students cannot come together around a touchstone experience, through which they can judge, argue and position their own design ideas. The experiences of students documenting their views using the CmyView methodology that has been outlined in the section above shows that there are valuable learning outcomes that can contribute to design studio learning, enabled by the process of walking, taking photographs and making audio recordings. How might the sharing of these walks be understood? Unlike the collecting part of the CmyView pilot, which produced tangible data, such as geo location, photographs and audio recordings, the *sharing* of walks can only be analysed by asking students how this experience changed their understandings of their initial CmyView walk.

After students had undertaken another person's walk they were asked to complete a short online survey that contained five open-ended questions. Initially they were asked to describe their experience of another student's CmyView walk. Overall, they commented that it was interesting to see and hear their peer's views of the surrounding areas of the university. In particular, they noted that seeing and hearing someone else's perspectives, distinct from their own, offered new insights, both about the built environment, but also about the way each person observes the world. One student commented:

It was a completely different experience to my own as different views were selected. Even if we were looking at the same views, this person clearly had a different perspective on what they saw. It just goes to show that there isn't one way of seeing things, and this theory is not exclusive to views.

This reveals that students can appreciate their distinct ways of seeing, and to value the opportunity to engage with other ways of seeing the world. They described the *sharing* experience as intimate and being an opportunity to "enter into someone else's headspace and see things the way they do." Further it affected and changed their understanding of their own walk – one student stated "Considering it was a similar walk to the one I completed I found their views to be different to mine. It made me reconsider again why I chose the views I did." They also expanded their concepts of what constituted the built environment.: "Something that was interesting with the other person's walk that I completed was that a lot of what was captured was not specifically buildings. It broadened my under-standing of built environment towards how we shape our natural environment also." These comments are particularly interesting because these students had already spent approximately six to eight weeks working together in the design studio on the assigned project brief. They had already formed collegiate relationships and shared experiences within the studio. Yet in undertaking a CmyView walk they were able to engage with each other in new ways that offered broader but significant learning outcomes for them. So how can such learning experiences be theorized?

Extending the Design Studio through Informal Learning Networks

Scholarship on informal learning networks is founded on the notion that learning is not limited to formal educational settings but that it can also take place through the social and material interactions of everyday life. While research on informal learning has emerged alongside the rise of internet and communication technologies, as a consequence of Web 2.0, social media and the participatory turn, Lucila Carvalho and Peter Goodyear observe in their book *The Architecture of Productive Learning Networks,* that it has a much longer history in pre-digital forms (2014, p. 4). Carvalho and Goodyear define learning as a change of behaviour that results from a particular experience. However, they propose that such an explicit definition is limiting; "learning may lead to a richer understanding of some phenomenon, or to experience change in one's sense of self, without anyone else being able to detect a change in behaviour" (2014, p. 5). Carvalho and Goodyear argue that learning can be a direct consequence *or* incidental to some other activity, but that neither form should be marginalised.

Carvalho and Goodyear analyse several social media platforms in terms of their value as informal learning networks (2014). They take an activity centred approach that focuses on what people are actually doing, both in physical space and in the online environment (or combinations of the two). In *The Architecture of Productive Learning Networks* they offer a framework for the analysis of media platforms such as *iSpot, Virtual Choir* and *Diseña el Cambio* as informal learning networks. The framework is centred on the tasks, emergent activities and resulting outcomes, but importantly incorporates the physically situated spaces and places, artefacts, tools and texts, and the dyads, groups, communities and social structures, as essential elements of the learning experience (Carvalho & Goodyear, 2014, p. 59). Their emphasis on sharing and interaction offers a theoretical framework though which to understand, develop and investigate the potentials of CmyView as enabling teamwork around the reception of the built environment. While students were not formally engaged in teamwork, collaborating and sharing are essential components of the CmyView methodology. Collecting views opened students to new perspectives on familiar environment, and sharing views enabled them to understand others' views and that there are a diverse range of experiences, but the effects beyond the exercise in terms of developing student's ability to interact and discuss aspects of the built environment in face to face interactions was an unexpected yet important outcome. When asked in the survey completed after undertaking one of their peers walks, whether participating in the CmyView pilot had prompted any conversations, all four students responded that it had. They commented on both pragmatic aspects of the research – the configuration of the tools, the app interface and problems that were encountered – and about the way sharing the experience enabled them to acknowledge their differing approaches to the same task. One student said "we were all enlightened that even though we are situated in the same area and exposed to the same areas, we are provoked and drawn to different details and aspects." There was a sense of surprise and discovery in finding out what they had each achieved. They noted that the experience "was more than just a photo, people liked the way that the audio voiced the meaning behind the view." Students' responses clearly indicate that participating in the CmyView pilot enriched their understanding of the built environment around their campus, of their own visual approach to the built environment and to the approach of others. Such feedback is promising in terms of developing ways that students can draw on their existing knowledge and experience of the built environment while collaborating to document their reception of places. Importantly, these skills develop not in isolation or individually, but together though sharing, in an informal form of teamwork. Complementing the design studio, through informal experiences that connect students formal experiences with their own informal learning, perhaps offers a means to address critiques about the design studio's emphasis on production and individual notions of authorship and to incorporate broader views and social issues such as equity, inclusivity and social justice into student learning outcomes (Anderson, 2014, p. 16; Elger & Russell, 2006, p. 112).While CmyView is in its initial stages of development, the pilot study demonstrates how sharing can be understood as an informal form of teamwork, when enabled through mobile digital technologies, and one that can contribute to the pedagogy of the design studio.

FUTURE RESEARCH DIRECTIONS

CmyView, discussed in this chapter is a small pilot study. However, its innovative approach and methodology connects informal learning to the reception of architecture thereby making a significant contribution to the topic of the book. The CmyView app will be completed in 2016 and there are plans to gain funding for a series of larger evaluation studies, both within an architectural educational setting, and with general public and with the heritage sector. Comments and contributions from readers are welcome.

CONCLUSION

Mobile digital technologies are sometimes touted as the panacea for all problems. But like previous shifts in media, initial polarised reactions soon make way for more complex and nuanced understandings of the potential they bring to existing practices. The design studio is a highly contested but unique pedagogical space in architectural education. Here, the historical and contemporary tensions between architectural practice, the profession and the academy are played out. While there are substantive critiques about the ambiguities within the pedagogy of the design studio this can also be seen as an opportunity to innovate by incorporating students' personal experiences of the built environment into the educational space. By integrating ideas from the studio, such as creative methods, with the potential that mobile communication technologies bring for embodied experiences, in situ, through representations, CmyView has the capacity to connect production to reception, individual work with collaboration and the space of the studio with the everyday.

CmyView, with its focus on mapping social values, sharing these through a digital platform, and engaging by experiencing places through the eyes of others, can be conceived of as an informal learning network focused on collaboration around the reception of the built environment. Such a digital platform can potentially increase the sense of community and participation within the design studio as well as contribute to improving the student's connection with their everyday observations and experiences. By emphasising *sharing*, as much as individual reflection-in-action, the app extends the boundaries of the studio into the lived experiences of students.

REFERENCES

Anderson, N. M. (2014). Public Interest Design as Praxis. *Journal of Architectural Education*, 68(1), 16–27. doi:10.1080/10464883.2014.864896

Architects Accreditation Council Of Australia (AACA). (2000a). *Competency Based Assessment in Architecture*. Retrieved from http://www.aaca.org.au/wp-content/uploads/2014/01/APE-LOG-BOOK-INFORMATION-Jan-2014.pdf

Architects Accreditation Council Of Australia (AACA). (2000b). *The National Competency Standards in Architecture*. Retrieved from http://www.aaca.org.au/wp-content/uploads/2010/09/2009_NCSA.pdf

Armstrong, K., Sade, G., & Thomas, L. (2012). Long Time, No See? Retrieved from http://explore.long-time-no-see.org

Barnes, S. Sydney Sidetracks. Retrieved from http://www.abc.net.au/innovation/sidetracks/default.htm

Barns, S. (2011). Street Haunting: Sounding the Invisible City. In M. Foth, L. Forlano, C. Satchell, & M. Gibbs (Eds.), *From Social Butterfly to Engaged Citizen* (pp. 203–216). London: The MIT Press.

Bendiner-Viani, G. (2005). Walking, Emotion, and Dwelling: Guided Tours in Prospect Heights, Brooklyn. *Space and Culture*, *8*(4), 459–471. doi:10.1177/1206331205280144

Burgess, J. (2009). Remediating vernacular creativity: Photography and cultural citizenship in the Flickr photosharing network. In T. Edensor, D. Leslie, S. Millington, & N. Rantisi (Eds.), *Spaces of Vernacular Creativity: Rethinking the Cultural Economy* (pp. 116–126). London: Routledge.

Carvalho, L., & Goodyear, P. (2014). *The Architecture of Productive Learning Networks*. NY: Routledge.

Carvalho, L., Goodyear, P., & de Laat, M. (2016). *Place-based Spaces for Networked Learning*. NY: Routledge.

Chalfen, R. (1987). *Snapshot versions of life*. Bowling Green, OH: Bowling Green State University Popular Press.

Donaldson, B., & Morris, D. (2001). *Architecture Newcastle: Preserving Its Educational History*. Newcastle: NSW RAIA.

Elger, D., & Russell, P. (2006). Crisis? What Crisis? *International Journal of Architectural Computing*, *4*(1), 107–121. doi:10.1260/147807706777008966

Freeland, J. M. (1971). *The Making of a Profession: A History of the Growth and Work of the Architectural Institutes in Australia*. Sydney, NSW: Angus and Robertson.

Garduño Freeman, C. (2010). Photosharing on Flickr: Intangible heritage and emergent publics. *International Journal of Heritage Studies*, *16*(4), 352–368. doi:10.1080/13527251003775695

Garduño Freeman, C. (2013). Participatory Culture as a Site for the Reception of Architecture: Making a Giant Sydney Opera House Cake. *Architecture Theory Review*, *18*(3), 325–339. doi:10.1080/132648 26.2013.890008

Gauntlett, D. (2007). *Creative Explorations: New Approaches to Identities and Audiences*. London: Routledge.

Gauntlett, D. (2011). *Making is connecting: The social meaning of creativity, from DIY and knitting to YouTube and Web 2.0*. Cambridge, UK: Polity Press.

Gauntlett, D., & Holzwarth, P. (2006). Creative and visual methods for exploring identities. *Visual Studies*, *21*(1), 82–91. doi:10.1080/14725860600613261

Groundspeak Inc. (2000). Geocaching. Retrieved from http://www.geocaching.com

Heynen, H. (2012). Genius Gender and Architecture: The Star System as Exemplified in the Pritzker Prize. *Architectural Theory Review*, *17*(2-3), 331–345. doi:10.1080/13264826.2012.727443

Kinsella, E. A. (2007). Technical rationality in Schön's reflective practice: Dichotomous or non-dualistic epistemological position. *Nursing Philosophy*, *8*(2), 102–113. doi:10.1111/j.1466-769X.2007.00304.x PMID:17374071

Kirsh, D. (2013). Embodied cognition and the magical future of interaction design. ACM Transactions on Computer-Human Interaction. *ACM Transactions on Computer-Human Interaction, 20*(1), 3:1-3:20.

Lawson, B., & Dorst, K. (2009). *Design Expertise*. Oxford: Architectural Press.

MacKerron, G., & Mourato, S. (n. d.). Mappiness. Retrieved from http://www.mappiness.org.uk

CFC. Media Lab., (2003). Murmur. Retrieved from http://murmurtoronto.ca/index.php

Mewburn, I. (2009). *Constructing Bodies: Gesture, Speech and Representation at Work in Architectural Design Studios*. The University of Melbourne.

Mewburn, I. (2011). Lost in Translation: Reconsidering reflective practice and design studio pedagogy. *Arts and Humanities in Higher Education, 11*(4), 363–379. doi:10.1177/1474022210393912

Middleton, J. (2010). Sense and the city: Exploring the embodied geographies of urban walking. *Social & Cultural Geography, 11*(6), 575–596. doi:10.1080/14649365.2010.497913

NSW Board of Architects. (2014a). The AACA Architectural Practice Examination (APE). Retrieved from http://www.architects.nsw.gov.au/students-graduates/architectural-practice-examination

NSW Board of Architects. (2014b). Architects Act 2003 Information Sheet: Illegal Use of the Title 'Architect'. Retrieved from http://www.architects.nsw.gov.au/download/INFORMATION SHEET - ILLEGAL USE OF THE TITLE ARCHITECT February 2014.pdf

Oppezzo, M., & Schwartz, D. L. (2014). Give your ideas some legs: The positive effect of walking on creative thinking. *Journal of Experimental Psychology. Learning, Memory, and Cognition, 40*(4), 1142–1152. doi:10.1037/a0036577 PMID:24749966

Ostwald, M. J., & Williams, A. (2008a). *Understanding Architectural Education in Australasia*.

Ostwald, M. J., & Williams, A. (2008b). *Understanding architectural education in Australasia*.

Rattenbury, K. (2002). Introduction. In K. Rattenbury (Ed.), *This is not architecture: Media constructions* (pp. xxi–xxiv). New York: Routledge.

Schön, D. A. (1983). *The Reflective Practitioner: How Professionals Think in Action* (1995 ed.). Aldershot: Avebury, Ashgate Publishing Limited.

Schön, D. A. (1985). *The design studio: an exploration of its traditions and potentials*. London: RIBA Publications for RIBA Building Industry Trust.

Seisler, N., & Bosque, L. (2010). City Souvenirs. Retrieved from http://citysouvenirs.wordpress.com

Solnit, R. (2000). *Wanderlust: A History of Walking*. New York: Penguin Books.

Stead, N. (2006). Fabulous, Far Away and Gigantic: Myth in Australian Architectural Authorship. *Les Cahiers du CICLas, 7*(May), 45–57.

Stead, N., & Garduño Freeman, C. (2013). Architecture and "The Act of Receiving, or the Fact of Being Received": Introduction to a Special Issue on Reception. *Architectural Theory Review, 18*(3), 267–271. doi:10.1080/13264826.2013.902418

The Burra Charter: The Australia ICOMOS Charter for Places of Cultural Significance 2013, (2013).

Tucker, R., & Abbasi, N. (2012). Conceptualizing teamwork and group-work in architecture and related design disciplines. *Paper presented at the ASA 2012: Building on knowledge, theory and practice: 46th Annual Conference of the Architectural Science Association*, Gold Coast, Qld. http://hdl.handle.net/10536/DRO/DU:30051739

van Dijck, J. (2008). Digital Photography: Communication, identity, memory. *Visual Communication*, 7(1), 57–76. doi:10.1177/1470357207084865

van Dijck, J. (2011). Flickr and the culture of connectivity: Sharing views, experiences, memories. *Memory Studies*, 4(4), 401–415. doi:10.1177/1750698010385215

van Dijck, J. (2013). *The Culture of Connectivity: A Critical History of Social Media*. Oxford: Oxford University Press. doi:10.1093/acprof:oso/9780199970773.001.0001

Van House, N., & Ames, M. (2007). The Social Life of Cameraphones Images. *Paper presented at the CHI '07*, San Jose, California, USA.

Van House. N., Davis, M., Takhteyev, Y., Good, N., Wilhelm, A., & Finn, M. (2004, November 6–10). *From "What?" to "Why?": The Social Uses of Personal Photos*. Paper presented at the CSCW'04 Chicago, Illinois.

Van House, N., & Churchill, E. F. (2008). Technologies of Memory: Key Issues and Critical Perspectives. *Memory Studies*, 1(3), 295–310. doi:10.1177/1750698008093795

Webster, H. (2004). Facilitating critically reflective learning: Excavating the role of the design tutor in architectural education. *Art, Design & Communication in Higher Education*, 2(3), 101–111. doi:10.1386/adch.2.3.101/0

KEY TERMS AND DEFINITIONS

Creative Methodologies: Research at the intersection of creative disciplines and sociology that use less traditional approaches to social questions.

Design Studio: A central part of the architectural curriculum that emulates practice.

Informal Networked Learning: Describes learning outcomes through peer-to-peer, social media and participatory platforms that have emerged alongside Web 2.0.

Mobile Digital Technologies: Mobile phones and tablets where users can download small applications (apps).

Production of Architecture: Activities that precede the realisation of buildings e.g. commissioning, concept design, development, documentation and construction.

Reception of Architecture: How architecture is experienced after construction, directly and through media, in images, text, films and other types of representations.

Social Value: A form of place significance within the field of heritage which acknowledges the connections, uses and forms of attachment that people have with particular buildings, or sites in urban settings in contrast to forms of significance which require expert interpretation.

ENDNOTES

[1]   This observation is based on first-hand teaching experience and discussions with colleagues from other universities.

[2]   I acknowledge that such a statement might appear to exclude individuals who are unable to walk, however the same effects can perhaps be achieved by moving through space at a similar speed.

Chapter 10
Learning Design Through Facilitating Collaborative Design:
Incorporating Service Learning into a First Year Undergraduate Design Degree Course

Oliver Bown
UNSW Art & Design, Australia

Philip Gough
Design Lab, University of Sydney, Australia

Martin Tomitsch
Design Lab, University of Sydney, Australia

ABSTRACT

This chapter presents a project in which students taking an undergraduate course on Design Thinking participated in a university widening participation project, visiting local schools from a low socioeconomic status background and engaging the school students in a design exercise. The project aimed to draw on the value of service learning, learning through an engaged and socially meaningful task, with tertiary students learning to facilitate design, following principles of co-design, in a community of stakeholders, and secondary students gaining contact with university life, seeing an undergraduate perspective on design, and receiving education in design thinking. Tertiary students were asked to develop design thinking toolkits that would support their design facilitation process. The authors present the results of a study of the project, based on students' assignment submissions, and a focus group following the activity.

DOI: 10.4018/978-1-5225-0726-0.ch010

INTRODUCTION

This chapter presents the findings of a study into service learning for tertiary design students, and its potential benefit in giving students useful experience working in teams and facilitating collaborative design. Service learning is a method for teaching students by putting them into the context of a community service activity, with the aim of providing synergistic relationships between students' educational goals and members of the community benefitting from their support in some way, possibly also an educational outcome, and also to encourage deep reflection in learning through meaningful and real activities (for a discussion of definitions see (Billig, 2000; Billig & Waterman, 2014)). The service learning activity described in this chapter was developed in response to The University of Sydney's widening participation program, which sought to bring tertiary students in contact with secondary students from low socio-economic status (low SES) schools, giving school students who wouldn't normally consider university education opportunities to gain familiarity with a university pathway to the workplace.

This chapter outlines how the service learning paradigm was adapted to a design education context, fulfilling these dual goals of service learning in a way that is suited to the specific needs of the design discipline, including, in particular, the need for students to gain hands-on experience working with clients (Nicol & Pilling, 2005), the need to develop teamwork skills in groups of mixed expertise (Adamczyk & Twidale, 2007), and the need to observe and gain an in-depth understanding of design cognition and decision making in a teamwork context (Wright & Davis, 2014). The authors set out to study how service learning might bring mutual benefits to both tertiary and secondary students, in this context.

The chapter discusses the results of the project based on data gathered from the tertiary students' assessed work, documentation of the process, and a focus group with the tertiary students at the end of the project. It concludes by offering recommendations for using service learning in design education.

This chapter begins by looking at the background in teaching contemporary design thinking, widening participation and service learning. It then details the goals and design of the study, the results, and a discussion that takes into account design thinking education and guidelines for duplicating the activity. The chapter concludes by summarising the case for the effectiveness of the approach.

BACKGROUND

Teaching Contemporary Design Thinking

Design and design thinking are increasingly gaining traction not just as a way to create new artefacts but also as a method of innovation and management (Cross, 2011; Brown & Martin, 2015), following the recognised benefits to the wider population of education in the methods of design thinking (Cross, 1982; Waks, 2001). In addition to developing skills to manipulate physical materials, design and technology education is useful for developing general problem solving skills (Middleton, 2005; Cross, 1982). Technological literacy is another common theme in research on design and technology education (Williams, 2013). As Wells (2012) outlines, design thinking is important to technological literacy, as technology and the built environment take over a greater share of our daily interactions; technology education in school is already a given, and design thinking allows students to identify and define potential technological advancements and how they will play out socially and in terms of the built environment (Wells, 2012).

Many other areas, such as business, are looking to design methods to develop new approaches to running organisations, structuring client relationships, and creating customer services (Greene, 2010). This is having the effect of extending the scope of design education at both secondary and tertiary levels, for example by making it easier for non-design students to enrol in such subjects (as is the case at the Hasso Plattner Institute of Design at Stanford University). Anecdotal evidence shows that in industry, designers are being asked to run design-training workshops for managers, developers, and other staff members from non-design departments.

At the same time, design thinking methods have proliferated and diversified, with a wide variety of methods focusing on strategies for collaborative design, as well as the management of design communication among stakeholders (Dekker *et al.,* 2014). This includes methods such as participatory design, where non-designers' creative input is treated as valuable, and can be facilitated with the support of trained and experienced designers (Bjögvinsson *et al.*, 2012). Participatory design is particularly useful for gaining insights into language, beliefs, and practices of end customers in the early stages of a design project (Muller & Druin, 2003).

These various factors inform the training of students in the Bachelor of Design Computing, a three-year undergraduate program at The University of Sydney, which prepares students for a career in interaction design and user experience design. Through education in core principles of design thinking, along with a wide variety of more specific design practices, it is expected that students gain competence not only at designing things, or 'Things' (Bjögvinsson *et al.*, 2012), but also at working amongst diverse communities to solve problems and understand needs and possibilities in many different areas of application. This includes the important capacity to facilitate design in teams of designers and non-designers, partly by teaching design, but also by effectively applying the appropriate collaborative design methods. Facilitating design here relates to applying methods of participatory design or co-design. A critical underlying skill then is to genuinely understand design cognition and communication, not only as something the designer does herself, but as something she can recognise and nurture in others.

At The University of Sydney, these learning objectives are first introduced in a unit of study called *Design Thinking,* a first year core unit in the Bachelor of Design Computing, also available as an elective to other students. One of the challenges of this unit is providing real hands-on experiences at an early stage. These should involve design-oriented interaction with people from outside the student's cohort, including non-designers. This is challenging because first year students fresh from school are poorly equipped to take on substantial design briefs with real clients, particularly where this requires the teamwork experience, and associated degree of confidence, required to facilitate design amongst others. At the same time, in teaching the authors have come to believe that providing such social experiences early on is important to setting the foundations for design thinking that are central to the degree's learning outcomes.

The relevance of these hands-on experiences and interactions with non-designers during the design process are communicated to students through lectures delivered as part of the *Design Thinking* unit. The lectures also highlight the importance of teamwork, which is reinforced in the more practical tutorials that require students to form teams in order to work on design exercises during class time.

This approach to teaching design thinking is aligned with the key strategies for design education outlined in the introduction of this chapter and has been refined over the years based on feedback from students and feedback from teaching staff and industry representatives involved in the course.

These concerns surrounding the core skill requirements in design thinking provide the context to the approach to service learning for design education developed by the authors below.

Widening Participation and Service Learning

Like many universities in Australia, The University of Sydney has a commitment to social inclusion through widening participation in all aspects of its relation to the wider community, but in particular through a target student intake that reflects the socioeconomic demographic of Australian and global society.

In Australia, as in many OECD countries, differential access to tertiary education remains both indicative of, and a contributor to, social inequality. The increased burden of debt associated with contemporary tertiary education funding models has made the prospect of studying at university particularly unappealing for those from low SES backgrounds (Basit & Tomlinson, 2012). Such individuals are also less likely to have had parents, older siblings or friends who went to university, resulting in a lack of familiarity with university culture, and a lack of confidence in university as a path to a future career (Basit & Tomlinson, 2012). This has been identified as a key barrier to these students choosing to undertake tertiary education (Archer *et al.*, 2005; Shavit & Gamoran, 2007). Financial issues aside, an important part of the social inclusion process lies in breaking down barriers of culture, expectation, uncertainty and lack of familiarity with the world of the university, for those for whom this is an unknown or uninviting direction. Of relevance to design, this may also include a possible misconception about what subjects are taught at university, with the possibility that design is not seen as an academic subject.

To help encourage Australian secondary students from low SES backgrounds to consider tertiary studies as an option, The University of Sydney uses funds from the Australian Government Higher Education Participation and Partnerships Program (University of Sydney, 2016; Australian Government Department of Education and Training, 2016) to run a social inclusion initiative. The objective of this approach is to increase awareness of, and more generally a sense of contact and connectedness to, university life, culture and career pathways amongst school students from low SES backgrounds, addressing the issues described above: serving a public good objective at the same time as aligning with the university's recruitment goals.

Essential to running such an activity with tertiary students as part of their studies, the program also requires that it be of clear educational benefit to the tertiary students as well as serving these other goals. This can be addressed by following established practices of *service learning*, where teaching is situated in community service contexts where mutual benefit can be established between learning outcomes and a public service.

Bringle & Hatcher (1996) state that in successful service learning design "meaningful service activities are related to course material through reflection activities such as directed writing, small group discussions, and class presentation" (p.222). Thus a real world activity can form the basis for critical thinking and the application of theory learnt in the lecture theatre. More generally, an observed educational benefit of service learning lies in stimulating students to discuss and thus effectively process the experience, more so than regular educational contexts (Astin *et al.*, 2000). Astin *et al.* also note that "the single most important factor associated with a positive service-learning experience appears to be the student's degree of interest in the subject matter", indicating that the alignment between social and learning objective needs to be carefully conceived and not tenuous.

Jerome (2012) lists other benefits for service learners, including confronting complex problems in complex settings, deeper learning because results are immediate and uncontrived, tasks that are more likely to be personally meaningful, and cooperative rather than competitive experiences. Gradoville &

Budny (2013) add to this the teaching of team dynamics and the engagement in a community. Jerome also mentions benefits in terms of 'social capital', improving attitudes towards others and strengthening local community connections, as well as a range of problems of resistance from participants, including rejection of deep reflection, frustration and misunderstanding about roles, and outright resistance to the activity. Brewster *et al.* (2016) discuss the challenges of balancing education and service goals to find mutually valuable outcomes.

The Sydney College of the Arts (SCA) and the Sydney Conservatorium of Music (SCM), both faculties of The University of Sydney, were previously awarded one of these grants and followed a service-learning model in fulfilling the aims of the grant. In both cases this took the form of an educational relationship in which the tertiary students taught skills to the secondary students and mentored them in music or art activities. In some cases, the tertiary students were studying to be educators, in which case the relevance of the engagement task was immediately obvious. In other cases, the value to the tertiary students lay more generally in developing communication skills around the techniques and practice in question. To achieve this, and also to create a common format that could work across disciplines, a common assessment was designed that involved the development of a "toolkit" of concepts and techniques. Each tertiary student developed their toolkit for use in the engagement, and evaluated it upon completion of the task.

This program provided funding for tertiary students from the SCA and SCM to engage with local schools whose students are from low SES background, commencing in 2013. The Faculty of Architecture, Design and Planning joined the program in 2014. As part of their participation in this program, the authors responded to the various concerns described in this section and the previous section to develop a service learning based engagement activity that was specifically tailored for design thinking education in the context of a contemporary design degree, and in a way that was compatible with the existing format developed by the SCA and SCM.

Service Learning in Design Education

Service learning for designers may involve performing a design service in their community. However, the specific aim was in engaging school students. One approach to service learning between tertiary and secondary students lies in giving tertiary students experience at being educators. Compared to art and music, Design Computing students at The University of Sydney are very much industry-focused, and an educational experience motivation was not suitable. More generally, service learning in an educational context needn't focus on teaching, but can be about any form of social engagement. The authors therefore set out to achieve mutual benefit by offering the engagement as an exercise in collaborative design (co-design) for tertiary students, with the secondary students as clients. The requirement of mutual benefit in service learning was addressed by drawing on the learning objectives in the first year of the bachelor's degree to engage students in understanding design processes, particularly those with a social component such as co-design and participatory design, through immersion and reflection using real design scenarios. Those methodologies involve the "end user" in the design process, and see designers and people not trained in design working together in the design development process (Sanders & Stappers, 2008). The end user, as the person who will eventually benefit from the designed outcome, is viewed as an *expert* because of her experience (Bødker, 1996). The process of co-design is facilitated through tools prepared by the designer, and allowing the end user to ideate, embody and express ideas and concepts (Sanders & Stappers, 2008; van Rijn & Stappers, 2008). This idea of using a set of tools that can facilitate co-design informed the design of the engagement activity and the underlying assessment task for the tertiary design students. The task required students to develop a design thinking toolkit consisting of methods for engaging their target audience in the design process.

The tertiary students were therefore not required to teach explicitly, even though many of the activities involved an educational component, but to facilitate a design task for a group of secondary students, guiding the design process using methods learnt in *Design Thinking*. Tertiary students were expected to reflect on what methods worked, and how. This placed secondary students into the role of the designer, working collaboratively with the tertiary students, aiming to achieve both the desired awareness of tertiary education and also an improved understanding of and relation to design thinking themselves (Cross, 1982; Middleton, 2005). In fact, this relationship also satisfies educational objectives (tertiary teaching secondary) according to Cross' approach to design education (Waks, 2001). The subsequent engagement therefore includes design teaching as part of a wider process of collaborative design facilitation.

THE STUDY

A study was carried out across the three participating faculties, with a common format for gathering data. This chapter only discusses the component of the study conducted at the Faculty of Architecture, Design and Planning. The primary aim of the study was to understand the impact of this activity on the design thinking education of the tertiary students. Is it possible to satisfy the goals of the social engagement activity whilst enhancing the design thinking education experience?

Service Learning in Design Education

The common assessable task given to tertiary students from the three faculties was to create a toolkit to help them either teach their practice or facilitate engagement in their practice – music, art or design – to high school students. The design students were instructed to specifically develop a design thinking toolkit to help them collect data and address the requirements for a given design brief. The approach they took was therefore not as an educator, but as a designer and facilitator, working within a brief, with high school students as prospective end users. The design thinking toolkit was intended to provide the framework for engaging high school students in a co-design process. Students were also given the option to find a user group of their own choice instead of the school user group.

Where design students did choose the secondary students as end users, the brief given to the design students was to engage the secondary students in the design of a bike hire station as part of a bike hire scheme for their local area, specifically taking into account the transportation needs of the students themselves. This brief was arrived at and considered suitable for a number of reasons, as follows.

A wide number of bike hire schemes, using automated stations, exist throughout the world; there are several variants on the hire station design available for comparison (after the activity), and advancing technology provides opportunities for new designs. The home city of the students, Sydney, does not have a bike hire scheme and the school students may never have had direct experience of such a system, but would have been familiar with all of the component parts required (bikes, pay kiosks, etc.). Such schemes touch on a suitably diverse range of components and aspects, such as the design of the bicycles themselves, issues of road safety, payment management systems, mobile mapping applications, and the geographical layout of stations. Such schemes have a clear rationale and utility, backed up by their global popularity, particularly in areas of poor public transportation, as in this case in the city in question. The project area is more public good focused than commercially focussed, giving clear objective value and minimising distracting discussions around the ethics of who benefits. Also, although the students are reinventing something that already exists (which enables comparison of designs) there is great potential for innovation and improvement across the various parts.

The engagement experience was expected to be valuable to tertiary students in first year studies as a catalyst for the crystallisation of their understanding of the concepts of design thinking. By repurposing techniques they had learned in class, it was expected that this would provide an opportunity to demonstrate a detailed understanding of the processes of design thinking.

Service Learning in Design Education

During the first half of the semester students were introduced to a wide range of design thinking techniques. The task itself took place in the second half of the semester. The brief for the tertiary students included a schedule of two two-hour sessions with their chosen end users, separated by two weeks.

At the beginning of the task, groups of tertiary students worked together in a group studio session to devise the tools they would use in the first contact session. The students then worked in the same groups to reflect upon and revise their methods between sessions, and after the second session. Tertiary students were evaluated on the resulting design thinking toolkit and an accompanying report, reflecting on the engagement. Secondary students were not formally evaluated, and their outputs and reflections were not included in the data collection.

Approximately 70 students took the subject, within which the activity was embedded. Of these students, 19 students chose to work on the provided brief and volunteered to participate in the school engagement activity. These students attended schools in three groups, with the groups consisting of 6, 11 and 2 students, comprising smaller groups of 2-4 formed at will by the students. Each of the groups was assigned a target high school by the authors. These numbers are typical for group sizes in the Design Computing degree and in the authors' experience make for effective teamwork. One of the authors, Gough, was also a tutor in the Design Thinking subject, and both Gough and Bown accompanied the design students during their visits to the high schools.

Six students — two from each of the three groups visiting separate high schools — participated in a one-hour post study focus group. The focus group facilitated open-ended discussion and reflection on the experiences of the tertiary students. The interaction between the tertiary students and school students was also covered in the discussion. Questions addressed whether the experience shifted student perceptions of design thinking, what their reactions were to the secondary students' design outcomes and team dynamic, how the experience influenced their understanding of the role of designer, what difficulties they had with the implementation of the task, and more specifically what worked and didn't work in their toolkits, and how they reflected on and modified the design of the toolkits throughout the process. All of the tertiary students were also filmed before going to the school in an exercise where they tested their prototype designs. These data were analysed to obtain the tertiary students' description of their interaction with the school students, and the changes in their perception of the activity between its start and finish.

RESULTS

The main criterion for success on the side of the tertiary students was how successfully the task enabled the tertiary students to gain a hands-on understanding of how design methods can stimulate and influence design outcomes. The main criterion for success on the side of the secondary students was how successfully the engagement changed their thinking about tertiary education as a possible pathway, and about design as a career option and/or valuable general skill. In this study there was no attempt to directly evaluate success on the side of the secondary students except indirectly through the responses gathered from the tertiary students. A number of the tertiary students were brought together in a focus group after the activity to respond to questions on the perceived benefit of the activity. Their assignments were also used as data to support the findings.

The key results are summarised here. In the following subsection the outcomes are discussed in finer detail. Given the nature of the data – qualitative focus group results across a very small number of participants – it is important to emphasise that this study is a first step towards understanding the potentials of service learning in design education and further research is needed to better support the claims. In summary, the data indicated that:

- A design engagement task was perceived to differ from a teaching task in terms of how both parties appreciated and approached the activity. It offered tertiary students the opportunity to experiment with and reflect on design strategies and design communication in a real context, and observe the creative processes of the secondary cohort both as individuals and as a group. For example, respondents expressed how valuable it was to work with a group who were not your university lecturers, and have to adapt on the spot.

- Tertiary students indicated that the secondary school provided a suitable context for such experience development, identifying it to be a familiar environment, situated in a social relationship scenario in which they could confidently direct the process, showing a combination of respect for the school students and also the need to take leadership. In this respect the setting was seen to be particularly effective for first year tertiary students at the early stages of learning about design thinking, with fresh memories of high school. In the words of one respondent: "It was nice that we were straight out of school, or a year or two out of school... we can have a connection with what school was like".

- Time management and coordination between the various parties and their complex timetabling constraints presented the most considerable challenge and risk to effective execution of the task, and placed additional demands on tertiary students' performance. A number of focus group comments addressed the challenges of time management, involving both time issues imposed upon them and time issues caused by their own planning.

- More tentatively, there was some evidence that secondary students were engaged and proactive in the task, and an effective division of roles was achieved between tertiary students as facilitators and secondary students as the primary contributors of design ideas. In some cases the school-teacher was also actively engaged in the task, though they were not required to be. This could be the focus of further research as it would provide further detail on how any mutual benefit is managed. Relevant comments from the focus group include: "The group we had, there was a lot of cliques. There were groups that were really interested in it, and others that were less interested in it."; and "When we left the first time, they continued on with our flash cards and did the whole project. So when we came back it was finished, and they had followed out steps."

- Following the process, though not necessarily before, at least one of the secondary school teachers recognised the potential to extend the activity through use of the design tools and methods introduced by the tertiary students. This included asking for copies of resources created by the tertiary students, furthering the tertiary students' appreciation of the value of these resources. Being a single instance, this is anecdotal evidence, but indicates at least the potential for a strong mutual benefit between tertiary and secondary student learning.

- Although the activity offered a real-world experience, the tertiary students' work was ultimately tailored to school children, and it was not clear how well their thinking was transferrable to professional design contexts.

Design Toolkits

As part of their assessment, the six groups of students (two groups at each of three high schools) each created a toolkit to help secondary students develop an understanding of design thinking. Each of these designs were developed after the first activity with the secondary students. The designs of the toolkits took the form of card decks, games and activity packages with instructions for a classroom context, inspired by the various design thinking tools experienced by students during their education in the *Design Thinking* unit. As expressed by one respondent, it was important to try "to make the whole activity more visually stimulating, something more exciting for them". This section discusses some features of the toolkits.

Gamification of the design process was used by students who wished to create an engaging activity for younger classes. One group took loose inspiration from a board game (Figure 1), where the participants worked their way around a wheel-shaped board through design exercises: developing user-scenarios, bodystorming and roleplaying, sketching, prototyping, testing and evaluation. The secondary students didn't find this model very engaging in the first encounter, and so the tertiary students responded by developing a more literal model of a board game (Figure 2). This required that the players construct a character for whom they will design, and play through several realms, to develop a product. These realms were "The Land of the Needy" where players used bodystorming and scenarios to build up their

Figure 1. Initial gamified concept for a design thinking toolkit developed by one of the groups of tertiary students

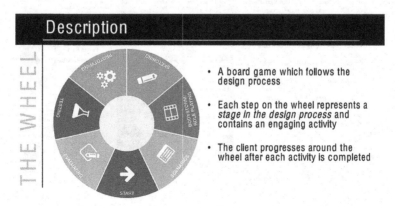

Figure 2. Full game version used in the revised design thinking toolkit, based on feedback received on the first iteration depicted in Figure 1

user-needs, "Idea City" where players used sketching and prototyping (which was the secondary students' favourite part of the original design), and "The Valley of Faults", where players evaluated their concepts. This was tested and proved to be more engaging for the younger audience. Other gamified toolkits included a mixed model that taught players about design iteration by challenging them to create the tallest possible tower using an entire set of wooden blocks, and card games.

Other card decks were also used without a game theme. Similar in practice to method card decks (e.g., IDEO, 2016), these gave instructions for activities that make up the design process (Figure 3). These included a very brief rationale for the process, so the secondary student understands the purpose, and the amount of time to complete the task, in order to fit into a school class period. Other method kits were developed which did not take the form of card decks (Figure 4). These were mostly used with

Figure 3. More traditional method cards used in one of the other design thinking toolkits

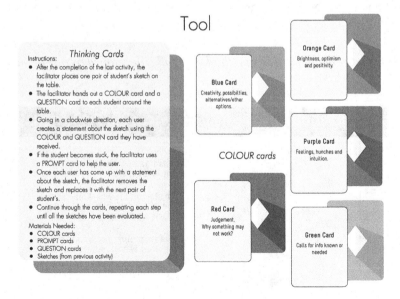

senior secondary students. Tertiary students selected design activities they had learned in class, which they thought would be appropriate for a high school-age user group. Concept development tools included brainstorming exercises, and novel activities, such as "Bin It!" where participants write down an idea, and throw it in a garbage bin, in order to generate a lot of unique ideas. Most groups also included tools to help facilitate investigation of the end-user, as well as sketching prototypes. All method kits included revision and evaluation techniques, such as bodystorming concepts, and critical exercises that identify positive, negative and interesting aspects of design concepts. A tertiary student reflecting on the effectiveness of the critical exercises noted: "That helped them understand visually and physically different potholes that they didn't see beforehand when they just drew up the model". Most of the toolkits focused on collaboration. For example, the brainstorming method used in Figure 4 required secondary students to evaluate each other's ideas.

The tertiary students noted that the secondary students didn't necessarily produce "good" designs, but nevertheless school students were able to engage with a design thinking process using these toolkits. For example: "The designs that came out of our [group] were basically copies of the reference material"; "We had a lot of very extravagant ideas… we had to refine it for those groups and talk to them realistically about what was best, and they decided what was more realistic". The design outcomes became a key point of discussion. Metaphors were observed to be common in the collaborative development and communication of design ideas. For example, one group ended up weighing up between two designs for storage of bikes: a large cheese wheel with a wedge cut out that bikes would revolve into; and a large mushroom that bikes would be lifted up into.

Focus Group

The results of the focus group can be broken down into the benefits to the tertiary students, benefits to the school students, and difficulties.

Figure 4. Method processes for groups combining brainstorming and analysis in their design thinking toolkit

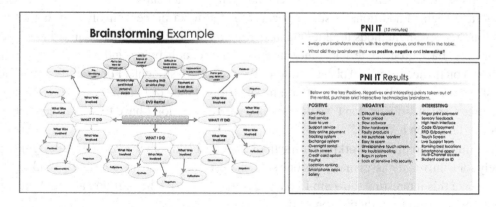

Perceived Benefits to Tertiary Students

The tertiary students outlined their experience in a way that can be separated into four general areas of benefit: motivation, learning environment, practise and role.

Motivation

The tertiary students expressed how they felt that they were motivated by the nature of the engagement with school students. For example: "When you are presenting to someone who is marking you, you have a captive audience, you've got somebody who is going to listen to you regardless... but when you are presenting to young adults, you're presenting to someone who has no obligation to listen to you, so the way you do it, the way you deliver what you're trying to deliver is everything." "You're constantly thinking 'how am I going to keep them listening?'" Such comments suggest that the engagement provided a positive incentive to perform, in addition to indications that the other stakeholders, the school students, seemed genuinely able to benefit from the activities that the tertiary students ran. This implied that as they developed the activities, the tertiary students became focussed on their own performance as designers and design facilitators, rather than as students, and to think about design cognition issues. In order to communicate effectively with the school students, it was necessary for the tertiary students to establish a clear understanding of design thinking processes. The tertiary students' responses and actions indicated that they understood this to be a necessary part of their process, helping them establish a clear comprehension of the content taught in the subject.

Learning Environment

Other responses indicated that the context was well suited to helping students develop their design thinking skills. In contrast to the students involved in similar programs at the SCA and SCM, the tertiary students from the Bachelor of Design Computing are not at all education focused, and instead of approaching the exercise as a teacher instructing a class, it was more appropriate for the tertiary students to approach the exercise as designers working with a potential user group. Within this context, the tertiary students were able to utilise design thinking methods that were part of the subject they were studying. One student described this as "taking what you have learned and doing it practically."

The context seemed additionally suited because of the meta process involved in both facilitating design through a design methods toolkit, and *designing the toolkit*. The latter included iterative design and user testing. Each group of tertiary students visited the schools twice, and were able to modify their designs based on the feedback and observations of the secondary students. For example: "We found that in the first session, generally speaking, after a bit of struggle they did get into it a bit... their attention span was pretty small, so why don't we do a toolkit where they don't have to sit and concentrate for a long time?... let's keep it simple."

Tertiary students contrasted working with school students in this environment with designing projects exclusively for a university assessment. As one student describes: "You are constantly thinking: how am I going to make this interesting, how am I going to bring them back in?... if you are pitching an idea to someone, your job is to keep them interested."

These principles are transferrable to other design areas, where, for example, a user interface must keep people interested.

Practise

What it teaches you that you need to tailor what you're trying to do to the audience you're doing it for.

Putting learning into practice is always beneficial to students. Tertiary students expressed that the engagement activity was a good opportunity to exercise the use of design thinking activities: bodystorming and low-fi paper prototyping. Also, secondary students had to develop an informed understanding for how to select the most appropriate tasks for the activity.

Secondary students often came up with wild design ideas, using the activities that the tertiary students facilitated. Though this often didn't result in "good" design, it challenged the preconceptions tertiary students had about idea generation, as well as user-centred design processes.

Role

Tertiary students reported that the relationship between the two student groups was beneficial because they had an informal, but structured role to play. The tertiary students described the school students as a "captive audience," though one which was not strictly required to take interest in their activities, since the work the school students produced was not assessed. One idea that emerged from the focus group was that the role they were playing at the school was different to one they would expect to play if they were engaged with a business.

"I think that for first year students, particularly for younger students, it's not the ideal scenario. You're going to walk into an environment where there are people who have been doing this for years, who are going to say 'what's he doing here, I'm not a university project'. Where if you go into a school, you're on the other side of the fence, you're the older person who is at a further level of education than they are."

In this way students indicated that engaging with a business might have been more intimidating. Tertiary students from the same subject who did not wish to be involved with a school visit were required to develop a toolkit to help someone with design thinking in a business context, and find their own client. The tertiary students who went to the schools reported that the role they were playing gave them confidence because they were the ones who knew more about the subject they were discussing; in a school setting, they were more educated, putting them in a position of relative expertise. "We found that the 'teacher role' just didn't work. So we tried to become more on the same level."

Since the tertiary students are not studying education, they were not engaging the school students as teachers, but in a consultant role. This allowed the tertiary students to engage with the students on a less formal level, which had some benefits for the school students through process and social connection.

Teamwork

In the case of teamwork, students expressed that they had gained an understanding of how they worked as a group, the social dynamics involved in the school cohort, and the different personality traits, and social and cognitive factors involved in group design and decision making. Tertiary students identified secondary students who were not engaged in design thinking processes. For example, one student was described as having an idea immediately, and then defending her idea in light of all further discussion. The tertiary students described how they worked with that situation, and used problem identification techniques to critically evaluate her design and help her to broaden her view.

Perceived Benefits to Secondary Students

This study did not involve recording any first-hand data from secondary students, as this added additional ethics requirements that were not deemed necessary to the design education outcomes. The tertiary students were able to report on their interactions with the secondary students to give indirect pointers to how the secondary students can benefit from this engagement activity.

The goal of the Widening Participation Grant is ultimately to broaden engagement with university education and diversify The University of Sydney's student cohort. These social inclusion goals are difficult to measure in the context of a single engagement program, as, for some secondary students, it will be a few years before they are even considering which university courses they want to attend, and because the sample size is very small. In addition to this, choosing a tertiary course to study is a complex decision, with factors that are beyond the scope of this article.

From the feedback in the focus group with the tertiary students, there are two broad areas in which the school students were perceived to have benefitted. These have not been directly tested, and further research would be needed to do so. These are engagement with a design process, for the sake of designing instead of for assessment, and social interaction between the two student groups.

Process

The first proposed process benefit was that students were given the opportunity to work through a guided co-design process. The tertiary students engaging with a different mode of designing to traditional methods, working with the secondary students, forms a novel learning space.

The school students were given the autonomy to work on the project within their context. Tertiary students reported that within the design brief some students naturally moved towards different design challenges: some students working on user interface design, some working on visual or industrial design, others experimenting with user scenarios. Secondary students had not yet been formally introduced to design language and terminology, and so were able to express themselves in ways that were natural to them and their experience. The tertiary students then had the task of integrating the results of the various processes followed by the secondary students, which they did with more or less success.

Social

Another suggested benefit to the tertiary students was the opportunity for social interaction with tertiary students. The tertiary students felt that their first semester was an ideal time to engage with the secondary students, as they found it easy to relate to their experience—particularly for senior secondary students who were considering options for further study. Some tertiary students were able to stay after the activity had formally finished, and discussed various aspects of applying to university, and university life. The Bachelor of Design Computing course would have been a reasonable goal for many of the secondary students interested in studying design at university. The tertiary students noted that university study was the goal of some of the students they worked with.

Afterwards, we stuck around, we spoke to the year 12 kids… they were working on their own projects and they had a vested interest in what we were saying… That 1-on-1, or 1-on-3 engagement, where you're talking to somebody on a more level playing field about design processes, was quite good for them, and quite good for us.

DIFFICULTIES

Though the engagement appeared successful, given the positive responses from the focus group, it was not without difficulties. The process of synchronising availability of tertiary students with rigid high school timetables was not simple, and the tertiary students expressed some of the ways they were able to learn from these challenges. One substantial challenge for tertiary students was to shift timing at short notice. This was an unavoidable change that the tertiary students had no choice but to learn to adapt to, and may, or may not, be a fairly realistic scenario for working with clients who have their pressures and deliverables outside the design process.

Tertiary students expressed difficulty keeping some secondary students engaged with the task. As they were not assuming the role of teachers, their relationship relied, at least in part, on the tertiary students providing an engaging activity for the secondary students. This proved to be a valuable activity for the tertiary students after the first visit, as one student commented "nothing benefited [us] more than going to the school for the first time." Before the second visit, the tertiary students were able to update their design to the needs of the intended audience, to make it more engaging. This reflected a realistic design scenario, where design iteration is used to refine the designed product, based on the user needs and feedback.

There was one significant difference between the school groups, which was reported during the focus group. As is expected for junior secondary school students, they were organised by their teacher, and did not find it unusual to take part in a novel activity. Senior secondary school students are used to less rigid direction, and seemed unprepared for the workshop with the tertiary students. This was not seen as a bad thing, but it did require that some time was taken up to orient the secondary students to the task that was being conducted.

If there is some more personal talking time, and maybe we learn about what they're doing... if they' have that project-based learning that they're doing, maybe there should be an initial point where we can help with what they're doing. And that way we're coming in, when we start doing these design tools, we're coming in with a pre-established relationship... rather than as the people who are trying to play the role of authority, rather than teaching.

DISCUSSION

Overall, tertiary students attending the focus group were enthusiastic about the way that the engagement experience supported their learning, and the above outcomes lend support to the view that this type of engagement provides valuable hands-on experience with design thinking in practice. They were most critical of the time management of the project: due to timetabling considerations for schools there were some last minute changes to the engagement times, and this was disruptive for students, particularly when this involved a reduction in the time available between encounters. This timetabling organisation was also the biggest administration overhead involved in the project.

In this section broader theoretical issues of design education, introduced at the beginning of the chapter, are considered. Suggestions for developing the concept are also discussed.

Implications for Design Education

The intended learning outcomes of the engagement was for tertiary students to (a) develop a better understanding of design through a process of facilitating design, implementing a constructive learning approach, and (b) to gain experience in facilitating design activities for non-designers, which will become an increasingly important skill in its own right for the next generation of design graduates.

The achievement of these goals through a service learning approach supports wider principles of design thinking education. The approach satisfies principles of constructivist learning. Furthermore, the task aims to enable tertiary students to:

- Structure a collective design process.
- Observe and understand the psychology of design in practice, particularly social and teamwork aspects, including issue such as dogmatism, conflict, introvert and extrovert characters, disruption and so on.
- Communicate design ideas, needs and problems, and help others better communicate these as well, including seeing first-hand the value of drawing, arranging, building, bodystorming and so on.
- Spread the word about design thinking: even if secondary students don't take design as a university path they may still learn to recognise powerful creative thinking strategies that can work in other fields.
- Learn to be less attached to their own ideas. Through a task in which they are not the ones expected to produce the ideas, tertiary students were able to become familiar with how ideas emerge and how they are best treated. By seeing the way that others become attached to certain ideas or perspectives they can recognise that in their own behaviour.

Finally, as well as being about design facilitation, an interesting observation is that the students approached the project using their newly learnt design principles themselves. They themselves used brainstorming, prototyping, user testing methods, personas, and so on in the development of their tools, and were able to understand and adapt to the user experiences and needs of the secondary students.

In other words, this was a metadesign activity with a complex level of social understanding. This might have been confusing to students had they been presented with the task of using design thinking to discover methods to facilitate design thinking, but this was not made explicit to the students. Instead they naturally applied these methods in their work, following the philosophy of design thinking becoming an integral aspect not only of a designer's work but all her actions (Howard *et al.*, 2015).

Recommendations for Further Iterations

This chapter has shown how tertiary design thinking courses can benefit from using service learning in secondary schools to give students the opportunity to experience hands-on the process of *facilitating* design. All universities have a nearby school community that could benefit from a closer engagement with the world of the university and the field of design. There is therefore good reason to believe that exploring such models may be of value to others. With this in mind, the following are some pointers, based on the experience with the engagement:

- Assess tertiary students on development of a design toolkit. Tertiary students must not be responsible for the designs themselves, but must only facilitate designs by others. This distinction can be drawn out in the introductory teaching.
- Tertiary students work in groups of three or four, with 10-15 secondary students. Although the effect of group size was not studied, satisfactory group dynamics were oberved with these numbers.
- The approach appears to work well with first year students as an early opportunity to get them working outside of the classroom in a context in which they feel comfortable.
- Use the second half of semester for the engagement activity, devoting the first half of semester to learning core design thinking principles and introducing the activity.
- Allow a good amount of contact time: such as three or four visits of around 3 hours each. Use an icebreaker method such as the "Marshmallow Challenge" on the first encounter. The Marshmallow Challenge requires teams of students to build the tallest tower they can, capable of holding up a marshmallow, using only a packet of dried spaghetti and some tape. It creates some energy in the room and gets people thinking about collaboration and design processes.
- Try to allow two weeks between visits (at least between the first and second visits). This allows more time to reflect, including in-class discussion time in the alternating weeks. It also means that secondary students revisit their design ideas with fresh eyes.
- Prepare students to expect the unexpected on the first visit, including widely varying levels of engagement.
- Get students to conduct observations and make notes during the activity (for example get one student at a time to observe while the others are working). Get them to think about how ideas are formed and how evaluation takes place. Get them to look at the group dynamics and think about how they can be made more conducive to design outcomes and cohesion.
- Aim to build a long-term relationship with schools, and work directly with specific teachers where possible, so that teachers can become familiar with the benefits of the exercise. Be adaptive to teacher needs. Work with other faculties, and central university services, to build a relationship between the university and the school across disciplines. Make a strong and clear case to the teachers as to what the benefit is.
- Plan well ahead as the coordination between timetables of the two institutions can be difficult and needs to be locked in with certain fixed deadlines. This is even harder if you are working with multiple schools.
- Allow a round-up event at the end of semester. This can be a chance for the school students to visit the university.

FUTURE RESEARCH DIRECTONS

The approach to service learning described in this chapter brings a new research-led perspective to teamwork within the context of design education. Rather than focusing on challenges associated with teamwork within a unit of study, the chapter puts forward a model for facilitating interactions and teamwork across tertiary and secondary students structured around the concept of co-design. This approach allows students to experience not only how to design in teams but also to communicate their knowledge to others. The study demonstrated that the implemented approach to service learning led to effective teamwork and interactions between the tertiary and secondary students.

However, the specific context within which this study was executed and the relatively small number of study participants, there is a need for further research to evaluate and strengthen the findings presented in this chapter. To better support these findings, future research should extend the approach to other design disciplines, such as industrial design, visual design, etc. In this study, the core participants were tertiary students in their first year of study at a university. It would be interesting to evaluate whether and how the effectivenss of the proposed approach to service learning would vary in senior units of study. Future research investigating these areas would help to better understand the value of service learning to tertiary design students, leading to a more in-depth knowledge about potentials and implications. Such knowledge could inform a framework to guide future implementations of service learning in design education.

The research presented in this chapter was limited to the evaluation of the implemented approach through the perspective of the tertiary students. The authors were therefore not able to evaluate the effect of the engagement activity on the secondary students. This opens up opportunities for further research that investigates the short- and long-term implications of service learning for secondary students. To that end, it would also be valuable for future research to include students from a range of secondary schools, rather than only focusing on low SES schools as was the case for this study.

Finally, future research should also evaluate the effect of the service learning approach on students' assessment and academic performance. In this area, it would also be valuable to study any effects of the interactions between tertiary and secondary students on the performance of tertiary students working in teams. Research in this direction would contribute new knowledge to the area of teamwork within the context of design education.

CONCLUSION

This project has offered preliminary evidence to show that a service learning engagement between university design departments and schools can mutually benefit tertiary and secondary students, teaching core design thinking skills to first year undergraduates. Despite the apparent risks of running such a project with new students at a very early stage in their design thinking education, the project has provided some evidence that this is a good way to bring practice-based, socially grounded learning in at an early stage. As Astin *et al.* (2000) note, students' interest in the subject is the single most critical factor in a successful service learning experience. Combined with constructivist learning principles and the challenges of a live collaborative experience working with non-designers and strangers, this produces a powerful learning experience, as evidenced in the focus group results. These results feed into the discussion of design thinking education, offering one way that students can benefit from social interaction at an early stage in preparation for more intimidating and demanding professional experience situations. Lastly, the authors have noted that design students are less education focused. Of course, this needn't be the case. Obviously some graduates go on to be design teachers, and the growth of design thinking may mean a diversification of design teaching opportunities. This engagement may have planted the seeds of interest in a career in design education for tertiary students as well.

ACKNOWLEDGMENT

We thank the team members and team leaders on this University of Sydney Widening Participation Grant from the SCA and SCM, as well as Lian Loke, coordinator of the Design Thinking unit, and all of the students and schools who participated in this project.

REFERENCES

Adamczyk, P. D., & Twidale, M. B. (2007). Supporting multidisciplinary collaboration: requirements from novel HCI education.*Proceedings of the SIGCHI conference on Human factors in computing systems* (pp. 1073-1076). ACM. doi:10.1145/1240624.1240787

Archer, L., Hutchings, M., & Ross, A. (2005). *Higher education and social class: issues of exclusion and inclusion*. Routledge.

Astin, A. W., Vogelgesang, L. J., Ikeda, E. K., & Yee, J. A. (2000). How service learning affects students. University of Nebraska, Omaha.

Australian Government Department of Education and Training. (2016, January 15) Retrieved from https://education.gov.au/higher-education-participation-and-partnerships-programme-heppp

Basit, T. N., & Tomlinson, S. (2012). *Social inclusion and higher education*. Policy Press.

Billig, S. (2000). Research on K-12 school-based service-learning: The evidence builds. *Phi Delta Kappan*, 2000, 658.

Billig, S. H., & Waterman, A. S. (Eds.), (2014). *Studying service-learning: Innovations in education research methodology*. Routledge.

Bjögvinsson, E., Ehn, P., & Hillgren, P. A. (2012). Design things and design thinking: Contemporary participatory design challenges. *Design Issues*, *28*(3), 101–116. doi:10.1162/DESI_a_00165

Bødker, S. (1996). Creating conditions for participation: Conflicts and resources in systems design. *Human-Computer Interaction*, *11*(3), 215–236. doi:10.1207/s15327051hci1103_2

Brewster, A. B., Pisani, P., Ramseyer, M., & Wise, J. (2016). Building a university-community partnership to promote high school graduation and beyond: An innovative undergraduate team approach. *Journal of Applied Research in Higher Education*, *8*(1), 44–58. doi:10.1108/JARHE-10-2014-0093

Bringle, R. G., & Hatcher, J. A. (1996). Implementing service learning in higher education. *The Journal of Higher Education*, *67*(2), 221–239. doi:10.2307/2943981

Brown, T., & Martin, R. (2015). Design for Action. *Harvard Business Review*, September, 56–64.

Cross, N. (1982). Designerly ways of knowing. *Design Studies*, *3*(4), 221–227. doi:10.1016/0142-694X(82)90040-0

Cross, N. (2011). *Design Thinking*. Bloomsbury Academic.

Dekker, A., Worthy, P., Viller, S., Zimbardi, K., & Robinson, R. (2014). Designer-client communication in web design: a case study on the use of communication in practice.*Proceedings of the 26th Australian Computer-Human Interaction Conference on Designing Futures: the Future of Design* (pp. 440-443). ACM. doi:10.1145/2686612.2686681

Ehrlenspiel, I. K., Giapoulis, A., & Günther, J. (1997). Teamwork and design methodology—Observations about teamwork in design education. *Research in Engineering Design, 9*(2), 61–69. doi:10.1007/BF01596482

Gradoville, R., & Budny, D. (2013). Undergraduate Service-Learning Engineering Design Projects In Ecuador.*Proceedings of COPEC World Congress* (Vol. 5).

Greene, J. (2010). *Design Is How It Works*. Portfolio Hardcover.

Howard, Z., Senova, M., & Melles, G. (2015). Exploring the role of mindset in design thinking: Implications for capability development and practice. *Journal of Design Business and Society, 1*(2).

IDEO. (2016). Method Cards. Retrieved from https://www.ideo.com/work/method-cards

Jerome, L. (2012). Service learning and active citizenship education in England. *Education. Citizenship and Social Justice, 7*(1), 59–70. doi:10.1177/1746197911432594

Middleton, H. (2005). Creative thinking, values and design and technology education. *International Journal of Technology and Design Education, 15*(1), 61–71. doi:10.1007/s10798-004-6199-y

Muller, M. J., & Druin, A. (2003). Participatory design: the third space in HCI. In *Human-computer interaction: Development process, 4235*.

Nicol, D., & Pilling, S. (Eds.), (2005). *Changing architectural education: Towards a new professionalism*. Taylor & Francis.

Preece, J., Sharp, H., & Rogers, Y. (2015). *Interaction Design - beyond human-computer interaction*. John Wiley & Sons.

Sanders, E. B. N., & Stappers, P. J. (2008). Co-creation and the new landscapes of design. *CoDesign, 4*(1), 5–18. doi:10.1080/15710880701875068

Shavit, Y., Arum, R., & Gamoran, A. (2007). *Stratification in higher education: A comparative study*. Stanford University Press.

University of Sydney. (2016, January 15). Social Inclusion. Retrieved from http://sydney.edu.au/social-inclusion/grants-program/index.shtml

van Rijn, H., & Stappers, P. J. (2008). Expressions of ownership: motivating users in a co-design process. *Proceedings of the Tenth Anniversary Conference on Participatory Design 08* (pp. 178-181). Indiana University.

Waks, L. J. (2001). Donald Schon's philosophy of design and design education. *International Journal of Technology and Design Education, 11*(1), 37–51. doi:10.1023/A:1011251801044

Waterman, A. S. (2014). *Service-learning: Applications from the research*. Routledge.

Wright, N., & Davis, R. (2014). Educating the creative citizen: Design education programs in the knowledge economy. *Techne Series: Research in Sloyd Education and Craft Science A, 21*(2), 42–61.

KEY TERMS AND DEFINITIONS

Collaborative Design (Co-Design): An approach to design in which other individuals besides the designers are brought into the design process, typically because as the target users they have knowledge that can contribute to the design.

Design Thinking: Design thinking primarily refers to the ways designers solve problems, as compared to other groups such as scientists, involving a greater role for creatively probing and reframing problems. It can also refer to the total suite of thinking methods involved in design.

Service Learning: An educational approach that places students in real world situations that support their learning at the same time as benefitting some other members of society.

Socioeconomic Status: Defined by the Australian Bureau of Statistics as a measure of access to material and social resources and ability to participate in society.

Widening Participation: Government and university initiatives that attempt to increase involvement in higher education amongst a wider section of the population.

Chapter 11
Intercultural Dialogue through Design (iDiDe):
A Model of Intercultural Collaboration and Student Engagement

Susan Ang
Deakin University, Australia

ABSTRACT

Intercultural dialogue through design, globally known as "iDiDe" (pronounced i-dee-dee) was initiated by an Australian university in 2011 for architecture and built environment disciplines. Set within the context of international education and internationalisation, which are the focus of Australian universities this century, iDiDe offers a model of intercultural collaboration and student engagement. iDiDe is more than a generic international study tour. Firstly, there is collaborative academic leadership that comes from institutional partnerships between Australia and five Asian nations (Malaysia, Thailand, India, Indonesia, Sri Lanka), secondly, intercultural dialogue and intercultural understanding underpin the pedagogical approach, and thirdly, iDiDe projects extend discipline specific learning into the realms of reality. This chapter is an expose of iDiDe. It seeks to determine what elements of the model contribute to intercultural collaboration and student engagement. Findings are evaluated for their impact upon participants. The potential for transformative learning and response to global citizenship are discussed along with future research.

INTRODUCTION

The Australian government under Julia Gillard, Prime Minister of Australia 2012-2013 published a White Paper titled "Australia in the Asian Century" to provide a plan for Australia's future success. It called upon Australia and Australians to "play our part in becoming a more Asia-literate and Asia-capable nation" (Australia & Gillard, 2012). Ms. Gillard's message is a reversal of perspective of Australia being the dominant provider of international education that began with the Colombo Plan. The Colombo Plan, first introduced in 1950s saw deserving scholars from underdeveloped countries receive educational

DOI: 10.4018/978-1-5225-0726-0.ch011

scholarships in developed countries, such as the United Kingdom and Australia. The New Colombo Plan (NCP), launched in 2014, is the Australian Government's signature initiative with the specific agenda of building a knowledge base of Asia to ensure Australian undergraduates have the skills and work-based experiences, to contribute to domestic and wider regional economy in the century marked as the "Asian century". $100 million has been committed towards global student mobility (over five years) that includes internships/mentorships, flexible mobility programs, both short and longer-term, practicums and research. Significantly, NCP is intended to be transformational, deepening Australia's relationships in the region, at the individual level and through expanding stakeholder links (Department of Foreign Affairs and Trade, 2014).

This chapter introduces an Australian case study of a model of global student mobility for architecture and built environment education called "Intercultural Dialogue Through Design" (globally known as "iDiDe" and pronounced i-dee-dee) iDiDe). iDiDe was initiated in 2011 through leveraging of academic alumni global connections formed in the 1980s, under the auspices of international education, specifically involving Australian graduates from Malaysia who are now academics employed in universities in both countries. It subscribes to the specific agenda of the NCP to achieve transformative and deep authentic learning experiences through a framework of intercultural learning. To date iDiDe has expanded and sustained partnerships to include five Asian nations (Malaysia, Thailand, India, Indonesia, Sri Lanka). The letters that spell the acronym "iDiDe" are an abbreviated play on the words "Intercultural Dialogue Through Design". High levels of participant engagement exist intrinsically in a study tour because of the appeal of travel. iDiDe has drawn upon this appeal and activated enriched learning environments through cultural immersion and collaboration with international peers. The learning objectives and graduate learning outcomes are aligned with discipline specific curriculum, and strategies for an international-ized syllabus. iDiDe acts as an intercultural collaborative platform and carries the vision to infuse future architects and built environment professionals with the essential skillset of a global citizen. Worldwide, the professions of architecture and design of the built environment look to teamwork and collaboration to achieve sustainable solutions. National and cultural boundaries are traversed as a matter of practice. Spaces that transcend cultural spheres of understanding offer learning opportunities. What is the nature of engagement that occurs in these "intercultural spaces"; how do they impact students who experience them? This chapter offers a research study of the iDiDe model in three parts. The first provides context to the rationale of the model. It provides an overview to internationalisation of higher education and introduces definitions of intercultural dialogue and intercultural understanding, as well as how these are used towards developing theory that underpins intercultural collaborative learning. The second part explains the iDiDe intentions, academic content, teaching and learning strategy, and the structure of delivery. Each iDiDe has both common and unique elements. A chronological history of iDiDe is presented as a comparative overview of the elements and the direction the programme has taken in the period 2011 – 2015. Each programme has been reflected upon as a trajectory of maturity. The outcomes have been substantiated through evaluation of participant testimonials. The final part of this chapter discusses the lessons learnt. The chapter concludes with direction for further research on future iDiDe offerings that will seek to validate these findings and to consolidate the theoretical framework for a best practice model of intercultural collaboration and student engagement for design.

BACKGROUND

iDiDe founder and academic programme leader, Susan Ang, is a qualified architect and senior academic at Deakin University Australia. The idea for international collaboration, mutual exchange and partnership activity evolved through collaborative discussion with alumni academic colleagues from two Malaysian universities and was formalised through memorandums of understanding (MOU). Deakin University took the lead in setting up the programme with foundation partners, the International Islamic University of Malaysia and the University Teknologi MARA, Malaysia. It was agreed that the programme would install one institution as "host" and that the academic schedule would drive the programme and allow cultural immersion activities that add learning value to the academic content to be included. Deakin University remains the executive lead and provides overall coordinator-ship of the theme, project and programme schedule. This is achieved through collaboration with partners at all times. Each partner governs formal alignment and assessment towards coursework within their own institution. The overall educational approach makes this a unique initiative in terms of its immersive pedagogical phases of collaborative intercultural learning experiences that focus upon transcultural design collaboration. The pilot iDiDe comprised of seminars, field trips, workshops, lectures, and a public exhibition by the Australian Government International Education. A further six programmes were delivered within Australia and Asia involving five new Indo-Pacific/Asian partners (Thailand, India, Malaysia Borneo, Indonesia). This expansion brought rich cultural diversity (Figure 1).

Figure 1. iDiDe students from Australia and India engaged in intercultural collaborative design studio on the project "Cultural Interventions for the Informal Settlements of Lal Kwan, Gurgaon, India". (Photo by S.Ang, 2013)

GLOBALISATION AND INTERNATIONALISATION OF HIGHER EDUCATION

In this century of globalisation, there are increasing movements of people, capital, goods and services across national boundaries. It is common to meet a colleague who will say they were born in one country, educated in a second, pursued employment in a third and may be contemplating further opportunities in a fourth. As regional economies and societies become more integrated and interdependent, this exchange driven by information communication technologies has evolved a knowledge-based society. In particular, "Generations X, Y, and Z are e-literate, they think and act globally" (Hope, 2008). Tertiary institutions have seen an increase in the cultural diversity of students and staff, and face the challenge of preparing their community to be "both consumers and producers of knowledge". Cultural diversity brings "creative friction", where strategic utlisation of global connections occurs where there are conversations across difference (Tsing, 2011). Tsing (2011) describes this as being in the "grip of worldly encounter", where collaboration is more than a simple sharing of information, rather it is capable of creating new interest and identities, though not to everyone's benefit. The term internationalisation is often confused with the word globalisation, though both are used interchangeably. Globalisation refers to the forces affecting the world such as the production of services and information technology whereas internationalisation is the playing out of such forces by people and ideas in the context of nation states (Webb, 2005). Since early 2000s, the concept of internationalisation of higher education has been debated and discussed in many different disciplines (Harman, 2005). Knight (2004) defines it as "the process of integrating international, intercultural or global dimension into the purpose, functions or delivery of post-secondary education". Four rationales for internationalisation are offered by Knight (2004): political, economic, academic and cultural. Political refers to the preservation of a nation's individual identity. Cultural and social rationales serve to improve intercultural understanding and communication. The academic rationale is the traditional role of universities to strive for the highest academic standards of scholarship and research. However, economic rationale tends to drive the internationalisation agenda in most universities, as they compete to export educational services and attract increasing numbers of students (Altbach & Knight, 2007). In a study with De Wit (1999), Knight describes two approaches to internationalisation in higher education. The 'activity' approach focuses on internationalising the curriculum, student exchanges and international students, while the 'competency' approach recognizes that students and staff need to develop new skills, knowledge and attitudes. To provide intercultural teaching and learning, institutions providing design education need to take proactive measures which enhance and facilitate the complex processes involved (Teekens, 2000). Leask (2003) argues that internationalisation in different regions has to develop separate and unique approaches due to differing political, economic and social cultural factors. Institutions in Europe might aim to increase mobility of students and staff across national borders while those in the Oceanic region seek to foster relations with Asian neighbours.

GLOBAL MOBILITY AND INTERCULTURAL COMPETENCY

The view that greater accessibility to international travel is the path to profound transformation is backed by academics that will have drawn upon their own lived experience. The Australian academic workforce is regarded as a highly mobile one. Australia has experienced a net increase in academics through migration in recent decades (Bexley, James & Arkoudis, 2011). 30.8% of academics in Australia had taken steps to find an academic position in another country, compared with an international average of 20.5% across the countries taking part in the Changing Academic Profession (CAP) survey, placing Australia second only to Italy in terms of academic staff mobility (Coates et al. 2009a cited in Bexley et al., 2011). The flow on effect suggests that Australia benefits from inflows of academics from other countries with the Australian Bureau of Statistics data showing 40.5% of Australian academic staff born overseas (Hugo 2008 cited in Bexley et al., 2011). In the development of intercultural competency, engagement with the study aspect is critical. With high intercultural profiles of academics, there is potential to further understandings of intercultural competency and to ground it as a practice at universities.

Whilst it can be said younger people experience greater influence on their curiosity about other cultures from travel, the extent to which transcends into intercultural sensitivity depends on the amount of cultural interaction which occurs in their home country (Cushner & Karim, 2004). The term "global student mobility" was used as an all-encompassing version of international learning, regardless of the actual mode by which it has been gained. Education in this century is about sensitising students to cultural diversity and expanding curriculum in response to preparedness for "global citizenship". To be a global citizen suggests a status and identity that is part of an emerging world community and having interests that reside with whole of community concerns.

One successful vehicle of global student mobility is a study tour. Freeman (1964) stated: "All travel is education." There are variations determined by duration of study tour undertaken, focus of the programme, destination of travel, types of activities and levels of engagement, presence or absence of external partners or sponsors, and others that contribute to the experience and outcomes. International study tours typically involve immense resources and dedicated staff. There is also risk management, financial accountability and complex planning required. Of note is the matter of ensuring the "right" kind of students are recruited – ideally, students whose personal goals may be aligned with the aims of the programme; students whose academic track performance warrant participation and endorses their contribution to the programme outcomes. A tangential outcome are students who gain the most from the experience will be motivated toward inspiring others to participate and be ambassadors for their institution. The most significant outcome is that it sparks a transformative experience at some level. The learning experience is implicit in the act of immersion in an environment different to one's natural environment. Even so, the depth and type of engagement determine the extent of impact. A one-dimensional programme relies solely upon observational style of learning and there is minimal "active" learning. Participants in group study tours reported that travel experiences have greater impact on self-awareness than formal education programs, as they need to negotiate tasks such as travelling times, acquiring food and finding their way around.

Sweet and Horman (2012) reported that their field school that saw Australian students engage in the Kelabit community in Bario, Malaysia facilitated a powerful cross-cultural learning experience for students. Findings suggested the incorporation of collaborative projects with local students is a contributing factor (Guest, Livett & Stone, 2006). Others suggested that the web could be used to establish discussion and networks with students in another country prior to the tour itself (Duke, 2000). Due to varying understandings of student mobility and what it entails, and impacts varying from individual to individual, the experience and impact have been difficult to document (Flom, 2014; Wells, 2014). Landis, Bennett & Bennett (2004) argue that these experiences will be of benefit if they are followed by a period of self-reflection. Joubert & Whitford (2006) established that there are rich educational opportunities in cross-cultural learning programs in architecture. They highlighted challenges of "whole of faculty buy in" with regards timetabling, funding, and bilateral collaboration. Over the last five years there have been some international activity in the field of design education including Swinburne Faculty of Health, Arts and Design (short term study tours to Vietnam, Hong Kong, Taiwan), University of Western Sydney (Exchange programs to Australia and Canada and Chile), Chinese School of Architecture, Tsinghua University of Beijing, and the Faculty of Architecture, Building, and Planning at the University of Melbourne (design collaboration programme between Turkey and Japan). Study tours provide a controlled and regulated environment for learning to take place in an overseas destination. The model of integrating and developing a project with a host institution combined with industry visits and excursions to places of cultural significance has worked well in Europe and provides a suitable framework for expanding and diversifying the international student experiences into Asia. A three-week study tour may seem small in the scheme of international exposure; however, it provides an influential introduction to the necessities of a successful transnational design career." (Kuys and Thompson-Whiteside, 2012). Opportunity to exchange ideas between Australia and Asia through action research methods of role-playing and reflective learning are being promoted. This is as much perceived as a response to issues of globalisation as it is the university's role as gatekeeper of professional standards, new methodologies and processes of teaching and learning in the global century (Novoa 2010). Increasingly, intercultural sensitivities gained by promoting appreciation of cultural difference are one of the most important issues thought to be an integral part of architectural education (Kuys and Thompson-Whiteside, 2012).

INTERCULTURAL DIALOGUE AND INTERCULTURAL LEARNING

Intercultural dialogue is a concept involving communication and mediation that emerged from political landscapes. No universal definition is in use by public or private sectors, yet the term is readily understood when broken down to its root words: "Dialogue" and "Intercultural". "Dialogue" is a form of articulated communication that sees an exchange of opinions, thoughts, and ideas between two parties. It is the oldest and most fundamental mode of democratic conversation. It works as antidote to rejection and violence. Its objective is to enable us to live together peacefully and constructively in a multicultural world and to develop a sense of community and belonging. "Intercultural" involves two or more cultures and infers exchange of something of value that belongs to each culture. Intercultural dialogue is defined by the European Union as:

A process that comprises an open and respectful exchange or interaction between individuals, groups and organisation with different cultural background or world views. In this sense, intercultural dialogue processes or encounters are to go beyond a mere 'tolerance of the other' and can involve creative abilities that convert challenges and insights into innovation processes and into new forms of expression. The "shared space" in which such processes take place can be located outside of physical spaces, situated in the media or in a virtual environment. (Council of Europe, 2014)

Equitable exchange and dialogue among civilizations, cultures and peoples, based on mutual understanding and respect, and the equal dignity of all cultures is the essential prerequisite for constructing social cohesion, reconciliation among peoples and peace among nations. Intercultural dialogue is inscribed as one of UNESCO's (United Nations Education, Scientific and Cultural Organisation) founding principles:

In a globalised world with interconnected societies, intercultural dialogue is vital if we are to live together while acknowledging our diversity. (United Nations Educational, Scientific and Cultural Organization, 2015)

The experience of distinctive global boundaries is increasingly becoming blurred effecting changes in our engagement with the diversity of cultural environments.

Cultural diversity is an essential condition of human society, brought about by cross-border migration, the claim of national and other minorities to a distinct cultural identity, the cultural effects of globalisation, the growing interdependence between all world regions and the advances of information and communication media. More and more individuals are living in a 'multicultural' normality and have to manage their own multiple cultural affiliations. (Council of Europe, 2014)

Collaboration and teamwork are synonymous across professional disciplines. Collaborative learning is a pedagogical pillar of design and built environment education and for all problem-based learning (De Graaf & Kolmos, 2003). Peer learning is consistent within higher education (Boud, Cohen & Sampson, 2014). A learning outcome of the disciplines of architecture and built environment is to develop team-working skills (team-mindedness) essential for professional practice (Nicol & Pilling (eds.), 2005; Nicol & Pilling, 2002). Real world experiential learning prepares students to make sense of, engage with and contribute to the ever expanding, complex and dynamic landscape of professional practice in the built environment disciplines. Collaborative learning enriches this process. Intercultural dialogue offers a starting block fundamental to intercultural education. The shift from interacting with more than one culture (multicultural) to "intercultural" informs a collective body of research, study and knowledge referred to as "intercultural learning". Discovery, personal engagement and questioning are key features. The understanding of intercultural dialogue as an open and respectful exchange of views between individuals and groups belonging to different cultures, presents the case for intercultural collaboration. It advocates an inclusive approach to education that moves beyond harmony, respect, appreciation and tolerance, all of which are emblems of intercultural understanding. In another sense, starting with the "other" brings about a shift in thinking from the personal to the interpersonal, focusing on what happens between people rather than simply who they are, a distinction Kalantzis and Cope (2005, pp. 24) described as follows:

The personal is about shaping oneself in the image of others, recognizing oneself in one's similarity with other models of gender or national identity, and making oneself into one person. The interpersonal is about negotiating differences, and in a world of growing differences this is about strategies for finding common ground, collaborating with strangers and the morality of compromise.

Architecture and built environment education should expose students to a sense of understanding and re-framing of known paradigms. Rather than presenting a problem, design education could start with an exercise on understanding which leads to architectural responses that are above the notions of problem solving.

Much of what we know of institutions, the distribution of power, social relations, cultural values, and everyday life is mediated by built environment. To make architecture is to construct knowledge, to build vision. (Dutton & Mann, 1996)

Architects have been criticized for ignoring social issues, and for valuing formal expression over cultural and social-behaviour needs of the users (Rapoport, 2005). Creativity should be expanded to include outside factors like culture, society and environment (Salama, 2007). Built environment stakeholders need to work responsibly together. Diversity and learning from other cultures and their solutions may be the way forward to a more sustainable future. Design teaching is open ended with no right answer. The creative design process is described as first "defining the problem, brain-storming in a group (typically about 5 in a group), evaluation and synthesis of the solution" (Salama, 1995). Teachers adopt the role of facilitators of learning, guiding the learning process. An example is a culturally relevant design exercise by Sanoff (cited in Salama, 2007) who runs "community-based design learning" field classes, where students collaborate with community members to design and implement projects aimed at meeting the communities' needs. Students learn to identify problems from data collection in a self-directed group process, and collaboration with the community develops empathy rather than competition. By "using the built environment as a text book", students have to address political issues, social networks and sustainable challenges (Eldeen, 2003). Slimbach's (2005) approach to intercultural learning borrows heavily from social anthropology, intercultural communication and international education. Slimbach's (2005) transcultural person model comprises a 6-point transcultural competency that includes "perspective consciousness, ethnographic skill, global awareness, world learning, foreign language proficiency and affective development" and suggests this be achieved outside the realms of conventional classroom learning where authentic cultural conditions can be experienced live. Individuals embarking upon a transcultural journey as a group might discover differences as well as commonalities before discovering the route to unity through difference, thereby making the intercultural journey the perfect catalyst for design collaboration.

ACADEMIC CONTENT INTENTIONS

Collaborative pedagogy in architecture and built environment education are the aims of iDiDe. The learning objectives aimed to equip students with intercultural understanding and intercultural communication skills alongside design collaboration skills. Learning objectives (LO) were: Identify and appreciate diverse cultural perspectives in design approach and outcomes (LO1); Exchange cultural knowledge and nuances through intensive collaborative and culturally immersive experiences (LO2); Reflect upon individual cultural identity and social practices and compare these with different cultures and social practices encountered (LO3); Extend discipline knowledge and skills in international context (LO4); and Practice intercultural communication (LO5). All learning objectives are linked to respond to graduate learning outcomes (GLO) which are: Discipline specific knowledge and capabilities: appropriate to the level of study related to a discipline or profession (GLO1); Communication using oral, written and interpersonal communication to inform motivate and effect change (GLO2); Digital literacy using technologies to find use and disseminate information (GLO3); Critical thinking: evaluating information using critical and analytical thinking and judgement (GLO4); Problem solving, creating solutions to authentic (real world and ill defined) problems (GLO5), and; Self-management, working and learning independently; and taking responsibility for personal (GLO6). Table 1: iDiDe Intercultural collaboration strategies in iDiDe programme below, identifies four strategies: 1) Diversity in student teams 2) Team identity 3) Intercultural project and 4) 3-phased academic structure.

INTERCULTURAL COLLABORATION STRATEGIES

Each partner university accommodates the programme structure independently within their university course structure and timetable and delivers a three-phased structure through both formal and informal learning environments. Deliverables include fieldwork research, proposals in mixed media formats that may include drawings, videos, reports, and journals (Figures 2-5).

Table 1. iDiDe Intercultural teaching and learning

Strategy and Method	Intentions	Example	Learning Objective (LO) Linked to Graduate Learning Outcomes (GLO)
1. Diversity in teams. Each student is allocated to a team with a diverse profile.	To create an intercultural learning environment.	2-3 Australian students and 2-3 non-Australian students. Refer Figure 2. Cultural diversity in student groups.	LO2 (GLO 1,) LO3 (GLO 2,4,6) LO5 (GLO 2, 6)
2. Team identity. Teams collaborate for the first time to complete a small group task that initiates "ice breaking" works towards team building.	This first small group task initiates "first contact" and encourages tolerance and confidence within teams • To respect individual contribution • To be conscious of self-identify, and increase cultural awareness. • To communicate respectfully. • To engage sensitive exchange. • To increase mindfulness of "other"	"Ice breaker and team manifesto". Refer example in Figure 3. The Ice Breaker Activity example of intercultural team building	LO1 (GLO 1, 5, 7, 8) LO2 (GLO 1) LO3 (GLO 2,6 LO4 (GLO 1,2,6) LO5 (GLO 2,6)
3. Intercultural project Projects developed collaboratively between Deakin and partners. Projects that respond strongly to considerations of "interculturality" and were set in an international setting (to Australian participants) were adopted.	• To challenge and extend knowledge. • To achieve authentic learning experiences. • To reimagine ways of seeing. • To achieve a group endeavour greater than the individual's.	Islamic Museum Geelong. Refer example shown in Figure 4. Geelong Museum of Islamic Art, a collaboratively developed transcultural design brief	LO1 (GLO 1, 5, 6) LO4 (GLO 1,2,6) LO5 (GLO 2, 6)
4. 3–phased structure Academics collaborate with partners throughout.	The programme is conducted via online and face-to-face platforms. External guests from industry are invited to participate. Academic content draws upon discipline specific such as design research, and communication and construction technology.	Academic content. Readings and lectures. Summative assessments. Refer example shown in Figure 5. Faculty staff engaged in intercultural and inter-university collaboration.	LO1 (GLO 1,5,6) LO2 (GLO 1,6) LO3 (GLO 2,0) LO4 (GLO 1,2,6) LO5 (GLO 2,6)

Figure 2. iDiDe 1 Malaysian students collaborate in a group comprising of culturally diverse members from Australia and Malaysia. (Photo by S.Ang, 2011)

Figure 3. iDiDe 3 Australia intercultural group outcome of icebreaker activity (Photo by S.Ang, 2013)

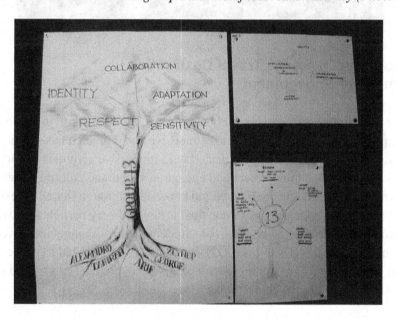

Phase 1: Preparation for First Contact

Student engagement is effected through seminars and workshops. This phase inducts a student. Each university uses this phase to prepare their own students. Inter-university and cross-national collaboration are initiated during this time with diverse team formation of 4-6 students. Groups engage in intercultural dialogue and commence engagement with the academic content. Teamwork and online communication allow students to identify and appreciate diverse cultural perspectives in design approaches and outcomes (UL01) and practice intercultural communication (ULO5).

Figure 4. Geelong Islamic Art Museum, A collaboratively developed iDiDe transcultural project brief (Photo by S.Ang, 2013)

Phase 2: In-Country (Overseas Travel Destination Culturally Immersive Engagement

The second phase (14 – 21 days duration) is a study tour format. Students travel in a group to international partner university premises. Student engagement is intensive and delivered face-to-face in-group workshops, field and site visits. Learning is supplemented with immersive activities that inform and inspire the students. Participants work on the project and engage in social and cultural activities. Participants actively engage in teamwork, building confidence and knowledge through shared experiences. Spending time in close proximity and working to a common goal is key. Industry participants who offer valuable professional mentorship are invited to be involved. Students learn to appreciate diverse perspectives and exchange cultural knowledge (ULO 1, ULO2). Students are encouraged to reflect upon individual identity and social practices and compare these with others encountered; (ULO3) and extend discipline knowledge and skills in international contexts. (ULO4)

Phase 3: Post Travel Debrief and Reflection

Student engagement is delivered though group debriefing. This reflective phase takes place on the final day prior to returning home. Once home, students use this phase to work on individual work that reflects upon, summarises and journals the whole learning experience. This phase is for students to extend and apply new/adjusted ideas into their own work and allows for reflection-on-action and self-critique (Schön, 1983).

Figure 5. Faculty staff from Australia and India collaborating in iDiDe 5 India (Photo by S.Ang, 2013)

EVOLUTION AND REFLECTION OF LESSONS LEARNT FROM iDiDe PROGRAMMES DELIVERED BETWEEN 2011-2015

- **2011 iDiDe 1 Kuala Lumpur, Malaysia (pilot):** The pilot programme was delivered in 2011 in partnership with two Malaysian universities (the International Islamic University of Malaysia and the University Teknologi, MARA). The Malaysian Institute of Architects facilitated the involvement of their professional members in various roles of guest presenters, reviewers and professional mentors. The design project was hypothetical based upon real conditions (Australian Art Centre). There was minimal Phase 1 engagement, rushed academic content, no cultural activity and ad hoc student recruitment processes. The largest challenges were identifying compatible timetabling between partners, managing resources, student recruitment and funding to enable the cost of the programme to be viable for students to take up. The use of Skype was unsuccessful, as Malaysian partners had restricted access. Too much emphasis was placed upon outcomes and the experience itself was overlooked. The 9-day itinerary was too intensive and almost all Australian students were affected adversely in terms of being overwhelmed and exhausted from unfamiliar cultural and climatic conditions. Dress code and code of conduct of Australian students visiting Malaysian university campuses came into question and it was a case of reacting to protocols as opposed being prepared. Students delighted in discovering many things that were the same about each other more than they did about things that were different. This notion of "same but different" became the inspiration for one of the teams design concepts. The success of this pilot must be attributed to the commitment and solidarity of the partnerships between universities. The hosting university helped define the role and responsibilities of a host. Feedback from participants at all levels were overwhelming in their praise.
- **2012 iDiDe 2 Kuala Lumpur, Malaysia:** The same three universities participated in 2012 with a different host. Recruitment of students became more streamlined with selection processes and

preparation briefings embedded into timelines. Professional members were approached to take on a more active involvement and invited to offer up their offices for student groups to spend 1-2 days to experience professional office environments and to work on their project under the stewardship of a combined mentor team of academic and professional tutor. This added another level of logistics in regards inviting, briefing and managing the involvement of the architects and their office environments. The design project was for an Australian Malaysian Art Centre in a riverfront site in Kuala Lumpur. This project was similarly hypothetical and based upon real conditions. The Australian Government International Education Counselor in Malaysia sponsored a reception for the exhibition. The implementation of Phase 1 engagement made a difference in preparing students. There were deliberate formation of inter-university teams, targeted lectures and reading lists developed. A single cultural immersion activity being a day trip to a cultural heritage town of Malacca, 60kms outside of Kuala Lumpur was organised. The cultural activity was a welcome inclusion. Student feedback attested to the value in having a social environment in which students from each university could socialise and get to know one another informally to build relations and help cross the cultural bridges. Recruitment of student participants was largely still ad hoc but the process benefited immensely from testimonials of students who participated the year before. A disparity in learner engagement behaviors were keenly observed between Australian students and Malaysian students from the pilot experience which prompted Malaysian partners to request a Malaysian cultural element be integrated into the brief arguing for cultural familiarity and local advantage for their students to counteract the lack of confidence they felt their students carried when collaborating with more confident and articulate English language speakers. The overall travel itinerary increased to 13 days to allow study free time. Participant entry and exit questionnaires were initiated and helped to document student feedback.

- **2013a iDiDe 3 Geelong-Melbourne, Australia:** The International Islamic University of Malaysia (IIUM) in partnership with Deakin University Australia (Deakin) applied and were successful in attracting a grant from the Australian Malaysian Institute (AMI) that enabled the Malaysian team to travel to Australia to experience an iDiDe programme in Australia, with Deakin University's School of Architecture and Built Environment taking up the role of host. The Australian Institute of Architects were invited to be involved in a project set as a hypothetical design project that allowed the examination of cross cultural identities within the proposed design of an Islamic Museum for Geelong, Victoria. Both Deakin and IIUM were keen to provide cultural engagement for the students and collaborated on the design brief to ensure an equitable engagement could be experienced. Team building activities (later referred to as "Ice Breaker Activity) were introduced for the first time as an effort towards facilitating students in getting to know one another through less threatening and less confronting circumstances. The Ice Breaker Activity was designed to initiate intercultural understanding, exchange of personal and cultural background knowledge and to build an intercultural team identity. Students from both Malaysia and Australia especially found time spent with practices and professionals a rewarding experience and rated this highly.

- **2013b iDiDe 4 Bangkok, Thailand:** New partner King Mongkut University of Thailand, Thonburi School of Architecture and Design (KMUTT) joined the iDiDe community along with the Siamese Institute of Architects. With students and staff from three countries (Australia, Malaysia and Thailand), the programme was considered to have evolved and expanded in its offering of enriched intercultural learning experiences. Key features that distinguish the iDiDe programme such as pre travel preparation, ice breaker activities, professional members active involvement alongside academics, jointly developed design project, high profile government event and public exhibition of student outcomes and a balance of study and cultural immersion activities and assessment through reflection were now well embedded into the study tour programme. The project (Community Art Gallery) was the first community based design project and addressed issues of preservation of local heritage and cultures of the river-based communities. The cultural collaboration and community engagement married well into iDiDe's transcultural agenda (Figure 6).

- **2013c iDiDe 5 Gurgaon-Delhi, India:** In line with Deakin University's international strategy to engage with India, Ansal University, India was identified as a strategic host. The Indian partner introduced the project, as it was one their 3rd year studio was already engaged with. The project was large in scope and groups were encouraged to develop their own brief within the context of the project, to offer cultural interventions for the improvement of an informal settlement. The new focus upon social architecture was highly rated with students valuing the social considerations as issues integral to architecture education. The programme trialled inter-year level students (3rd year and 4th year) and discovered benefits to students learning through mixed level exchange. Higher level students gained leadership and lower level students benefited from the mentoring of senior level team members.

- **2014 iDiDe 6 Miri-Bario-Kuching, Sarawak, Borneo, Malaysia:** With the growing reputation for community based design and cultural sensitivity in Asia, iDiDe attracted a special assignment project whereby The Rurum Kelabit Sarawak (RKS) approached Deakin University with a brief to visualize and design an Eco Live Museum for the Kelabit Highland Community. The community was located in a remote rural highland location with difficult access. The project addressed community concerns of preservation of intangible culture and heritage. The project demanded multiple travel destinations and a travelling schedule of presentation, community consultation to reach all the community that resided in these multiple sites. With additional challenges of a real life community, this was a coming of age in the iDiDE experience. The community participatory

Figure 6. Tri-national intercultural design collaboration iDiDe 4 Bangkok, Thailand involved participants from Australia, Malaysia and Thailand. (Photo by S.Ang, 2013)

design processes and designing on the go in unconventional areas such as street stalls, coffee shops, longhouses, rice fields and at airport lounges, proved the model to be adequately robust in its innovative teaching and learning of design, embedded study tour features and transformative experiences for students.

- **2015 iDiDe 7 Bali-Jogjakarta-Jakarta, Indonesia and 2016 iDiDe 8 Colombo-Ampara-Sri Lanka:** BINUS University Indonesia joined as the seventh iDiDe partner. Scheduling of cultural immersion activities are now offered ahead of the design studio scheduled in the final week of the tour programme to provide opportunity to acclimatise to appreciate and understand something of the local culture and context affect participants in positive ways can be seen in the design outcomes as well as in the student experience of the deign collaboration. Multi-sited, multi-national and inter-level participation through the power of academic, professional/industry and government partnerships and a focus on cultural and community based design are the hallmarks of the iDiDe model. iDiDe has successfully established and delivered a transcultural agenda over a sustained period of five years. At the time of writing this chapter, iDiDe programme planning is in place for delivery of the eight iDiDe in Sri Lanka, its fifth Asian destination and its seventh partner university.

SUMMARY OF EVALUATION OF PARTICIPANTS TESTIMONIALS

The strongest impacts live in the reflective voices of participants attested to in the written testimonials received. Formal evaluation of teaching was not available due to the small number enrolments. Participants were not obligated to complete any evaluation however many volunteered their feedback and provided testimonials. Twenty testimonials from 2012 – 2014 offering qualitative data were collected through invitation to participants to provide them on a volunteer basis. The qualitative data was analysed utilising a thematic-synthesis method drawn from a number of sources on qualitative thematic analysis methods (Lillyman & Bennet, 2014; Aronson, 1995 and Merriam, 1988) to identify the themes in relation to student participant experiences and their impacts upon intercultural learning and design collaboration. Prevalent themes of intercultural collaboration and student engagement were identified as "high impact", "moderate impact" and "low impact" dependent upon the frequency of key words extracted from the testimonials. Three categories of student participants described below provided qualitative data. Two examples of each category of participant testimonials are included in the sections below. A further category of participant is category D: "Non-student, partner representative, academic/professional/industry representative, government representative, others" is included to evidence the impact upon non-student participants which will be discussed more under further research.

Testimonials of Student Participant Category A: Australian Student from Deakin University Australia

Working in a group of 6 meant that we were subjected to five other perspectives and ideas. It teaches you to see things differently, altering priorities and exploring options to unify the main design intention. The programme was a great introduction to international collaboration and I feel much more comfortable with the idea of working beyond my own country borders, something that is inevitable to form part of a future career in Architecture. This experience has reinforced the idea that we're no longer confined to one city but instead, are part of a global community and engage in a bigger dialogue. I envision myself working on a global scale and am more transient as an aspiring professional. I've gained more confidence practicing in an international arena. Learning to adapt to new environments, be culturally sensitive, nurture human relationships, and overcome barriers. With the state of globalisation, we will inevitably cross paths with different cultures and this has allowed us to see the value in cultural diversity. Working internationally requires new understanding of cultural issues, practices, and knowledge and standards. Understanding foreign clients is more difficult than domestic clients, and sometimes it's about asking the right questions to offer the right solutions. Culture is ever evolving, and architecture responds to these changes to accommodate human life. Nearing the end of our architectural education is the time to forge our own path and pursue our personal interests in architecture. The best part about going away is coming back home and being eternally grateful for all that we have. (A1)

There many different ways you can learn. As tertiary students we do spend part of our time listening to others in university lectures, or reading journals and books, but it is the unique learning experience of the design studio that differentiates the education of architecture students. Education through doing is undoubtedly the most effective way to learn. The iDiDe programme has provided a unique 'doing' experience through the fusion of culture and design. The design process has been condensed into a week- long event, and as such we have learnt as much as we might in an entire semester within an extremely short time frame. However, it is not that we have simply learnt faster, the lessons are ones that you cannot teach, they cannot be replicated in a classroom but instead must be experienced through the iDiDe format. It is something I will recommend all students back home to be involved in. The sentiment I felt at the time of the closing are still true when I returned home and will resonate with me for a long time to come. (A2)

Testimonials from Student Participant Category B: International Student from Deakin University Australia

The programme is brilliant! It creates prospects for international students like myself to experience diverse environments in design. The part that impressed me the most is the opportunity of working in a group where almost all participants have different cultural and social backgrounds. It creates a situation that forces me to learn to think and make decisions quickly and amicably. It made me realise how much respect, patience and understanding is required. My perspectives towards design totally changed and grew. If I were to describe my experience in a word it would be "ENRICHMENT". (B1)

I wish to pen my gratitude for the opportunity Deakin gave me. I truly valued and appreciated the opportunity provided by the IDiDe programme to an international student like me. The cultural interaction in a different country to solve a design problem in a short period gave me valuable experience. I truly hope that the iDiDe continued and more students gain this invaluable experience. I think international students benefit so much from taking part in an intercultural study tour like this. It makes it special there is focus on intercultural issues. (B2)

Testimonials of Student Participant Category C: Non Australian Student from International Partner University in Asia

The collaboration between students from different institutions enabled me to communicate and exchange ideas between different types of cultures. Besides, it challenges my creative potential culminating in the formulation of my own design. Most importantly, I learnt how to adapt quickly within a short space of time on developing design between groups of students who had very little time to know each. Exposure. Networking. These two elements are some of the vital catalysts for every architecture student to develop and evolve towards becoming a great architect. I believe that Intercultural Dialogue through Design (iDiDe) is the best platform for me to search for exposure and networking between different kinds of culture, background and races other. In fact, architectural language and knowledge help a lot, as it is the main aspect that we have in common. From that, we managed to respect each other's opinion and ideas. (C1)

I was really affected by the way the programme works. How you interact with several people you never met before and together in one group, designing a significant, cultural building in such a short period of time. Working with several people who possess their very own forte made me paid more respect towards everyone's idea and opinion and I think that is how architecture world works. iDiDe shows me that communication is architect's greatest tool weather by your own drawings or your verbal messages. I found the worth and value towards the preparation of future graduates like me into global practice environment. To cap off my write up, I'd regard this programme as highly MOMENTOUS. (C2)

Testimonials of Participant Category D: Other Non-Student, Partner Representative, Academic and/or Professional/Industry Representative, Government Representative, Others

I am writing to congratulate Deakin University on the student mobility programme conducted in Malaysia in November and December 2011 for Australian and Malaysian architecture students. The "Intercultural Dialogue through Design is a particularly innovative example of international student engagement and mobility. I was pleased to attend the judging ceremony to meet the Australian and Malaysian students and the architects who hosted the student design teams. Australian universities have benefitted from the long history of engagement with Malaysia, recruiting undergraduate students in large numbers. With the growth in worldwide competition for students, Australia now faces increased demands for a deeper engagement on education that goes beyond student recruitment. Initiatives such as the Intercultural Dialogue through Design showcase the best of Australian education, and cultivate deeper ties between academics and students from both countries. I do hope Deakin will continue to lead such an impressive mobility project and congratulations on an excellent student mobility initiative. (D1)

iDiDe is an innovative programme of cultural exchange for university students studying architecture. It is successful in establishing closer ties between Australian and South East Asian architects through the engagement of academia in partnership with practitioners and professional associations within the region. The positive opportunities provided by iDiDe to the wider profession have been recognised as a key ingredient as it provides a template for engagement with other professional associations throughout the region. I have been involved in this programme since its inception in 2010. I am now based in Kuala Lumpur and attached to my own design firm who continue to support iDiDe. I can attest to its the real and ongoing benefits already generated, not only for students themselves but critically also for partici-pating practitioners and academics. The opportunity to meet face to face within a workshop setting has been invaluable, at the same time, providing the rare opportunity to raise significant issues of national global importance within a setting of exchange. This type of cultural exchange needs to be ongoing for the wider benefits to be felt in the profession and the in the future. iDiDe has already proven itself to be the right vehicle to enable this. (D2)

ETHICS AND APPROVALS

Approvals to conduct this research have been sought and received from Deakin University's Human Research Ethics Committee, ethics approval references HA 113-114 from 26 November 2013 till 26 November 2017 and 2010-4 from 3 November 2010 till 3 November 2014.

DISCUSSION AND SUMMARY OF ANALYSIS OF FINDINGS

From the content analysis performed, themes of intercultural collaboration and student engagement in relation to the impacts of grass roots collaborative design relations were identified amongst Australian student participants. Themes regarded as "high impact" were identified as those of highest frequency amongst participants (by 50% or more), "moderate impact" being those of moderate frequency (Between 25% and 50%), and "low impact" being those of least frequency (less than 25%).

High Impact Themes

High impact themes identified included: 1) Opportunity to experience collaborative engagement and be exposed to an international environment. Students felt it was of direct benefit to future practice and career prospects in the international arena; 2) The challenge and experience of collaborating and learning teamwork skills with people from diverse cultural and educational backgrounds. When initially daunted by fears of the unknown and the unfamiliar, students found it rewarding when called upon to reflect upon how at first they found something quite hard to do and then by doing it, found that it was not so hard to do and eventually gaining confidence from the experience of "doing". The tight time frames of the programme schedule actually worked to this advantage as it afforded little time to dwell on the "cannot do's" to a working approach of "just do it" and then to eventually discover that one has "done it" with-out overthinking. Many students carried preconceived expectations of having communication barriers and language problems. The nature of the intercultural environment levels the playing field for both parties on either side of the cultural fence. The expectations of the programme set the tone and attitude of participants such that they become mentally prepared to navigate these barriers despite expecting difficulties. The varied spectrum of resources made available through equal exchange amongst peers from different nationalities and cultural backgrounds as well as academics and professional participants as "living resources" within a rich and diverse learning pool from which Australian students found motivating. A crucial factor was the learning environment became 100% active. Students thrived in environments where there is respect and value for the knowledge they bring to the table and they became motivated to both divulge and absorb knowledge more hungrily than they would in an ordinary learning environment where some of the time spent is in the passive. 3) The opportunity of direct exposure to real scenarios and real world opportunities where students were pushed to further develop design ability and expand upon their architectural knowledge through intercultural practice of communication and culturally and socially responsive design parameters. Students found the design parameters set within the projects rewarding, as it afforded challenges they felt were globally relevant. The projects that were set in real situations gave this factor a realistic pressure and could definitely be seen to "bring out the best" in the students' performance. Working in teams meant that they had spent time building through new cultural friendships also added to the strong desire for individual students to perform to their ultimate best, no individual student was keen be perceived as letting down their new team members; with each student wearing the mark of individual and collective national pride and commitment to the task at hand. 4) The creation of unique and enriched learning experience where students believed they learnt a lot in a short timeframe. They were learning in a multitude of ways and formats. During down time, students continued to be engaged in learning conversations with peers from both within Australian and from outside Australia. Students discovered more about themselves as much as they learnt about others. 5) Students identified a deeper respect for cultural identity, intercultural peers and culture, were more culturally aware and felt that they were better prepared global practice, with many expressing desire to pursue employment in Asia.

Moderate Impact Themes

Moderate impact themes had to do with recommending the experience to future students and feelings of achievements. Students expressed satisfaction in successfully navigating through personal challenges they never thought they were capable of. Some students described the experiences as "edifying" and "momentous".

Low Impact Themes

Students expressed the forward hope and expectation of catching up with their new friends from other countries and discussed future plans to travel and visit these destinations. Some spoke of pursuing newfound desire to seek employment prospects and spoke about how they no longer felt the same fear of unfamiliarity, which could be read as new confidence to take on unknown global challenges.

Findings from Non-Student Participants (Faculties, Profession and Governments)

Majority of the feedback described iDiDe to be "innovative and collaborative" and that it enriches the knowledge of students through collaborative education and learning from each other". There was formal endorsement of how the programme contributed towards cultural understanding and deeper ties between Australia and Asia. It was regarded to be a successful model for "international collaboration being a benefit to student learning"; "Collaboration and working with diverse members"; "Developing discipline specific skills and knowledge" and "deeper respect for cultural identity, and "being more culturally aware". The innovative aspects of teaching and learning of intercultural competency and intercultural understanding are key strategies and the elements incorporated into iDiDe structure, academic content and overall programme can be judged to be successful from the outcomes of the feedback and from the sustained successful deliveries. The longevity and expansion into six countries whilst retaining key features and elements have worked successfully to enrich knowledge of students through collaborative design education and a mantra of learning from each other. Government and professional participants have offered their impressions of how valuable the intercultural nature of the learning environment serve to embody cultural considerations in design. The value of linkages into Asia and building deeper ties between Australia and Asia through mutual respect and basic friendships are well recognised. These innovations set the tone for education for life and produce not just memorable but deep and transformative experiences.

FURTHER RESEARCH DIRECTIONS

This chapter provided research on the iDiDe model by explaining its concept, the theory that underpins the teaching and learning, and how the programme was developed from its conception. It explained the essential elements, the most crucial being the Australian-Asian university partnerships. The research relied upon critical reflective methods of inquiry to gain insight into lessons learnt. Qualitative evaluations were performed to determine how relevant the elements were to intercultural collaboration and student engagement. Positioning and branding iDiDe as a model of global mobility in Asia has allowed it to be successful in attracting Australian Government global mobility grant funding in the century dubbed "The Asian Century". iDiDe was successful on three occasions (2014, 2015 and 2016). Moreover, it has demonstrated how global mobility has successfully integrated intercultural design collaboration as an essential component of architecture education in the 21st century. No opportunity has arisen to test the model in a different discipline however it could be tweaked to apply to any professional discipline that demands its future graduates be equipped with collaborative skills and readiness for intercultural global practice. In relation to how learning outcomes have responded to the desired international profile of Australian graduates, different criteria would have had to be used to evaluate those. The research enquiry was similarly interested to discover the potential for longer-term transformative learning. No data was collected beyond the immediate post-mortem phase and makes a case for further research to investigate these. One insight is that a measure of success of the impacts is the manner in which experiences are gained and how long lasting they remain to influence the individuals. The findings do suggest there is potential to continue. Observational evidence of postings amongst past participants on the iDiDe Global Facebook page suggests that ongoing connections have continued. The research question to ask might be "Are there connections made through iDiDe that may facilitate longer term connection between participants in Australia with Asia?" There are evidence of connections and communication being maintained through social media space such as Twitter and Instagram. However existing resources available in addition to the research methodology and ethics approval that accompanies such variable public domains of enquiry are not resolved at this time. An area of enquiry also excluded was academic staff engagement. Some findings suggested that the experience of teaching staff and of professionals who participated had profound influence upon the quality and success of the student learning. An example is the opportunity to bridge the divide in the nexus of education and practice. This chapter focused principally upon iDiDe model from the Australian (Deakin University) perspective. What of the perspectives of the international partners? How do the different cultural perspectives combine to our knowledge of this subject?

It is acknowledged that non-variable as well as variable elements are inherent in the model. Non-variable elements include academic intentions; content and pedagogical approach. The variables were the international participants, travel destinations, nature of project, involvement of external participants, as was the example of the Kelabit Highlands Cultural Museum project. In this example the added element of community participatory process involved in-depth community dialogue sessions, community presentations and feedback opportunities conducted with individuals and community groups. As the community participatory process went deeper, it became increasingly apparent Malaysian partners added invaluable intrinsic local design knowledge and expertise of local environment. The design process was greatly enriched by intercultural collaborative engagement. The Malaysian team not only contributed valuable climate appropriate strategies, knowledge of local construction techniques and sources of local material, they aided in the Australian team's understanding of the cultural nuances. This case study offers many more lessons. Refer Figures 7, 8 and 9.

CONCLUSION

The journey of a transcultural learner begins with cross-cultural conversation and aims for empathetic understanding. The capacity to "put oneself in another's shoes"—to apprehend their point of view and felt experiences—is prerequisite to finally taking responsibility as citizens of the global community." (Slimbach, 2005). From its pilot year of offering in 2011 to 2015, iDiDe has provided opportunities for intercultural collaboration and student engagement to fifty-five Australian students and eighty-five

Figure 7. Kelabit Highlands Community Museum, Miri-Bario-Kuching, Sarawak, iDiDe 6 Borneo Malaysia Project (Photo by S.Ang, 2014)

Figure 8. Community dialogue Kelabit Highlands Community Museum, Miri-Bario-Kuching, Sarawak, iDiDe 6 Borneo Malaysia Project (Photo by S.Ang, 2014)

Figure 9. Field visit and study of longhouses of Kelabit Highlands, Bario, Sarawak, iDiDe 6 Borneo Malaysia Project (Photo by S.Ang, 2014)

non-Australian students from the Asia and the Indo Pacific nations. The diversity and nationality of participants represent five nations - Australia (55) Malaysia (33), Thailand (9), India (31) and Indonesia (12). In 2016 Sri Lanka will host an iDiDe and a minimum of 20 Sri Lankan students will interact with new cohorts of iDiDe participants from Australia and Asia. The iDiDe Global Facebook group shows almost 200 members are globally connected. Australia is the only non Indo-Pacific nation and this is an important initiative in the context of the Australian Government's plan to build relations with its Asian neighbors. This chapter presented research on iDiDe for the first time hence it is not surprising that such a volume of further research has been identified. This is in no small part due to the enormous amounts of time, dedication, resources and effort invested over the last six years to achieve the iDiDe experience. What is apparent is that there is so much richness in the existing data that can be examined. With future iDiDe programmes, there will be further data that can offer itself to a longitudinal study. The "organic" nature is likely to be a defining characteristic of iDiDe. In so many ways, this quality also defines intercultural dialogue and intercultural understanding. This is the first paper on iDiDe. It is weighty in original content, and should be viewed as an opening of a doorway to intercultural collaboration and student engagement. There are three areas this chapter sought to inform a reader about iDiDe. The first is the framework in the global mobility study tour programme operates, the second is how this framework has evolved, grown, matured and adapted to suit any Asian context and the third provides guidance for those who wish to develop a study tour that may lead to successful outcomes. The objective was to introduce iDiDe to a global audience as an Australian model of global student engagement. This model has shown that it not only subscribed to the Australian Government's NCP agenda but has also demonstrated a vast potential for teaching deep and transformative learning through intercultural design collaboration. This objective, whilst it can be said has been achieved remains an open and evolving one. Refer Figures 10 and 11.

Figure 10. Group photo of students from Indonesia, Malaysia and Australia during site visit to Betawi village, iDiDe7 Bali-Jogjakarta-Jakarta, Indonesia. (Photo by S.Ang, 2015)

Figure 11. Public exhibition of student projects at Indonesian Institute of Architects, Jakarta, Indonesia, iDiDe7 Bali-Jogjakarta-Jakarta, Indonesia. (Photo by A.Prawata, 2015)

ACKNOWLEDGMENT

The author would like to thank all iDiDe participants represented, all iDiDe institutional partners, the Australian Government, representatives and staff of the Australian Embassies in Malaysia, Thailand, India and Indonesia, Australian Institute of Architects, The Malaysian Institute of Architects, Siamese Institute of Architects, Indian Institute of Architects, Indonesian Institute of Architects, and individuals who have supported and participated in iDiDe.

REFERENCES

Altbach, P., & Knight, J. (2007). Internationalisation of Higher Education: Motivations and Realities. *Journal of Studies in International Education, 11*(3-4), 290–305. doi:10.1177/1028315307303542

Aronson, J. (1995). A pragmatic view of thematic analysis. *Qualitative Report, 2*(1), 1–3.

Bexley, E., James, R., & Arkoudis, S. (2011). *The Australian Academic Profession in Transition: Addressing the Challenge of Reconceptualising Academic Work and Regenerating the Academic Workforce.* Centre for the Study of Higher Education.

Boud, D., Cohen, R., & Sampson, J. (Eds.). (2014). *Peer Learning in Higher Education: Learning from and with each other.* London: Routledge.

Council of Europe. (2014) *New Colombo Plan.* Retrieved from http://www.coe.int/t/dg4/intercultural/concept_EN.asp

Cushner, K., & Karim, A. (2004). Study Abroad at the University Level. In D. Landis, M. Bennett, & J. Bennett (Eds.), *Handbook of Intercultural Training*. Thousand Oaks, CA: Sage. doi:10.4135/9781452231129.n12

De Graaf, E., & Kolmos, A. (2003). Characteristics of problem-based learning. *International Journal of Engineering Education, 19*(5), 657–662.

Department of Foreign Affairs and Trade. (2014) *New Colombo Plan*. Retrieved from http://dfat.gov.au/people-to-people/new-colombo-plan/Pages/new-colombo-plan.aspx

Duke, C. (2000). Study Abroad Learning Activities: A Synthesis and Comparison. *Journal of Marketing Education, 22*(2), 155–165. doi:10.1177/0273475300222010

Dutton, T. A., & Mann, L. H. (Eds.). (1996). *Reconstructing architecture: Critical discourses and social practices*. Minnesota: University of Minnesota Press.

Eldeen, H. (2003). Ethics for Architecture: Imperative Approach for Integrating Sustainable Thinking in Design Education. Proceedings of the Scientific Conference on Sustainable Architectural and Urban Design, Cairo, Egypt.

Flom, N. A. (2014). *There and Back Again: Perceived Long-Term Effects of a High School Immersion Abroad Experience*. Education Doctoral Dissertations in Leadership.

Freeman, S. (1964). International Study at Home and Abroad. *The Annals of the American Academy of Political and Social Science, 356*(1), 133–141. doi:10.1177/000271626435600118

Gillard, J. (2012). *Australia in the Asian Century* (White Paper). Australian Government.

Guest, D., Livett, M., & Stone, N. (2006). Fostering International Student Exchanges for Science Students. *Journal of Studies in International Education, 10*(4), 378–395. doi:10.1177/1028315306287632

Harman, G. (2005). Internationalization of Australian Higher Education: A Critical Review of Literature and Research. In Internationalizing higher education (pp. 119-140). Netherlands: Springer.

Hope, J. (2008). The Language Teacher as an International Educator. *Paper Presented at the Developments in the Pedagogy of International Languages: A Gateway for Practitioners*, Kuala Lumpur, Malaysia.

Joubert, L., & Whitford, S. (2006). Bilateral Learning and Teaching in Chinese-Australian Arts and Architecture. *Journal of Studies in International Education, 10*(4), 396–408. doi:10.1177/1028315306288819

Kalantzis, M., & Cope, B. (2005). *Learning By Design*. Melbourne, Victoria, and Victorian: Schools Innovation Commission and Common Ground.

Knight, J. (2004). Internationalization Remodeled: Definition, Approaches and Rationales. *Journal of Studies in International Education, 8*(1), 5–31. doi:10.1177/1028315303260832

Knight, J., & De Wit, H. (1999). *Quality and Internationalisation in Higher Education*. Paris: OECD Publishing.

Landis, D., Bennett, J., & Bennett, M. (Eds.). (2004). *Handbook of Intercultural Training, Thousand Oaks*. CA: Sage.

Leask, B. (2003). Beyond The Numbers - Levels and Layers of Internationalism to Utilise and Support Growth And Diversity. *Proceedings of the17th IDP Australian International Education Conference*, Melbourne: Australia.

Lillyman, S., & Bennett, C. (2014). Providing a positive learning experience for international students studying at UK universities: A literature review. *Journal of Research in International Education, 13*(1), 63–75. doi:10.1177/1475240914529859

Merriam, S. B. (1988). *Case study research in education: A qualitative approach*. Jossey-Bass.

Nicol, D., & Pilling, S. (2002). Architectural Education and the Profession. In *Changing Architectural Education: Towards a New Profession* (pp. 1-22).

Nicol, D., & Pilling, S. (Eds.). (2005). *Changing Architectural Education: Towards A New Professionalism*. New York: Taylor & Francis.

Rapoport, A. (2005). Culture, Architecture and Design. Chicago, IL: Locke Science Publishing Co.

Salama, A. (1995). *New Trends in Architectural Education: Designing the Design Studio Raleigh*. NC: Tailored Text and Unlimited Potential Publishing.

Salama, A. (2007). An Exploratory Investigation into the Impact of International Paradigmatic Trends on Arab Architectural Education. *Global Built Environment Review, 6*, 31–43.

Schön, D. A. (1983). *The reflective practitioner: How professionals think in action*. Basic books.

Slimbach, R. (2005). The Transcultural Journey. *Frontiers: The Interdisciplinary Journal of Study Abroad, 11*, 205–230.

Sweet, J., & Horman, T. (2012). Museum Development and Cross-Cultural Learning in the Kelabit Highlands, Borneo. *Museums Australia Magazine, 21*(1), 23–26.

Teekens, H. (2000). Teaching and Learning in the International Classroom. *Internationalisation at Home: A Position Paper.*

Tsing, A. L. (2011). *Friction: ethnography of global connection*. Princeton University Press.

United Nations Educational, Scientific and Cultural Organization. (2015) *Introducing UNESCO*. Retrieved from http://en.unesco.org/about-us/introducing-unesco#sthash.xym89aT2.dpuf

Webb, G. (2005). Internationalization of Curriculum: An Institutional Approach. In J. Carroll & J. Ryan (Eds.), *Teaching International Students: Improving Learning for All*. London: Routledge.

Wells, A. (2014). International Student Mobility: Approaches, Challenges and Suggestions for Further Research. *Procedia: Social and Behavioral Sciences, 143*, 19–24. doi:10.1016/j.sbspro.2014.07.350

KEY TERMS AND DEFINITIONS

Australian Student: In the iDiDe context (in our data set), a student is an Australian student participant if they are enrolled in Deakin University Australia and holds an Australian citizenship or residency status.

iDiDe: Intercultural dialogue through design, globally known as "iDiDe" (pronounced i-dee-dee) is a model of intercultural collaboration and student engagement for architecture and built environment disciplines. It was initiated in 2011 by an Australian university in partnership with two Malaysian universities through leverage of Australian-Malaysian alumni connections formed in 1980s. To date it has expanded and sustained partnerships to include five Asian nations (Malaysia, Thailand, India, Indonesia, Sri Lanka). The letters that spell the acronym "iDiDe" are an abbreviated play on the words "Intercultural Dialogue Through Design".

International Student from Australia: In the iDiDe context (in our data set), a student is an International student participant from Australia if they are enrolled in Deakin University Australia and holds a temporary resident (visa status) of Australia; or a permanent resident (visa status) of New Zealand, or a resident or citizen of any other country.

Non-Australian Student: In the iDiDe context (in our data set), a student is a non-Australian student participant if they are enrolled in an international partner university in Asia regardless of their citizenship or residency status.

Chapter 12
Collaborative Spectra:
Mille Feuille Design Workshop – Teaching Individuals Design through Group Work

Ammon Beyerle
Here Studio, Australia & The University of Melbourne, Australia

Greg Missingham
The University of Melbourne, Australia

ABSTRACT

Two teaching experiences that structured individual student learning through the designed variation of group work opportunities are examined: a graduate architectural design studio and a repeated undergraduate course focused on methods and approaches for designing. The teaching approaches draw on participatory design and group learning theories. Group work was structured as a series of overlapping layers to bring about an individual learning experience and a shared studio experience of creativity. Various outcomes are read against an excerpt from Nancy's "The Inoperative Community" in Bishop's Participation (2006b). The discussion is a means to further explore common interests in designing design processes, in particular through developing collaborative learning in design, and a social-reflective practice in students. The authors are figuring yet another way of developing creativity wherein a student's skills, projects, and ideas come out of, and are intersected by a complexity of social processes, oppositions and the spectra that define them.

INTRODUCTION

Learning emerges because of interactive mechanisms, where individual knowledge is shared, disseminated, diffused and further developed through relational and belonging synergies. Collective learning can therefore be conceived as an evolutionary process of perfecting collective knowledge. (Rieger & Young, 2015, p. 60, citing SpringerReference.com)

DOI: 10.4018/978-1-5225-0726-0.ch012

Since the turn of the century there have been many calls for teaching collaboration in design studios, and the value of collaborative approaches to design. The authors' common interest is in teaching of and research into design processes where development of student designers' selves occurs within group processes in the world – one author's interest emphasizing participation and the other's reflective thinking. This chapter is an opportunity to connect these threads.

A review of calls for how to teach architecture and, specifically, design studios, follows. For our chapter, these seem to reveal three concerns: awareness of communication and transdisciplinarity, becoming self through engagement in group processes and situated, applied design and tacit learning. Where the profession of design teaching as a whole has commented on the value to students of collaboration, in specific design studio examples, exploration of concepts of collaboration, and how to structure it, have both instrumentalized and explicitly integrated collaboration in the creative process.

From 2000, the American Institute of Architects Students (AIAS) Studio Culture Task Force investigated studio culture in architectural education in the United States. The AIAS suspected studio culture was somewhat wanting in the workloads expected of students, how students were being treated (especially in reviews of projects) and, as the principal vehicle at the core of architectural education, whether it actually prepared students for the world of professional practice. Two aspects of what the Task Force found – among twelve – bore particularly on the last point, whether studio culture prepared students for the world of professional practice. These were phrased as:

Collaboration is the art of Design ("students would be better served by learning about the value of collaboration"), and ...

Design is inherently an Interdisciplinary act (Koch et al, 2002, pp. 12-13).

Two years later, the AIAS examined progress toward more sustainable, equitable and relevant studio cultures in schools of architecture. Among characteristics of studio culture was 'competition vs. collaboration' (Kellogg, 2005, p. 11). In other words, both should be assumed. In the next AIAS report, among *10 Best Practices, Guidelines and Recommendations*, item 10 included the development of 'successful team collaborators' and item 5 asked for 'cross-disciplinary educational environments' (The Second AIAS Task Force on Studio Culture, 2008, p. 17).

In Australia, the most comprehensive review of studio teaching in art, design and architecture was driven by a concerned group of academics, funded by a federal government grant. Like the AIAS, this review based its findings on interviews with deans, heads of schools and focus groups of academics, but also on two-day workshops with interested academics in a number of cities (Zehner et al, 2009).[1] One of the aims of the review was to uncover effective studio practice in each discipline. Among the *Benchmarks for Studio Teaching,* 'effective collaboration among students' was noted and 'multidisciplinary' projects (v. 1, p. viii) for more positive student and staff experiences. Volume 4 of the Report (Case Studies of Effective Practice) provides twenty-seven examples of good studio teaching practice, a number of which are 'multidisciplinary'/'cross-disciplinary'/'transdisciplinary' (for varieties of teamwork, teaching or practice) and a few which are explicitly 'collaborative'. The evidence of student opinions of good studio teaching practice is highlighted. Item 1 was: "Students appreciate opportunities to work collaboratively with their peers" (v. 4, p. 12).

A more recent text variably covers nineteen schools of architecture, how they see themselves now and into the future regarding pedagogy, issues to focus on, preparation for practice and so on. Examples are included from four UK schools, nine US schools, three continental European schools, two Chinese schools and one from Australia. Deans, heads of schools or noted senior academicsprovided the texts (Spiller & Clear, 2013). Collaborative studios are noted explicitly, in terms of: 'collaboration across interdisciplinary (computer) networks' – rather than between students (in Brett Steele's piece on the Architectural Association, p. 57, and in Mark Wigley's piece on Columbia University, p. 225); necessary transdisciplinarity of dealing with housing and ecology or valuable cross-fertilization in a very brief way; 'contamination' of ideas across disciplines (in Mohsen Mostafavi's piece on Harvard's GSD, pp. 196, 197); or 'transdisciplinarity' as a fundamental of useful contemporary design studios and practices (in RUR Architecture's piece on their studios at Columbia, p. 212, and in Mark Burry's piece on the Spatial Information Architecture Laboratory at RMIT University, Melbourne, emphasizing higher degree design research, p. 328). Notably, studio collaboration with 'client' bodies outside the school is noted (in Anthony Vidler's piece on the Cooper Union, p. 233, and Salomon Frausto's piece on the Berlage Institute, particularly, p. 271+). From the text of nineteen schools, only at one school is about teaching design, and this is introduced with a presumption of both individual and small group project work as a matter of course (in Hani Rashid's piece on the University of Applied Arts Vienna, p. 288).

Now, in all but one of the texts, there's a curious omission of one key type of studio (with the clear exception of Ian McArthur's paper in Zehner et al, 2009, v. 4, pp. 69+). At the authors' school (the Melbourne School of Design), this type is called the 'Travelling Studio'. In the Travelling Studio students and staff travel to a host school overseas, (or at least interstate), work intensively (for up to two weeks, full time) in mixed groups with students from the host school, and develop a project set by the host school and/or with local community representatives. Each school organizes its own students' prior preparation and work after the overseas intensive engagement with assessment, exhibition and any publication. Such studios have occurred for decades at most schools known to the authors and the Melbourne School of Design currently runs up to six a semester, interstate, on the subcontinent, in Europe, North and South America and East and South-East Asia. Such studios are inherently *collaborative* and most often interdisciplinary in the student bodies, staffing, tasks, issues to be addressed, outcomes and even assessment.

To this, most recent review of architectural design studio teaching in Australasia includes a specific design studio example which treats collaboration in a rich way. Reiter and Young (2015) discuss Studio Christchurch which "emerged as a collaborative teaching and design platform for architecture and related disciplines" (p. 59). The studio brought together seven schools from across New Zealand to design responses to the 2010-2011 Christchurch earthquakes. The concepts of transdisciplinarity and collaborative design were critically poignant choices that were relevant to the challenges inherent in the redevelopment of Christchurch from a community-wide perspective and thus, for the studio, integral to design processes that should be applied in working on those challenges.

The Christchurch example and the travelling studios exhibit a number of features that are interesting to this chapter: awareness of communication and transdisciplinarity, becoming self through engagement in group processes and situated, applied design and tacit learning (as noted above). What is especially seen as valuable to both the Christchurch and the travelling studios is the dynamic relation between the students' learning and the community, where otherness is *the* asset, and the development of identity (both of the community and the student) is an explicit topic of design. Group work plays a key part.

Studio Christchurch's vision is to educate innovative professionals with the knowledge and confidence to shape the built environment with respect to a common global future (Reiger & Young, 2015, p. 65, with our emphasis).

The discussion that follows is laid out in three parts: the first a theoretical background that outlines snippet themes of participation in architecture, social practice and tacit learning that were intrinsic to the authors' own teaching experiences, the second, a presentation of two case studies, which were teaching experience by the authors, and third, comparisons of the case studies and conclusion.

This discussion is necessarily retrospective because the value of the comparison became clear well after the completion of the original studio. Accordingly we have focussed on:

- What does this mean?
- What were we doing?
- What questions arise?

We have used the materials available to us (student feedback, student work, design reviews, moderation, material in reflective journals, course materials, discussion between teaching staff), rather than application of a specific research method.

BACKGROUND

Creating the Individual in Community

Reading Jean-Luc Nancy's difficult essay "The Inoperative Community" reveals a number of themes that put in doubt the mythology of community, and highlight that this same mythology can be studied in conceptions and destructions to define community and the relationship to the individual. Importantly, to excavate an understanding of community, Nancy starts with the individual. Instead of seeing a community defined and gathering together because of a sense of "whole" or "commonality" that might be implied in the concept of communing, in focusing on the horizons of conception (birth) and destruction (death), he regards community as all about positive difference. Community is fundamentally immanent. Community is brought about through, is made up of and produces differences. (For a synopsis of Gilles Deleuze's concept of positive difference, see Colebrook, 2002, Chpt. 1-2.) This point is interesting for a study of teaching design through group work.

Of further interest in Nancy's essay is the particular definition of the production of an individual. Nancy highlights this as the philosophical dilemma met when a member of a community actually reaches immanence through death. The experience and expression of this death is a loss that manifests itself not in the community as a whole but through different individuals, and, in reflection of each individual about the gap between that meaningless loss and the experience of the fundamentally immanent concept of community. (In this context, meaningfulness and meaning, more generally, are explored productively in Lefebvre, 1969, and Muecke, 1994, through the concept of 'horizon'.) Although Nancy does not pause to examine birth in as much depth, he clearly implies that the experience of community is actually about the conception of the individual. Might teaching individuals how to be creative through experiencing the immanence(s) of community and therefore effectively and actively to produce themselves be possible? This question sits behind the exposition of the teaching structures explored here.

The History of Architecture as a History of Lone Egos

Architecture has a mythology of individual egos – the 'starchitects', lone geniuses, Howard Roarks – to explain the production of important modern architectural revolutions. (On the origins of this and the very idea of the architect as artist, see Saint, 1983.) This is not only a mythology but a political culture that similarly assigns authorship and privilege to individual architects and proliferates as hierarchical organizational structures in architectural practices and people-less photographs of architecture (see Bonta, 1979, on the Barcelona Pavilion, for example, and Godber, 1998). It has also defined languages and styles of architecture itself – order and mess, straight lines and meandering ones, pre-conceived and emergent (Ingraham 1991, 1992).

Recently, Philip Plowright (2014) argued that there are three dominant frames within which the discipline of architecture thinks about architectural design itself: as patterns (particularly spatial patterns), as the resolution of (systems of) forces and/or as (systems of) concepts or ideas. There are other, less dominant frames. Over recent decades post-structural movements have looked to alternative forms and practices of power and Being, suggesting entirely different ways of conceiving architecture through social processes. Some of these movements blame preceding individual-architect approaches for the environmental and social degradation of the World. Architecture's interaction with Second and Third-Wave Feminism, urbanity and approaches to the Everyday have been productive foundations for this, and, have arguably brought architecture to connect with its extremities. People, place and process are key terms now, as is participation.

Plowright would probably wish to think of such approaches as resolving cultural, political and economic forces. Denise Costanzo's text (2016), aimed at beginner students of architecture, shows how very far the shift has been made in her rich yet succinct exposition of issues of Feminism, class, power, authority and the architect. Her treatment of the fictional Howard Roark in comparison with Louis I Kahn to summarize her argument is particularly cogent (pp. 251-253). (See, also: Chase (2008); Colomina (1996); De Certeau (1984); de Solà-Morales (1997); Wigglesworth (1996, 1998).)

To the judgement of architecture and ego, what Nancy's text suggests is that the role of the ego is important, because it is a paradox. Creativity in this instance is the expression of ego, but always in *clinamen* to community (p. 56).

Architecture and Participation

Architecture has a long history of participation (Beyerle 2014). There are a number of renowned architectural practitioners and theorists that have explored the valuable relationship between other people, designers and the design process and these inform our aspirations for teaching design.

Instead of the architect making all the decisions, principal examples such as John Turner ("Housing as Verb"), Eilfried Huth and Teddy Cruz describe the social, psychological and economic benefits of encouraging clients to participate in building (Turner and Fichter 1972). Similar examples that reframe the role of the architect include Walter Segal's 'Frame and infill' and Nicholas Habraken's 'Supports' and 1980s Herman Hertzberger's 'unfinished' (Habraken 1972). Architects Lucien Kroll and Giancarlo de Carlo explore this in terms of important public processes that continue (Blundell Jones, 2005; De Carlo, 2005; Obrist, 2006).

Today, it is expected that a successful and responsible architect must be able to work constructively with many other people in design, and still critically consider the social effects of their architectures. This goes further. Industry requires consortia of multiple disciples working together, engineers, economists, cost planners, community development workers, communicators, politicians and the active participation of clients themselves. Architects are faced with having to interact, form and act from and with experiences of community. It follows that learning critical participation ought to be a requirement of all graduating architecture students.

Social Practice

A turn toward architecture as a social practice was already intimated in the critiques of post-war Modernism, when modern architecture was commonly referred to as 'meaningless' and 'sterile' (Blake, 1977; Blundell-Jones, 2005; Brolin, 1976).

Contrasting the sense of meaninglessness when reflecting on death as mused by Nancy, in design participation processes the meaning (and value) is made through argument, tacit action and reflective practice. These processes are available to assume the inherent benefit of interaction and build upon them (Lefebvre, 1984).

Some of the theories that underpin attitudes to these processes stem from political theory and art praxis. Particular examples include Chantal Mouffe's agonistic pluralism and Claire Bishop's critical theories on participation and relational aesthetics (Mouffe 2000).

Both Mouffe's and Bishop's theories not only emphasise the value of interaction but, furthermore, emphasise the recognition and judgement of outcomes through processes of conception. One explicit reading useful to this discussion is that (social) engagement, with its tensions and difficulties, is key and a key opportunity. Another reading is that of meaninglessness, where social practice finds depth through the act of synthesising within a project and critical understanding across projects (Beyerle 2014).

(The historiography of architectural judgement and criticism does not have a long or relatively rich history. See, for example: Attoe (1978); Collins (1971); Hayes (2002); Hubbard (1980); Missingham (1986); Pattabi and Coyne (2000).)

Tacit Learning

This loosely described direction in architectural thinking, attempts to recognise the social aspects of architecture, first, with a respect for social processes and it prefigures the particular need to teach *architecture* through social learning. There is ample literature that establishes and explores the benefits and methods of social learning more generally (for example: Bandura, 1963, 1977; Kumpulainen & Wray, 2002; Miller, 2011). The emphasis of this chapter is then on those benefits and methods in teaching architecture. Notwithstanding, there are challenges because of the latent culture of architecture.

In design teaching we endeavour to set tasks that are complex and difficult, and encourage learning through social processes, osmosis, triangulation, processes of power and distraction (Stevens, 2007; Missingham, 2015). Students and their projects are subjected to complex situations and the students must somehow, within themselves, manage their own being through expression of themselves, and expression of a design object. This is delivered through a suite of assignments and/or performative self-examination. Exposure to the dilemma of the individual in community is key because we want to train reflective practitioners.

Overcoming Adversity or Difficulty as a Precondition for Creativity

The creative process itself hovers around key agonistic moments between individuals and community wherein an individual ego drives the expression of an artefact out of, because of and in spite of, a community. There is an inherent paradox in the desire to build and develop social processes and the expression of learning creativity. Although in reflection of different cultures of architecture, it is also true that social learning can have different politics. In the typical design studio that seeks to build a "studio culture" and engages in peer-to-peer learning or group work, this tension between social processes and expression of individual ego(s) is carefully utilised and designed into the structure and schedule of a design subject (Tregloan, 2015).

CASE STUDIES

Case Study 1: Mille Feuille

This case study concerns a postgraduate design studio in 2012. At the University of Melbourne, first, second and third-semester Master of Architecture students choose from of pool of 24-36 different design Studios, each run by practitioners and/or researchers (individually or in small teams) who independently design project tasks, schedules and assessments for the semester. (The number of pre-Thesis studios depends on the Semester and the number of graduate students undertaking their final Thesis, independently or in Thesis studios.)

Mille Feuille was a Studio run by Ammon Beyerle and Tim Derham in 2012, concerning the retrofit of a large site and heritage buildings under consideration by Arts Victoria, as part of the relocation of Circus Oz to Collingwood, in inner suburban Melbourne. (See Figure 1.) The studio was also supported by heritage architect Richard Falkinger and urban geographer Dr Kate Shaw. In *Mille Feuille*, students designed their own specific brief in direct consultation with hypothetical stakeholders, site visits, guest critiques and class discussions. The class comprised 14 Master of Architecture students spread from first to second year.

The semester was divided in three parts:

- First, a series of research projects and precedents;

Figure 1. Studio Mille Feuille concerned adaptive reuse of the 1930 Collingwood Technical School. Students visited the headquarters of Circus Oz and individual art studios at School House Studios

- Second, two interim proposals; and
- Third, design development and final presentation.

As a studio, the students were encouraged to share ideas with each other as they developed. Students shared their early research in weekly in-vivo group presentations followed by class discussion, feedback and publishing of final reports on a shared online folder. The whole studio distributed a share of precedents that the tutors pre-prepared regarding adaptive reuse, arts spaces, incubator spaces, community organisations and participatory design. The tutors also gave mini seminars in class on these topics, and arts and gentrification, economics, creative clusters and urban mapping.

In their journals, students were asked to focus on describing their own design process, their studio experience and how they improved the group work. Reflections about group work were shared in class each week, followed by discussion about how group work works. This was a particular opportunity for the tutors to direct discussion class wide on both general issues of design, and more specific issues of design in groups or community development principles. The class worked to develop a reflective, communicative and semi-structured space about creativity and working in groups.

Design responses in the form of a diagram, images and presentation were a step-by-step requirement for each layer of the research each week. The Studio met twice a week for three hours at a time. One weekly class focused on generative thinking called "tasting mouth" – where discussion was focused around many ideas, gathering, innovation and exploration. This was called "mess". The other weekly class focused on representing and communicating back to the whole studio called "speaking mouth" – where discussion was focused around few key ideas, synthesis, making-practical and critique. This was called "order". The pattern of tasting mouth versus speaking mouth, mess and order, attempted to frame different thinking roles as a cycle. (The relevant author now cannot recall where the "tasting mouth/speaking mouth" metaphor originated. It came from a reference provided by Darko Radovic, though not necessarily written by him. The metaphor of "mess and order" was developed by Ammon Beyerle in a series of design studios, the first co-coordinated with Simon Wollan.)

A third of the way into the semester, contacts with hypothetical clients and site visits were arranged with real arts and community organisations that had collectives running existing spaces around Melbourne. (See Figure 1.) These organisations had a variety of missions, metiers, interactions with the public, funding models, governance structures, and ages. The tutors formed new groups of 4-5 students who then chose multiple clients from a pre-prepared list that was designed to overlap, in which each group had a different set of clients, but at least one was common with another group. Students were given the initiative to visit "clients" themselves and report back to the Studio. The intention was that each group had specific major and minor clients to accommodate in their designs.

ASSESSMENT(S)

Mid semester presentations included open art installations as a fifth layer to preceding layers of research set by the tutors, in the form of a *"Mille Feuille* synthesis". (See Figure 2.) An immersive experience was arranged for guest critics, who included Arts Victoria, practicing architects, hypothetical clients and other design teachers. At mid semester the tutors met with students individually and discussed group work experiences, in particular focusing on each student's own role, strengths and how they could improve.

Figure 2. Studio Mille Feuille interim presentations included an art installation and discussion with hypothetical clients

The remainder of the semester continued the cycle of tasting mouth versus speaking mouth, mess and order. However, it included less whole of class discussion and more small group, pair and individual discussions, face to face with design tutors. Finally, students' work was assessed either in small groups, individually, or a combination of both. The final assessment included three deliverables produced and presented through an overlapping mix of group and individual experiences:

- **Master Plan "Whole Cake":** A 4-5 member group work.
- **Process Proposal "Large Piece":** A 2-3 member group work project.
- **Detailed "Small Piece":** An individual or pair design.

Many Groups

In fact, the individuals or pairs came out of the 2-3 member groups. These, in turn, derived from the 4-5 member groups. That is, after the research work, students did work towards their own final individual projects or project completed as a pair, but actually in successively smaller subsets of the initial, master planning group. (See Figure 3.) Grouping or teamwork was in practice nested. Finally, the students had to also submit an individual reflective journal.

The complexity of group work combinations (marked strictly as groups), together with individual components, meant that overall assessment was nuanced for each student, and required that students learned to get the best out of their team each opportunity. The other key aspect was that there were design ideas shared across the Studio as a whole, shifted, altered, and tailored specific to each student. In the students' final presentations verbal references were frequently made to combinations of different ideas that acknowledged the input of others in the Studio at different times.

COMMENTS

There were a number of turning points in the semester. These were moments of major change brought on by the tutors 'shaking things up' by altering the teaching style, asking students to present others' work, the introduction of 'clients' after the precedent work, separating the site visit to the derelict site in two

Figure 3. Tutors organised Studio Mille Feuille in layers; both themes for discussion and groupwork experiences. The students reflected on their various experiences and roles in text and diagrams.

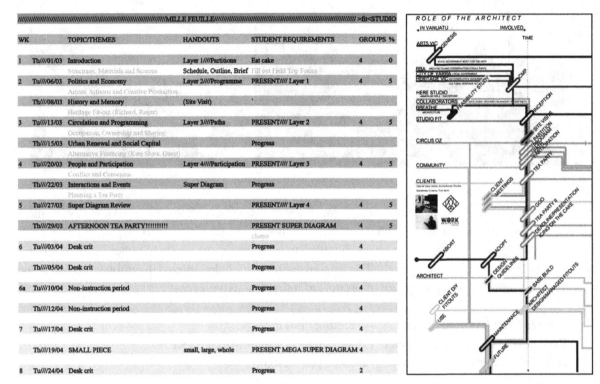

parts, one outside, and then later, one inside, and of course the forced changes in groups. These points were associated with a discussion about intentions and usually a surprise.

More generally the Studio developed a strong sense of collaborative culture where even if tutors were working one to one with someone or one group, the remainder of the class clustered in small groups and critiqued and encouraged each other. Collaborative document sharing was run by the students, themselves. Students often shared dinner in the evening classes and created their own Facebook page. In presentations the students were encouraged to note input from other people or groups, and by the end of the semester it was common practice for the students to suggest to the tutors to meet in clusters of similar ideas, or even, in the final presentation, quoted each other's comments or conceiving ideas from moments with each other. The tutors also encouraged the students to take an active part in the guest critiques.

The tutors found the final work at a high level, and this was commented upon by tutors of other studios in final moderation. Almost the whole class received second or first class honours, with different grades made up by a combination of their group work experiences, their individual projects, their individual journal and their participation more generally. Some students went so far as to build 1:1 prototype models of some parts of the project (these students were employed by one of the hypothetical clients to do some subsequent design work). Arts Victoria and Circus Oz also referenced the student projects and the many ideas in the Studio in their real architectural development that opened in 2012, and subsequent projects. One guest critic architect was contracted to reproduce a very similar concept for the site to that which was the premise for *Mille Feuille*.

Case Study 2: Design Workshop

First offered in 2013, Design Workshop is an undergraduate, elective design course, focusing on design methods, primarily for second- and third-year students in the architecture, landscape architecture and urban design Majors of the Bachelor of Environments at the University of Melbourne, intended to complement design studios. Enrolments have been substantial at 128, 141 and 135 in 2013, 2014 and 2015, respectively, with approximately 60% of students in their second year of study and 40% in their third.

The course Learning Objectives are:

- To enhance design and problem-solving skills through focused study of varied approaches to design, problem-solving and planning, and ...
- To provide an overview of approaches and methods that might otherwise be explored in planning for future environments.

The course is delivered through a system of lectures at which homework is issued and followed up in three-hour workshops some days later. No Workshop is to have more than fourteen students.

Teams

In designing the course, the principal concern was how to best allow students to explore and to structure their explorations of the plethora of materials, techniques and approaches available. For example, over the last decade or so, business and management with an interest in innovation have discovered creativity and value in design thinking and writers have catered to the demand: Adair (2009); Bielefeld and El Khouli (2007); Cornell (2012); Cross (2006, 2008, 2011); Csikszentmihalyi (1996, 2004); Curedale (2012, 2013); Dorst (2006, 2015), Gray, Brown and Macanufo (2010); Jormakka (2007); Koskinen et al (2011); Kumar (2013); Laurel (2003); Lawson & Dorst (2009); Lidwell, Holden and Butler (2010); Martin and Hanington (2012); Michalko (2006); Michel (2007); and Pürto (2004). Most of these authors come from industrial or product design and interface design backgrounds rather than from the larger-scale design disciplines of architecture, landscape design, engineering and urban design.

In *Design Workshop*, a key decision was to try to expose students to as much of the materials available as possible – not only to the more recent literature (as above) but also to material from key work since the Second World War (including Alexander, 1964; Alexander et al, 1977; Gordon, 1961; Halprin, 1969; Jones, 1970; McHarg, 1969; Polya, 1957; and Ulmer, 1994). Clearly, however, there is too much information available for any one student to digest.

So, how to manage the plethora? Is it better to provide selected digestible chunks (perhaps varying from year to year) or a scaffolding on which students could hang their own understandings of the imperfect selections that they might encounter, or to leave it to the students? (See Figure 4.)

The first step was to structure consideration of topics across the semester according to a very common pattern: using a three–part division of the act of designing. (See Figure 5.) Lectures bookend the semester, introducing the course and examining design thinking and concluding with a lecture on arguing a case for one's design and a summary of the semester's program. The nine topics between, in three groups of three, covered Generating, Exploring and Evaluating design ideas. This structure followed that of the graduate design elective *Design Approaches and Methods*. However, where *Design Workshop* concen-

Figure 4. To work through the diversity of information, Design Workshop required students to work in groups in class through different hands-on activities.

Figure 5. The coordinator divided Design Workshop into three parts, with subsequent lecture topics exploring the act of designing.

SEMESTER SCHEDULE

The timetable allows eleven weeks of contact, distributed so:

	LECTURE Fridays	WORKSHOP Wednesdays
INTRODUCTION: **The Subject**	August 02	August 07 Introductory Workshop
A: FRAMING **DESIGNING**		
Models of Designing, Design Thinking and Design Agendas	August 09	August 14
Contexts of Designing and Designers' Frames of Reference [Professor Emeritus Graham Brawn]	August 16	August 21
	August 23	August 28
B: GENERATING **IDEAS**		
Generating Ideas	August 30	September 04 & Submission A
Exploring Ideas	September 06	September 11
Communicating Ideas, Diagrams	September 13	September 18
C: DEVELOPING **IDEAS**		
	September 20	September 25 & Submission B
Developing Ideas	September 27	Non-Teaching Period
Non-Teaching Period	Non-Teaching Period	October 09
Evaluating and Selecting between Ideas	October 11	October 16
CONCLUSION: Arguing a Case and Presenting	October 18	October 23 The last class session
FINAL SUBMISSION		November 06 Submission C + Reflective Journal

trates on methods and skills acquisition, the graduate course focuses on developing students' thinking about their own designing (Missingham, 2003; Tregloan & Missingham, 2010).

The second step was to recognize that the forms in which materials that could focus Homework could come in a great many forms, but certainly including text, videos, models and examinations of actual sites or buildings or visits to exhibitions.

A third step was to remember that a venerable tradition in architectural design thinking was to characterise the architectural design task according to Henry Wootton's recasting of Vitruvius: Firmness, Commodity and Delight.

But, the fourth and most important feature of the approach taken in the course to this issue of excess plenty, was the adoption of a Team structure to division of the apparent workload. Within any Workshop ('tutorial') group, teams of at most three students were to explore each topic emphasising one of …

- **Firmness:** Technical and material aspects of designs;
- **Commodity:** Functional or programmatic, operational aspects of designs; or
- **Delight:** Aesthetic, experiential and symbolic aspects of designs).

The three divisions served to treat different aspects of designing. Firmness (Firmitas), Commodity (Utilitas) and Delight (Venustas) famously are the terms used in the Renaissance Englishman Henry Wootton's famous selective emphasis of the Roman Vitruvius's ideas about the major issues in architectural design. In being interested in urban design, infrastructure, building construction, architecture and the education of building and planning professionals, Vitruvius himself had a much longer list of issues he thought should be addressed (on which, see Costanzo, 2016, pp. 90-99).

But, expecting any one student to investigate design methods from only one of these perspectives across the whole semester would clearly be both pedagogically inappropriate and unfair, and to avoid any one student being disadvantaged by the behaviour of particular other students, structured mixing of team memberships was employed. Accordingly, teams changed membership and emphasis for each block of topics (Generating, Exploring or Evaluating design ideas). The ideal was to have no two students work in two Teams together.

The model for this approach to teamwork was adapted (it was thought) from the model adopted in *Mille Feuille*. A clear mistake was never explicitly addressing skills for working in teams.

In 2014, the names of the Team emphases were changed to Technology, Amenity and Poetry, respectively. The principal impetus for the change might surprise. Many students persistently managed to read "commodity" as a term from economics, despite repeated explanations, readings, and references to its specific architectural meaning and history.

ASSESSMENT(S)

Within a constructivist alignment pedagogy, the key question arose of how to assess the course against the defined intended learning outcomes (Biggs & Tang, 2007).

Initially, in 2013, assessment was determined from teamwork and individual components, across three instruments: Homework (reports), Job Files and Reflective Journals.

Homework

Homework was to be prepared in teams on behalf of the wider Workshop group and presented to it at the beginning of each Workshop – individual team members taking it in turns to present their team's work. Each Week, reports were to be distributed to every member of the Workshop group.

Homework tasks set at the end of each lecture for each team emphasis were usually of three kinds: various readings, a number of shorter or longer videos/film clips (YouTube, TED Talks, for example) and an activity (site visit, modelling task or equivalent). A curious feature of student responses noted in discussions with a number of tutors at coordination meetings was the number of expressed preferences for reading tasks over watching videos. The teaching staffs' conjecture was that this related to students' relative familiarity with reflecting on written texts compared with writing about video.

Job Files

The creative problem-solving literature suggests that working in teams is more fun, that you learn efficiently and effectively from others and that you learn best when you are having fun. (See Figure 6.) Importantly, professional designing is very rarely conducted other than in teamwork environments (despite the way in which design studios commonly and historically have been required to be run and be assessed in universities). Learning collaborative skills is crucial.

Teams were to keep annotated Job Files of their explorations and deliberations in Workshop sessions – just as if they were in an office and the file notes were to remind themselves of what had taken place, of decisions taken and to inform absent members of project teams (here meaning other student groups, for example).

But, the Job File was found to be too complicated for most students. They had real difficulty distinguishing between writing on their own experience of Workshops and writing about the exercises in the Workshop from the point of view of their team emphasis. Further, as undergraduates, usually without office work experience, most teams missed the point entirely of thoroughly documenting experiences for (hypothetical) others.

Accordingly, thinking it a simplification, in 2014, assessment employed two instruments, Team Submissions (one per topic group) and Reflective Journal. In actual practice, as the Team Submissions had to include the Homework for each team together with Workshop notes, they differed little from the actual Job Files produced in the previous year (although they did differ from the Job Files as originally

Figure 6. In class, Design Workshop focused on interactive activities, often led by the students themselves, moving around the room.

desired). The real difference in acceptance appeared to result from the perception that there was less work to do overall with two assessment tasks rather than three and that less of it apparently depended on teamwork. This, too, nevertheless provoked a relatively negative student response.

So, in 2015, collaborative work was assessed only through the Reflective Journal. Assessment of teamwork, directly, was abandoned. Teams were still to be formed and to work on behalf of the whole Workshop group, as before, and to have the team emphases in doing this work. But, members were no longer to be assessed within their teams. Materials from Homework, Workshop notes and reflections were to appear in each student's Reflective Journal in their own words.

COMMENTS

The design of the course was complex: after lectures, students studied in separate Workshops partici-pating in three kinds of teams covering three phases of design methods approaches and literature (and changing their membership each time), undertaking three kinds of Homework each week with, initially, three kinds of assessment tasks.

It may have been this inherent complexity that exacerbated the usual difficulties students commonly have with teamwork and assessment: objections to perceived unequal effort within teams and vulner-ability to key person absence (especially when teams could have as few members as two or, as was designed, three).

The assessment in 2015 partly recognised that written team feedback to Workshop groups was highly variable in quality across groups and frequently not provided whereas team engagement in providing activities for their Workshop fellows, based on the team's homework, has proved particularly successful.

Discussion

As a first written discussion about the Studio and the Workshops, the possibility of a theoretical framework by starting to expose particular themes that have emerged between the authors is explored as follows. The latter course, *Design Workshop*, sought to develop the premise of the framework of the graduate studio *Mille Feuille* that teaching creativity through multiple and changing group work experiences can be valuable. Any of our findings in this discussion are thus the result of critical conversations of many parts: story-telling what was and was not done, moderating outcomes through design critique sessions with guests against agreed criteria, discussing with students formally and informally, marking reflective journals, and workshopping modifications with other tutors in weekly meetings during the semesters. The following discussion is our own, ethnographic emphasis derived through lived-in comparisons and assertive reflection back to and forward from theory.

Returning to Nancy's individual in community, there are a number of theoretical aspects to consider that are probably at play. The first is that community (a group work, Studio, Workshop) is a myth, that it is unattainable yet the inherent goal of the individual (the student), and that paradoxical process gen-erates a moment of recognition of both community and individual. Second – which somewhat flows out of the first – is that a community is made up of positive differences, furthering that what makes up a community is actually a collection of different creative individuals and tangents, thus the production of creative individuals in the striving(s) for community. Third, is immanence, that in the coming and going of community, the extremities of flowing into and out of being is productive. This would suggest that students learn their own creativity in their starting and ending of group work –*when entering and leaving* multiple group works and multiple definitions between individual and group requirements.

In design-based work the myth of a single author – *even of* a singular group – expresses an impossibility of singularity in design. It does so too in assumption of the individual that their design work is entirely their own creation or came out of their own ego. Perhaps, more accurately, it is that in the noticeable crossover of students' ideas, skills and energies, the ego that an architecture student requires is more fundamentally a formation of a social process, rather than a lone and spontaneous necessity.

Behind the process of bombarding students with complexity and over-information (albeit in ways thought to be thoroughly scaffolded), is one hypothesis that there is a valuable learning process in the coming and going of the individual to and from group work. First, the authors seek to maximize the individual student's experience through a filtered experience of too much information – where through group work an individual is able (and unable) to access more information and perspectives. (See Figure 7.) Second, the authors seek to teach individuals how to work with different people – and develop different parts of themselves. Inherently, the experience continues in all but its limit through the imposed requirement that students are assessed in groups, and their total grade is the accumulation of group assessments. Notably, the undergraduate students had a difficulty with this, where most of the postgraduate students embraced it.

The authors are effectively bringing together a number of aspects into contextually-individuated experiences. Both *Mille Feuille* and *Design Workshop* set the scene for production of different architects, who produce architecture out of social processes both explicitly and implicitly. Pedagogically, both experiences are underpinned by necessitating the students to develop a reflective process – a personal design journal – throughout the semester. This arguably makes for more sensitive architects – sensitive to the exigencies of other people and different conceptions and destructions of ideation rather than simply assuming pre-conceived structurings.

With a purpose of also informing approaches to participation in architecture, or taking on social practices, the Studio and the Workshop course provide foundations. Production and synthesis through layered – and serial – group-work requires negotiation, argument and critical situation in the depth of a moment which is simultaneously a crossing of different scales and projects. Therein a student not only must produce valuable work, but is given a scaffold from which value can be considered in different ways: agonistically and antinomously (– both autonomously and heterogeneously). It is a somewhat impossible task but a perfect attempt at simulation.

Figure 7. Sometimes in Design Workshop two student groups were combined, within which the individual students had to listen and also articulate their views for a larger synthesis.

Perhaps one question to ask is how to describe these group processes in a way that can be managed in the context of an educational institution. Where the design is about producing immanent moments for the sake of producing creativity and simultaneous individual and community recognitions, in a manner that is positively about differences, then how does a teacher communicate and assess a start and a finish, or expectation and measurement of quality across a course? Some of the perceived difficulties of the undergraduate students in handling the group work seems to be as much a consideration of maturity, as it appears to be cultural. It behooves a teacher to hold the space – perhaps ideologically – and line towards (and out of) community through group work.

Second question (more constructively): if the purpose and principles of these immanent-embracing group processes are taken as foundation, are there more specific ways of critically reading and then developing these approaches as a methodology? What works, what doesn't work? What could be made to work better?

Where the first question might be attempted through theory, to answer this second there is an opportunity to make some comparisons of the two teaching experiences.

COMPARISONS

Three classes of comparative observations are worth making: first, to do with graduate versus undergraduate student expectations; secondly, to do with studio teaching and adjunct, generalist design teaching; and, thirdly, to do with project outcomes versus 'mere' skills or knowledge acquisition.

Graduates vs. Undergraduates

Graduate students are more tolerant of pedagogical flexibility and, simply, more tolerant of their educations, being more mature and better able to take what they want from what is offered. They are practiced learners compared with the more strategic learner undergraduates wishing to get good grades to get into graduate school, for example. For the graduate students of *Mille Feuille*, teamwork can quickly be seen as an advantageous way to achieve desirable outcomes. For the undergraduates of *Design Workshop*, working in teams is, at best, a barely tolerated way of getting to the desired outcome, seen often to be beset by the possibility of personally disadvantageous 'slacker' teammates and absenteeism.

So, there are issues of self-educational maturity and of learning styles that played out in these two learning experiences.

Studio vs. Course

Mille Feuille was a small, single class of fourteen that worked as a single studio, where *Design Workshop* entailed a lecture series, homework, workshops and multiple tutors (one per fourteen or fewer students, with from seven to nine different workshop leaders, depending on the year) for a cohort ten times the size. This had consequences both for students' experience and for staff roles in the education offered.

From the pedagogical framing perspective, *Mille Feuille* was readily able to focus on the ideology of group work as a purpose in itself, rather than as an application from without, more or less extrinsic to the learning task. And, additionally, the group's collective work with the (hypothetical) client body contributed to the sense of a design studio as a whole. The student experience was of a 'we-feeling' conjointly and on behalf of/with the client. This was not available to *Design Workshop* students.

Further, staff roles differ in the two educational circumstances: *Mille Feuille* staff had much greater control of the program delivery compared with program design and, therefore, of authority. *Design Workshop* staff, by comparison, were, rather, primarily facilitators for student learning of a program set by another, the subject coordinator. This bears on staff satisfaction both with their contributions to students and with the studio outcomes, regardless of how much freedom they could exercise in individual workshop sessions.

From an outcome perspective, next, *Mille Feuille* students worked toward 'tangible' products rather than toward vaguer notions of personal knowledge and skills development (quite literally, for the team that produced prototype flat pack furniture from plywood). The single, although nested suite of outcomes – master plan, process and individual proposition – makes for an ultimate horizon that necessitates students reaching a complex synthesis in *Mille Feuille*: the final design project. By comparison, in *Design Workshop*, assessments sit somewhat apart from each other and are only linked chronologically through relatively loose journal reflection and audition of the lecture series over the semester. A comparison can be made between the relative success of the nested and relatively linear aims of *Mille Feuille* and the frustrations engendered with the cyclic and multiple intangible outcomes of *Design Workshop*.

Although it may be taken as a prejudice towards instrumentalization of design and therefore at odds with the goal of developing understanding in participation, individuation and communion, the differences in the schedules of the two subjects is notable. This sense of a goal versus a suite of goals is a key difference to consider. Somewhat continuing on with the tropes of layers, the key difference is the chronological and nested nature of the *Mille Feuille* schedule as opposed to the *Design Workshop* scheme. Where a rhythm and clarity of immanence is achieved in *Design Workshop* – perhaps in a somewhat mechanical repetition, *Mille Feuille* required the students to be at once both in and out of different groups and scales of group, and somehow still to manage to express themselves. In *Design Workshop*, individuals had much more scope to avoid full participation in a group, and to become absorbed in their own thoughts and processes, and even to develop a (repeatable) method for how to undertake group work without real engagement.

The idea of collaborative learning or designing, of teamwork in design studios, seems excellent on many grounds. However, certain issues arose that were not expected or were not thought of in the first place – this is before any judgement of what was actually done or achieved. In its pedagogical practicality, the idea of collaborative learning does raise many issues that are spread out as spectra or as oppositions, two ends of what might be a spectrum between: mess and order, class size, student experience versus pedagogical design, undergraduate versus graduate, outcome focus versus self-growth, student development versus staff experience and satisfaction, assessment versus learning, delivery schedule versus collaborative engagement with third parties, comprehensiveness of content versus scaffolding or bones, among others. Valuation of the outcomes, it would seem, is also collaborative.

FUTURE RESEARCH DIRECTIONS

In the original call, contributors to this book were asked, where they could, to comment on three issues requiring research-led solutions:

First, many students leave academia without having been taught the knowledge and skills of how to design in teams;

Second, the design of teaching, feedback mechanisms and assignments needs to be informed by a clear understanding of what leads to effective teamwork and student interaction; and

Third, in academic contexts there is a need to individually assess students, which means that most design assignments require individual submissions or, when students work in teams, require evaluation of individual contribution (R. Tucker, personal communication, March 24, 2015).

In this Chapter, we have touched on all three issues, if to differing degrees.

Beyerle's professional practice and research drives his interest in the first issue (Beyerle, 2016), Missingham's teaching and research his interest in the third. We foresee greater emphasis on the second in our school and in recognition of the realities of present professional practice and trends in, at the least, greater poly-disciplinarity in all its forms.

Systematic investigation of poly-disciplinary studios, for example, necessarily incorporating teamwork, will further the interests of all disciplines involved. They do occur already, particularly in Travelling Studio form, but they are rarely framed, conducted and investigated from a pedagogical design perspective.

Finally, both authors conduct design studios as collaborative teams as a matter of course, even when students are expected to develop individual projects. But, design methods have usually been developed as collaborative tools that are commonly taught in workshops with an emphasis on development of individual skills and individual design thinking. Clearly, there's a pedagogical and implicit professional disjunction: the tools used in development of designs are mostly understood individually though they ought to be directed to design tasks in collaborative ways and from collaborative means. There are research opportunities, here, for examining fruitful transfers from one to the other kind of learning and practice.

CONCLUSION

For our chapter we have related our discussions to three concerns for teaching group work in design: awareness of communication and transdisciplinarity, becoming self through engagement in group processes and situated, applied design and tacit learning. What seems to emerge from our specific design teaching examples is that teaching group work in design is about framing, constraining and enabling dynamic processes. In our examples of *Mille Feuille* and *Design Workshop* we explored different approaches to this. In both examples we set up situations, tensions and transdisciplinary communications, through changing individual and group work structures, layering and staging. In reflection what is common to both approaches rehearses Nancy's philosophy that group (community) is made up of processes of becoming self and group. This may also suggest how student learning can make a collective contribution to the world.

As well as developing lessons for teaching design, we have learnt that there are some possible lessons regarding understanding the conception of community and inherently of the individual through creativity. They are (with some phrasing admittedly in Nancy-like terms):

- Community is the communion of differences (differences are contributed by individual students, groups and clients);
- Creativity in architecture revolves around formation and expression of the ego (which process can be be productive);
- The creative individual is birthed by community (and group processes);
- Community is a receptacle that allows creative realisation and action (both birth and death of egos);
- Design of complexity that can only birth recognition of self out of difference (community) simultaneously must and cannot recognise itself as an author (creativity and identity is more complex);
- Layering subsequent and nested experiences necessitate individual syntheses (this is unavoidable although it may not be easy to navigate);
- What to and how to navigate oneself in community processes are key learning experiences (these processes are 'immaterialised' into a design and expressed in change); and
- The process of community makes the formation of an individual designer immanent (both in a productive and a destructive sense).

The authors understand architecture as a necessarily collaborative practice. In practice one must synthesise many competing ideas in pursuit of a finite design outcome (time, budget and location) and as such design work is complex, involves many stakeholders and connects multiple expertises. To prepare for design practice, architecture students need to find reflective and social methods that are creative and productive. The authors understand that learning is done both directly and indirectly and can see complimentary parallels between individual creative processes and group work processes.

Collaboration needs space to go back and forth between one individual and another – or others. Teaching collaboration or design through collaboration, thus necessities the creation of dynamic learning structures to go back and forth on. We can call these collaborative spectra.

REFERENCES

Adair, J. (2009). *The Art of Creative Thinking: How to be Innovative and Develop Great Ideas*. London: Kogan Page.

Alexander, C. (1964). *Notes on the Synthesis of Form*. Cambridge, MA: Harvard University Press.

Alexander, C., Ishikawa, S., & Silverstein, M. (1977). *A Pattern Language: Towns - Buildings - Construction*. New York: Oxford University Press.

Attoe, W. (1978). *Architecture and Critical Imagination*. Chichester: Wiley.

Ballesteros, M. (Ed.). (2008). *Verb crisis*. Barcelona: ACTAR.

Bandura, A. (1963). *Social Learning and Personality Development*. New York: Holt, Rinehart and Winston.

Bandura, A. (1977). *Social Learning Theory*. Oxford: Prentice-Hall.

Bates, D., Mitsogiannini, V., & Ramirez-Lovering, D. (Eds.). (2015). *Studio Futures: Changing trajectories in architectural education*. Melbourne: uro publications.

Beyerle, A. (2014). Agonistic Participation: A political and architectural opportunity. *Journal of Arts and Communities*, *5*(2-3), 147–169.

Beyerle, A. (2016 forthcoming). *Participation in Architecture: Agonism in Practice* [Doctoral Dissertation]. The University of Melbourne, Parkville, VIC.

Bielefeld, B., & El Khouli, S. (2007). *Basics: Design Ideas*. Basel: Birkhäuser.

Biggs, J., & Tang, C. (2007). *Teaching for Quality Learning at University: What the student does* (3rd ed.). Maidenhead, Berks: Open University Press/McGraw Hill Education.

Bishop, C. (2006a). Letters: Claire Bishop responds. *Artforum*, *44*(May), 24.

Bishop, C. (2006b). *Participation, Documents of contemporary art*. Whitechapel. London and Cambridge, MA: The MIT Press.

Bishop, C. (2006c). The Social Turn: Collaboration and Its Discontents. *Artforum*, February, 179–183.

Blake, P. (1977). *Form Follows Fiasco: Why Modern Architecture Hasn't Worked*. Boston: Little Brown.

Blundell Jones, P. (2005). Sixty-eight and after. In P. Blundell Jones, D. Petrescu, & J. Till (Eds.), *Architecture and Participation* (pp. 127–139). London, New York: Spon Press.

Bonta, J. P. (1979). *Architecture and its Interpretation: a study of expressive systems in architecture*. New York: Rizzoli.

Bourriaud, N. (2002). *Relational aesthetics*. France: Les presses du réel.

Brolin, B. (1976). *The Failure of Modern Architecture*. London: Studio Vista.

Broome, J. (2005). Mass housing cannot be sustained. In P. Blundell Jones, D. Petrescu, & J. Till (Eds.), *Architecture and Participation* (pp. 65–75). London, New York: Spon Press.

Broome, J., & Richardson, B. (1995). *The self-build book. Rev. & updated edn*. Totnes, Devon: Green Earth Books.

Centre of Cultural Partnerships. (2013). *Spectres of Evaluation* (L. MacDowall et al., Eds.). Parkville, VIC: The University of Melbourne.

Chase, J., Crawford, M., & Kaliski, J. (Eds.). (2008). *Everyday Urbanism*. New York: The Monacelli Press.

Colebrook, C. (2002). *Understanding Deleuze*. Crows Nest, NSW: Allen & Unwin.

Collins, P. (1971). *Architectural Judgement*. Montreal: McGill-Queen's University Press.

Colomina, B. (Ed.), (1992). *Sexuality and Space*. New York: Princeton Architectural Press.

Cornell, A. (Ed.), (2012). *Breakthrough! 90 Proven Strategies to Overcome Creative Block & Spark Your Imagination*. New York: Princeton Architectural Press.

Costanzo, D. (2016). *What Architecture Means: Connecting Ideas and Design*. New York: Routledge/Taylor & Francis.

Cross, N. (2006). *(2007). Designerly Ways of Knowing. Rprt*. Basel: Birkhaüser.

Cross, N. (2008). *Engineering Design Methods: Strategies for Product Design (4th ed.)*. Chichester, West Sussex: Wiley.

Cross, N. (2011). *Design Thinking: Understanding How Designers Think and Work*. Oxford: Berg.

Csikszentmihalyi, M. (1996). *Creativity: Flow and the Psychology of Discovery and invention*. New York: Harper Collins Publishers.

Csikszentmihalyi, M. (2004). *Good Business: Leadership, flow, and the making of meaning*. London: Penguin.

Curedale, R. (2012). *Design Methods 2: 200 more ways to apply design thinking*. Topanga, CA: Design Community College.

Curedale, R. (2013). *Design Methods 1: 200 ways to apply design thinking*. Topanga, CA: Design Community College.

Davenport, T., & Prusak, L. (2000). *Working Knowledge: How Organizations Manage What They Know*. Cambridge, MA: Harvard Business School Press.

De Carlo, G. (2005). Architecture's public. In P. Blundell Jones, D. Petrescu, & J. Till (Eds.), *Architecture and Participation* (pp. 3–22). London, New York: Spon Press.

De Certeau, M. (1988). *The Practice of Everyday Life* (S. Rendall, Trans.). Berkeley, CA: University of California Press.

De Solà-Morales, I. (1997). Weak architecture. In I. De Solà-Morales (Ed.), *Differences: topographies of contemporary architecture* (trans G. Thompson). Cambridge, MA: The MIT Press.

Dorst, K. (2006). *(2003). Understanding Design: 175 Reflections on Being a Designer (Rev edn.)*. Corte Madera, CA: Gingko Press.

Dorst, K. (2015). *Frame Innovation: Create New Thinking by Design. Design Thinking/Design Theory*. Cambridge, MA: The MIT Press.

Elemental (2014). Projects – elemental. Retrieved from http://www.elementalchile.cl/en/projects/

Godber, B. (1998). The Knowing and Subverting Reader. In J. Hill (Ed.), *Occupying Architecture*. London: Routledge.

Gordon, W. J. J. (1961). *Synectics: the development of creative capacity*. New York: Harper and Row.

Gray, D., Brown, S., & Macanufo, J. (2010). *Gamestorming: A Playbook for Innovators: Rulebreakers, and Changemakers*. Sebastopol, CA: O'Reilly Media.

Habraken, N. J. (1972). *Supports: An alternative to mass housing*. London: Architectural Press.

Habraken, N. J., & Wiewel, W. (1976). *Variations: the systematic design of supports*. Cambridge, MA: Laboratory of Architecture and Planning at MIT.

Halprin, L. (1969). *The RSVP Cycles: Creative Processes in the Human Environment*. New York: Braziller.

Hayes, W. H. (2002). Architectural Criticism. *The Journal of Aesthetics and Art Criticism, 60*(4), 325–329. doi:10.1111/1540-6245.00079

Hertzberger, H. (2000). *Space and the Architect: Lessons in Architecture 2*. Rotterdam: 010 Publishers.

Hubbard, W. (1980). *Complicity and Conviction: Steps toward an Architecture of Convention*. Cambridge, MA: The MIT Press.

Huth, E. (2005). Fragments of participation in architecture, 1963-2002: Graz and Berlin. In P. Blundell Jones, D. Petrescu, & J. Till (Eds.), *Architecture and Participation* (pp. 141–148). London, New York: Spon Press.

Ingraham, C. (1992). The Burdens of Linearity. In J. Whiteman, J. Kipnis, & R. Burdett (Eds.), *Strategies in Architectural Thinking* (pp. 131–147). Cambridge, MA: The MIT Press.

Jaormakka, K. (2007). *Design Methods. Basics.* Basel: Birkhäuser.

Jones, J. C. (1970). *Design Methods: Seeds of Human Futures.* London: Wiley.

Kellogg, C. (2005). *The Studio Culture Summit: An Overview Report.* Washington, DC: The American Institute of Architecture Students.

Koch, A., Schwennsen, K., Dutton, T. A., & Smith, D. (2002). *The Redesign of Studio Culture: A Report of the AIAS Studio Culture Task Force.* Washington, DC: American Institute of Architecture Students.

Koskinen, I., Zimmerman, J., Binder, T., Redström, J., & Wensveen, S. (2011). *Design Research Through Practice from the Lab, Field, and Showroom.* Amsterdam: Morgan Kaufman/Elsevier.

Kumar, V. (2013). *101 Design Methods: A Structured Approach for Driving Innovation in Your Organization.* Hoboken, New Jersey: Wiley.

Kumpulainen, K., & Wray, D. (2002). *Classroom Interaction and Social Learning: From Theory to Practice.* New York: RoutledgeFarmer.

Laurel, B. (Ed.), (2003). *Design Research: Methods and Perspectives.* Cambridge, MA: The MIT Press.

Lawson, B., & Dorst, K. (2009). *Design Expertise.* Oxford: Architectural Press/Elsevier.

Lefebvre, H. (1984). *(1991). The Production of Space* (D. Nicholson-Smith, Trans.). Oxford: Basil Blackwell.

Lidwell, W., Holden, K., & Jill Butler, J. (2010). (2003).*Universal Principles of Design: 125 Ways to Enhance Usability, Influence Perception, Increase Appeal. Make Better Design Decisions, and Teach through Design* (Rev. ed.). Beverly, MA: Rockport Publishers.

Lyons-Reid, J., Kuddell, C., Beyerle, A., & James, M. E. (2014). Typology of Harm (Creative Work). In FCAC and The Centre for Cultural Partnerships (Ed.), *Spectres of Evaluation: Rethinking: Art Community Value.* Parkville, VIC: The University of Melbourne. Retrieved from http://www.spectresofevaluation.com/conference-ebook.html)

Martin, B., & Hanington, B. (2012). *Universal Methods of Design: 100 ways to Research Complex Problems, Develop Innovative Ideas, and Design Effective Solutions.* Beverly, MA: Rockport Publishers.

McHarg, I. L. (1969). *Design with Nature*. Garden City, New York: Doubleday/Natural History Press.

Michalko, M. (2006). *(1991). Thinkertoys: a handbook of creative-thinking techniques (2nd ed.).* Berkeley, CA: Ten Speed Press.

Michel, R. (Ed.). (2007). *Design Research Now: Essays and Selected Projects*. Basel: Birkhäuser. doi:10.1007/978-3-7643-8472-2

Miessen, M., & Mouffe, C. (2008). Violating Consensus: Markus Miessen interviews Chantal Mouffe. In M. Ballesteros (Ed.), *Verb crisis* (pp. 168–180). Barcelona: ACTAR.

Miller, P. H. (2011). *Theories of Developmental Psychology*. New York: Worth Publishers.

Missingham, G. (1986). Dao Nunda: A metacritical frame, Drew on Murcutt, and on Australianness in Architecture. *Transition*, 4(4), 41–46.

Missingham, G. (2003). Figuring Ariachne's Gardens: Reflecting on Research-led Teaching in Design. In C. Newton, S. Kaji-O'Grady, & S. Wollan (Eds.), *Design + Research: Project Based Research in Architecture*. Melbourne: Association of Architecture Schools of Australasia- http://www.arbld.unimelb.edu.au/events/conferences/aasa/papers

Missingham, G. (2015). Wicked Deliberations: research and design studios. In R.H. Crawford & A. Stephan (Eds.), *Living and Learning: Research for a Better Built Environment: 49th International Conference of the Architectural Science Association 2015* (pp. 846-855). Melbourne: The Architectural Science Association.

Mouffe, C. (2000). *The democratic paradox*. New York: Verso.

Mouffe, C., Deutsche, R., Joseph, B. W., & Keenan, T. (2001). Every Form of Art Has a Political Dimension. *Grey Room*, (2): 99–125.

Muecke, S. (1994). From Honey moon Gap to Millions of Stars: 'Aboriginal' Landscape and the Aesthetics of Disappearance. In H. Edquist & V. Bird (Eds.), *The Culture of Landcape Architecture*. Melbourne: Edge Publishing with RMIT (pp. 68-84; 267).

Obrist, H. U. (2006). Preface: participation lasts forever. In M. Miessen & S. Basar (Eds.), *Did someone say participate?: an atlas of spatial practice: a report from the front lines of cultural activism looks at spatial practitioners who actively trespass into neighbouring or alien fields of knowledge*. Cambridge, MA: The MIT Press.

Plowright, P. D. (2014). *Revealing Architectural Design: Methods, Frameworks and Tools*. Abingdon, Oxon: Routledge.

Polya, G. (1957). *How to Solve It: A New Aspect of Mathematical Method (2nd ed. reprint)*. Penguin Mathematics. Harmondsworth: Penguin Books.

Pürto, J. (2004). *Understanding Creativity*. Scottsdale, Arizona: Great Potential Press.

Raman Pattabi, G., & Coyne, R. (2000). The Production of Architectural Criticism. *Architectural Theory Review*, Journal of the Department of Architecture, Planning and Allied Arts. *The University of Sydney*, 5(1), 83–103.

Reiger, U., & Young, C. (2015). Design Through Collective Learning. In D. Bates, V Mitsogiannini & D. Ramirez-Lovering (Eds.), *Studio Futures: Changing trajectories in architectural education* (pp. 59-65). Melbourne: uro publications.

Saint, A. (1983). *The Image of the Architect*. New Haven, Conn: Yale University Press.

Spiller, N., & Clear, N. (Eds.), (2014). *Educating Architects: How tomorrow's practitioners will learn today*. London: Thames & Hudson.

The Second AIAS Task Force on Studio Culture. (2008). *Toward an Evolution of Studio Culture: A Report of the Second AIAS Task Force on Studio Culture*. Washington, DC: American Institute of Architecture Students.

Tregloan, K. (2015). *Design Epiphany and the Opportunities of Wickedness: constructions of insight, perspective and design* [Unpublished Doctoral Dissertation]. The University of Melbourne, Parkville, VIC.

Tregloan, K., & Missingham, G. (2010). Designing "Designing Environments". In G. Forsyth (Ed.), *ConnectED 2010 International Conference on Design Education*. Sydney: Faculty of the Built Environment, UNSW.

Turner, J. F. C. (1972). Housing as a verb. In J.F.C. Turner & R. Fichter (Eds.), *Freedom to build; dweller control of the housing process* (pp. xvi, 301). New York: Macmillan.

Turner, J. F. C., & Fichter, R. (1972). *Freedom to build; dweller control of the housing process*. New York: Macmillan.

Ulmer, G. L. (1994). *Heuretics: The Logic of Invention*. Baltimore: John Hopkins University Press.

Wigglesworth, S., McCorquodale, D., & Ruedi, K. (Eds.), (1996). *Desiring Practices: Architecture, gender and the interdisciplinary. Proceedings of the Desiring Practices Symposium*. London: Black Dog Publishing.

Wigglesworth, S., & Till, J. (Eds.). (1998). *The Everyday and Architecture. Architectural Design Profile no. 134*. London: Academy Editions, July/August.

Zehner, R., Forsyth, G. G., Musgrave, E., Neale, D., De La Harpe, B., … , K Warson, K. (2009). *Curriculum Development in Studio Teaching. Sydney: Australian Learning and Teaching Council*.

KEY TERMS AND DEFINITIONS

Becoming: Here, that immanent, developing nature and a comprehension of it, perhaps only half-grasped, of purpose, project, its design, self or community.

Design Studio: The term for the dominant pedagogical circumstance in architectural and cognate disciplines since the late eighteenth century. It encompasses simultaneously notions of a smallish group with instructor, physical environments, kinds of design task and forms of assessment.

Identity: Here, the sense of self of young designers, while learning or beginning practice especially of themselves *as designers*, and of the collective selves, the 'we-feeling' engendered through communally working on joint and mutually beneficial projects.

Participatory Design: Where designers tend to be knowledgeable facilitators or coaches of a community group in designing rather than entirely in command.

Poly-Disciplinarity: A catch-all term for what is described variously as cross-disciplinarity (with ideas, methods and practices transferred from one discipline to another), multi-disciplinarity (with a number of disciplines, cognate or otherwise, working in parallel and sometimes collaboratively on the same issue), trans-disciplinarity (where the focus on the task or issue so dominates the collective effort that the fact of differences in participants' professional disciplines almost passes unnoticed) and hybrids of these.

Social-Reflective Practice: Educational and professional practice (and practices) where students and educators reflect on the process and outcomes of teaching and learning experiences, as usual, but within a framework of acting for the betterment of socio-cultural and client-orientated circumstances as part of their own evaluations of success.

Tacit Learning: Learning unselfconsciously, often through physical activity or participation in a group activity and, if recognized, recognized as having occurred much after the fact.

ENDNOTE

[1]   Support for the original work was provided by the Australian Learning and Teaching Council Ltd, an initiative of the Australian Government Department of Education, Employment and Workplace Relations.

Chapter 13
Embracing Non–Traditional Partnerships in Design Education:
Breaking Down Myths and Stereotypes

Traci Rose Rider
North Carolina State University, USA

Elizabeth Bowen
North Carolina State University, USA

ABSTRACT

This chapter reviews the outline, process, and structure of the LEED Lab course at North Carolina State University (NCSU), which has engaged students from multiple colleges across the University. This chapter will specifically address NCSU's particular approach to teamwork in design education, using an existing building on NCSU's campus and an established assessment framework to provide context. With the LEED for Existing Buildings Operations and Maintenance as a guide, interdisciplinary teams of students worked together to establish recommendations for future operations. Additional teamwork opportunities included the engagement of a number of NCSU facilities departments, including Repairs and Renovation, Energy Services, Waste Reduction and Recycling, and others. Using examples of team-building exercises, integration with NCSU's Facilities Division, in-class hands-on exercises, and in-process photographs, this chapter will walk the reader through the opportunities and challenges of integrating non-traditional teamwork exercises into design education processes.

INTRODUCTION

One of the many challenges in design education, is providing opportunities for students to work meaningfully in interdisciplinary groups. Many design disciplines have historically been insulated in ivory towers, with the most likely possibility for integrated groups being limited to other design disciplines. These partnerships might include planning or landscape design students teamed with architecture stu-

DOI: 10.4018/978-1-5225-0726-0.ch013

dents, or possibly the inclusion of interior design. However, beyond being in the same room for a large lecture, such as art history, which affords no means for a collaborative experience, opportunities rarely exist to develop meaningful inter-collegiate and interdisciplinary partnerships in design - either within or external to the studio context. With the prevalence of interdisciplinary teams and integrated processes growing in architecture and design fields, practicing and future designers are encouraged to expand their current dialogues and vocabularies to better collaborate with other disciplines (Keeler, 2009; Moe, 2008; Yudelson, 2009; Deutsch, 2011; Reed, 2009). It has been found that courses emphasizing teamwork with interdisciplinary groups in fact engage students in a simulation of communications and projects in the working world (Smit and Tremethick, 2013; Fixson, 2009; Rhee, 2010). These types of educational experiences can have implications for students past graduation, as most projects involving both new and existing construction - as well as in other design fields - are most likely to be interdisciplinary challenges.

One difficulty in engaging design disciplines in interdisciplinary and intercollegiate projects is rooted in the studio culture of design education. If there is a possible partner discipline that can address similar course topics, such as civil engineering, it would be preferred to engage engineering students in a studio setting for collaboration, where much of the meaningful connections are provided (Kurt, 2009; Schon, 1984). However, the credit hour structure in other disciplines, such as engineering, does not often translate, or provide allowance for, a 6-credit hour studio course that meets three times per week for multiple hours per day. If students from other disciplines do arrange their schedule to attend studio, they lack the experience and context to understand what actually happens in a studio space for those extended hours, without a lecture or structured exercise. While this can be overcome, it is a deterrent nonetheless.

Though some design programs are beginning to establish successful processes and methods for interdisciplinary learning in the studio setting, there are additional opportunities for design students to work with other disciplines on campus outside of studio. Using the campus as a living laboratory to provide real world experience while impacting the operations of the campus has the potential to create a particularly meaningful opportunity for design and non-design disciplines alike. The goals for this chapter include: reviewing one successful seminar format for an interdisciplinary course at a major university; mapping the possibilities for partnerships between diverse colleges and facilities divisions; and providing suggestions for building rapport between students of differing expertise and backgrounds.

Background

At North Carolina State University in Raleigh, North Carolina, United States, Fall semester 2015 marked the second semester of a LEED Lab course. This specific approach is based on a program of the U.S. Green Building Council (USGBC) called Leadership in Energy and Environmental Design (LEED). The LEED program is one of the most popular green building certification programs used worldwide. While the bulk of the projects are found in the United States, many countries around the globe are establishing parallel organizations, such as the Green Building Council of Australia (GBCA) and the Indian Green Building Council (IGBC), and as a result either adopting or adapting the LEED rating system.

The particular seminar reviewed in this chapter makes use of the LEED Lab course, which has been developed by the USGBC's Center for Green Schools. As noted on the Center's website, "LEED Lab is a multidisciplinary immersion course that utilizes the built environment to educate and prepare students to become green building leaders and sustainability-focused citizens." USGBC's goal for the course is to simultaneously provide hands-on, practical experience in green building operations and maintenance to future design professionals, while enabling campuses with large existing building portfolios to work toward, and hopefully achieve, LEED green building certification to illustrate their commitment to the environment.

Taking this framework as a starting point, the primary goal of North Carolina State University's (NCSU) LEED Lab course is not necessarily to achieve LEED certification for the target building, but to engage NCSU students in meaningful interdisciplinary work. Rarely do design students take courses with other disciplines, particularly as non-lecture courses. However, in this particular course at NCSU, students from three different colleges are consistently involved in outreach and engagement activities on campus, including a waste audit, Indoor Air Quality assessment demonstrations, energy assessments, facilitating occupant surveys, and a final charrette exercise with building and campus stakeholders. These exercises not only engaged students in the specific issues being addressed, but also engaged other students on campus outside the class, university leadership, facility departments, faculty and staff beyond those directly involved in the course. This additional engagement increased both the meaning and impact of the course for the students, which will be discussed later.

The NCSU LEED Lab course was designed to focus on interdisciplinary collaboration in an approachable seminar setting to address specific learning outcomes connected to problem solving and the design assessment process. Substantial literature focusing on the benefits of interdisciplinary collaboration in higher education exists, and addresses increasing student production and cultivating professional skills (Blackburn & Chapin, 1994; Chapman, 2006; Hackett & Rhoten, 2009; Sawyer, 2007; Robinson, Sherwood & Depaolo, 2010), attending to realistic teamwork issues including communication barriers and knowledge expertise (Fleischmann, 2010; Kim, Ju & Lee, 2015; Spelt, Van Boekel & Mulder, 2014; Shattuck, 2001), the notion that interdisciplinary understanding can increase through disciplinary understanding (Johnston, 2014), and the need for interdisciplinary work to support the growing emphasis on sustainability and complexity (O'Rafferty, Curtis & O'Connor, 2014). The design of this specific course addressed many of these issues primarily through class exercises and group reflections on process (Rider, 2016), and is the focus of this chapter.

Harnessing the Local Context for Teambuilding

The North Carolina State University approach to the LEED Lab concept is unique in the way that it uses the LEED framework as a benchmarking tool without emphasizing certification, but instead using the system as a framework to facilitate the goal of interdisciplinary collaboration and teamwork between students from differing fields. Other LEED Lab programs often range in size from approximately ten students to nearly twenty-five students, as regularly seen at NCSU. Some peer LEED Lab courses are hosted in architecture departments, while others may not be in design disciplines at all, such as business schools or university facility groups. NCSU chose to use the LEED Lab framework as a tool for facilitating an often difficult, and at times nebulous, interdisciplinary teamwork structure, and specifically reached out to various disciplines for involvement. From the outset, one of the primary goals of this course was creating substantial links between students of different backgrounds, hoping to add support to debunking the myth that interdisciplinary work is too difficult to facilitate in a design program.

The LEED Lab course at NCSU is hosted out of the School of Architecture in partnership with the University Sustainability Office and the University Facilities Division. Structured with co-instructors from each of the two departments, the leadership for the course includes both meaningful learning objectives and experiences for the students, as well as potential impacts for the operations of the campus over time. An exercise in teamwork itself, the hosting of the course brought two differing perspectives to the classroom leadership: one primarily interested in interdisciplinary teamwork and partnering between differing disciplines, and another primarily interested in student engagement using the campus as a learning laboratory. This duality provided an interesting depth to the expectations and meaning for the students; this course was not about individuality or book learning. Logistically, the partnership helped to address the notion that an institutional commitment to service learning is a barrier to success (Bringle & Hatcher, 2000; Morton & Troppe, 1996).

In line with the opportunity to align the course project with an actual project on campus, another primary goal for this seminar was to afford opportunities for students to participate in real-world, environmentally-focused projects to better develop skills and experience for their future employment in a sustainability-focused field. The benefits of including real-world and service learning projects in university courses (Afacan, 2013) and the importance of experience with interdisciplinary workings in industry (Blair, 2012; Bryson, Crosby & Stone, 2006) are well documented. Asking students to focus on critical, reflective thinking in service learning projects also helps to develop personal and civic responsibility (American Association of Community Colleges, 2015). Billig et al. (2005) noted that using service-learning projects to explain course content was one of the most solid predictors of all academic outcomes, while Astin & Sax (1998) state that engaging in service learning projects significantly increases the student's growth in academics, life skills, and sense of civic responsibility.

Students in this course were able to meaningfully contribute to the holistic assessment of existing buildings at NCSU, through an interdisciplinary lens, with the goal to enhance both the learning objectives of the course as well as the students' notions of environmental responsibility as a service-learning project. By strategically selecting a building on the students' campus, in their own backyard, the course immediately provides a common goal and a common foundation for team building. As stakeholders in the project itself, and the campus, the students already have a common ground to build from, despite being from differing disciplines. This inward approach impacts the outlook of the students, as attitudes would have been different if a company in an office park had, for example, owned the topic building instead of a building in which they have investment. The integration of a real-world project on campus is seen as a key element to the success of the course, and particularly as it facilitates active teamwork. By choosing to use a project on campus, the team-making foundation was effectively set before the first class met.

Case Study Methodology

This study is approached as an explanatory case study, which seeks to understand how or why something happens (Yin, 2009). Using a pragmatic approach, the interest is looking more closely at how teamwork might be facilitated in a seminar format in design education. When using the case study methodology, it is understood that the context is important to the findings of the study (Yin, 2009). The case study explores interest areas in the natural context, collecting data within the real-world settings as opposed to contrived, laboratory settings.

Qualitative data was gathered directly in the form of direct observations and unstructured interviews. Indirect secondary data was gathered vain online pre- and post tests, as well as through online questionnaires focusing on teamwork, hosted by the university survey service. The team assessment survey consisted of both Likert scale questions addressing the perceived efficacy of teammates, as well as open-ended questions for further comment on teamwork. The primary purpose of the data gathering was to gain insight into the students' perception of their teamwork, as well as their opinions on the need for teamwork in this type of academic, interdisciplinary setting.

ENHANCED COLLABORATION FROM THE BEGINNING

The NCSU LEED Lab course is a transdisciplinary immersion course engaging design, environmental sciences, business, and engineering students in team projects with tangible results. Strategically organized so that each team of students within the course is interdisciplinary, seminar students are given the opportunity not only to work constructively with other fields, but also to learn to view environmental challenges and opportunities from different perspectives. This is the only course known of at NCSU that simultaneously establishes interdisciplinary relationships, uses hands-on service learning exercises, and actively affects the broader environmental impact of the university.

To capitalize on the different opportunities and facets of knowledge provided to the students, and to provide a foundational sense of collaboration and teamwork, intentional project selection and user engagement were established as values at the beginning of the course.

Intentional Project Selection and Leadership Commitment

Nelson Hall, the subject building of the first semester of the course, functions primarily as an office building. Home to the NCSU Poole College of Management, the hours and operations for Nelson Hall are similar any office building. Nelson Hall had been renovated recently in 1994 and 1999, compared to other renovation dates on campus, and was thought by facility partners to be one of the more appropriate buildings to consider pursuing LEED for Building Operations and Maintenance certification. This proximity to LEED certification was helpful, but more helpful still was the presence of the NCSU College Business Sustainability Collaborative, previously known as the NCSU College Sustainability Initiative, which is described as the following on its website:

The Business Sustainability Collaborative is an academic initiative that connects students, faculty, and the business community through experiential learning, career development, academic and applied research, and partnership opportunities. We develop leaders who can apply research, technology, and critical thinking to drive and measure sustainable business practices. The Collaborative works with faculty to integrate environmental, social, and financial responsibility into curricula throughout the NCSU College of Management. We engage industry to advance and share innovative sustainability practices that lead to positive business results. (http://bsc.poole.ncsu.edu/about-bsc/)

Course leaders felt strongly that an invested "client" or user group is key to facilitating a meaningful semester for the students in the course. With a goal to dive deeply into the holistic workings of the building, support from the users is important, with an emphasis on leadership investment. Not only was the Director of the Business Sustainability Collaborative engaged in the course, other College leadership was also informed, invested and supportive, including both the Dean and the University Chancellor.

The second building to host the course at NCSU was Bragaw Hall, one of the older residence halls on campus. Built in the 1960s, selecting Bragaw Hall for the second LEED Lab course was strategic for a number of reasons. First, Bragaw Hall is host to the EcoVillage, one of the University's Living and Learning Villages under University Housing, hosting approximately seventy-five students annually. Similar to other NCSU Villages such as the Engineering Village, the Arts Village, and the Scholars Village, which cater to specific student interests, the EcoVillage "welcomes students from all disciplines, thereby creating an interdisciplinary educational experience that prepares students for life-long sustainable living! Students go beyond the classroom to lead, serve, create, problem-solve and engage in complex issues facing the local and global energy and environmental challenges of society to advance sustainability." (http://housing.ncsu.edu/ecovillage) By partnering with the EcoVillage, the students enrolled in the class can not only gain a users' perspective on the facility, but also increase engagement and share knowledge with the occupants of the building.

A second key consideration to selecting Bragaw Hall was the important engagement of University Housing, or Campus Life. A separate entity and a receipts-based enterprise, University Housing is much more client-based and client-responsive than other physical structures on campus, such as classroom buildings, lab buildings, or studio buildings. University Housing, as an entity, also has a significantly larger reach across campus than a singular college. So, while some of the recommendations from the second semester of the course are particular to Bragaw Hall, much of the data, such indoor air quality and landscaping strategies, can be generalized to other University Housing buildings around campus. The Director of Facilities and IT in University Housing participated directly in the course, welcoming the students to the project and expressing how important this type of in-depth and interdisciplinary exploration was for University Housing as an enterprise. Representatives from University Housing also participated in the final event of the semester, providing feedback and validity to the information collected and analyzed by the students.

Each semester, the course opened with an official welcome to the students from the "client" for the semester. The first semester students were welcomed by the Director of the Business Sustainability Collaborative, and the students in the second semester heard a welcome from the Director of Facilities, IT, and Asset Management for Campus Life, along with the Director of the EcoVillage. The involvement of this leadership was crucial to establishing a team mentality within the class, and across disciplines, that the projects being addressed by the course groups were important and valuable to their university. The projects were not simply academic exercises, but could and would have a real-world impact at their alma mater. An important part of the course was subtly instilling this communal goal in the class as a whole, consistently, establishing a foundation for productive teamwork.

User Engagement

In all design processes, it is imperative to know your "client," your audience, and your users. Each of the buildings selected for the course were chosen with this in mind. For Nelson Hall, the first building, having the Poole College Business Sustainability Collaborative on board and excited about the project was imperative. As mentioned previously, the Director of the College of Management Sustainability Collaborative addressed the class and shared their organization's excitement about the project. Similarly, one of the student groups in the College of Management also became involved in reviewing the information and putting forth comments and recommendations to the University for follow through. In year two, students from the EcoVillage were also included in a number of the exercises. The entirety of the Village population was invited to the kick-off class, a number of in-class exercises, and to the final assessment and reporting event.

This engagement of other stakeholders outside of the class emphasized the importance of the teams' tasks and findings when planning and developing their course deliverables. The participation of these additional stakeholders highlighted to the students in the course that the problems being addressed were not simply an academic endeavor, but a meaningful problem worthy of their best work and attention, which in turn necessitates good teamwork.

COURSE GOALS

Because of the partnership vested in establishing this course, there were effectively two sets of goals for the course. One set of goals was addressed from the academic side, and was primary for the students of the course and for the topic of this chapter. There were, however, also Facility Division goals. The projects selected were within the boundary of the department's purview, and they had committed time and resources to the effort. Both sets of goals were complementary, and are reviewed here.

Interdisciplinary Learning and Academic Goals

From the academic perspective, the focus of the course was primarily for the development of student knowledge and experience in interdisciplinary teams, focusing on opportunities for teamwork that are not typically accessible to students. The primary goal of this course was to facilitate new teamwork structures around a common course project. By using the on-campus, real world project as described in detail above, the foundation was set for the students to embark up on a semester-long journey of understanding how other disciplines might approach the same project, and how those perspectives could be used to work together synergistically.

A secondary goal for the course was to use the existing, proven, organized structure of LEED to give the students a framework in which to think about complex issues surrounding building operation and maintenance after occupancy. As noted in endless literature (Espinosa & Walker, 2011; Kay, et al., 1999; Waltner-Toews, et al., 2008; Zellner, 2008), sustainability and green building is an overwhelming problem that is too intricate and detailed for one field alone, let alone one individual student, to tackle. But comprehending this complexity, and the primary components of this topic, is exactly what is asked of design students and future practitioners, as well as those colleagues with whom these students will collaborate in the real world.

To make the most sense of such an enormous topic, the LEED rating system was used as a structure for organizing issues. While none of the students had any experience with the LEED rating system specific to Operations and Maintenance, some students did have exposure to other versions of the LEED rating system, such as Building Design and Construction or Commercial Interiors. At the very least, many had heard the term LEED in conversations around the profession, in media, and in conversations with other faculty. Capitalizing on this familiarity with LEED systems, this course attempted to use the clear structure for students to get their minds around the variety of issues and tasks being asked of them. This tool helped to develop a scaffold for the immense amount of information that was being communicated and built upon over the course of the semester. The tool also helped the students identify key terms to used in their teams, helping to facilitate conversations and collaborations. This system was used to ultimately streamline communications and make the teamwork more efficient, which is identified as a recurring issue in the literature (Hall, et al., 2004; Minssen, 2006; Dayton & Henriksen, 2007).

University Facilities Division Goals

From the perspective of the university facilities department, this course was focused on documenting and analyzing data addressing the comprehensive operations of the University's building stock, helping the University itself move toward more sustainable operations. As a partner in the course, and coming from a different perspective, the NCSU Facilities Division has its own set of goals for partnering with the School of Architecture to deliver this course. However, many of these goals do not directly apply to this chapter emphasizing teamwork, and will not be elaborated. These goals center on exploring opportunities for Facilities to assess their building portfolio while providing valuable experience to the students. Some of the goals of the Facilities Division include: (1) the need to assess the process for funding existing building issues; (2) addressing the sheer amount of square footage on campus, which is a barrier to utilizing best practices; and (3) the lack of exposure for staff members to regular training on best practices in operations and maintenance, as found in systems such as LEED. While these goals are campus-centric, and not specifically related to the development and education of students in the class, the deep involvement of the University Facilities Division does provide a unique opportunity to look more closely at teamwork processes.

Unique Partnership Opportunities

Relative to this book's focus on teamwork, the third goal of the University Facilities Division as outlined above provides a unique opportunity on which the course design attempted to capitalize. The way this LEED Lab course is structured, the students are acting as educators to Facilities staff and educate them on best practices in the industry using established frameworks like LEED, and the industry terminology that is included. Facilities staff members are likewise regarded as experts in their particular fields, which promotes morale and pride in the organization. This balance is very important, as the students must regard the Facilities staff as experts, and the Facilities staff must be open to regarding the students as educators in order to have an ideal outcome. As these relationships develop over the course of the semester, the scope of the class "teams" expands to incorporate university staff as well.

This goal works in tandem with many of the academic goals for the course. The inclusion of not only other disciplines but staff input into team structures certainly assisted in establishing new teamwork structures for the students. Because many of the staff is aware of the LEED framework, it also helped to structure communications between the experiential differences between the teams of students and the expertise of the staff, but allowed for somewhat streamlined communications.

COURSE STRUCTURE

Working toward the overall academic goals for the course, and only committing for one semester, the course was designed to allow students to focus on two groups of specific individual credits, or considerations, over the entirety of the course. Because of both the breadth and depth of the LEED rating system, the course was divided into two phases across the semester, which were called Module 1 and Module 2. This phased module structure provides the students two opportunities to go in-depth with credits and considerations. It is possible that in one module, students could address credits applicable to their discipline while addressing other considerations that fall outside their expertise areas in the other module. This phasing and experience could then help to build an expertise outside of their field.

The module design for the course was established to support both individual flexibility and group collaboration between fields. Within each module, five interdisciplinary student groups were established that were dedicated to researching and assessing different credits in the rating system, as shown in Table 1.

Table 1. Module chart showing the division of credits and considerations across the semester

Group 1	Group 2	Group 3	Group 4	Group 5
Sust Sites/Location & Transport	**Water Efficiency**	**Materials & Resources**	**Energy & Atmosphere**	**Indoor Environmental Quailty**
PR: Site Mgmt Policy	PR: Indoor Water Use Reduction	PR: Ongoing Purchasing and Waste Policy	PR: Energy Efficiency Best Mgmt Practices	PR: Minimum Indoor Air Quailty Performance
Site Development/ Protect or Restore Habitat	PR: Building-level Water Metering	PR: Facility Maintenance & Renovations	PR: Minimum Energy Performance	PR: Environmental Tobacco Smoke control
Rainwater Management	Outdoor Water Use Reduction	Purchasing: Ongiong	PR: Building Level Energy Metering	Indoor Air Quality Management Program
Heat Island Reduction	Indoor Water Use Reduction	Purchasing: Lamps	Optimize Energy Performance	Enhanced Indoor Air Quailty Management Program
Site Management	Cooling Water Tower Use Reduction	Purchasing: Facility Management & Renovation	Advanced Energy Metering	
Sire Improvement Plan	Water Metering	Solid Waste Management: Ongoing	Demand Response	
		Solid Waste Management: Facility Management and Renovation		
Group 6	**Group 7**	**Group 8**	**Group 9**	**Group 10**
Indoor Environmental Quality	**Indoor Environmental Quality**	**Energy and Atmosphere**	**Energy and Atmosphere**	**Innovation & Regional Priority**
PR: Green Cleaning Policy	Thermal Comfort	PR: Fundamental Refrigeration Management	Existing Building Commissioning: Analysis	Innovation
Green Cleaninng: Custodial Effectiveness Assessment	Interior Lighting	Renewable Energy and Carbon Offsets	Existing Building Commissioning: Implementation	Regional Priority Credits
Green Cleaning: Products & Materials	Daylight and Views	Enhanced Refrigeration Management	Ongoing Commissioning	
Green Cleaning: Equipment	Occupant Comfort Survey	Light Pollution Reduction (SS)		
Integrated Pest Management				

Individual credits were grouped with similar credits as much as possible, with the intent to use credit synergies to make the students' work over the course of the semester more efficient, and at the same time more detailed. Individual credits and the comprehensive groups such as Group 1, Group 2, etc., were also organized in an attempt to balance the overall effort needed from each group. That is to say, the students with the heavier, more complicated energy analysis credits would not have exceptionally more research and analysis to do than groups addressing credits with varying levels of qualitative and quantitative work, which may be already addressed in a developed university policy.

Establishing Groups

In the third class session of each semester, the students were asked to provide their top three preferences for groups in both Module 1 and Module 2. Instructors decided to make every effort to try to support these choices, as opposed to pre-selecting the groups without student input. Because one of the primary goals of the course is to provide hands-on experiences in a real world setting that will support the students in their future workplace, instructors felt that providing students a choice in their detailed research topics was important. While not every preference could be accommodated, the vast majority were give their first or second choices of credits and considerations to explore throughout the semester. If one was not given their first or second choice in Module 1, they were certain to be placed in their first choice for Module 2.

Groups were arranged not only based on the individual preferences of the students, but to ensure that an equal number of students were in each group. Within those two boundaries, it was also a goal to make sure that the distribution of students within each group was balanced. In other words, each group needed to have at least one representative from each discipline or background, but no more than two from each discipline. By adhering to these established guidelines for groups, the five groups for each of the modules were as well balanced as possible within the makeup of the course itself.

Delivering Content

Each week, while student teams work on gathering documentation for their specific credits and considerations outside of class time for the final course deliverable, larger topics are covered in class and presented to all students. While each student group was given specific topics to explore in depth with their Module group assignments and teams, each student still needs to be exposed to a broader sample of issues, categories, and considerations that are included in the maintenance and operations of a building. This is designed to pick up the baton from a typical architect and designer's role - turning over the completed building at the end of construction. With this layer of direct (from module work) and indirect (from class lectures) information gathering, each group should be knowledgeable about all considerations, such as indoor air quality, energy consumption, waste management and recycling, and other issues. This layering of information, and the complementary delivery, speaks to the breadth and complexity of topics addressed in working toward a greener built environment. Using the LEED framework for the structure helps the students relate the content received in class back to the pertinent credits in their teamwork.

When possible, a representative from the University Facilities Division is brought in to be a guest speaker. For example, one class period is dedicated to the issues of Indoor Environmental Quality. Content addressing the larger concepts pertaining specifically to indoor air quality was provided in the first half of class. During the second half of class, a representative from the University's Environmental Health and Safety team spoke to the students about the daily activities of the job, including the typical issues seen on campus and in different types of buildings. This provides students valuable background on real-world processes while also providing all the students with information needed to support productive teamwork throughout the semester.

The totality of the content provided across the duration of the course is continually linked back to the LEED rating system structure, and the concepts therein. As the core structure of the course, all of the different themes and divergent information provided through readings, lectures, and guest speakers could be related back to the initial, foundational structure provided to the students. Through this consistency and framework, the divers groups are able to communicate efficiently in their teams.

Integrating with Campus

With the course structured as a strategic and meaningful partnership between multiple parties on campus, all groups involved in the course were engaged in a number of different ways, and at multiple times. The variations on engagement attempted to make the most efficient use of both the staff's time, respecting their other - and primary - responsibilities on campus, while bringing the most value to the students. Through the in-class exercises addressed earlier and detailed below, integrated student teams are involved in critically assessing green building and sustainability strategies on campus, taking part in energy audits, waste audits, and occupant satisfaction and comfort surveys. "We were tasked with researching the credits, coming up with action plans, and coordinating with professionals to solve problems we faced," said one student. "The ability to work with students from varying disciplines, apply critical thinking skills and engage in a professional project that improves our university was very rewarding. [This] has been my favorite course at NC State."

With a co-instructor with a role in both the University Sustainability Office and the University Facilities Division, the course strived to engage all appropriate departments dealing with operations and maintenance on campus (see Figure 1). These departments include Building Maintenance and Operations, Repair and Renovation, University Housekeeping, Energy Management, Waste Reduction and Recycling, Environmental Health and Safety, Energy Solutions, Purchasing, Grounds Management, and the Building Maintenance and Operations' Commissioning Team. Representatives from each of these University departments addresses the class individually, with the intent to communicate to the students their daily concerns and processes. Though these individuals are not typically in front of students, or even interacting with them, the purpose in their presenting to the class is to relay their operations and maintenance concerns to the students.

This two-way interaction not only provides a basic level of knowledge for all of the students enrolled in the class, but helps to establish a partnership between the students and the University staff. Through

Figure 1. Indoor air quality testing demonstration in Nelson Hall

this interaction, though typically less than an hour, the students engage in discussions with the staff member, asking questions about their world, their concerns and their perceptions. This brief time unifies the two sides as they move toward the same goal, which for this course is working toward a better, more sustainable and more efficient campus. The performance of the university facilities is extremely important to the staff members, particularly those that are asked to speak to the class. Bringing these staff into the class to talk with students that are just as interested in their daily goals seems to energize the staff themselves, providing additional kudos, information and energy to their roles and tasks on campus. This simple gesture helps to establish a common ground and goal, helping to further develop the extended notion of a team between the students and university staff.

TEAM BUILDING EXERCISES

Because students came from a variety of disciplines across campus, some of which rarely intersect, the course was designed to include a series of in-class exercise to begin to build a sense of camaraderie between the students. One key to improving deliverables and process in student team projects is the inclusion of team building exercises (Hansen, 2006). In addition, a situated sense of an entity, or investment in a group, is key to establishing powerful teams (Albert, Ashforth & Durron, 2000). Given this background, a series of exercises were integrated into the course to help to establish a sense of teamwork, entity, and common ground. The goal of the first few classes is to make the course a "safe place" where students feel comfortable with their peers, and aware of other expertise and value.

Identifying Myths and Breaking Down Stereotypes

The first class includes a *Myths and Stereotypes* exercise, where students are gathered into groups from their home Colleges, and asked to list three myths and stereotypes about each group, including their own. The results were largely entertaining and humorous. Responses about Design students included, "They have a lot of free time, but are always stressed," and "Often forget to shower." Stereotypes relating to the Natural Resources students included, "They hate to wear shoes," and "They all work on grass and things…?" and "We don't really know WHAT they do…" Engineers were viewed as, "Detail oriented and snobby," and also "So stressed – ALL the time."

Reporting these myths and stereotypes out to the larger group provided a safe venue to look critically at the perceptions that other disciplines brought to the course, and created a level playing field for all backgrounds involved in the class. By leveling the playing field in terms of identifying absurdities in engrained viewpoints This established and nurtured ease between students with different backgrounds of expertise gave each the opportunity to learn to view environmental challenges and opportunities from different perspectives.

Specifically, this exercise was one of the best-received and most effective teambuilding exercises in the course. This may have been because it was presented to the class first, and there was more stratifying ground to cover than later exercises. Of course, as the course progressed through each class period, the students became closer as a unit and more comfortable with each other and the different backgrounds found in the class. However, this exercise specifically lowered the tone of the room from a level of wariness and hesitation immediately toward a level of comfort.

Hands-On Exercises

As stated previously, one of the fundamental goals of the course, more basic even than learning objectives, is to establish a comfort level in non-traditional partnerships with design students. While this is addressed directly through the icebreaker activity described previously, it is also addressed through in-class activities, briefly mentioned earlier. These activities are strategically designed, or arranged, to establish a common understanding of processes and terms. These common understandings then serve to help establish a common vocabulary, centered on existing building and operations, that goes beyond the abstract, design-centered vocabulary of the architecture students. This new (to the students) language speaks beyond the harder science terminology of environmental sciences students, and brings the precision and efficiency terms from the engineering students into the realm of application. The following in-class exercises designed into the course are not only to allow the students to witness the actual process being discussed, but also are framed and executed to build relationships and interactions between often disparate fields in academia.

The class's indoor air quality testing exercise is one of the most realistic activities done in class. For this session, the staff representative from Environmental Health and Safety brings his standard equipment for the class to use. After orienting the class to the issues of indoor environmental quality through a thorough lecture, the staff focuses in on the issues of indoor air quality. With significant years of experience in indoor air quality testing, the staff shares stories of indoor air quality gone wrong, ranging in context from moldy ducts to rotten fruit to fresh air intakes right next to exhaust vents. After understanding the complexity and breadth of issues that can be found in indoor air quality, students are better prepared to understand the most common types of indoor air quality issues, and as such, the tools that measure them. Demonstrations were given by the staff member on each of the pieces of equipment, and then each piece of equipment was passed around for the students to try on their own.

Measurements were taken and basic thresholds were discussed based on the types of space being addressed at that moment. This activity gave each of the students hand-on experience with indoor air quality tools and equipment, allowing them to better understand the issues at hand, as well as the process it takes to thoroughly understand each issue. Knowing that indoor air quality can be a problem, the students are often not aware of how pervasive and invasive these types of issues can be in built environments. While only a handful of the students were looking at the IAQ credits in depth, the entire class was able to gain a deeper appreciation for both the issues themselves, as well as the methods and processes it takes to identify and mediate the problems in existing buildings. By establishing common terms, witnessing other students' ambiguity relating to the concepts of air quality, and laughing together as they struggled to make the equipment perform correctly, also helped to establish a feeling of solidarity between students from different disciplines.

The energy audit is the most technical of the three focused hands-on activities, led by on-campus partners each semester. Each semester, the course follows the structure of an ASHRAE (American Society of Heating, Refrigerating, and Air-Conditioning Engineers) Level I Energy Audit. The goal of this audit, as required by LEED, is primarily to review utility data and perform a walk-through of the site, checking equipment, maintenance and performance.

In the course, students participate in an "Energy Audit Lite." Given that there is only one class period allotted for the exercise, effectively capping the activity at three hours, there is not time to execute a full Level I Energy Audit with all the students. However, the goal of the hands-on session is for all students to understand the process, contributions, variables, and measurements needed for this type of energy verification. By giving all students exposure to the setting, experts and process affiliated with a Level I Energy Audit simulation, they will be better equipped to talk about it in the context of a whole building assessment - even if it is not their area of focus. As with other topics, a smaller group of students will work with the energy coordinator or appropriate staff to go more in-depth on the topic, and more fully address the Level I Audit requirements.

Similar to the indoor air quality testing exercise, the energy audit helped to demystify a commonly cumbersome concept in green building - energy use. It is often difficult to make the jump from understand the concepts of energy consumption and usage to moving into details and measurements as needed during an audit. Even those students in environmental sciences that may be familiar with renewable energy technologies are not always well-informed of energy management and monitoring at the building scale. By taking a detailed, foreign, and all-around difficult concept and bringing it into practice in the classroom, the exercise enable students to share in their struggling, information processing, and epiphanies as they began to grasp the new knowledge presented in the class (see Figures 2 and 3).

One of the most anticipated, and engaging, hands-on activities throughout the course is the waste audit. For this exercise, the students meet at the building, outside, in a previously prepared space. The Facilities Division's Waste Reduction and Recycling team was deeply engaged in this exercise, helping to prepare a meaningful and enlightening waste audit experience. In the first semester, the exercise included a full waste audit, assessing two days worth of trash from the dumpsters serving Nelson Hall, as shown in Figure 4. The primary goal of this exercise was to go through the trash that was headed for the landfill and separate what should be diverted to another stream, such as recycling or compost, which could be diverted from the landfill. This would help to establish a target diversion rate, enabling facilities and maintenance to see how much trash should actually be going to the landfill, envision methods to potentially minimize that amount, and better comprehend what kind of user education might be helpful to decrease material actually heading to the landfill. At the same time, there was also a smaller recycling

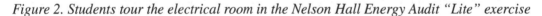

Figure 2. Students tour the electrical room in the Nelson Hall Energy Audit "Lite" exercise

Figure 3. Students assess the mechanical rooms in the existing facilities being addressed

audit that addressed the material found in the recycling dumpster. This was to see if that material actually belonged in the recycling or in a different stream. In other words, how much to the material to be recycled was actually recyclable? And how much of the material should be elsewhere, like compost?

This exercise took all of the three hours allotted for the weekly class time. With twenty-five students, three full dumpsters of garbage and recyclables could be assessed and divided. This exercise not only

Figure 4. Students sort trash from two dumpsters outside of Nelson Hall. Image © NCSU Sustainability Office

helped bond the students in a unique - and somewhat memorable - experience, but also revealed that 77 percent of Nelson Hall's waste is recyclable or compostable. The experience of digging through and categorizing trash was proven to be an experience that the students continue to bond over.

Concluding the Semester

The final collaborative exercise in the course, and arguably the most important, is a session designed to review all the documentation that each group had gathered over the course of the semester, in partnership with stakeholders. Both semesters saw the event structured as a workshop, or charrette, taking approximately two-to-three hours. Users of the building, including representatives from the College of Management Sustainability Collaborative in the first year, and residents in the second year, as well as facilities departments were invited to and involved with the session. After an initial presentation providing a summary of all the credits, the time was broken down into two sessions, modeling the Module structure. Student groups sat with representative from their aligned Facilities Division departments, as well as a small group of users and other stakeholders, as seen in Figure 5 and Figure 6. The first session in the room facilitated discussions about the credits assessed in Module 1, while the second hour discussed the credits addressed in Module 2. With each round, the student groups presented the findings and suggestions for next steps to their table of stakeholders, and received feedback. Stakeholders were given the opportunity to provide comments and concerns, and critically discuss the proposed solutions and implementations with the student groups.

This focused activity allowed the students to understand the systems thinking behind the identified strategies and proposed changes, from the perspectives of design, engineering, natural resources, facilities management, and the owner. These conversations worked both ways, letting students understand more

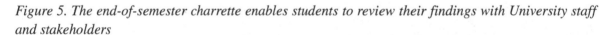

Figure 5. The end-of-semester charrette enables students to review their findings with University staff and stakeholders

Figure 6. Students share their recommendations and receive feedback from the Director of the Sustainability Office and other staff

in-depth issues pertaining to facilities division considerations and users, while bringing opportunities to the stakeholders through fresh eyes.

Through the initial overview presentation, this comprehensive workshop also allowed all facility divisions to review the reports and recommendations for all other credits and considerations - not just the ones that directly address their divisions. This is particularly important given the emphasis on a holistic approach to green building strategies, even in operations and maintenance. Many of the credits and considerations are linked with synergies and trade-offs. Though not covered explicitly here, one section of the course, as well as an assignment, is dedicated specifically to these types of partnerships and synergies. With this exercise, the students can take their conceptual understanding of synergies toward an applied, interdisciplinary understanding, with the help of the staff and other stakeholders. The closing workshop event allows the ideas, documented data, and possible design interventions to be looked at holistically for a more collaborative approach to an established problem – specifically the operations of an existing building on campus.

CONTRIBUTION OF GROUP WORK TOWARD LEARNING OBJECTIVES

The learning objectives for the course, which focus on skill development, enhanced understanding of complex issues, experience on an actual project, and data gathering and analysis, are more sufficiently achieved by using a collaborative teamwork approach in the course. As the primary goal of the course, establishing interdisciplinary relationships and a sense of teamwork was critical for delivery of the final course assignment. One student noted, "The biggest strength of the course is giving students access to knowledge and interdisciplinary experiences not typically available to students, making them more valuable in their future job-hunting endeavors." Another noted that, "The interdisciplinary work between the three schools was beneficial and helped us all to grow as students and helped prepare us for working after school." The primary goal of the course could not have been met without a teamwork approach.

Feedback received from students indicate that they have not been in such an interdisciplinary, collaborative, project-based academic setting before coming to this class, and have thoroughly enjoyed it. One student notes, "I also liked that there were other students from different majors in the class. I think having the variety of different majors in the class helped us learn from different perspectives." The teamwork arrangement of the class helped to establish an enhanced understanding of the complex issues in both building and sustainability, and exposed students to differing perspectives on frequently seen topics in construction and building maintenance. By approaching the issues addressed in class from a multi-disciplinary perspective, students were better able to prepare for their futures in the workplace, as well as begin to understand the importance of complexity (Johnson, Alexiou & Zamenopoulos, 2010; Rapoport & Kantor, 1967).

Similarly, the overall design of the course, emphasizing teamwork and exploratory processes, was undoubtedly beneficial to establishing a foundational structure for the course. As one graduate student notes, "Rather than being taught at us, which is usually the case, the students played an integral part in providing data and analysis. Having spent nearly half a decade in school, I have grown tired of teachers leading us down a winding road. One in which our skills are not tested and we are not challenged to excel and progress. This progression is not so for this course. We had the opportunity to learn from professionals outside of our fields. This challenged me to be comfortable communicating with my peers as well as the university faculty." The common structure recognized early in the semester helped the teams be able to communicate more effectively, and work more efficiently toward a meaningful deliverable at the end of the semester. In this way, the teamwork element of the course addressed the issues of challenging communication in interdisciplinary teams (Hall, et al., 2004; Minssen, 2006; Dayton & Henriksen, 2007).

FUTURE RESEARCH DIRECTIONS

As noted, there is an increased emphasis on interdisciplinary work in design practice, though the translation is more difficult to make into academia, particularly into design education. However, the LEED Lab program established by USGBC, and as hosted at NCSU, provides a legitimate model for crossover projects between academic disciplines surrounding the design field. Future research could specifically address LEED Lab participants, beyond just NCSU, and distribute pre- and post-tests across the wide range of LEED Lab hosts, helping to assess the different models, processes and structures being used for the courses.

Additional research could also be completed on the topic of interdisciplinary teamwork, exploring different methods for team building in a design course, and particularly with interdisciplinary teams. While often design teams are arbitrarily thrown together with instructions on a team project, there is considerable literature on team development that could support the future efforts of the students (Dyer and Dyer, 2013; Thompson, 2009; Way and Bordass, 2005), both in school and in the profession.

Still further research could address different icebreaker exercises, exploring which provide the most opportunity for engaging design students and their peers from other disciplines. There are a variety of possibilities to take into account the uniqueness of design students and education, which comparing and contrasting it with the standard education for engineers, environmental scientists, and business students.

Last to mention here, but certainly not the end of the list of possibilities, is the opportunity to assess different approaches to interdisciplinary courses in different settings, potentially comparing the opportunities for a studio setting with those of a seminar setting. This chapter outlined one possibility for a seminar, though there are certainly endless others that could be viable. How these shorter and more transferrable opportunities compare with the intense setting of a studio could provide further enlightenment.

CONCLUSION

As reviewed here, the NCSU LEED Lab course is a viable model for meaningful, collaborative relationships on college campuses using the LEED rating system as a both a conceptual and applied framework. The first two offerings of the NCSU LEED Lab course resulted in multiple positive outcomes, one of the most important of which was building rapport between previously disparate and seemingly distant student disciplines. In addition, NCSU's Facilities Division was provided with real-world feedback, which enabled them to reevaluate policies and procedures. This partnership enabled both the students - from a variety of different disciplines - to work with the facilities staff members to move toward a more sustainable campus, city and region. The University staff members and larger student population on campus were actively engaged in gathering data across the different credits, criteria and considerations, and continue to be appraised of discoveries and outcomes as both projects move forward through the Facilities Division on LEED Lab student recommendations. The findings from these projects are also being used to generalize across campus, impacting considerations on other buildings of similar type. Used in this instance as a model for student engagement, environmental stewardship, policy management, and interdisciplinary collaborations, it is possible that NCSU's LEED Lab can become implemented across all NCSU campus precincts and to similar institutions in the region.

The primary educational goal of the NCSU LEED Lab course is for all participating students to acquire a well-rounded understanding of the considerations for maintaining and operating a building after construction and into occupancy. This understanding of maintenance and operations allows design students to ultimately deliver better building designs, and to capitalize on the opportunities available for collaborations - both in school and in the workforce. This case study has shown that interdisciplinary projects are possible in a seminar setting within a design program, showing that students from different backgrounds can establish meaningful teams despite any stereotypes disseminated about peer programs in other programs.

REFERENCES

Albert, S., Ashforth, B. E., & Dutton, J. E. (2000). Organizational identity and identification: Charting new waters and building new bridges. *Academy of Management Review*, *25*(1), 13–17. doi:10.5465/AMR.2000.2791600

Bringle, R. G., & Hatcher, J. A. (2000). Institutionalization of Service Learning in Higher Education. *The Journal of Higher Education*, *71*(3), 273. doi:10.2307/2649291

Dayton, E., & Henriksen, K. (2007). Teamwork and Communication: Communication Failure: Basic Components, Contributing Factors, and the Call for Structure. *Joint Commission Journal on Quality and Patient Safety*, *33*(1), 34–47. PMID:17283940

Deutsch, R. (2011). *BIM and integrated design strategies for architectural practice*. Hoboken, N.J.: Wiley.

Dyer, W., & Dyer, J. (2013). *Team building proven strategies for improving team performance* (5th ed.). San Francisco: Jossey-Bass, A Wiley Imprint.

Espinosa, S. A., & Walker, J. (2011). *A complexity approach to sustainability: Theory and application*. London: Imperial College Press.

Fixson, S. (2009). *Teaching Innovation Through Interdisciplinary Courses and Programs in Product Design and Development: An Analysis at Sixteen U.S. Schools*. Babson College Center for Entrepreneurship Research Paper No. 2009-13.

Hall, P., Keely, E., Dojeiji, S., Byszewski, A., & Marks, M. (2004). Communication skills, cultural challenges and individual support: Challenges of international medical graduates in a Canadian healthcare environment. *Medical Teacher*, *26*(2), 120–125. doi:10.1080/01421590310001653982 PMID:15203520

Johnson, J., Alexiou, K., & Zamenopoulos, T. (2010). *Embracing complexity in design*. New York: Routledge.

Kay, J. J., Regier, H. A., Boyle, M., & Francis, G. (1999). An ecosystem approach for sustainability: Addressing the challenge of complexity. *Futures*, *31*(7), 721–742. doi:10.1016/S0016-3287(99)00029-4

Keeler, M. (2009). *Fundamentals of integrated design for sustainable building*. Hoboken, N.J.: John Wiley & Sons.

Kurt, S. (2009). An analytic study on the traditional studio environments and the use of the constructivist studio in the architectural design education. *Procedia: Social and Behavioral Sciences*, *1*(1), 401–408. doi:10.1016/j.sbspro.2009.01.072

Meadows, D., & Wright, D. (2008). *Thinking in systems: A primer*. White River Junction, Vt.: Chelsea Green Pub.

Minssen, H. (2006). Challenges of Teamwork in Production: Demands of Communication. *Organization Studies*, *27*(1), 103–124. doi:10.1177/0170840605056400

Moe, K. (2008). *Integrated design in contemporary architecture*. New York, N.Y.: Princeton Architectural Press.

Morton, K., & Troppe, M. (1996). From the margin to the mainstream: Campus Compact's Project on Integrating Service with Academic Study. *Journal of Business Ethics*, *15*(1), 21–32. doi:10.1007/BF00380259

Rapoport, A., & Kantor, R. E. (1967). Complexity and Ambiguity in Environmental Design. *Journal of the American Institute of Planners*, *33*(4), 210–221. doi:10.1080/01944366708977922

Reed, B. (2009). *The integrative design guide to green building: Redefining the practice of sustainability*. Hoboken, N.J.: Wiley.

Rhee, J. (2010). Pilot Implementation of an Interdisciplinary Course on Climate Solutions. *International Journal of Engineering Education (Special Issue)*, 391.

Schon, D. A. (1984). The Architectural Studio as an Exemplar of Education for Reflection-in-Action. *Journal of Architectural Education (1984-)*, *38*(1), 2.

Smit, E., & Tremethick, M. (2013). Development of an international interdisciplinary course: A strategy to promote cultural competence and collaboration. *Nurse Education in Practice*, *13*(2), 132–136. doi:10.1016/j.nepr.2012.08.006 PMID:22964472

Stibbe, A. (2009). *The handbook of sustainability literacy: Skills for a changing world*. Totnes, UK: Green Books.

Thompson, J. (2009). Building Collective Communication Competence In Interdisciplinary Research Teams. *Journal of Applied Communication Research*, *37*(3), 278–297. doi:10.1080/00909880903025911

Waltner-Toews, D., Kay, J., & Lister, N.-M. (2008). *The ecosystem approach: Complexity, uncertainty, and managing for sustainability*. New York: Columbia University Press.

Way, M., & Bordass, B. (2005). Making feedback and post-occupancy evaluation routine 2: Soft landings – involving design and building teams in improving performance. *Building Research and Information*, *33*(4), 353–360. doi:10.1080/09613210500162008

Yin, R. K. (2009). *Case study research: Design and methods*. Los Angeles, CA: Sage Publications.

Yudelson, J. (2009). *Green building through integrated design*. New York: McGraw-Hill.

Zellner, M. L., Theis, T. L., Karunanithi, A. T., Garmestani, A. S., & Cabezas, H. (2008). A new framework for urban sustainability assessments: Linking complexity, information and policy. *Computers, Environment and Urban Systems*, *32*(6), 474–488. doi:10.1016/j.compenvurbsys.2008.08.003

KEY TERMS AND DEFINITIONS

Benchmark: The current state of some measurement, or an established standard pertaining to some measurement, against which improvements can be assessed.

Design Fields: Academic disciplines and professional fields focused on making, representation, and creation.

Framework: A conceptual structure for organizing a complex set of information, around which the information can be ordered and new information can be understood.

Interdisciplinary: An effort combining two or more facets of knowledge, each with different focus areas, in an attempt to understand a concept better or generate new perspectives.

Partnerships: An agreement between parties that they will work together towards a common, previously established goal.

Stereotype: A simple, but often stable, perception of another individual, group or thing.

User: One who uses a building or facility, often for extended periods of time but also in short time increments, which would be impacted by the built environment they inhabit.

Section 3

Preparing for Collaboration:
Learning for Teamwork in Professional Practice

Chapter 14
Group Work and the Externally-Oriented Capstone:
Opening Students to the Challenges of Professional Practice

Nicole Wragg
Swinburne University of Technology, Australia

Carolyn Barnes
Swinburne University of Technology, Australia

ABSTRACT

Professional learning, where students gain skills and attributes relevant to their future work, is currently emphasised in tertiary education. Group work is promoted here for preparing students to work with clients and colleagues. We report on two capstone projects undertaken for external clients by teams of design students. In discussing the curricula and pedagogy of professional design education, the chapter addresses the value of group projects in developing graduates' work-readiness and insight into professional practice. Variances in approach, knowledge and perspective between colleagues, combined with differing needs and expectations across the designer-client-end-user divide, make goal setting and project resolution challenging in design. Project work approached from an expanded sense of the group and which delivers implementable proposals for clients provides graduating students with authentic learning around the demands of practice, stressing collaborative problem-solving based on knowledge of the design context and the wider relational systems surrounding industry practice.

INTRODUCTION

Capstone projects, so-called for their role as the culmination of undergraduate study, allow final year students to consolidate and test the diverse practical and intellectual knowledge gained at university in preparation for work. Capstone projects can be individual or group assignments. They can be real or simulated. For design students, work-readiness includes the capacity to work within the challenging

DOI: 10.4018/978-1-5225-0726-0.ch014

environment of client issues and problems, user needs and interests, and mixed projects teams that span different disciplinary knowledge and practices. This chapter discusses two capstone projects where groups of communication and digital media design students in the final year of their four-year Honours degree collaborated on demanding, client-supplied briefs with the expectation that implementable design proposals would be provided. For the clients, the projects offered access to design teams with the scope and motivation to engage intensely with the design task. This benefit was exchanged for significant mentoring for the students in a range of professional skills and expectations.

The two cases show that the group nature of the enterprise, which included an extended stakeholder group, combined with projects involving significant creative, intellectual and technical challenges fostered deep contextual learning around the exigencies of professional practice. To prepare students to manage ongoing, dynamic change in the nature of cultural production and consumption, the selected projects sought to extend, not simply model, industry practice. A tangible objective was to give the students an experience of design leadership. This being possible because most students had spent the third year of their degree in an Industry Placement (IP) program working as junior designers in leading design studios. The combination of a major project and the interaction of peers and diverse project stakeholders formed a virtuous circle in which students were supported to rehearse and reflect on the challenges of work.

BACKGROUND

The design industry's expectation for work-ready graduates has long encouraged the use of client-supplied and simulated professional project briefs in tertiary curriculum, but the nature of practice in contemporary creative industries like design is changing. The rise of service industries, the culture of co-creation and the spread of digital technologies have made many established ideas about design practice irrelevant. Designers now need to design from the perspectives of the consumer rather than focusing on the qualities of the designed artefact. Clients and employers expect a steady stream of design invention geared to commercial and social contexts in a state of flux. Communication design and digital media design are fields focused on conceptual and stylistic invention, but entrenched beliefs in designers' innate creativity, intuitive understanding of the design task and myth of the designer as lone creative genius, have made both fields resistant to new approaches such as user-centred design, with its requirement to base design on knowledge of people's situation and preferences.

Interdisciplinary and multidisciplinary professional practice is increasingly the norm in design with the rise of projects delivered across multiple platforms, both digital and print. Designers typically work in teams, engaging in the brainstorming, banter, critical feedback, discussion and negotiation that drives the process of conceptualisation, proposal making, design development and implementation, reflecting growing understanding that creativity is mostly a collective process (Sawyer, 2007). A design program that lacks group work, especially in its final year, misrepresents contemporary design practice. The capstone projects discussed here challenged students to connect the heterogeneous requirements, approaching their project as emerging from a community of practice in which differences of knowledge, meaning and practice must be actively brokered.

Case One, the '*Parents, Tweens and Sex*' (*PT&S*) project, partnered students with a psychologist and sexologist to create an application to help parents and tweens discuss sensitive sexual issues, the app merging experience design and innovative technology. The case shows how deep collaboration between a client and peers can see communication strategy flourish and students grow in confidence. In Case

Two, the 'Communicating Care in a Clinical Setting' project (*CCCS*), students worked with diverse stakeholders in a care organisation to explore how innovation in brand, information and systems design might enable institutional transformation, enhancing experiences and outcomes for clients and frontline staff. The inclusion of robust user research in the design process in the *CCCS* project encouraged students to understand design as 'creativity applied for a specific purpose' (Cox 2005, p. 2), the needs and interests of staff and clients having a constant presence in the designing.

Group Work In Tertiary Education

A range of writers discuss the benefits of group work in developing university students' industry readiness (Wageman & Frederick, 2005; Scott-Ladd & Chan, 2008), fostering shared understanding of tasks and learning objectives through formal and informal learning activities (Boud & Cohen, 2013), enabling collaborative skills development (Yazici, 2005), boosting student productivity (Sampson & Cohen, 2014) and allowing students to demonstrate the skills of teamwork to future employers (Phillips, 2005; Chapman, 2006; Sawyer, 2007; Kachra & Schnietz, 2008; Robinson, Sherwood & Depaolo, 2010). Alternatively, group work is seen as problematic due to the complex, human dynamics at play around group cohesion, communication, division of work, engagement, leadership, structure, time management and work ethic (Hellström, 2005; Kozlowski & Ilgen, 2006; O'Sullivan, Rice, Rogerson & Sauders, 2013).

Relevant literature focuses on how to support students to contribute in meaningful ways to the group effort. Different case studies explore student perspectives on group work (Rafferty, 2012), the nature and structuring of roles within groups (Hellström, 2005; Denton & McDonagh, 2005), providing students with training in managing group activity (Scott-Ladd & Chan, 2008), scaffolding of peer assessments (Fellenz, 2006; Willcoxson, 2006), strategies around group emails (Alpay, 2005), systems for virtual collaboration (Denton & McDonagh, 2005) and group work to enable teaching and learning beyond the physical classroom (Ganser, Kennel, & Kunz, 2007). University students' focus on individual achievement and outcomes (Scott-Ladd & Chan, 2008) is seen to clash with the use of group work to foster skills of cooperation and collaboration for future employment (Costigan, John & College, 2009; O'Sullivan, Rice, Rogerson & Sauders, 2013; Kiernan & Ledwith, 2014). This discussion identifies four challenges for academics conducting group work: 1) the need to teach the necessary practical skills to ensure group work is successful; 2) the need to develop students' social skills to enable them to collaborate with peers; 3) the need to develop scaffolded curriculum over students' university education that introduce and developed these skills; and 4) the need for suitable projects that effectively model the transition to industry.

A range of writers stresses the need to introduce group management practices before starting work (Kemery & Stickney, 2014; Scott-Ladd & Chan, 2008). Establishing ground rules or a roadmap for group work is recommended to avoid conflict and promote focused, constructive collaboration (Costigan, John & College, 2009) and a positive group experience (Surowiecki, 2004). Kolb (2013) argues that issues of power can have positive and negative effects on groups, the use of strategies to help students identify and manage behaviours that cause conflict having a critical bearing on the outcomes and value of group work. Folger, Pooles and Stutman (2009) argue that effective leadership can make a group more capable. Ferrante, Green and Forster (2006) contend that the misuse of power can undermine group effectiveness. Within the notion of group work, there is discussion of the difference between group and teamwork; Thornton (2010) stresses the importance of collaboration in successful group work, describing a team as a 'work group with shared goals or tasks' (p.12).

Ylikoski (2012) discusses the mounting pressure to provide professional learning in tertiary education through collaborative partnerships between industry and universities, some universities have reaccredited entire programs around major, externally-oriented group projects (Mendoza, Bernasconi & MacDonald, 2007). The literature strongly links academics' ability to coach and manage student teams a to positive group experience (Kozlowski & Ilgen, 2006; Sargent, Allen, Frahm & Morris, 2009; O'Sullivan, Rice, Rogerson & Sauders, 2013; Sampson & Cohen, 2014) and to departments' effectiveness in co-ordinating this activity (Hillyard, Gillespie & Littig, 2010). Delayed response in identifying negative behaviours is seen to intensify conflict (Rothwell & Kolb, 1999; Kolb & Rothwell, 2000). However, Denton and McDonagh (2005) report that conducting well-managed group projects is an intense experience for staff, recommending that staff be strongly supported here and limits placed on how often individual staff oversee group projects. To conduct group projects, particularly where external stakeholders are involved, Thornton (2010) argues academics require explicit knowledge of group dynamics and the interpersonal skills to understand students' psychological needs and responses.

Group Work In Design Education

Sawyer (2007) typifies contemporary design as defined by the rise of the collaborative organisation and team, creating the expectation that designers approach design with a collaborative outlook. The literature on group work in design education mainly discusses its use in industrial design and interdisciplinary design (Hellström, 2005, 2007; Denton & McDonagh, 2005; Ganser, Kennel & Kunz, 2007; Wodehouse & Maclachlan, 2010; Inns, Baxter & Murphy, 2015). Discussion focuses on the authenticity of teaching and learning and includes knowledge transfer within groups (e.g. Jerrard, 2006: Crabbe, 2008; Inns, Baxter & Murphy, 2015), which mirrors the focus on the dynamics of project teams in the new product development literature.

Since the commercial availability of digital media in the mid-1990s, many communication design and digital media design projects have become large in scale and implemented across multiple platforms, with projects completed by mixed teams of business specialists, marketers and programmers and creative practitioners with expertise in interface designer, motion graphics, photography and video (McCoy, 1995; Myerson & Vickers, 2002; Crawford, 2005; Lupton, 2006; Drucker and McVarish, 2009; McCarthy, 2015). The communication and digital media design education literature omits discussion of how to prepare graduates for group work in interdisciplinary projects, reflecting its paucity in the literature on curricula and pedagogy for professional practice. Some writers argue that industry requires graduates who can balance their individual creative approaches with the needs of peers and clients (Denton & McDonagh, 2005; Roberts, 2007; Sill, Harward & Cooper, 2009), but generally the literature has little to say on the how group work might foster this.

Capstone Projects

The capstone projects literature stresses the need to connect and build on the skills and knowledge final year students have gained during their degree (Kachra & Schnietz, 2008; Hauhart & Grahe, 2010; Robinson, Sherwood & DePaolo, 2010; Rafferty, 2012; Webb, 2012; Inamdar & Roldan, 2013). Levine (1998) identifies integration, breadth, application and transition as the four pedagogical tenets of this process. The main theorists, Lee and Loton (2015) have developed a framework of captone projects and outline six pedagogical objectives for capstone units: 1) integration and extension of prior learning; 2) authentic and contextualised learning experience; 3) challenging and complex scenarios; 4) student independence and agency; 5) a concern for creativity and critical inquiry; and 6) active dissemination and celebration of knowledge. They define six types of capstone project: 1) externally- and professionally-oriented projects where students develop a solution for a client; 2) academic inquiry projects that provide a research apprenticeship; 3) practice-oriented simulations that recreate the working conditions of the professional environment; 4) practice-based consultancies, where students gain a type of work experience through in-house university consultancies; 5) task-oriented simulations that focus on a defined set of activities with a specific goal; and 6) placements of students within industry.

The primary division here is between actual and simulated projects. Simulated projects are often judged as deficient in reflecting only some industry conditions and expectations (E.g. Marsden & Luczkowski, 2005; Roberts, 2007), although others acknowledge their scope to link theoretical understanding and practical skills through application (E.g. Sutliff, 2000; Evans & Spruce, 2005). Externally-oriented projects are seen to provide more authentic and comprehensive experience, several authors noting the multifaceted opportunities they provide in respect of networking (Denton & McDonagh, 2005; De Janasz & Forret, 2007; Ylikoski, 2012), project management (Whyte & Bessant, 2007) and team work (Kern, 2006). A number of case studies report on the use of externally-oriented group projects in the final year of study to address the transition between university and industry (E.g., Denton & McDonagh, 2005; Halls, 2005; Phillips, 2005; Fellenz, 2006). These studies come from varied fields including business education (Halls, 2005), design education (Marsden & Luczkowski, 2005), engineering education (Cano, Lidon, Rebollar, Roman & Saenz, 2006), management education (Carson, 2006; De Janasz & Forret, 2007) and university-workplace partnerships (Ylikoski, 2012).

In design education, simulated client work based around emblematic client briefs is included at all stages of an undergraduate degree. Design students participate in a range of group learning activities that mirror those in industry, including peer conceptualisation, presentations, feedback and reflection (Lee, 2009). To model industry conditions, teaching and learning for final year design students are often based in whole, or in part, on projects provided by external clients, with students often being located in in-house design studios (Denton & McDonagh, 2005; Walker, 2008; Ganser, Kennel & Kunz, 2007; Chiu, 2010). Roberts (2007) stresses the value of single major projects in the final year of study to extend earlier, industry-focused educational experiences to produce graduates with consolidated disciplinary and professional attributes, knowledge and skills. What is largely missing from the design education literature is substantial identification and discussion of the pedagogical parameters, characteristics and practical effects and benefits of capstone projects, that is, exactly how they prepare students for design practice.

McNamara et al, (2012) argue capstone projects in design should enable students 'to look back on their undergraduate study in an effort to make sense of what they have accomplished, and...look forward to a professional existence where they can build on that foundation' (p.2). Sill, Harward and Cooper (2009) see capstone projects as potentially transforming 'ways of knowing' (p.50), although they note they can be challenging and even disorientating for students. They attribute this to an abrupt shift from prescriptive briefs in the early years of design education to open-ended capstone briefs, which see student-led parameters determine the way forward. Case studies in various disciplines in the capstone literature discuss the structure of classes, the type and format of projects, required resources and final outcomes. Authenticity is seen as inherent to capstone projects, but the nature and value of group work is rarely examined in detail. Ball (2002, p. 10) argues that tertiary design education aims to develop 'capable, flexible, adaptable, lateral thinking and creative individuals'. Exposure to group work is part of this. The lack of comprehensive investigation into group capstone projects in tertiary design education, including externally-oriented ones, is necessary to understand if and how they enhance student outcomes. The two cases reported here explore these questions by providing detaned detailed accounts of events and attitudes around each project.

Research Design and Methods

To examine the use of externally-oriented, group projects in preparing students for professional practice, the study used an exploratory research design grounded in interview. The interviews followed Kvale's (1996) schema for informal conversational interviews, which holds that interviewees should be encouraged to provide descriptions of specific situations of relevance to the research topic. The interviews were short 30 to 40 minute conversations discussing the capstone project, its intentions, group dynamics and the role and input of the clients and other project stakeholders. Questions pursued specific themes, as set out below, but discussion was also open to other directions.

- Please describe the project in which you were involved?
- What was the scope of the project brief and did you have to set project parameters?
- Please describe the level, character and quality of interaction with the other students?
- Did you share roles across the groups or assume one role over the entire project?
- Please describe the level, character and quality of interaction with the client?
- Were there any constraints on the design process or outcomes as a result of student/client involvement?
- Capstones are seen to develop industry readiness. Did this project deliver on this perceived benefit of a capstone experience? In what way?
- The ideal capstone project is perceived as leveraging the amalgamation of previous student learning and experience? Having been on Industry Placement, did the skills required for this project offer higher learning? If so, in what ways?
- What aspect of the project was the most rewarding for you?
- Were there any aspects of the project that were frustrating for you?
- Did you discover a particular way that you like to work in design?

The study was carried out with the approval of the Research Ethics Committee of Swinburne University of Technology with due consideration to the requirements of informed consent and confidentiality.

Participants

Fifteen participants from three capstone units in Honours design programs at Swinburne University of Technology, Melbourne, were interviewed for the study between February and April 2015. Table 1 sets out the background of the participants.

CASE SELECTION AND DATA ANALYSIS

The two cases were selected from a range of possible projects for their comprehensive range of points of interest. In their inclusion of group work, the projects provided maximum educational benefit and design

Table 1. Details of participants

Participants	Background
Student A: Alice	Communication Design student, *PT&S*
Student B: Brett	Digital Media Design student, *PT&S*
Student C: Claudia	Communication Design student, *PT&S*
Student D: Daisy	Communication Design student, *PT&S*
Student E: Edward	Digital Media Design Honours student, *PT&S*
Client F: Fiona	Psychologist and Sexologist, *PT&S*
Student G: Grace	Communication Design student, *CCCS*
Student H: Hugh	Communication Design student, *CCCS*
Student I: Isabelle	Communication Design student, *CCCS*
Student J: Julie	Communication Design student, *CCCS*
Client K: Kate	Marketing and Development Manager, *CCCS*
Student L: Lillie	Communication Design student, *CCCS*
Student M: Mary	Communication Design student, *CCCS*
Student N: Nicole	Communication Design student, *CCCS*
Student O: Olivia	Communication Design student, *CCCS*

opportunity to final year students, being completed to a high level of creative achievement while enabling students' to develop and demonstrate a broad range of professional skills and attributes. Data analysis began from the perspective that how people talk about things matters, seeing a list of high-frequency words and themes created from the interviews. The comparison of emergent themes with issues and ideas from the capstone literature, particularly Lee and Loton's (2015) six pedagogical objectives for capstone projects, allowed new sets of questions to be asked of the data in an iterative approach leading to concept formation and the drawing of causal inference (Strauss & Corbin, 1998).

CASE STUDY ONE: PARENTS, TWEENS AND SEX

The *PT&S* project (2012) involved 33 Communication Design and Digital Media Design students. 'Fiona', a sexologist running her own psychology practice, supplied the brief for an eBook based on content she had developed to help parents discuss sensitive sexual issues with children aged 10 to 13 years. From her practice, Fiona had found that children wanted to speak to their parents about sex and sexuality, but didn't know how to formulate their questions. An alumnus of the University, Fiona had previously worked on a publishing project with the university's final year design students. Impressed by the innovative result, she sought to work with them again. The encompassing capstone unit sought to consolidate students' prior learning around creative strategy, the design process and technical knowledge by challenging students to use independent judgement in its application. The *PT&S* project with its multifaceted conceptual and technical challenges made it ideal for group work at Honours level. The addition of tight budgetary and time constraints enhanced the authenticity of the project.

The capstone unit spanned three hours of class contact a week over a twelve-week semester. In Week One, the students divided themselves into teams of four or five. In Week Four, all groups presented a prototype chapter of the e-Book to Fiona, delineating creative strategy and interactive characteristics and supported by their research into visual communication, media formats and audience needs and behaviour. In Week Six, Fiona provided detailed feedback on each project and the reasons for selecting one for development. The successful group of five students then worked solely on *PT&S*. The other 28 students moved on to different briefs. Part of their assessment, however, was allocated to a contribution to *PT&S* if the successful project team needed their expertise, seeing students from outside the group undertake tasks including coding, editing, icon design, illustration, photography, typesetting and video production as would happen in industry where understanding the design abilities in a consultancy, delegating work and engaging freelancer are important capacities. The main project team committed to an additional five weeks work after the semester to complete the design, after which they worked with a specialist, coding consultancy on production (Figure 1).

CASE STUDY 2: COMMUNICATING CARE IN A CLINICAL SETTING

The *CCCS* project was undertaken for Queen Elizabeth Centre (QEC). Located in the south-eastern suburbs of Melbourne, QEC provides parenting education and support for families with children up to the age of four through residential and outreach programs. QEC's client base is culturally, socially and linguistically diverse and mostly struggling with parenting. Senior managers were concerned that clients arrived at the centre in an anxious state with young children to face a lengthy admissions process requiring the completion of multiple forms. The research brief sought an investigation of the admissions system and

Figure 1. The contents page of the app, demonstrating the amalgamation of diverse design skills, including communication design, motion design and post production and coding

printed and electronic communications to see if things could be done better. Three self-formed student groups, comprised of five (*Initiate*), six (*Re.Think*) and five students (*Weaving Diversity*), elected to take on the *CCCS* project. Five remaining student groups chose projects for other clients.

The mixed teams of Communication Design and Digital Media Design students undertook the *CCCS* in 2014 in successive units with five hours of class contact a week across two semesters in 2014. The units' sought to give students experience in research for design practice and for academic purposes, the projects being simultaneously externally-oriented capstones and academic inquiry projects to provide a research apprenticeship (Lee & Loton, 2015). In completing the projects, the students experienced all aspects of an applied research project, beginning with literature review, preparing informed consent instruments, contextual and user research, and data analysis. The research activity was interwoven with the key stages of a design project from proposing a design strategy and early prototyping to design testing to culminate in the delivery of a proof-of-concept prototype to the client (Figure 2).

As research-driven projects, the client brief did not establish the parameters for design, only the context and focus, challenging the students to take full ownership of problem-identification, problem-definition and design response. Following a program of preliminary research comprising observation of the admissions process, interviews with staff and clients, and the review of QEC's admissions forms and printed and online communications, each group proposed an individual response to the research brief. *Initiate* investigated the research question 'How do we introduce a cultural change at QEC that reflects a sense of care within the organisational process?' *Re.Think* developed the research question 'How can QEC's brand act as a catalyst for institutional transformation through empowering all: clients, frontline staff, management and community?'. *Weaving Diversity* considered the research question 'How can design bridge the communication gap between QEC and families with culturally and linguistically diverse backgrounds?'.

Figure 2. A workshop that examined the brand mark and the affect of colour on perceptions of the brand mark

RESEARCH FINDINGS

The tertiary education literature promotes group projects for developing generic graduate attributes around communication and teamwork. That specifically discussing group work often emphasises the problems of group projects. The findings from the *PT&S* and *CCCS* cases suggest that close involvement of a client, in extending the scope and nature of the group to reflect industry practice, dissipates much of the perceived dysfunction. The further enlargement of the group to include project stakeholders such as technical specialists in the *PT&S* case and staff and clients of the sponsoring organisation in the *CCCS* case saw student teams focus on the challenge of communicating and working collaboratively with a diversity of people to achieve consensus on the determinants and final form of their design. The interviews indicate that interaction between experienced and novice professionals in the comparatively safe, but still challenging setting of the group capstone project (Scott-Ladd & Chan, 2008, pp. 231-232) fosters collaborative skills development around initiative, leadership, negotiation and problem-solving, preparing students for work and demonstrating that readiness to prospective employers.

Further, a complex, major group project with an external client offers authentic learning in key professional attributes for design beyond the usual body of disciplinary knowledge and skills. Effective creative and intellectual collaboration, exercising initiative, negotiation skills and perseverance came to the fore here, along with fostering future professional networks and the recognition of learning provided by completing a challenging project to a high standard to the satisfaction of a client. The following six sections present the findings in relation to Lee and Loton's (2015) six pedagogical objectives for capstone projects.

Integration and Extension of Prior Learning

For the students, prior learning spanned disciplinary knowledge gained in the first two or three years of their degree, this being consolidated and complemented for most students through the experience of practice during Industry Placement, Lee and Loton's (2015) sixth variant of capstone activity. The nature of the capstone projects required students to harness a wide range of knowledge, while extending it through the direction of a major project, a new expectation for them that amplified their existing industry experience. This was recognised by the students, Daisy commenting of her experience in *PT&S*, 'I think it was definitely good to have previous IP experience as we were building on something that we already knew about.' Lillie saw a difference in the group member without industry exposure, commenting they were 'always in the position of learning something new', where the Industry Placement students 'spoke to the client in more of a professional tone'.

In the *CCCS* case, the inclusion of research activity extended student knowledge and experience into areas new to the disciplines of communication and digital media design, reflecting an alliance of the twin imperatives of professional learning and research literacy in contemporary tertiary education. Here, Julie commented, 'Although I had done branding projects of a similar scale, they didn't have such a massive research component. I think the extra skills that were learnt such as the research component and the report writing were really beneficial.' Research for a branding project typically encompasses collecting and analysing the visual identity of competitor products or organisations. Julie's *Re.Think* team significantly expanded this by adding design workshops with staff and clients of QEC to identify major issues with the existing visual identity, ideas for a new identity and later to test design prototypes. In *PT&S*, the communication designers had their knowledge significantly extended by the interdisciplinary nature of the project, learning much about the narrative structures underpinning video and motion design. For Daisy, working in this area was an 'eye opener', especially the design constraints imposed by hypertext mark-up language (HTML), finding the opportunity to propose, question, interpret and negotiate possibilities with design colleagues from different backgrounds an important benefit of the capstone project. For Alice, working with Justin, the coding consultant, on the production of the *PT&S* app was an exceptional learning experience, commenting, 'He would work with us to develop the back end…That was a steep learning curve, but important for us to know how to work with different people and that not everything that we wanted to design could actually happen in an app'.

Consolidated learning was extended in the *CCCS* project by teams working in service and systems design—areas of design new to them—to find they were highly amenable to their design skills and knowledge. Grace, for example, discussed the use of design to reduce the complexity of gathering and managing data at QEC, commenting, 'this was an area that I've never experienced before, information systems and systems design. Getting to do it, you do see how design is logical. It makes sense that information systems would benefit from design philosophy'. The group dimension of the CCCS project was fundamental to allowing the students to tackle a large, multi-faceted project and thereby experience learning that enlarged upon a broad range of previous knowledge. For Daisy, the group work was 'challenging, but also the most rewarding part' of the unit. Important here was the perception that the group extended to organisational stakeholders, Nicole commenting, 'It wasn't until we presented all our research findings after six months and the CEO was there that it felt like we sort of crossed a trust barrier…then things became a lot easier. We felt like we were all on the same team'.

Learning how to connect with clients and work collaboratively with professionals from other fields were major skills developed. Ensuring QEC gave them sufficient access and information in the research phase required the students to act authoritatively and professionally. Julie discussed the marker of success here, commenting, 'The shift in perception about our role and our potential for change meant we'd have other staff members who we'd never met before coming up to us and giving us tips about what we need to be looking for, things they'd like to see changed and really using us as a mediator'. As the research and design activity unfolded in close collaboration with QEC staff, the students gained significant experience and confidence in professional consultancy. Mary comments, 'the client responded really well to the feedback that we gave them…they were glad that we were open and honest with them and we didn't hold back. I think it created a lot of excitement within QEC. It made all of the staff excited about the future and to start making change and being open to make change'. The main contact with QEC, Kate, confirms the first round of presentations were a turning point in the organisation's engagement with the groups due to the 'hard hitting' nature of the research results, commenting, 'You know they didn't hold back, but they did it with diplomacy…There were three teams. They all had a slightly different approach, but they all came back with very similar, well-founded themes…There was no denying the quality of the information…so I went back and presented that to the CEO.'

Being embedded in QEC to observe the work of nurses and administrators in the research phase of the project, followed by designing with staff and clients, built empathy and knowledge on both sides to enrich outcomes while giving students privileged insight into the world of work. Table 2 sets out how the students from both *CCCS* and *PT&S* perceived their knowledge and skills were applied and extended through the capstone projects, this being notable in the area of project management, synonymous with group work, where the requirement for leadership fostered new appreciation of designers' responsibility to clients and end-uses.

Table 2. Integrating and extending prior learning though project management

Student	Comments
Claudia	It was a different experience. We bought our design skills and learnt different things. The project was more about making sure we could get what we had to get done in the time, so it integrated project management learning with design.
Hugh	Higher, deeper learning in a group and trying to manage that with five other people that are your friends, but also work colleagues. Yeah, it was difficult at times, but it was exceptionally fulfilling when it came together. So it was a completely unique experience from anything we'd done at Swinburne and in IP.
Edward	It was a lot of team as well as separate sections. I was a motion designer, video person as well as a team member…where I was doing my IP, it was more one team where we worked together. It was nice heading up an element of this, then taking everyone else through it and combining as a whole.
Brett	In my industry placement, I mostly did web layout and web design…When it came this project, it was like my perfect role. I pretty much got to play with what I wanted, integrating my web knowledge with motion. Leading a specific path in the project, just focusing on the motion for this big project was awesome.
Mary	I think just the responsibility. Within a studio you might be delegated to a task that is part of the project, but with the capstone project you were required to go and meet with the client. You communicate with the client…It pushed you to think beyond the finished artwork. It made you think about how will the design impact their business. I think it's quite easy when you're in a studio situation to just design that poster or business card, but with the capstone project you really understood why you were doing it and who you were doing it for.
Nicole	I learnt a lot in unexpected ways. Managing a project involved managing people and expectations. What I found most beneficial was how to integrate research methods into the design process. In a design studio, you just need to get it done. I could never get my head around how research would work outside university. This project showed me how the research and design practice were so incredibly linked and how I could use design research within my actual studio life.
Olivia	Everybody, except for one person in our group, did Industry Placement. It was great because we knew about time frames and budgets and what sort of people we needed or where we could get things printed. If we had never done IP, we wouldn't know. Even creating all our mock-ups, we were all really quick in making everything because we knew what we were doing having already experienced this sort of thing.

Authentic and Contextualised Learning Experience

The interviews suggest that the demands and constraints of an actual project inspired student engagement. Brett, for example, commented, 'the opportunity to work on a real project with a real client – that would actually get produced – was motivational. PT&S was a project that was actually going to get made and the client was there and interested'. Daisy explained that 'we all wanted to do an awesome job. We all were passionate and we all pushed ourselves to do the best we could'. The students' Industry Placement year gave them a yardstick to judge the authenticity of professional learning, Claudia and Edward describing the experience as 'very similar to industry'. Table 3 sets out the main words the students used to describe their projects, their preference for the term 'industry' linking teaching and learning to vocational experience. Table 4 shows the extent of references to the client, the fewer mentions of Kate explained by the fact that the students had contact with many staff members in the *CCCS* project.

Underscoring the importance of direct engagement with a client to the students' regard for teaching and learning, Brett commented that although previous university assignments had been presented as 'real', the lack of client contact and feedback made him sceptical and diminished the value of the project for him. The student participants in both cases saw the need to understand what the client and other stakeholders were looking for, the context for their needs while delivering a relevant design within the

Table 3. Terms used to describe the project

Term	Frequency
'Real' project	22
Industry project	29

Table 4. Frequency of references to the client

Term	Frequency
Client	199
Fiona	54
Kate	18

timeframe as expressions of authenticity, providing incentive to focus on project goals and delivery. For Alice, this dimension saw her PT&S team getting quickly getting down to work. As she put it, 'there was no time to procrastinate.'

Lave and Wenger (1990), in their discussion of learning in communities of practice, argue that linking students' learning to their future vocation sustains and reinforces curricula. The conception, development, production and dissemination of communication and digital media design are increasingly bound up in interdisciplinary processes with a range of stakeholders, focusing design practice on managing the processes of distributed creativity and the relationships on which these are based. Modeling the interdisciplinary and multidisciplinary world the students were about to enter was perceived by students as adding to the authenticity of teaching and learning. Experience in forging the links and relationships that sustain professional life began with group formation. In both cases, the composition of design teams was the choice of the students, but all were advised to form groups with a mix of skills and interests. Even though they were in their final year of university, no student knew every other student in their class and very few knew others well. As the students negotiated who would be in each group, the capstone projects provided vital networking opportunities, an important skill in the creative industries where creative workers, especially those in freelance roles, have to constantly link with other creative workers and creative agencies to sustain a career (Lange, 2011, p. 216). Once formed, the group members needed to quickly build rapport with each other to form effective teams. Brett commented that, 'It would be good if more projects were like PT&S at university. Different people assigned to different roles, collaborating between communication designers, multimedia, film and game designing in every project'.

The pedagogical aim of the capstone units, however, was to transcend the characteristics of standard industry practice. The fact that the projects were undertaken in a university context enabled exposure to emerging and potentially disruptive trends in design, including around human relations. In the *CCCS* project in particular, working within an expanded stakeholder group over the key phases of a design project sought not only to develop job-ready skills of team work and collaboration, it aimed to prepare the students to be 'citizen designers' (Marshall, p. 2) aware of why audience needs and interests should have a strong presence in the design process, this feasibly extending to the audience members themselves. For Hugh, the extent of immersion in the design context, combined with the two semester duration of the project, made the learning feel genuine, seeing him comment, 'having that extra six months to sort of build on your proposal and the amount of new information and new approaches and attitudes that came out of it was actually quite incredible because you finished it and then you came back to it and then you built really far upon it. That was important to make it real I think, that longevity'.

Challenging and Complex Scenarios

Esteemed design educator Meredith Davis (2008) argues that most design education is lacking in emphasising know-how rather than awareness of the socio-cultural and economic relations that mould design. In 2008, the Visionary Design Council, an initiative of the American Institute of Graphic Arts, identified six emerging challenges for designers counter to design's primary involvement with the simple use or appearance of things (http://www.aiga.org/designer-of-2015-trends/). We had these six criteria in mind when choosing capstone projects, aiming to expose students to 1) meta-disciplinary design practice, requiring them to harness knowledge from diverse disciplines in order to respond to 2) the expanded scale and complexity of contemporary design projects, which demand 3) messages targeted to specific audiences due to the rise of narrow-casting and mass customization in new media, potentially achieving this through 4) co-creation approaches that involve audiences in design or robust audience research to align design with people's needs, situation and wants and 5) cut through a crowded media space to claim audiences attention, while 6) exercising leadership and ethical choices around designers' prominent role in the use of resources and influence over the nature of material and virtual environments (http://www. aiga.org/designer-of-2015-trends/).

Our findings suggest that the pedagogical value of externally-oriented capstone projects relates to their scope to foster critical insight into design by allowing students to encounter and navigate complexity, group work being valuable here in allowing students to tackle multiplex factors at scale. *PT&S* required students to investigate and make decisions around emergent technologies. It demanded they think about designing for social interaction spanning the different motivations, technological literacy and cognitive capacities of parents and children. Fiona thought an e-book was the right platform for her content. Broad and deep research by the student team into the provision of rich media through the range of available digital platforms, combined with the ways in which adults and children perceive and use technology, saw the students advise that e-books were soon to be displaced by mobile devices. In experiencing this strategic, advising role, again facilitated by the group nature of the project, the students learned that few designs today are independent entities. Learning that electronic information is famed by dynamic, technological systems while linking to people's cognitive and mental outlook highlighted the range of knowledge current designers must identify and consider (Figure 3).

Student Independence and Agency

The capstone and group work literature stresses the need to formally introduce group management practices to students. Our findings indicate that client involvement has a positive bearing on group relations, the level of conflict within the groups being minimal. The group work literature accentuates issues such as poor work ethic and participation, differences of opinion and problematical power relations in group projects and the negative affect of these on group learning and outcomes (Hellström, 2005; Kozlowski & Ilgen, 2006; O'Sullivan, Rice, Rogerson & Sauders, 2013). Only two students in the *CCCS* case discussed conflict within their team, attributing this to incompatible personalities. For both students, the active presence of the client mitigated such effects due to the need to present a unified position in

Figure 3. Stills from motion graphic section introductions and a Q&A page on the app

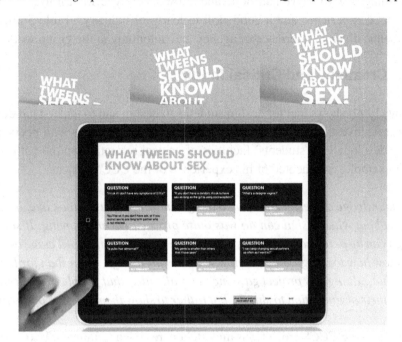

consultations and presentations. The scope and scale of the capstone projects had a similar effect, Lillie venturing that the experience was very different to group projects earlier in her degree; the need to clarify concepts and receive feedback from diverse project stakeholders encouraged the group members to take 'ownership' of project management and work as a team.

With the majority of students having worked in the design industry for a year, the students took responsibility for day-to-day management of their project. We worked in the background to support the students to experience autonomy, shoring up lines of communication and brokering expectations, perceptions and relations between clients and students. For Claudia, working on *PT&S* exposed the team's lack of knowledge in certain areas. She was aware that lecturing staff were there to provide a 'safety net', but saw working in group as equally important to being able to move outside her comfort zone into new aspects of design. Students also found the clients, carefully selected for this quality, to be nurturing and motivating. For Isabelle, as the stages of the project unfolded, the dynamics of group and client relations and the importance of their active management became apparent, suggesting the contribution of the group context to independent work-ready learning.

Themes of leadership arise throughout the interviews, with students discussing reframing questions and devising strategies to positive affect to negotiate with clients and other stakeholders around access to conduct research, project deadlines and production issues. Delegation was an important component that revealed the students taking responsibility for their actions and choices within their project teams. For Edward, sourcing expertise and delegating tasks across a range of design professionals provided experience in leadership, seeing him comment, 'the team had separate sections, so I was a motion designer, video person as well as a design team member. It was kind of nice working in that environment…having leadership roles in different areas'. Brett also commented on the experience of delegation, stating, 'it was basically just me and another student working on the motion graphics…learning how to brief him to complete something that you have half done and know where you want it to go and directing how, that was a really good experience and a good skill to learn for industry.' Table 5 provides a range of comments on students' diverse experience of agency and autonomy in the group work.

A Concern for Creativity and Critical Inquiry

A study by Ulusoy (1999) shows that for design students to design and to understand design are related, but distinct processes. Investigating the context for client needs and issues with peers and an extended stakeholder group developed the students' faculties of critical reflection on the nature and purpose of design. Hugh, for example, commented of his experience of the *CCCS* project:

There was all the knowledge on design, how to do things and what designs look like, but going into Honours and learning about what design can do was quite provocative and moving. It sort of changed my view of how design can be perceived. That was really quite a powerful thing...I came out of the third year thinking, "Aw, I know how to design. I don't know what it's for though, other than for laying out things." I knew I could do that...doing this project gave me the realisation that people are willing to have you on board and not tear their organisation to shreds, but rather to show them areas of opportunity to improve.

In the units in which the *CCCS* project was undertaken, research training and experience intertwined with designing to foster an evidence-based, evaluative approach to professional practice. Interaction with QEC staff and clients, in forming the larger stakeholder group around the project, introduced varied, sometimes conflicting factors to be navigated. It challenged the three student teams to see the people they were designing for, both QEC clients and staff, as contributors to the design process or at least an important focus within it. The extended group dimension of the project responded to the expectation that work-ready graduates will approach client problems as 'unique', exercising sound decision-making to propose innovative responses forged of advanced knowledge and thinking, not resort to formulaic solutions (Litchfield, Frawley & Nettleton, 2010, p. 523). Hugh and Julie recollect how the many conversations with QEC staff and clients helped their group to frame and refine their initial design proposal and subsequent prototype work.

Heightened awareness of the context for design though wide-ranging qualitative research highlighted the divergent behaviors, objectives and values of project stakeholders in the *CCCS* case, prompting considerable diversity of response across the teams. Critical to capitalising on the access afforded to QEC's systems and practices was the scope within each group to divide, share and reflect on activities. Grace highlighted the insight and value produced from the detailed research undertaken by the group, commenting, 'Through extensive observation of how the [admission] system worked, going through it ourselves to work out what fuels it, we worked out how many questions were being asked more than once; it was over 500 questions.' (See Figure 4) The extent of research into the design context facilitated by the group activity was important to the students' ability to apply their problem solving, critical thinking and creative skills and design knowledge later in the project. Grundin (1993, p.111) argues that 'designers... tend to be young, rationalistic, idealistic and the products of relatively homogeneous academic environments. They often have little experience or understanding of the different work situations and attitudes of the users.' This is exacerbated by the fact that orthodox design practice stresses the rapid delivery of aesthetically and conceptually resolved designs. By contrast, the *CCCS* project emphasised investment in process and the difficulty in resolving a tangle of issues in a single design.

Table 5. Experiencing independence and agency

Known Group Work Issues	Student Comments
Leadership	…in the second semester we had six people, three of whom wanted to be the leaders, all at once, and that caused a little bit of tensions at different stages, but even with that, the three of them still were very considerate of each other. (Isabelle)
Project management	this project was probably the best group I've ever worked in. This was the only one where we all managed to work together and get everything done. (Olivia)
Communication	We were really lucky. We all got along really well. We worked well as a group. We were good friends by the end of it. And we understood each other's capabilities and what each team member could bring. And, yeah, we never had any problems, like everyone was in it for the same reason and we're all relatively dedicated to the same level. (Mary)
Group dynamics	Some of the group had a lot of preconceptions about what things should be. One was very determined to do her own thing and it was a little bit difficult…I had to get her to focus. So that was a bit tricky and caused some stress, but I think we managed it well. (Grace)
Workload	I think it was a really good team project because there were five of us and we all had different strengths. I think we worked well together and made sure work was allocated evenly and for our strengths. (Claudia)
Time management	Clients have expectations. They want to see something within a week or two and you've got to put it together. In non-client projects, procrastination comes into it as well, but working for a client, things just need to get done. (Daisy)
Compromise	This was the first time I had to work with a group and compromise on certain things because of budget and timelines. The project was definitely about compromise for most of us…because we're working with other people and not designing things for ourselves. (Alice)

Figure 4. Visual summary of research findings regarding the questions asked of clients

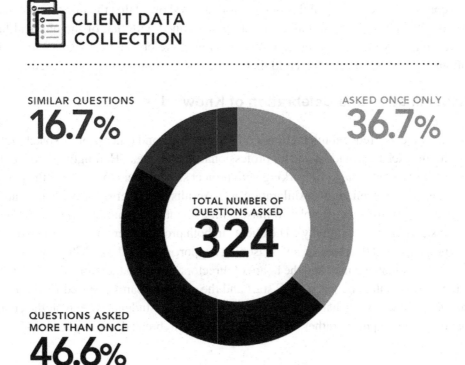

The introduction of reflexivity into the design process through the addition of research was frame changing at times. After experiencing the admissions process themselves, Grace's *Initiate* team recognised that the extent and repetition of questions, combined with the very direct nature was needless and poorly timed in coinciding with clients' first real contact with the organisation. The research activity stressed the students' responsibility as designers to go beyond visual appearance to find ways to imbue the gathering of patient information with positive values, including by acknowledging the diverse background of clients. Julie, for example, commented on interacting with QEC's refugee clients, explaining how she 'learnt a lot about lifestyle norms…it wasn't about you must do things our way, the western way…I supposed I'd never thought about it before. They're coming here. They want to learn our ways, but what can we learn from them? That was really rewarding for me to change my way of thinking and create that bond with the Sudanese women'. Working as a team to understand the needs and expectations of people with backgrounds very different to their own through immersion in an context far removed from the design studio addressed the criticism that a shortcoming of graduates in many professional fields is a lack of 'worldliness' (Litchfield, Frawley & Nettleton 2010, p. 522).

A range of writers argue that consulting or conducting meaningful research enhances design outcomes (Chu, Paul, & Ruel, 2009; Cooke, 2006), boosts creativity (Storkerson, 2006) and validates design decisions and outcomes from the perspective of clients and end-users (Bolton & Green, 2007), raising graphic design's credibility as a discipline (Bennett, 2006). In the *CCCS* project, the extent and depth of the groups' research prompted both insight and creativity, producing varied ideas to develop more client-centred processes at QEC. Initiate provided a blueprint for streamlining admission and communications, rebuilding the admissions process around a welcome pack received before arrival. Weaving Diversity found that a one-size-fits-all approach to communications neglected the differences in cultural perspectives and needs between clients in their different engagements with the organisation. They chose to focus on the needs of specific client groups, using redesigned visual communications to weave cultural diversity into communications. Re.Think's design workshops showed that the institutional look and feel of visual identity and printed and digital information, combined with that of the physical facility saw clients experience the organisation as anonymous. *Re.Think* developed a new visual identity emphasising the relationship between parent and child that staff could customise to express their individuality.

Active Dissemination and Celebration of Knowledge

In both capstone projects, frequent interaction with peers, clients and other project stakeholders offered opportunities for the exchange of ideas and for professional development. Hanington (2007, p. 14) reports design students' initial nervousness in working with project stakeholders to establish the parameters for design, but the subsequent feelings of 'exhilaration at the results that emerge from dynamic and inspiring research sessions'. For Olivia, being able 'to liaise with a client first hand' enabled her to demonstrate skills and understanding 'professionally'. The clients in both projects were highly responsive to the students' design proposals and the research and reasoning supporting it. In the CCCS project, presentations to general staff, senior management and the board of directors validated the groups' efforts and abilities. Kate noted how close contact between QEC staff and the students teams inspired long serving staff to embrace change, commenting 'what we found was as soon as the students were in at the centre and the staff saw that they were inquiring rather than telling, it started to break down any fears and we got much more support from staff'. For Hugh, presenting their final design prototypes proposal to a board meeting at the end of the year-long project was highly affirming, showing that QEC 'clearly valued the research and by that point knew that what we were doing was useful, not just a university project. We were giving them proper insights into their organisation and areas that they could improve on'.

Innovation motivated Fiona to work with students on *PT&S*, as reflected in her comment, 'I wanted creative, fresh thinkers. I didn't want them to copy what had been done. I wanted them to be able to think entirely outside the box'. The students' creativity exceeded her expectations. She found the Week Four presentations of early proposals exhilarating, explaining, 'it was this extraordinary thing, a physiological process I could identify. I was so overwhelmed I actually started to hyperventilate. They had taken this idea of mine and represented it in seven different contexts. It was awesome'. Despite initial hesitation regarding too much client involvement—reflecting the design industry's frequent disdain for clients—Fiona's positive endorsement of the students' work motivated the successful team to strive for excellence. Fiona reported that close contact with the students fostered knowledge flow in both directions, enabling all to experience ownership of the design process. She commented, 'it gave me an opportunity to be curious myself, not to impose something, to work with, to suggest, to complement, rather than to dictate or be dictated to. It was a very unique situation. It was a true collaboration'.

The projects discussed here have been or are in the process of being implemented in whole or in part. *PT&S* was officially launched in April 2013 at an event attended by specialists in health, design and education and the media. The project received an excellence award at the Faculty graduate exhibition (2012) and through selection as a finalist in the Victorian Premier's Design Awards (2013). The app is being used in schools nationally and internationally and can be purchased through iTunes. Four years later, Edward still includes video material from *PT&S* in his professional show reel, leveraging the awards *PT&S* received to stress the professional endorsement of his abilities. On graduation, the Re.Think team formed a design consultancy to develop their branding proposal for implementation by QEC, allowing a group of junior designers to work at a level and scale suggestive of senior designers in leading design consultancies. The client implemented key aspects of the other CCCS team's work, with some instigated during the course of the project.

The students from both cases used their project to launch their careers. Kate became a referee in Isabelle's résumé. Hugh and Nicole put their capstone project first in their portfolios to demonstrate their design abilities and experience in design leadership and collaboration with clients, peers and other knowledge specialist. For Alice, now an account manager in advertising, the close work with a client alerted her to the potential in a strategic rather than a 'hands-on' involvement in design. She commented that 'working directly with Fiona...presenting ideas and explaining the background, rather than the designing was more interesting to me. That was a massive turning point. I don't really know if I would have ended up where I am if I didn't work in this project'. Mary and Claudia's gravitation to client liaison organisational and leadership roles in their respective teams steered them towards design management roles on graduation. Looking back, Brett regards PT&S as a 'good opportunity to define his future direction.' Having a major, high quality project in his graduate portfolio allowed him to move into his desired field of motion graphics with an internationally-renowned creative agency. For Daisy, presenting the PT&S app on an iPad in interviews showed she could produce an impressive, commercial product. She commented that, 'a lot of people interviewing me thought PARENTS, TWEENS AND SEX was brilliant and that they wouldn't expect that sort of project to be done through university'.

FUTURE RESEARCH

This paper has compared two case studies on externally-oriented group projects with the six pedagogical objectives that Lee and Loton (2015) identify as attributes of capstone projects. The findings highlight that a more authentic experience within a design context motivates and inspires the students. Greater accessibility to the client provides autonomy and leadership opportunities and in these cases dissolved many of the issues pertaining to group projects. Although Lee and Lotan (2015) define six types of capstone project, this study focuses on one type with overlapping attributes from other capstone projects. Given our findings, there are many factors that could be applied to the development of authentic group projects in the earlier years of undergraduate design education, such as client engagement, delegation, leadership, autonomy and communication. In regard to the other types of capstone projects, future studies should address the authenticity of any group project and specifically investigate under what circumstances a project becomes authentic from a student perspective.

CONCLUSION

This chapter has discussed the content and pedagogy of professional design curricula with a focus on the value of group work within the context of capstone units at Honours level. Becoming an experienced and effective practitioner requires relevant skills and knowledge and the ability to apply them in real situations, group projects offering contextualised work-ready learning around teamwork, collaboration, communication and leadership. As we have shown, using externally-oriented projects that introduce clients and other stakeholders into the mix expands the constitution and sense of the group for students, with positive benefits for group cohesion and productivity and the development of students' professional skills and attributes. For design students, interaction with diverse project stakeholders has the specific added benefit of developing their consideration of the context for and recipients of design in the design process, a growing expectation for all designers.

In Australian universities, an Honours year is mostly a pathway to a research degree (Kiley, Boud, Cantwell & Manathunga 2009, p. 2). Outside the areas of science and technology, research training in Honours typically focuses on individual scholarship rather than group activity or broader skills development around graduate employability through the application of research skills and knowledge in industry and community contexts (Blaj-Ward, 2011). As a vocationally-oriented field, the Honours year in design education often departs from this model to focus on deeper engagement with disciplinary practices to the exclusion of research training and critical engagement with design. Despite the collaborative nature of contemporary communication design and digital media design practice, group projects are often not included at Honours because of problems in establishing individual team member's contribution when group projects are included in graduate's portfolios or entered for graduate design awards.

Offering research experience as professional learning to design students has potential benefits for design, a vocational field where knowledge is mostly practice-driven, with designers lacking access to systematically produced evidence to support decision-making. What stands as research in design is often a by-product of the rapid turnover of designs in the marketplace, designers being trained to find the unique points of differentiation in a project by quickly surveying competitors' offerings. This path presents problems for the design industry. Bolton and Green (2007, p. 6) identify a lack of recognition of design's scope to deliver value to the market and end users with clients often seeing design as a basic, undemanding craft that adds costs, not an intellectual or professional activity that creates economic, cultural and social value. The capstone units in which the *PT&S* and *CCCS* projects took place were framed to consciously close this gap by having students follow a research-informed design process to develop explicitly articulated and evidenced design proposals. Producing deep and robust insight into the multi-dimensional facets of a complex design project is by nature a group activity. The requirement to consult or conduct research, combined with a major, client-supplied project and the interaction of peers and diverse project stakeholders formed a challenging context in which students were enabled to rehearse and reflect on the nature of contemporary design practice and its emergent trends.

Within both projects, student teams became agents of innovation in productively adapting emerging design methods and thinking to a context formed of client and end-user needs and issues. This experience positioned the students to transfer vital practical and theoretical knowledge to industry on graduation. The primary innovation in the *CCCS* project was the use of research-led designing, rare in design practice for a range of reasons including a lack training in research processes, constrained budgets and time lines to attitudes about design and designers. The addition of robust contextual and audience research in the *CCCS* project saw design less focused on material outcomes and more on using design to develop a caring and collaborative communications and service culture for their client. In the *PT&S* project, extensive secondary research into media platforms and human-computer interaction extended the students' engagement with design, showing that design is not a fixed thing, but rather involves continual exploration, analysis and adaption, the success of projects for clients depending on this.

In both case studies, group work was critical to enabling the scope, depth and authenticity of learning and outcomes. The students' comments show that externally-oriented, group capstone projects consolidate skills and knowledge in multiple dimensions while fostering the development of higher professional attributes such as self-awareness and the capacity to learn and grow from experience. Neff, Wissinger and Zukin (2005) argue that employment in creative industries requires significant intellectual independence and self-investment, early career designers needing to quickly show they have the right stuff in terms of disciplinary and professional aptitudes, with interpersonal skills being a priority. The capstone projects described here were challenging, but enabled the students to develop and demonstrate heightened awareness of the changing nature of design practice, including the need to communicate and collaborate with a range of people and the capacity to be innovative, open-minded and reflective. Navigating varied stakeholder requirements and preferences as a team, without the insulating abstraction of a pre-determined design brief, to shape new solutions for socially progressive ends saw the potential difficulties in group work set aside for higher purposes to the students' benefit.

REFERENCES

Alpay, E. (2005). Group dynamic processes in email groups. *Active Learning in Higher Education*, *6*(1), 7–16. doi:10.1177/1469787405049942

Ball, L. (2002). Preparing graduates in art and design to meet the challenges of working in the creative industries: A new model for work. *Art. Design & Communication in Higher Education*, *1*(1), 10–24. doi:10.1386/adch.1.1.10

Blaj-Ward, L. (2011). Skills versus pedagogy? Doctoral research training in the UK Arts and Humanities. *Higher Education Research & Development*, *30*(6), 697–708. doi:10.1080/07294360.2010.535507

Bolton, S., & Green, L. (2007). *Getting Design Off the Substitute Bench: Reframing and realigning design processes for the business development game. Emerging Trends in Design Research.* International Association of Societies of Design Research, The Hong Kong Polytechnic University School of Design.

Cano, J. L., Lidon, I., Rebollar, R., Roman, P., & Saenz, M. J. (2006). Student groups solving real-life projects. A case study of experiential learning. *International Journal of Engineering Education, 22*(6), 1252–1260.

Carson, L. (2006). Raising the Bar on Criticality: Students' Critical Reflection in an Internship Program. *Journal of Management Education, 30*(5), 700–723. doi:10.1177/1052562905284962

Chapman, K. J. (2006). Can't We Pick our Own Groups? The Influence of Group Selection Method on Group Dynamics and Outcomes. *Journal of Management Education, 30*(4), 557–569. doi:10.1177/1052562905284872

Chiu, S. H. (2010). Students' knowledge sources and knowledge sharing in the design studio-an exploratory study. *International Journal of Technology and Design Education, 20*(1), 27–42. doi:10.1007/s10798-008-9061-9

Costigan, R. D., John, S., & College, F. (2009). Developing The Great Eight Competencies with Leaderless Group Discussion. *Journal of Management Education, 33*(5), 596–616. doi:10.1177/1052562908318328

Cox, G. (2005). *Cox Review of Creativity in Business: Building on the UK's Strengths.* London: HM Treasury.

Crabbe, A. (2008). The value of knowledge transfer collaborations to design academics. *Design Journal, 11*(1), 9–28. doi:10.2752/175630608X317887

Crawford, C. (2005). *Chris Crawford on interactive storytelling.* Berkeley, CA: New Riders.

Davis, M. (2008). Toto, I've Got a Feeling We're Not in Kansas Anymore…. *Interaction, 15*(5), 29–34.

De Janasz, S. C., & Forret, M. L. (2007). Learning The Art of Networking: A Critical Skill for Enhancing Social Capital and Career Success. *Journal of Management Education, 32*(5), 629–650. doi:10.1177/1052562907307637

Denton, H., & McDonagh, D. (2005). An exercise in symbiosis: Undergraduate designers and a company product development team working together. *Design Journal, 8*(1), 41–50. doi:10.2752/146069205789338315

Deuze, M. (2007). *Media Work.* Cambridge: Polity Press.

Drucker, J., & McVarish, E. (2009). *Graphic design history: A critical guide.* Upper Saddle River, NJ: Pearson Prentice Hall.

Evans, M., & Spruce, J. (2005, September 15-16). Knowledge Networks: Collaboration between Industry and Academia in Design. *Proceedings for the Engineering and Product Design Education Conference.* Napier University, Edinburgh, UK.

Fellenz, M. R. (2006). Toward Fairness in Assessing Student Groupwork: A Protocol for Peer Evaluation of Individual Contributions. *Journal of Management Education, 30*(4), 570–591. doi:10.1177/1052562906286713

Ferrante, C. J., Green, S. G., & Forster, W. R. (2006). Getting More out of Team Projects: Incentivizing Leadership to Enhance Performance. *Journal of Management Education, 30*(6), 788–797. doi:10.1177/1052562906287968

Folger, J. P., Pooles, M. S., & Stutman, R. K. (2009). *Working through conflict: Strategies for relationships, groups, and organizations.* Pearson Education.

Ganser, C., Kennel, T., & Kunz, A. (2007). Digital support for net-based teamwork in early design stages. *Journal of Desert Research, 6*(1/2), 150. doi:10.1504/JDR.2007.015567

Griffiths, R. (2004). Knowledge production and the research-teaching nexus: The case of the built environment disciplines. *Studies in Higher Education, 29*(6), 709–726. doi:10.1080/0307507042000287212

Grudin, J. (1993). Obstacles to Participatory Design in Large Product Development Organizations. In D. Schuler & A. Namioka (Eds.), *Participatory Design: Principles and practices* (pp. 99–122). New Jersey: Lawrence Erlbaum Associates.

Halls, J. (2005). Theory wrapped in context: Bridges between academic and industrial worlds. *Industrial and Commercial Training, 37*(6), 279–285. doi:10.1108/00197850510617541

Hanington, B. (2007). *Generative Research in Design Education. Emerging Trends in Design Research.* International Association of Societies of Design Research, The Hong Kong Polytechnic University School of Design.

Hauhart, R. C., & Grahe, J. E. (2010). The Undergraduate Capstone Course in the Social Sciences: Results from a Regional Survey. *Teaching Sociology, 38*(1), 4–17. doi:10.1177/0092055X09353884

Healey, M., & Jenkins, A. (2006). Strengthening the teaching-research linkage in undergraduate courses and programmes. In C. Kreber (Ed.), *Exploring Research-based Teaching* (pp. 45–55). San Francisco: Wiley.

Healey, M., & Jenkins, A. (2009). Developing undergraduate research and inquiry. York: Higher Education Academy. Retrieved from http://www.heacademy.ac.uk/assets/York/documents/resources/publications/DevelopingUndergraduateFinal.pdf

Hellström, T. (2005). Role-Taking, Role-Breaking and Role-Shaking Amongst Designers: A Qualitative Study of a Team Effort. *The Design Journal: An International Journal for All Aspects of Design, 8*(2), 25–37. doi:10.2752/146069205789331592

Hellström, T. (2007). The individual vs. the group? Individualization and collectivity among students in collaborative design. *International Journal of Technology and Design Education, 17*(3), 305–321. doi:10.1007/s10798-006-9004-2

Hillyard, C., Gillespie, D., & Littig, P. (2010). University students' attitudes about learning in small groups after frequent participation. *Active Learning in Higher Education, 11*(1), 9–20. doi:10.1177/1469787409355867

Inamdar, S. N., & Roldan, M. (2013). The MBA Capstone Course: Building Theoretical, Practical, Applied, and Reflective Skills. *Journal of Management Education, 37*(6), 747–770. doi:10.1177/1052562912474895

Inns, T., Baxter, S., & Murphy, E. (2006). Transfer or Emergence: Strategies for Building Design Knowledge Through Knowledge Transfer Partnerships. *The Design Journal*, *9*(3), 34–44. doi:10.2752/146069206789331429

Jerrard, B. (2006). Design-based knowledge transfer partnerships. *Design Journal*, *9*(3), 1–2. doi:10.2752/146069206789331410

Kachra, A., & Schnietz, K. (2008). The Capstone Strategy Course: What Might Real Integration look like? *Journal of Management Education*, *32*(4), 476–508. doi:10.1177/1052562907300811

Kemery, E. R., & Stickney, L. T. (2014). A Multifaceted Approach to Teamwork Assessment in an Undergraduate Business Program. *Journal of Management Education*, *38*(3), 462–479. doi:10.1177/1052562913504762

Kern, A. (2006). *Survey Results Reveal What the Industry Really Expects from Graduates.* Retrieved from http://www.aiga.org/content.cfm/survey-results-reveal-what-the-industry-really-expects-from-graduates

Kiernan, L., & Ledwith, A. (2014). Is Design Education Preparing Product Designers for the Real World? A Study of Product Design Graduates in Ireland. *The Design Journal: An International Journal for All Aspects of Design*, *17*(2), 218–237. doi:10.2752/175630614X13915240576022

Kiley, M., Boud, D., Cantwell, R., & Manathunga, C. 2009. *The Role of Honours in Contemporary Australian Higher Education,* A report commissioned by the Australian Learning and Teaching Council Ltd, an initiative of the Australian Government Department of Education, Employment and Workplace Relations. Retrieved from http://www.aushons.anu.edu.au

Kolb, J. A. (2013). Conflict management principles for groups and teams. *Industrial and Commercial Training*, *45*(2), 79–86. doi:10.1108/00197851311309516

Kolb, J. A., & Rothwell, W. J. (2000). Challenges and Problems Reported by Small Group Facilitators. *Performance Improvement Quarterly.*, *13*(4), 122–136. doi:10.1111/j.1937-8327.2000.tb00195.x

Kozlowski, S., & Ilgen, D. (2006). Enhancing the Effectiveness of Work Groups and Teams. *Psychological Science in the Public Interest*, *7*(3), 77–124. PMID:26158912

Kvale, S. (1996). *Interviews: An introduction to qualitative research interviewing.* Thousand Oaks, CA: SAGE.

Lange, B. (2011). Professionalization in space: Social-spatial strategies of culturepreneurs in Berlin. *Entrepreneurship & Regional Development*, *23*(3–4), 259–279. doi:10.1080/08985620903233978

Lave, J., & Wenger, E. (1990). *Situated learning: Legitimate peripheral participation.* Cambridge: Cambridge University Press.

Lee, N. (2009). Project methods as the vehicle for learning in undergraduate design education: A typology. *Design Studies*, *30*(5), 541–560. doi:10.1016/j.destud.2009.03.002

Lee, N., & Loton, D. (Eds.). (2015) *The Capstone Principles.* Retrieved from http://www.capstonecurriculum.com.au/the-capstone-principles/

Levine, A. (1998). A president's personal and historical perspective. In J. Gardner & G. Van der Veer et al. (Eds.), *The senior year experience: Facilitating integration, reflection, closure, and transition* (pp. 51–59). San Francisco: Jossey-Bass.

Litchfield, A., Frawley, J., & Nettleton, S. (2010). Contextualising and integrating into the curriculum the learning and teaching of work-ready professional graduate attributes. *Higher Education Research & Development, 29*(5), 519–534. doi:10.1080/07294360.2010.502220

Lupton, E. (2006). 2004]). The Birth of the User. In M. Bierut, W. Drenttel, & S. Heller (Eds.), *Looking closer five: Critical writings on graphic design* (pp. 23–25). New York: Allworth Press.

Marsden, K., & Luczkowski, J. (2005). Implementing work-based learning within masters' courses in design: A research evaluation of curriculum. *Art. Design & Communication in Higher Education, 4*(2), 135–146. doi:10.1386/adch.4.2.135/7

Marshall, T. (2009, January). *Designing design education.* Retrieved from http://www.icograda.org/education/education/articles1397.htm

McCarthy, M. (2015). Clear and Nishi. *Design + Business.Lecture presented at theAustralian Graphic Design Association (AGDA) business series.*

McCoy, K. (1995). Graphic Design in a Multicultural Word. In A. Bennett (Ed.), *Design studies: theory and research in graphic design* (pp. 200–205). New York: Princeton Architectural Press.

McNamara, J., Kift, S. M., Butler, D., Field, R. M., Brown, C., & Gamble, N. (2012). Work-integrated learning as a component of the capstone experience in undergraduate law. *Asia-Pacific Journal of Co-operative Education, 13*(1), 1–12.

Mendoza, H. R., Bernasconi, C., & MacDonald, N. M. (2007). Creating new identities in design education. *International Journal of Art & Design Education, 26*(3), 308–313. doi:10.1111/j.1476-8070.2007.00541.x

Myerson, J., & Vickers, G. (2002). *Rewind 40 years of design and advertising.* London: Phaidon.

Neff, G., Wissinger, E., & Zukin, S. (2005). Entrepreneurial Labor among Cultural Producers: ''Cool'' Jobs in ''Hot'' Industries'. *Social Semiotics, 15*(3), 307–334. doi:10.1080/10350330500310111

Nettleton, S., Litchfield, A., & Taylor, T. (2008). Engaging professional societies in developing work-ready graduates.*Proceedings of the 31st Annual International HERDSA Conference*, Rotorua, New Zealand, (pp. 241–251)

O'Sullivan, T., Rice, J., Rogerson, S., & Saunders, C. (2013). *Successful Group Work A Practical Guide for Students in Further and Higher Education.* Hoboken, NJ: Taylor and Francis.

Phillips, A. (2005). Working in groups in an international publishing class. *Art. Design & Communication in Higher Education, 4*(3), 173–187. doi:10.1386/adch.4.3.173/1

Rafferty, P. D. (2012). Group Work in the MBA Classroom: Improving Pedagogical Practice and Maximizing Positive Outcomes With Part-Time MBA Students. *Journal of Management Education, 37*(5), 623–650. doi:10.1177/1052562912458644

Ragin, C. C. (2013). *The comparative method: Moving beyond qualitative and quantitative strategies: with a new introduction*. Oakland, CA: University of California Press.

Roberts, J. L. (2007). *The Future of Academic-Industry Collaboration. Presented* at IASDR07, International Association of Societies of Design Research. Hong Kong Poly Technic University, November.

Robinson, D. F., Shersood, A. L., & Depaolo, C. A. (2010). Service-Learning by Doing. *Journal of Management Education, 34*(1), 88–112. doi:10.1177/1052562909339025

Rothwell, W. J., & Kolb, J. A. (1999). Major workforce and workplace trends influencing the training and development field in the USA. *International Journal of Training and Development, 3*(1), 44–53. doi:10.1111/1468-2419.00063

Sampson, J., & Cohen, R. (2014). In D. Boud, R. Cohen & J. Sampson (Eds.), Peer learning in higher education: learning from and with each other.

Sargent, L. D., Allen, B. C., Frahm, J., & Morris, G. (2009). Enhancing the Experience of Student Teams in Large Classes: Training Teaching Assistants to be Coaches. *Journal of Management Education, 33*(5), 526–552. doi:10.1177/1052562909334092

Sawyer, K. (2007). *Group Genius: The Creative Power of Collaboration*. Cambridge, MA: Basic Books.

Scott-Ladd, B., & Chan, C. A. (2008). Using action research to teach students to manage team learning and improve teamwork satisfaction. *Active Learning in Higher Education, 9*(3), 231–248. doi:10.1177/1469787408095848

Sill, D., Harwood, M., & Cooper, I. (2009). The Disorienting: The senior capstone as a transformative experience. *Liberal Education, 95*(3).

Strauss, A., & Corbin, J. (1998). *Basics of qualitative research* (2nd ed.). Thousand Oaks, CA: SAGE.

Surowiecki, J. (2004). *The wisdom of crowds: why the many are smarter than the few and how collective wisdom shapes business, economies, societies, and nations*. New York: Doubleday.

Sutliff, K. (2000). Integrating Academics and Industry: A Challenge for Both Sides. *ACM Journal of Computer Documentation, 24*(1), 33–38.

The Boyer Commission on Educating Undergraduates in the Research University. (1998). *Reinventing Undergraduate Education: A Blueprint for America's Research Universities*. Princeton: Carnegie Foundation for the Advancement of Teaching. Retrieved from http://naples.cc.sunysb.edu/Pres/boyer.nsf/

Thornton, C. (2010). *Group & Team Coaching The Essential Guide*. Hoboken, NJ: Taylor and Francis.

Tynan, J., & New, C. (2009). Creativity and Conflict: How theory and practice shape student identities in design education. *Arts and Humanities in Higher Education, 8*(3), 295–308. doi:10.1177/1474022209339959

Ulusoy, Z. (1999). To Design Versus to Understand Design: The role of graphic representations and verbal expressions. *Design Studies, 20*(2), 123–130. doi:10.1016/S0142-694X(98)00030-1

Wageman, R., & Frederick, M. G. (2005). As the Twig is Bent: How Group Values Shape Emergent Task Interdependence in Groups. *Organization Science, 16*(6), 687–722. doi:10.1287/orsc.1050.0146

Walker, S. (2008). Following Will-O'-The-Wisps and Chasing Ghosts: Design-Centred Research, Sustainability and the Bottom Line. *The Design Journal: An International Journal for All Aspects of Design*, *11*(1), 51–64. doi:10.2752/175630608X317904

Webb, M. (2012). *Outduction: Enhancing the final year experience. Final report to the HE Academy.* Kingston: Kingston University.

Whyte, J., Bessant, J. (2007). *Making the most of UK design excellence: equipping UK designers to succeed in the global economy.* Tanaka Business School, Imperial College London.

Willcoxson, L. E. (2006). "It's not Fair!": Assessing the Dynamics and Resourcing of Teamwork. *Journal of Management Education*, *30*(6), 798–808. doi:10.1177/1052562906287964

Wodehouse, A., & Maclachlan, R. (2014). An Exploratory Model for Understanding Culture in Student Design Team Idea Generation. *The Design Journal*, *17*(4), 488–514. doi:10.2752/17563061 4X14056185479980

Yazici, H. J. (2005). 'A Study of Collaborative Learning Style and Team Learning Performance'. *Education + Training*, *47*(2/3), 216–229. doi:10.1108/00400910510592257

Ylikoski, T., & Kortelainen, M. J. (2012). A new approach for managing university-workplace partnerships. *Industrial and Commercial Training*, *44*(6), 349–356. doi:10.1108/00197851211254798

Chapter 15
Identity Transformation through Collaboration:
Narratives of 'Becoming an Architect'

James Thompson
University of Washington, USA

ABSTRACT

Presenting narratives of three recent graduates of a U.S. Master of Architecture program, this study employs an interpretative-narrative approach to access and evoke the role that collaboration plays in the process of 'becoming a design professional'. Whereas ontological learning has been recognized as fundamental to life-long learning and development, research has yet to explore themes of self-authorship in relation to collaborative design experiences. In representing authentic voices of learners, the research presented in this chapter contributes to a deeper understanding of the ways in which aspiring design professionals make sense of their transformation from academic to professional selves. This will ultimately inform how design educators value and structure team-based design projects by providing a more holistic understanding of the role such projects might play in shaping individuals' identities.

More than in many other jobs, being a successful architect means not only knowing but being. (Stevens, 1999: p. 55)

INTRODUCTION

Educators, scholars, and professional bodies have long been concerned with the transition from school to work, from the standpoints of competency, socialization, and the public good (see Boyer & Mitgang, 1996; Merton, 1968; Tierney & Bensimon, 1996). This passage from disciplinary outsider to member is a critical period of meaning-making and introspection during which aspiring professionals are con-

DOI: 10.4018/978-1-5225-0726-0.ch015

fronted with questions of who they are and who they wish to become (see Baxter Magolda, 2001; Case, 2013; Chickering, 1969). Sullivan (2012, p. 104) writes, "Professional education presents students with the knowledge, skills, and purpose of the field they seek to learn. It also frames how students relate the demands and possibilities of the profession to their developing sense of self and purpose." Thus, professional education marks a period when students undergo marked changes to their 'ways of being' (see Barnett, 2000; Sandberg & Pinnington, 2009). Supporting and encouraging this process of transformation, which educational theorists call 'ontological development', is increasingly considered a primary aim of higher education across disciplines (see Barnett, 2000; 2004; Baxter Magolda, 2001; Dall'Alba & Barnacle, 2007; Hanson, 2014; Harrell-Levy & Kerpelman, 2010).

The potential 'transfer of learning' from academic to professional contexts is one of the most commonly touted benefits of collaboration in higher education (see Cuseo, 1996; Ettington & Camp, 2002). Ettington and Camp (2002) argue that students need to perceive the relevance of collaboration in order to transfer teamwork skills from the classroom to professional applications. Student perceptions toward collaboration is thus a chief concern for educators and professional bodies alike. As Gale, Martin, Martin, & Duffey (2014, p. 27) warn: "Negative attitudes toward collaborative learning could have a significant impact on the success of emerging professionals." However, prior studies on this topic in design-based fields are not designed to examine how collaborative learning experiences contribute to ontological development within students' broader life histories. Using primarily questionnaires, they tend to consider student attitudes only within the scope of specific courses, projects, or learning outcomes (see Byun, Kim, & Duffey, 2012; Gale et al., 2014; Hynes, 2015; Kim, LaFleur, & Schaeffer, 2008; Russ & Dickinson, 1999; Webb & Miller, 2006). The study presented in this chapter takes a holistic, phenomenological approach by exploring what role collaborative experiences play in wider narratives of self that constitute the process of 'becoming a design professional.' This follows Hanson's (2014, p. 8) claim that,

Any thorough study of how people change in college would seem to require an analysis of the narratives that students use to develop identities—a sense of what they were like before they started and how they became during the course of their education.

In this ongoing study, recent graduates of a Master of Architecture (M.Arch) program based in the United States participated in a series of in-depth interviews that sought to situate graduate school experiences within personal life histories. Adopting an interpretative approach informed by interdisciplinary theories of ontological learning, student agency, and narrative identity, analysis procedures ultimately produced a series of passages evoking the transformative potential of designing in teams. Thus, results from this study suggest ways in which narrative reflections of collaborative learning experiences can prompt transformations of self-identity. This work builds upon scholars' attempts to better understand and promote ontological development amongst undergraduates in liberal arts contexts using the concept of 'self-authorship' (see Barber, King, & Baxter Magolda, 2013; Baxter Magolda, 2001; Case, in press; Pizzolato, 2003; Torres & Hernandez, 2007). While further research is required to convincingly link collaborative learning to the development of self-authorship in aspiring design professionals, this project serves as a revealing graduate-level and professional case study and opens up a promising area for scholarship on design education.

BACKGROUND

The uncertain and complex challenges associated with contemporary life have prompted scholars in the field of education to call for an 'ontological turn' in higher education (see Barnett 2012; Dall'Alba & Barnacle, 2007). As these scholars argue, epistemological qualities alone (i.e., knowledge and skills) are considered inadequate for becoming successful citizen-practitioners. Barber et al. (2013, p. 867) argue: "The complex challenges college graduates face are not just technical challenges that require skill acquisition but adaptive challenges that require transforming one's mindset to a more complex way of making meaning." Or as Sandberg and Pinnington (2009, p. 1162) put it, professional competence "is not primarily defined by scientific knowledge, tacit knowledge, knowing-in-action, understanding of work or practice as such. Instead, professional competence is constituted by specific ways of being." In reconsidering curricular and pedagogical aims of universities, learning is conceptualized broadly as primarily a process of meaning-making intended to foster critical thinking and self-authorship (Kegan, 1994). A separate but related area of research suggests that a chief means by which individuals construct meaning from their experiences is through narratives of self (see Eakin, 2008; McAdams, 1993; Somers, 1994; Wortham, 2001). This section briefly reviews aspects of self-authorship and narrative identity that informed the present study, as well as how these concepts relate to design education and collaboration, specifically.

Identity and Self-Authorship in Higher Education

For decades, social scientists in sociology, anthropology, psychology, social work, and education have concerned themselves with how individuals construct meaning from life events, as well as how one's identity develops over various life stages (Goodson, 2001). In an early attempt to theorize the transformation of college students, Chickering (1969) posited seven major dimensions of development: competence, emotions, autonomy, identity, interpersonal relationships, purpose, and integrity. Together, these qualities foreground student experience and wellbeing within higher education contexts. In the process of 'learning', students are "actively experimenting with and consolidating a sense of identity: who they are, what they can do well, what is important to them, how they want others to see them, and so forth" (King & Kitchener, 1994, p. 203). Based on their personal life histories, as well as self-assessments of their learning and development, students cognitively develop 'identity horizons' to reconcile their professional goals with their emerging sense of self (Côté, Skinkle, & Motte, 2008). This raises questions regarding how educators might support and encourage processes of self-knowing. The notion of self-authorship provides a conceptual and analytical framework for linking meaning-making and development across cognitive, intrapersonal, and interpersonal domains to narratives of personal experience (see Baxter Magolda, 2001; Kegan, 1994). According to Barber et al. (2013, p. 868), self-authorship is "the internal capacity to define one's beliefs, values, identity, and social relations, thus taking responsibility for one's actions and life decisions, not simply relying on the advice or actions of others." The authors expound further on their definition:

Individuals who are 'self-authoring' consider multiple perspectives, reflect on their own values and motivations, and utilize goals and perspectives that are internally grounded and evaluated as a foundation for meaning making. (pp. 869-70)

Connecting the concept to the broader purpose of higher education, *Case (in press*, p. 1) writes:

Self-authorship as a goal for the university student is centred on building a person who can align their intellectual growth with their personal and social commitments, and thus take up the roles in society that might be expected of a college graduate.

Longitudinal studies using in-school and post-graduation interviews have found that, whereas self-authorship development rarely occurs in the timeframe of college itself, it can be detected over time by considering learning more holistically across life history contexts (see Baxter Magolda, 1992; 2001). Qualitative analysis revealed that certain students underwent 'developmentally effective experiences', expressed in particular by a shift from an external to an internal voice (Barber et al., 2013). Other themes tied to self-authorship included a sense of belonging and peer support, working through personal difficulties, and experiencing dissonance in terms of one's worldview. In relating narratives of student experience to an individual's ontological development, we can begin to see what this type of research might offer educators seeking to improve teaching and learning practices:

Understanding the factors that trigger these substantial shifts could help faculty design more powerful learning experiences [and]…help administrators make decisions about supporting educational initiatives… (Barber et al., 2013, pp. 868-9)

We also might begin to imagine the potential ways that team-based activities might be involved in the development of self-authorship, given the typical features of collaborative design processes and experiences. For instance, students might engage in certain modes of professional role-playing, allowing them to compare their present and possible future selves. Or they might encounter diverse and/or incompatible worldviews and social commitments, prompting them to reflect upon their own. The present study seeks to explore this possible relationship between collaborative experiences and aspiring design professionals' developing senses of self.

The Role of Narrative

The work presented in this chapter presumes a certain role of narrative and storytelling in the everyday lives of individuals and learning communities. First, as the late Marco Frascari (2012, p. 228) argues, "The education of architects has always followed a curriculum based on storytelling." Indeed, storytelling represents a central element of design culture, used by students and practitioners alike: from developing user scenarios as part of the design process (Parkinson & Bohemia, 2012a), to constructing narratives as a way of making sense of or explaining one's design process (Parkinson & Bohemia, 2012b), to describing and analyzing the ways in which we experience a completed design product (Coates, 2012; Ro & Bermudez, 2015). In a less palpable way, narrative remains the primary means through which individuals ascribe and communicate coherence to their everyday experience: "Stories are…explanatory devices that help us make sense of the random and inexplicable happenings of everyday life" (Frascari, 2012, p. 229). A more profound role of narrative is its potential for aiding in the construction and transformation of the self: "Stories not only help us make sense of the actions of others, they serve to shape our own identities" (Frascari, 2012, p. 228). This echoes the work of researchers who claim that identity is narratively constructed, and that narrative is not simply a way of describing past events but has an ontological dimension—meaning that we become who we are through internal and external narrative practices (see Eakin, 2008; McAdams, 1993; Somers, 1994; Wortham, 2001). Though it is important to remember that our particular social context places limits on how we perform these stories and what we are able to say through them (i.e., narrative structure and content), narratives of self are inherently tied to processes of social agency, as they grant us the opportunity to construct and reinvent our past, present, and future identities.

From a practical as well as an epistemological standpoint, narrative practice and narrative inquiry relate long-held pedagogical traditions in design culture to themes of ontological learning, identity, and agency. For this reason, storytelling occupies a central place in this study, as a methodological framework and representational strategy.

Socialization and Enculturation in Architecture

Long-preoccupied with its future standing and role in society, the profession of architecture has also been plagued by "myths and illusions about what architects do" (Gutman, 1997; 2010a, p. 44). Likewise, architecture culture has been said to function as a 'black box', with socialization occurring via the telling of fables and anecdotes mysterious to the outside world (Banham, 1990; 1996). Historically, architectural educators were quite transparent in their objective of cultivating a certain class of 'professional gentlemen' (see Cret, 1941; Esherick, 1977). Necessary while problematic, processes of enculturation came to, over the decades, constitute the 'hidden' (Dutton, 1987) or 'invisible' (Stevens, 1999) facet of architectural curricula. In his seminal work on reflective practice, Schön (1983, 1987) proposed that a chief function of architecture school was training students to 'think-like-an-architect', achieved by students modeling behavior of their design tutors. In this way, the traditional master-apprenticeship relationship represents contemporary studio pedagogy's historical foundation. Critiques of Schön's pedagogical model and studio culture from feminist and critical pedagogues (see Anthony, 1991; Dutton, 1987; Mewburn, 2010; Webster, 2008; Willenbrock, 1991), as well as various cultural shifts beyond the discipline, eventually led to more student-centered teaching practices. And as part of architecture's ongoing attempt to define what makes practicing designers 'successful' in changing professional contexts and demands, educators began questioning common pedagogical practices and seeking alternatives.

As part of this shift, enculturation processes returned as a chief concern for those researching design education. Rather than simply training graduates in 'design skills', scholars argued that certain, revised modes of studio pedagogy could aid in cultivating critical thinking skills and dispositions through 'independent design decision-making' (Bose, Pennypacker, & Yahner, 2006) or that 'practical communication strategies' and community-based projects might promote an ethical framework of practice as opposed to egocentricism (Monson, 2005). The underlying critique of this line of research was that common practices of studio-based socialization (i.e., those that reproduced the myth of individualism, see Cuff 1991; Stevens, 1998; Till, 2009) were not producing 'successful' graduates and/or that outmoded professional ways of being were inadequate for meeting the demands of contemporary society (see Schneider & Till, 2009; Speaks, 2002). Amidst this rise of pedagogical criticism and innovation, collaborative learning strategies emerged as a potential means for socializing students into transformed modes of practice, such as one based on 'design agency' (see Schneider & Till, 2009). Till (2009), for example, recognizes 'dependency' as a defining feature of contemporary architectural practice and proposes reformulating our notion of architecture to introduce non-architects into the processes and products of practice. He advocates for *a move from the idea of architect as expert problem-solver to that of architect as citizen sense-maker; a move from a reliance on the impulsive imagination of the lone genius to that of the collaborative ethical imagination; from clinging to notions of total control to a relaxed acceptance of letting go. (p. 151)*

Thus, collaborative ways of being are currently considered by certain design scholars to represent a central feature of the ideal design professional. In this way, calls for more (and more meaningful) opportunities for collaboration in educational contexts are fundamental to projects seeking to ontologically reshape the profession itself.

While research on the learning outcomes of school-based collaboration has increased in recent years, its promotion is certainly not a new trend. A half-century ago, Walter Gropius (1962) called for teamwork in architecture schools as a way to reduce the rift between the academy and the profession, referring to resolving this schism as "an urgent task lying before the new generation, not only in the field of architecture but in all our endeavors to create an integrated society" (p. 78). While noting "the advantages and difficulties of collaborating in groups", he asserted that students "had to learn to collaborate without losing their identity" (p. 78). In a radical revision of Gropius' dictum, this chapter's study of student narratives suggests that collaborative learning and one's sense of self need not be considered opposing forces, and that aspiring designers should learn to collaborate *in order to* encourage and support a transformation of their identities.

METHODS

Research studies on teaching and learning practices like collaboration most commonly employ Likert-scale surveys in order to gauge student attitudes. What these studies potentially yield in terms of informative and comparative data, they lack in richness—namely, authentic student voices understood within a particular historical and cultural context. In fact, collecting narratives of learners remains somewhat marginalized in higher education scholarship:

The stories that students use to make sense of who they are do not fit into charts or graphs. They clash with the culture of positivism that we maintain in the academy. Many scholars feel bound to use the methods of science as opposed to those of the humanities. We see stories as 'soft', and thus we find one reason why faculty rarely assess the meaning of the college experience. Administrators and policy makers have also paid scant attention to the web of narrative that students inhabit. (Hanson, 2014, p. 8-9)

This chapter's study borrows from the interdisciplinary methodological tradition of life history and narrative inquiry most commonly used by social scientists for empirically exploring themes of self-authorship and identity in learning communities. Though the historic application and acceptance of this suite of methods has waxed and waned (Goodson, 2001), the recent quantity of publications on self-authorship and student identity suggests we are in the midst of a resurgence.

As is common in narrative inquiry, a case study approach was employed, focusing on a small selection of participants using in-depth, semi-structured interviews in concert with other data sources to capture the social and institutional context. The vignettes presented in the following section are passages gleaned from interviews with aspiring architects who graduated between 2013 and 2015 from the M.Arch program at the University of Washington (UW) in Seattle, USA. They form part of a larger case study of the program that sought to examine the ways in which aspiring architects construct meaning and a sense of self from their recollections of experiences as students and emerging design professionals. Two separate cohorts of four alumni, each interviewed one-on-one, served as primary participants. The two participant cohorts were conceived to represent distinct points in the educational-professional identity development timeline. The first cohort graduated from the program within two months of being interviewed, a similar time point to typical program exit interviews. The second cohort of alumni graduated between six and 18 months prior to being interviewed, and thus were able to candidly speak about their experience in graduate school from some distance. For this second cohort, then, recollections of their experiences as students should be understood as being narratively constructed from a professional, if still emerging, identity. Much like a recent longitudinal study by Case (in press), the objective was for participants to be "able to look back on their university experiences from some distance, and also to locate these within the broader developments in their working and personal lives" (p. 3). Thus, interview content covered life circumstances, design-related learning, and perceptions towards the profession of architecture before, during, and after the graduate program. Participants were given the chance to delve into details of particular events, relationships, and courses, effectively assembling their personal histories into a holistic narrative, supported by briefer, experiential narratives. With considerable time separating given educational activities from interviews (at least one year for those presented in this chapter), recollections ought to represent more persistent attitudes than those collected, say, immediately following a course or project. Regarding the topic of collaboration, this more mature pool of participants may explain the lack of concern expressed about assessment or 'free-riders', a frequent theme in undergraduate surveys following team-based activities (see for instance Webb & Miller, 2006).

Overall, participants ranged in terms of program track/length and employment status. In terms of characteristics like age, national origin, ethnic and gender identity, and sexual orientation, participants were recruited in an attempt to achieve a level of diversity reflective of the program's current student body. Common amongst graduates from this particular program, each alumni participant had some level of professional experience prior to graduating, and each participated in some form of collaborative work as students in design studios (ranging from site analysis activities to a nine-month thesis project). Each alumni participant yielded three to four hours of dialogue, recorded over three separate interviews, as proposed by Seidman (2013). To provide a better understanding of participants' cultural and institutional context, other data sources included interviews with four faculty members, two focus group sessions with four current M.Arch students, as well as program-related documents and histories.

Researcher power, privilege, and positionality represents the central ethical concern associated with narrative inquiry. As researcher and interviewer, my own insider-outsider position (as someone who recently completed a different M.Arch program before undertaking doctoral studies and teaching duties within the same college as the participants) afforded me a certain level of access to participants' life stories and educational experience by way of trust and parity. In other words, this study's narratives cannot be dissociated from my performance as an interviewer and my identity as interpreted by participants. A similar study conducted by a faculty member or administrator would have undoubtedly yielded different narratives. Other ethical concerns include colonizing participant stories and the issue of textual closure inherent in 'the move from life story to life history' (see Goodson, 2001, pp. 137-139). Such problematic issues should not be disregarded, and yet the ethical paradox of representation cannot be avoided in the retelling of others' stories.

Approaching the analysis and subsequent representation of participant histories includes both phenomenological and interpretative objectives (see Larkin, Watts, & Clifton, 2006). Phenomenologically, the aim is to understand and describe what the participants' world is like, whereas the interpretative aim is to speculate on "what it means for the participants to have made these claims, and to have expressed these feelings and concerns in this particular situation" (Larkin, Watts, & Clifton, 2006, p. 104). These aims correspond to first- and second-order analysis, respectively, the former represented in narrative form as a conversation between interviewer and participant and the latter through the author's discussion that links these narratives to relevant theories. Through a close reading of all interview transcripts, first-order analysis involved inductively identifying content themes. Here, collaboration, which had not been specifically targeted as an interview topic in protocols, emerged as a theme across all eight alumni participants. The next phase of analysis consisted of constructing 'profiles' of each participant by reducing and reorganizing transcripts to first-person narrative form (see Seidman, 2013). Passages previously coded with the theme of 'collaboration' were then evaluated in relation to each participant's profile to determine whether or not these passages fit into their broader narratives of development. Passages that met this criterion, meaning those interpreted as 'developmentally effective experiences' (Barber et al., 2013) that fell within broader 'information-rich narratives' (see Baxter Magolda & King, 2007; Case, in press), are presented in this chapter. Extended interview passages are included to provide readers the opportunity, however limited, to 'hear' participants' voices. Real names, identifiable content, and everyday speech patterns that might detract considerably from the reading experience were removed, while attempts were made to remain true to what I understood to be participants' intended meaning. Thus, the passages should be read as life histories co-constructed by researcher and participant, rather than stories as told directly via interview.

PROGRAM CONTEXT

To frame the subsequent participant narratives, this section outlines the institutional context that forms the social structure of participants' academic life histories. Despite some similarities owing perhaps to accreditation requirements and pedagogical lineage, the culture of architecture programs can vary significantly, even within a particular geographic region. Thus, it is important to briefly describe the cultural milieu co-produced by the participants represented in this chapter and from which their attitudes emerged. This is also intended to help readers consider the applicability and transferability of findings to their own contexts, as case study-based inquiry demands (Lincoln & Guba, 1985).

The University of Washington is located in Seattle, the Pacific Northwest's primary urban and cultural hub and home to a growing number of software- and web-related corporations, as well as several design firms internationally renowned for their environmentally conscious approaches to regional modernism. The Department of Architecture, which recently celebrated its centennial, is housed within UW's College of Built Environments alongside units in allied fields, such as landscape architecture, construction management, urban design and planning, and real estate. Owing to its relative geographic isolation from other centers of architectural culture, members of the department have long considered its provincial character a mixed blessing (see Johnston, 1991; Ochsner, 2007). As a nationally accredited professional degree program, the M.Arch program meets the standards set by the National Architecture Accreditation Board (NAAB), meaning its graduates are eligible for obtaining state licensure as practicing architects following completion of the National Council of Architectural Registration Boards' (NCARB) Intern

Development Program (IDP) and the Architect Registration Examination (ARE). On average, about 50 students graduate from the program each year (Miller, Anderson, Young, & Cauce, 2013). Departmental administrators maintain that, "Most of our students intend to become practicing architects" (Miller et al, 2013, p. 17). From faculty, student, and alumni interviews, it was clear that working in a local architecture firm after graduation was considered both normal and expected, though there was no assumed 'typical' firm type or size. Recent statistics tracking the professional status, discipline, or location of program alumni were not available; however, ARE pass rates by UW alumni averaged 79% from 2010-2014, with between 25 and 50 passing the exam in each of those years (NCARB, 2015).

In the administrators' words, the Department seeks to cultivate "students who understand their ethical responsibilities in professional practice, including obligations to the traditions of the discipline, the mores of the profession, and the needs of clients and society" (Miller et al., 2013, p. 25). This, paired with the strong connection between the program and the local community of design professionals (evident in the presence of local design practitioners serving as faculty members, guest lecturers, and guest critics) means that students are poised to join and contribute to this community soon after graduating. And as the program's recent NAAB Report put it, "Since most graduates stay in the Seattle area, the values and skills taught in the Department ultimately make their way back into the professional community" (Chronister, Ameri, Golden, McEnroe, & Malek-Aslani, 2014, p. 1).

From departmental documents and histories, accreditation reports, and interviews with faculty, alumni, and current students, there is a remarkably consistent discourse concerning the program's characteristic qualities. Here, architecture is considered first and foremost a craft that ultimately leads to the assemblage of tangible materials in real space. As a faculty member stated in a history lecture to students, "Architects have to be practical. Buildings have to get built" (May 11, 2015). Students are frequently encouraged to defer to the practicalities of the profession and real-world constraints, with most design projects located on feasible building sites in the Seattle area. Two of the Department's most recognized and longest-standing courses are the Neighborhood Design-Build Studio and Furniture Studio (see Ochsner, 2012), together reflecting the school's ethos of architecture as fundamentally concerned with making.

As is typical in architecture programs worldwide, studio lies at the center of the curriculum and student life. The studio's pedagogical and cultural character is intended to foster a supportive environment, where "students benefit from peer feedback and a sense of common purpose unusual in other university courses" (Miller et al., 2013, p. 5). Thus, even if projects are completed individually by students, the studio is intended to function as a collaborative learning community. The claim frequently made, and boasted nearly universally in studio-based programs, is that, upon fully embracing studio culture, students often learn as much from each other as from their instructors. With the M.Arch program including a three-year track for students with non-architecture undergraduate degrees, student backgrounds can range substantially within each cohort—not only in terms of professional and academic design experience but as far as experience related to collaboration in their prior academic, professional, and personal lives. Upon graduation, however, nearly all students have first-hand experience working in the profession, thanks in part to a recently implemented initiative with local firms that guarantees a supervised, paid summer internship for all three-year students following their first year. This opportunity is meant, in part, to ease the school-to-work transition by providing mentored professional experience within the graduate-level curriculum ("UW Master of Architecture Student Internship Program," 2014).

RESULTS: PARTICIPANT NARRATIVES

For the participants presented in this section, collaborative experiences played a central role in the meaning-making process of their professional education. As discussed in the section on methods, these three participants are being represented in particular because their narratives of 'developmentally effective experiences' were considered 'information-rich.' In analyzing their narratives, it became clear that these participants considered the value of collaboration not simply as translatable skills or knowledge for working in teams but for the ways that it shaped how they understood themselves as designers in the process of becoming. Thus, their narratives suggest that, for some, collaborative experiences play an important role in long-term projects of self-authorship, primarily by prompting self-reflection on issues of agency, identity, and wellbeing.

Irene

Irene moved to the United States from overseas initially to study interior design—partly because, in her own assessment, she lacked the aptitude and confidence to enter an architecture program directly from high school. After completing her undergraduate degree and feeling out of place in the culture of interior design, she was encouraged by her family to reconsider architecture as a field of study. When I spoke with her, two months had passed since she completed the three-year M.Arch program, and she was in the process of searching for employment. At the time, she remained skeptical about whether she was committed enough to architecture to succeed in the profession.

Irene admitted to struggling throughout graduate school when it came to engaging in design criticism. As was true for every participant interviewed for this study, the ebb and flow of self-confidence was a central theme of Irene's graduate education. Once she became comfortable seeking feedback from instructors, her tendency, as she explained it, was to take their criticism personally and judge the success or failure of her designs (and herself as a designer) purely on the comments of instructors or guest critics. In other words, by conflating her design work with her own self, she was vulnerable to perceiving design criticism as a reflection of her identity and self-worth, reminiscent of the experiences in an undergraduate architecture program described by Willenbrock (1991, p. 102-103):

We were to wrap ourselves completely in our work until the day of critiques, and then divorce ourselves completely from it...The identification we naturally made with our work rendered us vulnerable to destructive comments and made objective distance virtually impossible in our early critiques. We later learned to toughen our skins.

Similarly, in her last interview, Irene noted that she eventually improved her ability to cope with criticism:

I think I've gotten a little better trying to decide for myself if it's a good or a bad design. I mean, if I like it, I like it. And someone else is gonna hate it, but how can I do anything about that?

Probing this, I asked Irene to identify the moment when she noticed this shift beginning to happen.

Well, I noticed when I actually did a studio project with a partner—I noticed that I was more influenced by the professor than my partner was. She was very strong-minded—like, she knew what she wanted, she knew what was good. Regardless of whether people hated it or not!

So every time we had a desk crit [with the instructor], we would come outta there like, 'Did he like it?' 'I don't know.' 'What the hell's going on?'

And our design was just totally different from everybody else's.

And I would come outta there, and I'd be like, [whispering] 'Shouldn't we change it? Should we do what he says? Should we not make this angle?'

And she would be like, 'No! We're makin' the angle! We're stickin' with it!'

And I'd be like, 'Ok! Are you sure?'

And she'd just be like, 'Yes! It's fine! We're going to stick with it.'

So that's when I noticed, Oh! You can actually just say, 'No, I don't really want to listen to you. I'm gonna do it my way.'

And I don't think I was brought up that way. 'Cause my mom usually suggests things, and I'm like, 'Ok, I'll do it.' So I was brought up just doing things—whatever anyone told me to do.

And then when I worked with [my studio partner], it was an interesting experience 'cause I was like, 'Oh! Ok!' I could not have gone against the professor's advice if she wasn't there and telling me like, 'No, it's fine. Just leave it.' So I think that's when I noticed—and that's when I started to try and do it myself.

I don't do as good of a job as her, but…Not blindly taking someone else's advice and thinking for myself, I think, is a good thing to learn.

Irene's reflection on this topic suggests that, at some point, she became aware of the potential misalignment between her cultural upbringing and the ideal of objective, dialogical criticism considered such a fundamental value in contemporary studio-based pedagogy. Through this experience, she recognized an ontological gap leading up to this point in time between her self-image and the image she held of being a successful designer. In her recounting of this story, Irene makes it clear that the experiences of designing with a partner granted her the opportunity for self-reflection on her own agency as a designer, to the point where she could imagine herself challenging the opinions of her 'superiors', whether inwardly or outwardly. In constructing her own framework for meaning-making and not depending on authority figures, she began shifting from an external to an internal voice, a hallmark of self-authorship (Barber et al., 2013). We can infer that this experience and Irene's willingness to adopt the traits of her peer for the sake of self-improvement was made possible largely through the collaborative structure of the project which granted her a level of joint responsibility and decision-making power. In her reconstructed dialogue, Irene conveys how her reluctance to defy instructor criticism was challenged by her partner, granting

Irene the opportunity to undergo an experience she would not have otherwise—namely, determining her own criteria for a 'good' design. In this way, she considers her collaborative experience as providing a unique opportunity to transform her previously held identity of being 'someone who did what she was told' to 'someone sufficiently strong-minded to think and act for herself'.

As a narrative of meaning-making, whether or not the instructor's criticism was externally 'valid' or 'appropriate' is irrelevant, as is whether or not the groupmate's reaction to instructor criticism was justified. What matters in the context of this study is Irene's belief that this experience affected her personal development, and that she was able to weave this experience into her personal narrative. Whereas the experience did not necessarily increase the confidence she had in her design ability, it did allow her to participate in, and ultimately adopt herself, a more autonomous identity as a designer. Although Irene's narrative is not a full expression of self-authorship, it reveals that she considers the experience a significant event in shaping her current personal identity. Later in the same interview, Irene spoke of how this experience of discovering her agency as a student and as a designer influenced how she carried out her thesis project. In the process of developing her thesis project, she relied less on her instructors for design guidance: "I didn't really have people to depend on but myself." This project thus became a process of self-discovery, in which her disciplinary agenda and professional ambitions were sharpened. At the time of her interviews, she was attempting to enter the workforce with some hesitation, although this had more to do with concerns about finding fulfillment professionally than with doubting her competence.

Robin and Monica

Though interviewed separately one year after they graduated, the narratives of two other study participants are very much intertwined, having developed a particularly significant collaboration with each other while in graduate school. Robin and Monica each entered the 2-year track of the M.Arch program with similar agendas regarding expanding architecture's social responsibility, which had been cultivated in undergraduate architecture programs at other institutions. Though their backgrounds and paths to graduate school differ, their journeys through school share many parallels. They each described their first studio experience at UW as 'disenchanting' and 'miserable'. As Monica put it, "I thought I'd made a huge mistake coming back". In both of their cases, this was because the way that the studio was being operated by the instructor was "tightly controlled" and therefore did not match their personal philosophies toward design (in which design problems ought to emerge from how the designer interprets the particular project's conditions, not *a priori*) or what they considered to be the purpose of architectural education (for instance, Monica believes school should be a time and place to "formulate ideas about what *you* want it to mean to be an architect", whereas Robin believes school should be a time and place that fosters self-exploration by encouraging students to practice what he calls 'radical creativity'). Robin discussed these convictions in relation to his first studio experience at UW:

I think there were a lot of negative dynamics in that studio. One of them was about keeping people disconnected. It wasn't a studio about collaboration. I didn't get to know people for a long time because it was so individualistic. It felt like being isolated from community! Even though we were in one big room together…

That studio…rubbed me the wrong way because it felt very constraining…I felt like we were just practicing to do the work we were gonna do when we got out of school…And I think it leaves out a lot of self-exploration and developing some self-knowing about what's important to you and what you really want to do. And I think that's part of the positive side of the individualism that I see is developing an internal compass, in a sense of what I want to be doing, what I value...

Prompted by their negative feelings in their first studios, both Monica and Robin described finding other dissatisfied students and joining a 'niche community' of what Robin referred to as the "bad kids who had been analyzing, critiquing the program for years already". While this cemented their identities at the margin of the program's dominant culture, it provided them with a peer support network they considered crucial to their livelihoods as students.

When they reached the thesis stage, a sequence of research and design courses that represents the culmination of the program's curriculum and encompasses a full calendar year, Robin and Monica discovered they had common interests and decided to undertake a collaborative thesis project. Thesis projects, typically conducted independently, are oftentimes the one opportunity for students in the program to choose their own project site, building type, and theoretical topic—and therefore can be a particularly significant moment of freedom and discovery for young designers. Because theses are not conceived as team-based design projects in the program's curriculum, Monica and Robin had to receive permission from their advisors to work collaboratively. In their case, it is clear that Monica and Robin's shared identities as outsiders were largely what led to the formation and success of their partnership. Part of what also drew them together was the potential to form a deeper working relationship than is possible in typical studios—particularly at UW, where academic terms span only ten weeks.

In describing their experience carrying out a thesis project together, both Monica and Robin noted the non-instrumental values of collaboration. As Monica said, "Sharing the burden of something like that goes a long way, I think, psychologically to making it feel like it's something that you're actually gonna finish or get to a point where you're happy with it". Or as Robin put it,

Just feeling like other people have my back and that I have their back...that we're a team, is just a way in the world that I feel most comfortable...

And actually, hard things in life were happening in different points during...thesis. And having someone else be in the back and forth, and to actually feel supported—I saw so many people working individually—And this happens a lot, I think, in architecture, that it's psychologically unhealthy and people having breakdowns. Y'know, you can see on their face, so just drained and anxious.

Building on our discussion of 'being collaborative' and his thesis experience, I raised the familiar argument for collaborative processes, that they actually generate higher-quality design products. To this, he countered:

I don't think that it necessarily is better.

I just feel better in myself and in a community and in the world if I'm seeing people do things collaboratively.

I think there's all these benefits that aren't tangible, and maybe are benefits to the practitioners more than the clients sometimes. Where you're actually just building community and exploring ideas and doing

all this work on yourself that I think does trickle down or is reflected in the work you actually produce that other people experience.

But I find the experience of isolated work by myself is—in the communal sense of being human—dehumanizing.

The potential that collaborative design projects have for improving psychological wellbeing is something Robin and Monica each identified as one of the chief benefits of their thesis experience. However, here, we can recognize Robin beginning to apply the 'non-tangible benefits' of collaboration to a professional context, where social relations and expectations of efficiency tend to differ from academic contexts. After graduating, both Robin and Monica found employment with sole practitioners and are attempting to build a foundation of professional skills. At the time of their interviews, they continue to collaborate with each other on design competitions outside of their jobs.

Ultimately, their thesis process granted Monica and Robin the time and freedom to explore a site and their own working relationship sufficiently enough to meet the standards of their converging philosophies of design. Collaborating strengthened not only each of their critical convictions about coventional architectural practice but also their beliefs that their identities—however marginalized they considered them to be in their disciplinary context—could operate successfully within the profession. Working together on their thesis offered Monica and Robin a performative opportunity to embody identities that they later would develop in a professional context. Now working for an architect whom she considers a 'counterexample' role model, Monica expressed the enduring conflict between her own self-image and that of an architect: "Even once I get my license, I'm not sure I'm gonna feel like an architect". As she put it,

I don't wanna wake up one day and be the entity that I was criticizing ten years ago...

I do wanna continue to be employed. But I think it's gonna be largely about finding avenues on which I can actively be that and challenge it at the same time.

Thus, rather than attempting to suppress the 'instigator' identity she had developed over the years for pragmatic purposes, Monica attributes graduate school with providing her the opportunity to construct an 'insider-instigator' identity (what she calls a 'counterexample') that she carried with her to the professional world. In this sense, Monica might well be considered either a 'purifying simulator' or 'simulating purifier' in Whiting's (2010, pp. 314-315) hybridization of Gutman's (1985, 2010b, pp. 268-269) original conceptualization of architecture's two academic camps: the 'purifiers' (those who sought to maintain the autonomy of the academy) and the 'simulators' (those who sought to integrate the academy with professional modes of design). Through reflective, creative, and performative experiences over the course of her M.Arch education, Monica was ultimately able to construct an 'identity horizon' (Côté, Skinkle, & Motte, 2008) that positioned her values and ethical commitments within the broader culture of architectural practice.

Robin, who also works for a sole practitioner, sees the value of learning through an apprenticeship model for his own development and goal of professional autonomy. As he put it,

I value knowing everything I need to know so that I don't have to work for a big firm that might not be doing what I want.

I think I want more control over how and with whom I work and collaborate.

Robin ended his final interview by noting a recent shift in his outlook toward the future:

I feel like I don't know how to predict what will be next [in my career]...

Being in school, there's this conception or curiosity of what professional life is going to be like. And getting out of this long process of education that was, in a way, encapsulated. And then now to be in sort of the open range of professional life where I really want to encapsulate and figure out what are the phases. Like, are there gonna be stages of growth, or phases of interests?

I've been experiencing a bit of an overwhelming feeling...It feels like this expansive, nebulous place now. That either I could just do what I'm doing now forever. Or things will change along the way.

And I'm sure there'll be happenstance, and there'll be opportunities that'll just be out of my control. But now, I'm starting to feel like, 'Wow, I have a lot more responsibility to take those changes, make those shifts.'

Because hopefully I'm not just gonna get fired or laid off or whatever, [which would] just force me to totally reevaluate. I would rather choose like, 'Ok, I want to start a firm with a collaborative basis. Or join one at some point when I'm ready to. Or shift my focus of interest when I'm ready.'...

I think I'm seeing more that it's my responsibility to continue my evolution. Where I think I saw school and grad school as supporting me, doing that for me—like it was challenging me, it was telling me to change...And I think that that's a big shift, where now it's my job to do that.

Here, Robin is expressing how his development within a professional context demands self-authorship. Rather than depending on institutional structures for opportunities to reinvent himself, which he considers essential for professional growth, he believes this is now his responsibility. He describes this feeling as 'overwhelming', but his recognition of this shift in itself suggests he is up to the challenge. By knowing himself, knowing that he must change, and considering himself responsible for supporting these change, Robin has journeyed most of the way towards self-authorship. While he did not relate these realizations directly to his experience collaborating in school, it undoubtedly played a central role in his transition from school to work.

In fact, both Robin and Monica's interview transcripts revealed clear evidence of meaning-making processes, and their parallel experiences comprise many of the themes of self-authorship illuminated by Barber et al. (2013), including: experiences of dissonance, the significance of belonging, working through personal difficulties, and taking ownership of their beliefs. As the catalyzing force behind their identities shifting from academic to professional selves, their collaborative thesis project represents a significant chapter of their respective narratives.

CONCLUSION

The preceding narratives evoke various ways in which an individual's encounter with collaboration in a design studio ultimately became woven into their personal narrative of ontological development: from prompting reflection on one's own agency as a designer (Irene), to demonstrating the affective benefits of being collaborative (Robin), to providing an opportunity to embody a 'dissonant' professional identity (Monica). In this way, these participants' collaborative experiences shaped their student narratives, which then became prologues to their narratives as emerging architects. In other words, they are examples of how, by recollecting their experiences as students, emerging professionals might make meaning and ultimately themselves. This study thus helps broaden our understanding of how aspiring design professionals transition from school to work by expanding the focus beyond skills and knowledge to 'ways of being' and, specifically, narrative processes. How individuals construct meaning from significant events in their lives is considered a major determinant of their future wellbeing (Cox, 2015). So while there is certainly nothing inherently life-changing about collaborating in school, certain learning experiences invariably help determine how we construct our past, present, and future selves. Therefore, it is important to recognize the potential role that collaborative opportunities might play in the life histories of college students and emerging design professionals.

All this leads to the question of how educators might support or encourage ontological development, particularly as it relates to collaborative design, as well as what directions future research on this topic might take. First, it is important to recognize that self-authorship does not typically occur within the timeframe of an academic program (Barber et al., 2013). Because it cannot thus be considered a learning outcome for a single course, project, or instructor, this would suggest that self-authorship itself cannot be assessed as such. However, educators can promote self-exploration by helping students "work on themselves" over the course of their education (Tennant, 2012). As Harrell-Levy and Kerpelman (2010) argue, teachers can serve as 'agents of identity formation' by deliberately adopting 'transformative pedagogy'. This would imply extending one's role beyond simply 'supporting' students by structuring courses, projects, assessment, and entire curricula in ways that encourage self-exploration and explicitly recognize aspects of ontological learning as broader educational outcomes (Dall'Alba & Barnacle, 2007, p. 687). Opportunities for students to participate in 'autobiographical practices' (see Miller & Morgan, 1993), like exit interviews or reflection journals, can provide opportunities for them to narratively illuminate their individual journeys of 'becoming a design professional', while improving their chances for future success (Ghassan & Bohemia, 2011). Among numerous other prospects, engaging students in 'learning conversations' or role-playing exercises with peers and/or practitioners can prompt self-reflection regarding, for instance, how their emerging identities relate to others', as well as to professional social norms (Westrup & Planander, 2013). Finally, considering collaborative design practices as 'ways of being' means that educators should also recognize that cultivating the emotional aspects of collaborative design requires training, just as does learning the practical aspects of working in teams. As Byun, Kim, and Duffey (2012) argue, emotional learning "is a critical component of collaborative learning outcomes" (p. 202).

FUTURE RESEARCH DIRECTIONS

The lack of research relating collaborative learning to ontological development means there is much to be gained from future studies on this topic. However, it is important to consider possible reasons for the scarcity of research thus far. One is that modes of phenomenological/interpretative research such as this study employed are still not widely accepted in certain scholarly communities, as the results yielded are not, strictly speaking, generalizable or considered 'valid' under dominant epistemological frameworks. However, it remains the most accepted approach for life history research, and its acceptance appears to be growing. A second reason, as already noted, is that the timeframe by which transformations like self-authorship take place extends beyond the timeframe of educational assessment. Therefore, research studies limited to classroom contexts would prove insufficient for exploring more holistic development processes. There is, on the other hand, much more work to be done in classroom-based inquiry to understand the relative strengths of the pedagogical strategies discussed above. Future studies could begin to assess the potential of these various strategies to operate as a 'transformative pedagogy' in the context of collaborative design.

To expand on this case study, future research should also investigate other institutional and disciplinary contexts using longitudinal studies, as it remains unclear to what degree design collaboration as a meaning-making opportunity differs depending on one's sociocultural context. With a wider set of examples of how collaborative learning has encouraged self-exploration in design students like those presented in this study, further thematic features and conceptual frameworks will ostensibly emerge, which could inform metrics for identifying and evaluating learning outcomes related to self-development in studio collaboration. Finally, there is much to be explored within the realm of narrative-based inquiry on this topic in terms of data collection techniques and representational strategies. Future research could take more creative approaches to gathering and depicting collaborative learning experiences within particular, contextualized life histories.

REFERENCES

Anthony, K. (1991). *Design juries on trial: The renaissance of the design studio*. New York: Van Nostrant Reinhold.

Banham, R. (1996). A black box: The secret profession of architecture. In M. Banham, P. Barker, S. Lyall, & C. Price (Eds.). A critic writes: Essays by Reyner Banham (pp. 292-299). Berkeley: University of California Press. (Originally printed in New Statesman and Society 12 October 1990).

Barber, J. P., King, P. M., & Baxter Magolda, M. B. (2013). Long strides on the journey toward self-authorship: Substantial developmental shifts in college students' meaning making. *The Journal of Higher Education, 84*(6), 866–896. doi:10.1353/jhe.2013.0033

Barnett, R. (2000). *Realizing the university in an age of supercomplexity*. New York: Open University Press.

Barnett, R. (2004). 2012). Learning for an unknown future. *Higher Education Research & Development, 31*(1), 65–77. doi:10.1080/07294360.2012.642841

Baxter Magolda, M. B. (1992). *Knowing and reasoning in college: Gender-related patterns in students' intellectual development*. San Francisco, CA: Jossey-Bass.

Baxter Magolda, M. B. (2001). *Making their own way: Narratives for transforming higher education to promote self-development*. Sterling, VA: Stylus.

Baxter Magolda, M. B., & King, P. M. (2007). Interview strategies for assessing self-authorship: Constructing conversations to assess meaning making. *Journal of College Student Development*, *48*(5), 491–508. doi:10.1353/csd.2007.0055

Bose, M., Pennypacker, E., & Yahner, T. (2006). Enhancing critical thinking through 'independent design decision making' in the studio. *Open House International*, *31*(3), 33–42.

Boyer, E. L., & Mitgang, L. D. (1996). *Building community: A new future for architecture education and practice*. Carnegie Foundation for the Advancement of Teaching.

Byun, S.-E., Kim, H., & Duffey, M. (2012). A multicourse collaborative project within a global context: Multidimensional learning outcomes for merchandising and interior design majors. *Clothing & Textiles Research Journal*, *30*(3), 200–216. doi:10.1177/0887302X12453646

Case, J. M. (2013). *Researching student learning in higher education: A social realist approach*. New York: Routledge.

Case, J. M. (in press). Journeys to meaning-making: A longitudinal study of self-authorship amongst young South African engineering graduates. *Journal of College Student Development*.

Chickering, A. W. (1969). *Education and identity*. San Francisco: Jossey Boss.

Chronister, L. M., Ameri, A., Golden, D., McEnroe, R., & Malek-Aslani, C. (2014, February 26). *University of Washington Department of Architecture National Architectural Accrediting Board (NAAB) Visiting Team Report (VTR)*. Retrieved from http://arch.be.washington.edu/sites/default/ files/pdf/ UW_NAAB_2014_VTR_%5BFinal%20Draft%5D.pdf

Coates, N. (2012). *Narrative architecture*. Hoboken, NJ: Wiley.

Côté, J., Skinkle, R., & Motte, A. (2008). Do perceptions of costs and benefits of post-secondary education influence participation? *Canadian Journal of Higher Education*, *38*(2), 73–93.

Cox, K. (2015). Meaning making in the life story, and not coherence or vividness, predicts well-being up to 3 years later: Evidence from high point and low point stories. *Identity*, *15*(4), 241–262. doi:10.10 80/15283488.2015.1089508

Cret, P. (1941). The Ecole des Beaux-Arts and architectural education. *The Journal of the American Society of Architectural Historians*, *1*(2), 3–15. doi:10.2307/901128

Cuff, D. (1991). *Architecture: The story of practice*. Cambridge, MA: MIT Press.

Cuseo, J. (1996). *Cooperative learning: A pedagogy for addressing contemporary challenges*. Stillwater, OK: New Forums Press.

Dall'Alba, G., & Barnacle, R. (2007). An ontological turn for higher education. *Studies in Higher Education*, *32*(6), 679–691. doi:10.1080/03075070701685130

Dutton, T. A. (1987). Design and studio pedagogy. *Journal of Architectural Education*, *41*(1), 16–25. doi:10.1080/10464883.1987.10758461

Eakin, P. J. (2008). *Living autobiographically: How we create identity in narrative*. Ithaca, NY: Cornell University Press.

Esherick, J. (1977). Architectural education in the Thirties and Seventies: A personal view. In S. Kostof (Ed.), *The architect: Chapters in the history of the profession* (pp. 238–279). New York: Oxford University Press.

Ettington, D., & Camp, R. (2002). Facilitating transfer of skills between group projects and work teams. *Journal of Management Education*, *26*(4), 356–379. doi:10.1177/105256290202600404

Gale, A., Martin, D., Martin, K., & Duffey, M. (2014). The burnout phenomenon: A comparative study of student attitudes toward collaborative learning and sustainability. *Journal of Interior Design*, *39*(1), 17–31. doi:10.1111/joid.12022

Ghassan, A., & Bohemia, E. (2011). Notions of self: Becoming a 'successful' design graduate. In N.F.M. Roozenburg, L.L. Chen, & P.J. Stappers (Eds.), *Diversity and unity: Proceedings of IASDR2011, the 4th world conference on design research* (pp. 1-9). Delft University of Technology: Delft, Netherlands.

Goodson, I. (2001). The story of life history: Origins of the life history method in sociology. *Identity*, *1*(2), 129–142. doi:10.1207/S1532706XID0102_02

Gropius, W. (1962). *Scope of total architecture*. New York: Collier Books.

Gutman, R. (2010a). Professions and their discontents: The psychodynamics of architectural practice. In Cuff, R. & Wriedt, J. (Eds.) *Architecture from the outside in: Selected essays by Robert Gutman* (pp. 43-58). New York: Princeton Architectural Press. Originally published in Practices 5/6 Spring, 1997.

Gutman, R. (2010b). Educating architects: Pedagogy and the pendulum. In Cuff, R. & Wriedt, J. (Eds.) *Architecture from the outside in: Selected essays by Robert Gutman* (pp. 258-286). New York: Princeton Architectural Press. (Originally published in Public Interest 80 Summer, 1985, pp. 67-91).

Hanson, C. (2014). Changing how we think about the goals of higher education. In C. Hanson (Ed.), *In search of self: Exploring student identity development: New directions in higher education, no. 166* (pp. 7–13). San Francisco: Jossey-Boss. doi:10.1002/he.20090

Harrell-Levy, M. K., & Kerpelman, J. L. (2010). Identity process and transformative pedagogy: Teachers as agents of identity formation. *Identity*, *10*(2), 76–91. doi:10.1080/15283481003711684

Hynes, W. (2015). Impacting student attitudes towards teamwork. In Vande Zande, R., Bohemia, E., & Digranes, I. (Eds.), *Learn x design:Proceedings of the 3rd International Conference for Design Education Researchers* (pp. 1002-1015). Aalto, Finland: Aalto University.

Johnston, N. J. (1991). *The college of architecture and urban planning: Seventy-five years at the University of Washington: A personal view*. Seattle: University of Washington College of Architecture and Urban Planning.

Kegan, R. (1994). *In over our heads: The mental demands of modern life*. Cambridge, MA: Harvard University Press.

Kim, H.-S., LaFleur, R., & Schaeffer, K. (2008). A multi-course collaborative project: Using technology to learn. *Journal of Family and Consumer Sciences*, *100*(3), 34–41.

King, P., & Kitchener, K. (1994). *Developing reflective judgment*. San Francisco, CA: Jossey-Bass.

Larkin, M., Watts, S., & Clifton, E. (2006). Giving voice and making sense in interpretative phenomenological analysis. *Qualitative Research in Psychology*, *3*(2), 102–120. doi:10.1191/1478088706qp062oa

Lincoln, Y. S., & Guba, E. G. (1985). *Naturalistic inquiry*. Beverly Hills, CA: SAGE.

McAdams, D. P. (1993). *The stories we live by: Personal myths and the making of the self*. New York: The Guildford Press.

Merton, R. K. (1968). *Social theory and social structure*. New York, NY: The Free Press.

Mewburn, I. (2010). Lost in translation: Reconsidering reflective practice and design studio pedagogy. *Arts and Humanities in Higher Education*, *2*(4), 363–379.

Miller, D. E., Anderson, A. T., Young, M. K., & Cauce, A. M. (2013). *University of Washington Architecture Program Report (APR)*. Retrieved from http://arch.be.washington.edu/sites/default/ files/pdf/ UW_2013_APR.pdf

Miller, N., & Morgan, D. (1993). Called to account: The CV as an autobiographical practice. *Sociology*, *27*(1), 133–143. doi:10.1177/003803859302700113

Monson, C. (2005). Practical discourse: Learning and the ethical construction of environmental design practice. *Ethics Place and Environment*, *8*(2), 181–200. doi:10.1080/13668790500237070

National Council of Architectural Registration Boards. (2015). *ARE Pass Rates by School* [Data file]. Retrieved from http://www.ncarb.org/ARE/ARE-Pass-Rates/Pass-Rates-by-School.aspx

Ochsner, J. K. (2007). *Lionel H. Pries, architect, artist, educator: From Arts and Crafts to the Modern Movement*. Seattle: University of Washington Press.

Ochsner, J. K. (2012). *Furniture studio: Materials, craft, and architecture*. Seattle: University of Washington Press.

Parkinson, D., & Bohemia, E. (2012a). Developing the design storytelling impact-approach framework. In Bohemia, E., Liedtka, J., & Rieple, A. (Eds.). *Leading innovation through design:Proceedings from the Design Management Institute's International Research Conference* (pp. 803-810). Boston.

Parkinson, D., & Bohemia, E. (2012b). Designer storytelling. In Buck, L., Frateur, G., Ion, W., McMahon, C., Baelus, C., de Grande, G., & Vervulgen, S. (Eds.). *Design education for future wellbeing:Proceedings from the International Conference on Engineering and Product Design Education* (pp. 742-747). Antwerp.

Pizzolato, J. E. (2003). Developing self-authorship: Exploring the experiences of high-risk college students. *Journal of College Student Development, 44*(6), 797–812. doi:10.1353/csd.2003.0074

Ro, B., & Bermudez, J. (2015). Understanding extraordinary architectural experiences through content analysis of written narratives. *Enquiry, 12*(1), 17–34.

Russ, R., & Dickinson, J. (1999). Collaborative design: "Forming, storming, and norming". *Journal of Interior Design, 25*(2), 52–58. doi:10.1111/j.1939-1668.1999.tb00344.x

Sandberg, J., & Pinnington, A. H. (2009). Professional competence as ways of being: An existential ontological perspective. *Journal of Management Studies, 46*(7), 1138–1170. doi:10.1111/j.1467-6486.2009.00845.x

Schneider, T., & Till, J. (2009). Beyond discourse: Notes on spatial agency. *Footprint, 4*, 97–112.

Schön, D. A. (1983). *The reflective practitioner: How professionals think in action.* London: Temple Smith.

Schön, D. A. (1987). *Educating the reflective practitioner: Toward a new design for teaching and learning in the professions.* San Francisco: Jossey-Bass.

Seidman, I. (2013). *Interviewing as qualitative research: A guide for researchers in education and the social sciences* (4th ed.). New York: Teachers College Press, Columbia University.

Somers, M. (1994). The narrative constitution of identity: A relational and network approach. *Theory and Society, 23*(5), 605–649. doi:10.1007/BF00992905

Speaks, M. (2002). Theory was interesting…but now we have work. *Architectural Research Quarterly, 6*(3), 209–212. doi:10.1017/S1359135503001714

Stevens, G. (1998). *The favored circle: The social foundations of architectural distinction.* Cambridge: MIT Press.

Stevens, G. (1999). How the invisible stays that way. *Thresholds, 19*, 54–56.

Sullivan, W. M. (2012). Professional education: Aligning knowledge, expertise, and public purpose. In E. C. Lagemann & H. Lewis (Eds.), *What is college for? The public purpose of higher education* (pp. 104–131). New York: Teachers College Press, Columbia University.

Tennant, M. (2012). *The learning self: Understanding the potential for transformation.* San Francisco: Jossey-Boss.

Tierney, W. G., & Bensimon, E. M. (1996). *Promotion and tenure: Community and socialization in academe.* Albany, NY: State University of New York Press.

Till, J. (2009). *Architecture depends.* Cambridge, MA: MIT Press.

Torres, V., & Hernandez, E. (2007). The influence of ethnic identity on self-authorship: A longitudinal study of Latino/a college students. *Journal of College Student Development, 48*(5), 558–573. doi:10.1353/csd.2007.0057

UW Master of Architecture Student Internship Program. (2014). University of Washington Department of Architecture, Professional Advisories Council.

Webb, J., & Miller, N. (2006). Some preparation required: The journey to successful studio collaboration. *Journal of Interior Design*, *31*(2), 1–9. doi:10.1111/j.1939-1668.2005.tb00407.x

Webster, H. (2008). Architectural education after Schön: Cracks, blurs, boundaries and beyond. *Journal for Education in the Built Environment*, *3*(2), 63–74. doi:10.11120/jebe.2008.03020063

Westrup, U., & Planander, A. (2013). Role-play as a pedagogical method to prepare students for practice: The students' voice. *Högre utbildning*, 3(3), 199-210.

Whiting, S. (2010). Welcome to the banquet (or, how to increase the relative happiness of the M.Arch Thesis student). In Cuff, D., & Wriedt, J. (Eds.), *Architecture from the outside in: Selected essays by Robert Gutman* (pp. 131-17). New York: Princeton Architectural Press.

Willenbrock, L. L. (1991). An undergraduate voice in architectural education. In T. A. Dutton (Ed.), *Voices in architectural education: Cultural politics and pedagogy* (pp. 97–119). New York: Bergin & Garvey.

Wortham, S. (2001). *Narratives in action: A strategy for research and analysis*. New York: Teachers College Press.

KEY TERMS AND DEFINITIONS

Agency: The capacity of individuals to act independently and make their own free choices. Structure, agency's dialectical complement, is those factors of influence that determine or limit an agent and his or her decisions.

Life History: A method employed in social science and humanities research that studies autobiographical accounts, often to examine the relationship between a person's life story (its content, structure, or some combination) and their sociocultural structure.

Narrative Identity: The notion that we come to be who we are (however ephemeral, multiple, and changing) by being located or locating ourselves (usually unconsciously) within social narratives rarely of our own making.

Ontological Learning: A way of conceptualizing learning that foregrounds how 'ways of being' transform within a given social/disciplinary context. This is in contrast to the predominant conceptualization of learning that focuses exclusively on skill/knowledge transfer/acquisition.

Self-Authorship: The internal capacity to construct one's beliefs, identity, and social relations. A growing number of scholars and educators consider the transition from dependence on authority to self-authorship as crucial to successfully navigating adult life.

Compilation of References

Aarnio, M., Nieminen, J., Pyörälä, E., & Lindblom-Ylänne, S. (2010). Motivating medical students to learn teamwork skills. *Medical Teacher*, *32*(4), e199–e204. doi:10.3109/01421591003657469 PMID:20353320

Adair, J. (2009). *The Art of Creative Thinking: How to be Innovative and Develop Great Ideas*. London: Kogan Page.

Adamczyk, P. D., & Twidale, M. B. (2007). Supporting multidisciplinary collaboration: requirements from novel HCI education.*Proceedings of the SIGCHI conference on Human factors in computing systems* (pp. 1073-1076). ACM. doi:10.1145/1240624.1240787

Adams, R. S., Daly, S. R., Mann, L. M., & Dall'Alba, G. (2011). Being a professional: Three lenses into design thinking, acting, and being. *Design Studies*, *32*(6), 588–607. doi:10.1016/j.destud.2011.07.004

Adams, S., Simon, L., & Ruiz, B. (2002). A pilot study of the performance of student teams in engineering education. *Proceedings of the American Society for Engineering Education Annual Conference and Exposition,Montreal*.

AE International. (2010). International student numbers, 2009. Retrieved from http://aei.gov.au/AEI/PublicationsAndResearch/Snapshots/2010022610_pdf.pdf

Aggarwal, P., & O'Brien, C. L. (2008). Social Loafing on Group Projects: Structural Antecedents and Effect on Student Satisfaction. *Journal of Marketing Education*, *30*(3), 255–264. doi:10.1177/0273475308322283

Agouridas, V. (2007, June 11-14). Towards the systematic Definition of Project-Based Design Modules. *Paper presented at the 3rd International CDIO Conference*, MIT, Cambridge, Massachusetts, USA.

Ahern, A. (2007). What are the perceptions of lecturers towards using cooperative learning in civil engineering? *European Journal of Engineering Education*, *32*(5), 517–526. doi:10.1080/03043790701433152

Ahmed, S., Wallace, K. M., & Blessing, L. M. (2003). Understanding the differences between how novice and experienced designers approach design tasks. *Research in Engineering Design*, *14*(1), 1.

Akin, Ã., & Lin, C. (1995). Design protocol data and novel design decisions. *Design Studies*, *16*(2), 211–236. doi:10.1016/0142-694X(94)00010-B

Al-Abdeli, Y., & Bullen, F. (2006, December 10-13). Connecting teaching and research through problem based learning in thermal and automotive engineering. *Paper presented at the17th Annual Conference of the Australasian Association for Engineering Education*, Auckland.

Albert, S., Ashforth, B. E., & Dutton, J. E. (2000). Organizational identity and identification: Charting new waters and building new bridges. *Academy of Management Review*, *25*(1), 13–17. doi:10.5465/AMR.2000.2791600

Alexander, C., Ishikawa, S., & Silverstein, M. (1977). A Pattern Language: Towns - Buildings - Construction. New York: Oxford University Press.

Alexander, C. (1964). *Notes on the Synthesis of Form*. Cambridge, MA: Harvard University Press.

Alfonseca, E., Carro, R. M., Martín, E., Ortigosa, A., & Paredes, P. (2006). The impact of learning styles on student grouping for collaborative learning: A case study. *User Modeling and User-Adapted Interaction, 16*(3-4), 377–401. doi:10.1007/s11257-006-9012-7

Alge, B. J., Wiethoff, C., & Klein, H. J. (2003). When does the medium matter? Knowledge-building experiences and opportunities in decision-making teams. *Organizational Behavior and Human Decision Processes, 91*(1), 26–37. doi:10.1016/S0749-5978(02)00524-1

Alpay, E. (2005). Group dynamic processes in email groups. *Active Learning in Higher Education, 6*(1), 7–16. doi:10.1177/1469787405049942

Altbach, P., & Knight, J. (2007). Internationalisation of Higher Education: Motivations and Realities. *Journal of Studies in International Education, 11*(3-4), 290–305. doi:10.1177/1028315307303542

Amabile, T. M. (1983). *The social psychology of creativity*. New York: Springer-Verlag. doi:10.1007/978-1-4612-5533-8

Amason, A. (1996). Distinguishing effects of functional and dysfunctional conflict on strategic decision making: Resolving a paradox for top management teams. *Academy of Management Journal, 39*(1), 123–148. doi:10.2307/256633

Amason, A., & Sapienza, H. (1997). The effects of top management team size and interaction norms on cognitive and affective conflict. *Journal of Management, 23*(4), 496–516. doi:10.1177/014920639702300401

Amatullo, M., Becerra, L., & Montgomery, S. (2011). Design matters case studies: Design education methodologies as a tool for social innovation. *Paper presented at theAnnual Conference of the National Collegiate Inventors and Innovators Alliance*, Washington, D.C.

American Association of Colleges and Universities [AAC&U]. (2010a). *Valid Assessment of Learning in Undergraduate Education*. Retrieved from https://www.aacu.org/value

American Association of Colleges and Universities [AAC&U]. (2010b). *Teamwork VALUE Rubric*. In T.L. Rhodes (Ed.), *Assessing Outcomes and Improving Achievement: Tips and tools for Using Rubrics*. Association of American Colleges and Universities. Retrieved from https://www.aacu.org/value/rubrics/teamwork

American Society of Interior Designers [ASID]. (2015). *Becoming an interior designer*. Retrieved from https://www.asid.org/content/becoming-interior-designer#.VgcaLKSFOM8

Anderson, D. (1988). The process of learning. 2nd ed. Sydney: Prentice- Hall, 1987: review. Forum of Education; 47(2), 103-105.

Anderson, N. M. (2014). Public Interest Design as Praxis. *Journal of Architectural Education, 68*(1), 16–27. doi:10.1080/10464883.2014.864896

Anthony, K. (1991). *Design juries on trial: The renaissance of the design studio*. New York: Van Nostrant Reinhold.

Archer, L., Hutchings, M., & Ross, A. (2005). *Higher education and social class: issues of exclusion and inclusion*. Routledge.

Architects Accreditation Council Of Australia (AACA). (2000a). *Competency Based Assessment in Architecture*. Retrieved from http://www.aaca.org.au/wp-content/uploads/2014/01/APE-LOG-BOOK-INFORMATION-Jan-2014.pdf

Architects Accreditation Council Of Australia (AACA). (2000b). *The National Competency Standards in Architecture*. Retrieved from http://www.aaca.org.au/wp-content/uploads/2010/09/2009_NCSA.pdf

Armstrong, K., Sade, G., & Thomas, L. (2012). Long Time, No See? Retrieved from http://explore.long-time-no-see.org

Arnett, B. (1993). Education and human development at future workstations. *Paper presented at theTeleTeaching '93 Conference*, Trondheim, Norway.

Aronson, J. (1995). A pragmatic view of thematic analysis. *Qualitative Report, 2*(1), 1–3.

Astin, A. W., Vogelgesang, L. J., Ikeda, E. K., & Yee, J. A. (2000). How service learning affects students. University of Nebraska, Omaha.

Atman, C. J., Adams, R. S., Cardella, M. E., Turns, J., Mosborg, S., & Saleem, J. (2007). Engineering Design Processes: A Comparison of Students and Expert Practitioners. *The Journal of Engineering Education, 96*(4), 359–379. doi:10.1002/j.2168-9830.2007.tb00945.x

Atman, C. J., Cardella, M. E., Turns, J., & Adams, R. (2005). Comparing freshman and senior engineering design processes: An in-depth follow-up study. *Design Studies, 26*(4), 325–357. doi:10.1016/j.destud.2004.09.005

Atman, C. J., Chimka, J. R., Bursic, K. M., & Nachtmann, H. L. (1999). A comparison of freshman and senior engineering design processes. *Design Studies, 20*(2), 131–152. doi:10.1016/S0142-694X(98)00031-3

Atman, C. J., Kilgore, D., & McKenna, A. (2008). Characterizing Design Learning: A Mixed-Methods Study of Engineering Designers' Use of Language. *The Journal of Engineering Education, 97*(3), 309–326. doi:10.1002/j.2168-9830.2008.tb00981.x

Attoe, W. (1978). *Architecture and Critical Imagination*. Chichester: Wiley.

Augustin, S. (2014). Designing for Collaboration and Collaborating for Design. *Journal of Interior Design, 39*(1), ix–xviii. doi:10.1111/joid.12020

Australian Government Department of Education and Training. (2016, January 15) Retrieved from https://education.gov.au/higher-education-participation-and-partnerships-programme-heppp

Bacon, D. R., Stewart, K. A., & Silver, W. S. (1999a). Lessons from the Best and Worst Student Team Experiences: How a Teacher can make the Difference. *Journal of Management Education, 23*(5), 467–488. doi:10.1177/105256299902300503

Bacon, D. R., Stewart, K. A., & Stewart-Belle, S. (1998). Exploring predictors of student team project performance. *Journal of Marketing Education, 20*(1), 63–71. doi:10.1177/027347539802000108

Badke-Schaub, P., & Frankenberger, E. (2002). Analysing and modelling cooperative design by the critical situation method. *Le Travail Humain, 65*(44), 293–314. doi:10.3917/th.654.0293

Baird, F., Moore, C. J., & Jagodzinski, A. P. (2000). An ethnographic study of engineering design teams at Rolls-Royce Aerospace. *Design Studies, 21*(4), 333–355. doi:10.1016/S0142-694X(00)00006-5

Baker, D. (2008). Peer assessment in small groups: A comparison of methods. *Journal of Management Education, 32*(2), 183–209. doi:10.1177/1052562907310489

Ballard, B., & Clanchy, J. (1991). *Teaching students from overseas: a brief guide for lecturers and supervisors*. Melbourne: Longman Cheshire.

Ballesteros, M. (Ed.). (2008). *Verb crisis*. Barcelona: ACTAR.

Ball, L. (2002). Preparing graduates in art and design to meet the challenges of working in the creative industries: A new model for work. *Art. Design & Communication in Higher Education, 1*(1), 10–24. doi:10.1386/adch.1.1.10

Bandura, A. (1963). *Social Learning and Personality Development*. New York: Holt, Rinehart and Winston.

Bandura, A. (1977). *Social Learning Theory*. Oxford: Prentice-Hall.

Banham, R. (1996). A black box: The secret profession of architecture. In M. Banham, P. Barker, S. Lyall, & C. Price (Eds.). A critic writes: Essays by Reyner Banham (pp. 292-299). Berkeley: University of California Press. (Originally printed in New Statesman and Society 12 October 1990).

Barab, S. A., Thomas, M. K., Dodge, T., Squire, K., & Newell, M. (2004). Critical design ethnography: Designing for change. *Anthropology & Education Quarterly*, *35*(2), 254–268. doi:10.1525/aeq.2004.35.2.254

Barber, P. (2004). Developing and assessing group design work: a case study. *Paper presented at the International Engineering and Product Design Education Conference*, DELFT, Netherlands.

Barber, J. P., King, P. M., & Baxter Magolda, M. B. (2013). Long strides on the journey toward self-authorship: Substantial developmental shifts in college students' meaning making. *The Journal of Higher Education*, *84*(6), 866–896. doi:10.1353/jhe.2013.0033

Barnes, S. Sydney Sidetracks. Retrieved from http://www.abc.net.au/innovation/sidetracks/default.htm

Barnett, R. (2000). *Realizing the university in an age of supercomplexity*. New York: Open University Press.

Barnett, R. (2004). 2012). Learning for an unknown future. *Higher Education Research & Development*, *31*(1), 65–77. doi:10.1080/07294360.2012.642841

Barns, S. (2011). Street Haunting: Sounding the Invisible City. In M. Foth, L. Forlano, C. Satchell, & M. Gibbs (Eds.), *From Social Butterfly to Engaged Citizen* (pp. 203–216). London: The MIT Press.

Baron, R. A. (1990). Conflict in organizations. In K. R. Murphy & F. E. Saal (Eds.), *Psychology in organizations: Integrating science and practice* (pp. 197–216). Hillsdale, NJ: Lawrence Erlbaum Associates Inc. Publishers.

Barrett, E., & Lally, V. (1999). Gender differences in an on line learning environment. *Journal of Computer Assisted Learning*, *15*(1), 48–60. doi:10.1046/j.1365-2729.1999.151075.x

Barron, B. (2000). Achieving Coordination in Collaborative Problem-Solving Groups. *Journal of the Learning Sciences*, *9*(4), 403–436. doi:10.1207/S15327809JLS0904_2

Barron, B. (2003). When smart groups fail. *Journal of the Learning Sciences*, *12*(3), 307–359. doi:10.1207/S15327809JLS1203_1

Barron, B. J., Schwartz, D. L., Vye, N. J., Moore, A., Petrosino, A., Zech, L., & Bransford, J. D. (1998). Doing with understanding: Lessons from research on problem-and project-based learning. *Journal of the Learning Sciences*, *7*(3-4), 271–311. doi:10.1080/10508406.1998.9672056

Barros, B., & Verdejo, M. F. (2000). Analysing student interaction processes in order to improve collaboration. The DEGREE approach. *International Journal of Artificial Intelligence in Education*, *11*(3), 221–241.

Barr, T. F., Dixon, A. L., & Gassenheimer, J. B. (2005). Exploring the "Lone Wolf" Phenomenon in Student Teams. *Journal of Marketing Education*, *27*(1), 81–90. doi:10.1177/0273475304273459

Basit, T. N., & Tomlinson, S. (2012). *Social inclusion and higher education*. Policy Press.

Bates, D., Mitsogiannini, V., & Ramirez-Lovering, D. (Eds.). (2015). Studio Futures: Changing trajectories in architectural education. Melbourne: uro publications.

Baxter Magolda, M. B. (1992). *Knowing and reasoning in college: Gender-related patterns in students' intellectual development*. San Francisco, CA: Jossey-Bass.

Baxter Magolda, M. B. (2001). *Making their own way: Narratives for transforming higher education to promote self-development*. Sterling, VA: Stylus.

Baxter Magolda, M. B., & King, P. M. (2007). Interview strategies for assessing self-authorship: Constructing conversations to assess meaning making. *Journal of College Student Development*, *48*(5), 491–508. doi:10.1353/csd.2007.0055

Beer, D. F. (2002, September 17-20). Reflections on why engineering students don't like to write - and what we can do about it. *Paper presented at theIEEE International Professional Communication Conference*, Portland, Oregon. doi:10.1109/IPCC.2002.1049119

Behfar, K. J., Peterson, R. S., Mannix, E. A., & Trochim, W. M. K. (2008). The critical role of conflict resolution in teams: A close look at the links between conflict type, conflict management strategies, and team outcomes. *The Journal of Applied Psychology*, *93*(1), 170–188. doi:10.1037/0021-9010.93.1.170 PMID:18211143

Bendiner-Viani, G. (2005). Walking, Emotion, and Dwelling: Guided Tours in Prospect Heights, Brooklyn. *Space and Culture*, *8*(4), 459–471. doi:10.1177/1206331205280144

Bexley, E., James, R., & Arkoudis, S. (2011). *The Australian Academic Profession in Transition: Addressing the Challenge of Reconceptualising Academic Work and Regenerating the Academic Workforce*. Centre for the Study of Higher Education.

Beyerle, A. (2016). *Participation in Architecture: Agonism in Practice* [Doctoral Dissertation]. The University of Melbourne, Parkville, VIC.

Beyerle, A. (2014). Agonistic Participation: A political and architectural opportunity. *Journal of Arts and Communities*, *5*(2-3), 147–169.

Bhika, R., Francis, A., & Miller, D. (2013). Faculty professional development: advancing integrative social pedagogy using ePortfolio. *International Journal of ePortfolio, 3*(2), 117-133.

Bielefeld, B., & El Khouli, S. (2007). *Basics: Design Ideas*. Basel: Birkhäuser.

Biggs, J. (1986). Assessing student approaches to learning *'Research and development in higher education: volume 8: papers presented at the eleventh annual conference of the Higher Education Research and Development Society of Australasia, University of Auckland, Auckland, New Zealand, 24th-27th August 1985' edited by J Jones and M Hornsburgh, pages 241- 246. Sydney: Higher Education Research and Development Society of Australasia.*

Biggs, J., & Tang, C. (2007). Teaching for Quality Learning at University: What the student does (3rd ed.). Maidenhead, Berks: Open University Press/McGraw Hill Education.

Biggs, J., & Watkins, D. (1996). The Chinese learner in retrospect. In D.A. Watkins & J.B. Biggs (Eds.), The Chinese learner: cultural, psychological and contextual influences (pp. 269-285). Hong Kong: Comparative Education Research Centre (CERC) and Melbourne: Australian Council for Educational Research (ACER).

Bilda, Z., & Demirkan, H. (2003). An insight on designers' sketching activities in traditional versus digital media. *Design Studies*, *24*(1), 27–50. doi:10.1016/S0142-694X(02)00032-7

Billig, S. (2000). Research on K-12 school-based service-learning: The evidence builds. *Phi Delta Kappan*, *2000*, 658.

Billig, S. H., & Waterman, A. S. (Eds.), (2014). *Studying service-learning: Innovations in education research methodology*. Routledge.

Bishop, C. (2006a). Letters: Claire Bishop responds. *Artforum*, *44*(May), 24.

Bishop, C. (2006b). *Participation, Documents of contemporary art. Whitechapel.* London and Cambridge, MA: The MIT Press.

Bishop, C. (2006c). The Social Turn: Collaboration and Its Discontents. *Artforum*, February, 179–183.

Björgvinsson, E., Ehn, P., & Hillgren, P. A. (2012). Design things and design thinking: Contemporary participatory design challenges. *Design Issues*, *28*(3), 101–116. doi:10.1162/DESI_a_00165

Blaj-Ward, L. (2011). Skills versus pedagogy? Doctoral research training in the UK Arts and Humanities. *Higher Education Research & Development*, *30*(6), 697–708. doi:10.1080/07294360.2010.535507

Blake, P. (1977). *Form Follows Fiasco: Why Modern Architecture Hasn't Worked.* Boston: Little Brown.

Blosiu, J. O. (1999). Use of synectics as an idea seeding technique to enhance design creativity. *Paper presented at the IEEE SMC '99 Conference on Systems, Man, and Cybernetics,* Tokyo. doi:10.1109/ICSMC.1999.823365

Blundell Jones, P. (2005). Sixty-eight and after. In P. Blundell Jones, D. Petrescu, & J. Till (Eds.), *Architecture and Participation* (pp. 127–139). London, New York: Spon Press.

Boden, M. A. (2004). *The Creative Mind: Myths and Mechanisms* (2nd ed.). London: Routledge.

Bødker, S. (1996). Creating conditions for participation: Conflicts and resources in systems design. *Human-Computer Interaction*, *11*(3), 215–236. doi:10.1207/s15327051hci1103_2

Bolton, S., & Green, L. (2007). *Getting Design Off the Substitute Bench: Reframing and realigning design processes for the business development game. Emerging Trends in Design Research.* International Association of Societies of Design Research, The Hong Kong Polytechnic University School of Design.

Bonta, J. P. (1979). *Architecture and its Interpretation: a study of expressive systems in architecture.* New York: Rizzoli.

Boroditsky, L. (2001). Does Language Shape Thought?: Mandarin and English Speakers' Conceptions of Time. *Cognitive Psychology*, *43*(1), 1–22. doi:10.1006/cogp.2001.0748 PMID:11487292

Bose, M., Pennypacker, E., & Yahner, T. (2006). Enhancing critical thinking through 'independent design decision making' in the studio. *Open House International*, *31*(3), 33–42.

Boud, D., Cohen, R., & Sampson, J. (Eds.). (2014). *Peer Learning in Higher Education: Learning from and with each other.* London: Routledge.

Boud, D., & Falchikov, N. (1989). Quantitative Studies of Student Self-Assessment in Higher Education: A Critical Analysis of Findings. *Higher Education*, *18*(5), 529–549. doi:10.1007/BF00138746

Boud, D., & Feletti, G. (1998). *The challenge of problem-based learning* (2nd ed.). London, Stirling: Psychology Press.

Bourriaud, N. (2002). *Relational aesthetics.* France: Les presses du réel.

Bowerman, M. (1996). Which way to the present? Cross-linguistic differences in thinking about time. In J. Gumperz & S. Levinson (Eds.), *Rethinking linguistic relativity* (pp. 145–176). Cambridge, MA: Cambridge Univ. Press.

Boyer, E. L., & Mitgang, L. D. (1996). *Building community: A new future for architecture education and practice.* Carnegie Foundation for the Advancement of Teaching.

Bradley, J. H., & Hebert, F. J. (1997). The effect of personality type on team performance. *Journal of Management Development*, *16*(5), 337–353. doi:10.1108/02621719710174525

Bradley, J., White, B. J., & Mennecke, B. E. (2003). Teams and tasks: A temporal framework for the effects of interpersonal interventions on team performance. *Small Group Research, 34*(3), 358–387. doi:10.1177/1046496403034003004

Brandt, C. B., Cennamo, K., Douglas, S., Vernon, M., McGrath, M., & Reimer, Y. (2013). A theoretical framework for the studio as a learning environment. *International Journal of Technology and Design Education, 23*(2), 329–348. doi:10.1007/s10798-011-9181-5

Bravo, C., Redondo, M. A., Ortega, M., & Verdejo, M. F. (2006). Collaborative environments for the learning of design: A model and a case study in Domotics. *Computers & Education, 46*(2), 152–173. doi:10.1016/j.compedu.2004.07.009

Brereton, M., & McGarry, B. (2000). An observational study of how objects support engineering design thinking and communication: implications for the design of tangible media. *Paper presented at theSIGCHI conference on Human Factors in Computing Systems*, The Hague, The Netherlands. doi:10.1145/332040.332434

Brewster, A. B., Pisani, P., Ramseyer, M., & Wise, J. (2016). Building a university-community partnership to promote high school graduation and beyond: An innovative undergraduate team approach. *Journal of Applied Research in Higher Education, 8*(1), 44–58. doi:10.1108/JARHE-10-2014-0093

Bringle, R. G., & Hatcher, J. A. (1996). Implementing service learning in higher education. *The Journal of Higher Education, 67*(2), 221–239. doi:10.2307/2943981

Bringle, R. G., & Hatcher, J. A. (2000). Institutionalization of Service Learning in Higher Education. *The Journal of Higher Education, 71*(3), 273. doi:10.2307/2649291

Brolin, B. (1976). *The Failure of Modern Architecture*. London: Studio Vista.

Brooks, C. M., & Ammons, J. L. (2003). Free riding in group projects and the effects of timing, frequency, and specificity of criteria in peer assessments. *Journal of Education for Business, 78*(5), 268–272. doi:10.1080/08832320309598613

Broome, J. (2005). Mass housing cannot be sustained. In P. Blundell Jones, D. Petrescu, & J. Till (Eds.), *Architecture and Participation* (pp. 65–75). London, New York: Spon Press.

Broome, J., & Richardson, B. (1995). *The self-build book. Rev. & updated edn*. Totnes, Devon: Green Earth Books.

Brown, R. W. (1995, November 1-4). Autorating: Getting Individual Marks from Team Marks and Enhancing Teamwork. *Paper presented at the25th Annual Frontiers in Education Conference*, Atlanta, Georgia. doi:10.1109/FIE.1995.483140

Brown, T., & Martin, R. (2015). Design for Action. *Harvard Business Review*, September, 56–64.

Bucciarelli, L. L. (1988). An ethnographic perspective on engineering design. *Design Studies, 9*(3), 159–168. doi:10.1016/0142-694X(88)90045-2

Bucciarelli, L. L. (2002). Between thought and object in engineering design. *Design Studies, 23*(3), 219–231. doi:10.1016/S0142-694X(01)00035-7

Buckenmyer, J. A. (2000). Using Teams for Class Activities: Making Course/Classroom Teams Work. *Journal of Education for Business, 76*(2), 98–107. doi:10.1080/08832320009599960

Burgess, J. (2009). Remediating vernacular creativity: Photography and cultural citizenship in the Flickr photosharing network. In T. Edensor, D. Leslie, S. Millington, & N. Rantisi (Eds.), *Spaces of Vernacular Creativity: Rethinking the Cultural Economy* (pp. 116–126). London: Routledge.

Burleson, B. R., & Caplan, S. E. (1998). Cognitive complexity. In J. C. McCroskey, J. A. Daly, M. M. Martin, & M. J. Beatty (Eds.), *Communication and personality: Trait perspectives* (pp. 233–286). Cresskill, NJ: Hampton Press.

Burningham, C., & West, M. A. (1995). Individual, climate, and group interaction processes as predictors of work team innovation. *Small Group Research, 26*(1), 106–117. doi:10.1177/1046496495261006

Burns, R. B. (1991). Study and Stress Among First Year Overseas Students in an Australian University. *Higher Education Research & Development, 10*(1), 61–77. doi:10.1080/0729436910100106

Burry, M. (2011). *Scripting Cultures: Architectural Design and Programming*. London: John Wiley and Sons.

Busby, J. R. (2001). Error and distributed cognition in design. *Design Studies, 22*(3), 233–254. doi:10.1016/S0142-694X(00)00028-4

Byun, S.-E., Kim, H., & Duffey, M. (2012). A multicourse collaborative project within a global context: Multidimensional learning outcomes for merchandising and interior design majors. *Clothing & Textiles Research Journal, 30*(3), 200–216. doi:10.1177/0887302X12453646

Campion, M. A., Medsker, G. J., & Higgs, C. A. (1993). Relations between work group characteristics and effectiveness: Implications for designing effective work groups. *Personnel Psychology, 46*(4), 823–850. doi:10.1111/j.1744-6570.1993.tb01571.x

Campion, M. A., Papper, E. M., & Medsker, G. J. (1996). Relations between work team characteristics and effectiveness: A replication and extension. *Personnel Psychology, 49*(2), 429–452. doi:10.1111/j.1744-6570.1996.tb01806.x

Cano, J. L., Lidon, I., Rebollar, R., Roman, P., & Saenz, M. J. (2006). Student groups solving real-life projects. A case study of experiential learning. *International Journal of Engineering Education, 22*(6), 1252–1260.

Cárdenas, C. (2009, October 18-21). Social design in multidisciplinary engineering design courses. *Paper presented at the 39th IEEE Frontiers in Education Conference*, San Antonio, Texas. doi:10.1109/FIE.2009.5350878

Carey, T. (2015). Defining learning outcomes is just the beginning: Exploring a learning outcomes value cycle for KPU. *Teaching Matters@KPU, 8*. Retrieved from http://www.kpu.ca/sites/default/files/ Teaching_and_Learning /INSTL-newsletter_Sep2015_Issue4.pdf

Carmel-Gilfilen, C. (2012). Uncovering pathways of design thinking and learning: Inquiry on intellectual development and learning style preferences. *Journal of Interior Design, 37*(3), 47–66. doi:10.1111/j.1939-1668.2012.01077.x

Carson, L. (2006). Raising the Bar on Criticality: Students' Critical Reflection in an Internship Program. *Journal of Management Education, 30*(5), 700–723. doi:10.1177/1052562905284962

Carvalho, L., & Goodyear, P. (2014). *The Architecture of Productive Learning Networks*. NY: Routledge.

Carvalho, L., Goodyear, P., & de Laat, M. (2016). *Place-based Spaces for Networked Learning*. NY: Routledge.

Case, J. M. (2013). *Researching student learning in higher education: A social realist approach*. New York: Routledge.

Case, J. M. (in press). Journeys to meaning-making: A longitudinal study of self-authorship amongst young South African engineering graduates. *Journal of College Student Development*.

Caspersen, J., Frølich, N., Karlsen, H., & Aamodt Per, O. (2014). Learning outcomes across disciplines and professions: Measurement and interpretation. *Quality in Higher Education, 20*(2), 195–215. doi:10.1080/13538322.2014.904587

Casperz, D., Wu, M., & Skene, J. 2003. Factors influencing effective performance of university student teams. *Paper presented at the Learning for an unknown future:proceedings of the 2003 Annual International Conference of the Higher Education Research and Development Society of Australasia (HERDSA)*, Christchurch, New Zealand.

Centre of Cultural Partnerships. (2013). *Spectres of Evaluation* (L. MacDowall et al., Eds.). Parkville, VIC: The University of Melbourne.

CFC. Media Lab., (2003). Murmur. Retrieved from http://murmurtoronto.ca/index.php

Chai, K.-H., & Xiao, X. (2012). Understanding design research: A bibliometric analysis of Design Studies (1996-2010). *Design Studies*, *33*(1), 24–43. doi:10.1016/j.destud.2011.06.004

Chalfen, R. (1987). *Snapshot versions of life*. Bowling Green, OH: Bowling Green State University Popular Press.

Chan, C. K. K. (2001). Promoting learning and understanding through constructivist approaches for Chinese learners. In D.A.W. & J.B. Biggs. (Eds.), Teaching the Chinese learner: psychological and pedagogical perspectives (pp. 181-203.). Hong Kong: Comparative Education Research Centre Melbourne Vic: Australian Council for Educational Research.

Chandrasekaran, S., Stojcevski, A., Littlefair, G., & Joordens, M. (2013). Project-oriented design-based learning: Aligning students' views with industry needs. *International Journal of Engineering Education*, *29*(5), 1109–1118.

Chapman, K. J. (2006). Can't We Pick our Own Groups? The Influence of Group Selection Method on Group Dynamics and Outcomes. *Journal of Management Education*, *30*(4), 557–569. doi:10.1177/1052562905284872

Chapman, K. J., & Auken, S. V. (2001). Creating Positive Group Project Experiences: An Examination of the Role of the Instructor on Students' Perceptions of Group Projects. *Journal of Marketing Education*, *23*(2), 117–127. doi:10.1177/0273475301232005

Chase, J., Crawford, M., & Kaliski, J. (Eds.). (2008). *Everyday Urbanism*. New York: The Monacelli Press.

Chickering, A. W. (1969). *Education and identity*. San Francisco: Jossey Boss.

Chiocchio, F., Forgues, D., David, C., & Iordanova, I. (2011). Teamwork in integrated design projects: Understanding the effects of trust, conflict, and collaboration on performance. *Project Management Journal*, *42*(6), 78–91. doi:10.1002/pmj.20268

Chiu, M. (2002). An organisational view of design communication in design collaboration. *Design Studies*, *23*(2), 187–210. doi:10.1016/S0142-694X(01)00019-9

Chiu, S. H. (2010). Students' knowledge sources and knowledge sharing in the design studio-an exploratory study. *International Journal of Technology and Design Education*, *20*(1), 27–42. doi:10.1007/s10798-008-9061-9

Choi, S. H. J., & Nieminen, T. A. (2012). Factors influencing the higher education of international students from Confucian East Asia. *Higher Education Research & Development*, *32*(2), 161–173. doi:10.1080/07294360.2012.673165

Christiaans, H.C.M. (2002). Creativity as a design criterion. *Communication Research Journal,* 14(1), 41-54.

Chronister, L. M., Ameri, A., Golden, D., McEnroe, R., & Malek-Aslani, C. (2014, February 26). *University of Washington Department of Architecture National Architectural Accrediting Board (NAAB) Visiting Team Report (VTR)*. Retrieved from http://arch.be.washington.edu/sites/default/ files/pdf/UW_NAAB_2014_VTR_%5BFinal%20Draft%5D.pdf

Cicek, J. S., Ingram, S., Sepehri, N., Burak, J. P., Labossiere, P., & Mann, D. Topping A. (2015). Rubrics as a Vehicle to Define the Twelve CEAB Graduate Attributes, Determine Graduate Competencies, and Develop a Common Language for Engineering Stakeholders. *Proceedings of the Canadian Engineering Education Association*. Winnipeg MB: Canadian Engineering Education Association.

Coates, N. (2012). *Narrative architecture*. Hoboken, NJ: Wiley.

Coffield, F., Moseley, D., Hall, E., & Ecclestone, K. (2004). *Learning styles and pedagogy in post-16 learning: a systematic and critical review.* London: The Learning and Skills Research Centre.

Cohen, E. G. (1994). Restructuring the Classroom: Conditions for Productive Small Groups. *Review of Educational Research, 64*(1), 1–35. doi:10.3102/00346543064001001

Cohen, S. G. (1997). What Makes Teams Work: Group Effectiveness Research from the Shop Floor to the Executive Suite. *Journal of Management, 23*(3), 239–290. doi:10.1177/014920639702300303

Colebrook, C. (2002). *Understanding Deleuze.* Crows Nest, NSW: Allen & Unwin.

Coley, F., Houseman, O., & Roy, R. (2007). An introduction to capturing and understanding the cognitive behaviour of design engineers. *Journal of Engineering Design, 18*(4), 311–325. doi:10.1080/09544820600963412

Collins, P. (1971). *Architectural Judgement.* Montreal: McGill-Queen's University Press.

Colomina, B. (Ed.), (1992). *Sexuality and Space.* New York: Princeton Architectural Press.

Cornell, A. (Ed.), (2012). *Breakthrough! 90 Proven Strategies to Overcome Creative Block & Spark Your Imagination.* New York: Princeton Architectural Press.

Costa, R., & Sobek, D. K. (2004). How process affects performance: an analysis of student design productivity. *Paper presented at theASME '04 International Design Engineering Technical Conferences and Computers and Information in Engineering Conference,* Salt Lake City, Utah USA. doi:10.1115/DETC2004-57274

Costanzo, D. (2016). *What Architecture Means: Connecting Ideas and Design.* New York: Routledge/Taylor & Francis.

Costigan, R. D., John, S., & College, F. (2009). Developing The Great Eight Competencies with Leaderless Group Discussion. *Journal of Management Education, 33*(5), 596–616. doi:10.1177/1052562908318328

Côté, J., Skinkle, R., & Motte, A. (2008). Do perceptions of costs and benefits of post-secondary education influence participation? *Canadian Journal of Higher Education, 38*(2), 73–93.

Council for Interior Design Accreditation. (2015). *Final draft professional standards 2017: August 2015.* Retrieved from http://accredit-id.org/wp-content/uploads/2014/10/Professional-Standards-2017-final-draft-August-2015.pdf

Council for Interior Design Qualification [CIDQ]. (2004). *Definition of interior design.* Retrieved from http://www.ncidqexam.org/about-interior-design/definition-of-interior-design/

Council of Europe. (2014) *New Colombo Plan.* Retrieved from http://www.coe.int/t/dg4/intercultural/concept_EN.asp

Coventry, K. R., & Garrod, S. C. (2004). *Saying, seeing and acting: The psychological semantics of spatial prepositions.* Psychology Press.

Cox, G. (2005). *Cox Review of Creativity in Business: Building on the UK's Strengths.* London: HM Treasury.

Cox, K. (2015). Meaning making in the life story, and not coherence or vividness, predicts well-being up to 3 years later: Evidence from high point and low point stories. *Identity, 15*(4), 241–262. doi:10.1080/15283488.2015.1089508

Crabbe, A. (2008). The value of knowledge transfer collaborations to design academics. *Design Journal, 11*(1), 9–28. doi:10.2752/175630608X317887

Crawford, C. (2005). *Chris Crawford on interactive storytelling.* Berkeley, CA: New Riders.

Cret, P. (1941). The Ecole des Beaux-Arts and architectural education. *The Journal of the American Society of Architectural Historians, 1*(2), 3–15. doi:10.2307/901128

Crosby, A. L., Hromek, M. J., & Kinniburgh, J. (2015, August). Making space: Working together for Indigenous design and architecture curricula. *Paper presented at theIndigenous Content in Education Symposium.* Adelaide, Australia.

Crossley, T. (2006). Letting the drama into group work: Using conflict constructively in performing arts group practice. *Arts and Humanities in Higher Education, 5*(1), 33–50. doi:10.1177/1474022206059996

Cross, N. (1982). Designerly ways of knowing. *Design Studies, 3*(4), 221–227. doi:10.1016/0142-694X(82)90040-0

Cross, N. (2006). *(2007). Designerly Ways of Knowing. Rprt.* Basel: Birkhaüser.

Cross, N. (2008). *Engineering Design Methods: Strategies for Product Design* (4th ed.). Chichester, West Sussex: Wiley.

Cross, N. (2011). *Design Thinking.* Bloomsbury Academic.

Cross, N. (2011). *Design Thinking: Understanding How Designers Think and Work.* Oxford: Berg.

Cross, N., & Clayburn Cross, A. (1995). Observations of teamwork and social processes in design. *Design Studies, 16*(2), 143–170. doi:10.1016/0142-694X(94)00007-Z

Cross, N., & Clayburn-Cross, A. (1996). Observations of teamwork and social processes in design. In N. Cross, H. Christiaans, & K. Dorst (Eds.), *Analysing design activity* (pp. 291–318). Chichester, US: John Wiley & Sons Ltd.

Crowther, P. (2013). Understanding the signature pedagogy of the design studio and the opportunities for its technological enhancement. *Journal of Learning Design, 6*(3), 18–28. doi:10.5204/jld.v6i3.155

Csikszentmihalyi, M. (1996). *Creativity: flow and the psychology of discovery and invention.* New York: Harper Collins Publishers.

Csikszentmihalyi, M. (1996). *Creativity: Flow and the Psychology of Discovery and invention.* New York: HarperCollinsPublishers.

Csikszentmihalyi, M. (2004). *Good Business: Leadership, flow, and the making of meaning.* London: Penguin.

Cuff, D. (1991). *Architecture: The story of practice.* Cambridge, MA: MIT Press.

Cummings, T. G. (1981). Designing effective work groups. In P. C. Nystrom & W. H. Starbuck (Eds.), *Handbook of organizational design.* New York: Oxford University Press.

Curedale, R. (2012). *Design Methods 2: 200 more ways to apply design thinking.* Topanga, CA: Design Community College.

Curedale, R. (2013). *Design Methods 1: 200 ways to apply design thinking.* Topanga, CA: Design Community College.

Cuseo, J. 2000. Collaborative and cooperative learning: Pedagogy for promoting new-student retention and achievement. *Paper presented at thePreconference workshop delivered at the 19th Annual Conference on The First-Year Experience,* Columbia, SC.

Cuseo, J. (1996). *Cooperative learning: A pedagogy for addressing contemporary challenges.* Stillwater, OK: New Forums Press.

Cushner, K., & Karim, A. (2004). Study Abroad at the University Level. In D. Landis, M. Bennett, & J. Bennett (Eds.), *Handbook of Intercultural Training.* Thousand Oaks, CA: Sage. doi:10.4135/9781452231129.n12

Dacey, J. S., & Lennon, K. H. (1998). *Understanding creativity: the interplay of biological, psychological, and social factors.* San Francisco: Jossey-Bass.

Dall'Alba, G., & Barnacle, R. (2007). An ontological turn for higher education. *Studies in Higher Education*, *32*(6), 679–691. doi:10.1080/03075070701685130

Das, M., Mpofu, , Dunn, , & Lanphear, . (1998). Self and tutor evaluations in problem based learning tutorials: Is there a relationship? *Medical Education*, *32*(4), 411–418. doi:10.1046/j.1365-2923.1998.00217.x PMID:9743805

Davenport, T., & Prusak, L. (2000). *Working Knowledge: How Organizations Manage What They Know*. Cambridge, MA: Harvard Business School Press.

Davies, P. (2000). Computerized Peer Assessment. *Innovations in Education and Teaching International*, *37*(4), 346–355.

Davis, D.C., & Ulseth, R.R. (2013, June). Building Student Capacity for High Performance Teamwork. *Paper presented at 2013 ASEE Annual Conference*, Atlanta, Georgia. Retrieved from https://peer.asee.org/19274

Davis, D. C., Gentili, K. L., Trevisan, M. S., & Calkins, D. E. (2002). Engineering Design Assessment Processes and Scoring Scales for Program Improvement and Accountability. *The Journal of Engineering Education*, *91*(2), 211–221. doi:10.1002/j.2168-9830.2002.tb00694.x

Davis, D., Trevisan, M. S., Davis, H. P., Beyerlein, S. W., Howe, S., Thompson, P. L., & Khan, M. J. et al. (2011). IDEALS: A model for integrating engineering design professional skills, assessment and learning.*Proceedings of the American Society for Engineering Education Annual Conference*. Vancouver, Canada: ASEE.

Davis, D., Trevisan, M., Gerlick, R., Davis, H., McCormack, J., Beyerlein, S., & Brackin, P. et al. (2010). Assessing team member citizenship in capstone engineering design courses. *International Journal of Engineering Education*, *26*(4), 771.

Davis, D., Trevisan, M., Leiffer, P., McCormack, J., Beyerlein, S., Khan, M. J., & Brackin, P. (2013). Reflection and metacognition in engineering practice. In M. Kaplan, N. Silver, D. LaVaque-Manty, & D. Meizlish (Eds.), *Using reflection and metacognition to improve student learning: Across the disciplines, across the academy*. Sterling, VA: Stylus Publishing, LLC.

Davis, M. (2008). Toto, I've Got a Feeling We're Not in Kansas Anymore…. *Interaction*, *15*(5), 29–34.

Dayton, E., & Henriksen, K. (2007). Teamwork and Communication: Communication Failure: Basic Components, Contributing Factors, and the Call for Structure. *Joint Commission Journal on Quality and Patient Safety*, *33*(1), 34–47. PMID:17283940

De Carlo, G. (2005). Architecture's public. In P. Blundell Jones, D. Petrescu, & J. Till (Eds.), *Architecture and Participation* (pp. 3–22). London, New York: Spon Press.

De Certeau, M. (1988). *The Practice of Everyday Life* (S. Rendall, Trans.). Berkeley, CA: University of California Press.

de Dreu, C. K. W. (1997). Productive conflict: The importance of conflict management and conflict issues. In C. de Drew & E. Van de Vliert (Eds.), *Using conflict in organizations* (pp. 9–22). London: Sage. doi:10.4135/9781446217016.n2

de Dreu, C. K. W., & Vianen, A. E. M. V. (2001). Managing relationship conflict and the effectiveness of organizational teams. *Journal of Organizational Behavior*, *22*(3), 309–328. doi:10.1002/job.71

De Dreu, C. K. W., & Weingart, L. R. (2003). Task versus relationship conflict, team performance, and team member satisfaction: A meta-analysis. *The Journal of Applied Psychology*, *88*(4), 741–749. doi:10.1037/0021-9010.88.4.741 PMID:12940412

De Graaf, E., & Kolmos, A. (2003). Characteristics of problem-based learning. *International Journal of Engineering Education*, *19*(5), 657–662.

De Janasz, S. C., & Forret, M. L. (2007). Learning The Art of Networking: A Critical Skill for Enhancing Social Capital and Career Success. *Journal of Management Education, 32*(5), 629–650. doi:10.1177/1052562907307637

de Solà-Morales, I. (1997). Weak architecture. In I. De Solà-Morales (Ed.), Differences: topographies of contemporary architecture (trans G. Thompson). Cambridge, MA: The MIT Press.

De Vita, G. (2001). *The use of group work in large and diverse business management classes: Some critical issues.* Paper presented at the The International Journal of Management Education. doi:10.3794/ijme.13.11

De Vita, G. (2007). Taking stock: An appraisal of the literature on internationalising HE learning. In *Internationalising higher education* (pp. 154-167).

De Vita, G. (2002). Does assessed multicultural group work really pull UK students' average down? *Assessment & Evaluation in Higher Education, 27*(2), 153–161. doi:10.1080/02602930220128724

De Wit, F. R. C., Greer, L. L., & Jehn, K. A. (2012). The paradox of intragroup conflict: A meta-analysis. *The Journal of Applied Psychology, 97*(2), 360–390. doi:10.1037/a0024844 PMID:21842974

Deeter-Schmelz, D. R., Kennedy, K. N., & Ramsey, R. P. (2002a). Enriching our understanding of student team effectiveness. *Journal of Marketing Education, 24*(2), 114–124. doi:10.1177/0273475302242004

Dekker, A., Worthy, P., Viller, S., Zimbardi, K., & Robinson, R. (2014). Designer-client communication in web design: a case study on the use of communication in practice.*Proceedings of the 26th Australian Computer-Human Interaction Conference on Designing Futures: the Future of Design* (pp. 440-443). ACM. doi:10.1145/2686612.2686681

Delahaye, B. L. (2005). *Human Resource Development: Adult Learning and Knowledge Management.* Brisbane: John Wiley & Sons.

Denton, H., & McDonagh, D. (2005). An exercise in symbiosis: Undergraduate designers and a company product development team working together. *Design Journal, 8*(1), 41–50. doi:10.2752/146069205789338315

Department of Foreign Affairs and Trade. (2014) *New Colombo Plan.* Retrieved from http://dfat.gov.au/people-to-people/new-colombo-plan/Pages/new-colombo-plan.aspx

Deutsch, R. (2011). *BIM and integrated design strategies for architectural practice.* Hoboken, N.J.: Wiley.

Deuze, M. (2007). *Media Work.* Cambridge: Polity Press.

DiSalvo, C. (2009). Design and the construction of publics. *Design Issues, 25*(1), 48–63. doi:10.1162/desi.2009.25.1.48

Dochy, F., Segers, M., & Sluijsmans, D. (1999a). The use of self-, peer and co-assessment in higher education: A review. *Studies in Higher Education, 24*(3), 331–350. doi:10.1080/03075079912331379935

Doise, W. (1990). The development of individual competencies through social interaction. In H. C. Foot, M. J. Morgan, & R. H. Shute (Eds.), *Children helping children* (pp. 43–64). Chichester: J. Wiley & sons.

Dommeyer, C. J. (2007). Using the diary method to deal with social loafers on the group project: its effects on peer evaluations, group behavior, and attitudes. *Journal of Marketing Education, 29*(2), 175–188. doi:10.1177/0273475307302019

Dommeyer, C. J., & Lammers, H. B. (2006). Students' attitudes toward a new method for preventing loafing on the group project: The team activity diary. *Journal of College Teaching and Learning, 3*, 15–22.

Donaldson, B., & Morris, D. (2001). *Architecture Newcastle: Preserving Its Educational History.* Newcastle: NSW RAIA.

Donato, R. (2004). 13. Aspects of Collaboration in Pedagogical Discourse. *Annual Review of Applied Linguistics, 24*, 284–302. doi:10.1017/S026719050400011X

Dong, A. (2005). The latent semantic approach to studying design team communication. *Design Studies, 26*(5), 445–461. doi:10.1016/j.destud.2004.10.003

Dool, R. (2010). Managing conflict in online multicultural student teams. *Journal of Education, Information, and Cybernetics, 2*(2).

Doppelt, Y. (2005). Assessment of Project-Based Learning in a MECHATRONICS Context. *Journal of Technology Education, 16*(2), 7–24.

Dorst, K. (2003). *Understanding design. 150 reflections on being a designer.* Amsterdam, Netherlands: BIS Publishers.

Dorst, K. (2006). *(2003). Understanding Design: 175 Reflections on Being a Designer* (Rev edn.). Corte Madera, CA: Gingko Press.

Dorst, K. (2015). *Frame Innovation: Create New Thinking by Design. Design Thinking/Design Theory.* Cambridge, MA: The MIT Press.

Dorst, K., & Cross, N. (2001). Creativity in the design process: Co-evolution of problem-solution. *Design Studies, 22*(5), 425–437. doi:10.1016/S0142-694X(01)00009-6

Dorta, T., Lesage, A., & Di Bartolo, C. (2012). Collaboration and design education through the interconnected HIS. *Physical Digitality:Proceedings of the eCAADe* (Vol. 2, pp. 97-105).

Drazin, R., & Auster, E. (1987). Wage differences between men and women: Performance appraisal ratings vs. salary allocation as the locus of bias. *Human Resource Management, 26*(2), 157–168. doi:10.1002/hrm.3930260204

Driskell, J. E., Hogan, R., & Salas, E. (1987). Personality and group performance. In C. Hendrick (Ed.), *Group processes and intergroup relations* (pp. 91–112). Newbury Park, CA: Sage.

Drucker, J., & McVarish, E. (2009). *Graphic design history: A critical guide.* Upper Saddle River, NJ: Pearson Prentice Hall.

Duke, C. (2000). Study Abroad Learning Activities: A Synthesis and Comparison. *Journal of Marketing Education, 22*(2), 155–165. doi:10.1177/0273475300222010

Dunne, A., & Raby, F. (2013). Speculative Everything: Design, Fiction, and Social Dreaming. Cambridge, MA, USA: MIT Press.

Dutson, A. J., Todd, R. H., Magleby, S. P., & Sorensen, C. D. (1997). A Review of Literature on Teaching Engineering Design Through Project-Oriented Capstone Courses. *The Journal of Engineering Education, 86*(1), 17–28. doi:10.1002/j.2168-9830.1997.tb00260.x

Dutton, T. A. (1987). Design and studio pedagogy. *Journal of Architectural Education, 41*(1), 16–25. doi:10.1080/10464883.1987.10758461

Dutton, T. A., & Mann, L. H. (Eds.). (1996). *Reconstructing architecture: Critical discourses and social practices.* Minnesota: University of Minnesota Press.

Du, X., & Kolmos, A. (2009). Increasing the diversity of engineering education – a gender analysis in a PBL context. *European Journal of Engineering Education, 34*(5), 425–437. doi:10.1080/03043790903137577

Dyer, W., & Dyer, J. (2013). *Team building proven strategies for improving team performance* (5th ed.). San Francisco: Jossey-Bass, A Wiley Imprint.

Dym, C. L., Agogino, A. M., Eris, O., Frey, D. D., & Leifer, L. J. (2005). Engineering Design Thinking, Teaching, and Learning. *The Journal of Engineering Education, 94*(1), 103–120. doi:10.1002/j.2168-9830.2005.tb00832.x

Eakin, P. J. (2008). *Living autobiographically: How we create identity in narrative.* Ithaca, NY: Cornell University Press.

Eastman, C. M. (1969). Cognitive processes and ill-defined problems: a case study from design*Proceedings of the 1st international joint conference on Artificial intelligence* (pp. 669-690). Washington, DC: Morgan Kaufmann Publishers Inc.

Eckert, C. M., & Stacey, M. K. (2001). Dimensions of communication in design. *Proceedings of the International Conference on Engineering Design, ICED01*, Glasgow (pp. 473-80).

Edward, N. S. (2004). Evaluations of introducing project-based design activities in the first and second years of engineering courses. *European Journal of Engineering Education, 29*(4), 491–503. doi:10.1080/03043790410001716284

Egea, K., McKenzie, J., & Griffiths, N. (2013). Achieving academic engagement: Supporting academics to embed first year transition pedagogies in the curriculum.*Proceedings of the 16th International First Year in Higher Education Conference.* Wellington, New Zealand.

Ehrlenspiel, I. K., Giapoulis, A., & Günther, J. (1997). Teamwork and design methodology—Observations about teamwork in design education. *Research in Engineering Design, 9*(2), 61–69. doi:10.1007/BF01596482

Eisenhardt, K. M., Kahwajy, J. L., & Bourgeois, L. J. III. (1997). Conflict and strategic choice: How top management teams disagree. *California Management Review, 39*(2), 42–62. doi:10.2307/41165886

Eldeen, H. (2003). Ethics for Architecture: Imperative Approach for Integrating Sustainable Thinking in Design Education. Proceedings of the Scientific Conference on Sustainable Architectural and Urban Design, Cairo, Egypt.

Elemental (2014). Projects – elemental. Retrieved from http://www.elementalchile.cl/en/projects/

Elger, D., & Russell, P. (2006). Crisis? What Crisis? *International Journal of Architectural Computing, 4*(1), 107–121. doi:10.1260/147807706777008966

Erez, M., & Zidon, I. (1984). Effect of goal acceptance on the relationship of goal difficulty to performance. *The Journal of Applied Psychology, 69*(1), 69–78. doi:10.1037/0021-9010.69.1.69

Esherick, J. (1977). Architectural education in the Thirties and Seventies: A personal view. In S. Kostof (Ed.), *The architect: Chapters in the history of the profession* (pp. 238–279). New York: Oxford University Press.

Espinosa, S. A., & Walker, J. (2011). *A complexity approach to sustainability: Theory and application.* London: Imperial College Press.

Etroo, F. (2011). *An assessment of teamwork among Ghanaian construction professionals.* Heriot-Watt University.

Ettington, D., & Camp, R. (2002). Facilitating transfer of skills between group projects and work teams. *Journal of Management Education, 26*(4), 356–379. doi:10.1177/105256290202600404

Evans, M., & Spruce, J. (2005, September 15-16). Knowledge Networks: Collaboration between Industry and Academia in Design.*Proceedings for the Engineering and Product Design Education Conference.* Napier University, Edinburgh, UK.

Falchikov, N. (1986). Product Comparisons and Process Benefits of Collaborative Peer Group and Self-assessment. *Assessment & Evaluation in Higher Education, 11*(2), 146–166. doi:10.1080/0260293860110206

Falchikov, N. (1988). Self and peer assessment of a group project designed to promote the skills of capability. *Programmed Learning and Educational Technology, 25*, 327–339.

Falchikov, N. (1991). Group process analysis: self and peer assessment of working together in a group. In S. Brown & P. Dove (Eds.), *Self and peer assessment.* Birmingham: SCED Publications.

Falchikov, N., & Goldfinch, J. (2000). Student Peer Assessment in Higher Education: A Meta-Analysis Comparing Peer and Teacher Marks. *Review of Educational Research, 70*(3), 287–322. doi:10.3102/00346543070003287

Falchikov, N., & Magin, D. (1997). Detecting gender bias in peer marking of students' group process work. *Assessment & Evaluation in Higher Education, 22*(4), 385–396. doi:10.1080/0260293970220403

Farh, J., Cannella, A., & Bedeian, A. (1991). The impact of purpose on rating quality and user acceptance. *Group & Organization Management, 16*(4), 367–386. doi:10.1177/105960119101600403

Feichtner, S. B., & Davis, E. A. (1984). Why some groups fail: A survey of students' experiences with learning groups. *The Organizational Behavior Teaching Review, 9*(4), 58–73.

Fellenz, M. R. (2006). Toward Fairness in Assessing Student Groupwork: A Protocol for Peer Evaluation of Individual Contributions. *Journal of Management Education, 30*(4), 570–591. doi:10.1177/1052562906286713

Ferrante, C. J., Green, S. G., & Forster, W. R. (2006). Getting more out of team projects: Incentivising leadership to enhance performance. *Journal of Management Education, 30*(6), 788–797. doi:10.1177/1052562906287968

Fiechtner, S. B., & Davis, E. A. (1992). Why some groups fail: A survey of students' experiences with learning groups. In A.S. Goodsell, M.R. Maher & V. Tinto (Eds.), Collaborative Learning: A Sourcebook for Higher Education. National Center on Postsecondary Teaching, Learning, & Assessment, Syracuse University.

Finke, R. A., Ward, T. B., & Smith, S. M. (1992). Creative cognition: Theory, research, and applications. Cambridge, MA: MIT Press (Bradford Book).

Fischer, G., Giaccardi, E., Eden, H., Sugimoto, M., & Ye, Y. (2005). Beyond binary choices: Integrating individual and social creativity. *International Journal of Human-Computer Studies, 63*(4-5), 482–512. doi:10.1016/j.ijhcs.2005.04.014

Fixson, S. (2009). *Teaching Innovation Through Interdisciplinary Courses and Programs in Product Design and Development: An Analysis at Sixteen U.S. Schools.* Babson College Center for Entrepreneurship Research Paper No. 2009-13.

Flom, N. A. (2014). *There and Back Again: Perceived Long-Term Effects of a High School Immersion Abroad Experience.* Education Doctoral Dissertations in Leadership.

Folger, J. P., Pooles, M. S., & Stutman, R. K. (2009). *Working through conflict: Strategies for relationships, groups, and organizations.* Pearson Education.

Fowler, A. (1995). How to build effective teams. *People Management, 1*(4).

Frank, M., Lavy, I., & Elata, D. (2003). Implementing the Project-Based Learning Approach in an Academic Engineering Course. *International Journal of Technology and Design Education, 13*(3), 273–288. doi:10.1023/A:1026192113732

Freeland, J. M. (1971). *The Making of a Profession: A History of the Growth and Work of the Architectural Institutes in Australia.* Sydney, NSW: Angus and Robertson.

Freeman, M., & McKenzie, J. (2001). Aligning peer assessment with peer learning for large classes: The case for an online self and peer assessment system. In. D. Boud, R. Cohen & J. Sampson (Eds.), Peer Learning in Higher Education: Learning from & with Each Other (pp. 156-169). London: Kogan Page.

Freeman, M., Hutchinson, D., Treleaven, L., & Sykes, C. (2006). Iterative learning: self and peer assessment of group work. *Paper presented at the Proceedings of the 23rd annual ascilite conference: Who's learning? Whose technology?,* The University of Sydney.

Freeman, K. A. (1996). Attitudes toward work in project groups as predictors of academic performance. *Small Group Research, 27*(2), 265–282. doi:10.1177/1046496496272004

Freeman, L., & Greenacre, L. (2011). An examination of socially destructive behaviors in group work. *Journal of Marketing Education*, *33*(1), 5–17. doi:10.1177/0273475310389150

Freeman, M., & McKenzie, J. (2002). SPARK, a confidential web-based template for self and peer assessment of student teamwork: Benefits of evaluating across different subjects. *British Journal of Educational Technology*, *33*(5), 551–569. doi:10.1111/1467-8535.00291

Freeman, S. (1964). International Study at Home and Abroad. *The Annals of the American Academy of Political and Social Science*, *356*(1), 133–141. doi:10.1177/000271626435600118

Fry, T., Dilnot, C., & Stewart, S. (2015). *Design and the Question of History*. London: Bloomsbury.

Furnham, A., & Stringfield, P. (1994). Congruence of self and subordinate ratings of managerial practices as a correlate of supervisor evaluation. *Journal of Occupational and Organizational Psychology*, *67*(1), 57–67. doi:10.1111/j.2044-8325.1994. tb00549.x

Gale, A. J., Martin, D., Martin, K., & Duffey, M. A. (2014). The burnout phenomenon: A comparative study of student attitudes toward collaborative learning and sustainability. *Journal of Interior Design*, *39*(1), 17–31. doi:10.1111/joid.12022

Gamero, N., González-Romá, V., & Peiró, J. M. (2008). The influence of intra-team conflict on work teams' affective climate: A longitudinal study. *Journal of Occupational and Organizational Psychology*, *81*(1), 47–69. doi:10.1348/096317907X180441

Ganser, C., Kennel, T., & Kunz, A. (2007). Digital support for net-based teamwork in early design stages. *Journal of Desert Research*, *6*(1/2), 150. doi:10.1504/JDR.2007.015567

Gardner, B. S., & Korth, S. J. (1998). A framework for learning to work in teams. *Journal of Education for Business*, *74*(1), 28–33. doi:10.1080/08832329809601657

Garduño Freeman, C. (2010). Photosharing on Flickr: Intangible heritage and emergent publics. *International Journal of Heritage Studies*, *16*(4), 352–368. doi:10.1080/13527251003775695

Garduño Freeman, C. (2013). Participatory Culture as a Site for the Reception of Architecture: Making a Giant Sydney Opera House Cake. *Architecture Theory Review*, *18*(3), 325–339. doi:10.1080/13264826.2013.890008

Gatfield, T. (1999). Examining student satisfaction with group projects and peer assessment. *Assessment & Evaluation in Higher Education*, *24*(4), 365–377. doi:10.1080/0260293990240401

Gauntlett, D. (2007). *Creative Explorations: New Approaches to Identities and Audiences*. London: Routledge.

Gauntlett, D. (2011). *Making is connecting: The social meaning of creativity, from DIY and knitting to YouTube and Web 2.0*. Cambridge, UK: Polity Press.

Gauntlett, D., & Holzwarth, P. (2006). Creative and visual methods for exploring identities. *Visual Studies*, *21*(1), 82–91. doi:10.1080/14725860600613261

Gerlick, R., Davis, D., Brown, S., & Trevisan, M. (2010). Reflective practices of engineering capstone design teams. *Proceedings of the American Society for Engineering Education Annual Conference*. Louisville, KY: American Society for Engineering Education.

Gero, J. S. (1996). Creativity, emergence and evolution in design. *Knowledge-Based Systems*, *9*(7), 435–448. doi:10.1016/S0950-7051(96)01054-4

Gero, J. S., & Neill, T. M. (1998). An approach to the analysis of design protocols. *Design Studies*, *19*(1), 21–61. doi:10.1016/S0142-694X(97)00015-X

Ghassan, A., & Bohemia, E. (2011). Notions of self: Becoming a 'successful' design graduate. In N.F.M. Roozenburg, L.L. Chen, & P.J. Stappers (Eds.), *Diversity and unity: Proceedings of IASDR2011, the 4th world conference on design research* (pp. 1-9). Delft University of Technology: Delft, Netherlands.

Giaccardi, E. (2004). *Principles of Metadesign: Processes and Levels of Co-creation in the New Design Space. (PhD).* Plymouth, UK: University of Plymouth.

Gillard, J. (2012). *Australia in the Asian Century* (White Paper). Australian Government.

Gladstein, D. (1984). Groups in Context: A Model of Task Group Effectiveness. *Administrative Science Quarterly*, *29*(4), 499–517. doi:10.2307/2392936

Glanville, R. (1999). Researching design and designing research. *Design Issues*, *15*(2), 80–91. doi:10.2307/1511844

Gleitman, L., & Papafragou, A. (2005). Language and thought. In K. J. Holyoak & R. G. Morrison (Eds.), *Cambridge handbook of thinking and reasoning* (pp. 633–661). New York: Cambridge University Press.

Godber, B. (1998). The Knowing and Subverting Reader. In J. Hill (Ed.), *Occupying Architecture*. London: Routledge.

Goff, L., Potter, M. K., Pierre, E., Carey, T. T., Gullage, A., Kustra, E., . . . Van Gaste, G. (2015). Learning outcomes assessment: A practitioner's handbook. Higher Education Quality Council of Ontario, Research Report 13/14- 008. Retrieved from http://www.heqco.ca/SiteCollectionDocuments/heqco.LOAhandbook _Eng_2015.pdf

Gokhale, A. (1995). Collaborative Learning Enhances Critical Thinking. *Journal of Technology Education*, *7*(1), 22–30. doi:10.21061/jte.v7i1.a.2

Goldfinch, J. (1994). Further developments in peer assessment of group projects. *Assessment & Evaluation in Higher Education*, *19*(1), 29–35. doi:10.1080/0260293940190103

Goldfinch, J., & Raeside, R. (1990). Development of a Peer Assessment Technique for Obtaining Individual Marks on a Group Project. *Assessment & Evaluation in Higher Education*, *15*(3), 210–231. doi:10.1080/0260293900150304

Goldschmidt, G. (1990). Linkography: Assessing Design Productivity. In R. Trappl (Ed.), *Cybernetics and system '90, World Scientific* (pp. 291–298). Singapore: World Scientific.

Goldschmidt, G. (1995). The designer as a team of one. *Design Studies*, *16*(2), 189–209. doi:10.1016/0142-694X(94)00009-3

Goldschmidt, G., & Tatsa, D. (2005). How good are good ideas? Correlates of design creativity. *Design Studies*, *26*(6), 593–611. doi:10.1016/j.destud.2005.02.004

Goltz, S. M., Hietapelto, A. B., Reinsch, R. W., & Tyrell, S. K. (2008). Teaching teamwork and problem solving concurrently. *Journal of Management Education*, *32*(5), 541–562. doi:10.1177/1052562907310739

Gómez Puente, S. M., van Eijck, M., & Jochems, W. (2011). Towards characterising design-based learning in engineering education: A review of the literature. *European Journal of Engineering Education*, *36*(2), 137–149. doi:10.1080/0 3043797.2011.565116

Gómez, C., Kirkman, B., & Shapiro, D. (2000). The impact of collectivism and in-group/out-group membership on the evaluation generosity of team members. *Academy of Management Journal*, *43*(6), 1097–1106. doi:10.2307/1556338

González-Fernández, M. J., García-Alonso, J. M., & Montero, E. (2014). The Use of a Rubric-Based Method to Assess Teamwork Skill Development. A Case Study in Science and Engineering Courses. *Proceedings of the New perspectives in science educationConference* (p. 409). Rome: Edizioni Libreriauniversitaria.

Goodson, I. (2001). The story of life history: Origins of the life history method in sociology. *Identity*, *1*(2), 129–142. doi:10.1207/S1532706XID0102_02

Gordon, W. J. J. (1961). *Synectics: the development of creative capacity*. New York: Harper and Row.

Gorla, N., & Lam, Y. (2004). Who should work with whom? Building effective software project teams. *Communications of the ACM*, *47*(6), 79–82. doi:10.1145/990680.990684

Gosenpud, J. J., & Washbush, J. B. (1991). Predicting simulation performance: Differences between individuals and groups. In W. J. Wheatley & J. Gosenpud (Eds.), *Developments in business simulation & experiential exercises* (pp. 44–48). Stillwater, OK: Association for Business Simulation and Experiential Learning.

Gradoville, R., & Budny, D. (2013). Undergraduate Service-Learning Engineering Design Projects In Ecuador.*Proceedings of COPEC World Congress* (Vol. 5).

Graen, G. B., Hui, C., & Taylor, E. A. (2006). Experience-based learning about LMX leadership and fairness in project teams: A dyadic directional approach. *Academy of Management Learning & Education*, *5*(4), 448–460. doi:10.5465/AMLE.2006.23473205

Gray, P. J. (2013). Developing Assessment Rubrics in Project Based Courses: Four Case Studies. *Proceedings of the9th International CDIO Conference, Cambridge, Massachusetts*.

Gray, D., Brown, S., & Macanufo, J. (2010). *Gamestorming: A Playbook for Innovators: Rulebreakers, and Changemakers*. Sebastopol, CA: O'Reilly Media.

Greene, J. (2010). *Design Is How It Works*. Portfolio Hardcover.

Griffee, D. T. (1995). *A Longitudinal Study of Student Feedback: Self-Assessment*. Course Evaluation and Teacher Evaluation.

Griffiths, R. (2004). Knowledge production and the research-teaching nexus: The case of the built environment disciplines. *Studies in Higher Education*, *29*(6), 709–726. doi:10.1080/0307507042000287212

Gropius, W. (1962). *Scope of total architecture*. New York: Collier Books.

Groundspeak Inc. (2000). Geocaching. Retrieved from http://www.geocaching.com

Grudin, J. (1993). Obstacles to Participatory Design in Large Product Development Organizations. In D. Schuler & A. Namioka (Eds.), *Participatory Design: Principles and practices* (pp. 99–122). New Jersey: Lawrence Erlbaum Associates.

Grudin, J. (1994). Computer-supported cooperative work: History and focus. *Computer*, *27*(5), 19–26. doi:10.1109/2.291294

Guerin, D., & Martin, C. (2010). *The interior design profession's body of knowledge and its relationship to people's health, safety, and welfare*. Retrieved from http://www.idbok.org/PDFs/IDBOK_2010.pdf

Guest, D., Livett, M., & Stone, N. (2006). Fostering International Student Exchanges for Science Students. *Journal of Studies in International Education*, *10*(4), 378–395. doi:10.1177/1028315306287632

Guilford, J. P. (1967). *The Nature of Human Intelligence*. New York: McGraw-Hill.

Gürel, M. Ö. (2010). Explorations in teaching sustainable design: A studio experience in interior design/architecture. *International Journal of Art & Design Education*, *29*(2), 184–199. doi:10.1111/j.1476-8070.2010.01649.x

Gutman, R. (2010a). Professions and their discontents: The psychodynamics of architectural practice. In Cuff, R. & Wriedt, J. (Eds.) Architecture from the outside in: Selected essays by Robert Gutman (pp. 43-58). New York: Princeton Architectural Press. Originally published in Practices 5/6 Spring, 1997.

Gutman, R. (2010b). Educating architects: Pedagogy and the pendulum. In Cuff, R. & Wriedt, J. (Eds.) Architecture from the outside in: Selected essays by Robert Gutman (pp. 258-286). New York: Princeton Architectural Press. (Originally published in Public Interest 80 Summer, 1985, pp. 67-91).

Habraken, N. J. (1972). *Supports: An alternative to mass housing.* London: Architectural Press.

Habraken, N. J., & Wiewel, W. (1976). *Variations: the systematic design of supports.* Cambridge, MA: Laboratory of Architecture and Planning at MIT.

Hackman, J. R. (1987). The design of work teams. In J. W. Lorsch (Ed.), *Handbook of organizational behavior* (pp. 315–342). Englewood Cliffs, NJ: Prentice Hall.

Hackman, J. R., & Morris, C. G. (1975). In L. Berkowitz (Ed.), *Group tasks, group interaction process, and group performance effectiveness: A review and proposed integration* (pp. 47–99). Advances in experimental social psychologyNew York: Academic Press.

Hackman, J. R., & Oldham, G. R. (1980). *Work redesign. MA.* Reading: Addison-Wesley.

Hackman, J. R., & Walton, R. E. (1986). Leading groups in organizations. In P. Goodman (Ed.), *Designing effective work groups* (pp. 72–119). San Francisco: Jossey-Bass.

Haigh, M. (2008). Internationalisation, planetary citizenship and Higher Education Inc. *Compare: A Journal of Comparative Education, 38*(4), 427–440. doi:10.1080/03057920701582731

Hales, C. (1993). *Managing engineering design.* Harlow, UK: Longman Scientific & Technical.

Hall, P., Keely, E., Dojeiji, S., Byszewski, A., & Marks, M. (2004). Communication skills, cultural challenges and individual support: Challenges of international medical graduates in a Canadian healthcare environment. *Medical Teacher, 26*(2), 120–125. doi:10.1080/01421590310001653982 PMID:15203520

Halls, J. (2005). Theory wrapped in context: Bridges between academic and industrial worlds. *Industrial and Commercial Training, 37*(6), 279–285. doi:10.1108/00197850510617541

Hall, W., Palmer, S., & Bennett, M. (2012). A longitudinal evaluation of a project-based learning initiative in an engineering undergraduate program. *European Journal of Engineering Education, 37*(2), 155–165. doi:10.1080/03043797.2012.674489

Halprin, L. (1969). *The RSVP Cycles: Creative Processes in the Human Environment.* New York: Braziller.

Halualani, R. T., Chitgopekar, A., Morrison, J. H. T. A., & Dodge, P. S.-W. (2004). Who's interacting? And what are they talking about?—intercultural contact and interaction among multicultural university students. *International Journal of Intercultural Relations, 28*(5), 353–372. doi:10.1016/j.ijintrel.2004.08.004

Hamlyn-Harris, B. J., Hurst, B. J., Baggo, K. V., & Bayley, A. J. (2006). Predictors of team work satisfaction. *Journal of Information Technology Education, 5,* 299–315.

Hanesian, D., & Perna, A. J. (1999, November 10-13). An evolving freshman engineering design program- The NJIT experience. *Paper presented at the29th Annual Frontiers in Education Conference,* San Juan, Puerto Rico. doi:10.1109/FIE.1999.839284

Hanington, B. (2007). *Generative Research in Design Education. Emerging Trends in Design Research.* International Association of Societies of Design Research, The Hong Kong Polytechnic University School of Design.

Hanrahan, S. J., & Isaacs, G. (2001). Assessing Self- and Peer-assessment: The students' views. *Higher Education Research & Development, 20*(1), 53–70. doi:10.1080/07294360123776

Hansen, R. S. (2015). *The relationship between task conflict, task performance and team member satisfaction: the mediating role of relationship conflict.* (Master), University of Oslo. Retrieved from https://www.duo.uio.no/bitstream/handle/10852/44744/The-relationship-between-task-conflict--task-performance-and-team-members-satisfaction---the-mediating-role-of-relationship-conflict--Hansen-2015.pdf?sequence=11&isAllowed=y

Hansen, R. S. (2006). Benefits and problems with student teams: Suggestions for improving team projects. *Journal of Education for Business*, *82*(1), 11–19. doi:10.3200/JOEB.82.1.11-19

Hanson, C. (2014). Changing how we think about the goals of higher education. In C. Hanson (Ed.), *In search of self: Exploring student identity development: New directions in higher education, no. 166* (pp. 7–13). San Francisco: Jossey-Boss. doi:10.1002/he.20090

Harman, G. (2005). Internationalization of Australian Higher Education: A Critical Review of Literature and Research. In Internationalizing higher education (pp. 119-140). Netherlands: Springer.

Harper, S. R., & Nagel, R. L. (2014). A study on conflicts during an interdisciplinary capstone design experience. *International Journal of Collaborative Engineering*, *1*(3-4), 256–273. doi:10.1504/IJCE.2014.063354

Harrell-Levy, M. K., & Kerpelman, J. L. (2010). Identity process and transformative pedagogy: Teachers as agents of identity formation. *Identity*, *10*(2), 76–91. doi:10.1080/15283481003711684

Harrison, D., Price, K., Gavin, J., & Florey, A. (2002). Time, teams, and task performance: Changing effects of surface and deep-level diversity on group functioning. *Academy of Management Journal*, *45*(5), 1029–1045. doi:10.2307/3069328

Hasirci, D., & Demirkan, H. (2007). Understanding the effects of cognition in creative decision making: A creativity model for enhancing the design studio process. *Creativity Research Journal*, *19*(2-3), 259–271. doi:10.1080/10400410701397362

Hastie, C., Fahy, K., & Parratt, J. (2014). The development of a rubric for peer assessment of individual teamwork skills in undergraduate midwifery students. *Women and Birth; Journal of the Australian College of Midwives*, *27*(3), 220–226. doi:10.1016/j.wombi.2014.06.003 PMID:25042349

Hauhart, R. C., & Grahe, J. E. (2010). The Undergraduate Capstone Course in the Social Sciences: Results from a Regional Survey. *Teaching Sociology*, *38*(1), 4–17. doi:10.1177/0092055X09353884

Hayes, W. H. (2002). Architectural Criticism. *The Journal of Aesthetics and Art Criticism*, *60*(4), 325–329. doi:10.1111/1540-6245.00079

Healey, M., & Jenkins, A. (2009). Developing undergraduate research and inquiry. York: Higher Education Academy. Retrieved from [REMOVED HYPERLINK FIELD]http://www.heacademy.ac.uk/assets/York/documents/resources/publications/DevelopingUndergraduateFinal.pdf

Healey, M., & Jenkins, A. (2006). Strengthening the teaching-research linkage in undergraduate courses and programmes. In C. Kreber (Ed.), *Exploring Research-based Teaching* (pp. 45–55). San Francisco: Wiley.

Hegarty, M., & Kozhevnikov, M. (1999). Types of visual–spatial representations and mathematical problem solving. *Journal of Educational Psychology*, *91*(4), 684–689. doi:10.1037/0022-0663.91.4.684

Helle, L., Tynjälä, P., & Olkinuora, E. (2006). Project-Based Learning in Post-Secondary Education – Theory, Practice and Rubber Sling Shots. *Higher Education*, *51*(2), 287–314. doi:10.1007/s10734-004-6386-5

Hellström, T. (2005). Role-Taking, Role-Breaking and Role-Shaking Amongst Designers: A Qualitative Study of a Team Effort. *The Design Journal: An International Journal for All Aspects of Design*, *8*(2), 25–37. doi:10.2752/146069205789331592

Hellström, T. (2007). The individual vs. the group? Individualization and collectivity among students in collaborative design. *International Journal of Technology and Design Education, 17*(3), 305–321. doi:10.1007/s10798-006-9004-2

Hennessey, B., & Amabile, T. (1999). Consensual assessment. In M. Runco & S. Pritzker (Eds.), *Encyclopedia of creativity* (pp. 346–359). San Diego, CA: Academic Press.

Hertzberger, H. (2000). *Space and the architect: lessons in architecture 2*. Rotterdam: 010 Publishers.

Heufler, G. (2004). *Design basics*. Zurich: Niggli Verlag.

Heynen, H. (2012). Genius Gender and Architecture: The Star System as Exemplified in the Pritzker Prize. *Architectural Theory Review, 17*(2-3), 331–345. doi:10.1080/13264826.2012.727443

Hillyard, C., Gillespie, D., & Littig, P. (2010). University students' attitudes about learning in small groups after frequent participation. *Active Learning in Higher Education, 11*(1), 9–20. doi:10.1177/1469787409355867

Ho, C.-H. (2001). Some phenomena of problem decomposition strategy for design thinking: Differences between novices and experts. *Design Studies, 22*(1), 27–45. doi:10.1016/S0142-694X(99)00030-7

Holzer, D., Hough, R., & Burry, M. (2007). Parametric Design and Structural Optimisation for Early Design Exploration. *International Journal of Architectural Computing, 5*(4), 625–643. doi:10.1260/147807707783600780

Honey, P., & Mumford, A. (1992). *The manual of learning styles*. Maidenhead: Peter Honey.

Hope, J. (2008). The Language Teacher as an International Educator. *Paper Presented at the Developments in the Pedagogy of International Languages: A Gateway for Practitioners*, Kuala Lumpur, Malaysia.

Hörnig, R., Oberauer, K., & Weidenfeld, A. (2006). Between reasoning. *Quarterly Journal of Experimental Psychology, 59*(10), 1805–1825. doi:10.1080/17470210500416151 PMID:16945861

Howard, Z., Senova, M., & Melles, G. (2015). Exploring the role of mindset in design thinking: Implications for capability development and practice. *Journal of Design Business and Society, 1*(2).

Howard, T. J., Culley, S. J., & Dekoninck, E. (2008). Describing the creative design process by the integration of engineering design and cognitive psychology literature. *Design Studies, 29*(2), 160–180. doi:10.1016/j.destud.2008.01.001

Hubbard, W. (1980). *Complicity and Conviction: Steps toward an Architecture of Convention*. Cambridge, MA: The MIT Press.

Hubka, V., & Eder, W. E. (1987). A scientific approach to engineering design. *Design Studies, 8*(3), 123–137. doi:10.1016/0142-694X(87)90035-4

Hughes, R. L., & Jones, S. K. (2011). Developing and assessing college student teamwork skills. *New Directions for Institutional Research, 2011*(149), 53–64. doi:10.1002/ir.380

Huth, E. (2005). Fragments of participation in architecture, 1963-2002: Graz and Berlin. In P. Blundell Jones, D. Petrescu, & J. Till (Eds.), *Architecture and Participation* (pp. 141–148). London, New York: Spon Press.

Hyatt, D. E., & Ruddy, T. H. (1997). An examination of the relationship between work team characteristics and effectiveness: A replication and extension. *Personnel Psychology, 50*, 553–585. doi:10.1111/j.1744-6570.1997.tb00703.x

Hynes, W. (2015). Impacting student attitudes towards teamwork. In Vande Zande, R., Bohemia, E., & Digranes, I. (Eds.), *Learn x design:Proceedings of the 3rd International Conference for Design Education Researchers* (pp. 1002-1015). Aalto, Finland: Aalto University.

Hynes, W. (2015). Impacting student attitudes towards teamwork.*Proceedings of the 3rd International Conference for Design Education Researchers* (p. 1002). Alto Finland: Cumulus Association.

Ibrahim, R., & Rahimian, F. P. (2010). Comparison of CAD and manual sketching tools for teaching architectural design. *Automation in Construction*, *19*(8), 978–987. doi:10.1016/j.autcon.2010.09.003

IDEALS Learning System. (2015). *Integrated Design Engineering Assessment and Learning System (IDEALS)*. Retrieved from https://ideals.tidee.org/

IDEO. (2016). Method Cards. Retrieved from https://www.ideo.com/work/method-cards

IML. (2002). *Enhancing Experiences of Group Work: A Resource Kit for Managing and Motivating Student Groups. Sydney*. Sydney: Institute for Interactive Media and Learning, University of Technology.

Inamdar, S. N., & Roldan, M. (2013). The MBA Capstone Course: Building Theoretical, Practical, Applied, and Reflective Skills. *Journal of Management Education*, *37*(6), 747–770. doi:10.1177/1052562912474895

Ingham, A. G., Levinger, G., Graves, J., & Peckham, V. (1974). The Ringelmann effect: Studies of group size and group performance. *Journal of Experimental Social Psychology*, *10*(4), 371–384. doi:10.1016/0022-1031(74)90033-X

Ingraham, C. (1992). The Burdens of Linearity. In J. Whiteman, J. Kipnis, & R. Burdett (Eds.), *Strategies in Architectural Thinking* (pp. 131–147). Cambridge, MA: The MIT Press.

Inns, T., Baxter, S., & Murphy, E. (2006). Transfer or Emergence: Strategies for Building Design Knowledge Through Knowledge Transfer Partnerships. *The Design Journal*, *9*(3), 34–44. doi:10.2752/146069206789331429

Interior Designers of Canada. (2013). *An interior designer's scope of work*. Retrieved from http://www.idcanada.org/english/for-the-public/an-interior-designers-scope-of-work.html

Iordanova, I. (2007). Teaching Digital Design Exploration: Form Follows. *International Journal of Architectural Computing*, *5*(4), 685–702. doi:10.1260/147807707783600807

Jalajas, D. S., & Sutton, R. I. (1984-1985). Feuds in student groups, coping with whiners, martyrs, saboteurs, bullies, and deadbeats. *Organizational Behavior Teaching Review*, *9*(4), 217–227.

James, R., McInnis, C., & Devlin, M. (2002). *Assessing Learning in Australian Universities*. Melbourne: Centre for the Study of Higher Education and The Australian Universities Teaching Committee.

Janis, I. L. (1972). *Victims of 'Groupthink*. Boston: Houghton Mifflin.

Jaormakka, K. (2007). *Design Methods. Basics*. Basel: Birkhäuser.

Jara, C. (2014). Verbal literacy in the design process: Enthusiasm and reservation. *Paper presented at theARCC/EAAE 2014 International Conference on Architectural Research Conference*, Honolulu, USA.

Jehn, K. A. (1994). Enhancing effectiveness: An investigation of advantages and disadvantages of value-based intragroup conflict. *The International Journal of Conflict Management*, *5*(3), 223–238. doi:10.1108/eb022744

Jehn, K. A. (1995). A Multimethod Examination of the Benefits and Detriments of Intragroup Conflict. *Administrative Science Quarterly*, *40*(2), 256–282. doi:10.2307/2393638

Jehn, K. A. (1997). A qualitative analysis of conflict types and dimensions in organizational groups. *Administrative Science Quarterly*, *42*(3), 530–557. doi:10.2307/2393737

Jehn, K. A., & Bendersky, C. (2003). Intragroup conflict in organizations: A contingency perspective on the conflict-outcome relationship. *Research in Organizational Behavior*, *25*, 187–242. doi:10.1016/S0191-3085(03)25005-X

Jehn, K. A., Chadwick, C., & Thatcher, S. M. (1997). To agree or not to agree: The effects of value congruence, individual demographic dissimilarity, and conflict on workgroup outcomes. *The International Journal of Conflict Management*, *8*(4), 287–305. doi:10.1108/eb022799

Jehn, K. A., & Chatman, J. A. (2000). The Influence of Proportional and Perceptual Conflict Composition on Team Performance. *The International Journal of Conflict Management*, *11*(1), 56–73. doi:10.1108/eb022835

Jehn, K. A., & Mannix, E. A. (2001). The Dynamic Nature of Conflict: A Longitudinal Study of Intragroup Conflict and Group Performance. *Academy of Management Journal*, *44*(2), 238–251. doi:10.2307/3069453

Jerome, L. (2012). Service learning and active citizenship education in England. *Education. Citizenship and Social Justice*, *7*(1), 59–70. doi:10.1177/1746197911432594

Jerrard, B. (2006). Design-based knowledge transfer partnerships. *Design Journal*, *9*(3), 1–2. doi:10.2752/146069206789331410

Johnson, D.W., & Johnson, R.T. (1992). Positive interdependence: Key to effective cooperation. In *Interaction in cooperative groups: The theoretical anatomy of group learning* (pp. 174-199).

Johnson, C., & Smith, F. (1997). Assessment of a complex peer evaluation instrument for team learning and group processes. *Accounting Education*, *2*, 21–40.

Johnson, D. W., & Johnson, F. P. (1994). *Joining together: Group Theory and Group Skills*. Needham Heights, MA: Allyn and Bacon.

Johnson, J., Alexiou, K., & Zamenopoulos, T. (2010). *Embracing complexity in design*. New York: Routledge.

Johnston, L., & Miles, L. (2004). Assessing contributions to group assignments. *Assessment & Evaluation in Higher Education*, *29*(6), 751–768. doi:10.1080/0260293042000227272

Johnston, N. J. (1991). *The college of architecture and urban planning: Seventy-five years at the University of Washington: A personal view*. Seattle: University of Washington College of Architecture and Urban Planning.

Jonassen, D., & Reeves, T. C. (1996). Learning with technology: Using computers as cognitive tools. In D. Jonassen (Ed.), *Handbook of research for educational communications and technology: a project of the Association for Educational Communications and Technology*. New York: Macmillan Library Reference.

Jones, J. C. (1992). Design methods (2nd ed.). New York: Van Nostrand Reinhold.

Jones, A. (2013). There is nothing generic about graduate attributes: Unpacking the scope of context. *Journal of Further and Higher Education*, *37*(5), 591–605. doi:10.1080/0309877X.2011.645466

Jones, J. C. (1970). *Design Methods: Seeds of Human Futures*. London: Wiley.

Joubert, L., & Whitford, S. (2006). Bilateral Learning and Teaching in Chinese-Australian Arts and Architecture. *Journal of Studies in International Education*, *10*(4), 396–408. doi:10.1177/1028315306288819

Jules, C. (2007). *Diversity of Member Composition and Team Learning in Organizations*. Case Western Reserve University.

Kachra, A., & Schnietz, K. (2008). The Capstone Strategy Course: What Might Real Integration look like? *Journal of Management Education*, *32*(4), 476–508. doi:10.1177/1052562907300811

Kalantzis, M., & Cope, B. (2005). *Learning By Design*. Melbourne, Victoria, and Victorian: Schools Innovation Commission and Common Ground.

Kane, J. S., & Lawler, E. E. (1978). Methods of peer assessment. *Psychological Bulletin*, *85*(3), 555–586. doi:10.1037/0033-2909.85.3.555

Kan, J. W. T., & Gero, J. S. (2008). Acquiring information from linkography in protocol studies of designing. *Design Studies*, *29*(4), 315–337. doi:10.1016/j.destud.2008.03.001

Kankanhalli, A., Tan, B. C. Y., & Wei, K.-K. (2007). Conflict and performance in global virtual teams. *Journal of Management Information Systems*, *23*(3), 237–274. doi:10.2753/MIS0742-1222230309

Kaufman, D., Felder, R., & Fuller, H. (2000). Accounting for individual effort in cooperative learning teams. *Journal of Engineering Education-Washington*, *89*(2), 133–140. doi:10.1002/j.2168-9830.2000.tb00507.x

Kay, J. J., Regier, H. A., Boyle, M., & Francis, G. (1999). An ecosystem approach for sustainability: Addressing the challenge of complexity. *Futures*, *31*(7), 721–742. doi:10.1016/S0016-3287(99)00029-4

Keeler, M. (2009). *Fundamentals of integrated design for sustainable building*. Hoboken, N.J.: John Wiley & Sons.

Kegan, R. (1994). *In over our heads: The mental demands of modern life*. Cambridge, MA: Harvard University Press.

Kellogg, C. (2005). *The Studio Culture Summit: An Overview Report*. Washington, DC: The American Institute of Architecture Students.

Kemery, E. R., & Stickney, L. T. (2014). A Multifaceted Approach to Teamwork Assessment in an Undergraduate Business Program. *Journal of Management Education*, *38*(3), 462–479. doi:10.1177/1052562913504762

Kern, A. (2006). *Survey Results Reveal What the Industry Really Expects from Graduates*. Retrieved from http://www.aiga.org/content.cfm/survey-results-reveal-what-the-industry-really-expects-from-graduates

Khodadad, N. (2013). Fostering the connection: examining the impact of team-teaching and collaboration within an interdisciplinary design studio (Panel session). *Proceedings of Interior Design Educators Council 2013 Annual Conference*, Indianapolis, IN: Interior Design Educators Council.

Kidder, D. L., & Bowes-Sperry, L. (2012). Examining the influence of team project design decisions on student perceptions and evaluations of instructors. *Academy of Management Learning & Education*, *11*(1), 69–81. doi:10.5465/amle.2010.0040

Kiernan, L., & Ledwith, A. (2014). Is Design Education Preparing Product Designers for the Real World? A Study of Product Design Graduates in Ireland. *The Design Journal: An International Journal for All Aspects of Design*, *17*(2), 218–237. doi:10.2752/175630614X13915240576022

Kift, S. (2009). *Articulating a Transition Pedagogy to Scaffold and to Enhance the First Year Student Learning Experience in Australian Higher Education: Final report for ALTC Senior Fellowship Program*. Strawberry Hills, NSW: Australian Learning and Teaching Council.

Kiley, M., Boud, D., Cantwell, R., & Manathunga, C. 2009. *The Role of Honours in Contemporary Australian Higher Education,* A report commissioned by the Australian Learning and Teaching Council Ltd, an initiative of the Australian Government Department of Education, Employment and Workplace Relations. Retrieved from http://www.aushons.anu.edu.au

Kim, H.-S., LaFleur, R., & Schaeffer, K. (2008). A multi-course collaborative project: Using technology to learn. *Journal of Family and Consumer Sciences*, *100*(3), 34–41.

Kimmel, K., & Volet, S. (2012). University Students' Perceptions of and Attitudes Towards Culturally Diverse Group Work Does Context Matter? *Journal of Studies in International Education*, *16*(2), 157–181. doi:10.1177/1028315310373833

King, P., & Kitchener, K. (1994). *Developing reflective judgment*. San Francisco, CA: Jossey-Bass.

Kinsella, E. A. (2007). Technical rationality in Schön's reflective practice: Dichotomous or non-dualistic epistemological position. *Nursing Philosophy*, 8(2), 102–113. doi:10.1111/j.1466-769X.2007.00304.x PMID:17374071

Kirchmeyer, C., & Cohen, A. (1992). Multicultural Groups Their Performance and Reactions with Constructive Conflict. *Group & Organization Management*, 17(2), 153–170. doi:10.1177/1059601192172004

Kirsh, D. (2013). Embodied cognition and the magical future of interaction design. ACM Transactions on Computer-Human Interaction. *ACM Transactions on Computer-Human Interaction*, 20(1), 3:1-3:20.

Klein, M. (1991). Supporting conflict resolution in cooperative design systems. IEEE Systems Man and Cybernetics, 21(6).

Knight, J. (2004). Internationalization Remodeled: Definition, Approaches and Rationales. *Journal of Studies in International Education*, 8(1), 5–31. doi:10.1177/1028315303260832

Knight, J., & De Wit, H. (1999). *Quality and Internationalisation in Higher Education*. Paris: OECD Publishing.

Koch, A., Schwennsen, K., Dutton, T. A., & Smith, D. (2002). *The Redesign of Studio Culture: A Report of the AIAS Studio Culture Task Force*. Washington, DC: American Institute of Architecture Students.

Koehne, N. (2005). (Re) construction: Ways international students talk about their identity. *Australian Journal of Education*, 49(1), 104–119. doi:10.1177/000494410504900107

Kolarevic, B. (2003). *Architecture in the Digital Age: Design and Manufacturing*. London, New York: Spon Press.

Kolb, J. A. (2013). Conflict management principles for groups and teams. *Industrial and Commercial Training*, 45(2), 79–86. doi:10.1108/00197851311309516

Kolb, J. A., & Rothwell, W. J. (2000). Challenges and Problems Reported by Small Group Facilitators. *Performance Improvement Quarterly.*, 13(4), 122–136. doi:10.1111/j.1937-8327.2000.tb00195.x

Kolmos, A. (2002). Facilitating change to a problem-based model. *The International Journal for Academic Development*, 7(1), 63–74. doi:10.1080/13601440210156484

Koskinen, I., Zimmerman, J., Binder, T., Redström, J., & Wensveen, S. (2011). *Design Research Through Practice from the Lab, Field, and Showroom*. Amsterdam: Morgan Kaufman/Elsevier.

Kozlowski, S. W. J., & Ilgen, D. R. (2006). Enhancing the Effectiveness of Work Groups and Teams. *Psychological Science in the Public Interest*, 7(3), 77–124. PMID:26158912

Kozlowski, S., & Ilgen, D. (2006). Enhancing the Effectiveness of Work Groups and Teams. *Psychological Science in the Public Interest*, 7(3), 77–124. PMID:26158912

Kravitz, D. A., & Martin, B. (1986). Ringelmann Rediscovered: The original article. *Journal of Personality and Social Psychology*, 50(5), 936–941. doi:10.1037/0022-3514.50.5.936

Kruger, C., & Cross, N. (2006). Solution driven versus problem driven design: Strategies and outcomes. *Design Studies*, 27(5), 527–548. doi:10.1016/j.destud.2006.01.001

Kuh, G. D. (2003). What we're learning about student engagement from NSSE: Benchmarks for effective educational practices. *Change: The Magazine of Higher Learning*, 35(2), 24–32. doi:10.1080/00091380309604090

Kumar, V. (2013). *101 Design Methods: A Structured Approach for Driving Innovation in Your Organization*. Hoboken, New Jersey: Wiley.

Kumpulainen, K., & Wray, D. (2002). *Classroom Interaction and Social Learning: From Theory to Practice*. New York: RoutledgeFarmer.

Kurt, S. (2009). An analytic study on the traditional studio environments and the use of the constructivist studio in the architectural design education. *Procedia: Social and Behavioral Sciences, 1*(1), 401–408. doi:10.1016/j.sbspro.2009.01.072

Kurtzberg, T. R., & Mueller, J. S. (2005). The influence of daily conflict on perceptions of creativity: A longitudinal study. *The International Journal of Conflict Management, 16*(4), 335–353.

Kvale, S. (1996). *Interviews: An introduction to qualitative research interviewing.* Thousand Oaks, CA: SAGE.

Kvan, T. (2000). Collaborative design: What is it? *Automation in Construction, 9*(4), 409–415. doi:10.1016/S0926-5805(99)00025-4

Landis, D., Bennett, J., & Bennett, M. (Eds.). (2004). *Handbook of Intercultural Training, Thousand Oaks.* CA: Sage.

Langan, A., Wheater, C., Shaw, E., Haines, B., Cullen, W., Boyle, J., & Lockey, L. et al. (2005). Peer assessment of oral presentations: Effects of student gender, university affiliation and participation in the development of assessment criteria. *Assessment & Evaluation in Higher Education, 30*(1), 21–34. doi:10.1080/0260293042003243878

Lange, B. (2011). Professionalization in space: Social-spatial strategies of culturepreneurs in Berlin. *Entrepreneurship & Regional Development, 23*(3–4), 259–279. doi:10.1080/08985620903233978

Larkin, M., Watts, S., & Clifton, E. (2006). Giving voice and making sense in interpretative phenomenological analysis. *Qualitative Research in Psychology, 3*(2), 102–120. doi:10.1191/1478088706qp062oa

Larson, C. E., & LaFasto, F. M. J. (1989). *Teamwork: What Must Go Right/What Can Go Wrong.* Newbury Park, CA: Sage.

Lauche, K., Bohemia, E., Connor, C., & Badke-Schaub, P. (2008). Distributed collaboration in design education: Practising designer and client roles. *Journal of Desert Research, 7*(3), 238–258. doi:10.1504/JDR.2008.024193

Laurel, B. (Ed.), (2003). *Design Research: Methods and Perspectives.* Cambridge, MA: The MIT Press.

Laurillard, D., & McAndrew, P. (2002). Virtual Teaching Tool: Bringing academics closer to the design of e-learning. In S. Banks, P. Goodyear, V. Hodgson and D. McConnell (Eds.) *Network Learning 2002: A Research Based Conference on e-Learning in Higher Education and Lifelong Learning.* Retrieved from http://kn.open.ac.uk/public/document.cfm?docid=7243

Laurillard, D. (2002). *Rethinking university teaching: A conversational framework for the effective use of learning technologies* (2nd ed.). London, New York: Routledge. doi:10.4324/9780203304846

Lave, J., & Wenger, E. (1990). *Situated learning: Legitimate peripheral participation.* Cambridge: Cambridge University Press.

Law, J. (2009). Actor network theory and material semiotics. In B. S. Turner (Ed.), *The New Blackwell Companion to Social Theory* (pp. 141–158). Chichester, England: Wiley-Blackwell. doi:10.1002/9781444304992.ch7

Lawson, B. (1980). *How designers think* (E. ed.). Westfield, NJ: Architectural Press.

Lawson, B., & Dorst, K. (2009). *Design Expertise.* Oxford: Architectural Press.

Leask, B. (2003). Beyond The Numbers - Levels and Layers of Internationalism to Utilise and Support Growth And Diversity. *Proceedings of the17th IDP Australian International Education Conference*, Melbourne: Australia.

Leask, B., & Carroll, J. (2011). Moving beyond 'wishing and hoping': Internationalisation and student experiences of inclusion and engagement. *Higher Education Research & Development, 30*(5), 647–659. doi:10.1080/07294360.2011.598454

Lee, J. H., Gu, N., & Ostwald, M. J. (2013). Architectural Design using Algorithmic Scripting: An Application of Linkographic Analysis Techniques. In *Cutting Edge:47th International Conference of the Architectural Science Association* (pp. 133-142). Hong Kong: Architectural Science Association.

Lee, J. H., Ostwald, M. J., & Gu, N. (2015). Multi-cultural design communication: Exploring both cognitive and linguistic characteristics in the design process. In Y. Ikeda, C. M. Herr, D. Holzer, S. Kaijima, M. J. Kim. M, A, Schnabel (Eds.), CAADRIA 2015: Emerging Experience in Past, Present and Future of Digital Architecture (pp. 531-540). Hong Kong: The Association for Computer-Aided Architectural Design Research in Asia (CAADRIA).

Lee, N., & Loton, D. (Eds.). (2015) *The Capstone Principles.* Retrieved from http://www.capstonecurriculum.com.au/the-capstone-principles/

Lee, J. H., Gu, N., & Ostwald, M. J. (2015). Creativity and parametric design? Comparing designer's cognitive approaches with assessed levels of creativity. *International Journal of Design Creativity and Innovation, 3*(2), 78–94. doi:10.1080/21650349.2014.931826

Lee, J. H., Gu, N., & Williams, A. (2014). Parametric design strategies for the generation of creative designs. *International Journal of Architectural Computing, 12*(3), 263–282. doi:10.1260/1478-0771.12.3.263

Lee, N. (2009). Project methods as the vehicle for learning in undergraduate design education: A typology. *Design Studies, 30*(5), 541–560. doi:10.1016/j.destud.2009.03.002

Lefebvre, H. (1984). *(1991). The Production of Space* (D. Nicholson-Smith, Trans.). Oxford: Basil Blackwell.

Lejk, M., & Wyvill, M. (2002). Peer Assessment of Contributions to a Group Project: Student attitudes to holistic and category-based approaches. *Assessment & Evaluation in Higher Education, 27*(6), 569–577. doi:10.1080/0260293022000020327

Lennon, S. (1995). Correlations between tutor, peer and self assessments of second year physiotherapy students in movement studies. *Enhancing student learning through peer tutoring in higher education. Section, 3,* 66–71.

Levine, A. (1998). A president's personal and historical perspective. In J. Gardner & G. Van der Veer et al. (Eds.), *The senior year experience: Facilitating integration, reflection, closure, and transition* (pp. 51–59). San Francisco: Jossey-Bass.

Levinson, S. C. (1996). Frames of reference and Molyneux's question: Crosslinguistic evidence. In P. Bloom & M. Peterson (Eds.), *Language and space* (pp. 109–169). Cambridge, MA: MIT Press.

Levinson, S. C. (2003). *Space in Language and Cognition: Explorations in Cognitive Diversity.* Cambridge University Press. doi:10.1017/CBO9780511613609

Li, M. (2003, November 29 – December 3). Culture and classroom communication: a case study of Asian students in New Zealand language schools 'Educational research, risks and dilemmas. *Proceedings ofNZARE/AARE Conference,* Auckland New Zealand. Association for Research in Education.

Lidwell, W., Holden, K., & Jill Butler, J. (2010). *(2003). Universal Principles of Design: 125 Ways to Enhance Usability, Influence Perception, Increase Appeal. Make Better Design Decisions, and Teach through Design* (Rev. ed.). Beverly, MA: Rockport Publishers.

Lillyman, S., & Bennett, C. (2014). Providing a positive learning experience for international students studying at UK universities: A literature review. *Journal of Research in International Education, 13*(1), 63–75. doi:10.1177/1475240914529859

Lincoln, Y. S., & Guba, E. G. (1985). *Naturalistic inquiry.* Beverly Hills, CA: SAGE.

Lind, D., Rekkas, S., Bui, V., Lam, T., Beierle, E., & Copeland, E. III. (2002). Competency-based student self-assessment on a surgery rotation. *The Journal of Surgical Research, 105*(1), 31–34. doi:10.1006/jsre.2002.6442 PMID:12069498

Lindström, L. (2006). Creativity:What Is It? Can You Assess It? Can It Be Taught? *International Journal of Art & Design Education*, *25*(1), 53–66. doi:10.1111/j.1476-8070.2006.00468.x

Lira, E. M., Ripoll, P., Peiró, J. M., & González, P. (2007). The roles of group potency and information and communication technologies in the relationship between task conflict and team effectiveness: A longitudinal study. *Computers in Human Behavior*, *23*(6), 2888–2903. doi:10.1016/j.chb.2006.06.004

Litchfield, A., Frawley, J., & Nettleton, S. (2010). Contextualising and integrating into the curriculum the learning and teaching of work-ready professional graduate attributes. *Higher Education Research & Development*, *29*(5), 519–534. doi:10.1080/07294360.2010.502220

Liu, Y.-T., & Lim, C.-K. (2006). New tectonics: A preliminary framework involving classic and digital thinking. *Design Studies*, *27*(3), 267–307. doi:10.1016/j.destud.2005.11.008

Lloyd, P. (2000). Storytelling and the development of discourse in the engineering design process. *Design Studies*, *21*(4), 357–373. doi:10.1016/S0142-694X(00)00007-7

Lloyd, P., & Scott, P. (1994). Discovering the design problem. *Design Studies*, *15*(2), 125–140. doi:10.1016/0142-694X(94)90020-5

Locke, E. A., & Latham, G. P. (1990). Work motivation and satisfaction: Light at the end of the tunnel. *American Psychological Society*, *1*(4), 240–246.

Longenecker, C. O., Scazzero, J. A., & Stansfield, T. T. (1994). Quality improvement through team goal setting, feedback, and problem solving. *International Journal of Quality & Reliability Management*, *11*(4), 45–52. doi:10.1108/02656719410057944

Loughry, M. L., Ohland, M. W., & DeWayne Moore, D. (2007). Development of a theory-based assessment of team member effectiveness. *Educational and Psychological Measurement*, *67*(3), 505–524. doi:10.1177/0013164406292085

Lou, Y. (2004). Learning to solve complex problems through between-group collaboration in project-based online courses. *Distance Education*, *25*(1), 49–66. doi:10.1080/0158791042000212459

Lovelace, K., Shapiro, D. L., & Weingart, L. R. (2001). Maximizing cross-functional new product teams' innovativeness and constraint adherence: A conflict communications perspective. *Academy of Management Journal*, *44*(4), 779–793. doi:10.2307/3069415

Lumsdaine, E., Shelnutt, J. W., & Lumsdaine, M. (1999, June 20-23). Integrating Creative Problem Solving and Engineering Design. *Paper presented at theASEE Annual Conference & Exposition*, Charlotte, NC.

Lupton, E. (2006). 2004]). The Birth of the User. In M. Bierut, W. Drenttel, & S. Heller (Eds.), *Looking closer five: Critical writings on graphic design* (pp. 23–25). New York: Allworth Press.

Lyons-Reid, J., Kuddell, C., Beyerle, A., & James, M. E. (2014). Typology of Harm (Creative Work). In FCAC and The Centre for Cultural Partnerships (Ed.), *Spectres of Evaluation: Rethinking: Art Community Value*. Parkville, VIC: The University of Melbourne. Retrieved from http://www.spectresofevaluation.com/conference-ebook.html)

Macías-Guarasa, J., Montero, J. M., San-Segundo, R., Araujo, A., & Nieto-Taladriz, O. (2006). A project-based learning approach to design electronic systems curricula. *IEEE Transactions on Education*, *49*(3), 389–397. doi:10.1109/TE.2006.879784

MacKerron, G., & Mourato, S. (n. d.). Mappiness. Retrieved from http://www.mappiness.org.uk

Maher, M. L. (2010). Evaluating Creativity in Humans, Computers, and Collectively Intelligent Systems. *Paper presented at the DESIRE'10: Creativity and Innovation in Design*, Aurhus, Denmark.

Maher, M. L., & Poon, J. (1996). Modeling Design Exploration as Co-Evolution. *Computer-Aided Civil and Infrastructure Engineering*, *11*(3), 195–209. doi:10.1111/j.1467-8667.1996.tb00323.x

Maldonado, H., Lee, B., Klemmer, S. R., & Pea, R. D. (2007). Patterns of Collaboration in Design Courses: Team dynamics affect technology appropriation, artefact creation, and course performance. *Proceedings of the 8th international conference on Computer supported collaborative learning* (pp. 490-499). International Society of the Learning Sciences. doi:10.3115/1599600.1599690

Marsden, K., & Luczkowski, J. (2005). Implementing work-based learning within masters' courses in design: A research evaluation of curriculum. *Art. Design & Communication in Higher Education*, *4*(2), 135–146. doi:10.1386/adch.4.2.135/7

Marshall, T. (2009, January). *Designing design education*. Retrieved from http://www.icograda.org/education/education/articles1397.htm

Martin, E., & Paredes, P. 2004. Using learning styles for dynamic group formation in adaptive collaborative hypermedia systems. *Paper presented at the Proceedings of the 4th international conference on web-engineering*, Munich.

Martin, B., & Hanington, B. (2012). *Universal Methods of Design: 100 ways to Research Complex Problems, Develop Innovative Ideas, and Design Effective Solutions*. Beverly, MA: Rockport Publishers.

Martin, R. M., Maytham, B., Case, J., & Fraser, D. (2005). Engineering graduates' perceptions of how well they were prepared for work in industry. *European Journal of Engineering Education*, *30*(2), 167–180. doi:10.1080/03043790500087571

Mattessich, P. W., & Monsey, B. R. (1992). *Collaboration: What Makes It Work*. St. Paul, MN: Amherst H. Wilder Foundation.

Matthews, T., Whittaker, S., Moran, T., & Yuen, S. (2011). Collaboration personas: A new approach to designing workplace collaboration tools. *Proceedings of the SIGCHI Conference on Human Factors in Computing Systems* (pp. 2247-2256). ACM: New York.

May, G., & Gueldenzoph, L. (2006). The effect of social style on peer evaluation ratings in project teams. *Journal of Business Communication*, *43*(1), 4–20. doi:10.1177/0021943605282368

McAdams, D. P. (1993). *The stories we live by: Personal myths and the making of the self*. New York: The Guildford Press.

McCarthy, M. (2015). Clear and Nishi. *Design + Business. Lecture presented at the Australian Graphic Design Association (AGDA) business series*.

McCormack, J., Beyerlein, S., Davis, D., Trevisan, M., Lebeau, J., Davis, H., & Leiffer, P. et al. (2012). Contextualizing professionalism in capstone projects using the IDEALS professional responsibility assessment. *International Journal of Engineering Education*, *28*(2), 416.

McCoy, K. (1995). Graphic Design in a Multicultural Word. In A. Bennett (Ed.), *Design studies: theory and research in graphic design* (pp. 200–205). New York: Princeton Architectural Press.

McGourty, J., Dominick, P., & Reilly, R. R. (1998, November 4-7). Incorporating Student Peer Review and Feedback into the Assessment Process. *Paper presented at the 28th Annual Frontiers in Education Conference*, Tempe, Arizona. doi:10.1109/FIE.1998.736790

McGourty, J., & De Meuse, K. P. (2001). *The Team Developer: an assessment and skill building program / Student guidebook*. New York: Wiley.

McGrath, J. E. (1964). *Social psychology: A brief introduction.* New York: Holt, Rinehart & Winston.

McGrath, J. E. (1984). *Groups: Interaction and performance.* Englewood Cliffs, NJ: Prentice-Hall.

McHarg, I. L. (1969). *Design with Nature.* Garden City, New York: Doubleday/Natural History Press.

McKendall, M. (2000). Teaching groups to become teams. *Journal of Education for Business, 75*(5), 277–282. doi:10.1080/08832320009599028

McKenzie, J., & Egea, K. (2015, July). Sustaining an institutional first year experience strategy: A distributed leadership approach. *Paper presented at the Students, Transitions, Achievement, Retention & Success (STARS) Conference,* Melbourne, Australia.

McNamara, J., Kift, S. M., Butler, D., Field, R. M., Brown, C., & Gamble, N. (2012). Work-integrated learning as a component of the capstone experience in undergraduate law. *Asia-Pacific Journal of Cooperative Education, 13*(1), 1–12.

Meadows, D., & Wright, D. (2008). *Thinking in systems: A primer.* White River Junction, Vt.: Chelsea Green Pub.

Meier, R. L., Williams, M. R., & Humphreys, M. A. (2000). Refocusing our efforts: Assessing non-technical competency gaps. *The Journal of Engineering Education, 89*(3), 377–385. doi:10.1002/j.2168-9830.2000.tb00539.x

Mello, J. A. (1993). Improving individual member accountability in small work group settings. *Journal of Management Education, 17*(2), 253–259. doi:10.1177/105256299301700210

Menchaca, M., Resta, P., & Awalt, C. (2002). Self and Peer Assessment in an Online Collaborative Learning Environment.

Mendoza, H. R., Bernasconi, C., & MacDonald, N. M. (2007). Creating new identities in design education. *International Journal of Art & Design Education, 26*(3), 308–313. doi:10.1111/j.1476-8070.2007.00541.x

Merriam, S. B. (1988). *Case study research in education: A qualitative approach.* Jossey-Bass.

Merton, R. K. (1968). *Social theory and social structure.* New York, NY: The Free Press.

Mewburn, I. (2009). *Constructing Bodies: Gesture, Speech and Representation at Work in Architectural Design Studios.* The University of Melbourne.

Mewburn, I. (2010). Lost in translation: Reconsidering reflective practice and design studio pedagogy. *Arts and Humanities in Higher Education, 2*(4), 363–379.

Mewburn, I. (2011). Lost in Translation: Reconsidering reflective practice and design studio pedagogy. *Arts and Humanities in Higher Education, 11*(4), 363–379. doi:10.1177/1474022210393912

Michaelsen, L. K., Knight, A. B., & Dee Fink, L. (2002). *Team-based learning: A transformative use of small groups.* Praeger Pub Text.

Michalko, M. (2006). *(1991). Thinkertoys: a handbook of creative-thinking techniques* (2nd ed.). Berkeley, CA: Ten Speed Press.

Michel, R. (Ed.). (2007). *Design Research Now: Essays and Selected Projects.* Basel: Birkhäuser. doi:10.1007/978-3-7643-8472-2

Middleton, H. (2005). Creative thinking, values and design and technology education. *International Journal of Technology and Design Education, 15*(1), 61–71. doi:10.1007/s10798-004-6199-y

Middleton, J. (2010). Sense and the city: Exploring the embodied geographies of urban walking. *Social & Cultural Geography, 11*(6), 575–596. doi:10.1080/14649365.2010.497913

Miessen, M., & Mouffe, C. (2008). Violating Consensus: Markus Miessen interviews Chantal Mouffe. In M. Ballesteros (Ed.), *Verb crisis* (pp. 168–180). Barcelona: ACTAR.

Miller, D. E., Anderson, A. T., Young, M. K., & Cauce, A. M. (2013). *University of Washington Architecture Program Report (APR)*. Retrieved from http://arch.be.washington.edu/sites/default/ files/pdf/UW_2013_APR.pdf

Miller, N., & Morgan, D. (1993). Called to account: The CV as an autobiographical practice. *Sociology, 27*(1), 133–143. doi:10.1177/003803859302700113

Miller, P. H. (2011). *Theories of Developmental Psychology*. New York: Worth Publishers.

Mills, J. E., & Treagust, D. F. (2003). Engineering Education – Is Problem-Based or Project-Based Learning the Answer? *Australasian Journal of Engineering Education, 3*(2), 2–16.

Minssen, H. (2006). Challenges of Teamwork in Production: Demands of Communication. *Organization Studies, 27*(1), 103–124. doi:10.1177/0170840605056400

Missingham, G. (2015). Wicked Deliberations: research and design studios. In R.H. Crawford & A. Stephan (Eds.), *Living and Learning: Research for a Better Built Environment: 49th International Conference of the Architectural Science Association 2015* (pp. 846-855). Melbourne: The Architectural Science Association.

Missingham, G. (1986). Dao Nunda: A metacritical frame, Drew on Murcutt, and on Australianness in Architecture. *Transition, 4*(4), 41–46.

Missingham, G. (2003). Figuring Ariachne's Gardens: Reflecting on Research-led Teaching in Design. In C. Newton, S. Kaji-O'Grady, & S. Wallan (Eds.), *Design + Research: Project Based Research in Architecture*. Melbourne: Association of Architecture Schools of Australasia; http://www.arbld.unimelb.edu.au/events/conferences/aasa/papers

Moe, K. (2008). *Integrated design in contemporary architecture*. New York, N.Y.: Princeton Architectural Press.

Moggridge, B. (2010). Design Thinking: Dear Don. *Core 77 online design journal*. Retrieved from http://www.core77.com/posts/17042/design-thinking-dear-don-17042

Monson, C. (2005). Practical discourse: Learning and the ethical construction of environmental design practice. *Ethics Place and Environment, 8*(2), 181–200. doi:10.1080/13668790500237070

Montuori, A. (2005). Literature review as creative inquiry: Reframing scholarship as a creative process. *Journal of Transformative Education, 3*(4), 374–393. doi:10.1177/1541344605279381

Morgan, P. (2002). Supporting staff to support students: the application of a performance management framework to reduce group working problems. Retrieved from http://www.business.heacademy.ac.uk/resources/reflect/conf/2002/morgan

Morris, R., & Hayes, C. (1997). Small group work: are group assignments a legitimate form of assessment? *Paper presented at the Learning Through Teaching:Proceedings of the 6th Annual Teaching Learning Forum*, Perth, Australia, Murdoch University.

Morris, R., & Hayes, C. (1997, February). Small Group Work: Are group assignments a legitimate form of assessment? In Pospisil, R. and Willcoxson, L. (Eds.), Learning Through Teaching (pp. 229-233). *Proceedings of the 6th Annual Teaching Learning Forum,* Murdoch University, Perth.

Morton, K., & Troppe, M. (1996). From the margin to the mainstream: Campus Compact's Project on Integrating Service with Academic Study. *Journal of Business Ethics, 15*(1), 21–32. doi:10.1007/BF00380259

Mouffe, C. (2000). *The democratic paradox*. New York: Verso.

Mouffe, C., Deutsche, R., Joseph, B. W., & Keenan, T. (2001). Every Form of Art Has a Political Dimension. *Grey Room*, (2): 99–125.

Muecke, S. (1994). From Honey moon Gap to Millions of Stars: 'Aboriginal' Landscape and the Aesthetics of Disappearance. In H. Edquist & V. Bird (Eds.), The Culture of Landcape Architecture. Melbourne: Edge Publishing with RMIT (pp. 68-84; 267).

Mulder, R. A., & Pearce, J. M. (2007). *PRAZE: Innovating teaching through online peer review.Paper presented at the24th Annual Conference of the Australasian Society for Computers in Learning in Tertiary Education*, Singapore.

Mulder, R. A., & Pearce, J. M. 2007. PRAZE: Innovating teaching through online peer review. *Paper presented at the24th Annual Conference of the Australasian Society for Computers in Learning in Tertiary Education*, Singapore.

Muller, M. J., & Druin, A. (2003). Participatory design: the third space in HCI. In *Human-computer interaction: Development process, 4235.*

Munnich, E., Landau, B., & Dosher, B. A. (2001). Spatial language and spatial representation: A cross-linguistic comparison. *Cognition, 81*(3), 171–208. doi:10.1016/S0010-0277(01)00127-5 PMID:11483169

Myerson, J., & Vickers, G. (2002). *Rewind 40 years of design and advertising*. London: Phaidon.

National Council of Architectural Registration Boards. (2015). *ARE Pass Rates by School* [Data file]. Retrieved from http://www.ncarb.org/ARE/ARE-Pass-Rates/Pass-Rates-by-School.aspx

Neff, G., Wissinger, E., & Zukin, S. (2005). Entrepreneurial Labor among Cultural Producers: ''Cool'' Jobs in ''Hot'' Industries'. *Social Semiotics, 15*(3), 307–334. doi:10.1080/10350330500310111

Nelson, L. M. (2013). Collaborative Problem Solving. In C. M. Reigeluth (Ed.), *Instructional-design theories and models: A new paradigm of instructional theory 2* (pp. 241–267). Hoboken, Pennsylvania: Taylor and Francis.

Nettleton, S., Litchfield, A., & Taylor, T. (2008). Engaging professional societies in developing work-ready graduates. *Proceedings of the 31st Annual International HERDSA Conference*, Rotorua, New Zealand, (pp. 241–251)

Nicol, D., & Pilling, S. (2002). Architectural Education and the Profession. In *Changing Architectural Education: Towards a New Profession* (pp. 1-22).

Nicol, D., & Pilling, S. (Eds.), (2005). *Changing architectural education: Towards a new professionalism.* Taylor & Francis.

Nicol, D., & Pilling, S. (Eds.). (2005). *Changing Architectural Education: Towards A New Professionalism.* New York: Taylor & Francis.

Nonaka, I., & Takeuchi, H. (1995). *The knowledge-creating company: How Japanese companies create the dynamics of innovation.* Oxford: Oxford university press.

NSW Board of Architects. (2014a). The AACA Architectural Practice Examination (APE). Retrieved from http://www.architects.nsw.gov.au/students-graduates/architectural-practice-examination

NSW Board of Architects. (2014b). Architects Act 2003 Information Sheet: Illegal Use of the Title 'Architect'. Retrieved from http://www.architects.nsw.gov.au/download/INFORMATION SHEET - ILLEGAL USE OF THE TITLE ARCHITECT February 2014.pdf

O'Brien, W., Soibelman, L., & Elvin, G. (2003). Collaborative design processes: An active and reflective learning course in multidisciplinary collaboration. *Journal of Construction Education, 8*(2), 78–93.

O'Leary-Kelly, A. M., Martocchio, J. J., & Frink, D. D. (1994). A review of the influence of group goals on group performance. *Academy of Management Review*, *37*(5), 1285–1301. doi:10.2307/256673

O'Sullivan, T., Rice, J., Rogerson, S., & Saunders, C. (2013). *Successful Group Work A Practical Guide for Students in Further and Higher Education*. Hoboken, NJ: Taylor and Francis.

Oakley, B., Felder, R. M., Brent, R., & Elhajj, I. (2004). Turning student groups into effective teams. *Journal of Student Centered Learning*, *2*(1), 9–34.

Oakley, B., Felder, R. M., Brent, R., & Elhajj, I. (2004). Turning Student Groups into Effective Teams. *Journal of Student Centered Learning*, *2*(1), 9–34.

Obrist, H. U. (2006). Preface: participation lasts forever. In M. Miessen & S. Basar (Eds.), *Did someone say participate?: an atlas of spatial practice: a report from the front lines of cultural activism looks at spatial practitioners who actively trespass into neighbouring or alien fields of knowledge*. Cambridge, MA: The MIT Press.

Ochsner, J. K. (2007). *Lionel H. Pries, architect, artist, educator: From Arts and Crafts to the Modern Movement*. Seattle: University of Washington Press.

Ochsner, J. K. (2012). *Furniture studio: Materials, craft, and architecture*. Seattle: University of Washington Press.

Ohland, M. W., Loughry, M. L., Woehr, D. J., Bullard, L. G., Felder, R. M., Finelli, C. J., & Schmucker, D. G. et al. (2012). The comprehensive assessment of team member effectiveness: Development of a behaviorally anchored rating scale for self-and peer evaluation. *Academy of Management Learning & Education*, *11*(4), 609–630. doi:10.5465/amle.2010.0177

Oliver, B. (2011). *Good practice report: Assuring graduate outcomes*. Australian Learning and Teaching Council. Retrieved from http://www.olt.gov.au/resource-assuring-graduate-outcomes-curtin-2011

Oliver, B. (2015). *Assuring Graduate Capabilities*. Retrieved from http://www.assuringgraduatecapabilities.com/about.html

Oliver, B. (2013). Graduate attributes as a focus for institution-wide curriculum renewal: Innovations and challenges. *Higher Education Research & Development*, *32*(3), 450–463. doi:10.1080/07294360.2012.682052

Oppezzo, M., & Schwartz, D. L. (2014). Give your ideas some legs: The positive effect of walking on creative thinking. *Journal of Experimental Psychology. Learning, Memory, and Cognition*, *40*(4), 1142–1152. doi:10.1037/a0036577 PMID:24749966

Orr, S. (2010). Collaborating or fighting for the marks? Students' experiences of group work assessment in the creative arts. *Assessment & Evaluation in Higher Education*, *35*(3), 301–313. doi:10.1080/02602931003632357

Ostergaard, K. J., & Summers, J. D. (2009). Development of a systematic classification and taxonomy of collaborative design activities. *Journal of Engineering Design*, *20*(1), 57–81. doi:10.1080/09544820701499654

Ostwald, M. J., & Williams, A. (2008a). *Understanding Architectural Education in Australasia*.

Ostwald, M. J., & Williams, A. (2008b). *Understanding architectural education in Australasia*.

Ostwald, M. J., & Williams, A. (2008). *Understanding architectural education in Australasia. Retrieved from Strawberry Hills, N.S.W.: Schön, D. A. (1987). Educating the Reflective Practitioner*. San Francisco: Jossey-Bass.

Palmer, P. J. (2010). *The courage to teach: Exploring the inner landscape of a teacher's life*. New York, NY: John Wiley & Sons.

Palmer, S., & Hall, W. (2011). An evaluation of a project-based learning initiative in engineering education. *European Journal of Engineering Education*, *36*(4), 357–365. doi:10.1080/03043797.2011.593095

Parkinson, D., & Bohemia, E. (2012a). Developing the design storytelling impact-approach framework. In Bohemia, E., Liedtka, J., & Rieple, A. (Eds.). *Leading innovation through design:Proceedings from the Design Management Institute's International Research Conference* (pp. 803-810). Boston.

Parkinson, D., & Bohemia, E. (2012b). Designer storytelling. In Buck, L., Frateur, G., Ion, W., McMahon, C., Baelus, C., de Grande, G., & Vervulgen, S. (Eds.). *Design education for future wellbeing:Proceedings from the International Conference on Engineering and Product Design Education* (pp. 742-747). Antwerp.

Pashler, H., McDaniel, M., Rohrer, D., & Bjork, R. (2008). Learning styles concepts and evidence. *Psychological Science in the Public Interest*, *9*(3), 105–119. PMID:26162104

Pea, R. D. (1993). Practices of distributed intelligence and designs for education. In G. Salmon (Ed.), *Distributed cognitions: Psychological and educational considerations* (pp. 47–87). Cambridge: Cambridge University Press.

Peeters-Baars, M. A. G. (2006a). *Design teams and personality: effects of team composition on processes and effectiveness*. TechnischeUniversiteit.

Peeters, M. A. G., Rutte, C. G., van Tuijl, H. F. J. M., & Reymen, I. M. M. J. (2008). Designing in teams: Does personality matter. *Small Group Research*, *39*(4), 438–467. doi:10.1177/1046496408319810

Peeters, M. A. G., Van Tuijl, H. F. J. M., Rutte, C. G., & Reymen, I. M. M. J. (2006b). Personality and Team Performance: A Meta-Analysisy. *European Journal of Personality*, *20*(5), 377–396. doi:10.1002/per.588

Pelled, L. H. (1996). Demographic diversity, conflict, and work group outcomes: An intervening process theory. *Organization Science*, *7*(6), 615–631. doi:10.1287/orsc.7.6.615

Pelled, L. H., & Adler, P. S. (1994). Antecedents of intergroup conflict in multifunctional product development teams: A conceptual model. *IEEE Transactions on* Engineering Management, *41*(1), 21–28.

Pelled, L. H., Eisenhardt, K. M., & Xin, K. R. (1999). Exploring the black box: An analysis of work group diversity, conflict, and performance. *Administrative Science Quarterly*, *44*(1), 1–28. doi:10.2307/2667029

Perkins, D. N. (1981). *The mind's best work*. Cambridge, MA: Harvard University Press.

Peterson, J. F., Frankham, N., McWhinnie, L., & Forsyth, G. (2015). Leading creative practice pedagogy futures. *Art. Design & Communication in Higher Education*, *14*(1), 71–86. doi:10.1386/adch.14.1.71_1

Pettigrew, T. F. (1998). Intergroup contact theory. *Annual Review of Psychology*, *49*(1), 65–85. doi:10.1146/annurev.psych.49.1.65 PMID:15012467

Pfaff, E., & Huddleston, P. (2003). Does it matter if I hate teamwork? What impacts student attitudes toward teamwork. *Journal of Marketing Education*, *25*(1), 37–45. doi:10.1177/0273475302250571

Phillips, A. (2005). Working in groups in an international publishing class. *Art. Design & Communication in Higher Education*, *4*(3), 173–187. doi:10.1386/adch.4.3.173/1

Pizzolato, J. E. (2003). Developing self-authorship: Exploring the experiences of high-risk college students. *Journal of College Student Development*, *44*(6), 797–812. doi:10.1353/csd.2003.0074

Plowright, P. D. (2014). *Revealing Architectural Design: Methods, Frameworks and Tools*. Abingdon, Oxon: Routledge.

Podsakoff, P. M., Aheame, M., & MacKenzie, S. B. (1997). Organizational citizenship behavior and the quantity and quality of work group performance. *The Journal of Applied Psychology*, *82*(2), 262–270. doi:10.1037/0021-9010.82.2.262 PMID:9109284

Poggenpohl, S. H. (2004). Practicing collaboration in design. *Visible Language, 38*(2), 138–157.

Polya, G. (1957). How to Solve It: A New Aspect of Mathematical Method (2nd ed. reprint). Penguin Mathematics. Harmondsworth: Penguin Books.

Pope, N. K. L. (2005). The impact of stress in self- and peer assessment. *Assessment & Evaluation in Higher Education, 30*(1), 51–63. doi:10.1080/0260293042003243896

Potur, A. A., & Barkul, Ö. (2009). Gender and creative thinking in education: A theoretical and experimental overview. *Journal of ITU A|Z, 6*(2), 44-57.

Prather, L. J., & Middleton, K. L. (2002). Are N+1 heads better than one?: The case of mutual fund managers. *Journal of Economic Behavior & Organization, 47*(1), 103–120. doi:10.1016/S0167-2681(01)00172-X

Preece, J., Sharp, H., & Rogers, Y. (2015). *Interaction Design - beyond human-computer interaction*. John Wiley & Sons.

Prince, M. J., & Felder, R. M. (2006). Inductive Teaching and Learning Methods: Definitions, Comparisons, and Research Bases. *The Journal of Engineering Education, 95*(2), 123–138. doi:10.1002/j.2168-9830.2006.tb00884.x

Pürto, J. (2004). *Understanding Creativity*. Scottsdale, Arizona: Great Potential Press.

Quintrell, N., & Westwood, M. (1994). The influence of a peer-pairing program on international students' first year experience and use of student services. *Higher Education Research & Development, 13*(1), 49–58. doi:10.1080/0729436940130105

Raban, R., & Litchfield. (2006, December 3-6). Supporting peer assessment of individual contributions in groupwork. *Paper presented at the 23rd Annual Conference of the Australasian Society for Computers in Learning in Tertiary Education*, Sydney.

Rafferty, P. D. (2012). Group Work in the MBA Classroom: Improving Pedagogical Practice and Maximizing Positive Outcomes With Part-Time MBA Students. *Journal of Management Education, 37*(5), 623–650. doi:10.1177/1052562912458644

Ragin, C. C. (2013). *The comparative method: Moving beyond qualitative and quantitative strategies: with a new introduction*. Oakland, CA: University of California Press.

Rahim, M. A. (2015). *Managing conflict in organizations*. Transaction Publishers.

Raman Pattabi, G., & Coyne, R. (2000). The Production of Architectural Criticism. *Architectural Theory Review*, Journal of the Department of Architecture, Planning and Allied Arts. *The University of Sydney, 5*(1), 83–103.

Rapoport, A. (2005). Culture, Architecture and Design. Chicago, IL: Locke Science Publishing Co.

Rapoport, A., & Kantor, R. E. (1967). Complexity and Ambiguity in Environmental Design. *Journal of the American Institute of Planners, 33*(4), 210–221. doi:10.1080/01944366708977922

Rattenbury, K. (2002). Introduction. In K. Rattenbury (Ed.), *This is not architecture: Media constructions* (pp. xxi–xxiv). New York: Routledge.

Reed, B. (2009). *The integrative design guide to green building: Redefining the practice of sustainability*. Hoboken, N.J.: Wiley.

Rees, C. (2003). Self assessment scores and gender. *Medical Education, 37*(6), 572–573. doi:10.1046/j.1365-2923.2003.01545.x PMID:12787384

Reiger, U., & Young, C. (2015). Design Through Collective Learning. In D. Bates, V Mitsogiannini & D. Ramirez-Lovering (Eds.), Studio Futures: Changing trajectories in architectural education (pp. 59-65). Melbourne: uro publications.

Rhee, J. (2010). Pilot Implementation of an Interdisciplinary Course on Climate Solutions. *International Journal of Engineering Education (Special Issue)*, 391.

Riener, C., & Willingham, D. (2010). The myth of learning styles. *Change: The magazine of higher learning, 42*(5), 32-35.

Ro, B., & Bermudez, J. (2015). Understanding extraordinary architectural experiences through content analysis of written narratives. *Enquiry*, *12*(1), 17–34.

Roberts, J. L. (2007). *The Future of Academic-Industry Collaboration. Presented* at IASDR07, International Association of Societies of Design Research. Hong Kong Poly Technic University, November.

Robinson, D. F., Shersood, A. L., & Depaolo, C. A. (2010). Service-Learning by Doing. *Journal of Management Education*, *34*(1), 88–112. doi:10.1177/1052562909339025

Rothwell, W. J., & Kolb, J. A. (1999). Major workforce and workplace trends influencing the training and development field in the USA. *International Journal of Training and Development*, *3*(1), 44–53. doi:10.1111/1468-2419.00063

Ruel, G., & Bastiaans, N. (2003). Free-riding and team performance in project education. *International Journal of Management Education*, *3*(1), 26–37.

Russ, R., & Dickinson, J. (1999). Collaborative design: "Forming, storming, and norming. *Journal of Interior Design*, *25*(2), 52–58. doi:10.1111/j.1939-1668.1999.tb00344.x

Sadowska, N., Griffith, S., & Morgan, T. (2009, April). Mind the gap: A collaboration in design teaching and learning between UK and Australia.*Proceedings of the 8th European Academy Of Design Conference*. Aberdeen, Scotland: The Robert Gordon University.

Safoutin, M. J., & Thurston, D. J. (1993). A communications-based technique for interdisciplinary design team management. *IEEE Transactions on* Engineering Management, *40*(4), 360–372.

Saint, A. (1983). *The Image of the Architect*. New Haven, Conn: Yale University Press.

Salama, A. (1995). *New Trends in Architectural Education: Designing the Design Studio Raleigh*. NC: Tailored Text and Unlimited Potential Publishing.

Salama, A. (2007). An Exploratory Investigation into the Impact of International Paradigmatic Trends on Arab Architectural Education. *Global Built Environment Review*, *6*, 31–43.

Salas, E., Rozell, D., Mullen, B., & Driskell, J. E. (1999). The effect of team building on performance, an integration. *Small Group Research*, *30*(3), 309–329. doi:10.1177/104649649903000303

Salas, E., Stagl, K. C., & Burke, C. S. (2004). 25 Years of Team Effectiveness in Organizations: Research Themes and Emerging Needs. In C. L. Cooper & I. T. Robertson (Eds.), *International Review of Industrial and Organizational Psychology* (pp. 47–91). New York: Wiley.

Sale, D. (2001). Designing a 'Thinking Curriculum' in the Classroom. *Curriculum and Teaching*, *16*(1), 45–57. doi:10.7459/ct/16.1.04

Salter, A., & Gann, D. (2003). Sources of ideas for innovation in engineering design. *Research Policy*, *32*(8), 1309–1324. doi:10.1016/S0048-7333(02)00119-1

Sampson, J., & Cohen, R. (2014). In D. Boud, R. Cohen & J. Sampson (Eds.), Peer learning in higher education: learning from and with each other.

Sandberg, J., & Pinnington, A. H. (2009). Professional competence as ways of being: An existential ontological perspective. *Journal of Management Studies, 46*(7), 1138–1170. doi:10.1111/j.1467-6486.2009.00845.x

Sanders, E. B. N., & Stappers, P. J. (2008). Co-creation and the new landscapes of design. *CoDesign, 4*(1), 5–18. doi:10.1080/15710880701875068

Sargent, L. D., Allen, B. C., Frahm, J., & Morris, G. (2009). Enhancing the Experience of Student Teams in Large Classes: Training Teaching Assistants to be Coaches. *Journal of Management Education, 33*(5), 526–552. doi:10.1177/1052562909334092

Sawir, E. (2005). Language difficulties of international students in Australia: The Effects of prior learning experiences. *International Education Journal, 6*(5), 567–580.

Sawyer, K. (2007). *Group Genius: The Creative Power of Collaboration*. Cambridge, MA: Basic Books.

Schneider, T., & Till, J. (2009). Beyond discourse: Notes on spatial agency. *Footprint, 4*, 97–112.

Schon, D. A. (1984). The Architectural Studio as an Exemplar of Education for Reflection-in-Action. *Journal of Architectural Education (1984-), 38*(1), 2.

Schön, D. A. (1983). *The reflective practitioner: How professionals think in action*. Basic books.

Schön, D. A. (1983). *The Reflective Practitioner: How Professionals Think in Action*. New York: Basic Books.

Schön, D. A. (1984). The architectural studio as an exemplar of education for reflection-in-action. *Journal of Architectural Education, 38*(1), 2–9. doi:10.1080/10464883.1984.10758345

Schön, D. A. (1985). *The design studio: an exploration of its traditions and potentials*. London: RIBA Publications for RIBA Building Industry Trust.

Schön, D. A. (1987). *Educating the Reflective Practitioner*. San Francisco: Jossey-Bass.

Schön, D. A. (1987). *Educating the reflective practitioner: Toward a new design for teaching and learning in the professions*. San Francisco: Jossey-Bass.

Schubert, T. Jr, Jacobitz, F., & Kim, E. (2012). Student perceptions and learning of the engineering design process: An assessment at the freshmen level. *Research in Engineering Design, 23*(3), 177–190. doi:10.1007/s00163-011-0121-x

Schwartz, D. L., & Heiser, J. (2006). *Spatial Representations and Imagery in Learning. The Cambridge handbook of: The learning sciences* (pp. 283–298). New York, NY, US: Cambridge University Press.

Scott, K. D., & Townsend, A. (1994). Teams: Why some succeed and others fail. *HRMagazine, 39*(8), 62–67.

Scott-Ladd, B., & Chan, C. A. (2008). Using action research to teach students to manage team learning and improve teamwork satisfaction. *Active Learning in Higher Education, 9*(3), 231–248. doi:10.1177/1469787408095848

Scott, V. (2010). *Conflict Resolution at Work for Dummies*. Indianapolis, Indiana: Wiley Publishing, Inc.

Seidman, I. (2013). *Interviewing as qualitative research: A guide for researchers in education and the social sciences* (4th ed.). New York: Teachers College Press, Columbia University.

Seisler, N., & Bosque, L. (2010). City Souvenirs. Retrieved from http://citysouvenirs.wordpress.com

Senge, P. M., Scharmer, C. O., Jaworski, J., & Flowers, B. S. (2005). *Presence: An Exploration of Profound Change in People, Organizations, and Society*. New York: Doubleday.

Shaffer, D. W. (1997). Design, collaboration, and computation: The design studio as a model for computer supported collaboration in mathematics.*Proceedings of the 2nd international conference on Computer support for collaborative learning* (pp. 253-258). International Society of the Learning Sciences. doi:10.3115/1599773.1599804

Shannon, C. E. (1948). A mathematical theory of communication. *The Bell System Technical Journal, 27*(3), 397–423. doi:10.1002/j.1538-7305.1948.tb01338.x

Shavit, Y., Arum, R., & Gamoran, A. (2007). *Stratification in higher education: A comparative study.* Stanford University Press.

Shaw, J. D., Zhu, J., Duffy, M. K., Scott, K. L., Shih, H., & Susanto, E. (2011). A contingency model of conflict and team effectiveness. *The Journal of Applied Psychology, 96*(2), 391–400. doi:10.1037/a0021340 PMID:20939655

Shea, G. P., & Guzzo, R. A. (1987b). Groups as human resources. In K. M. Rowland & G. R. Ferris (Eds.), *Research in personnel and human resources management* (pp. 323–356). Greenwich, CT: JAI Press.

Sherrard, W. R., & Feraidoon, R. (1994). An empirical study of peer bias in evaluations: Students rating students. *Journal of Education for Business, 70*(1), 43–47. doi:10.1080/08832323.1994.10117723

Shih, S.-G., Hu, T.-P., & Chen, C.-N. (2006). A game theory-based approach to the analysis of cooperative learning in design studios. *Design Studies, 27*(6), 711–722. doi:10.1016/j.destud.2006.05.001

Shore, L., & Thornton, G. III. (1986). Effects of gender on self-and supervisory ratings. *Academy of Management Journal, 29*(1), 115–129. doi:10.2307/255863

Shore, T. H., Shore, L. M., & Thornton, G. C. (1992). Construct validity of self-and peer evaluations of performance dimensions in an assessment center. *The Journal of Applied Psychology, 77*(1), 42–54. doi:10.1037/0021-9010.77.1.42

Shreeve, A., Sims, E. A. R., & Trowler, P. (2010). A kind of exchange: Learning from art and design teaching. *Higher Education Research & Development, 29*(2), 125–138. doi:10.1080/07294360903384269

Shulman, L. S. (2005). Signature pedagogies in the professions.*Daedalus, 134*(3), 52–59. doi:10.1162/0011526054622015

Sill, D., Harwood, M., & Cooper, I. (2009). The Disorienting: The senior capstone as a transformative experience. *Liberal Education, 95*(3).

Simons, T., & Peterson, R. (2000). Task conflict and relationship conflict in top management teams: The pivotal role of intragroup trust. *The Journal of Applied Psychology, 83*(1), 102–111. doi:10.1037/0021-9010.85.1.102 PMID:10740960

Slimani, K., Ferreira Da Silva, C., Médini, L., & Ghodous, P. (2006). Conflict mitigation in collaborative design. *International Journal of Production Research, 44*(9), 1681–1702. doi:10.1080/00207540500445198

Slimbach, R. (2005). The Transcultural Journey. *Frontiers: The Interdisciplinary Journal of Study Abroad, 11*, 205–230.

Sluijsmans, D. M. A., Dochy, F., & Moerkerke, G. (1999). Creating a Learning Environment by Using Self-, Peer- and Co-Assessment. *Learning Environments Research, 1*(3), 293–319. doi:10.1023/A:1009932704458

Smart, J., & Dixon, S. (2002). The discourse of assessment: Language and value in the assessment of group practice in the performing arts. *Arts and Humanities in Higher Education, 1*(2), 185–204. doi:10.1177/1474022202001002005

Smit, E., & Tremethick, M. (2013). Development of an international interdisciplinary course: A strategy to promote cultural competence and collaboration. *Nurse Education in Practice, 13*(2), 132–136. doi:10.1016/j.nepr.2012.08.006 PMID:22964472

Smith, C. G. (1966). A comparative analysis of some conditions and consequences of intra-organizational conflict. *Administrative Science Quarterly*, *10*(4), 504–529. doi:10.2307/2391573

Smith, K. M. (2013). Recognition of problem insufficiency: A proposed threshold concept emergent in student accounts of memorable interior design educational experiences. *Journal of Interior Design*, *38*(4), 37–54. doi:10.1111/joid.12018

Solnit, R. (2000). *Wanderlust: A History of Walking*. New York: Penguin Books.

Somers, M. (1994). The narrative constitution of identity: A relational and network approach. *Theory and Society*, *23*(5), 605–649. doi:10.1007/BF00992905

Speaks, M. (2002). Theory was interesting…but now we have work. *Architectural Research Quarterly*, *6*(3), 209–212. doi:10.1017/S1359135503001714

Spiller, N., & Clear, N. (Eds.), (2014). *Educating Architects: How tomorrow's practitioners will learn today*. London: Thames & Hudson.

Stead, N. (2006). Fabulous, Far Away and Gigantic: Myth in Australian Architectural Authorship. *Les Cahiers du CICLas*, *7*(May), 45–57.

Stead, N., & Garduño Freeman, C. (2013). Architecture and "The Act of Receiving, or the Fact of Being Received": Introduction to a Special Issue on Reception. *Architectural Theory Review*, *18*(3), 267–271. doi:10.1080/13264826.2013.902418

Steiner, I. D. (1972). *Group Process and Productivity*. New York: Academic Press.

Steiner, I. D. (1972). *Group Processes and Productivity*. New York: Academic Press.

Stempfle, J., & Badke-Schaub, P. (2002). Thinking in design teams - an analysis of team communication. *Design Studies*, *23*(5), 473–496. doi:10.1016/S0142-694X(02)00004-2

Stevens, G. (1998). *The favored circle: The social foundations of architectural distinction*. Cambridge: MIT Press.

Stevens, G. (1999). How the invisible stays that way. *Thresholds*, *19*, 54–56.

Stibbe, A. (2009). *The handbook of sustainability literacy: Skills for a changing world*. Totnes, UK: Green Books.

Strauss, A., & Corbin, J. (1998). *Basics of qualitative research* (2nd ed.). Thousand Oaks, CA: SAGE.

Strober, M. H. (2010). *Interdisciplinary Conversations: Challenging Habits of Thought*. Palo Alto, CA: Stanford University Press.

Strong, J. T., & Anderson, R. E. (1990). Free-riding in group projects: Control mechanisms and preliminary data. *Journal of Marketing Education*, *12*(2), 61–67. doi:10.1177/027347539001200208

Stumpf, S. C., & McDonnell, J. T. (2002). Talking about team framing: Using argumentation to analyse and support experiential learning in early design episodes. *Design Studies*, *23*(1), 5–23. doi:10.1016/S0142-694X(01)00020-5

Sullivan, W. M. (2012). Professional education: Aligning knowledge, expertise, and public purpose. In E. C. Lagemann & H. Lewis (Eds.), *What is college for? The public purpose of higher education* (pp. 104–131). New York: Teachers College Press, Columbia University.

Sundstrom, E., & Altman, I. (1989). Physical environments and workgroup effectiveness. In L. L. Cummings & B. Staw (Eds.), *Research in organizational behavior* (pp. 175–209). Greenwich, CT: JAI Press.

Sundstrom, E., de Meuse, K. P., & Futrell, D. (1990). Work Teams: Applications and Effectiveness. *The American Psychologist, 45*(2), 120–133. doi:10.1037/0003-066X.45.2.120

Surowiecki, J. (2004). *The wisdom of crowds: why the many are smarter than the few and how collective wisdom shapes business, economies, societies, and nations.* New York: Doubleday.

Sutliff, K. (2000). Integrating Academics and Industry: A Challenge for Both Sides. *ACM Journal of Computer Documentation, 24*(1), 33–38.

Suwa, M., Purcell, T., & Gero, J. (1998). Macroscopic analysis of design processes based on a scheme for coding designers' cognitive actions. *Design Studies, 19*(4), 455–483. doi:10.1016/S0142-694X(98)00016-7

Sweet, J., & Horman, T. (2012). Museum Development and Cross-Cultural Learning in the Kelabit Highlands, Borneo. *Museums Australia Magazine, 21*(1), 23–26.

Tang, C. (1996). Collaborative learning: the latent dimension in Chinese students' learning. In D.A. Watkins & J.B. Biggs (Eds.), The Chinese learner: cultural, psychological and contextual influences (pp. 183-204). Hong Kong: Comparative Education Research Centre (CERC) and Melbourne: Australian Council for Educational Research (ACER).

Tannenbaum, S. I., Beard, R. L., & Salas, E. (1992). Team building and its influence on team effectiveness: An examination of conceptual and empirical developments. In K. Kelley (Ed.), *Issue, Theory, and Research in Industrial/Organizational Psychology* (pp. 117–153). Amsterdam: Elsevier. doi:10.1016/S0166-4115(08)62601-1

Taras, M. (2008). Issues of power and equity in two models of self-assessment. *Teaching in Higher Education, 13*(1), 81–92. doi:10.1080/13562510701794076

Tedeschi, J. T., Schlenker, B. R., & Bonoma, T. V. (1973). *Conflict, power and games.* Chicago: Aldine.

Teekens, H. (2000). Teaching and Learning in the International Classroom. *Internationalisation at Home: A Position Paper.*

Tekleab, A. G., Quigley, N. R., & Tesluk, P. E. (2009). A Longitudinal Study of Team Conflict, Conflict Management, Cohesion, and Team Effectiveness. *Group & Organization Management, 34*(2), 170–205. doi:10.1177/1059601108331218

Tenbrink, T., & Ragni, M. (2012). Linguistic Principles for Spatial Relational Reasoning. In C. Stachniss, K. Schill, & D. Uttal (Eds.), *Spatial Cognition VIII* (Vol. 7463, pp. 279–298). Springer Berlin Heidelberg. doi:10.1007/978-3-642-32732-2_19

Tennant, M. (2012). *The learning self: Understanding the potential for transformation.* San Francisco: Jossey-Boss.

The Boyer Commission on Educating Undergraduates in the Research University. (1998). *Reinventing Undergraduate Education: A Blueprint for America's Research Universities.* Princeton: Carnegie Foundation for the Advancement of Teaching. Retrieved from http://naples.cc.sunysb.edu/Pres/boyer.nsf/

The Burra Charter: The Australia ICOMOS Charter for Places of Cultural Significance 2013, (2013).

The Second AIAS Task Force on Studio Culture. (2008). *Toward an Evolution of Studio Culture: A Report of the Second AIAS Task Force on Studio Culture.* Washington, DC: American Institute of Architecture Students.

Thomas, J. W. (2000). *A Review of Project Based Learning.* San Rafael, California: The Autodesk Foundation.

Thomas, K. W., & Kilman, R. H. (1974). *The Thomas-Kilman Conflict Mode Instrument.* Tuxedo, NY: Xicom.

Thompson, D., & McGregor, I. (2009). Online self and peer assessment for groupwork. *Education + Training, 51(5/6),* 434 - 447.

Thompson, J. (2009). Building Collective Communication Competence In Interdisciplinary Research Teams. *Journal of Applied Communication Research, 37*(3), 278–297. doi:10.1080/00909880903025911

Thornton, C. (2010). *Group & Team Coaching The Essential Guide*. Hoboken, NJ: Taylor and Francis.

Tierney, W. G., & Bensimon, E. M. (1996). *Promotion and tenure: Community and socialization in academe*. Albany, NY: State University of New York Press.

Till, J. (2009). *Architecture depends*. Cambridge, MA: MIT Press.

Tjosvold, D., & Deemer, D. K. (1980). Effects of controversy within a cooperative or competitive context on organizational decision making. *The Journal of Applied Psychology, 65*(5), 590–595. doi:10.1037/0021-9010.65.5.590

Tonkinwise, C. (2014). What is Design Studies good for? *Design and Culture, 6*(1), 5–44. doi:10.2752/175470814X13823675225036

Toohey, S. (1999). *Designing courses for higher education*. Buckingham: Society for Research into Higher Education/Open University.

Topping, K. (1998). Peer Assessment between Students in Colleges and Universities. *Review of Educational Research, 68*(3), 249–276. doi:10.3102/00346543068003249

Torres, V., & Hernandez, E. (2007). The influence of ethnic identity on self-authorship: A longitudinal study of Latino/a college students. *Journal of College Student Development, 48*(5), 558–573. doi:10.1353/csd.2007.0057

Trahar, S., & Hyland, F. (2011). Experiences and perceptions of internationalisation in higher education in the UK. *Higher Education Research & Development, 30*(5), 623–633. doi:10.1080/07294360.2011.598452

Transferable Integrated Design Engineering Education [TIDEE]. (2006). *About the Project*. Retrieved from http://www.tidee.wsu.edu/

Tregloan, K. (2015). *Design Epiphany and the Opportunities of Wickedness: constructions of insight, perspective and design* [Unpublished Doctoral Dissertation]. The University of Melbourne, Parkville, VIC.

Tregloan, K., & Missingham, G. (2010). Designing "Designing Environments". In G. Forsyth (Ed.), *ConnectED 2010 International Conference on Design Education*. Sydney: Faculty of the Built Environment, UNSW.

Tsing, A. L. (2011). *Friction: ethnography of global connection*. Princeton University Press.

Tucker, R. (2012). *Collaboration Down Under: investigating team learning in Australia in architecture and related design contexts* Paper presented at the Canada International Conference on Education (2012: Ontario, Canada) Ontario, Canada Tucker, R., & Abbasi, N. (in press). The Architecture of Teamwork: Examining Relationships between Teaching, Assessment, Student Learning and Satisfaction with Creative Design Outcomes *Journal of Architectural Engineering & Design Management*.

Tucker, R., & Abbasi, N. (2012). Conceptualizing teamwork and group-work in architecture and related design disciplines. *Paper presented at the ASA 2012: Building on knowledge, theory and practice: 46th Annual Conference of the Architectural Science Association*, Gold Coast, Qld. http://hdl.handle.net/10536/DRO/DU:30051739

Tucker, R., & Abbasi, N. (2014). The architecture of teamwork: examining relationships between teaching, assessment, student learning and satisfaction with creative design outcomes. *Journal of Architectural Engineering and Design Management*.

Tucker, R., & Rollo, J. (2006). Teaching and Learning in Collaborative Group Design Projects. *Journal of Architectural Engineering & Design Management, 2*, 19-30.

Tucker, R., Abbasi, N., Thorpe, G. R., Ostwald, M. J., Williams, A. P., & Wallis, L. (2014). *Enhancing and Assessing Group and Team Learning in Architecture and Related Design Contexts.* Retrieved from http://www.olt.gov.au/system/files/resources/ID11_2004_Tucker_Report_2014.pdf

Tucker, R., Abbasi, N., Thorpe, G., Ostwald, M., Williams, A., Wallis, L., & Cashuk, S. (2014). Enhancing and assessing group and team learning in architecture and related design contexts. Office for Learning and Teaching, Department of Education. Sydney: N.S.W.; Retrieved from http://dro.deakin.edu.au/eserv/DU:30069902/tucker-enhancing-2014.pdf

Tucker, T., & Abbasi, N. (2014a). *Manual on teamwork in design for students.* Retrieved from http://www.teaching-teamwork-in-design.com/manual-on-teamwork-in-design-for-students.html

Tucker, T., & Abbasi, N. (2014b). *Manual on teamwork in design for teachers.* Retrieved from http://www.teaching-teamwork-in-design.com/manual-on-teamwork-in-design-for-teachers.html

Tucker, R. (2008). The Impact of Assessment Modes on Collaborative Group Design Projects. In S. Frankland (Ed.), *Enhancing Teaching and Learning through Assessment: Embedded Strategies and their Impacts* (pp. 72–85). Hong Kong: The Assessment Resource Centre, The Hong Kong Polytechnic University.

Tucker, R. (2011). The architecture of peer assessment: Do academically successful students make good teammates in design assignments? *Assessment & Evaluation in Higher Education*, 2011, 1–11.

Tucker, R. (2012). Collaboration down under: Investigating team learning in Australia in architecture and related design contexts, In C.A. Shoniregun, & G.A. Akmayeva (Eds.), *CICE 2012: Proceedings of the Canada International Conference on Education*, Guelph, Canada (pp. 324-329). Infonomics Society.

Tucker, R. (2013). Sex does not matter: Gender bias and gender differences in peer assessments of contributions to group work. *Assessment & Evaluation in Higher Education*, *39*(3), 293–309. doi:10.1080/02602938.2013.830282

Tucker, R., & Abbasi, N. (2012). Conceptualizing teamwork and group-work in architecture and related design disciplines, *in ASA 2012: Building on knowledge, theory and practice. Proceedings of the 46th Annual Conference of the Architectural Science Association*, Architectural Science Association, Gold Coast (pp. 1-8).

Tucker, R., & Abbasi, N. (2015). The architecture of teamwork: Examining relationships between teaching, assessment, student learning and satisfaction with creative design outcomes. *Architectural Engineering and Design Management*, *11*(6), 405–422. doi:10.1080/17452007.2014.927750

Tucker, R., Abbasi, N., Thorpe, G., Ostwald, M., Williams, A., Wallis, L., & Kashuk, S. (2014). *Enhancing and assessing group and team learning in architecture and related design contexts (D. o. Education, Trans.)* (p. 109). Sydney: Office of Learning and Teaching, Department of Education, Australian Government.

Tucker, R., Abbasi, N., Thorpe, G., Ostwald, M., Williams, A., Wallis, L., & Kashuk, S. (2014). Enhancing and assessing group and team learning in architecture and related design contexts. Sydney: Office of Learning and Teaching, Department of Education, Australian Government.

Tucker, R., & Ang, S. (2007). The Academic Acclimatisation Difficulties of International Students of the Built Environment. *The Emirates Journal for Engineering Research*, *12*(1), 1–9.

Tucker, R., Fermelis, J., & Palmer, S. (2009). Designing, Implementing and Evaluating a Self-and-Peer Assessment Tool for E-learning Environments. In C. Spratt & P. Lajbcygier (Eds.), *E-Learning and Advanced Assessment Technologies: Evidence-Based Approaches* (pp. 170–194). Hershey, PA, USA: IGI Global. doi:10.4018/978-1-60566-410-1.ch010

Tucker, R., & Reynolds, C. (2006). The impact of teaching models, group structures and assessment modes on cooperative learning in the student design studio. *Journal for Education in the Built Environment, 1*(2), 39–56. doi:10.11120/jebe.2006.01020039

Turner, J. F. C. (1972). Housing as a verb. In J.F.C. Turner & R. Fichter (Eds.), Freedom to build; dweller control of the housing process (pp. xvi, 301). New York: Macmillan.

Turner, J. F. C., & Fichter, R. (1972). *Freedom to build; dweller control of the housing process.* New York: Macmillan.

Tu, Y., & Lu, M. (2005). Peer-and-self assessment to reveal the ranking of each individual's contribution to a group project. *Journal of Information Systems Education, 16*(2), 197.

Tynan, J., & New, C. (2009). Creativity and Conflict: How theory and practice shape student identities in design education. *Arts and Humanities in Higher Education, 8*(3), 295–308. doi:10.1177/1474022209339959

Ulmer, G. L. (1994). *Heuretics: The Logic of Invention.* Baltimore: John Hopkins University Press.

Ulusoy, Z. (1999). To Design Versus to Understand Design: The role of graphic representations and verbal expressions. *Design Studies, 20*(2), 123–130. doi:10.1016/S0142-694X(98)00030-1

United Nations Educational, Scientific and Cultural Organization. (2015) *Introducing UNESCO.* Retrieved from http://en.unesco.org/about-us/introducing-unesco#sthash.xym89aT2.dpuf

University of Sydney. (2011). *Graduate Attributes Policy.* Retrieved from https://www.itl.usyd.edu.au/graduateAttributes/policy.htm

University of Sydney. (2016, January 15). Social Inclusion. Retrieved from http://sydney.edu.au/social-inclusion/grants-program/index.shtml

University of Technology Sydney. (2013). *Graduate Attributes and the UTS Graduate Profile Framework.* Retrieved from http://www.iml.uts.edu.au/learn-teach/attributes.html

UW Master of Architecture Student Internship Program. (2014). University of Washington Department of Architecture, Professional Advisories Council.

Valkenburg, R. (1998). Shared understanding as a condition for team design. *Automation in Construction, 7*(2-3), 111–121. doi:10.1016/S0926-5805(97)00058-7

Valkenburg, R., & Dorst, K. (1998). The reflective practice of design teams. *Design Studies, 19*(3), 249–271. doi:10.1016/S0142-694X(98)00011-8

van den Berg, I., Admiraal, W., & Pilot, A. (2006). Peer assessment in university teaching: Evaluating seven course designs. *Assessment & Evaluation in Higher Education, 31*(1), 19–36. doi:10.1080/02602930500262346

Van der Lugt, R. (2000). Developing a graphic tool for creative problem solving in design groups. *Design Studies, 21*(5), 505–522. doi:10.1016/S0142-694X(00)00021-1

van der Zee, E., & Slack, J. M. (2003). *Representing Direction in Language and Space.* Oxford University Press. doi:10.1093/acprof:oso/9780199260195.001.0001

van Dijck, J. (2008). Digital Photography: Communication, identity, memory. *Visual Communication, 7*(1), 57–76. doi:10.1177/1470357207084865

van Dijck, J. (2011). Flickr and the culture of connectivity: Sharing views, experiences, memories. *Memory Studies, 4*(4), 401–415. doi:10.1177/1750698010385215 van Dijck, J. (2013). *The Culture of Connectivity: A Critical History of Social Media*. Oxford: Oxford University Press. doi:10.1093/acprof:oso/9780199970773.001.0001

Van House, N., & Ames, M. (2007). The Social Life of Cameraphones Images. *Paper presented at the CHI '07*, San Jose, California, USA.

Van House. N., Davis, M., Takhteyev, Y., Good, N., Wilhelm, A., & Finn, M. (2004, November 6–10). *From "What?" to "Why?": The Social Uses of Personal Photos*. Paper presented at the CSCW'04 Chicago, Illinois.

Van House, N., & Churchill, E. F. (2008). Technologies of Memory: Key Issues and Critical Perspectives. *Memory Studies*, *1*(3), 295–310. doi:10.1177/1750698008093795

van Rijn, H., & Stappers, P. J. (2008). Expressions of ownership: motivating users in a co-design process. *Proceedings of the Tenth Anniversary Conference on Participatory Design 08* (pp. 178-181). Indiana University.

Visser, W. (1993). Collective design: A cognitive analysis of cooperation in practice. *Paper presented at the9th International Conference on Engineering DesignICED '93*, Zurich, Switzerland (*Vol. 1*).

von der Weth, R. (1999). Design instinct?—the development of individual strategies. *Design Studies*, *20*(5), 453–463. doi:10.1016/S0142-694X(99)00021-6

Vygotsky, L. S. (1978). *Mind in society: The development of higher psychological processes*. Cambridge, Massachusetts: Harvard university press.

Wageman, R., & Frederick, M. G. (2005). As the Twig is Bent: How Group Values Shape Emergent Task Interdependence in Groups. *Organization Science*, *16*(6), 687–722. doi:10.1287/orsc.1050.0146

Waks, L. J. (2001). Donald Schon's philosophy of design and design education. *International Journal of Technology and Design Education*, *11*(1), 37–51. doi:10.1023/A:1011251801044

Walker, A. (2001). British psychology students' perceptions of group-work and peer. *Psychology Learning & Teaching*, *1*(1), 28–36. doi:10.2304/plat.2001.1.1.28

Walker, S. (2008). Following Will-O'-The-Wisps and Chasing Ghosts: Design-Centred Research, Sustainability and the Bottom Line. *The Design Journal: An International Journal for All Aspects of Design*, *11*(1), 51–64. doi:10.2752/175630608X317904

Waltner-Toews, D., Kay, J., & Lister, N.-M. (2008). *The ecosystem approach: Complexity, uncertainty, and managing for sustainability*. New York: Columbia University Press.

Waterman, A. S. (2014). *Service-learning: Applications from the research*. Routledge.

Watkins, R. (2005). *Groupwork and assessment: The Handbook for Economics Lecturers*. Kingston University.

Watson, W. E., Johnson, L., & Zgourides, G. D. (2002). The influence of ethnic diversity on leadership, group process, and performance: An examination of learning teams. *International Journal of Intercultural Relations*, *26*(1), 1–16. doi:10.1016/S0147-1767(01)00032-3

Way, M., & Bordass, B. (2005). Making feedback and post-occupancy evaluation routine 2: Soft landings – involving design and building teams in improving performance. *Building Research and Information*, *33*(4), 353–360. doi:10.1080/09613210500162008

Webb, G. (2005). Internationalization of Curriculum: An Institutional Approach. In J. Carroll & J. Ryan (Eds.), *Teaching International Students: Improving Learning for All*. London: Routledge.

Webb, J. D., & Miller, N. G. (2006). Some preparation required: The journey to successful studio collaboration. *Journal of Interior Design, 31*(2), 1–9. doi:10.1111/j.1939-1668.2005.tb00407.x

Webb, M. (2012). *Outduction: Enhancing the final year experience. Final report to the HE Academy.* Kingston: Kingston University.

Webster, H. (2004). Facilitating critically reflective learning: Excavating the role of the design tutor in architectural education. *Art, Design & Communication in Higher Education, 2*(3), 101–111. doi:10.1386/adch.2.3.101/0

Webster, H. (2008). Architectural education after Schön: Cracks, blurs, boundaries and beyond. *Journal for Education in the Built Environment, 3*(2), 63–74. doi:10.11120/jebe.2008.03020063

Wells, A. (2014). International Student Mobility: Approaches, Challenges and Suggestions for Further Research. *Procedia: Social and Behavioral Sciences, 143*, 19–24. doi:10.1016/j.sbspro.2014.07.350

Wen, M., & Tsai, C. (2006). University students' perceptions of and attitudes toward (online) peer assessment. *Higher Education, 51*(1), 27–44. doi:10.1007/s10734-004-6375-8

West, M. A., Borrill, C. S., & Unsworth, K. (1998). Team effectiveness in organizations. In C. L. Cooper & I. T. Robertson (Eds.), *International Review of Industrial and Organizational Psychology.* Chichester: Wiley.

Westrup, U., & Planander, A. (2013). Role-play as a pedagogical method to prepare students for practice: The students' voice. *Högre utbildning, 3*(3), 199-210.

White, K. (1984). MIS Project Teams: An investigation of cognitive style implications. *Management Information Systems Quarterly, 8*(2), 85–101. doi:10.2307/249346

Whiting, S. (2010). Welcome to the banquet (or, how to increase the relative happiness of the M.Arch Thesis student). In Cuff, D., & Wriedt, J. (Eds.), *Architecture from the outside in: Selected essays by Robert Gutman* (pp. 131-17). New York: Princeton Architectural Press.

Whyte, J., Bessant, J. (2007). *Making the most of UK design excellence: equipping UK designers to succeed in the global economy.* Tanaka Business School, Imperial College London.

Wigglesworth, S., McCorquodale, D., & Ruedi, K. (Eds.), (1996). Desiring Practices: Architecture, gender and the interdisciplinary. *Proceedings of the Desiring Practices Symposium.* London: Black Dog Publishing.

Wigglesworth, S., & Till, J. (Eds.). (1998). *The Everyday and Architecture. Architectural Design Profile no. 134.* London: Academy Editions, July/August.

Willcoxson, L. E. (2006). "It's not Fair!": Assessing the Dynamics and Resourcing of Teamwork. *Journal of Management Education, 30*(6), 798–808. doi:10.1177/1052562906287964

Willenbrock, L. L. (1991). An undergraduate voice in architectural education. In T. A. Dutton (Ed.), *Voices in architectural education: Cultural politics and pedagogy* (pp. 97–119). New York: Bergin & Garvey.

Willey, K., & Gardner, A. (2007, December 9-13). Building better teams at work using self and peer assessment practices. *Paper presented at theEighteenth Annual Conference of the Australasian Association for Engineering Education,* Melbourne.

Williams, A., Askland, H. H., & Boud, D. (1996). Assessing creativity: Strategies and tools to support teaching and learning in architecture and design. *Resource Library, 1995*, 1994.

Willingham, D. T., Hughes, E. M., & Dobolyi, D. G. (2015). The scientific status of learning styles theories. *Teaching of Psychology, 42*(3), 266–271. doi:10.1177/0098628315589505

Willmot, P., & Crawford, A. (2004, October 16-21). Online peer assessed marking of team projects. *Paper presented at theInternational Conference on Engineering Education*, Gainesville, Florida.

Wodehouse, A., & Maclachlan, R. (2014). An Exploratory Model for Understanding Culture in Student Design Team Idea Generation. *The Design Journal, 17*(4), 488–514. doi:10.2752/175630614X14056185479980

Wong, J. (2004). Are the Learning Styles of Asian International Students Culturally or Contextually Based? *International Education Journal, 4*(4), Retrieved from http://iej.cjb.net

Wong, Y. K., Shi, Y., & Wilson, D. (2004). Experience, gender composition, social presence, decision process satisfaction and group performance. *Proceedings of theACM International Conference Proceeding Series.*

Wortham, S. (2001). *Narratives in action: A strategy for research and analysis.* New York: Teachers College Press.

Wright, L. (1995). All students will take more responsibility for their own learning. In S. Griffiths, K. Houston, & A. Lazenblatts (Eds.), Enhancing student learning through peer tutoring in higher education (Vol. 1, pp. 90-92). Coleraine, Northern Ireland: University of Ulster.

Wright, N., & Davis, R. (2014). Educating the creative citizen: Design education programs in the knowledge economy. *Techne Series: Research in Sloyd Education and Craft Science A, 21*(2), 42–61.

Wright, S., & Lander, D. (2003). Collaborative group interactions of students from two ethnic backgrounds. *Higher Education Research & Development, 22*(3), 237–251. doi:10.1080/0729436032000145121

Yazici, H.J. (2005). A study of collaborative learning style and team learning performance. *Education+ training,* 47(3), 216-29.

Yazici, H. J. (2005). 'A Study of Collaborative Learning Style and Team Learning Performance'. *Education + Training, 47*(2/3), 216–229. doi:10.1108/00400910510592257

Yeatts, D. E., & Hyten, C. (1998). *High-performing self-managed work teams: A comparison of theory to practice.* Thousand Oaks, CA, USA: Sage. doi:10.4135/9781483328218

Yellen, R. E., Winniford, M. A., & Sanford, C. C. (1995). Extroversion and introversion in electronically supported meetings. *Information & Management, 28*(1), 63–74. doi:10.1016/0378-7206(94)00023-C

Yin, R. K. (2009). *Case study research: Design and methods.* Los Angeles, CA: Sage Publications.

Ylikoski, T., & Kortelainen, M. J. (2012). A new approach for managing university-workplace partnerships. *Industrial and Commercial Training, 44*(6), 349–356. doi:10.1108/00197851211254798

Yudelson, J. (2009). *Green building through integrated design.* New York: McGraw-Hill.

Zehner, R., Forsyth, G. G., Musgrave, E., Neale, D., De La Harpe, B., … , K Warson, K. (2009). Curriculum Development in Studio Teaching. Sydney: Australian Learning and Teaching Council.

Zehner, R., Forsyth, G., Musgrave, E., Neale, D., de la Harpe, B., Peterson, F., & Frankham, N. with Wilson, S., & Watson, K. (2009). *Curriculum Development in Studio Teaching Volume One, STP Final Report.* Sydney: Australian Learning and Teaching Council. Retrieved from http://online.cofa.unsw.edu.au/studioteaching/

Zellner, M. L., Theis, T. L., Karunanithi, A. T., Garmestani, A. S., & Cabezas, H. (2008). A new framework for urban sustainability assessments: Linking complexity, information and policy. *Computers, Environment and Urban Systems, 32*(6), 474–488. doi:10.1016/j.compenvurbsys.2008.08.003

Zhang, X., Chen, Z., & Guo, C. (2009). The opening" black box" between conflict and knowledge sharing: A psychological engagement theory perspective. *Paper presented at the42nd Hawaii International Conference on System Sciences.*

Zhang, B., Johnston, L., & Kilic, G. B. (2007). Assessing the reliability of self- and peer rating in student group work. *Assessment & Evaluation in Higher Education, 33*(3), 1–12.

Zhen Hui, R. (2001). Matching teaching Styles with learning Styles in East Asian Context. *Foreign language College.* Retrieved from http:iteslj.org/Techniques/Zhenhui-TeachingStyles.html

About the Contributors

Richard Tucker has twenty years of experience as a teacher and researcher in the context of architectural education. He has over 50 publications to his name, reflecting an expertise in five interrelated areas: (1) sustainable design of urban ecologies; (2) the evaluation and perception of sustainable design; (3) teamwork in design; (4) education for the sustainable design of urban ecologies; and (5) built environment design education. Richard is a member of the Alfred Deakin Research Institute and the Centre for Memory Imagination and Invention (CMII). Richard has been a team member of grant-funded projects totalling over $1 million; eleven investigations including six as project leader. In 2007, Richard's teaching scholarship was recognised nationally by a Carrick Institute Citation for Outstanding Contributions to Student Learning. In 2011, Richard became only the 2nd teacher in the discipline of architecture in Australia to be awarded an ALTC Award for Teaching Excellence.

***

Neda Abbasi is a Research Fellow in School of Architecture and Built Environment at Deakin University. Her research interest and expertise focus on physical environments of learning and teaching i.e. planning, design and evaluation studies. She holds a Master of Architecture from the Faculty of Fine Arts, University of Tehran. Her master thesis examined adolescents' leisure time and its impacts on their psychosocial development and applied the theories of adolescent development within a project for a cultural and recreational centre. In 2006, she started a research project in the University of Melbourne on the role of school design in adolescent identity formation. In Deakin University, she has worked on the development of a Tool for Evaluation of Academic Library Spaces (TEALS) and was the project manager on an OLT funded project on Teaching and Assessing Team Learning (2011-2014).

Tom Allen is a Design and Business Strategist with extensive experience in Europe and Australia. His work at Strategic Design Consultancy Seven Positive focusses on empowering people, organisations and enterprise to create positive futures. He is a Sessional Academic at Queensland University of Technology (QUT) and Griffith University (QCA), passionately teaching Design and Business related subjects and the value of socially and environmentally responsible entrepreneurial activity. Tom is on the Board of the Design and Emotion Society (Australia Chapter).

Susan Ang is a senior academic with the School of Architecture and Built Environment. Susan teaches architecture design and design communication and is currently leading the universal design agenda in built environment education and is involved in research, teaching and learning that is concerned with social inclusion and designing inclusive environments. Susan was born in Kuala Lumpur, Malaysia and completed her Bachelor of Architecture degree at Deakin in 1986. Susan has practised as an architect for more than fifteen years with a special interest in community engaged projects. Susan's work is inspired by intrinsic personal transcultural heritage and identity, with aspirations for a sustainable future imbued with cultural harmony and social responsibility. Since 2011, Susan initiated and led Deakin University's iDiDE: Intercultural Dialogue Through Design, a collaborative design programme with established international partners in Malaysia, Thailand, India, Indonesia and Sri Lanka. The program is focused upon culturally immersive collaborative learning and practice in design and is concerned with sustainable design outcomes that contribute towards preservation of humanity, diversity and dignity. Susan is involved in development aid and rural community development projects in Sri Lanka utilizing collaborative integrated sustainable community principles.

Carolyn Barnes is Academic Director of Research Training in the School of Design, Swinburne University of Technology, Melbourne, where she teaches research methods for academic and practice purposes. Her research investigates the agency and knowledge bound up in individuals and groups to address their primary needs and interests. Using social research approaches, she works in two main areas: participatory design, examining how co-creation methods can mobilise stakeholder knowledge, and knowledge transmission within practitioner networks.

Ammon Beyerle teaches design and theory, and is currently completing a PhD by creative works in Architecture, Participation and Agonism at the University of Melbourne. He is also co-Director Here Studio, an architecture practice that focuses on participatory design in public projects.

Oliver Bown is a researcher in the fields of creative computing, interactive media, interaction design and computational creativity, with a broad academic background in computing, social sciences and interaction design. He is also a practicing musician and media artist. He is senior lecturer at the Faculty of Art & Design at the University of New South Wales.

Thomas Carey is a Visiting Senior Scholar in the Office of the Provost at Kwantlen Polytechnic University, a Research Professor in the Center for Research in Math and Science Education at San Diego State University and an executive consultant for higher education systems and institutions in strategy for exemplary teaching and learning. His previous faculty roles in Canada include leading teaching and learning centres in two Canadian research universities and serving as Associate Vice-President for teaching and learning support at the University of Waterloo. Tom has also been a Visiting Professor at the University of York and the Open University (U.K.) and a Visiting Senior Scholar for the Higher Educational Quality Council of Ontario (Canada), the California State University Office of the Chancellor and the Carnegie Foundation for the Advancement of Teaching (U.S.).

Alexandra Lara Crosby is the course director of Interdisciplinary Design, in the School of Design at the University of Technology Sydney. She studied Visual Communications and International Studies, completing a PhD in 2013 on local environmentalism enacted through site-based creative community events in contemporary Indonesia. Her research explores the role of creative practices in culturally-specific forms of activism with a focus on post colonial contexts. She has worked extensively on cross-cultural projects in the Asia-Pacific region. She was co-Director of the Gang Festival (2005-2008) and in 2009 was awarded the Ros Bower award for excellence in Leadership in Community Cultural Development by the Australia Council. In 2012 she was awarded the Creative Media Social Justice award at the UTS Human Rights Award for her work with EngageMedia and the Papuan Voices project.

Philip Crowther is Head of Architecture in the School of Design at Queensland University of Technology. Philip's research focuses on design for disassembly in an architectural context. He has studied the life cycle of buildings and the sustainable reuse of building materials. Through his research, Philip developed principles of Design for Disassembly (DfD) and theoretical models for environmentally sustainable construction. Philip is also researching in design education and the development of creativity. He is interested in the ways that creativity can be fostered and assessed within a university teaching environment.

Cristina Garduño Freeman is an academic in the fields of digital media, architecture and heritage. She has a forthcoming book titled Participatory Culture and the Social Value of an Architectural Icon: Sydney Opera House with Ashgate, UK and in 2014 received the International Visual Sociology Association Rieger Award for an Outstanding Doctoral Thesis. Her research work has been published in some of the world's leading international journals including: the International Journal of Heritage Studies (2010) and Architectural Theory Review (2013). In 2015 Dr Garduño Freeman co-edited Volume 27:3 of Historic Environment, a special issue titled Watermarks with Dr Ursula de Jong and in 2013 was Assistant Guest Editor for Volume 18:3 of Architectural Theory Review (2013) with Dr Naomi Stead. She is a graduate of the prestigious 'Oxford Internet Institute Summer Doctoral Program', which led to a collaborative publication in Nexus: New Intersections in Internet Research. Recent innovative work includes the Melbourne Lovability Index, in collaboration with Dr Fiona Gray, which seeks to measure people's connection with place. Dr Garduño Freeman is also a multidisciplinary designer and has practiced professionally in architecture, landscape architecture and urban design, and in visual communication design.

Paola Gavilanez has been an interior design practitioner and educator for over 15 years. Her body of professional work includes designing at the senior level for over 30 projects and she has authored articles for trade publications and newspapers in both Canada and Ecuador. Paola's design philosophy stems from the powerful emotional response humans have to design in nature. She believes the continued study of the principles and elements of design as they exist in nature can serve not only as inspiration but as a benchmark of quality and attention to detail. Paola obtained a Diploma in Interior Architecture and Design in Ecuador from Instituto Eurodiseño and is currently pursuing a Master of Arts in Interdisciplinary Studies at Royal Roads University with a focus on Sustainability and Communications. She is currently a faculty member in the CIDA-accredited Interior Design program at Kwantlen Polytechnic University's Wilson School of Design and her teaching experience includes positions in Canada and Ecuador, where she taught at the Universidad de Guayaquil's Faculty of Architecture. Paola is a Registered Interior Designer with the Interior Designer's Institute of BC (IDIBC) and Interior Designers Canada, and has served on IDIBC's Board of Management as both VP Education and VP Communications.

Phil Gough is a digital artist and designer. Phil works as a creative technologist in research, design and art contexts. Phil works visualising data using D3.js for research purposes, for scientists and non-expert users. He is a PhD candidate at The University of Sydney, employing qualitative, practice-based research to investigate user experiences with static, moving and interactive non-expert user visualisations (or NEUVis) using a research through design methodology. He currently is working for ACEMS at the Queensland University of Technology as a research associate, designing interactive, web-based visualisations for research and industry collaborations.

Ning Gu is a Professor of Architecture in the School of Art, Architecture and Design at the University of South Australia.. His most significant research contributions have been made towards research in architectural and design computing. The research outcomes have been documented in over 140 peer-reviewed publications. He has been a reviewer/guest editor for various international journals including Design Studies, Automation in Construction, Architectural Science Review, IJAC and ITCon. He was visiting scholar at MIT, Columbia University and Technische Universiteit Eindhoven.

Wayne Hall holds a PhD from the University of Warwick and a PGCert in Learning and Teaching from the University of Plymouth. He is a Corporate Member of the Institution of Mechanical Engineers (MIMechE) and a Chartered Engineer (CEng). He has held teaching and research appointments at the University of Warwick, University of Nottingham and University of Plymouth in the UK, and at Deakin University and Griffith University in Australia. He is currently Deputy Head of School (Learning and Teaching) in the Griffith School of Engineering at Griffith University. Dr Hall's research interests lie in the design and manufacture of lightweight and Fibre Reinforced Plastics (FRPs) and in engineering education related research. Most recently, his technical research has focused on the role of natural fibres as a sustainable alternative to man-made reinforcements in structural composites. His interest in engineering education is focused on the development and implementation of successful teaching and learning strategies for on- and off-campus (distance education) students, and on the implementation of Project-Based Learning (PBL) in the engineering curriculum.

Ju Hyun Lee is Senior Lecturer in the School of Architecture and Built Environment, the University of Newcastle, Australia. Dr Lee has made a significant contribution towards architectural and design research over the past 10 years in three main areas: design cognition, planning and design analysis, and design computing. His recent cognitive research, Design and Language, has a significant impact on breaking down the barriers to achieving efficient and sustainable interactions between people in design teams, particularly those in the Asia–Pacific region. Dr Lee was invited to become a visiting academic at the University of Newcastle in February 2011. His international contribution has been recognised as: Associate editor for a special edition of Architectural Science Review; Reviewer for many international journals and conferences; International reviewer for national grants.

Anthony Mills is Chair of Construction Management and Head of School of Architecture and Built Environment at Deakin University, Australia. He has published over 100 referred papers in international journals and conferences, and is a member of many local and international Boards related to construction, and quantity surveying, Including the Australian Council of Deans of the Built Environment and is also a founding member of the Australian National Construction Forecasting Committee. Prof Mills is world expert on construction procurement, and currently supervisors 5 PhD's in related fields.

Gregory K Missingham is an associate professor at the University of Melbourne and has a teaching and research focus on design methods and improving teaching and learning in architecture. He has published, additionally, on human-environment relations, Chinese gardens and recently on creativity.

Adam C. Morgan is a Lecturer at the Institute for Interactive Media and Learning (IML) at the University of Technology Sydney (UTS). He wrote the UTS handbook 'Enhancing Experiences of Groupwork: A Resource Kit for Managing and Motivating Student Groups'. Adam consults and runs workshops for academic staff on groupwork and collaborative learning. He also plays a major role supporting the use of the software SPARKPlus (www.sparkplus.com.au) at UTS. His PHD was in the area of teamwork, and he has a strong interest in collaborative learning and enhancing the student experience of groupwork.

Amber Ortlieb holds two Bachelor degrees one in Interior Design (from Brigham Young University) with the second in Education (from the University of Alberta) and a Master of Science in Consumer and Design Sciences (from Auburn University). With a focus on sustainability in the built environment, she is researching the impacts on human health and wellbeing to understand the benefits and future directions of optimal healthy interiors related to both the emotional and physical health parameters of occupants. For the past seven years, Amber has been employed in interior design education at the diploma and degree level. Recently, she joined the Interior Design faculty of Kwantlen Polytechnic University in Vancouver, BC. She is a Registered Interior Designer with Interior Designers of Canada, NCIDQ certified and a LEED Green Associate.

Michael J. Ostwald is Dean of Architecture at the University of Newcastle (Australia) and a Visiting Professor at RMIT University (Australia). Michael has a PhD in architectural history and theory and a higher doctorate (DSc) in design mathematics. He is Co-Editor-in-Chief of the Nexus Network Journal: Architecture and Mathematics and a member of the editorial boards of ARQ and Architectural Theory Review. Michael's more than 300 published research papers cover aspects of the history and theory of geometry and design, and applications of computing in architectural analysis.

Stuart Palmer is Associate Professor of Integrated Learning in the Faculty of Science, Engineering and Built Environment at Deakin University. He completed his undergraduate degree with distinction in electronics engineering. During nearly a decade of professional practice in consulting engineering he completed an MBA in technology management. In 1995 he joined the School of Engineering at Deakin University and lectured in the management of technology for 12 years. During that time he was awarded the Australasian Association for Engineering Education McGraw-Hill New Engineering Educator Award, completed his doctoral studies in engineering management education, and completed a Graduate Certificate in Higher Education. In 2011 he was awarded an ALTC Citation for Outstanding Contribution to Student Learning. His research interests include frequency domain image analysis and the effective use of digital/online technologies in learning and teaching. More recently he has taken a role in the Faculty of Science, Engineering and Built Environment at Deakin University. He maintains a strong interest, and active involvement, in engineering education.

Traci Rose Rider is the Coordinator for the Design Initiative for Sustainability and Health, and Research Associate at North Carolina State University's College of Design. Dr. Rider's research has focused on the relationship between the design culture and the notion of sustainability, exploring factors impacting environmental attitudes of designers including environmental education, learned associations and informal influences. Dr. Rider teaches courses focusing on sustainability for the Department of Architecture, including a Sustainability in Architecture Seminar and an interdisciplinary LEED Laboratory course focusing on the issues of existing buildings and operations. Her funded research projects include methods for introducing building science and health topics to middle school students in North Carolina through STEM exercises, as well as supporting the development of interdisciplinary focus areas for the NC State in the areas of Sustainable Cities. In her Extension role, Dr. Rider works with North Carolina communities that have a community development need, using participatory action research and student involvement to help facilitate the development of concept designs to help strengthen North Carolina's communities in terms of economy, human health, and the environment.

Andrew J Scott has been practicing and teaching industrial design for two decades. His experience as a design consultant has included work in industrial design, ergonomics, corporate identity and entertainment concepts for clients such as World Expo 88, the Civil Aviation Authority, Spectra Lighting and other businesses in the Brisbane area. He is Head of Studies for the School of Design, Creative Industries Faculty, responsible for the Bachelor of Design programme, catering to 1,500 students of architecture, industrial design, interior design and landscape architecture, Bachelor of Fine Arts (Fashion) and Bachelor of Fine Arts (Interactive and Visual Design). He completed his masters (research) investigating touch screen interface design and his PhD research focuses on product attachment and personal identity. Other interests include product aesthetics, graphical literacy and information design. Specialties: Industrial design, teaching, first year education, design and identity, material culture, touch screens, information design

James Thompson is a Doctoral Candidate in the PhD in the Built Environment Program and a Pre-Doctoral Teaching Associate in the College of Built Environments at the University of Washington, Seattle, USA.

Martin Tomitsch is Associate Professor in Design, and Director of the Design Computing program at the University of Sydney. He studied and worked in Vienna, Stockholm, Reykjavik, and Paris before moving to Australia, where he currently leads the Design Lab in the University of Sydney's Faculty of Architecture, Design and Planning. He is founding member of the Media Architecture Institute, state co-chair of the Australian Computer-Human Interaction Special Interest Group (CHISIG), and visiting lecturer at the Vienna University of Technology's Research Group for Industrial Software (INSO).

Nicki Wragg is a Senior Lecture at Swinburne University of Technology and Swinburne Online. Her in-depth knowledge and experience in the practice of Communication Design has been recognised and awarded in seven distinct awards. At Swinburne Online, Nicki has overseen the transformation from studio-based design curriculum to delivery that is fully online. She has reimagined and implemented innovative methods that ensure the ongoing relevance of design traditions within the context of technological change within design and society.

Index

Printed in the United States
By Bookmasters